GW01161687

RECORD AND SERVICES,

SATISFACTORY

On election to President of the Manchester Association of Engineers, 1973–74. (The chain carries the names of recent predecessors in the office).

Record and Services, Satisfactory*

WILLIAM JOHNSON

* For the origin of these words, see page 417.

M C

© William Johnson 2003

First published in 2003 by
The Memoir Club
Whitworth Hall
Spennymoor
County Durham

All rights reserved
Unauthorised duplication contravenes existing laws

British Library Cataloguing-in-Publication data
A catalogue record for this book is available from the British Library

ISBN 1–84104–059–2

The descriptions of events, incidents and characters featured in this book are true and correct according to the recollections of the author

Printed in the UK by CPI Bath

Dedication:
To Family and Friends

THREE ATTITUDES TO WRITING A MEMOIR

I thought I might obtain some help and guidance in developing this autobiographical memoir by examining some of the classic historical records I had encountered. I ended with the following three pieces of opinion and advice. First are some words tendered by Benvenuto Cellini (1500–1571), the celebrated Florentine precious metal-worker and sculptor. Second is a passage from Edward Gibbon's (1737–94) *Autobiography*, in the Everyman series, 1923. (Alas, he has a 200-page continuous *Memoir* without a section or chapter heading!) Finally, there is a typically provocative contribution from Charles Babbage (1792–1871).

THE LIFE OF BENVENUTO CELLINI (1571)
BOOK FIRST

All men of whatsoever quality they be, who have done anything of excellence, or which may properly resemble excellence, ought, if they are persons of truth and honesty, to describe their life with their own hand; but they ought not to attempt so fine an enterprise till they have passed the age of forty. This duty occurs to my own mind, now that I am travelling beyond the term of fifty-eight years, and am in Florence, the city of my birth. Many untoward things can I remember, such as happen to all who live upon our earth; and from those adversities I am now more free than at any previous period of my career.

GIBBON'S AUTOBIOGRAPHY (1794)

In the fifty-second year of my age, after the completion of an arduous and successful work, I now propose to employ some moments of my leisure in reviewing the simple transactions of a private and literary life. Truth, naked unblushing truth, the first virtue of more serious history, must be the sole recommendation of this personal narrative. The style shall be simple and familiar: but style is the image of character; and the habits of correct writing may produce, without labour or design, the appearance of art and study. My own amusement is my motive, and will be my reward: and if these sheets are communicated to some discreet and indulgent friends, they will be secreted from the public eye till the author shall be removed beyond the reach of criticism or ridicule.

From *The Life of a Philosopher* by Charles Babbage (1864)

PREFACE

Some men write their lives to save themselves from *ennui*, careless of the amount they inflict on their readers.

Others write their personal history, lest some kind friend should survive them, and, in showing off his own talent, unwittingly show them up.

Others, again, write their own life from a different motive – from fear that the vampires of literature might make it their prey.

I have frequently had applications to write my life, both from my countrymen and from foreigners. Some caterers for the public offered to pay me for it. Others required that I should pay them for its insertion; others offered to insert it without charge. One proposed to give me a quarter of a column gratis, and as many additional lines of éloge as I chose to write and pay for at ten-pence per line. To many of these I sent a list of my works, with the remark that they formed the best life of an author; but nobody cared to insert them.

XLIX

'Tis all a Chequer-board of
   Nights and Days
Where Destiny with Men
   for Pieces plays:
Hither and thither moves,
   and mates, and slays,
And one by one back in the
   Closet lays.

Contents

Three attitudes to writing a memoir — vi
Acknowledgements — xii

Part I FAMILY AND EARLY EDUCATION

I Background — 3
II Lower Openshaw — 21
III Grammar School — 35
IV The Start of the Second World War — 42
V Evacuation — 45
VI Political Opinion — 49

Part II THE ARMY

VII Selection Processes — 61
VIII From Primary Training to Commission — 66
IX The Prisoner's Guard — 73
X To Italy — 80
XI Central Purchase and Production — 88
XII The 492 Tank Transporter Company — 111
XIII Marriage — 117
XIV Austria — 123
XV Padova and Demobilisation — 127

Part III IN ACADEMIA

XVI A Civil Servant Remembers — 135
XVII Sheffield University — 139

XVIII	At 'Owens', Manchester University	157
XIX	Manchester College of Technology (later UMIST)	176
XX	Ridge Hall	213
XXI	Cambridge	230
XXII	Some Research Activities	241
XXIII	Varia	263
	1 I. Todhunter ... The Elements of Euclid	264
	2 I. Todhunter ... Textbook Writer, Scholar, Coach and Historian of Science	268
	3 An Engineer Hoist with his own Petard?	271
	4 Heat Lines	273
	5 Dr Moshe Barash: From the Technion to Purdue: the British Connection	275
	6 A Pair of Mechanical Innovators	279
	7 Unfinished Military History	280
	8 Edward Gibbon ... Early Historical Sciences ... and Maurist Erudition ...	285
	9 A University at Stamford	287
	10 The State Lottery	289
	11 The Taj Mahal	291
	12 Blenkinsop	292
	13 The Importance of Newton's Birthplace	294
	14 The New DNB	302

Part IV A Wandering Scholar

XXIV	The USSR and Russia	305
XXV	Japan	339
XXVI	China and Women in Mathematics	355
XXVII	Turkey, Greece and Mount Athos	367
XXVIII	Taiwan	382
XXIX	The USA: Two special visits	384
XXX	Australia	386
XXXI	Israel	388
XXXII	Nigeria	390
XXXIII	Singapore and Hong Kong	391
XXXIV	India	393

XXXV	Iran	397
XXXVI	Germany	403
XXXVII	Canada	406

Part V COMING TO REST?

XXXVIII	Removing to Cornwall	411
1	An Epitaph from Jonathan Swift (1667–1745)	414
2	The Book title derived from a letter of Yester-year	417
3	Errors and Author's Apologies	418
	Index	421

Acknowledgements

Primarily, I would like to thank my wife Heather for the great support she has rendered during the writing of this volume. She helped by reading, gently criticising and correcting many drafts of chapters and proofs. Foremost, however, was the effort she made in typing material when that task was no longer the easy job it once was, since she was approaching 80 years of age. Certainly, without her encouragement my efforts would not have been completed early in 2002.

I am also very grateful to my sons and daughters for presenting us with a Packard Bell personal computer. For the greater part of the production of the manuscript it was invaluable though to those unused to its complexities – the grandparent generation – it often seemed to possess a will of its own.

There are many references, quotations and excerpts from various publications of, notably, Elsevier and Pergamon Press. To them and others I am greatly indebted for permission to use their material.

The effort the staff of the Memoir Club have made to produce this volume has been immense: without their expertise the work would not appear as clear and accurate as it is.

PART I

Family and Early Education

CHAPTER I

Background

———◆———

I FIRST MAKE SOME REMARKS about my parents and their families in order to describe the background of circumstances of the Johnsons, and thereby establish what determined much of my early life. First, to the masculine side. My father, James Johnson, was the third or fourth son in his family: some children died in infancy, including twins, but I do not know how many; there were two Walters, I understand, 'big' and 'little', Thomas John and one daughter, Catherine ('Kit'); John was the youngest (and 'spoiled', they said) whilst Kit was 'damaged' because of my grandmother's unyielding preference for boys! Little Walter died in childhood, the other joined the Army and went to participate in the war in South Africa during the first years of this century. Alas, he never came back; he was either killed or died from disease and sickness.

Thomas was apprenticed at the time with the Manchester Corporation to become a paviour. (In the days before all our roads were made of concrete or 'macadam', streets and roads were carefully paved with large blocks of stone or 'setts', each a cube of about eight inches. All the roads in Manchester were beautifully crowned by tradesmen 'out of their time'. (But what a row the large, metal-wheeled traffic made when passing over them!) Thomas was said to be a fine military man who joined the St John's Ambulance Corps in the First World War, but was killed in 1916 in a rescue operation. His body was never found but his name is recorded on the cenotaph at Thiépval in France (see Figures 1 and 2).* He married just before he went out to France and thus never saw his son, Thomas, born after his death. His wife enjoyed a state pension and continued to live with her parents (Harrison by name) and family in an overcrowded terraced house. 'Young' Thomas was said to have grown up 'too soft and gentle', as indeed he was. His health was poor and many of his adolescent years were spent in hospitals. He contracted emphysema of which he later died. He was apprenticed in his dead father's trade but hardly even started work: the Manchester Corporation had accepted that it had a responsibility to treat him specially, due to the death of his father.

---

* My grandmother made the longest journey of her life by passing through London and going on to see the cenotaph in France. No one else in the family except my wife, Heather, and I have ever visited the latter – except grand-daughter, Rebecca Ryan in July 2003.

Figure 1.
The Cenotaph at Thiépval.

Young John became a paviour tradesman too, after seven years of apprenticeship, and then enjoyed a good wage. I used to watch him and his 'mates' at work, paving, in the area around my home. After his first wife died, in childbirth, he joined the Territorial Army and won prizes as the smartest recruit. Soon he met a young woman, Elsie Middleton, who was to raise his career sights so that he determined to try to better himself – working via a correspondence course for a Clerk of Works Certificate. I, then fifteen years old, used to help him with his mathematics (actually elementary geometry for road-builders) and he succeeded. With his Certificate he changed his occupation to become Clerk of Works in Chesterfield and when the Second World War started, his new job was declared to be a Protected Occupation. All his mates in the Territorials were called up into the Army and many were captured in France when it collapsed in 1940. He stayed in Chesterfield for the remainder of his life and did very well – in salary and in being allotted a corporation house. He died there aged 76. He was always good to me and frequently 'dropped' me two shillings which, pre-Second World War, was very, very helpful to a young student!

Kate was an employee at MacConnells' Cotton Mill in the centre of Manchester. She worked all her life in an extremely damp atmosphere full of cotton wool and dust and died at about fifty of a lung disease. She had little education, always

Figure 2. Thomas Johnson.

attended church, took me for airings in a perambulator (or a 'death wagon', said my grandmother) and attended to me when I was a baby. She had few boyfriends – my grandmother always chased them off! – and lived no real independent life, always being dominated by a very tough mother who destroyed any marriage prospects.

My father's father appears to have been a drunkard. All I ever heard was that it was not uncommon for them to find him in the street gutter, blind drunk and penniless. He died before he was forty. My grandmother really brought up the family alone: she cleaned each day at the Town Hall, starting at 5.30 a.m. She kept house for a minister of the church and washed the clothes of his family. She also made a little extra money as 'the lady in the area who laid out the dead'. My father, as a boy, was her invaluable aid. He kept the house clean when she was at work and he dragooned his younger brother and sister into going to school. He kept the fire alight, putting on shovelfuls of coal and removing the ashes: this was a pivotal job in all our houses which had but one cold water tap in the place. One boiled every drop of water on the fire one could and used the cooking and baking oven endlessly; the deep-grated narrow coal fires could give a wonderful red glow to a tiny living room as well as help to provide toast quickly; however, it always deposited ash on the few items of furniture they had. My father described his visits to the butcher for 'two pence worth of undercut' – which he used to cut up and cook for all four of them. (And ashes from the coal he frequently threw at my mother who, as a girl, was his neighbour and sat on the party wall taunting him!) He also had to pawn his father's one suit on Monday mornings and retrieve it on Fridays, ready for the weekend. I believe he was known at the pawn shop for being able to calculate sums owed to them as 'interest' as fast as they could. The minister tried to persuade my grandmother to let him put James forward for a place at Chetham's.* I understand he once spent several months in a convalescent home at Abergele, North Wales. He was notably under-nourished and when she married him my mother swore 'his number was nearly up' for 'he had a clear number eleven at the back of his neck'. I believe he used to sell newspapers every day and once remarked that he sold the most on the day after it became known that Captain Scott had died at the South Pole. About his activities at school I never knew him to utter a word. I judged from my mother's remarks that she left school at thirteen and he, at about twelve – he just ceased to attend. Apart from his convalescence, the only long regular activity he had was in the Royal Navy and even then he spent much time in hospital. At some point he was transferred to the Army but was soon taken back into hospital. He and my mother married in 1921 on New Year's Day, he 22, and she 21. I was born in April 1922.

I ought to say a few more words about my paternal grandmother, because of all my family – parents excepted – she was the one to whom I was closest. She was born Sarah Cartwright, 'of good family', and came from Macclesfield, Cheshire. When I began to know her it must have been about 1929 or 1930. My mother, Elizabeth, used to work casually in the Manchester Market for fruit, vegetables or fish. Essentially she was her father's stand-in. When he didn't want to go to work, or could not, she went: it was usually when he was away from home or suffering after drinking too much. All he (and she) did was to look after the horses and carts (and later the lorries) which came to buy fruit and fish at the early morning market. They caught the first tram car into town at about 5.30 a.m. – in all weathers – and their job consisted of parading up and down, watching for thieves stealing from vehicles left standing alone whilst their owners made their purchases, loaded and then paid for them. The vehicles would then be driven to their owners' stores and the latter would have the produce on sale to the public by 8 o'clock. My grandfather, and mother, would be 'tipped' (paid gratuities) by the vehicle owners. He always wore a large apron to and from the market and a large thick belt on which a three-inch circular medallion gave his registration number. He carried a large bag, strapped around his middle to take his cash and also wore a plain silk cravat and a flat cap – and walked slowly, with his feet apart (see Figure 3). During the war he suffered severe frostbite. His only interests were drinking and modest gambling on horses. When my mother had to go to the market she departed from the house early, two hours before my father, who left every day at 7.40 a.m. Thus my grandmother was set to come to our house to rouse me and get me off to school, washed, fully clothed, and breakfasted on porridge. Washing one's legs in cold water over the sink in the kitchen was a challenge in winter: I knew well what it was to suffer chapped fingers, hands and legs. 'Melrose Ointment' could be a godsend! For doing this, four mornings a week, my grandmother received two shillings. She would arrive

---

* Chetham's Hospital 'for the maintenance and education of poor boys' in Manchester was started in 1656, with a bequest left by the philanthropist Humphrey Chetham who had died three years previously. However, James' mother did not want him to go and he didn't want to leave her.

Figure 3. George Riley, extreme left.

at the house about 8.20 a.m., ensconced in a black shawl: we used to exchange many words – neither of us being short of the ability to explain why something should be done – or not! I was pushed out at 8.50 a.m. and usually ran to school. I had to cross the main road – Ashton Old Road – tram cars clanging up and down, lots of carts and horses, a few motor vehicles and many bicycles. It could be hazardous – especially as no one 'saw you across' the busy road, even at seven years of age.

I recall with much amusement my grandfather in our kitchen some years later gutting a fish in preparation for frying it. My young brother, then about fourteen, happened to be alongside him in the kitchen as he did this. He suddenly turned to him and said, at the same time pointing to it, 'Look, Grandad, there's its heart!' Grandfather glared at it, fingered it and then looked up and said, 'First time I knew a fish 'ad a bloody 'eart!'

It sometimes happened that there would be a certain 'coolness' in the family between my mother and grandmother. In that case, my grandmother ceased to act and Esther Wilshaw was substituted. She lived around the corner from us. Her technique was to enter our house, wrap me in a large coat, gather up my clothes and run me round to her house. Her house seemed always warmer than ours and I used to like it: she made a fuss of me, fed me toast and jam and always treated me ahead of her own two children. She was a softer and gentler person than my grandmother. With the latter I had fights! She would abandon me when I said I could do without her; like husband and wife we came to know each other very well. Despite these quarrels, I visited her often – she was but 200 yards away, up a series of 'back entries'. Monday afternoons she used to bake and after school I went to cadge a fresh barm cake – they were beautiful if well-buttered – and so fresh that indigestion would be the eventual outcome. Of course I also ran her errands – for barm, for bacon – to many different shops. She knitted continually: I have since thought she could hardly read; but a great and frequent treat were the pairs of woollen football stockings with two bright red rings she gave me. On Sundays, I recall, I used to visit her with a small medicine bottle which I smuggled up to her to fill up with beer – which I then took home and had with my Sunday dinner, my father protesting that she was teaching me bad habits. Evenings too I would call on her and find her alone by the fire, with a pint or two of beer in a jug, standing on the table alongside a large teacup. If I chose the right time I could be despatched to take and pay the (insurance) club money – a walk of about half a mile – it was always worth a penny to her. While I was away she would nip out for a 'quick one' with her second husband to the Clock Face pub. I could meet her on the way back: you had to know that under her large shawl she often carried a half-gallon jug of beer. I used to ask her about 'the old days' and the wall photos; in particular a large one, twenty inches square, with flags of decorated silk, showing a photo of Thomas, Walter and Jim. I thought that one day, when she died, I would take it, but I lost it, though I have seen its like in antique shops.

My grandmother hated Roman Catholics and much of this she tried to pass on to me. She literally would fight them – men as well as women. The street behind her house was almost entirely Catholic and to walk down it was to issue a challenge. She used to enjoy an encounter with Irishman Jimmy Duggan, whom she would assail and end up pushing him out of a mutual friend's house! The Whit-week walks in Manchester were an annual event: Whit Sunday, Protestant churches paraded and walked around the parish, but Whit Monday was the big day when they set off to walk two miles to Albert Square in the centre of Manchester.

Large portions of the town were blocked off and pedestrians crowded the main streets. These occasions were grand affairs. There were masses of flowers gathered by girls and banners abounded carried by stout men in their best suits. I was dressed up by my father as a sailor, in white, with a little hat placed firmly on my head with the name of the ship he had served in, over my right eye. I marched, not carrying the Union Jack but the White Ensign of the Royal Navy! (There must still be my large front-page photograph in the archives of the *Manchester Evening Chronicle* or *News*, parading myself when only six or seven!) The Roman Catholics walked around our parish on Whit Friday and the next Sunday, but then, I think, they too marched to Albert Square and back. As I was passing my grandmother on one occasion, during a parade, she thrust a large ice-cream cornet into my hand ... I was mad with her. Whoever saw a sailor carrying a flag and eating an ice-cream? She would also call out, 'Good old Irish face!' (Irish, because I was a rosy-cheeked, fresh-faced child then.) I stood with her once when the Roman Catholics' procession was passing and it was beginning to rain. 'Ah! God knows his own!' she shouted out … we had had no rain for *our* procession! She told me someone in her mother's family had been at Cambridge (before I had any knowledge of the place) and she knew of him marching in his academic dress.

More compelling than her previous escapades was her description of her father hitting her mother a blow which killed her – or led to her death. Her father was 'had up' for murder. There was 'another' in the case, it was hinted. In the trial, once on the stand, she perjured herself and said her father did not actually strike her mother, though he raised his arm. There were no other witnesses and he 'got off'. Her mother had initially run away with her joiner husband and my grandmother would refer to him as wearing a top hat and carrying tools in a bag he slung over his shoulder. He kept a large, three-foot-cube box of tools – upstairs now in my back bedroom – and which I have retained these many years.

My grandmother's rented home, at 4 Gorton Road, was an old decrepit house, up ten or twelve steps from the pavement. The front cellar was used for washing clothes, but there was no light in the back cellar. It was the home of the rats and at the foot of the cellar steps you could hear them and sometimes see their eyes gleaming. The outside lavatory was abominable and I tried never to use it. The kitchen, with stone floor, was miserably small and one foot lower than the dining room. I understood that when my parents married, the celebrants were so drunk that there was danger, during the dancing, of the floor collapsing and my mother and father (nearly teetotal all their lives) in their wedding clothes had to prop it up from the cellar below, using orange boxes. Folk lay about 'paralytic', they said – stretched out flat; one half in the kitchen, the other in the living room!

My grandmother, Sarah, and her second husband (we all called him Mr Taylor) used to take me on holiday with them – which was generally to Blackpool or Southport, except for one year when we went to the Isle of Man for a week. The sea crossing was very bad and it took many hours to travel from Fleetwood to Douglas. The boat was actually a huge paddle boat and we arrived at such a late hour that some shops stayed open for us. The seas were so high they broke over the deck and unprepared young women clad in flimsy dresses were wet through, the dye running and leaving them a sight to see! Most of the heavily-laden passengers were sick: vomit was continuously being swept overboard by crew who cleaned the decks every half-hour. The feather in my grandmother's hat was tipped over her face, whilst Mr Taylor's white, bristly moustache was thick with sea salt and stood out at right angles to his skin. A sailor came along and with the help of my grandmother explained to me that the sea water was being thrown up by another sailor … I wondered at how daft they thought I was. I remember, too, how well I did for 'wafer ice-creams' that summer. Either I got one penny for standing outside the pub while they nipped in for a half-pint, or they actually brought me a cornet as I was digging hard in the sand on the beach and then left me, having promised not to go away. In boarding houses too, I remember with distaste the women who made me give them a kiss when in the dining room, so that I could get at my bucket and spade from an inaccessible corner. I always enjoyed the Isle of Man, and remember going to the remote, tiny, restricted Calf of Man, near St Mary's, and Peel. In those days one walked over the headland between the small towns and saw St Patrick's footsteps carefully protected on the top: they are not there today. It was interesting to see all the young women packing barrels of fish in ice on the quays, newly-landed from fishing smacks that morning. One could also visit factories where fish were smoked – especially haddock. Again, all this has gone, as have the industrial ships and ports.

I later saw Mr Taylor when he had become unemployed: he was a painter with Crossleys' Motor Engineering Company, and there were a lot of attractive painter's materials in his house. But in early retirement he sat in front of the fire quietly smoking his pipe. Slowly he started dozing, became 'lost' and spoke little. He simply faded away. When they laid him to rest at Weaste Cemetery on a rainy day in winter, his coffin was put into a grave already inches deep in water. He had a horse-drawn hearse and carriage as did my grandmother, I believe. I remember, at this juncture, seeing Mr Molyneau's funeral – John's first wife's father. It took place out of Roman Catholic Clifford Street – a street 'in the pits' of Lower Openshaw (or was it Gorton there?). He had been in the Army all his life and retired as a sergeant. 'They' sent a horse-drawn gun carriage, draped with the Union Jack, to bear his coffin to the cemetery. It was a very impressive performance. I had never had much conversation with the old fellow; he was very withdrawn and struck me as being long dead before he died.

The Johnson side of the family, after grandparental marriage, seemed to have lived in Collyhurst, as did my mother's parents. This was the poorest suburb in Manchester, into which newcomers drifted. Many families left Ireland, especially after the Great Famine, and made for Liverpool. When that was overcrowded they headed up the River Mersey for Collyhurst, Manchester. They came to search for property and jobs in Cottonopolis and later 'flitted' (i.e. relocated) to better parts of Manchester.

Both my maternal grandfather and grandmother were named Riley, he George and she Elizabeth. All I know of his life as a boy was that he swam for coins tossed into the canal in the centre of the city. My mother used to observe, colourfully, that she wasn't brought up but 'dragged up' in Collyhurst. It was, apparently, the first physical resting place for many Catholics after leaving Ireland – as it was for my grandfather.

There is some doubt that my maternal grandparents were ever married, though my mother said she thought they got married when she was a little girl and that she was present. They had two children, William and Elizabeth. Their son was a 'tear-away'; he was apprehended by the police with the help of his father, because 'nothing could be done with him' and he was put into a Reformatory School. There he learned to play the cornet and became much acclaimed for 'the sweet notes he played'; the Reformatory band even won national prizes. But my mother remarked how, when 'on the loose', he did not come home – or if he did he climbed the walls at the rear of the house and knocked on her bedroom window to be let in – and had disappeared when she woke again and it was light. Willie joined the Army at eighteen and was 'blown to pieces' in the Battle of the Somme in July 1916, aged twenty. His name is on the same cenotaph as

Tommy Johnson's. I was named after him. A huge copper medallion – perhaps four inches in diameter – used to be at loose in our home in 16 Kay Street. It was to be displayed on a wall, in a home, so that a 'fallen one' should not be forgotten: it gave his brief details ... 'Private in the Lancashire Fusiliers ... ' (see Figure 4). But my mother was contemptuous of such practices: nothing substituted for his person; mementoes were fakes; the Government never otherwise recalled his death or his background. What was there to be grateful for? And no one on this side of the family ever visited the Cenotaph.

Among his kit, four private letters to a young Miss were found and forwarded by his Company's Adjutant, but no one knew her. My wife and I stayed one night at a hotel in Albert, France, near Thiépval in the 1980s and spent a day wandering through the area. There are very many small cemeteries still in the old First World War battle regions of France, in the middle of fields of vegetables and pasture with very small chapels attached. Gentle winds blow quietly across the countryside; the number of the cemeteries is amazing; and the scenes are heart-rending. There are still trenches around where fighting took place more than eighty years ago. It is all very touching. I have usually visited war cemeteries wherever they exist – in parts of the globe where fighting took place, and I am pleased that I have always found them to be very well looked after – without pretence and none but two or three local gardeners to look to their condition and, I suppose, with the War Graves Commission at a distance – whether in Singapore, Hong Kong, Jerusalem, Italy, Austria ... their condition is very well preserved.

My maternal grandfather was an average Englishman. I had few intimate conversations with him but when older he talked of Willie. He said that when he learned of his son's death, he went and joined up immediately, giving a false age. 'All I wanted to do was kill all the Germans ... I was sent to Saltash in Devon and I had the job of looking after the horses pulling the big guns ... I got myself to France ... and then began to realise how big the war was. My anger drained away and I became depressed; physical conditions were very bad; we could be in water or ice-bound in trenches for hours. Eventually I got frostbite and they discharged me ...' It was all very sad, especially the manner in which he related his own education in the matter of learning how vast was the impact of the War. (For a first-hand account of war in the trenches, the reader should obtain a copy of Robert Graves' autobiography, *Goodbye To All That*, published about 1929.)

When, as a child, I became aware of my grandfather, he actually lived with us because my grandmother, Isabella, died four days after I was born. She had a stroke – a cerebral haemorrhage – after a celebratory drinking bout. She was said to be overcome to have a grandson, and welcomed him too alcoholically. So, in a matter of ten days, they had a christening and a death in the family. Grandfather gave up responsibility for his two-bedroomed house to my father and mother who paid a rent of eight shillings and fourpence for 16 Kay Street. He paid them lodging money and thus became a source of help to the household – and my mother could keep an eye on him! He lived amidst our family of three, but mostly independently. I was always quite surprised at his independent

*Figure 4. Willie Riley,
on the right.*

treatment by his daughter (my mother); and how it was accepted by my father, never one to suffer injustice with ease, I do not know.

With my grandfather, I learned to fish with rod and line in canals and various 'meres'. I pestered him to teach me. I had to provide the bait – maggots. Joe Livesey was a relative of ours who owned a butcher's shop; I usually went to see him for bait and was then shown the large bins of fat and rotting meat, crawling with maggots, in his back yard. I had to bottle up any thoughts of revulsion and – ungloved – root around arm-deep in those cylinders for the biggest, fattest and whitest maggots, perhaps a centimetre long. A tin was filled in a quarter of an hour! Equipped with rod, line, worms and other bait, we carried a large empty steel fishing bucket on our journeys to lake or canal. When the day's events were over, this article was full of water and six- to eight-inch fish, i.e. carp and roach, and had to be got home on buses, railway trains and by strenuous walking. In our home tank, the fish generally lasted only a day or two, for want of a pump to bubble air through the water. As an active ten-year-old my patience only stretched to about eight trips. Once the line was cast, you sat watching the float for hours on end; my grandfather could do it, I couldn't. My first bite took place under the surface of my float: I was dreaming and my grandfather shouted, 'You've got a bloody bite!' Instantly, I yanked the rod and line up into the air and through sitting too near my grandfather, got my line tangled up in his. The air was 'blue' for the five minutes thereafter. But it was just too demanding to ask a youngster to sit and watch an inch-high, red bobbing float, waiting for the moment when it would be dragged below the water surface. I came to setting a line and then absconding for an hour in search of food, drink or any adventure. In the end, I learned not to fish for freshwater trout; we could lay bait all day and not even get a 'tickle' with these fish of quality.

My grandfather could, I now suppose, just about read. He used to sit and read in the only lavatory we had, at the bottom of the yard to our house. It was a large wooden box in a very small out-house; the seat was about three feet by two feet and always scrubbed clean – scrupulously so. By putting planks of wood and then newspaper over it, it made a desk! It was very successful except that, using a small chair or stool to sit on, it was difficult to know what to do with one's legs. More than once I transferred myself to write and draw down there. However, my grandfather spent half-hours shut in the privy: I asked my mother if he read all the advertisements in the *Daily Express* which he used to take in with him. He also used to carry in an extra half-sheet of newspaper which he always carefully cut into four parts. Again enquiry brought me no enlightenment – why four? – what drill did he follow? The only answer I got was a cuff around the ears for being 'nosy'.

I knew little about my mother's girlhood. She stayed in school until she was thirteen and went into the mill at fourteen. At some stage she was trapped in spinning machinery and very badly crushed in the stomach region. Soon after marriage she started to suffer with varicose veins and ulcers. The calves of her legs were always swollen, red and ulcerated. They were only cured after a heavy operation on her abdomen when she was taken into hospital during the second year I was at grammar school. She was anonymously written up in the medical/surgical literature by a distinguished surgeon; it seems the machine-crushing misfortune somehow heavily damaged the blood circulation in her middle region; her ulcerated legs were always a setback and a consideration in whatever we did. Of course there was never a thought of compensation – 'lots of blame but no compensation', to follow the style of modern-day television adverts.

My mother, 'Lizzy', was barely five feet high, large or amply fleshed out, of a good colour, with dark hair and eyes. Dressed in her thick black leather coat she substituted for my grandfather in Shude Hill Market, Manchester, minding the carts and trucks against theft, as I have remarked above.

As a small boy, walking home from school, I can remember my joy at seeing my mother coming towards me – and how I would rush into her welcoming arms. She would reach deep into her pocket and produce two Victoria plums. She knew I was hard to fill with fruit; and great she was whenever I was in trouble. She and my grandmother Taylor, standing side by side, bare arms folded, often declared in no pretty terms what they would do with Hitler if ever they got their hands on him! In an unaided struggle, Hitler would indeed have suffered.

I understand she did a lot of dancing at Belle Vue (see p. 29) during the First World War when she was engaged to my father. He didn't like it – certainly while he was away fighting for King and country and living a puritanical life, and he let her know it.

Elizabeth Riley was, as noted elsewhere, warm-hearted and a typical 'Lancashire cotton-girl'. She was thickset, had a fine bust – a veritable copy of her mother. She could be very tough. Once, I was sent to buy wool. I produced it: 'It cost twopence ha'penny,' I said. 'Twopence,' she said. 'Twopence ha'penny,' I replied. 'Where's the ha'penny?' 'I don't have one!' 'You've spent it!' 'No, I haven't.' 'I'll give you a last chance! Where's the ha'penny?' 'I didn't have one ...' I was being interrogated standing on the sofa. Then there was a crash as she delivered a blow to the right side of my face. 'What have you done with it?' 'I haven't got it!' The next blow came from the left. After half-a-dozen such blows, I capitulated. 'I spent it on toffees coming home.' 'You did? Well, don't do it again!' And with that, a final dismissive clout was dealt and she left me to recover. My mother could not argue or discuss. My father could – he did it all the time with my mother, until I was about eleven years old. She was fast in a disputation with her flat palm! She even kept a 'cat o' nine tails' hung on the door of the coal cellar. Fortunately it soon got mislaid. I wonder why? And my father too had to be careful, for she would detonate. One of my very earliest recollections was of him struggling to hold her off and of me clinging on to their legs, shouting, 'Stop, stop!' Arguments would break out and she couldn't hold her own. At some juncture attack would occur. She would use the nearest weapon – a fire iron – anything! On one famous occasion my father retreated upstairs and she chased him with a bottle in her hand. It was launched but unfortunately hit the ceiling over the stairs and bounced back to hit her, herself. But these were twice-yearly incidents and normally, the pair of them were as thick as thieves. I distinctly remember a Sunday tea once, when setting the table, they launched into singing 'Ramona' as a duet. But father would never 'mix it'. He was all talk and discussion. She went from negotiation to meaningful war in one bound. But she was great to have on one's side!

Freddy Bailey's family, neighbours of ours, were all boxers; i.e. the father and three sons, two actually performing in the ring. I got to fighting him for no real reason – with bare knuckles. He was tall and thin with long arms, but slow; I wasn't liked in the area – an only one and a little better looked after and nourished than most of the other kids in neighbouring families; I was compact and agile; he was head and shoulders taller than me. We started to fight and I got the best of it by far; I knocked out one of his teeth. A gang of unemployed men who used to stand at certain street corners came and formed a ring around us and urged us on, all for their own entertainment. However, once the fighting had stopped, we ambled back to Regent Street, fifty yards away. While doing this, jeering began and we were caused to start up again at the end of the street. The clamour brought out housewives who lived in that street. Seeing the pair fighting they supported their neighbour's boy but some outright interference stopped the performance. I was a little sad about the affair even though much the smaller because I really did not dislike my opponent. I was reviled by all the mothers and felt their rejection. My own mother suddenly appeared from nowhere and swept me into her arms and to her breast. I broke down, crying – I had a single

Figure 5. Grandfather Thornber and Grandson Christopher.

supporter out of a railing, accusatory group of men and women who should have known better.

For good health and full-blooded support there was never a better mother. I remember that she took me, aged five, to the local swimming baths for females. She had me climb on her back, dived in and completed a length of twenty-five yards. I had never seen a swimming bath, much less been in one before. I clung to her for dear life! I was once pushed into the pool where it was deeper than my height. As I struggled to reach the side of the pool, out of my depth, I panicked and started shouting. I eventually reached the side and some time afterwards recalled that my shouting consisted of calls for 'Mam, Mam, Mother ...!' I recollect being told, twenty years later, that injured air crew during World War II screamed for their mothers as their planes descended out of control. These events show how unsuspectingly intimate and close to our mothers we really are. I have recognised that at some critical points in my life I have gone to my mother rather than my father, to declare courses of action and although she was not sure about 'this education business' at its beginning with the grammar school, yet she followed my father and later on was very pleased she had done so. When I started courting my wife – a massive step in my parents' eyes and therefore mine – it was to my mother that I first made known my inclinations; again, not my father. I suppose there was always an element of fear with him.

I remember enrolment in the infant school in Grange Street; my mother had taken me to see a blue-gowned, straight-backed, iron-grey-haired headmistress,

Miss Lavery; I was just four and therefore being registered to start at the beginning of the next academic year. Thus, I would have started in the second class of four- and five-year-olds in the infant school. The only true recollection I have of the first year is that of threading large, different-coloured wooden bricks on to a long thick piece of string and thinking what a silly, pointless activity it was. I recollect, too, the curiosity and attractiveness of the little girls around me at the play table. They were a scarce commodity in my world and differed somehow from boys!

There is little further I recall until the years in which I was six or seven. Amusingly, I recall reading aloud to a young teacher who was sitting on the warm hot-water pipes in the classroom. I came to the word 'sod': I was reading well up to that time, but stopped suddenly on being confronted with the (to me) swear-word, 'sod'. It took her some time to coax me to speak that word but she succeeded only by saying, 'It means a piece of grassy soil, Willie.' I also remember at this time being thumped on the back by the teacher, thin, shrewish Miss Brown who was conducting our singing in the hall. I must have been daydreaming. She used to talk about a box in the throat which created sounds. I really did think it was a silly idea – I remember to this day contemplating the notion. Also, that five minutes after the incident I was called for by a plump Miss Hill. A few of us were usually pulled out of the class to attend for a chat about our raffia work by our class teacher. On this occasion it was about my raffia pin-cushion – indeed it was below average condition. But really, I think I was one of Miss Hill's favourites; we always liked each other.

I remember too at this time, intending to write a letter. I recall how puzzled I was, to know where to send it to. You could not write, 'Mr X, Our House', could you? It was then that I noticed the use of the names of streets and of the numbers on doors, and understood how and why they were needed.

An incident I also remember concerned the development of the sense of number, and the coming of memory. Newly attached to school and therefore four-plus, I remember observing to my mother when I had been waiting for her on the school steps, 'It seems I must have been here about twelve years!' and immediately reflecting how silly was the remark, seeing as I was aged only four.

I had a sister, Bella, born eighteen months after me, I am told, but who died after some weeks, in 1923. It is hard to write that when God took her, my parents were, apparently, relieved. My father had become unemployed and on going to 'the Guardians', as the Government Support Office was then called, to ask for monetary help, was offered one shilling and sixpence (7½p in today's terms). He told them to 'keep it!', adding that he would not accept such a minor charitable sum. Many times later on, Bella was remembered by all of us for what she might have brought us – both as daughter and sister.

My younger brother, John, was born to us, at home, in January 1930. I well remember his arrival, just after midday. Arriving home from school, I was taken upstairs to see the small bundle – he was nearly eight years younger than me. There was never any competition between us. When we moved to a semi-detached house in *Higher* Openshaw in September 1934, we moved up a social class or two as my father had been promoted from labourer to charge-hand or deputy foreman. John was then four and in Newhaven Avenue we started to share a double bed in the back bedroom. I had a small desk (a bureau in fact, which we pronounced 'burroo') in a corner with a bookcase on top. For nine years these arrangements prevailed, until I graduated and went into the Army in 1943, aged 21.

John went to the same grammar school as I did at eleven years of age. Biology was his great interest, which – with a career in prospect – changed to the reading of Medicine at Manchester University in 1948, a great challenge then for a youngster from so humble a background. Of course, he did well; not only did he graduate, but he went on to achieve consultant status in psychiatry at the early age of 32 – and co-authored a short but very interesting book on *Impotence* in particular in boxers.

In 1947, a large fraction of the intake to the Manchester University Medical School was ex-Servicemen and as John's Higher School Certificate (HSC) results were very good (with distinctions), the Department had no hesitation about putting him straight into second year Medicine. He described to me how, on his first day of term, he was shown into the Anatomy-Surgical laboratory, to find that his allotted task was to dissect a leg. Without previous experience and with no time to adapt to such matters, he was certainly thrown in at the deep end.

In my fifth year at elementary school I took the grammar school examination. In accordance with my own desire, I succeeded in gaining a place. My father had had an interview with the school headmaster, Mr Holmes, who counselled against my going to grammar school. Long experience with a few other youngsters and their working-class parents had taught him that they gave up when they reached fourteen years of age and went 'to work for money'. However, talks with teachers Mr Henry and Mr Lamb supported the notion of my going to grammar school.

On the day of the grammar school examination, which was held in a school two miles away, we were sent off with only fifteen minutes to spare; we had to take a tram car at the cost of a ha'penny, which sum most of us were lucky enough to have on us. We arrived twenty minutes late, to find the school silent as a grave. We crept around and finally found the rooms in which the places corresponding to our examination numbers were reserved. We were quietly seated and given the first examination paper – Mental Arithmetic. This meant only one thing to us; solving problems *in your head* and then writing down the answer. Only when I heard a boy asking for more paper did I realise that the workings of each problem should have been shown. I was probably very lucky to pass. There had been no special preparation, or even interest in seizing such an opportunity. Competition for entry to *the* Manchester Grammar School never even presented itself. A letter arrived some weeks later saying that I had secured a place at the Central High School for Boys. My father and I thought, at first, the pass was to a central school. (There were four grammar schools, numerous 'central' schools and a few technical schools.) It was 36 hours later that we realised it was the oldest of Manchester City Council's grammar schools in Whitworth Street, in the city centre. The school's charge of fees was varied according to a parent's income. The greatest requirement was for six pounds and six shillings; lower incomes attracted fees of four and two guineas, then nothing, and maybe you would be entitled to receive free books and sometimes free uniform and even free dinners. I remember being called to the school to collect my free books. I opened a letter addressed to my father from the Education Committee and saw that I had to present myself at the school that same morning. I quickly dressed and then went to his 'works'. I spoke to the man on the gate and asked him to pass a message inside that I was at the front gate and wished to speak with my father. He came out, I showed him the letter and we talked. I was bid, 'Go and take a tram into town. Go to the fish market and find your mother. Tell her you have come from me and that she must buy you a satchel right away.' This was done, successfully. I found her sitting in a corner with a colleague, Molly, 'plaiting' parsley. She took me off to one of the close-by 'swag shops' and we bought a satchel. I then set off back, across the city to the school, sporting my new empty leather bag. All I can remember is having a larger number of books (new ones) on my hands than I could fit into the satchel – and an outsize atlas. It was a difficult struggle home on the tram car, carrying so much knowledge! As I was about to depart from the school, the Secretary had announced to us all, 'I *advise* you to be present in the Hall ten minutes early on Monday morning.' I mentioned this to my father who asked, 'He used the word "advise", did he?' I assured him that he had. 'Mm ...', he responded, 'Yes.' We both noted the discretion in the choice of words and that I was entering a new culture.

For the sake of history I should now mention my wife's family. My father-in-law, John B. Thornber (see Figure 5), was born into a poor family in Blackburn, Lancashire. At some time in the 1880s, his mother, who had been widowed very soon after his brother Billy's birth, went to India with a Mr Baldwin, who was a master weaver and manager of a cotton mill in Bombay, leaving John and Billy with their grandparents. In 1900, at fourteen years of age, John ran away from home and took a job on board a ship bound for India. Arriving in Bombay, he soon found his mother, settled in with her, and later was introduced to the cotton-weaving industry by his 'new father', Mr Baldwin.

We know that, when a young man, he visited Australia, either on a matter of business or to spend time with other members of his family who had emigrated there. We know too that he spent some time whilst there as an out-rider on one of the large sheep farms in Queensland, where his younger half-sister Queenie was born.

John Thornber would also recount to the family how he had once spent several months as a pearl-fisher in the seas between Ceylon and the tip of southern India. I only half-believed the description of this latter activity but changed my opinion when I became better acquainted with the story behind the opera, 'The Pearl Fishers'. On reading this story, I was astonished to find that it included mention of actual pearl fishing in the region I have described (Bombay was once the chief market for Oriental pearls) and where there was supposed to be a religious shrine.

John was trained to be a manager in the cotton-weaving factory and did this until 1926 when he returned to Stockport, England where his brother was living. John had married Heather's mother, Mildred, in 1915 and she was their only child; it was to improve her health that he moved back to his own country.

Mildred was the daughter of an Italian mining engineer who was naturalised as British, taking the surname Baker (see Figure 6). I believe her mother's forebears were Portuguese, from Goa. Heather's father arrived in England at a time of

Figure 6. Grandmother Milly and Grandaughter Sarah.

economic depression and he had many jobs before he took the offer of a sub-post office in Abbey Hey, Gorton, Manchester in 1932. The independence this gave him suited him well and he remained the local postmaster until he died in 1953. The Thornber family of three lived quietly in a pleasant semi-detached house in Abbey Hey. Heather was born in 1922 and grew up an athletic girl and especially an avid reader and writer of poetry* and diaries. She was a pupil at the Central Grammar School, Manchester, between 1934 and 1938 (in the same years as myself), leaving school near the beginning of the Second World War to join her father as his assistant in the post office. During her years at grammar school I frequently encountered her when we travelled to school on the same tram car and bus. Though the boys' and girls' schools were on the same site, they were single sex schools. She was a well turned-out little person, always in full school uniform (light in summer and heavier in winter) with a bright round face, light blue eyes and black hair with a fringe. The only items of uniform I sported were the mandatory cap and badge, and her neat attire contrasted sharply with my own working-class, economical clothes. See Figure 7.

The latter type of encounter between myself and my wife-to-be had, in fact, a relationship which is well-known in Italian literature! Thus ...

By frequently trying to win a little money in newspaper competitions, I came to know the name of Dante when I was still at the elementary school, but I did not know what he had written. Thus I asked my Irish schoolmaster, Mr Henry, as he left the classroom one lunchtime, 'Sir! Who was Dante?'

---

* To be published.

Figure 7. Heather Thornber, schoolgirl.

'Dante, Willie?' he answered. 'He was Dante Alighieri, author of *The Divine Comedy, The Inferno, Paradise and Purgatory*!'

In later years, I read about Dante and his Beatrice. Dante (1265–1321) had a mature man-young girl affinity for Beatrice. This affection was not reciprocated and each married another; they met in 1274, but she died young in 1290. However, Dante did not forget Beatrice and in 1292–3 she was the inspiration for his *Vita Nuova* ('New/Young Life'). My own affection grew from a boy-girl relationship, but it ended more successfully than that of Dante!

After we were married, I came to know Heather's cousin, Jack B. Thornber, who served as a sergeant in the Royal Marine Commandos during the Second World War.

Heather also had an aunt, Nell Baldwin, an experienced Nursing Sister working overseas in the QAs – the Queen Alexandra's Military Nursing Service. At the end of the war she emigrated to Australia, having married a Polish infantry sergeant, Jan Piatrowski, en route. (She had arranged to marry when younger but it was called off when her groom learned she had been born out of wedlock.) I met the two of them some years later in Sydney, Australia when Jan presented me with an historical volume written in Italian from the seventeenth century. He had been presented with it by an Italian nobleman, some time after Cassino had fallen, but it turned out not to be of great value. Letters of friendship still pass between the Piatrowski family in Poland and the Thornber family in England, especially at Christmas time.

CHAPTER II

Lower Openshaw

———•———

SHAW IS SWEDISH IN ORIGIN and refers to a small thicket, wood or area, so the whole name Openshaw* refers, it would seem, to a not-so-dense wood. When cleared of trees, the area was probably first covered, in about 1850, with rows and rows of densely packed terraced houses. When I knew it there were only a few trees left in the parks: it was a miserable area, chock-full of industrial factories – Whitworth's, Vaughan's, Armstrong's, the Tank, Ferguson's and Crossley's – engineering firms and places of residence cheek-by-jowl, with an awfully polluted atmosphere. However, my mother always spoke with great warmth of her first house as her 'little palace'.

My birth occurred after sixteen months of married life and I seemed to be very welcome even if unsolicited. My mother expressed surprise that I was born in good health since she ate a bunch of celery just before my arrival, whilst watching a football match. Her house, No. 22, looked out over a 'croft' – a piece of waste ground large enough to be a full-sized football pitch. The bottom side was limited by the huge, high, blank wall of one of Joseph Whitworth's factories. Later, I learned that it was a favourite lovers' station on cold, dark nights.

It must have been only a year or two after I was born in that old terraced house in Kay Street, Lower Openshaw, Manchester, that my parents moved from No. 22 to a larger property, No. 16 (and later, No. 20). It had two rooms at ground level and two bedrooms upstairs. There was, as well, a short corridor – good for parking bicycles or toys in – and a scullery. This contained a sink, a boiler for washing all clothes and bed linen etc., and also a gas stove. One washed in, or from, the sink at all times, except when one was very small, when a small trough or metal bath was placed on the living room table and filled with kettle-boiled hot water heated on the fire. A tot of three or four like me could just get into the bath, but getting out naked in front of the family always embarrassed me. There was but one fire in the house (although there were grates in all the other rooms) which was kept going all day (and often night) long – if my parents were lucky and in pocket. Hot water for tea came by boiling water on the living-room fire in one large kettle, which always contained two sea-shells

---

* 'Openshae' was first listed in 1237 whilst 'Mamecaester' was the name in Anglo-Saxon Chronicle records of 925 AD for a Roman fort, referenced in the Domesday Book of 1087 as applying to Manchester.

(for scale prevention) brought back from holidays in Blackpool. Since little boys had short trousers then (in the 1920s and 1930s) every morning I had to wash hands, face and legs in cold water.

The fireplace in the living room was absolutely pivotal to our existence. It always had my grandfather in his rocking-chair on the left, my father on the right and mother, wherever she could get in. I usually sprawled on the mat between their feet. The fire was deep, glowed red and this depth made it marvellous for toasting bread. Beside the hob for the kettle, there was an oven and in it, all bread, cakes, pies, etc., were baked. In the early years, we had no rugs or mats, just plain scrubbed boards or 'oil-cloth' (cheap linoleum). Then, my parents suddenly started to make mats, or carpets, about 3 ft. × 2; they cut up dresses and coats selecting small bright pieces and attached them to a black 'wrapper' backing. They looked lovely and colourful, especially on Friday evenings (when weekly pay-packets were produced) in front of freshly polished brass fire-irons. Polishing was usually performed on Monday evenings, the fire-irons set on the couch, with newspaper over and under them – where they were left until late Friday afternoon when they were transferred again to the front of the fire and where I also used to wrestle with our mongrel dog, Judy. The whole of the fireplace was usually 'black-leaded' and polished to improve its appearance for the weekend. A fine brass screen across the 'ash-hole' always completed the scene. The fire, however, seemed to need endless poking and the accumulated ash beneath needed to be removed to the large dust-bin in the yard. On the opposite side from the 'coal place', were two cupboards, the top one contained all our comestibles: we 'set the table' from it. The second, lower cupboard was a disgrace. All the old newspapers were consigned to its shelves but found their way into the bottom. The lower walls were everywhere cracked and beetles lived in them – mixed with fallen plaster. Saturday nights when my parents and I returned from a visit to the Manchester open street market, immediately we entered the house and put on the gas light, on looking into the fireplace hearth we saw a gathering of one-inch long black beetles; some were pale white, having become covered with white plaster dust. I suppose they were attracted by the heat of the fire.

Lighting in these houses was by gas mantle; only our main living room and the 'parlour' had these, very fragile, mantles. I remember the installation of a wall switch for gas for the first time. In the bedrooms we simply had a small naked jet of gas.

My grandparents I never knew to 'bath'. There was a small, pantry-like cell, off our living room and under the stairs, into which coal was brought; if it was delivered by the hundred-weight (cwt.) sack, by a 'coalman', his big dirty step-marks to this cell from the front door through the living room drew many lusty reproofs. The coal cell stored, perhaps, three cwt. of coal and served as the spot to which Father Christmas delivered his presents. I had to pretend surprise to find chocolate figures on newspaper on the floor in this place, once a year.

On occasion, we might run out of coal and then I would be sent off to the coal yard, about 100 yards away, clutching one shilling and eight pence for 1 cwt. of 'nuts' – small pieces of best burning coal. This might be already contained in a sack, but if not it was shovelled out into a large dirty sack, placed on one pan of a very large steel-yard (balancing machine) and weighed out. It was heaved off the pan and put into a small truck – a box on two wheels with a handle – which I had then to pull home; and it was no easy matter negotiating pavement edgings, up or down! But so young, you learned about kinds of coal and coke and saw the principle of the steel-yard in action.

Almost opposite our house was 'The Mission' – sent by Higher Openshaw to us in Lower Openshaw – a simple building or hall equipped with chairs and tables, stage and curtains, some lavatories and kitchens – in which meetings could be held. They held funeral dinners in it, Sunday school meetings, prize-giving ceremonies, put on plays, congregated scholars for Whit-week walks and held weekly temperance meetings, with a little singing and a strong advocacy of temperance. I remember a Mr Underhill, a large speaker, being introduced by the church minister. 'Mr Underhill has come to talk to you about not drinking when you get older. He has a very large heart as you can see, with a lot of little places in it for everyone.' He was speaking to a collection of perhaps 30–40 ten-year-olds.

The Salvation Army also held meetings here from week to week and showed silent films about their work in foreign parts. As these affairs were free to all-comers, you could bank on getting in although it was always a fight to do so and to secure a front seat.

Throughout the week there were also Scout and Cub meetings and the equivalent for girls. Later in the evening there was a practice in drilling and marching, and for an hour, a band practice, all bugles and drums. For the young cubs, earlier in the evening there was marching and working for badges to win and wear. On the table there were jerseys, neckerchiefs, caps and woggles to be bought and for the church there were small subscriptions to be paid. On average, we paraded as one unit around the neighbourhood about every other week. Once a year too, we marched and paraded at Belle Vue Zoological Gardens and took part in the All-Manchester competition for band and parade. On 11 November we paraded similarly around the several war-memorials in our home district. At the various rolls of honour for those killed in the First World War, a march was played and the 'last post' sounded, followed by the laying of a wreath of poppies. A two-minutes silence was observed. The names of the local men who had died were often simply chipped into a stone slab and mounted on the side of a house, a few feet off the ground. (And I remember when I newly joined the troop – aged seven – as a marching member, our group marched from church, across the main road, up the street of my home and past its front door – presumably for my mother's benefit!)

In these years I was allowed to go to the 'pictures' (cinema) alone. Monday night I always went to 'The Roy', known as 'the bug hut', admission price 2*d*., where I used to sit on one of the wooden forms right at the front almost under the screen. Of course, this was the era of the silent movie. Poor, old and retired folk predominated in the 'tuppennies'. I recall that any conversation in the film appeared as a typed-in caption on the screen. Some of the old folk could not read and friends would read out the captions for them aloud, quietly – but you would hear it if you were sitting near them. It became comical when a screen enemy was about to strike the hero in the back; they would utter their warnings, calling to him, 'Watch that bugger behind you!', when they got too excited.

On the right hand side of the Mission was Knott's Iron Yard. Scrap iron was collected there and anything useful was selected from it before it was passed on for smelting down. It had a huge, horizontal plate-weighing machine which measured loads on entry. A child could wander into the office and play with balancing machinery or typewriters; there would be nobody about to intervene! The firm was run by three brothers, one of whom they said was 'daft'. If you asked him for half-a-crown, he would likely give it to you, whilst the eldest brother would more likely throw you out. On Saturday night, Harry Knott would call into their house a party of children and cook sausages for them! (It was all innocent enough.) Many a journal-bearing did I hammer to get at the brasses within or in a search for ball-bearings which could be used in playing marbles. It was also a marvellous place for finding balls which had been kicked (football) or knocked (cricket) over the wall to land, lost, among the scrap metal. Being a little chap, I could wriggle under the back gate and spend a quiet half-hour when all had gone home, searching for anything interesting. The two crofts on the sides of Knott's premises, full of bricks, stones and other detritus, were our best playing fields for daily cricket and football. (I believe England's best footballers were nurtured on these, pre-Second World War!)

At seven-and-a-half years of age I entered Johnson Street, Elementary School – a gothic building on the edge of a recreation area, which constituted our playground and which was otherwise a park; there were about half a dozen thin-trunk trees along two sides of it. It was surrounded by railings perhaps five feet high, with only two entry points for gates. At the opposite end to the school was a bowling green and two tennis courts. The street which ran along the short side of the school was Barmouth Street Opposite the school end, along and across Barmouth Street, were the public swimming and personal cleaning baths; for 4d. one could have a large bath all to one's self. People used it mostly to have one of their few baths of the year, prior to going on holiday, i.e. to Blackpool, Southport, Morecambe or New Brighton. For 2d., a tot like myself could bathe for ten minutes. This was sheer luxury. Do not forget we had no such entity as a bathroom in those days, in 1929, in our terraced houses. The baths for males and those for females were strictly separated. The female baths were on the first floor whilst the ground floor accommodated single sex swimming pools. These bathing arrangements were conducted by the Manchester Corporation as were the clothes-washing arrangements. I was never allowed to enter the latter lay-out; I simply remember peering into the hot, thick, steamy atmosphere where women with their sleeves rolled-up seemed to be in hell, tending the boilers and stoves and feeding them with personal clothes and bed linen.

Our school consisted of seven classrooms, plus toilets, a headmaster's office, a congregation hall for the whole school and a separate teachers' room for taking meals, writing, exercise marking, and storing their coats.

Regarding school-teaching, I well remember the names of those un-married women who managed classes of just under *sixty*. What magnificent women they were! Pity the poor teachers who can't manage a statutory thirty today. We sat at ancient desks for two, in several parallel lines. No lying down writing with exercise books on the floor, no sitting on the floor or writing on your knee! In the infant school we did have small tables for groups of four or six, but not in the 'big' (elementary) school. Thus we learned to do our sums, to read one after the other along the rows, and silently but determinedly. The female teachers focused attention on what was read out aloud. There was tough Miss Broderick for Standard 1, good-looking Miss Philips for Standard 2 and Miss Mather, like a giant octopus glowering over and dominating Standard 3. *She* wore a wig – so we youngsters thought. Who could love her? No prettiness, no oil-painting! Yet Mr Wimeraugh used to have lunch with her in the classroom from 12 to 1.30 p.m. They used to do newspaper crossword puzzles and you could find pencil markings on the tablecloth showing how they had tried out solutions to clues.

Miss Philips was a winner with the boys; we all liked her. Young, good figure, bright smiling blue eyes. Of course she was quite good at dealing out punishments. She would thump your back – hard – as you sat in your double-desk and to reduce the force you bent out of the way of her fist. She often had to lean heavily to the far side of the desk and alas, her skirts would then rise showing her legs and even her knickers. But it was she who first told us the story of the Spanish Armada with such vividness we sat rivetted on the top of our desks as Drake set off from his game of bowls on Plymouth Hoe to confront the Spanish dons – first lesson in spirited nationalism!

Whilst in her class, we once had to have the headmaster stand-in to teach when she was ill. We learned about Northwich, Nantwich and Middlewich as centres for salt-mining in Cheshire. He wrote these facts immaculately in chalk on a blackboard. We were required to copy them neatly into our books. (I remember it was in this class or year that we first learned to do joined-up writing – and something of a fuss it was about very little!) Alas, I made more than six copying errors and, along with two or three other pupils I had later to report to the headmaster's office where our copying had been marked. We were given six strokes with a leather strap for this. It left an impression on me. Old Holmes, our headmaster, always appeared in well-pressed trousers, wearing spats and dark spectacles. He would march up corridors, feet splayed – or as the boys said, 'set at ten to two' – his hands clasped behind him – a veritable terror. In my last year at his school I used to take the official school mail for posting. I read what I could of his mail, usually postcards to the Manchester Education Committee. Typically, he told them that he would need, '... Two new Cleaners, scrubbing brushes and buckets', and described the painting he required to be done and windows to be repaired, etc., etc. It gave me a useful insight into the running of a school. His job was not all teaching!

In this primary or elementary school I was first introduced to examinations and, to this day, can recall class positions, so important were they made to seem. There were two examinations per year, one before Christmas and the other at the academic year's end, in July. Once marked, we wrapped our foolscap-sized examination scripts in newspapers we had brought in from home for the purpose.

These assembled, a summary form for the results was added: parents were required to sign this and add any opinions they might have. This lot was bundled up and carefully taken home. The very first one I took home – I was third, in Standard 1, was duly signed by my father, with his added comment, 'All mistakes due to carelessness'. There was never room for sentiment in the Johnson household. (I remember one poor boy's parents objecting that not enough ink had been provided for their son to answer all the questions! As a monitor, I collected returned parents' signed sheets and took the opportunity to read them all.)

I ought to record something that should give the post-Second World War generations something to think on. As the monitor for several of my class teachers, I often called and marked (but did not counter-sign) the class register. On average, out of a class of 50 or 60 pupils, no more than three would be marked as 'absent'. About twice a year on a Friday morning, the headmaster's messenger would take a note to each class teacher for him or her to read aloud to all the class, saying, 'The headmaster wants all boys to be present this afternoon. If you do this the whole school (over 400) will have had no absences this week and will be top of all the schools in Manchester.' And the school usually made it! About the only event I can recall of Standard 3, apart from being slightly afraid of the tentacular (or so it seemed) Miss Mather, was of being given a single lecture on Nature – simple biology. I found it fascinating: it was the only mention of this topic in five years at that school. I remember too that I had some weeks off school around Christmas, with mumps. Confined to bed, my grandmother took over, as usual. There was little medicine, but her own medical treatment was to blow powdered sulphur down my throat – with near lethal consequences for me, it seemed! Her cure for a cold on the chest was to fasten to it brown paper on which candle grease had been rubbed. At this time, I recall consuming jars and jars of cod-liver-oil and malt.

In Standard 4 we changed over to male teachers and my first one was a splendid Irishman of about 30, Mr Henry: over six feet tall and well-proportioned, he had strong features and always presented himself well in a suit, a stiff white collar and tie. He was a fine example to the undersized and underfed lot we were. We had a variety of things on our feet, galoshes, Wellingtons and boots. No 'low-quarters' or shoes: a few came in little football boots. Short trousers could be all kinds of lengths: knees were well-washed to different degrees of whiteness. Jerseys, with little scruffy ties, well sucked at the ends, covered our upper bodies. No one wore any underpants, and vests were a rarity; hair was lucky to have been combed. So, Mr Henry taught us Measures – tons, hundredweights, quarters, pounds, and ounces; then inches, feet, yards, fathoms, rods, perches, poles and chains (22 yards – a cricket pitch length), furlongs (220 yards), miles and leagues. We also had guineas but largely pounds, shilling and pence, and farthings, often to be multiplied by three-figure numbers, as were quantities in the other units. Most of us knew the multiplication tables up to the twelve times table (and at that time there were 12*d.* (pence) in one shilling) off by heart – and had done since the end of Standard 2. Teachers might try to trick you. 'What are the factors of 23?' Miss Mather would ask. No answers. You were chancing your arm (or life) to give one! If you were wrong she would come down on you like the proverbial ton of bricks. So, you hesitatingly put up your hand. 'There aren't any, Miss'. In Standard 4 I remember, we 'did' areas – and I had an argument with schoolmaster Mr Henry as to whether you found the area of two contiguous rectangles as the sum of the two pieces or by using differences. I opted for the former, arguing that addition is always easier than subtraction.

It was in this class that on Monday afternoons we went to Every Street Museum. We walked a mile – a long line of little pairs – crossing the Red Rec(reation) over the railway bridge and into Ancoats, another of the 'pits' of Manchester. In the museum we had a magnificent lady teacher: we sat around a copy of a Greek sculpture and she told us the usual connected mythology. She also talked, I remember, specifically of how swift-footed Atlanta had lost a race to Milanion who had deliberately dropped golden apples which she stopped to pick up – and thus had to become his wife. For every story she told, we were taken and shown an appropriate sculpture. I thought then and still do today, what a splendid innovation it was. At the end of the term, for my age, I knew a lot about the Greek gods and goddesses and what they stood for, about Homer, Ulysses, Troy and the Wooden Horse. I felt I had real contact with Athens, Sparta and Greece. And for the last few weeks of our term we went on to listen to stories of the Norse Gods, of Beowulf including its famous dragon, Grendell and 'bad man Loki'. A useful half day each week was also spent in a nearby special school learning how and when to make certain carpentry joints, practising with chisels, saws and the like, and learning the importance of establishing a reference 'face side' to the wooden block one worked on. 'Manual' was the title of this activity. Some schools, in the winter evenings, were opened up and turned over to youngsters who were interested enough to go along and make useful objects such as aspidistra plant-stands. Some of the classes were set aside for board games and there were others where one could play handball. And all at no charge!

As a small boy I played football and cricket for my elementary school and on Saturday mornings competed with similar schools. Our under-eleven (years of age) cricket team won the Manchester School Championship in 1933. I fielded at square leg and was a change-bowler. But in football we were often beaten – physical size (or maturity) was a very important factor.

I went to Old Trafford, Manchester too, to see Lancashire Cricket Club at the time when Eddie Paynter was a national hero for scoring 90 runs for England in a test match even though he was ill. I was not taken with test cricket, one was too far from the pitch to be able to see the action clearly. Much more attractive was following Manchester City Football Club in their great years just before the Second World War. I remember they lost in the Cup Final to Everton one year, won the Cup the next year and then the Championship of League Division 1 after that. I used to know the names of all the members of the teams. Games were much better attended then than they are now. At City's ground, Maine Road, I was present when they packed in 84,000 – nearly all standing. It was a Cup round and the game played was against Stoke City. Boys were passed or toppled forward over the heads of men, by hand from the rear of the standing crowd of men down to the edge of the pitch. It was rough handling as I well knew, being once subject to it. I heard tell, but never experienced it, that as men were unable to get out of such a crowd to go to the toilet, one could experience a warm liquid trickling down one's leg coming from a neighbour. It was very interesting too to watch a 'wave' pass downward from the top of a crowd to the pitch. Standing on the edge of a terrace, one could be carried forward off it, this loss of potential energy becoming kinetic energy in the wave, the pressure inside it suddenly mounting to a heavy crush with a downwards surge of several feet. In later life I often thought about how to calculate that wave speed. It seems that later on crash barriers were introduced to prevent this phenomenon. In those days, incidentally, Manchester United were 'nowhere'. As kids we said they were the strongest team in the second division — firmly at the bottom holding up all the other teams!

I may add that boys from working class families throughout the country tended to play football with almost any size or kind of available ball on the paved streets of the communities they lived in. The professional players in the first division Football League were then all paid at the same rate — £8 per week — two or three times as much as they would make as journeymen, or 'fitters', in a factory.

In Standard 4 in school we were offered, occasionally, visits to hear the Hallé Orchestra in the Free Trade Hall, for a few pence. It wasn't a success, for none of us had any familiarity with Beethoven or Bach, etc. Better was the opportunity to be taken into Manchester to see and hear for the first time, Godfrey Tearle in a wonderful production of *Julius Caesar*, and later, just a little less so, in a production of *As You Like It*. Many years later, I met him in 1947, performing before the troops in Milan, Italy.

Perhaps the school's finest effort was the offer of free tickets for the warm, well-furnished Children's Reading Room and Library in the adjacent district of Bradford. That year, I believe I spent most of my evenings between 5 and 8 p.m., reading all Percy Westerman's books about life with Drake on the Spanish Main as well as books by G. H. Henty. My father recommended my reading *Masterman Ready*, but I found it dull.

This is a suitable point at which to describe a street event that could only take place in areas of terraced housing where the population is dense. It concerns an annual experience in Lower Openshaw which has now declined — Guy Fawkes night. For days before 5 November, youngsters collected anything that would burn from shops and homes and piled it high against a blank wall amid the houses in the street. My father was looked-to to produce some small coils of wire from his company, for free. This was stretched across the street at a height of about ten feet, as tightly as possible. A Guy Fawkes effigy would be hung from the sagging cable over the fire, late in the evening when it was at its brightest. Making a Guy Fawkes model was quite a task. I made one for each of three years, between the ages of ten and twelve. I learned to construct the effigy by starting with a wooden frame (five pieces) and a sack. Then, using the best male cast-off clothing one could lay one's hands on, the arms, legs and body were stuffed and a mask was fastened to the top of the frame. Exclamations were common, observing that the figure which was to be burned in your father's old clothes, looked very much like him! These were always great occasions, as many mams and dads turned out – roasting potatoes and chestnuts in the fire. I never knew a single person to be hurt or burned by the fireworks, yet we lighted and threw around halfpenny 'little demons' and 'rip-raps'.

When we first moved to Higher Openshaw, to an estate of semi-detached properties, I endeavoured to preserve contact with my friends in Lower Openshaw who were three miles down the road, nearer to Manchester centre, by fashioning a rather large-size Guy Fawkes. This I transported by tram car. The guard would not allow me to take it in among the passengers but directed me to place it on the running platform behind a highly surprised driver. There this large figure could be seen by passers-by as we sped along, lying there like a drunken man. Halfway through the journey, the car was stopped and a policeman appeared, intending to arrest the semi-reclining drunken lout at the front with the driver. However, the figure had a right to be there, since I had paid for it as luggage.

Guy Fawkes nights were seldom seen in the new lower middle class districts. As with football, there was no such action possible in the 'avenues' in the new area. With smaller families and less dense housing, outside team play was very difficult.

Monday was washing-day. When I came home from elementary school at dinner (now lunch) time, the streets were difficult to negotiate. There would be large sheets and blankets etc. hung out to dry. (And of course there were no cars, so traffic was not a problem.) Dinner would consist of whatever was left over from Sunday dinner. At grammar school I used to have to take sandwiches. In that case lunch was two rounds of bread and Sunday's meat – invariably surrounded with hard white fat; and therefore frequently not eaten by me. On Monday evenings it was either go to the dog track with my parents or visit my Grandma.

On the occasions I did go to the dog track I generally had little to do except watch the greyhounds chase the hare around the track once every half hour. I learned about 'prices' or the odds in betting. I used to follow 'favourites' – 'Great Chum' was mine – he frequently won. You could collect betting cards to form number sequences, or you could stand back and watch the book-makers and their assistants changing the prices offered as the amounts laid on a dog changed around the ground. My turn came at the end of the evening's racing when we left the track; we had the back of our hands stamped with the date and then left one section of Belle Vue to go to another for the fireworks display (see Figure 1). To be let in you had to roll up your sleeve and show the date stamp. We gathered together around the edge of the lake. First there was a simple display of fireworks, rockets, 'flowers', pin-wheels, big bangs and Roman candles. That finished, quietness descended until broken by martial music. We had a place on the edge of the lake with a wooden exhibition floor behind – on which open-air dancing could take place, military works bands and bugle bands played, and other kinds of parades were performed at different times. Alongside this latter were 'stands'. The upper floors (open air) were all seats and for a price you could watch a parade from on high or the firework displays from a distance. No matter, we ignored the stands and stood to see, over to the other side of the lake, fort scenery; it was usually French, with lots of blue flags. It filled with

Figure 1. Aerial view of Belle Vue, 1957.
This Belle Vue picture/diagram was made up after 1957 when some changes had been made to it after the end of the Second World War. It still gives a good impression of how it looked in pre-war days.

soldiers in blue and white uniforms, a few on horses. They carried arms and seemed to be firing at an enemy in the distance. After a few minutes there would be movement on the extreme right and slowly the red and white soldiers would appear and return the fire. The next action was the carrying of boats, into which the troops loaded themselves. Then followed the oars, and there was a rowing across the lake and landing alongside the fort. They seemed to get mixed up with the French as in-fighting developed. Meanwhile the music – brass band style – continued and the air became literally blue with gunsmoke (fireworks of course). At some time later the General arrived with a British flag, his party carrying it on high and marching through the fort. The French were beaten and capitulated! All this was advertised as General James Wolfe (1727–59) at the Battle of Quebec, Canada, and the Plains of Abraham, in 1759 – where he was, in fact, killed in battle. The ovation was always tremendous; it was all executed in half an hour and one learned a little 'history'.

For some reason, one evening I did not accompany my parents to 'the dogs' and for the want of something to do, took myself off to visit my grandma: she lived two hundred yards away, up some rather small 'entries' – passages between back-to-back houses – a short but unpleasant journey that was always a little threatening because the passages were so narrow. I found my Gran alone, sitting by the fire. She knew what I had come for – my weekly penny (1d) and a barm cake (muffin) baked earlier that day. She had her glass of beer at hand and was pleased to see me. The usual banter between us was exchanged.

While searching for the barm cake I looked through her copy of the Sunday issue of *The People* (at home we took the *Empire News*); I came across a puzzle in the children's section – a small black three-inch sided square, divided into about a dozen irregular pieces, which had to be cut out and reassembled to make a picture. Five prizes of two shillings and sixpence were to be given for the best efforts. I tore out the section from the newspaper and half-an-hour later went home. I had never before attempted such a puzzle but on this occasion thought to see what I could do. I cut out the pieces and played around with them for a few minutes, coming up with 'A coal man, carrying a sack of coal on his back'. It was easily recognisable as such, even though the individual pieces were straight-sided. The assembled picture was to be affixed to a postcard and despatched to Fetter's Lane, London. I was lucky to find a clean postcard in my home. (Written communications from our home didn't exceed half-a-dozen a year – just to book or reserve holiday bedrooms at Blackpool, to a friend in hospital, or for a very special birthday.) The pieces were to be stuck on, firmly. Of course, we did not have any true glue! And thus I went on to use the next best thing I knew, which was thick, tinned condensed milk, which dried hard; and the little picture was slightly warmed before the fire to make sure no part would fall off. In the half-hour remaining, my name and address was added and that to which the entry was to be sent. The 'post tram car' (it carried a mail bag and guaranteed delivery in London the following morning) ran up Ashton Old Road each evening, passing our street about 9.30 p.m. En-route to intercepting it, a one penny stamp had to be collected from the machine alongside the post-box, the post office having closed at 7 o'clock; so with the postcard stamped, I caught the tram car. Delivery from the post office pillar box would not get the card to London on time (first post Tuesday). The following Sunday, when I checked *The People*, my name was there, one of the five big prize winners of 2s. 6d.!

My family learned of 'the win' without congratulation – what did that long word mean in those days? – except for my grandfather, who commented to Grandma: 'So the little bugger won two shillings and sixpence for a penny's Saturday spends. And a better bloody return I'll bet than 'is Mam and Dad got on the whole of Monday night, betting at the dogs!'

Betting was a relatively big activity in our household. My parents and grandfather (my mother's father), George – or 'Enry – which was how my brother and I came to refer to him, would sit around the coal fire in the evening, George reading the section on racing in the *Daily Express*, my mother paying attention to *The One o'clock* (a 1d. single sheet, horse-racing newspaper obtainable only in the middle of the day), and, most frequently, my father of course studied the *Form Book* which covered the races run by horses and gave details of their performances throughout England, describing the prevailing weather on each course and the 'going', i.e. whether it was wet, cold or warm and the ground hard or soft. The expectation was that these studies could improve the predictability of a horse's performance.

Betting slips at my home were written out by my mother and grandfather and 3d. or (mostly) 6d. was backed on 'fancied' horses; they were prone to picking up tips at work in the market in the centre of the city, in the early morning. The name of a horse alone could recommend it – some tip – or a horse was often suggested to my mother by God! The name of the horse was stated and, I think, the place and time of the race. Betting slips usually carried a signature – my grandfather was just 'George', my mother signed as 'Willie' and my father, just 'J.J.'. The task of placing the bets was frequently my responsibility on return to afternoon school. I usually took two slips to Tommy Pearson. He was the book-maker and stood for an hour or so, between 12 and 2 o'clock, on the back steps of somebody's back doorway in a rear entry. I would take a quick glance up the entry, between the rows of terraced houses, to make sure there were no policemen or 'DIs' (Detective Inspector) in the vicinity, race up to Tommy or his man and *en passant*, place small coins and the betting slips, in his hand. There was always a 'look out' man of Pearson's on the prowl, as the police would 'pinch' a book-maker and his collector if they were caught receiving money. Rumour had it that Pearson actually agreed to be caught once or twice a year – the police got their arrest and Pearson was then left alone and without fear of being interrupted for the rest of the year, for the price of a small fine. When the *Evening Chronicle* or *News* arrived at my home about 5.30 p.m., the racing results were quickly found – including the STOP PRESS results – and the final odds noted. If we won at, say 7–1, a simple calculation on a sixpenny bet suggested our winnings were 7 x 6d plus the stake. I would be sent to collect the winnings, if there were any, at the same place as I had left the bet, though usually after dark. One simply arrived and asked for 'George's winnings', for example, and collected them – they were very trusting at the pay-out! My reward was to be paid one ha'penny for the afternoon and evening errand.

Some bets were complicated. Only achieving a 'place' (that is in coming in the first three) was bet upon, according to some simple rules. Daringly, some betting slips informed the bookie that if a placed bet was a win, then all the winnings were to be used as a stake on a certain horse in a subsequent race. It was not unknown for people to specify a further 'all up' on a third horse. In all this there was some elementary arithmetic to be practised and an elementary introduction to the laws of chance made plain. Stories circulated that a few punters had won one hundred pounds by this last route!

My grandfather went to horse-racing meetings at York and Grange-over-Sands once or twice a year. Apparently he assisted book-makers as a 'tic-tac' man. He would signal more text to other book-makers, or receive it from them, that the odds on a certain horse were changing. If the betting on a horse increased, the odds offered by a book-maker would be reduced to protect his 'bank', i.e. reduce his risk. I gathered that advantage could be taken of 'tic-tac' price movements, if one could 'read' or break into the 'arm' conventions being flashed around the course. I could usually tell if my grandfather had done well at a race meeting by his state of inebriation when he arrived home!

In a journey to the North in later life, I used to call into the ancient church at Grange-over-Sands, to look at the underside of the seats in the choir stalls, where one could find quite un-Christian grotesque carvings – the Misericordia. My interest in these came from a small leaflet my grandfather had brought home and passed on to me, saying he was sure it was 'the kind of thing' I would be interested in! I looked often for these sorts of items in the North of England but have never found more or indeed reference to any.

Still on the subject of betting, I venture the following story about how I used it to enlarge my library. In a Technical Library I had come across Sherwood Taylor's* *Inorganic Chemistry* and, to a degree, found it interesting. I was at the grammar school at the time, in my second year, and had just started Chemistry. Now, it so happened in my home that 'pool' betting on soccer had been taken up by my grandfather and mother. Littlewoods sent a sheet of the games football clubs in England and Scotland played against one another each weekend. The punter needed to predict their outcome – win, lose or draw. You marked '1' for a home win, '2' for an away victory and '3' for a draw. For, say, a dozen games selected by the book-maker, here Littlewoods, you filled in on a coupon your predictions and returned it with a postal order to pay for the bet. On Saturday evening, as results came in on the radio, you marked your sheet. Alas, my family had never won any prize, and there were five levels of dividend. All correct returns – the first dividend – could bring in thousands of pounds, whilst the fifth dividend was small. My grandfather allowed me to fill in two lines for him one weekend and on marking it some days later, found we had a fourth dividend in prospect. Not every week was there a winner and if so lower levels in total points might bring in higher dividends to lower totals. In the event, our dividend was very modest at £20. I received ten shillings, and my grandfather and mother shared the £19 10s. 'Sherwood Taylor' cost seven shillings and sixpence, so I became the proud possessor of a new volume! In the School Certificate Examination in Chemistry I attained a 'Good' – a B-level pass.

As I was born and lived in Kay Street for twelve years I was drawn to ask, 'Why Kay? Who was Kay?' At elementary school I remember the teacher encouraging us to reflect on street names because they could inform you about your past history. One of my favourites was Grey Mare Lane. Another was Pin Mill Brow. However, I seemed to know of the flying-shuttle, and that John Kay (1733–1764) had invented it, so I supposed it celebrated him as a local technical hero. Much later however I learned of a Kay (1804–1877) who was a Manchester-born, Edinburgh-trained doctor of medicine who did much to show that cholera and such diseases in Manchester were due to the contamination of drinking water with sewage. His help thus improved the situation. (This was twenty years before Sir Joseph Bazalgette (1819–91) got to work to do the same for London.) This same Kay was also very influential at the time in securing a start in education for the poor classes of people by establishing a training college for pupil-teachers, around 1840. He also wrote much on social issues and education and served on committees about scientific instruction and the advancement of

---

* Director of the Science Museum, London.

science. Kay was knighted for his work and when married in 1842 added to his name the surname of his wife. He is identified today as Sir James Phillips Kay-Shuttleworth and it is my guess that he it is after whom Kay Street was named, following his death. (The area today has been swept away and completely rebuilt.)

John Kay, on the other hand, died a pauper, in France.

CHAPTER III

Grammar School

MANY ASPECTS OF GRAMMAR SCHOOL EDUCATION are common to all of us and there is no need therefore to describe it as such, so I restrict myself to making specific observations.

The school I joined had about 700 pupils, arranged in four forms, up to and including the School Certificate (SC) year, a fifth form for SC repeaters, and two sixth forms for the two years at Higher School Certificate level. The first-formers in my year were in seven groups of about 30 boys in each – from 1A to 1G – an intake of about 200. Masters could be seen to be perturbed if there were more than 30 in a class. By the SC year, i.e., fourth year, there remained a 4A and 4B Science, 4 Modern and 4 Craft, so that roughly half the number that started three years previously had left by the time they were fourteen or fifteen – a startling statistic. 4A Science and the 'Arts' (or 4 Modern) pupils were expected to achieve their SCs; sadly, very little was expected of or achieved by the others. Again, scarcely one third of the entrants survived to gain the SC. (This was the origin of Headmaster Holmes' attitude, see p. 17. And we were very much a 'working class' grammar school.)

All teaching at the grammar school, I believe, was good – though there could be great differences. All teachers had degrees – and good degrees at that. I remember I was told that a new young teacher would be joining the staff to help in the mathematics teaching and that he had recently graduated with first-class honours. So said Mr J. P. Hindley, M.Sc., our Head of Mathematics, and a man who had clearly studied the principles of teaching. I found Mr Hindley to be an attractive lecturer in that he had a knowledge of the history of his subject too. I remember him describing how, when a cube of gold had been stolen from the temple at Delphi, the Oracle could only placate its god Apollo by replacing it with a cube twice as large. In restoring it, his devotees contributed a block eight times too large, through simply making the sides of the cube twice as long. They were reprimanded and commanded to do as bid. Of course, after thinking about it, they returned with a cube of side-length $\sqrt[3]{2}$ or about 1.26 units. This was sufficiently stimulating for twelve-year-olds! Geography was similarly taught. On my first trip to the USA, 25 years later, as the plane flew into North America over the Laurentian Plain, I looked down and instantly a phrase came into my mind: 'A bloody denudated peneplain!' and the visage of my old geography master, Mr 'Tubby' King, who had taught me that, appeared in my mind.

Literature and languages were not so well presented. I think they are harder to teach than the sciences. An excellent older teacher, 'Ikey' Lawrence, would enliven English by taking a word and following it through several languages with various comments, tracing how a word had come down into French, with variations, from the Latin, and also into Italian or Spanish. Physics and Chemistry were generally well taught and illustrated in labs with special equipment and in circumstances new to me. There was one very curious teacher who wrote and published poetry, plays, and essays on English Literature – and books on *Flame and Combustion*. He had a Manchester *D.Sc.* and his task was to infuse us 'scientists' with a little culture. His name was Oliver Coligny de Champfleur Ellis – and I have told a little more about him on p. 224 below. My overall impressions of the teachers were that they were very competent, hardworking and solidly middle class. I think they often found it hard to be teaching youngsters from such deprived backgrounds as I had.

'How to Decide Your Future Career' might well be the title of the next event! Towards the end of our fourth form year, the headmaster sent a letter to the parents of the ten boys at the head of 4 A Science and 4 Modern. He wrote that he advised parents to have their boys stay on into the sixth form to take HSC in two years, i.e. first year in form VIB and second year in VIA. If parents accepted his offer, he required them to so inform their sons and from them he would collect the information. My parents – and they were not alone – were in deep water. No one had ever 'stayed on' at school to such a great age, to their knowledge. But I was fully committed to it and pressed them. I told them I wanted to 'do' Maths, Physics and Chemistry. Then one afternoon, ten of us were called down to Headmaster E. F. Chaney's office. We lined up in the corridor at the open door. Quickly, boys went in and came out, having said whether or not they wished to prepare for HSC* and if they did, made known their choice to the Head. Before me, in the queue at the door, was short, thick-bodied Conway. I was listening to him respond to the Head's questions and heard him say, Pure Maths, Applied Maths and Physics. No Chemistry? Was that collection of subjects possible? School Certificate Chemistry had been misery to me, though basically I liked the subject. All those lists of properties of acids and gases one had to learn – for a cook or professional technician! ... with no theory behind them, it seemed. Between the door and Chaney's desk I made up my mind and registered with the Head for Pure Maths, Applied Maths and Physics. There were no questions – it was all over in two seconds – and my School Certificate results turned out good enough for me to be able to take the subjects. So that was great and I went forward happy. The way ahead was clear now, and had not been discussed with anyone! I only regretted later never to have read any organic chemistry, which everyone who took the subject later declared to be 'great'. However my overall choice suited me well and I never regretted it.

In the sixth form, in all, there were about eighteen lads. Not all ten invited to stay on did so. Of 4 Modern's ten, only three or four did so. The total in Pure Maths, Applied Maths and Physics was four: Willie Crooke joined us from

---

* The Higher School Certificate. (Today we have A-Levels.)

Ardwick Central School. He intended taking up teaching. Only John Bennett and I intended going to university. And Thurlough, our fourth member, disappeared before the end of the second year. Bennett was good intellectually: he went to Owens College at Manchester University to read mathematics but didn't survive the first year. He wanted to join the Army and entered the Tank Corps. I think he lost interest in working at mathematics which was a great misfortune. Later I heard he had been injured in the war but I never found out what further happened to him beyond the fact that he was farming in Cheshire. The Maths, Physics and Chemistry group was relatively large at about a dozen. A small number of lads joined us from the local central school but I didn't know them intimately. I do not believe there were any from this latter background who survived and went on to university. (One could not then better Manchester University for reputation, apart from Oxbridge. And the start of the Second World War was at hand which discouraged individuals from living away from home.)

Physics was taught by Messrs. Reynolds and Clayton. The latter also lectured us, under the heading of mathematics, on algebraic topics, e.g. permutations and combinations, and he was a physics master with a difference. He would enter the classroom and declare, 'I was in a private room earlier today and fell to calculating the length of a toilet roll.' He kept excellent notes of the historical aspects of some classical topics. (In physics he also used to teach of an evening 'across the road' at the College of Technology (CoT). I think, really, he was wasted in teaching elementary physics.)

As a consequence of the HSC results one youngster only went to Medical School. Two men went into medicine from the year ahead, and one from the year ahead of that – all Jewish – and all eventually became consultants. (I recall the humorous dialogue between two Jewish mothers – 'How does it feel, Mrs A., to have a son who is the President of the United States?' 'Fine! But you know, my eldest son is a doctor!')

Two of our colleagues went into the Faculty of Science at Manchester University, one to read geology and the other mathematics. The geologist I believe became a Reader at a Scottish university, whilst the mathematician left his course at the end of the first year as described above.

Six of us went to the Manchester College of Technology (MCoT), which comprised the Faculty of Technology in the university, one each to Electrical, Mechanical and Municipal Engineering, two to Chemical Engineering and one into Applied Chemistry. All graduated with good Honours degrees. At the time, the MCoT was rated lower than the Engineering Department at Owens College in the Faculty of Science. The great Osborne Reynolds, FRS (1842–1912), the first professor in the department (1868–1905) had brought it enormous prestige with his work on fluids and lubrication. (See *Osborne Reynolds and Engineering Science To-day*, Manchester University Press, 1970, 263 pp.)

The Municipal Engineering Department was somewhat different from the Civil Engineering Department at the 'other place'. The latter was heavily weighted towards structural engineering whilst the former was (humorously) known as 'shit engineering'.

To those who are not clear about what we owe to the latter group of engineers

Figure 1. The Central Grammar School, in 1935, from (a) above: The Park and (b) Whitworth Street.

it is only necessary for them to read Stephen Halliday's *The Great Stink of London*, (Dutton Publishing Ltd, Stroud, 1999, 210 pp.), which is an historical account of Sir Joseph Bazalgette's direction in turning 'the Thames from the filthiest to the cleanest metropolitan river in the world (and which it remains)', between 1858 and 1888. 'Cholera was eliminated from Victorian London by massive engineering works ... completed in the face of appalling difficulties.'*

This Faculty of Engineering at Manchester was housed almost entirely in one huge building across the road from the school, actually across (Sir Joseph) Whitworth Street. In the 1930s it catered almost exclusively for men studying for the Higher National Certificate (HNC) which gave them, when they had passed, registration as professional engineers (after several years in practice) with the Institution of Mechanical Engineers, or with the Civils or Electricals.

À propos the above topics I recall going all of 100 yards, on the spur of the moment, one empty lunch-time to the Registrar's Office in the College of Technology. I asked for a free prospectus; this was two hundred pages or so long but a beautifully turned-out paperback volume. It contained statements of the subject contents of all the courses for all departments, among many other things. A very helpful Deputy Registrar, Mr Coates, asked why I wanted it and I explained that I was from the Central High School and was hoping to join Mechanical Engineering. He thereupon telephoned the Professor (H. Wright-Baker), explained to him my interest, and was asked to bring me to him. In his huge office on the second floor, I met him. He was a fine looking fellow – fit, clearly energetic, nearly six feet tall and wearing a tweed suit with waistcoat and gold watch and chain, with brown boots to match, brightly polished. He gave me his whole attention, asked what I was studying for HSC and seemed delighted. I was with him for a full ten minutes! – and he impressed me very much. That evening I read through the contents of his courses and they seemed well-suited to my interests and inclinations. There were lots of mathematics and basic sciences though I rightly had some apprehensions about engineering design, particularly for the third year. Management, commercial law, production planning and the history of labour relations beckoned me – and later, I was not disappointed (though I had to go to the Industrial Relations Department of which Dr Fenelon was Head for these subjects and about which Wright-Baker was not over-pleased. (It was not *real* engineering science!) My father discerned my inclinations and sensibly did not intervene; he knew well my interest in politics. It was a good idea for me to live at home (cheaper too) whilst attending college; it was 1940 and the nation would soon be in the middle of a Blitz. As well, I (we) believed I must read engineering as it would be the only profession in which I would later be able to get a job, teaching excepted. Who wanted a mathematician, outside the class or lecture room?

It perhaps goes without saying that there were many much better grammar schools in the Manchester area than ours, with long traditions of success and it

---

* One cannot but compare the attitudes and concerns of *The (Oxbridge) Dons* (N. Annan, University of Chicago Press, 1999) with those of engineers in the nineteenth and early twentieth centuries.

was to these that knowledgeable and richer parents sent their offspring. The relative predominance of Jews in our classes was quite conspicuous, many of whose parents were tailors. No Roman Catholics seemed to be present. They had their own grammar school, St Gregory's, at Ardwick Green – and to judge from the outside, their premises were poor, as were the pupils themselves.

The Manchester Central Grammar School was one uniform building divided into two, to separate the sexes. Both halves of the school had minute recreational external areas but the boys were allowed out on the streets at lunch-time, the girls not. There was a coming together of the two schools only for the annual Play. Intercommunicating doors between the two sections were locked, except when the boys, as sixth formers, went for biology lessons with the female teacher, which implies that there was no biology or botany in the boys' school. (It was a general opinion that these few male visitors were made specially welcome by the biology teachers, many of whom were middle-aged spinsters. My brother held that they were women who had lost their prospective partners in the First World War.) Though the sexes were kept separate, in later life one found that many marriages had come about between boys and girls from the two halves of the school – both my brother and I and our wives being examples. We all – the males, for rugger, cricket and football and the females for hockey and rounders – had to take trains or buses out to Parrswood, perhaps four miles out of the city centre. From the dressing rooms to the playing fields was a distance of a kilometre. So there was some small expense and a big waste of time in travelling, leading to a loss of enthusiasm by the time one began to kick a ball. I used to travel into Manchester daily some years later, the train passing alongside Stockport Grammar School, and observed the sports field still adjacent to that school. The total separation of school and its playing field was seen to be a very poor idea when one's football team visited other grammar schools, such as Audenshaw, Bury and Manchester. Ours was a miserable arrangement.

The Central Grammar School was founded in about 1904, so it may have been that a sports field adjacent to the school was not then considered a necessity, though a visit to the independent schools would show the close association of the two to have always been the case. And putting the school in the centre of the town was not such a good idea because the price of land would be too high; see Figure 1. I may mention that only recently did I learn that some state schools had sold off their playing fields to raise funds for certain unspecified educational activities. That this could happen, I found astonishing.

A year or two after the Second World War finished, a collection was raised to purchase an organ in memory of those killed from the Central Grammar School; those of us who survived were pleased to contribute. About ten years ago, when passing my old school building, it occurred to me to enter and to enquire about the organ and to see the Roll of Honour, suspecting that many friends from my school days had been killed in the War and their names would be found on the Roll. It had often been observed that airforce crews were largely recruited from grammar school boys. The Labour Party in the intervening years had, of course, done away with the public grammar schools and my school was now named *The Shiela Simon College*. The Roll of Honour used to be in the school entrance hall, but it was not there now and there was no obvious sign of an organ. I wrote to the Manchester Reference Library, asking what had happened regarding the school and if a history of it had been written. The library acknowledged that, unfortunately, they had no information on these two points – an appalling admission.

CHAPTER IV

The Start of the Second World War

I REMEMBER HELPING MY FATHER to finish installing our air-raid shelter in the garden. It was hard work digging deep in thick, rain-saturated clay. We managed to put in an electric cable for a two-bar electric radiator and we were ready for the war when it came. Nothing much happened until perhaps May 1940. This was the month immediately preceding the Higher School Certificate examinations, when we learned that Holland and Belgium had fallen and the German Army had broken through into northern France. In the middle of a 'practical' in physics when the class of perhaps a dozen was occupied with experimental equipment, the door opened and in came a technician. He went up to Mr Clayton and said, loudly, 'France has fallen'. Everyone heard it. Silence fell on us as everyone stopped what they were doing. We all looked at one another but said nothing. I think it dawned on us all, simultaneously, that we were now quite alone. The war had suddenly become very close and we knew how uncertain the future was. France, alas, had never seemed reliable, with often four changes of government a year. Laval was a Fascist and the government had moved to Vichy; General Pétain, a highly regarded leader during the First World War was looked to to lead, but he was much too old. What happened south of Paris didn't matter to us, but the knowledge that all the coast opposite ours across the Channel was now in German hands, did. Somewhere along the line our own government jettisoned Chamberlain and we got Churchill. His 'We shall fight on the beaches ...' speech lifted us, till we thought, 'with what?' LDVs – Local Defence Volunteer groups – were started overnight, but, said some, all it meant was, 'Look, Duck and Vanish!' Drill was carried out with long brushes instead of rifles – anything of a similar shape sufficed. My father, at work, manufacturing barbed wire, worked through weekends as loads were dispatched to the South coast. All supply for foreign business had long since ceased.

The taking of examinations – HSC in June 1940 – came and went. I emerged in August with two 'Goods' and one 'Credit' (in Physics) in the Ordinary papers; in the Scholarship papers, I got an Unclassified in Applied Maths but a Distinction in Pure Maths. I took the Open (May) Scholarships competition at the University (of Manchester) but couldn't make much of the questions: they were first year degree work. When Mr Hindley, our maths master, wrote out the answers, I recognised that I could have done two questions. I had taught myself to do them – something about the value of the sum of high powers of the roots of cubic

Figure 1. Dr A. Peter Hatton (BSc Hons Mechanical Engineering 1943, and former Reader in the Department of Mechanical Engineering) wrote with this photograph 'Professor Bill Johnson at the 1943 degree ceremony: Left to right: Dr Ben Furber who spent some years on the staff in the Department of Mechanical Engineering and continued to a distinguished career in the nuclear power industry – Dr Peter Hatton, Jack Bell – with whom we lost touch, Professor Bill Johnson, and finally the late Professor Doug Elliott who became Professor of Mechanical Engineering at Aston University but sadly died at rather an early age.' (The author is indebted to Mainstream No.20, Spring, 1996, for the above copy photograph.)

equations – and I had even practised examples at home. But I didn't have the confidence to tackle or touch them in the Open Scholarship examinations. Later, I was interviewed by a small board of professors – as were all who subsequently went across Whitworth Street from school to 'The Tech'* – and somehow came out with a Scholarship for Part Time Students *and others*. It paid £90 a year and was given by Manchester Education Committee. The support was very welcome and I completed two years and nine months for a degree in Mechanical Engineering in June/July 1943. The upset in the universities caused by the war was immense. Some departments went out of existence and others doubled in size almost overnight. Nor was there any staying on and preparing for Oxbridge

---

* Some accounts of the origin of The Tech. (to UMIST) is given in Chapter XIX below.

Scholarships with a third year in the school's sixth form. Young masters were called up and their absence heavily felt.

I first registered for military service in 1940, when I was eighteen years of age, and opted to join the Royal Navy, as my father had done before me. This was not followed up, for on seeing that I was an engineering student, 'they' said, 'Stay where you are and then you will be more use to us after you have graduated.' So that was what I did, and the same thing happened to all my school colleagues of the same age and inclination.

I graduated at the end of July 1943 and joined up on 5 August 1943. I was one of four students who had been admitted to read Mechanical Engineering Honours in October 1940; it was the largest number in the first year since its inception. The following year that number jumped to twenty-three and State Scholarships were given to encourage potential army recruits. The degree awarded at the conclusion of the course was B.Sc.Tech. The degree of B.Sc. was awarded on graduation from the Engineering Department (Civil and Mechanical), in the Faculty of Science. (My school form-master once observed to my father, that this abbreviation 'Tech.' cheapened the degree!) In the year before I was admitted the number of undergraduates was three, and the year before that, one. (In my third year as lecturer at Sheffield University in 1955, there was only one honours graduate in Mechanical Engineering!) The first year work of my degree course was not hard but too often dreary and unexciting. Indeed after only two or three weeks I thought seriously of transferring to Mathematics, but decided that things had already gone too far to pursue that line. Subjects such as Engineering Design and Chemistry for Engineers hardly constituted thrilling material for Saturday morning lectures.

The second year of the degree course was also wearisome and uninspiring, e.g. in giving several methods for determining B.M. (Bending Moment) diagrams in Strength of Materials! These first two years seemed to prepare one to be a good designer-draughtsman. Our third year, however, was very different – more scientific and mathematical. I chose as my two options for the third year, (i) Internal Combustion Engines and (ii) Workshop Planning and Progressing, with the history of Trade Unionism and Mercantile Law.

I might observe that Thomas Bevan's *Theory of Machines*, specifically about chains of links, gears and cams, etc. (essentially the mathematics of different mechanisms), was, I believe, the outstanding volume on the subject for English-speaking students world-wide. Sir Charles Inglis's *Mechanics of Machines* (CUP), was an alternative volume. Bevan was our senior lecturer here at the CoT and Inglis was Professor of Engineering at Cambridge. Bevan's book, I believe, reflected its origins and final purpose, whilst Inglis's book was essentially, an extension of first year engineering mathematics. The two large volumes were very different in presentation and outlook. The point to observe here is that Bevan received no public accolade for having written a long, very well-received volume (549 pp.) which was accepted world-wide.

When in June 1943 my 'year' graduated there were five of us (Jack Bell stayed on from the Ordinary Degree Course). Figure 1 shows us all – it was rated quite a good year.

CHAPTER V

Evacuation

It was 1 September 1939; German armies, after three weeks, had occupied Poland, and Britain and France were under treaty obligation to go to her aid. Germany was informed that if she did not withdraw by 3 September, war would be declared.

On the Friday morning of the 1st I took my young brother, John, who was nine and two-thirds years old, to Varna Street school with his little suitcase and knapsack for 9 a.m. This was not his usual school – St Clements – that was half-a-mile away. I delivered him to the school entrance and said goodbye. He was being evacuated from Manchester. My mother did not take him, she was working in the market as usual. For half-an-hour or so I hung around expecting to see the school children leave for their new evacuation homes, but nothing was happening on the outside and as all was relatively quiet, I simply went home. It was another two weeks before I knew what had happened to him.

Come early Sunday morning the 3rd, I myself was in progress as a seventeen-year-old evacuee. I was half-way through my two-year HSC course: the date coincided with the end of our six-week midsummer vacation. We 'old' sixth formers were each allocated a group of eleven- or twelve-year-old youngsters and bussed with them from school to Manchester's Victoria Railway Station. I, like my pals, was in charge of one compartment of young boys – perhaps twelve. On boarding, a plaintive mother accosted me and begged me to look after her son. She did not know where we were going but I soon learned we were heading for Blackpool. The wholesale packing of a train for Blackpool seemed straightforward and there was no panic or distress. Arrived at Blackpool, we were delivered by bus to Blackpool grammar school where we received a carrier bag of supplies – milk, sandwiches, biscuits, etc., left to satisfy any hunger we had developed, and also re-grouped with our classmates to be delivered to lodging houses. Like common lodger-holidaymakers we were shown a bedroom! Most of us shared a double bed. In our dwelling there were five sixth-formers and three younger fifteen-year-olds. Rooms, linen, towels, toilets and bathrooms etc., were all very clean, but much of the time we did not know what to do with ourselves. My recollection is that the poor householder received about ten shillings and sixpence (it might only have been 7s. 6d.) per person to keep us fast-growing boys, per week. This situation – being on holiday effectively – lasted about two weeks when suddenly, at the weekend, we were transferred to another 'digs' at, I believe,

60 Caunce Street. There was not much difference in our hosts except that they were much younger. The meals provided followed the same pattern as previously – excellent during the first week and then collapsing to a very wearisome level. In particular at our new digs we had 'potato hash' each lunch-time at twelve o'clock; the potatoes were always only half-cooked. There, I first knew indigestion.

I had heard Neville Chamberlain's poignant announcement on the radio on 3 September, that ... as from 11 a.m. that day we were in a State of War with Germany. It was all very ominous. How could an island of 45 million people possibly defeat one of, perhaps 90 million (including Austria)? I remember looking out to sea on the promenade, listening to a mournful dance band tune and thinking that all the lights were indeed slowly being put out ... and wondering what it would bring. My father once remarked, 'If we come out of this lot as we went in we shall be very fortunate.' Things looked very bleak. Some children were sent away to the United States and some were lucky to fall into good 'digs'. Two of my friends, Edels and Raymond, had sumptuous conditions with a well-heeled couple and lived regally! But in view of the never-ending broadcasts and reports nowadays about paedophilia and attacks on small children, why is it that we have no recollection of such things happening in those days?

The severe cold weather in this exceptional year caused freezing and, in our case, the toilet clogged up. We were reduced, when in dire need, to climbing over the school wall to get to a toilet. I remember too that our first two weeks in September, on 'holiday' in Blackpool, were spent on the beach, swimming and playing football as well as visiting the library. Mr Hindley, our old maths master very occasionally came round to inquire how well we were surviving. Wives of schoolmasters appeared, little groups of them formed and could be seen at school, knitting woollies for the Forces or even darning socks for students. I clearly remember nice-looking Mrs Clayton: she must have had quite a time with her cantankerous senior-physics-master husband; they had no children. He told us, frequently, that he had been a captain in the First World War. I remember he took us for sixth form algebra too. He introduced us to the subjects of Complex Numbers and Series; (and he used to write on the blackboard *Bleeding Homework*, white chalk words dripping with red chalk streams in junior forms).

The winter of 1939 was very cold. Even the edge of the sea froze, in Blackpool in December. We used to swim for five minutes in the night's darkness on the beach in front of the Tower, in the nude. This was reported to our Supervisor, Mr Parker, but he didn't see fit to try to stop it. I also then played for the school's 1st eleven football team a few times, but otherwise remember nothing further about sport or lessons.

We shared Blackpool Grammar School with its 'owners', 'weeks about' – working mornings 9 a.m. – 12.30 p.m., or afternoons, 1 p.m. – 4.30 p.m., and six days per week, i.e. including Saturday. Homework was difficult – doing it in the digs' dining room which eight of us shared, all on the dining room table after dinner. The 'old man' in the second digs we had, joined our bridge school and thoroughly enjoyed himself: the game standard was high but it went on at the same time as doing HSC maths and physics homework! We older ones took to going to Blackpool library, which was not too far away, for peace and quietness to study in. The Reference Library was excellent and there were always places at the desks. The excellence of the library was a distraction: for my part I was tempted to browse in the books and remember large portions of Bishop Barnes's* *Science and Religion* and a favourite by Bernard Shaw, *The Quintessence of Ibsenism*. More immediate for me was finding the *Encyclopaedia Britannica* and reading the entry entitled *CURVES*. Now that I had a fair knowledge of the calculus under my belt, I marvelled at the many different plane curves there were, e.g. 'The Witch of Agnesi',† lemniscates, limacons, conchoids, etc., – quite a new world to me. However, as the evening light declined with the approach to Christmas, it could happen that on moonless nights I had to make my way 'home' from the library by feeling and stretching across buildings – remember the black-out was almost total.

The latter Blackpool-Manchester arrangement didn't seem very successful but at least it kept the mass of the school together. The total numbers began to dwindle and evacuation was thought needless, especially as no significant night bombing had occurred. Parents did remove children – not being sure how well looked-after were their little progeny! My parents sometimes sent postal orders for three shillings, to be given to our foster mother. Some parents even sent jars of jam or other items of food, recognising how small were the rations and upkeep rates. My parents visited me once in three months and that was all that was needed; obviously, they visited my younger brother frequently. He ended up with another child in a nice, caring household in the hills near Mossley – well fed and accommodated and barely ten miles from our home in Manchester!

My school returned officially to Manchester and opened up there again about the beginning of February 1940. The first portion of the War, September 1939 to the spring of 1940, is usually written off as the Phoney War, but night bombing came on after the Battle of Britain in the autumn. It interrupted night sleep and work in the daytime but no great damage was inflicted in the north of England. However, bombing did become a fact of every day life as the year went on.

There were bombing raids of some degree most nights, the whirr of the sirens told us so but, apart from a casual event the main aim was towns such as Liverpool, Sheffield and Hull. One such event for me was the evening when a 'stick' of six small 'whistling' bombs was dropped over our heads. As the bombs fell they did indeed whistle loudly – to try to terrorise people. I remember counting them as they hit the earth. The sixth bomb fell in a cricket field just outside my girlfriend-to-be Heather's home. But Manchester's really big night was the 23 December 1940. It began early, at about 6.30 p.m. and went on until 7.00 a.m the next morning. It was primarily an incendiary attack. The whole of the centre of Manchester seemed to be ablaze. It was where all the cotton warehouses were located. One railway bridge was brought down too so that traffic was stopped for two days until the rubble was cleared. The morning after the blitz I walked into the town centre to offer any help I could. As I walked I met a continuous

---

* Believed to have a Cambridge 'first' (i.e. to be a 'wrangler') in mathematics.
† 55 years later I was to write a paper on 'Some Women in the History of Mathematics', of whom Maria Agnesi was one! See *Journal of Materials Technology*, 40 (1994), 33–71.

stream of women pushing perambulators, containing small children and baskets of clothes. It looked as I had seen on film on the roads of France several months before. It was very much the intention to get away from the city centre. People knew the bombing would recommence on the 24th – it was always the pattern. And so it happened, the bombers came in at about 7.00 p.m. and it continued until midnight. Mercifully, the Germans then stopped and did not return on Christmas Day.

Throughout the winter of 1941 we had an occasional day air-raid of short duration, but mostly night after night there were long periods of 'alert' only. Typically, the siren would warn us about 7.30 p.m. and it might well be retained into the early hours of the morning. One slept as best one could in the air raid shelter.

Into this régime went a day or two of fire-watching duty each week and a day per week doing a Home Guard duty, or attending the OTC (Officers' Training Corps) when in the University. Nonetheless, these calls did not divert us from our university courses. As far as I know no allowance for these hiatuses was ever made – or asked for – in respect of examinations or syllabuses to be covered. It was too, no strange matter to pass on the way to the bus stop or tram for College in the morning, a roped-off crater in the middle of the road, displaying a notice, 'Unexploded Bomb' …

CHAPTER VI

Political Opinion

———◆———

POLITICS LOOMED LARGE in our domestic household. Until he had reached the age of forty, I believe my father regretted he had not endeavoured, more positively, to pursue politics as a career. After that age, I think he came to care much more about the future of his two sons. There had never been a certainty that politics would bring him any reasonable income, adequate for 'a married man with two kids', as my mother never let him forget in free exchanges when they had 'words'. Throughout this period of change I frequently argued with him but generally accepted his ideas about the necessity for a fairer Britain which seemed to us only obtainable through a socialistic society.

In 1938, as I went into Form VI Science, the year in which I became sixteen, I was aware of the growth of the ultra-nationalisms of Mussolini, Franco, Hitler and our own Oswald Mosley, to mention only Europe. It is curious how the growth of Fascism outside of Germany at that time hardly seems to be drawn upon by political commentators today, when it comes to discussing Hitler and the Second World War. Mussolini had began early in 1922 – the year of his march on Rome, and continued in the 1930s with the invasion of Abyssinia – using aerial bombs against the spears of Emperor Haile Selassi's troops to achieve a slight increase in the size of the Italian Empire; that also was his reason for invading Albania (not at all mentioned recently by commentators on the wars in the Kosovo region). Spain was undergoing a conquest by Franco, with the help of Mussolini, Hitler and, indirectly I believe, our own non-interventionist Foreign Minister, Lord Halifax. With Hitler's acquisitions of the Saar, the Polish Corridor and Austria, the build-up of Fascist successes caused an alert to be sounded from the far left in the UK and France. Their warnings were much louder than those emanating from Mr Churchill. The Americans were then preoccupied with the 'New Deal' and had no interest in Europe; they were simply very sensitive with respect to the Monroe Doctrine (which disappeared after the Second World War and gains no recollection today); it allowed no interference on the American continent by non-American states. Of course, South America was heavily influenced and still is in some parts by American capital. Outside of Europe, there was Japan, which also had had colonial ambitions in Manchuria and China since the mid-1930s. Even France had its difficulties with Fascism; as I have recalled elsewhere, throughout the 1930s it had three or four new governments each year – a state of affairs that made it incapable of mounting serious opposition to German aggression.

My growing awareness of the mounting troubles, especially in Western Europe, was similarly the concern of half a dozen of my school colleagues who emerged as Socialists and then, mostly, later on shifted into the Communist camp. Several of them were Jews, one of whom underwent a name change from Appenschlak to Appleton. Nearly all of them engaged in school debates to denounce the Fascists. There was also a much smaller tendency to note that Stalin was not beyond criticism. At the time of some of Stalin's mass murders (about which there was uncertainty), we were enraged by the report that several engineers installing equipment in Moscow, who were in the employ of the large and local Manchester electrical engineering firm, Metro-Vickers, were arrested and tried in Moscow in 1937, for alleged political misconduct and espionage. Thankfully, they were subsequently released.

In this year, Victor Gollancz's Publishing Company started the Left Book Club, and on behalf of my colleagues, I joined it for its monthly volume. I remember one such which had the arresting title, *Guilty Men* – with a red hard back. When I received it, I endeavoured to read it rapidly and then to pass it around our group. After some months, 'financial support' for it declined, so that I couldn't pay the subscription any longer, at which point my father seemed to take it over, and without comment, it was stopped.

In 1940 at the CoT, I joined Soc. Soc. (the Socialist Society) and became its Treasurer, but resigned in my third year because there was pressure on me to join the Young Communist League. At other universities, others were deeply into politics, and it is from this morass that Philby, Burgess and Maclean emerged. How they allowed themselves to be led so far astray and how they could be so de-coupled from their families and friends, is difficult to understand. Perhaps it owes much to school and to class?

Socialist meetings were held from month to month in a variety of small halls in the centre of the city. One heard comrades who had recently returned from Spain, having served in the International Brigade. Even priests in ecclesiastical garb were not afraid to appear on a platform, as were also a few professors, such as J. B. S. Haldane, at *Aid for Spain* meetings. I still have in my mind a picture of Haldane arriving, cap-in-hand, halfway through a meeting, having come up to Manchester from University College London (UCL), by train. One read his books on sound, popular, scientific subjects. He was quite an outstanding figure for youngsters like me who were preparing for HSC. There were appeals at these meetings for money for Spain to support socialist colleagues. I witnessed men holding up wage-packets to start up a collection – from pound notes down to a one penny piece.

At the CoT early on in 1942 or 1943 we had a political speaker – who was I believe – the communist Harry Pollitt, addressing an afternoon meeting when it was interrupted by an air raid warning. It was broken off and we all trooped into the College basement shelters, where, after a fashion, the meeting was continued. There was then a strong call to 'Open the Second Front Now!'. It was due to the fact that the pact made between Hitler and Stalin in 1939 had released Fascist war against the West. Germany felt free to attack Poland and then France and Britain. Of course, after failing to take Britain, Hitler had no hesitation about suddenly breaking the pact and assailing Russia. Somewhere in this period, probably in 1942 or 1943, at a meeting, I heard a young communist colleague speak from the floor of a hall, calling, 'What does it matter if we lose a million men and relieve Russia?' – which was certainly going a little far! I recall later, with amusement, that the speaker graduated and joined a research group in the armaments industry; he did not go in search of a place in the first invasion barge on 6 June 1944!

In these years Penguin books were new and still priced at 6d. or 9d., books which did a great deal to enhance the education of the masses, by such as Professor of Classics, Benjamin Farrington, author of *Greek Science* in the Pelican series. And one should never forget the excellent Everyman series, hardback classics at two shillings a time. For my part, I remember my first purchase for a sixteenth birthday, Karl Pearson's *The Grammar of Science*. He was a mathematician who followed and completed Isaac Todhunter's work on the history of elasticity and later on, one who developed statistical methods when in his professorial chair at UCL. He was a very distinguished scientific hero for me throughout the whole of my life, one whose name and reputation have always shone brightly.

I remember 'picking up' large thin books for a few pence from the Shude Hill market in Manchester and on bric-à-brac stalls across the main road from my home. I bought one book which was a translation of *The Theory of Recapitulation* by Professor Ernst Haekel (1834–1919), of the University of Jena. He had clearly been inspired by Darwin's work and his theme was, 'Ontology recapitulates Phylogeny', meaning loosely, that a present-day biological form as it develops in embryo, recapitulates the earlier forms of previous ages (which theme has never been totally accepted). Another book in the same series was *The Evolution of the Idea of God* (1911) by Grant Allen (1848–1899). The latter two books came, I believe, from the Rationalist Society – and so were science-political.

In the same category, a conspicuous and influential volume for me and one which had a certain notoriety, was Joseph McCabe's account of his *Twelve Years in a Monastery* (1897), written some years after he had become a lapsed Roman Catholic priest.

And yet another name of frequent occurrence was that of Ray Lancaster (b.1847), an author with 'progressive' views on popular biology.

A name very well received in the pre-war days was that of John Strachey. His pamphlet on '*Why you should be a Socialist*' struck a good note with many young people.

J. B. S. Haldane was a name which caught on and influenced us all greatly, as I have indicated elsewhere.

Very well regarded with us, and a biologist by profession, but truly an all-rounder, was Lancelot Hogben. His *Mathematics for the Million* and *Science for the Citizen* were of very great influences on the thinking man. Heather bought me Hogben's *Dangerous Thoughts* for a 21st birthday present. (And I bought her for her 21st, *Science for the Citizen*). The latter were outstanding volumes concerned with politics, mathematics, history and biology. (An excellent 40-page biography of Hogben which can be recommended is that by G. P. Wells in the *Biographical Memoirs of the Fellows of the Royal Society*, Vol. 74, 1978.)

H. G. Wells too was a great favourite of mine, not for his *War of the Worlds*, but for his *Work, Wealth and the Happiness of Mankind*, his *Outline of World History* and his large volume, *Outline of Biology* (with his son G. P. Wells and Julian Huxley). These were central to my education. If I had to select a personal/intellectual hero or father-figure in my formative years it would be the Wells of these three books. I remember determinedly reading his *Biology*, days before sitting my Finals.

There were many who influenced and guided my thinking – Bertrand Russell and C. E. M. Joad particularly – too many to mention.

In literature I remember that James Joyce's *Portrait of the Artist as a Young Man*, reflected my own inward feelings, and that somehow, by contrast, I acquired a great regard for Anatole France's literary prize winning French novels, e.g., *The Revolt of the Angels*, as well as Robert Graves's historical novels.

The task of reviewing the particular influence of all these writers is now beyond me but by the time I joined the Army they had all done their best for me. It strikes me as remarkable how I came to be so influenced by these men, in a close scientific way as well as in a broad literary fashion. It was not school that had any great depth of influence – a lot of it was ascribable to cheap second-hand book purchasing, a nearby library and having time to search and browse alone.

In mathematics I browsed in the *Recreations and Essays* of Rouse-Ball and read with deep interest *Men of Mathematics* by E. T. Bell, in the school library.

There was too the BBC's Third Programme where one could hear Bertrand Russell engage for an hour and more on scientific and philosophical questions. One also listened to the radio and could pick up Radio Centre Moscow, beamed to the UK, which had as its call sign, the hymn of the Red Flag, and from which I first heard Robbie Burns' *A Man's a Man for a' that* ('... the rank is but the guinea stamp, the man's the gold for a' that and a' that' etc.). (One rarely finds this poem of Burns in popular collections.)

À propos of politics, I recall the following unique treatment of a guilty man, *me*, for a deemed improper activity. I had quietly circulated one sheet of political literature (see Figure 1), during a three-hour Engineering Design session. The procedure was for a class held in a drawing office, to have a half day's problem outlined for perhaps fifteen minutes after which the lecturer would depart but return after an hour, to see if there were any questions. He would then depart again and return at the end of the allotted period, to collect our designs for marking. We were left alone, without anyone to maintain order, so boredom could set in and pranks take over (or 'nipping out' for tea and cakes or a 'smoke'). In one of the latter periods, I distributed my political literature. Two days later, I had a note to ask me to go and see the Principal at an assigned time. I was to be interviewed for my transgression by Sir John Myers, a noted chemist and head of our Institution. On presenting myself, I was ushered before him in his inner sanctum; he indicated to me to sit down alongside him in front of his fire. His first words were, 'What are your opinions of Gandhi's programme?' I replied to the effect that they were primitive and totally inadequate for seriously

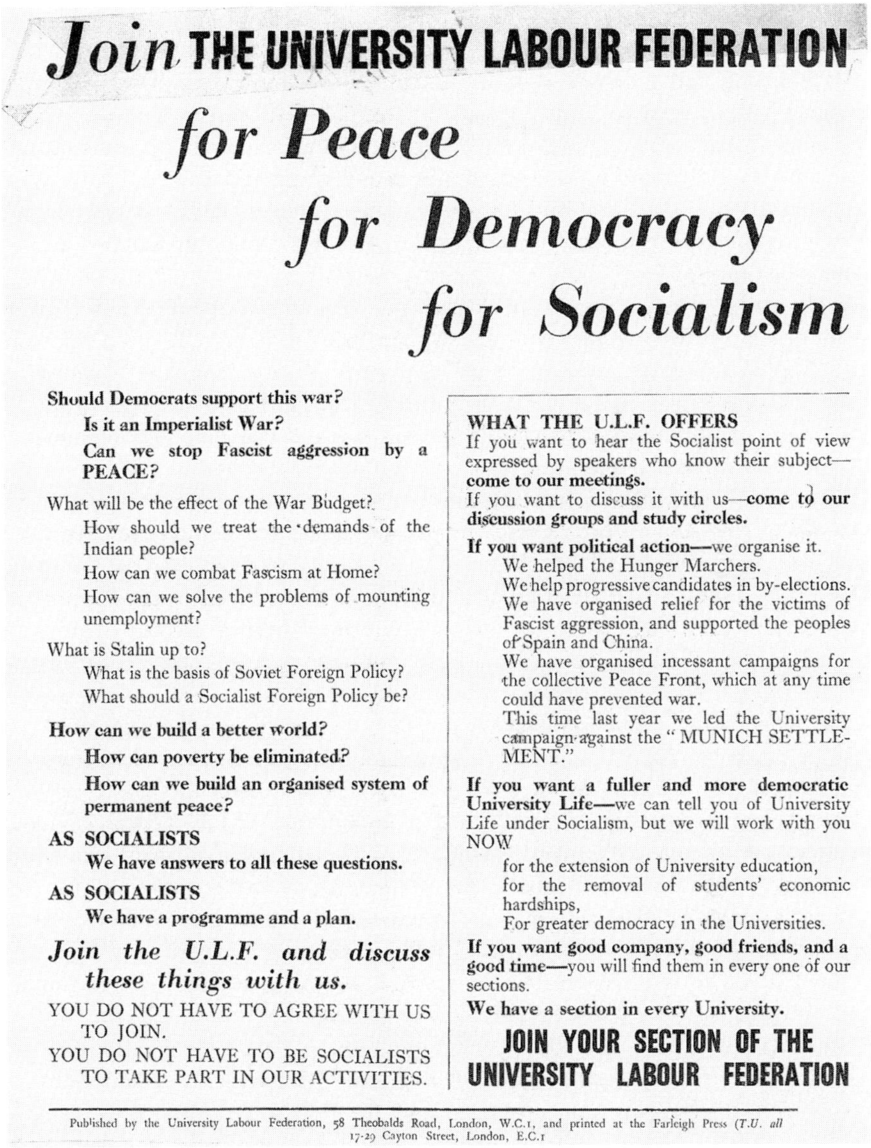

Join THE UNIVERSITY LABOUR FEDERATION
for Peace
for Democracy
for Socialism

Should Democrats support this war?
  Is it an Imperialist War?
  Can we stop Fascist aggression by a PEACE?

What will be the effect of the War Budget?
  How should we treat the demands of the Indian people?
  How can we combat Fascism at Home?
  How can we solve the problems of mounting unemployment?

What is Stalin up to?
  What is the basis of Soviet Foreign Policy?
  What should a Socialist Foreign Policy be?

How can we build a better world?
  How can poverty be eliminated?
  How can we build an organised system of permanent peace?

AS SOCIALISTS
We have answers to all these questions.

AS SOCIALISTS
We have a programme and a plan.

Join the U.L.F. and discuss these things with us.

YOU DO NOT HAVE TO AGREE WITH US TO JOIN.
YOU DO NOT HAVE TO BE SOCIALISTS TO TAKE PART IN OUR ACTIVITIES.

WHAT THE U.L.F. OFFERS
If you want to hear the Socialist point of view expressed by speakers who know their subject—**come to our meetings.**
If you want to discuss it with us—**come to our discussion groups and study circles.**

If you want political action—we organise it.
  We helped the Hunger Marchers.
  We help progressive candidates in by-elections.
  We have organised relief for the victims of Fascist aggression, and supported the peoples of Spain and China.
  We have organised incessant campaigns for the collective Peace Front, which at any time could have prevented war.
  This time last year we led the University campaign against the "MUNICH SETTLEMENT."

If you want a fuller and more democratic University Life—we can tell you of University Life under Socialism, but we will work with you NOW
  for the extension of University education,
  for the removal of students' economic hardships,
  For greater democracy in the Universities.

If you want good company, good friends, and a good time—you will find them in every one of our sections.

We have a section in every University.

JOIN YOUR SECTION OF THE UNIVERSITY LABOUR FEDERATION

Published by the University Labour Federation, 58 Theobalds Road, London, W.C.1, and printed at the Farleigh Press (*T.U. all* 17-29 Cayton Street, London, E.C.1

Figure 1. Undergraduate propaganda during my time at University – 1940–43.

improving the economic position of the majority of Indians. I said I thought that only modern Western manufacturing methods could possibly bring the Indians to a satisfactory state of modern living. The conversation went on for fifteen or twenty minutes while we worked through fascism, communism and Spain, and in between I was served with a cup of tea. His post was then brought in for signing, so he stood up and shook hands with me, saying, 'Nice to exchange views with you, Johnson. Good afternoon!' There was no mention of my error, so I say, 'God Bless Him!' By contrast, I remember some of our bolder spirits, trying to sell leftist booklets to the head of the mathematics department, at the end of a lecture!

It is fitting that I devote a closing section to my father, for it was he with whom I had, or grew to have, an early intellectual relationship. With the rest of my family I had common day-to-day experiences or exchanges but it was through my father that my mind was exercised, not in any systematic way but by dialogue or often dialectically – not that I knew then what that word meant. Essentially it was argument. From him I learned about ideas not commonly handled by my family or others.

I have told of him earlier but pick up here when he was about 30 and I, eight years of age. As I knew him, consciously, he was a labourer at Richard Johnson and Nephews Ltd (no relation to us), a wire-producing company founded in 1785. He was stern, highly moral and disciplined. He had done night-work in the cellars of his employer's firm for a few years and was pale in consequence; that was how I saw him.

There was a general strike in the country in 1926 and the number of unemployed was up to two million throughout the decade. Somehow he had come to take part in trade-unionism and was elected to be the works' secretary or representative. One Friday evening he arrived home and declared he had been 'sacked' and that he was going to Sheffield to see his full-time local branch secretary. He was reinstated the following week. Some little time later a strike occurred, it lasted for about two weeks, the workers went back to work but my father was sacked again. Apparently he had been much involved in the negotiations between workers and management. He was now out of work, but no one tried to have him restored and he was 'black-listed'. My mother was 'up in arms' about the neglect shown to him. Then, surprisingly, he was 'called in' and offered the job of 'charge-hand', in effect sub-foreman. The word was that he had shown management capability during the strike discussions; his wages went up from £2 15s. 0d. to £3 7s. 6d. and in a sense, he changed sides – though not in political conviction – ably pushed by my mother. Within two years he was raised to foreman of the warehouse at £5 5s. 0d.; he was responsible for despatching the company's output, home and abroad. The year was 1933, one before I went to grammar school.

In about 1935, my father's firm determined to implement the Bedaux plan of working; this was a system of efficient work organisation introduced by a Frenchman, in the same category as that by the well-known American ergonomicist, Gilbreth. It precipitated a strike. Strike-breaking by the company was successful – achieved by bussing in new labour from outside the immediate region. It led to ugly confrontations; my father regretted it all but was glad he was not part of it.

The parlour in the little home in which I lived was for entertainment, except that we hardly ever entertained anyone. It was mostly used for laying out the dead in their coffin under the window, near an aspidistra plant. It was used as an isolation chamber if one was ill with an infectious disease, and at one stage I used it for prayer. For five consecutive days I asked God to send me £5,000 and to put this in the 'Toby Jug' on a shelf at 1 p.m., but never did I find anything there. This did not increase my belief in the Bible! However in one corner of the room was a small cupboard carrying a bookcase of four rows of books. We had Darwin's *Voyage of the Beagle* and *The Origin of Species*, three of the four volumes of Macaulay's *History of England*, and another of his, *Essays and the Lays of Ancient Rome*, Thomas Carlyle's *Progress and Poverty*, one entitled *Protoplasm and the Matter of Life*, Marx's *Das Kapital*, and Meiklejohn's volume on geography. These volumes and a good many more I used to take down and try to read. I remember having difficulty with Carlyle's phrase 'complex fluctuating media' of which I never quite got the meaning. We also had one volume of selections from Gibbon's *Rise and Fall* and I remembered his account of sitting down in the midst of the ruins in Rome and deciding he would write a history of Rome. From the book on geography, I learned of the heliocentric theory of the solar system, that the sun was 93 million miles away and the moon 240 thousand. In my early teens I tried to read Marx, but did not get beyond page 48. A volume entitled *British Government*, made me realise there was a legislative, a judicative and an executive aspect to our way of political life. The *Last Days of Pompeii* I started but again did not finish. We had eight volumes of Cassell's *Encyclopaedia* of which I made good use, two large volumes of Webster's *Dictionary* containing articles about Assyrian cuneiform and Egyptian hieroglyphics. An exception pertained to mathematics and physical science – about which there was nothing special in the library.

I used to talk to my father about these things but I never saw him read or refer to any of them, I was turned 60 before I realised that most likely he had never really read any one of them.

I knew only that he had listened to public-spirited men, some of whom were university teachers, discussing these subjects in Platt Fields and Heaton Park and that he had attended a few WEA (Workers' Education Association) conferences.

I remember his making a point to me that there were *physical things* one could see, touch and hear etc., for example a table, and there were *ideas* that did not conform, for example thoughts and poems ... there was a philosophical realisation cast that I came truly to realise only later on reading Joad's *Guide to Philosophy*.

Once he was promoted to a higher wage my parents 'took the plunge' as they called it and bought a new semi-detached house in Higher Openshaw where we had a bathroom, an inside toilet and a small garden. The mortgage was £2 2s. 8d. per month; once a month I paid in this sum to the Leeds Building Society on Moseley Street in the centre of Manchester. The house had a 25 year repayment mortgage on it and I remember that it introduced me to the real world of business! It coincided with the school arithmetic we had been learning – buying and selling prices and rates of interest, simple and compound. It led me to try to check on the period of repayment my parents had signed up to, but I found the calculation too difficult and too long.

From 1934 on, my parents my young brother and I started to have an annual week's holiday in a boarding house in Blackpool (or sometimes Southport). These were the days when one queued up on the landing in the house to secure a place in the lavatory and when you paid for 'cruet' (salt and pepper on the table); when you handed in to the landlady the eggs and bacon to be cooked for your family's next day breakfast – and complained that what you received the following morning

Figure 2. My parents on the North Pier at Blackpool.

was not what you put in the previous day! But North Shore, Blackpool we thought was unbeatable for healthy recreation and Figure 2 shows my parents enjoying it.

Now I was 'growing up', I was taken and shown over the wire-manufacturing plant in which my father served; I was informed about wire-drawing dies and noted how hot wire racing from 'draw' to 'draw' decreased in diameter, got brighter as it progressed (i.e. heated up as it was thinned) to become bright red; it fractured sometimes and snaked violently and dangerously over the works floor. I became familiar with micrometers and gauges and learned there were tradesmen – wire drawers – who had 'served their time' of apprenticeship (seven years), and who therefore received wages on a different level from the labourers (and therefore also had a different trade union).

I came to learn from my father about capitalism and socialism, about profit and share prices, the connection of the shop floor to the banks and insurance companies, parliament, the newspapers (*Daily Express*, not *Manchester Guardian*!) and their relationship ultimately to the educational system – schools, universities and libraries, both local and big reference ones.

I learned to understand the difference between Labour and Conservative and to appreciate the controversy between them. My grandfather Riley was Tory 'blue', regarding all Labour supporters as 'reds'. He would argue riotously with my father, telling him, 'to get back to bloody Russia', and my father would respond with, 'If they took a bloody pig and tied a blue ribbon round its neck you lot would still vote for it!'

As I got well into my teens I started to attend the political meetings at the Free Trade Hall in the city or at Belle Vue; I even heard and saw Ernest Bevin and Clement Attlee deliver their political gospels.

I have tried to convey something of what had been a little island of scholarship in Lower Openshaw when my parents seriously changed their dwelling and with it our class. In the new region of Higher Openshaw there were no factories within half a mile. It contrasted with the street of my Lower Openshaw home in which there was a factory that manufactured printing machines and just around the corner a 'croft' on which was located a large 'rag and bone' yard where horses and carts lined-up to deposit their collections of rubbish. There was Robino's too which made musical instruments, especially pianos. A short walk up the road along a railway siding was Black Brook – an ink-dark, filthy stream of industrial effluent disappearing into a tunnel which one little boy would challenge another to enter.

My father's employer was in the district of Bradford, Manchester, a mile from our home and to get there he approached it alongside *the* colliery, obvious by its tower, large cage-lifting wheels and cables. The small library and reading room where I spent many of my evenings was close by, next to the large theatre where you could hear live shows – George Formby for instance – and then the gas works with the large gas holders alongside. I was actually taken as a member of a small school party to witness the emptying of coke from the huge iron ovens, when the 'mains gas' had been extracted from the coal. It was a tremendous sight to see the bright red hot coke cinders being pushed out of the ovens and into waggons. Last of all along the road was Phillips Park and its cemetery. The park was noted for its great floral display in late spring. My grandmother could describe at length the sight of coffins floating down the river on the occasion of a winter flood, when she was a young girl.

To make my point about how hard living was for most people in the neighbourhood of Lower Openshaw, I might just mention four adjacent families (problem families today?) in a row a few yards away from our house, though there was indeed something to be learned from all the families around us. The Woodwards were a large family with two of whom I played football. I would call to their house and wait for them to finish a meal – everyone had a cup for drink but no saucers or cups with handles to them. I sometimes met one of the boys in McGrath's provision shop at 8 a.m., sent for a penny-worth of jam; he would hold up a cracked cup and from a large pot Mr McGrath would scoop out a great quantity to fill it. The 'jam' was the black remains after the jam had been made and scooped from the bottom of the vats. No nicely presented jam in jars with bright labels! (But the Woodwards did draw acclaim when we stood on the main road and waved to Mr Woodward as he drove past us in his tram car.)

By contrast, the Hydes, also a large family, were always better dressed and fed than the Woodwards, though their father was unemployed. Mr Hyde was a man of initiative. He would send his children to some fields near Belle Vue to pick particular flowers and plants by the sackful. From these he produced lots of fine 4d. bottles of herb beer, for the neighbourhood families.

The Caseys were a family I visited. The father was an ex-serviceman, his wife incompetent and with a mouthful of the most awful gangrenous teeth; they died young and the family was divided. The three older children were adopted by an aunt in the same street whilst the three youngest were put into an orphanage; the former group was chosen because they would soon be of working age.

The Wilshaws were a small family and I have already mentioned them. The eldest, Kitty, competed in and won a dance competition for excellence in being able to do the Charleston whilst her brother Fred was put to training to be a draughtsman and had to attend night school. My mother recalled being present when Mr Wilshaw came home after his day's work, and his utterance, as his wife stood by awaiting praise for having wall-papered the living room. He observed, 'First bloody time I've seen flowers growing upside down!'

I think I have sketched enough of my early life in Lower Openshaw to show it was mainly coarse, hard living. But there was a modest intellectual dimension of a kind to it. I was a lucky child who had a good start even if there was a self-start element in it all. The essence of its interest was variety of activity. My father and I did 'walks' together and talked, despite the hours of work being 47 or five and a half days per week, 8 a.m. to 5.30 p.m. (or more likely 6.30 if an order had to be 'got out of the shop' to catch a boat out of London). Holidays were few – two days at Christmas (one finished work at 5.30 p.m. on Christmas Eve) and one for New Year's Day. The annual holiday then was one week, which was not paid leave unless you were on the staff. We went together over three successive years to see Manchester City football club, when they were cup finalists and then winners. Sport had its dimension too!

But good books – a matter of about 100 – were the life-line from industrial poverty to liberty and education, a father who could talk about most of his library and one to whom they meant gaining respect through learning.

PART II

The Army

CHAPTER VII

Selection Processes

WHAT TO DO WITH US, as regards employment on graduation in mid-1943 was to be settled for all five of us mechanical engineers from the Manchester College of Technology by a selection board of four, sitting for a few days and interviewing us in the University – a Chairman, our Professor W. H. Wright-Baker, the famous Dr C. P. Snow, and a psychologist.

A few days before the interviews, Dr C. P. Snow addressed all the students in science and technology on the country's need for good technical military officers. A subsidiary message seemed to foretell that we were all going to be recruited into the Army! It transpired that a few were indeed finally called-up for the Army, i.e., the Royal Engineers, the Royal Electrical and Mechanical Engineers (REME), the Royal Corps of Signals and perhaps, the Royal Artillery.

In fact, I think it was due to the failure of the Allies, in conflicts with the Germans in the Western desert of North Africa in the pre-El Alamein days that weaknesses and deficiencies in operating and repairing such military equipment as guns and tanks, led to a decision at a high level that some improvement had to be made in military technical staff.

Of our interviewed group, one was a conscientious objector, three were obviously classed as research scientists and likely to obtain at least a 2(i) degree (and so were to be channelled into a government research establishment), whilst the fifth, myself, who had manifested a major interest in production, management or industrial engineering, seemed an ideal recruit for REME workshops or the like. All I remember of the interview was that the psychologist sat in a dark corner and so was difficult to see, and that I engaged in an exchange of opinions with him, maintaining that there was too little experimental work done by psychologists to justify the theory or concepts held – especially those of Jung.

I did not learn about the outcome of the recommendations of the interviewing board, but during the Easter of 1943, a few weeks before Final Examinations started, I was required to present myself at REME War Office Selection Board (or WOSB) No. 6, Redhill in Surrey. It was the first time I had been to London or indeed further south than Cheshire, which I enjoyed, in itself, despite the war. Once there I was given a set of overalls and an arm band – no. 43 (a prime number!). I was there for three days. The first morning we were taken to an area on the edge of a wood where several 'obstacles' were in evidence. Two military officers clutching clip boards, called us forward one by one and ordered, 'Do any five of them!'

We asked, 'Do what?'

'It's up to you,' they replied. 'Get going, you've got about ten minutes.' I could only conclude that there was supposed to be some element of character revelation in all this which they were looking for. I can only remember clambering up and over an A-shaped frame, moving myself along a single horizontal rope stretched between two trees, about twenty feet above the ground, climbing a vertical rope ladder and sliding down an adjacent rope, and finally, walking along a swinging platform. One or two chaps slightly injured themselves in these tests. Later on, a small group of us had to work together in transferring a mythical 100 pound 'bomb', from one side of a stream to another without tilting or rotating it. I thought this had something to do with demonstrating capacity to work as part of a team. (Incidentally, we dropped our 'bomb' and lost it in the river!)

A remarkable test was when three of us were given a message to remember prior to having to get ourselves across a river where the bridge had been destroyed. Two pieces of timber were available to help achieve this, but were not long enough to span the opening. I suggested that we look around for some more timber, and on finding and using a third piece, we successfully achieved our purpose. In all, it took us eight minutes, and we were allowed ten. This, however, is only part of the story because our 'purpose' in crossing the river was to convey the message to the people on the other side, so the two officers asked us each to repeat the message. The message included a motor car licence number, and two map references. The supposition, I imagine, was that candidates would forget the details of the message in their anxiety to cross the river.

One set of interviews was devoted to examining our technical knowledge and I recall an officer asking me if I had any knowledge of the Theory of Machines. This astonished me, since to all mechanical engineering undergraduates this was a specialist branch of Applied Mechanics which was lectured upon in each of the three years of one's course. The question left me wondering how much my interrogator knew about the subject! Yet another officer was interested in testing one's knowledge of politics, and after discussing China we had to settle a point as to the location of Szechwan (China), a region of great mineral wealth. There were three discussion group meetings in which subjects were freely discussed by students, presumably to reveal their degree of ease and confidence in lecturing to groups of men, the officers listening in.

One long session was given over to Intelligence and Numerical Testing; there was also one special aural test, using head-phones, in which one had to recognise sounds of diminishing intensity – seemingly to identify men well-fitted for the Corps of Signals!

One day, we were pushed out on to the road immediately after lunch and ordered to run a mile, and our times were noted. Later that afternoon there was a fast, competitive walk of four miles. Presumably, this was some assessment of physical fitness. A ten-minute short lecture was also required of each member of the group, on the subject of his own choice – in the time between the physical events. Many other short tests were also delivered but at the conclusion one had to appear, solo, before a board of senior officers. The only question which seemed to have been asked of everybody was, 'Do you wish to take up a commission in REME?' As I was later recruited and processed to officer status, I suppose I passed the tests.

Some weeks later we had a medical examination and two of my Tech. colleagues failed it. Of course, the selection process should have only admitted men who were medically A1 in the first place; they did the tests the wrong way round!

I estimated that there were only about twelve of us from the CoT who finally went forward for engineering commissions.

Quite some time after I was called for the initial interview by the Board it came to light that Crossley's Gas and Oil Engine Co. Ltd (where I had spent the 1942 long vacation working on two-stroke, eight-cylinder diesel engines intended for certain fast ships – corvettes – co-operating in Atlantic convoy work) had sent a letter to the Board asking for me to be assigned to their company. However, the latter claim carried no weight. (Later, I learned that Crossleys had written to the Board about taking on another, named, undergraduate member of my year. They were refused both of us.)

As it turned out, on paper, I was perhaps well matched for what I subsequently met. My other three colleagues on the course were apolitical and interested in very little else but engineering. For contrary reasons I was diversely structured and probably better-suited to the Army than they were.

That year, as a member of the Home Guard and the OTC, I was tested for my (advanced) Certificate B and failed. Gaining the Certificate B was supposed to give immediate access to an Officer Cadet Training Unit, though I never knew it actually to do so. I had a dispute with my examining Major about an aspect of what one could learn from contoured maps, and I suppose, for this reason, I was failed – about the only person out of some three hundred! I had, of course, walked and tramped (solo) across the Kinder Scout moors and Bleaklow in all weathers, moving only with the aid of a map, and without getting lost! I had been maintaining with the major that by walking at the bottom of a peat 'dune' (the analogue of a sand dune) one could not be seen at a distance; I believe he really had no experience of the depth of the peat lands in this part of Derbyshire.

Two days after graduation, I was bound for Maidstone Barracks and the Queen's Own Royal West Kent Regiment – for six weeks' primary training, all white 'blanco', polish and unquestioning obedience!

I went through a Civil Service Selection Board four years later, but the characteristics tested were intellectual, not physical – yet the testing procedures followed those of the Army except for requiring essays on political issues.

A Different Selection Process

The Tech. Socialist Society organised a Saturday evening party to which men brought their girlfriends. I believe this happened in the late summer of 1941, when daylight prevailed into the late evening. I was involved in the arrangements of the party as the Treasurer of the Society. I booked the room at a local Co-operative Society, paid the fee and had the oversight of the provisions for the

Figure 1. Heather, young woman.

evening's food; I even paid a visit to the market for a 7lb slab of cake. At this meeting – notable for a little dancing, several games and much discussion – I met and talked to Heather Thornber for the first time – having arranged for one of her old friends to invite her. (See Figure 1.) And, as they put it, we immediately 'clicked'. From that evening onwards we met every Saturday and Sunday evening – and occasionally midweek. Her job in the Post Office, except for Sunday, always made for difficulty. The Post Office's hour of closing was 7.30 p.m. and even later when the day's account books did not balance. It could be a matter of hanging about for another twenty or thirty minutes. Our courting consisted of long evening walks through parks and around the reservoirs, ending back at her home at about 10.30 p.m. Once or twice, we were 'pulled in' by the police, air-raid wardens or the LDV (Local Defence Volunteers) and our identity cards were demanded! On Sundays we went to listen to speeches or political addresses, and to see foreign films near the town centre – *Sous les Toits de Paris* was one I recall. Just occasionally we went to a Wednesday afternoon university open lecture. Professor T. H. Pear we frequently heard discoursing on philosophy; his delivery was always clear but alas there was never anything of such importance that it made an imprint on our minds. We took to reading books and bought a lot of H. G. Wells, Bernard Shaw, Lancelot Hogben and J. B. S. Haldane. Heather bought me Hogben's *Dangerous Thoughts* for my 21st birthday whilst I bought her Liszt's *Hungarian Rhapsody*. We saw films we remembered – *Dr Mameluk*(?) – about a Jewish doctor and his intended bride, in Nazi Germany. We saw *the first* performance of Shaw's *The Golden Days of Good King Charles* at the Manchester Palace. And Sunday afternoon was a popular time for Hallé Concerts led by Sir John Barbirolli, in the Manchester Free Trade Hall. I also introduced Heather to the Peak District, especially climbing Kinder Scout from Edale and crossing the moors of Bleaklow from Glossop.

Once I was in the Army our periods of meeting were truncated and we took to exchanging very long letters about philosophy and politics during our separations.

CHAPTER VIII

From Primary Training to Commission

I JOINED the Primary Training Wing of the Queen's Own Royal West Kent Regiment, at Maidstone, Kent, but completed my introduction with the 'Beds(fordshire) and Herts(fordshire)', at Bury St Edmunds. At the Queen's Own, we were kitted out and then rammed together in huts for 60, that carried three-high bunk beds, about two feet apart. Each mattress consisted of a large bag filled with straw, obtained 50 yards away, packed to your own hoped-for degree of comfort. You lived out of your kit bag, which contained two pairs of boots, a groundsheet-cum-raincoat, pair of gaiters, large back-pack and small pack, gas mask, two or three pieces of underwear, and our uniform – trousers, blouse and great-coat all made of stiff serge material (with brass buttons) and a rifle and 'suit' of denims.

There was only one hot stove, in the centre of the hut, around which men congregated, argued and wrote letters home. (And there was one chap in the hut even trying to write a prize essay submission!)

There were lots of parades on the square – rifle drill, marching and formation changing. For the first week or two we were not allowed out of the barracks, being considered not fit to be seen. One of our upper-class, immaculately dressed officers, actually once addressed us on parade as 'scum'. But the few engineering graduates amongst us reckoned that he had read History at Oxford and couldn't 'do' calculus! There was no doubt about it that as a platoon we improved enormously in the six weeks allotted to the course – full marks to our father-sergeant. We had practice with live ammunition on three occasions: rifle and Bren gun firing, and grenade lobbing. (For practice with live grenades, three of us, a young eighteen-year-old, a sergeant and I, took up a position in a 4 ft. deep pit. When the youngster withdrew the pin of his grenade, he dropped it and the lever sprang free. The grenade, now live, was rapidly retrieved by the sergeant and lobbed into the depression alongside us. Grenades had fuses which gave either 4 seconds or 7 seconds of time to detonation: fortunately, the latter were always used with beginners, and thus we narrowly escaped death!

There was a weekly pay-parade – our pay was 3s. a day, but each week after smartly saluting the Officer, we drew 18s. The three shillings withheld was retained to build up a large sum to pay for a new pair of boots should we lose them or have them stolen. Each pair of boots was supposed to be worn on alternate days. The pair not used was required to be displayed (with the soles perfectly clean at the foot of your bed), so that a passing orderly officer could see them easily. Huts were rigorously inspected, every day except Sunday. Before falling-in for breakfast-parade, beds would have had to be 'made up'. Pillows were carefully wrapped up in blankets in an approved manner and set at the far end of the bed with boots alongside and with rifles on display. Cutlery and mess-tins, among other things, were all clearly laid out. Inspection of all these items made for tidiness and good order in a very cramped environment.

Whilst morning parades were in progress, men were called out to have their teeth examined, and some to suffer extractions – without pain-killing drugs, and no time wasted in recuperation! Medical examinations were similarly fitted in, especially the examination of genitalia. Sometimes it was done like a production process – as were vaccinations – when a long line of half-clad troops queued up to reveal themselves and be punctured, feeling the consequences for two days afterwards. (Some few of the men escaped at weekends to London, where they tried to make up for the sex they had missed; they had to get lucky, for they could achieve nothing by paying for it out of their army pittance!)

For a few days after the mass of the initial Primary Training intake had been despatched to their new postings, the graduates – bound for commissions, awaiting their postings – were used for auxiliary jobs such as filling in holes in the roads in the camp, or patching up target papers on the rifle range. Uniquely, I was used for bringing in a prisoner from Scotland Yard, London – as I have related in story form below. (See Chapter IX). When the order came through, we were despatched to the pre-OCTU (Officers Cadet Training Unit) at Wrotham in Kent. This experience was to prove a tough assignment, but one which only lasted for six weeks. (A good fraction of its intake over that period had no opportunity whatsoever to travel off the site of the Unit for recreational purposes.) The pre-OCTU seemed to be deliberately set up to put physical and psychological stress on the inmates; it aimed to remove the weaker ones and indeed, some 25% of each group put through its paces, failed to pass out after the six weeks. A lighter side of the Unit's work was that of teaching cadets how to drive motor cycles and personal utility vans – all in a matter of two or three days. (All the vehicles at this time were, incidentally, gear changed by double de-clutching.) Near to the end of the course, we had two battle-inoculation exercises, a day-time one and one in the late evening. On each occasion, arriving at the site where the exercises were to be conducted, we found two formidable 'blood wagons' (ambulances) with ambulance crews, waiting. Training officers and NCOs (non-commissioned officers), were directed to various points to observe, control and interact with the line of troops as they moved from start to finish. During an advance, sergeants would jump out and throw thunder-flashes in the way of a Section's advance past different kinds of obstacles strewn about and in some places, advance was by crawling. Machine guns chattered, firing live ammunition on 'fixed lines' – under which we had to crawl, dragging along our rifle and ammunition. We had once to negotiate a small river sporting the usual destroyed bridge. Typically, the course terminated with a requirement for us to run *up* a hill from the river to our final objective. Unfortunately, it had rained that day and the ground was churned up and very muddy. At the top of the hill over which it was difficult to run, we were required to loose off a few rounds at targets beyond us. I remember, at the end, pointing my rifle over a nearby protuberance and aiming it at a target without too much finesse, only to find that I could not immediately locate either the rifle bolt or the trigger. The whole area around the gun bolt was thick with muddy clay which I endeavoured to scrape clear with my fingers. This done, I moved my head well to one side and fired off half-a-dozen shots, and then, due to the reaction, gently slid down some yards of the incline. I recall that less than half the line of men reached the finish – no unusual fraction. For anyone who was fit and agile the exercise was not at all a bad one, especially as no one was hurt.

From pre-OCTU we moved, over a weekend, to OCTU, at Foremark Hall, near Derby, where we spent most of the final few weeks of our non-commissioned life. At this juncture, we had to wear a clear white hat-band which identified us as Officer Cadets. The high point of this week's course was about four days of exposure to supposedly realistic battle conditions in North Wales, near Snowdon and Llyn Ogwen. With this promotion to Cadetship however, there was a noticeable change in the manner of the lecturers who addressed us – our imminent status was evidently recognised and exchanges tended to be intelligent and measured. These exercises took place at the end of February and in the cold weather many of them were quite testing.

We alighted from the train at Penmaenmawr (or was it Llanfairfechan?) and after marching a mile or so towards our temporary camp encountered two 'German officers'. Fortunately, with some support from the keener cadets the Senior Cadet of the day made the right decision and ordered them to be arrested. (Was this something of a joke or British humour?)

On the first morning of this short adventure, after a welcome by the CO (Commanding Officer) to our group of about thirty, there were three gentle morning lectures. The first was on military law when we were recommended to read the short manual on the subject which I believe was actually supplied to us. For my part, I only ever had need of one section, and that related to prosecuting or defending in minor courts-martial. The follow-up talks dealt with medical matters, particularly as they applied to the ORs (Other Ranks, i.e., privates) and especially concerning VD, which in Italy was not uncommon among them – and not unknown even in the officer class. Finally, there was advice given about behaviour if one was captured, and some interesting tips referring to sending secret information! In the afternoon there was much activity or exercise in running with machine guns and ammunition, up hills and across rivers again. There were also some small exercises dealing principally with giving orders to troops during fighting. In giving orders to my section on one occasion I was censured for calling them out too loudly. The sergeant overlooking, remarked, 'Not so loud, the bloody enemy could hear you! Sir!'

On the second day we started by having the opportunity to familiarise ourselves with firing an army pistol at targets about twenty yards away. The British pistol was relatively large and those with small hands – like me – needed both to hold it firmly and fire it accurately when at arm's length. To achieve accuracy at more than a few feet seemed to me to require luck as well as ability so that I soon acquired a disrespect for all John Wayne's supposed heroic accomplishments! We went on to exercises in enemy 'house-clearing' using live ammunition. (I found that this kind of fighting in real action was of the bitterest sort at Cassino.) With an officer, two of us would rush into a deserted barn, and when he pointed and called out, 'There!', one of us would deliver a quick burst of machine-gun fire, at the hidden enemy. The supporting colleague always had to be alert and sharp, especially when another hidden enemy was suddenly indicated behind him! This action, too enthusiastically performed, could easily endanger his colleague, to say the least.

Typical infantry exercises started when a platoon was on the move with a burst of tracer fired into what was to be taken as the point to be attacked and not the position from which the tracer was fired. The exercise was usually contrived so that all three sections of a platoon played slightly different roles. We had one night-time exercise during which lots of fixed-line tracer and thunder-flashes were used. We crawled across muddy fields, a few feet below the bright line of the tracer fire (again!); seeing the latter so close above you there was no need for anyone to tell you to keep your head down! Crossing a fence on one occasion, we were surprised to hear some muttering and swearing: it turned out that a local priest had come with our Deputy Commander to view the exercise. Unfortunately, the two of them became lost in the darkness, were pounced upon by defending cadets and when the visiting cleric was heard to declare, 'I'm the Reverend Brown from St Asaph!' there came the reply, 'And I'm the bloody Archbishop of Canterbury!' Another notable exercise occurred at the end of our second day of operations when, having 'stooped' our way up a modest river, we were ordered to lie down on the right bank and be prepared to attack a nearby cottage. The order was given and the senior cadet for the operation led the attack. We had got little more than ten yards, when an irate voice boomed out, 'You're on the wrong side of the river, you should be attacking from the other bank!' A 180° error in the direction of progression! It was a poor performance when one remembered how long it had taken us to get into position with rifles held at breast height, well out of the water. Realism was added to that night because we were left to sleep out and had not come prepared for a winter's night on a bare mountain top. The final exercise involved marching over the hill-tops to a spot near Llyn Ogwen, where we were told that collapsible boats would be found at the water's edge. These we would erect, launch and paddle across the lake. Fortunately or unfortunately, strong winds had developed and even erecting the boats was very difficult. Amidst the usual clatter of machine-gun fire, and closely laid thunder-flashes, it became clear that even if launching was successful, once out in the middle of the lake, there was a high probability that one or two boats would be overturned. Fortunately, an order came to abandon the exercise. We had been briefed that once across the lake, we should attack and 'take' an obvious block of stables. Like all our exercises the final attack would be up hill and the point of consolidation even further up. And because the exercise finished early, the order was given to march several miles back to camp through the hail and rain, at a fast rate.

The last exercise was that of Rapid Dispersal From Moving Vehicles. Here, the aim was to give experience and offer suggestions for dismounting from the running board of a small truck, whilst carrying a rifle. We started dismounting with the truck moving at about four mph, its speed being repeatedly increased until it was something around twelve mph. The supposed mechanics of it were that, holding on to the vehicle with one arm and spread-eagled with the rifle, one lay back at an angle to the ground which was the smaller, the greater the vehicle's speed. There were more cadets injured in this exercise than on any other occasion, and I believe it was subsequently discontinued.

We returned to Foremark Hall and had a passing-out parade before a distinguished senior Officer. We all knew well that we could appear hereafter with one pip or star on each shoulder. That indicated we were Second Lieutenants for the next six months and 'except for accidents' we would then be promoted to First Lieutenants. Thus, after several months of continuous service we got a week's leave and instructions to report at REME Corps Headquarters, Arborfield, near Reading. During the week or two before the parade, optimists had visited local tailors and been measured for an officer's dress suit and some for a Sam Browne (a highly polished leather belt with diagonal shoulder strap).

Arborfield

I arrived at Arborfield in January 1944 and attended a short course of technical instruction on Armoured Fighting Vehicles – lectures in the morning and practice in the afternoon: most lectures were delivered by experienced senior technical non-commissioned officers. However, in truth, I have very few recollections of precisely what we heard and did. We were subject to a lot of description with much detail about tanks, Churchill, Sherman (and possibly Cromwell). There was an immense amount delivered about tank engines, about particular matters such as clutch clearances and the like – three-eighths of an inch here, and half an inch there, and trying to appreciate special items concerning gun turrets, etc. All this could not be assimilated and I fear that for much of the time, the mind of the class was switched off! The afternoons were spent on tanks in the field and in the workshop; I remember such operations as helping to substitute a new link in one of the tank caterpillar tracks, and lying almost upside-down out of a tank turret with my head in the engine compartment, and contemplating the compactness of all the fittings I saw. I also recall lying on my back underneath a tank belly and removing a heavy cover plate above me; it was no position of comfort! I gained some experience of driving the different tanks and appreciated especially the claustrophobic feelings of their crews. Across a field over which tanks had been driven in exercises, the viscous mud lay about a foot deep and I saw that if one got more than a few yards from your tank, you could be so firmly held down as to be unable to make the return journey – seriously!

Colchester Workshops

Commissioned in REME, four of us, Second Lieutenants, were sent to learn and follow the methods and procedures used in a large REME vehicle workshop as typified by the one in Colchester. It also offered us our first experience of a well-run mess which was very welcome after several training units. There was no structured course though I think one had been intended; our CO was an ex-car sales manager and garage owner, without any professional engineering background. It seemed to all four of us that the time we spent in Colchester could have been better used elsewhere, for to some degree we all sought out technical activity from any direction. We all helped with the workshop paper work and especially in the business of being Orderly Officer for 24 hours every few days. We also spent whole days out repairing and recovering army vehicles which were passing through our area, guessing that a sudden increase in movement was afoot when D-day was at hand. Whole Divisions seemed to be moving towards the South coast.

I remember with great humour during these days our workshop being inspected by a colonel from London. We passed him on return to the workshop after lunch one day, all four of us throwing him a salute. However, later in the afternoon we received a summons to present ourselves in our CO's office. Sitting regally behind the desk, he demanded to know why we were not 'properly dressed' – carrying a cane and wearing gloves! (Chief Constables still do this.) We were standing to attention in a line and I was all for challenging this practice of carrying objects which announced to the world that *you* (officers), don't use your hands for manual work; gloves and cane for an engineer would carry precisely the wrong message! A year before, at the university, I had read a volume by the American sociologist Vorsten Veblen (1857–1929), called *The Theory of the Leisure Class* (1899), in connection with a course of lectures on Workshop Psychology. Though emboldened to argue the point, I fortunately retained my silence. If I had not, I think I would have been quickly posted to some distant unit!

Another historic moment for me was to be ordered to attend a court martial, there to defend one of the young army fitters, who was charged with stealing a motor cycle. My experience with law was non-existent, and I had to try – with the aid of the *Manual of Military Law* – to do what was expected of me. I discussed the case with the youngster in jail. He claimed he had had a sudden impulse to ride the motor cycle, and – without thinking about how his action would be interpreted – he 'took off for a spin'. The court was a very simple affair, a Major (in Law) presiding over it. It was one of several cases and a few visitors were present. I persuaded 'the accused' to plead guilty, which made it easier for me to deal with. I had come prepared to deliver a few hundred words on his behalf. I spoke of his lack of experience of the Army's ways, of his youthfulness, his limited education and his previous good conduct. I asked that the court accept his apologies and his promise not to repeat the offence. The President of the court then delivered a solemn warning and dismissed the case.

Apart from a 'stir' which was caused in the Mess by a young Scots officer who very much wanted to marry a female Army clerk, I cannot claim that Colchester was alive with stirring events and good conversation. The Scot came along with a colleague when we borrowed bicycles and rode over to Cambridge and back, staying for the weekend. It proved a very pleasant tour of the colleges and churches. I remember on the next evening, getting into an argument with my CO (Commanding Officer) about the value of university education.

CHAPTER IX

The Prisoner's Guard

THE FOLLOWING DESCRIBES a rather unusual personal experience I had, written up in story form many years ago.

I was a seven weeks old Private who had completed his Primary Training and was awaiting posting instructions to pre-OCTU and, as you may know, much of a soldier's life is spent in waiting for things to happen.

For a week I had been reporting to Company office each morning at eight o'clock, there to be detailed for some odd job to occupy me for the day. There were two other men besides myself, and we were allotted the most diverse tasks, from road-mending by filling pot-holes with soil and pebbles, to pasting bits of paper over bullet holes in rifle targets.

It was a few days before Christmas 1943, and as we had finished decorating the dining hall with 'streamers', fir and tinsel, I took myself off to the reading room adjoining the NAAFI.

This was a solitary occasion on which the wireless was not blaring away or a one-fingered Paderewski trying to thump out the Warsaw Concerto; so as the only distraction was the slight chatter of my neighbours, I soon settled down to 'roast my shins' by the fire and read *Man, Microbe, and Malady*.

Alas, this heaven only remained for twenty minutes, when in rushed a Welshman, gasping – in that sing-song monotone peculiar to his race,

'Any of you blokes Thompson?'

'Why, what the devil's the matter?' I snapped.

'You 'im?' he asked, and gathering that I was, continued, 'You're wanted on escort duty, righ' away.'

I put my head on my hand as I sat there by the fire, gazed meditatively into it, and refrained from using expletives. I slowly gathered my wits from wondering whether or not there was peace on earth, raised up my body, and slowly directed it to the hut. On entering, corporal 'Smiff' was to be seen donning his great-coat and web-belt. Seeing me, he yelled, 'Come-on, you'.

'Where are we going?' I enquired.

'To London!' he replied. 'Get changed into serge immediately. You'll want your overcoat and respirator. Hurry up, and meet me at the office as soon as you can.' With these terse phrases he bustled himself out of our hut and away.

I changed, and whilst I did so, Spider and Johnnie prepared my greatcoat and knapsack and fitted into one of the pockets my huge volume, *War and Peace*. I gathered up my spectacles and my remaining shilling as I went out.

I quickly walked down to the office to meet the NCO, hardly having had time to curse my bad fortune. I met him holding two large parcels wrapped in newspaper. He thrust one of them at me, "Aversack rations,' he explained. 'It's 11.25 now and the train goes at 11.35. We can't get it now if it's on time. That lot of fools come and tell me to be at Company Office for 11 o'clock at ten-past eleven!'

So off we set, both hoping that we would miss the train, for we had to call at the police station on the way down to the railway station.

I soon learned that my superior wanted to miss the train in order to arrive in London after 5 p.m., for then the Military Police Station would not release the prisoners; we should not be able to travel back to Bury St Edmunds that night with a prisoner, and he (the corporal) would be able to go home to Hammersmith 'for a night with the wife', picking up the prisoner next day when the station released men after about nine o'clock.

For my part, I wanted to miss the train so that we could return to the barracks for a good dinner, for I dislike sandwiches and buns replacing normal 'iron' rations. And further, I thoroughly hate travelling in stuffy railway coaches and sitting in cramped and uncomfortable positions for hours on end. And anyway, it meant I would lose the quiet evenings I had come to value so much.

So firstly we went into the town and to the local police-station to borrow a pair of handcuffs. Two huge Samsonian specimens of masculinity served us with handcuffs after we had duly signed for them.

I looked at those handcuffs and reflected, somewhat apprehensively. The prisoner had to be handcuffed to a person of equal rank, and I was to be that person. I didn't fancy the idea of being so securely attached to a dangerous man! Never know what he might do! Things could be made awkward for me. Suppose, that whilst we were standing on the platform awaiting the train, he suddenly decided to commit suicide rather than face trial – and he flung himself in the track of the oncoming train – and me with him! What a fix! Suppose he was a tough-guy who thought he may as well be hanged for a sheep as a lamb, as the saying goes, and decided he might have some fun before he got penned up again and so took the opportunity of shady corners and streets to slosh me one!

I looked into shop windows and saw my figure. 'Fairly broad, you weigh about ten and a half stone,' I said to myself. 'Unless he is a really big fellow you should be able to give as much as you take. Anyhow, I don't fancy it, I hope there's no rough-house either ... Better be careful with him,' said Caution. 'Wish they'd picked someone else, all the same.'

And so my half-conscious misgivings went on. We arrived at the station at ten minutes to twelve. The train was late, and I was pleased, for the corporal had strongly offered me accommodation in his own home that evening and I could do little else but accept, possessing but one shilling and two-pence. I was rather dubious about this. No shaving tackle, no soap, no pyjamas with me. I tell you, I didn't like it; I preferred my own bed and Army barrack-room privacy.

I read my book from Bury to Cambridge and from Cambridge to London. I made a few attempts to open up a conversation with the corporal – but all in vain.

'What do you think of the Yanks?'

'Alright, but I've no time for 'em.'

'How long have you been in the Army?'

'Joined up in 1924. Was in the Army of Occupation.'

'What impression did you get of the German people?'

'They're very clean. Rather 'ave 'em any time than the French. Dirty lot of b——ds. Suppose it's all these Nazis – there's good and bad in 'em all.'

That exhausted the subject of Germany.

He bought a small dinner for each of us in the canteen at Bury; 'An eyeful of spuds and two —- sausages.'

'—— good job we grow spuds in this country, otherwise we'd starve,' he commented.

We greedily devoured the meal in the few minutes available, and I bought a couple of apples – but not without an amusing little incident occurring first.

An American Airforceman who was before us in the queue, after several attempts had managed to order his 'potatoes mashed and sausage', and then he came to the difficult task of borrowing a knife and fork. The attendant required a one shilling deposit and his hat. Poor lad – he couldn't have been in the country long, for it was obvious that he wasn't aware how valuable cutlery had become. He was so confused and bewildered because she demanded his hat as a security for the knife and fork. He couldn't understand it. He blushed, repeated his questions, thought he misunderstood the waitress, but eventually yielded up his hat.

He sat opposite us to eat his meal, and I suppose he felt that he must have someone to confide in. His face broke out into a huge good-natured smile.

'Say pal, ah couldn't understand why she wanted ma hat at first. Takes me long enough to order what ah want at the best of times, without having to do that as well.'

My corporal's face never altered a muscle. I looked up and smiled at him to make up for our seeming lack of friendliness.

As I have said, I tried often to make out some sort of conversation with my 'commander', but time and again I was simply returned a 'Hm.', which, meaning nothing in itself, yet in its intonation seemed to say, 'Shut up! I've something else to think about.' – Such a short, sharp, crisp 'Hm', so hurried and conclusive. I quickly learned that this was one specimen of humanity that couldn't be humoured. And so I forsook him intellectually, and trusted that God would see me home that night. God granted that wish and I hereby thank Him. But that is out of turn.

We arrived at King's Cross about 4.15 p.m., and of course visited the places all men and soldiers visit so frequently. Firstly the 'Gentlemen' and secondly the Canteen. We satisfied our hunger with more starchy food, and then headed for Whitehall. By now it was dusk and the Corporal, though he knew he would have to 'report in', was yet confident that 'they' would not wish him to take back to camp a 'prisoner', in the 'blackout'.

And so, Whitehall! A huge building whose wooden floors were scrubbed white – too obviously military.

We were directed to the Garrison sergeant-major's office and there found several NCOs and men. Our prisoner then, was not the only one contained here. Stern faced NCOs walked about. Occasionally, after a slamming and clanging of doors, a downcast individual would appear, be told to, 'Quick march, Left wheel. Inside there!'

My corporal argued and remonstrated with the 'Lance-jack' in charge about needing to pick up our man tonight – but all in vain. Our prisoner, Private P., had to be removed that evening. Already they were overcrowded and wanted to get rid of as many as possible.

The necessary paper-work was executed (that is to say, my NCO signed a slip of paper to the effect that he had received one prisoner), and the jailer – or whatever he was called, was despatched to prepare Private P. for transportation. Meanwhile, we sat on a form alongside many other escorts, and waited.

Out, first of all, came a tall, large-headed youth; deep sunken eyes, pale, badly in need of a hair cut. He was obviously physically weak. I supposed he was a 'conshi', for his fine-featured face had a suggestion of the delicate, sensitive timidity, usual with many of them. Was he our prisoner? No. He was taken into 'that' room, was inside a few minutes, and then 'carted off'.

No sooner had he gone, than another was brought out. He was big and sturdy, I should think with the strength of a bull. I surveyed him apprehensively. No, he wasn't ours! Thank God!

The next one was short, ragged-looking, with a typical 'downy' look about him. He looked the typical sneak, pilferer or petty thief. But alas, neither was he our prisoner!

When were the MPs (Military Police) going to bring ours?

Again the usual metallic thuds, and the sound of boots.

But for this fourth time an Air-Force youth appeared; fairly tall – three or four inches more than I – none too heftily built, head inclined forward, back-bone curved and shoulders forward. Hardly the kind that would give trouble when handcuffed. Ours? Into the office he went, and soon the call came for Corporal S. So this was our prisoner! Well, well, now I *was* a little happier.

Eventually Private P. and Corporal S. came out of the office, the former in a state of half undress – presumably he had been searched or medically examined. We waited till he dressed himself and soon the huge mass of a Military Policeman (M.P.) came along and guided us outside to an awaiting three-ton truck – but not before I had been handcuffed to the prisoner – quite a novel experience for me!

Our movements being somewhat restricted in consequence, we found it difficult to clamber on to the truck; soon we drove off, the handcuffed pair sitting on one side of the truck, the corporal on the other. It was a typical example of how the army usually obeys State injunctions – 'Save Transport' – so they use a three-ton truck to carry three people from Whitehall to Liverpool Street Railway Station.

At first, Private P. avoided looking me in the face, but after a trial glance or two he gave a weak smile and then retired into himself. His first request was for a cigarette; he hadn't had one for the past 36 hours; but even this couldn't be granted for it was illegal to smoke in trucks according to military law. Anyhow, this opened up the conversation and we learned the details – as he gave them. I cannot recollect the true conversational exchange, but I shall relate what I remember.

He had joined the RAF as a volunteer air-gunner. After a few months he had been 'grounded', found unfit for flying duties, and was eventually re-posted to the Army. He had an intense dislike for the Army, as many RAF men have, and on getting a few days leave prior to his Army 'call-up' he had submitted a false address on his pass and intended deserting, or 'losing' himself 'in the Metropolis'. His parents lived somewhere in the Midlands, but from about 14 years of age he had lived away from them. Indeed he had no real home.

He had had numerous jobs. His friend – or 'buddy' as he called him – was a cripple and unable to earn a living when he wasn't near, so in London he joined him and together they existed by doing all kinds of odd jobs. He had been a motor mechanic, sign-writer and so on, and the scarcity of such people then meant that he could find plenty of work. However, he had been absent from the Army for about 6 weeks, when someone 'shopped' him to a 'copper' on leaving a cafe. 'Someone' had been interested in a sign-writing job he had done for £3 and for spite had 'split' on him.

So, on that particular day in December, he found himself in Whitehall Military Police Station, with three blankets, a few boards to sleep on, and plenty of inmates – though not provided for company – without the privilege to smoke, nothing to read, awful grub to eat, and in general with the millstone Time about his neck. He had

had no idea of the time of day, his cell and ward having no clock; he had hoped and waited for us to fetch him.

The Corporal talked to him a good deal to begin with. I believe he said more to the prisoner in 5 minutes than he said to me the whole day. Between us we learnt his trouble, and we did our utmost to convince him that the Army was not half as bad as made out.

I offered him some plain chocolate I couldn't eat but he devoured it with gusto!

After alighting at Liverpool Street Station, we walked close together into the station, down a slippery incline on which our boots seemed to clang violently to attract the attention of passers-by, though it was almost fully dark by now.

Our train was scheduled for 6.17 p.m., so we had time to drop in at the YMCA for something to eat and drink. It was decided that the chained pair should remain outside and the Corporal should go inside, buy the food and bring it out to us. He brought out a couple of sandwich meat rolls and a cup of tea each. We sat on the stone floor like a couple of beggars just outside the YMCA door on the right and in the shadow. It was an altogether dangerous job holding a cup of tea in your left hand and trying to eat your roll from your handcuffed right. I quickly 'polished off' my grub and tea, but he could scarcely finish his second roll. He seemed very unhappy, forlorn, and I think glad to be with anyone who had a kind word to say to him. We sat there on the ground exchanging occasional statements and being the objects of close scrutiny by those passers-by who noticed us. Perhaps they thought we were a drunken pair and most people passed us by unconcernedly.

We waited on platform 6 some ten minutes or more. Again we stood close together in the darkness beneath the iron girders, much to the annoyance of a few amorous couples, but these we turned our backs on and chatted – the precise subject of which conversation I cannot recollect.

When our train came in we searched in vain for the carriage with a white 'Private' label on the window. Its absence was reported to the guard, who promptly ousted several people from a compartment and officiously stuck the necessary white label on the window.

So we had privacy at least – till another party arrived, and who should it turn out to be, but the other group from our Camp who had also set out about nine o'clock that morning to collect its prisoner from Kensington.

Well, now we were quite a happy little gathering, two corporals, two privates, and two prisoners, with six sandwiches between us and a two or three hours journey ahead of us.

But the second prisoner wasn't handcuffed at all – and what a happy, short, broad-shouldered, red-headed Irishman he was – with a beaming face that outshone our glum party, and a brogue that made his speech frequently unintelligible.

Private Murphy (the Irishman of course), had gone absent without leave (AWOL) eight times before and he was quite used to it. And what was his interesting story?

I was unable to make a complete continuity from his talk, but the threads, such as I gathered, were these.

In the first place he had been absent for over a month before he was apprehended by the civil police eventually, for assault and battery on his wife. It appears, that contrary to many of his associates' advice, he had married his wife who was known openly to be a prostitute, and that on return home one evening he had found a Canadian soldier in bed with her. He promptly knocked the Canadian out, 'threw him out of his house' (or so he said!), and then set about his wife, whose 'head I bashed in and she's now in hospital.' (True?)

After this episode he went off for a time but 'returned to the scene of his crime' where his mother-in-law asked him to see her. There he met her, and as soon as he saw the couple of policemen with her he began 'to let her have it too, for shopping me'.

Thus was friend Pte. M. taken into custody and locked away safely, but not before he had had the chance to tell the doctor that he would 'do her in and next time I'll slit her throat from ear to ear' – going through the motions as he told us. It seemed an immense joke to me and all the present company as he related his tale, for he didn't once betray any sorrow, and all the while he laughed and smiled apparently quite happy.

It was a great joke too, returning without the cuffs. He had been quite free to slip away if he had pleased, but instead he remained out of loyalty to this guard.

Coming up from Kensington, he laughingly told us, that one of his mates who had been released under escort a few hours before he himself had been, had met him on the Kensington platform on his way home. He had given his escort 'the slip' somehow! Quite funny in one way, but incomprehensible to me in another.

The prisoners had the usual exchange of confidences and questions.

Why had Private P. not been more successful?

'Well, I had no civvy clothes, and anyway, if I could have done another week's work I would have had enough to buy a set of cards – grade four medical category and ration and identity cards for only £10.'

We had all the windows of our compartment closed of course, a typical ill-ventilated railway compartment, stuffy and smelly, and so it wasn't long before Pte P. fell asleep, and Pte M. followed. The Corporals too, soon exhausted their mutual flatteries, and when I could not continue to read my *War and Peace* due to low light, I struck up a conversation with Pte L. – my opposite number with respect to Pte M. – who was destined (as I found out), for the Intelligence Corps and who spoke French and Italian fluently. He had been a student at the Paris Polytechnic in pre-war days, and lived in Milan, or Milano as he called it. Our talk was mutually enlightening. He spoke of contemporary French literature and life, and I of English Trade Unionism and Industrial Psychology.

On arrival at Bury St Edmunds, the two parties lost each other in the black-out. Whilst the train was in motion we had been unchained, but then again on alighting we were forced into very close proximity. We had arrived in Bury about eleven o'clock, and our search for a WVS canteen was not in vain. In there we could not hide the cuffs, for we couldn't circumnavigate the disorderly arrangement of tables and chairs so close together.

And then we got down to the root of the matter.

He didn't see why he should fight for 'the Government'; they had never done anything for him or his pal. How much worse off would he be if Jerry won? He would welcome the Germans and the chance to be a Gauleiter for them. How he would revenge himself on all those who had persecuted him!

To hear this saddened me. Somehow, to talk of 'democracy' and 'opportunity' to one who had seen only the roughest side of life seemed hypocritical and naive. I was acutely aware of my inability to answer his case. When he went up for trial by Court-Martial for desertion, I knew he would be convicted. It left me wondering how justice could be done. It seemed to me that the fundamental principles of right and justice, and a clear statement of what we were fighting for were the only real issues in his case, and never would he be reasonably dealt with by Army officialdom. One saw that in Private P. a social failure had been created and he alone was not to blame.

When last I saw Private M. he was eating anything and everything he could find in the Guard-room back at camp. So many times had he been in that Guard-room that he knew his way about it better than even the Military Police. He knew where they kept the cups and as I entered, to everyone's amusement, Pte. M. was searching the cupboard for the guard's midnight supply of cocoa and cheese.

As for Private P., he refused to eat. He 'didn't want to cost the Government any more'. He refused to sign all Army documents and put on Army clothing. What would you have done with him? I neither saw nor heard more of him again, since I left for pre-OCTU the next afternoon.

CHAPTER X

To Italy

I KNEW FROM THE TIME OF ARRIVAL at Arborfield that after attending the sixteen-week Armoured Fighting Vehicle Course, I would be given a short leave and then shipped abroad. Where? North West Europe, Central Mediterranean Forces (CMF), India and Burma, Pacific Far East? Whichever, I tell no lies when I say I prayed that it would be Italy.

My father and future wife saw me off from London Road Railway Station, Manchester. With my father I shook hands and he walked away without looking back, leaving Heather and me together for perhaps ten seconds before the train pulled out. Of course the train's departure broke up many such small groups. We travelled to Nottingham and then by lorry to the Mobilisation Centre where our overseas destinations were listed. The majority of young REME officers were bound for India. I found my name – and not for the first (or last) time, God noted my preference – W. Johnson, directed to Italy; there were just four of us, as against two or three dozen who went to hotter climes. I remember going into Nottingham town centre the following day but recall only the Trip to Jerusalem (the oldest ale house in Britain, they said) which was pointed out to me. We were assembled at 9 p.m. the same evening and with the ORs (Other Ranks), a body of perhaps 60, lined up and marched to the railway station. It is hard to believe but in our short march, women – mothers, wives and sweethearts – appeared from nowhere, to attach themselves to men for a few seconds, kiss and call out words of farewell; some produced bottles of beer for 'their boy' or 'their man'. At the station we formed up on the platform, quietly. The many-coached train arrived, some compartments being already labelled for officers and one of which was designated for the four of us. All went very easily. By 10.30 p.m. we were away. Slowly but steadily we soon noted we were going northwards – Scotland? – we stretched out and slept as best we could. There were many stops and starts as the train collected more troops, that is until 1 or 2 a.m. when, as the locomotive steamed into some small Yorkshire town, there was the enormous irruption of a military band playing with all the energy it could command. Startled, we peered out of the window and beheld the wonderful sight of an array of the KRRs (King's Royal Rifle Corps), all standing to attention. As the train came to a halt a well-formed platoon headed by four very young officers (their green caps set centrally over their foreheads) in front of a platoon of perhaps 30, were being shaken vigorously by the hand of their Colonel. The band was to one side of the platform with some non-boarding KRRs constituting companions. The goodbyes and best wishes finished, the group mounted the train. The music had stopped. Then, as the guard waved off the train, up struck the band again with their loud, vigorous regimental march and we were played to whilst drawing out of the station. Everyone was impressed with the display, so alive was it at such a God-forsaken time and situation. No further such event interrupted our onward journey to an obviously Scottish port.

We came up finally almost alongside a ship moored on the Clyde – I believe at Greenock.

Whilst waiting to board the ship we noticed a congregation of bedraggled troops, obviously of foreign origin. We were quite separate from them but knew somehow that they were not Allied troops – perhaps from their clothes and their 'herded' arrangement. I have since thought that many of them were anti-Russian troops from Yugoslavia.* Anthony Eden had consented to their return to Russia. (I believe they were disposed of subsequently by Stalin – several hundred, if not thousands. This subject is still talked of and is a matter in which Eden, and perhaps even Churchill, complied in a shameful agreement with Stalin when they well knew what was going to happen; it is a matter most people prefer to forget.)

On board ship we were well accommodated. I think we had one four-bunk compartment. In the bowels of the ship, the ORs were scattered among strung-up hammocks, in places as many as five deep. (Where sergeants were ensconced, I do not know – I don't recall seeing any.) We officers received first-class dining service: we were waited on at a table – the edges of which folded up (presumably so that nothing would spill). We had a printed menu daily (one is copied in Figure 1), each meal being of several courses. The ORs got, and always had, 'iron', prison-like meals, plain bread and jam, and food from large pots – possibly porridge. We sailed out of the Clyde after standing out in the Firth of Forth for three cold and blustery days and it seemed then that we went out straight into the mid-Atlantic, later changing to travelling due south. It was winter and the weather, rough. Sea-sickness was suffered by nearly everybody. We young officers each served an Orderly Officers' Duty Day; we were expected to visit the ORs in the hold to determine if they had any complaints. I only performed that task twice. I think tiny Lieut. Manson, hailing from one of the Scottish islands, once substituted for me. When I visited the hold, men in the top bunks were vomiting from a height of several feet. The food being swilled or 'served' was of the most primitive kind and the men's circumstances were appalling. I was ashamed at the difference in the conditions given to the 'men' and to the 'officers'. I never saw a senior officer to report or complain to, even in the last part of our voyage. The sight of those conditions under which the troops lived, has stayed with me ever since it occurred. I wondered why the troops themselves did not express their dissatisfaction vocally. I was reminded of the appalling conditions in which naval gunners lived on the gun decks of old wooden battleships.

At some point in mid-Atlantic we must have turned east and headed for Gibraltar. All that I recall is waking up early one morning, looking through the

---

* A few of the western Yugoslav states were Roman Catholic and pro-Hitler at the time.

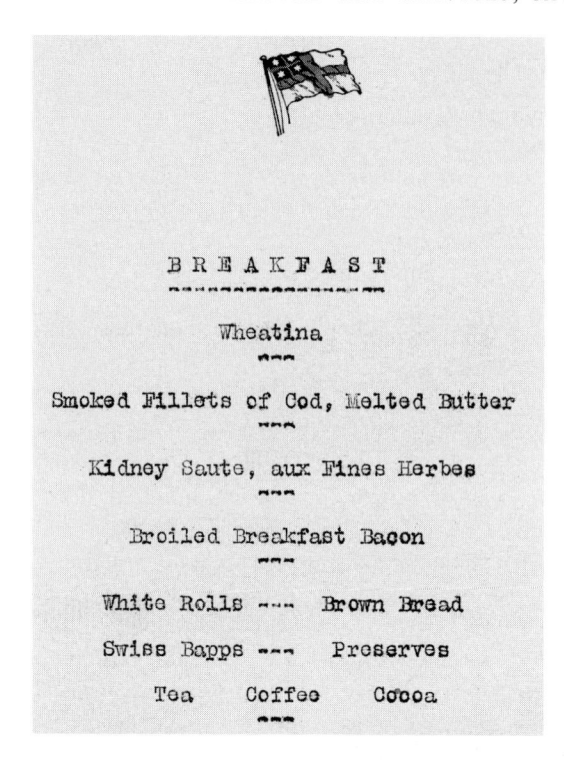

```
        B R E A K F A S T

            Wheatina

Smoked Fillets of Cod, Melted Butter

   Kidney Saute, aux Fines Herbes

       Broiled Breakfast Bacon

   White Rolls ---- Brown Bread

   Swiss Bapps ---  Preserves

      Tea   Coffee   Cocoa
```

Figure 1. Breakfast aboard ship to Italy – for officers – near to the end of the Second World War!

port-hole and seeing a small, gaily-painted boat moving by – and in the background there was the dear old Rock of Gibraltar as it is commonly seen, reclining grandly with the sun shining upon it. It was absolutely unforgettable. In the last few days all other ships had disappeared; there was no convoy protection. Then, through the Straits and onwards due east. For the past two weeks I had been reading Robert Graves' *I Claudius*; few other books in literature could better have matched my circumstances and indeed my heart took a great leap – Italy! (See Figure 2.) On our entering the Mediterranean, the weather had 'picked up' and it was lovely and fresh, though we were still in the very early part of the year. Thus we came to the magnificent Bay of Naples, with smoking Vesuvius in the background. One thought of Pompeii and Herculaneum around the Bay and Ischia and Capri in the distance. I recollected Graves' description of the later days of Tiberius, when performing his dark deeds ... What more could a man ask for?

We berthed in the ancient *Sinus Cumaenus*, not close at a dock-side but alongside another ship, on its side, sunken and fixed, over which we filed onto the dock-side. Italian labourers were having trouble unloading some equipment and goods. A large group of us watched their antics from above; a wooden packing-case became loose and rolled into the sea! It was an occasion for great humour ... Laurel and Hardy couldn't have done better.

We marched up through the town to a camp on a hillside with lots of 'bell' tents around.

Of the four of us young replacement officers, each with a degree in mechanical engineering, I was the only one who had made the acquaintanceship of Production

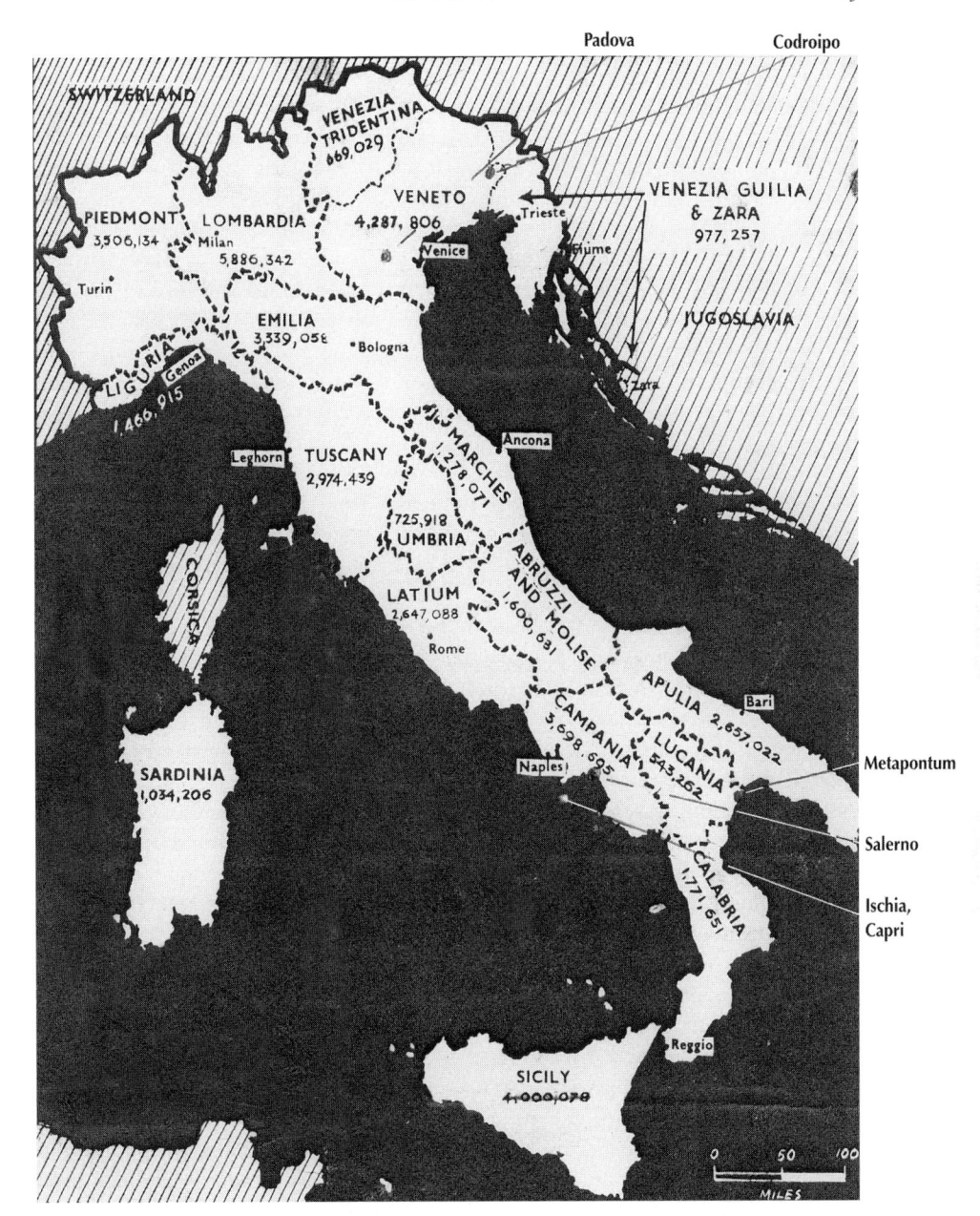

Figure 2. Italy showing the provinces and their populations (1936 Census).

Engineering. I was a graduate member of the Institution of Production Engineers, as well as the Institution of Mechanical Engineers. 'Production' was roughly equivalent to Production *Manufacture*, whereas Mechanical was concerned with the design and supply of specialist equipment.

I had had visions of a job to be filled in Italy which had been called for, at some time, by General Montgomery! (However I learned he had gone back 'home' to lead the Second Front, as it was called, in north-west Europe.)

So, looking back, I remembered my Professor (Wright-Baker) at the Tech., who disapproved or looked down upon, Production Engineering which, essentially, I had preferred when making it my second third-year Special Option.* I chose Internal Combustion Engines for my other Option – and, of course all the other usual ordinary subjects of a Mechanical Engineering degree – Mathematics, Design, Theory of Machines and Vibrations, Strength of Materials and Hydrodynamics, etc. The importance of Production Management had become very clear to me from the nature of my father's job as a foreman. He was engaged in the massive production of barbed wire, 'up to standard' in size and finish; after inspection it would have been coiled or rolled up and prepared for sending to designated places 'at home and abroad' – needed in abundance for defending the realm.

My father's out-of-date procedure in recruiting labour was to select from among men who simply hung about the firm's front gate! When a new method was introduced, i.e., of having a special new Office of Employment in his firm – a radical diversion – he was appalled at his exclusion from the selection process and the expense of the new office.

Majesterially, I came to believe that I knew well what was wanted in a Manufacturing Course and put together suggestions for individual subjects in connection with the Institution of Production Engineers' announcement of a Lord Austin (of Oxford) Essay Prize; there was a requirement for a three-thousand word essay. My submission was written in barrack rooms and army NAAFI (Naval, Army and Airforce Institute) canteens during the eight weeks at my Primary Training Centre at Maidstone, when I first joined up. In the essay a general case was first made and then one for individual subjects, with details of content, argued, the whole being typed out by my wife-to-be. It won me the prize and I promptly asked for the *three* volumes of Lipson's *Economic History of England*. In granting my request though, the Institution of Production Engineers asked me to send *them* three guineas 'by return', since each volume cost two guineas! I thought privately, Lord Austin might have been able to stretch to something slightly more than three guineas! The offices of the I.Prod.E., including its library, were burnt down during the Blitz. Their copy of my essay was lost (as I was informed when wishing to take a copy of it, later). This *is* true because they supplied me with a fine certificate for display!

Britain's long incapability in manufacturing engineering products economically and efficiently, by comparison with foreign competitors, is well brought to light by Norman Atkinson in his *Sir Joseph Whitworth (1803–1887): the World's Best Mechanician*. After visiting the USA, specifically, Whitworth wrote about how much better were the Americans in production engineering, even in the 1860s. We remember too how good are German and French motor car producers and

---

* In order to go to the Industrial Administration Department for reading material and supervision for this Second Option – I was in a class of one – I was not able to attend one of my two obligatory mathematics lectures.

that Japan has long since overhauled us, though it had not even started production in the mid-nineteenth century. Alas, we British have only ourselves and our culture to blame. Too highly was *The Don's* classical nineteenth-century culture valued and applauded!

In mentioning Gibraltar above – this is now quite out of chronological order – I paid a week's visit to it with my wife, after retirement, to view its military emplacements. We had returned from our few years at Purdue University in the USA, where I had written a long article about one eighteenth-century military episode of the Rock's history. As I am unlikely to be able to return to the subject of Gibraltar, I thought it worthwhile to mention here the article and its content. See Figure 3, *The Siege of Gibraltar (1779–83)* and related Figure 4 below.

The following article describes one of the most memorable of confrontations – yet is almost unknown in common British naval-military history – between Spanish and French fleets and the Gibraltar garrison. At the time of the battle, the stand-off between the American states and Britain was at its height.

Figure 3.

The Siege of Gibraltar: Mostly relating to the shooting of hot shot and setting fire to a besieging fleet

Delivered as a lecture at UMIST, 18 March, 1987 and published in the I.J.Impact Eng., 6, pp.175–310, 1987

Summary – The Siege of Gibraltar, 1779–1783, is generally regarded as one of the most memorable in military history yet it is hardly known by students of engineering impact. The paper concentrates mainly on describing artillery exchanges between the besiegers, Spanish and French, and the defenders, British. This great attack on the Gibraltar garrison was made by battering ships in September 1782. Also, topic by topic, e.g. Carcasses and Fire ships, etc., brief accounts are given of the use of these sorts of organs of attack in this protracted struggle; they have relevance to some present-day issues in the field of impact. Despite paying particular attention to professional impact engineering, the more human and dramatic aspects of this siege are not neglected.

Gibraltar

Gibraltar is very near to, but not at the tip of, the Iberian peninsula nearest to Africa; it forms one of the two historical *Pillars of Hercules* known in pre-Christian times as Calpe or Alybe and Abyla; the latter later became the name of the prominence Ceuta,* which is 14 miles south on the other side of the Straits of Gibraltar (or Gut as it was called in the nineteenth century). This pair of hills long marked the historical western limit of trading for ancient Mediterranean peoples. It only became occupied, by Arabs, at the period of Islam's rapid expansion in AD 711 when a force led by a certain

---

* Today Spain exercises a protectorate over north west Morocco and besides Ceuta, possesses Melitta, Alhucemas, Penon de Velez de la Gomera and the Chafarinas Islands off the Moroccan coast.

Tariq captured it and started the building of a castle on the face of the hill. It was completed in 725 and became known as Gibel-Tariq, Jebel Tariq or the mountain of Tariq; this was subsequently corrupted to Gibraltar.

A map of present-day Gibraltar is seen in Fig. 1(a) in the original article and indicates the old Spanish and British lines in the eighteenth and nineteenth centuries. Many marine, military and civil structures have, naturally, been demolished since 1779–1783 which is the period of concern in this paper. The Gibraltar peninsula is about three miles long and one mile wide but has a breadth at the isthmus of only 900 yards; the hill rises to nearly 1400 ft. Impressions of nineteenth century and modern Gibraltar appear in Fig. 1(b).

Gibraltar became part of the Spanish crown's domain in 1502 when Islamic influence in Europe was in decline. It was regarded as impregnable especially by virtue of the early fortification designs of Daniel Speckle* (1536–1589). However, the Rock was captured by the Dutch and British in July 1704 after a three-day siege.†

Unsuccessful sieges by Spain in 1720 and 1726 failed to recover it and negotiation did not succeed for the Spanish either. In July 1779 hostilities at Gibraltar began during the American War of Independence, when the Spaniards (mostly) and French besieged the British in their fortress. Most of the British military and naval forces were then principally preoccupied several thousand miles away with revolt of their American colonies. The four-year siege of Gibraltar, which it turned out to be, is generally regarded as 'one of the most memorable in history' according to an entry in the *Brittanica Encyclopaedia*, Vol. 10, 1946, p. 336. The Governor was to be General Sir George Augustus Elliot (or Eliot) (1717–1790), who got to Gibraltar shortly after the siege had started as part of Lord Howe's convoy. This had left Spithead on 11 September and despite violent storms arrived in Gibraltar with 34 ships of the line and more than 100 merchantmen.

A small naval assault force first engaged the Gibraltar garrison on 11 July, 1779, but was not successful. Afterwards, the siege was conducted by blockade, by attempting starvation and by naval attack with frigates, battering ships, fire ships, with mortars fired from bomb ketches, and from land bombardment and by infantry sorties and assaults. At some time during the four years of assault all these different methods and devices were employed. The siege was raised or ended in February 1783, the garrison not having yielded.

The British defenders on the Rock won the day in that February by firing hot cannon balls. The latter were well known at the time as Figure 4 confirms.

---

* A prestigious German military architect, see pp. 54–57 of C. Duffy's *Siege Warfare*, Routledge & Kegan Paul Ltd, 1979.
† The Catholic King yielded Gibraltar to England through the Treaty of Utrecht in 1713 and the Treaty of Versailles, in September 1783, confirmed it.

The siege of Gibraltar

THE

GREAT ART

OF

ARTILLERY

OF

CASIMIR SIMIENOWICZ,

Formerly LIEUTENANT-GENERAL of the
Ordnance to the King of *Poland.*

Translated from the FRENCH,
By *GEORGE SHELVOCKE,* Jun. Gent.

Illustrated with Twenty Three Copper Plates.

LONDON:
Printed for J. TONSON at *Shakespear's Head in the Strand.*
M DCC XXIX.

CHAP. XVII.
Of RED-HOT BALLS.

THE Practice of shooting *Red-hot Iron,* is far from being of modern Date; for long before the Invention of our *Artillery,* it was the Custom of the *Ancients* to defend themselves with *Red-hot Iron,* as is testified by *Diodorus Siculus,* who saith: *That the Tyrians threw great Bodies of Red-hot Iron into the Works of* Alexander the Great. An uncertain Author also speaks to this Effect in *Suidas: They threw from Eminencies whatever was Liquid or Fusible, scalding hot upon the Enemy. And amongst other Things* Red-hot Pieces *of* Iron, *which they kept ready for those who attempted to scale their Walls.* † *Vitruvius* also speaking of the People of the Town of *Marseilles,* saith, *That they threw Bars of* Red-hot Iron *from* Balistæ *to burn the Besiegers Works.* If you would be farther informed upon this Head, you may consult those Authors, whose Testimony we have all along recurred to. But to dwell much upon the great Request *Red-hot Balls* have been in since the Invention of *Gun-powder,* or to recount the Havoc they have made, or to relate their frightful Executions in the several Occurrences of *War,* would be giving of myself a needless Trouble; since none can be Strangers to this matter, but those who have never borne Arms, or never dealt in *History,* which does furnish us with many Examples of this kind:

The title page of the book of 1729 by General Simienowicz. (d) The beginning of the chapter on Red-hot Balls.

Behold, the French, amaz'd vouchsafe, a parle;
And now instead of *bullets wrapp'd in fire,*
To make a shaking fever in your walls,
They shoot but calm words folded up in smoke
To make a faithless error in your ears;....

Figure 4.

CHAPTER XI

Central Purchase and Production

THE WAR WAS EDGING TO A CLOSE though no one knew how long it would be before there was a German capitulation. The War for the Allies had consisted of campaigns – North African, Italian, Greek, (North West) European, Far East and so on. Each was different in that it had its own strongly-marked characteristics. My own experience was with the second, the Italian campaign: it was not going to have an easy end for the Allies. Now that they had fought their way up the Apennines of Italy (there were people who thought this campaign was a serious error*) and broken through the Hitler line, the next battle would be on the Lombardy plain, and after that the armies would sweep up into the Cis-Alpine regions to Austria and Bavaria. The fighting would be endless for it would be all struggle against an enemy for whom the mountains would be a great defensive help.

My part in it all was of no great value. Being a mechanical engineer with an interest in production or manufacturing engineering and Institution grade certificates in both subjects, meant that I would be of value in army equipment workshops and allied activities rather than in the infantry. From the camp in Naples I was the first of the four officers to be selected for a specific job – after being rapidly interviewed by a visiting REME major. Our tent in the Replacement Centre was at the edge of a cemetery which had been damaged and pillaged – one grave reputed to be that of the tenor, Gigli. Though the terrain was rough and overrun with small lizards, the weather was still warm and the conditions far from bad. I was there but one day, after talking to the Major, before being carried off with equipment, bedding roll and kit bag to a Mess in the centre of Naples. It was one floor of an old office block, with its several young officers boxed into one small bedroom. It never turned out to be unpleasant – after all I could have been dumped out in the countryside with a rough itinerant infantry unit! My unit-to-be was Central Purchase and Production (CP & P) a REME-RAOC (Royal Army Ordnance Corps) group, put together to obtain for the Army items in short supply from the UK. We had to seek out the tiny private workshops in and around Naples, which – using sweated labour and working in make-do premises – could supply, typically, petrol pump unions for cars, mess tins by the thousand, knives

---

* See *1943, The Victory that Never Was. The tragic mistake that delayed the end of the Second World War,* John Grigg, Methuen, 1980.

and forks as well as large crates for transporting damaged heavy tank engines back to the UK. I inspected working premises, discussed manufacture with employers, supplied metals or goods to them for conversion, gave out contracts and arranged a price, progressed the work, had it collected and inspected, and paid for if the product was satisfactory. (The tallest item we ever needed was a flag-pole and the smallest, baby clothes for our young ATS (Auxiliary Teritorial Service), women clerks who got themselves pregnant!)

Naples

My first posting with CP & P was to Naples where I remained for about two months. I was then transferred to Rome and functioned there for several months. during which time the war ended, before being moved back to Naples. Finally, I was moved up to the branch in Milan. Each location had its own very specific historical character. Below, I have given briefly some impressions of my work in these regions but there were many experiences which befell me which were not bound up directly with my main purpose. At a distance of 56 years I can only attempt to describe these events in simple terms.

Naples itself, towards the end of the war, was always full of troops of many nationalities. The city centre had many shabby streets and neighbourhoods. On the *via Roma* – once *via Toledo* when the kingdom of two Sicilies existed – little boys would run up beside one and ask, 'Want a woman, Johnny?' Shops were reappearing and selling goods of various kinds. I remember buying a tiny radio for instance, which lasted me for two years. (I had already exchanged a bottle of whisky for an ex-tank military radio but that was too large and relied on an uncertain accumulator.) Theft was very common in what was a big, militarily controlled port, in which all kinds of expensive goods could be had. I bought two dozen old '78' records of opera and Neapolitan love songs, produced before the start of the war, which the troops at home later introduced to the UK populace, as they did pasta-based dishes! Of course, we entertained ourselves with visits to the large Allied-controlled hotel for lunches, dinners and short respites from duty; the other ranks had their own massive canteens or clubs. When the Opera opened I was a frequent visitor, hearing for the first time in my life, Italian arias sung by star performers.

Most of my contracts for various military items were produced by small companies which mainly straddled the coast road south out of Naples down to Salvatore Annunziata and Torre del Greco. The road to these places passed by Herculaneum and Pompeii. At some point I took off a couple of hours to visit the latter – which then offered free entry to troops. But Bulwer Lytton's famous novel *The Last Days of Pompeii* was nowhere to be bought (or borrowed) in the area! This road led on to Sorrento and Amalfi.

Whilst contracts were fulfilled, mostly using juvenile labour, one company had been started up in the local Naples prison, where its chief executive appeared to be an inmate, serving several years for embezzlement! The latter I visited to 'progress' a contract placed there by one of my predecessors. When I arrived at the jail, the huge gates were always opened quickly to the *'militari'* – by brightly clad *carabiniere*. I was then conducted to a prison-cell-cum-office and after a few words, cakes and coffee would be served by a pretty young waitress. I often reflected that she was there for selection as much as the cakes were.

I once gave a small contract to one Angelino Antimo; it was the first time he had been awarded a contract with us, and he was so pleased that he called into our office a few days later with two large turkeys, freshly strangled, for our Mess dinner. (We were pleased to pass on one of them to the Sergeants' Mess). So, no hesitation about greasing the Unit's palm. A small memorandum I preserved from the Head of that company is seen in Figure 1.

One of my special operations was to supervise an Army timber yard. I was supposed to authorise all the timber which left the yard for contractors as per the contracts. A certain number of scantlings (flat, 20ft. lengths of timber to be made up into cases for large tank engines, then returned by ship to the UK) would be authorised and loaded on to a truck for delivery. However I knew that sometimes instead of 40, 41 would be loaded. That 'error' was an item which could be sold easily on the open market, for which they received an underhand sum from the company we were supplying.

Timber parks normally estimate their holdings in cubic feet, but the Army generally asked for monthly returns by *weight*. Largely this was fine and could be estimated, except when we had rain, which then caused our holdings to be suddenly increased. I remember on one occasion, taking a telephone call while visiting a company, to say that the Army guard in my timber yard was under assault. The yard was actually on a railway siding (possibly at Tuscolana), and being fired upon from the lower slopes of Vesuvius. Fortunately, no-one was hurt, but this did not happen only once. Recall that everything was in short supply for the Italian population at this time: there was little non-military transportation by road – there was no petrol and they were short of tyres and engine parts. Our transport was stolen from time to time by enterprising thieves. Incidentally, US soldiers supplied us with timber, by the truck-load from the docks, shipped up from the south of Italy, Lucania. See Figure 2, in Chapter X.

Mount Vesuvius, incidentally, was a smoking ash heap all the time I was there, though a year earlier, in 1944, there had been a serious eruption. On the route from central Naples out towards the north west, I noted a tunnel, said to be of ancient origin. Of most interest was the fact that this area was the once-historical town of Cuma. Particularly, I remember here a pre-Christian stone fort which looked out over the sea and was a most impressive construction. I walked through the fort noting that it seemed to have been used recently by the Germans for gun emplacements; and abandoned war material and wagons were spread over the site. I recall that in one location, an underground reservoir seemed to have been constructed out of solid stone. It was dank and dark and littered with small snakes.

This area was also that of the Phlegrean Fields, a volcanic area which gave off a distinctly sulphurous odour; I believe the modern name of the area is Solfetaro. Because the ground sported small craters it was thought in ancient times to be the entrance to the underground regions of Hell and Purgatory! Dante wrote in his *Inferno* of being led through these regions by Virgil. (See *In the*

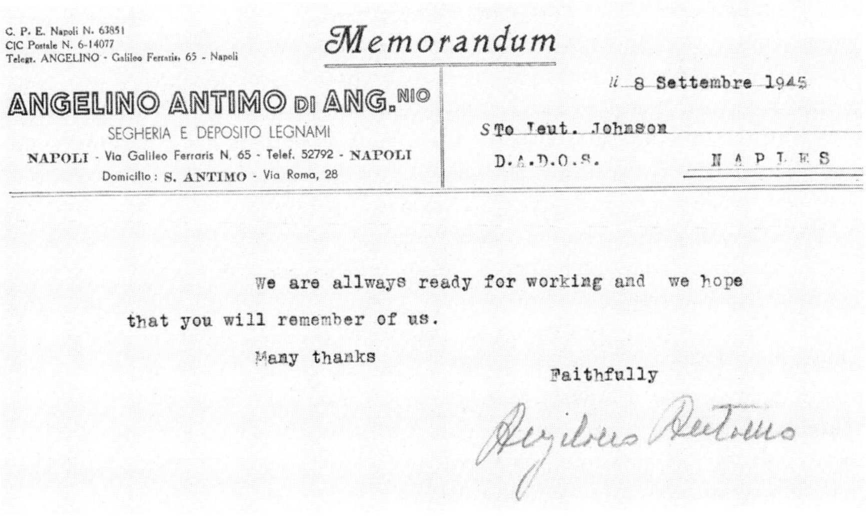

```
C. P. E. Napoli N. 63851
CIC Postale N. 6-14077
Telegr. ANGELINO - Galileo Ferraris, 65 - Napoli
```

ANGELINO ANTIMO DI ANG.NIO
SEGHERIA E DEPOSITO LEGNAMI
NAPOLI - Via Galileo Ferraris N. 65 - Telef. 52792 - NAPOLI
Domicilio: S. ANTIMO - Via Roma, 28

Memorandum

li 8 Settembre 1945

S To Leut. Johnson

D.A.D.O.S.   NAPLES

We are allways ready for working and we hope that you will remember of us.

Many thanks

Faithfully

Figure 1. Memorandum.

Footsteps of Orpheus, by R. F. Paget, Scientific Book Club, London. It deals with finding and identifying the lost entrance to Hades – the Oracle of the Dead, the River Styx and the Infernal Regions of the Greeks, 208 pp.).

The region of ancient Cuma was one of the first settlements in Europe made from the Eastern Mediterranean, Greece and Persia, dating back to about 1000 BC. This port was noted for its trade in precious metals, principally tin, with Cornwall, in England. Many ancient Roman buildings had visibly subsided into the sea and are today the subjects of marine archaeological investigations.

In the elevated area hereabouts was The Orange Club for officers, from which inebriated celebrations were said to be heard.

At the other side of Naples, in Sorrento, there was a large military hospital, which was spoken of with great respect.

It was amazing, incidentally, that one could tell if one of the larger battleships was in port, whether British or American, without actually seeing it, for then there would be long queues waiting outside the local VD centre. After intercourse, the British soldiers were required to follow certain procedures, in private. This done correctly, the men were supplied with a note which, when passed on in their own units, would ensure that their pay was not then 'docked' when made to their wives at home.

I recollect meeting up with a young French officer, who, like myself was greatly interested in visiting Paestum; it was reputed to have the finest specimens of Greek temples anywhere. Together we set out on a journey southwards, in great anticipation of seeing Paestum's treasure. En route we saw Capri across the sea. It was out of bounds to us, as was Ischia. After an interesting drive we arrived on the shore of Paestum and noted as we walked across the site, the remains of battle from the relatively recent landings on the Salerno beaches. The area was still littered with slit trenches and army equipment. Whilst examining the temples with great earnestness, we were suddenly surprised to see a senior British officer's car arrive and deposit four very English-looking ladies carrying baskets, at the site entrance. Without looking at anything archaeological at all, they proceeded to the finest temple and from their baskets withdrew table-cloths which they set out on the stone floor at its centre. Other items were there being laid out which we could not see. Some time later, when we looked again in their direction they were very much enjoying lunch – an incongruous sight.

From Paestum, we went on down the coast to look at Eboli, a name made famous by Carlo Levi, who had not long ago written his acclaimed *Christ Stopped at Eboli*. (He had been exiled there by Mussolini.) The book's title implied that beyond Eboli, Christianity had not yet penetrated the hinterland. The village was an appalling collection of untidy dwellings, having sewage flowing down the main street. Walking over a railway crossing, we encountered the horrible sight of an adult leading along a youth, using a halter; his face was repellant in being physically corrupt – probably suffering from leprosy, said my doctor brother years later.

I had begun to learn Italian and to speak a few words of the language to help communication with my contractors. It was largely left to me as to how I dealt with them. We had a captain about to be married to a lady who was the daughter of an Italian naval admiral and as may be surmised, he spoke fluent Italian. On the other hand, one or two of my colleagues would not attempt any communication using Italian at all. I suppose there were about ten of us on the same sort of job – RAOC officers dealing with non-technical purchases and REME officers for technical ones. Translators could be employed but they made exchanges long and complicated. As an illustration, I recall appearing in a military court as the prosecuting officer in a case concerning a driver in our unit who was accused of stealing eight 1-cwt. boxes of lead spelter bars, and passing them on to an American GI. He was so careless as to unload it in the same street as that in which the military police had a Mess (unknown to him and his assistant of course.) The driver was seen and apprehended at the conclusion of the spelter transfer. The case was brought up and it fell to me for a second time to be a prosecuting officer in court. However, acting for the prosecution was very different from being a defending officer. I found that it was up to me to make the case and to prove the charge. I had had no training in legal activities and now there was no time to learn. On the morning of the case, the driver was in the dock and I was calling witnesses for questioning in order to make the case against him. (The Italian labourer who had accompanied him on the truck had already been tried by an Italian court and was in prison, serving a sentence.) The labourer was produced so that he could be questioned and had been brought from prison by two large *carabinierie*. They stood at his side whilst he gave evidence. I addressed questions to him through an interpreter. As may be imagined, it was a slow and sometimes comical situation. Also, the American GI was put on the 'stand'. He it was who had been caught red-handed taking over the spelter. The GI here was accompanied by an American officer – I suppose to see fair play. In all, the proceedings took three hours. All I had to call upon for guidance was the Army *Manual of Military Law* and, occasionally, the judge-major in charge of all the proceedings. The driver was found guilty and went to prison for two months.

We had in CP & P an RAOC officer who was, in civilian life, a solicitor in the legal department of the LCC (London County Council). He was required to defend a soldier accused of murder. Presumably, I had operated at the very limit of what could be expected of a non-professional.

It was in Naples where I took on the jobs of Education Officer and being in charge of the running of our NAAFI unit, especially the bar. To build the latter in the basement of our office block I acquired timber from my own yard. However, the lounge bar was also the lecture room for a handful of men, perhaps a dozen, who were my responsibility as the Education Officer. The Education Corps produced fine, large maps and booklets to facilitate the discussion of issues then current in the UK, e.g. the Beveridge Report, and world problems; see, for example, Figure 2 overleaf which was reproduced from a poster of approximate original dimensions 30″ × 40″. They were used as accessories when debating and discussing political and social issues. The education lectures were held in the evening and attendance was optional. The job of volunteer Education Officer followed me to Rome and included making arrangements for the taking of men and their women to the open air opera in the Forum Romanum. *La Bohème*, *Aida* and *Madame Butterfly* were heard there by most of us, for the first time; in the long summer evenings, performances started about 9.30 p.m. and ended after 1 a.m. They were superb evenings.

It seems I tried too to promote serious thought about our country's future by inclining troops to save money (see Figure 3); it was to little effect.

I would not wish to forget that on the day that Pietro Mascani (1863–1945) died I happened to be at the Opera House. At the start of the evening's performance, a silence was observed and the orchestra remembered Mascani with a rendering of *Cavalleria Rusticana* – a man whose music is remembered almost only by the overture.

A most curious addition to our Naples Mess was that of a small number of RAF officers who came to stay in our billets from time to time. They flew out from somewhere in Norfolk, UK, to Naples with certain special supplies. They came to our Mess for two nights to be 'at home' with us. When they departed, as a *quid pro quo*, they took with them a collection of addressed small wooden, shoe-sized boxes, for posting when they got back to the UK. Some contained, for example, silk stockings, whilst others were packed with dried fruit or an occasional bottle of sherry, or figs, peaches and lemons with a little tree-branch attached, which the children in my family at home had not previously seen. This was therefore a good parcel post service, operated without authorities such as Customs and Excise (C & E) knowing anything about the irregularity. There was one Italian carpenter in our unit whose whole time was given over to manufacturing small boxes! An amusing practice at one time concerned the dodging of the censorship of mail which families operated using agreed simple codes with their sons, to say where they were.

The much praised Capri I never visited because it was said to be afflicted with malaria. I knew of it well from childhood, when working-class women of Lancashire were overwhelmed on hearing their much celebrated singer-comedienne Gracie Fields. She was heard on the radio and in all the music-halls,

TROUBLED BACKGR

N° 88 — FROM MARCH 11th TO MARCH 24th, 1946
(Published March 30th)

Mediterranean Sea

Key:
- PROVEN OIL FIELDS
- PIPE LINES
- INTERNATIONAL BOUNDARIES
- RAILWAYS (MAIN)
- PRINCIPAL ROADS

IMPACT OF THE OUTSIDE WORLD: THE OIL BASIN

★ SHADING SHOWS FOREIGN OIL CONCESSIONS - MOSTLY BRITISH AND AMERICAN

★ SHADING SHOWS AREA OCCUPIED BY MAIN MAP

ACCURATE CENSUS FIGURES NOT AVAILABLE FOR MUCH OF THIS AREA

EGYPT 17½ MILLION POPULATION

WORLD SETTING: W

MAP REVIEW No. 88. DRAWN AND COMPILED BY THE ARMY BUREAU OF CURRENT AFFAIRS

ROUND The Middle and Near East
ABCA MAP REVIEW

POLITICAL PATTERN: BACKGROUND TO ARAB ASPIRATIONS

> NOTICE
>
> NATIONAL SAVINGS.
>
> It is intended to start a Saving Group in this Unit to purchase National Savings Certificates.
>
> Though thrift is a commendable practice it is the lesser of the two reasons why we should save. Saving is deferred consumption and by buying Savings Certificates we put money into the hands of our Government for them to use on the finance of urgent social issues e.g. on Housing and to keep down direct and indirect taxation. Savings enables the Nation to use its productive power on the most urgent goods. Saving is a National Duty that is every bit as important during Reconstruction periods as during War periods. Much of the nations wealth and effort has been spent on the materials of war, but now, as we face Social Insurance, Education, Housing, Rehabilitation of Industry and Social Services, the Government needs as much financial support as ever it has had. The Finance of all State activities is either by Savings, Loans or Taxation. The later can only be reduced by increasing the former: By deferring our rights to less necessary goods (i.e, by saving) and by directing production on the most urgent needs of the country we are making an intelligent and practical effort to make a success of Post-War Problems.
>
> The Unit Educational Officer will see men who wish to be members of this Group. Contributions must be regular and the minimum weekly subscription is one shilling.
>
> (W. JOHNSON)

Figure 3. National Savings.

particularly touring the Manchester-Rochdale-Blackpool areas. Prior notice that Gracie would be on the radio was sufficient to keep most people indoors of an evening. At the height of her Lancashire acclaim it was suddenly announced in the papers that she was marrying an Italian and going to live in Capri. The people were astonished and neither got over the shock nor could understand her. She almost disappeared from view after this and her adoring audience had no more performances of *The Biggest Aspidistra in the World* or such typically comic songs. The populace shared with her the cotton mills of South Lancashire but the marriage between a little-known Italian and a working-class Lancashire lass was difficult to contemplate. (Around this time there was a popular dance-hall number called *It was on the Isle of Capri that I found you*.)

The only other knowledge I had of Capri then, in 1945, was through Robert Graves' Roman novel, *I Claudius*. I had also come to know Axel Munthe (1857–1949), the author of a world-class, semi-autobiographical best-seller, *The Story of San Michele* (1929) – it was a Swedish medical doctor's experiences when serving in the region around 1900. After the war, he returned to live in Capri, having acquired British citizenship.

From this time forward I became fascinated by the whole region of Southern Italy and only recently wrote about it in *Antient Philosophy-Science in Magna Graecia, Cassiodorus and Pythagorus, and twentieth-century literary travellers*

George Gissing and Norman Douglas' (IJMS, 42, 2075–97, 2000). English novelist George Gissing, a one-time Manchester University undergraduate, and writer Norman Douglas later travelled in this area, the latter writing several books about it. My own personal penetration into Southern Italy was only to the edge of Lucania at Eboli, to which I have already referred.

Rome

After a few months in Naples I was drafted to Rome and was there when the Second World War finished. Three recollections of my journey from Naples to Rome may be of interest. First, was the pausing en-route for lunch, outside a small village, when a crowd of children rapidly accumulated. They gazed so hard at our corned beef and 'Spam' sandwiches, cakes and hard biscuits, that all three in the party gave them up for the children to share. (True-to-style coffee and cakes could, I was told, be had freely from American stationary vans on some of the main roads, though I myself only ever encountered it once.) Secondly, my driver-colleague at some point in the journey remarked, 'You are now beginning to drive up the 'mad mile''. (This was an open mile of road reaching to the town of Monte Cassino and the hill behind it.) From around the monastery of Monte Cassino, at the top of a 1700ft. hill, German defences had bombarded roads and countryside, holding back the Allies for months, despite several efforts to take it. (The British and French each lost about 22,000 men and American and Polish losses were similarly large.) The hill and town of Cassino had been evacuated at the behest of the Germans, so that their position was nearly impregnable (Frank Majdalany has given one of the best accounts of the many allied assaults in his *The Battle of Cassino*, Ballantine Books Inc., NY, 1957.) When we had passed through the region my driver again remarked, 'You recognise that you have just passed through the town of Cassino?' (See Figure 4.) Some people were then living in caves along the banks of the Garigliano. Cassino was in fact the gateway to Rome up the adjacent River Liri. It was at Anzio that an allied sea-landing (slightly up the coast from Cassino) took place; it was 'touch and go' before the success of the landing was achieved.

And thirdly, realising I was entering Rome, I suddenly became aware of the walls of the Roman amphitheatre on my left. Then followed a short journey down the via Imperiale into the square, harbouring the famous balcony from which Mussolini harangued the masses. All this was memorabilia indeed, for it was my 23rd birthday!

Our technical offices in Rome were excellently located on the via Regina Elena but our billet, Mess and accommodation were very poor and equally poorly situated on the perimeter of the city. Our CO at the time was a gentle fellow – a major – who too easily accepted our miserable accommodation as satisfactory; he played the viola frequently and it accompanied him everywhere he was posted to. However, after a few weeks a very different, new CO took over and established for us a new Mess on the third floor of a block looking straight into the then-dry Fontana Trevi – a truly wonderful location (see Figure 5).

I recall well the ending of the Allied-Japanese war. Walking down a main

Monastery

Town

Figure 4. *Cassino: after the battle.*

street I saw on a newspaper stand a large headline, 'LA BOMBA ATOMICA'. For a day or two afterwards, I did not believe it, and thought it was incredible that nuclear physics had advanced so far. But true enough it was. A letter from my father at this time reminded me that it was not atomic bombs only that we should be thinking about. (See Figure 6.)

A notice had been circulated a few weeks earlier asking for men to go to the Far East theatre of war and in order to see the wonders of that part of the world, I had volunteered; that was now no longer applicable.

Life in the new Mess contained its usual typical comedies. Most of the officers had mistresses and indeed an older officer with whom I shared a room, more often than not, shared the bed with the female owner of our commandeered flat. On the floor below us it was alleged that a brothel existed which assured some American officers of a little joy. This was a summer of many pleasant days, which started for me after breakfast each morning by walking to the office up a narrow street where an early morning market was in progress. It was below the once royal Quirinale palace walls, where excited women sold small quantities of fruit, vegetables and the like. Along this street, small candle-lit statues of the Virgin Mary gave an aura of antiquity and peace to it all.

I assume that the job I was there to do for the Army I may take, now, to be understood by the reader! The short periods of leisure in which I sought education and pleasure at the same time, were similar to those just described. My first visit in Rome was to the Forum Romanum. I entered it as easily as if it was a public park, deliberately taking up a pose in the manner of Edward Gibbon. I well remember his description of going into the forum, and telling how he had seated

Figure 5. Quotation: The fountain of Trevi. Fontana di Trevi (Central part). Erected in 1735. Rome is the city of fountains. The Fontana di Trevi, erected by order of Pope Clement XII, in 1735, is the largest and most celebrated of the public fountains in Rome. Tradition goes that if on the eve of departure from Rome you throw a coin into the water, you cannot remain absent from Rome forever; destiny will bring you back. Fountains are to be seen everywhere in Rome; wherever you go you hear the pleasant sound of babbling waters. On every piazza, fountains, embellished with sculptures, elaborate marble basins, obelisks, etc., spit and splash streams of the most limpid and pure waters.

himself and decided that he would write on the Decline and Fall of Rome – not the Roman Empire until a year or two later. It was to Rome that my wife-to-be, Heather, sent, via Foyles in London, eight battered volumes of an early edition of Gibbon, published around 1800. I must confess to amazement that the Army Postal Service delivered two such heavy parcels at our offices on via Regina Elena, without demur! I thumbed the volumes well and read small excerpts, despite being confused by the use of the printed 'long s', (not 'f' but the German character) and being astonished at the clarity of Gibbon's own literary style. I proudly displayed these volumes on my desk in the office but my CO took exception to them and I was asked to put them out of sight on the window sill.

On VE day I was on duty touring the city as part of the military system for discouraging any 'troubles' should they arise. Everywhere was totally quiet except when we passed the locked entrance to the British Embassy where we saw a small gathering. Its members carried three flags, one the Union Jack, the Red Flag of the Soviet Union and the Italian flag/tricolor. With the help of a few musical instruments the gathering gave voice to 'God Save the King' and ended with 'The Red Flag'. It was an unbelievably incongruous situation.

A hundred yards from our Unit offices there was a fine cinema for the troops.

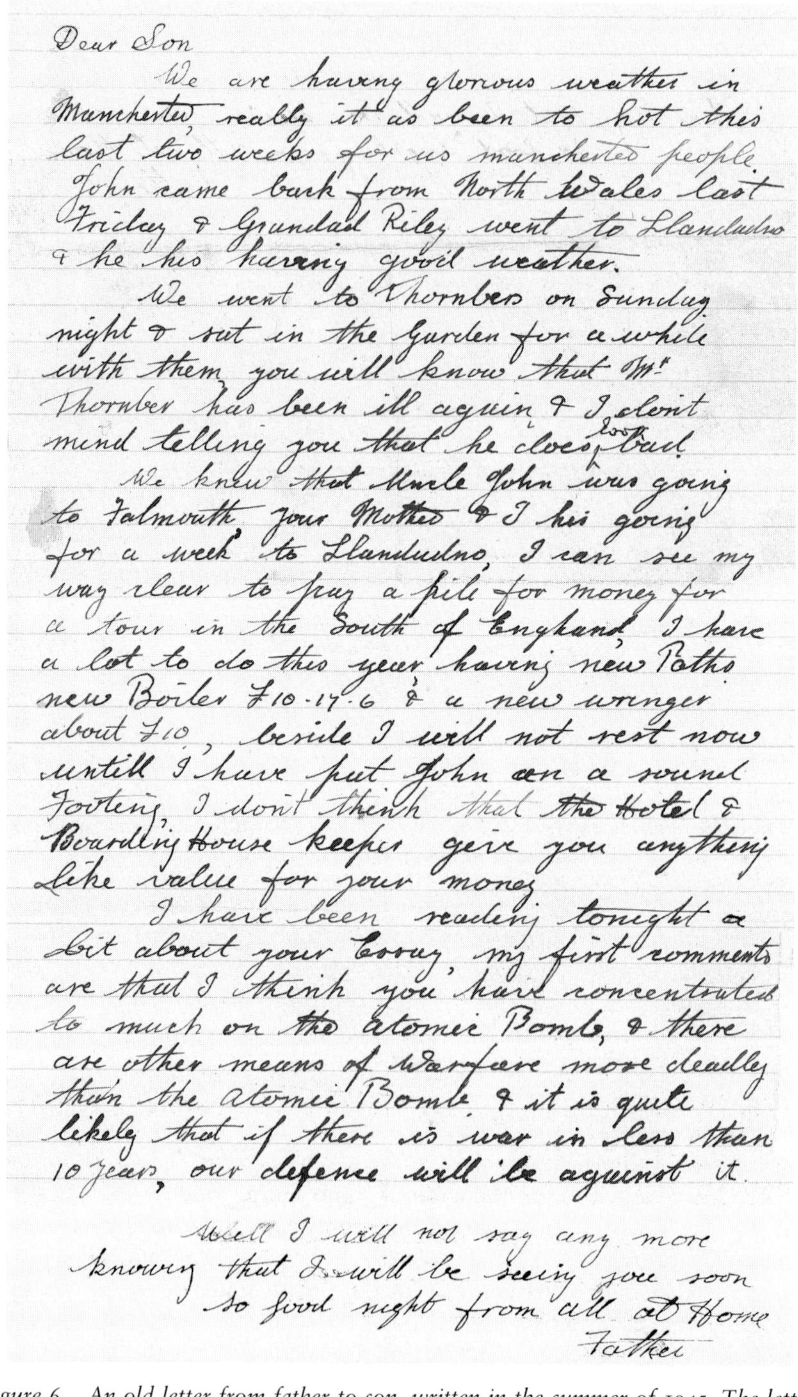

Dear Son

We are having glorious weather in Manchester, really it as been to hot this last two weeks for us manchester people. John came back from North Wales last Friday & Grandad Riley went to Llandudno & he his having good weather.

We went to Thornber on Sunday night & sat in the Garden for a while with them you will know that Mr Thornber has been ill again & I dont mind telling you that he does look bad.

We knew that Uncle John was going to Falmouth your Mother & I his going for a week to Llandudno, I can see my way clear to pay a pile for money for a tour in the South of England, I have a lot to do this year having new Paths, new Boiler £10·17·6 & a new wringer about £10, beside I will not rest now untill I have put John on a sound Footing. I don't think that the Hotel & Boarding House keeper give you anything like value for your money.

I have been reading tonight a bit about your Essay, my first comments are that I think you have concentrated to much on the atomic Bomb, & there are other means of Warfare more deadly than the atomic Bomb, & it is quite likely that if there is war in less than 10 years, our defence will be against it.

Well I will not say any more knowing that I will be seeing you soon so good night from all at Home
Father

Figure 6. *An old letter from father to son, written in the summer of 1945. The letter is notable for its style and interests rather than its pre-First World War orthography. His reference is to a long essay I had written about the atomic bomb.*

On each summer's evening, the roof would be drawn back and one looked up to the bright stars from the screen below. One evening, Laurence Olivier's version of Shakespeare's *Henry V* was shown. Unfortunately, the film was not well-received by the troops; it was loudly booed, then abruptly taken off. This was not quite as bad as the reception accorded to a film on the war in Burma in which all the military advances were led by conspicuously non-British senior officers, when chairs and beer bottles were hurled at the screen!

Late in the summer I discovered a nicely furnished coffee shop (for gentlemen-officers), in the basement of a 'ruin' on the edge of the forum which had been opened by a group of, so it seemed to me, Church of Scotland middle-aged ladies. It was a delight to call in for mid-morning coffee or lunch; such cleanliness, order and a desire to serve showed that civilised living was in process of restoration.

One of the books I had brought with me to Italy was the Penguin edition of Nicholas Pevsner's *European Architecture*. I followed this book in my little expeditions around Rome and, typically, I remember going one lunch-time to the small church of the Quattro Fontana (four fountains) and coming away believing that it was one of the most elegant ecclesiastical interiors I had ever encountered. It is not noted in most of the guide books in Rome. And one weekend later, I went to see St Paul's Outside the Walls, Figure 7(b). The ambulatory was, to my eyes, almost perfect in architectural form. These latter two items have stayed with me throughout life, as the most beautiful architecture I have ever seen. (About 18 years later my parents saw the St Paul's ambulatory – perhaps on my recommendation – when on a visit to Rome and sent me the postcard in Figure 7(a).) Thank you, Professor Pevsner, wherever you are! (Back in England at some time, between leaving one unit and joining another, I was assigned an office job in Leicester for a week, and fortunate to be able to attend an evening lecture that Pevsner was giving in the city museum. It turned out to be very enjoyable, just as I had expected.) Later, I also had the good fortune – in Padova (see Ch.15) where our military workshop was situated – to be close to the Arena Cappella where there were some large frescoes by Giotto and his pupils, from about 1304. In the words of the caption in one guide book, 'There are Saints, Prophets and Doctors'. On the lower part of the wall are allegorical figures of the seven Virtues and their opposite Vices. (The 'goings on' in Hell were much more interesting than those in Heaven!) As these kinds of events occurred to me many times in Italy I am not surprised that the Italian people have such excellent artistic taste. They see it every day and live surrounded by it from birth to death.

Rome was the only office in which we had Italian translators appointed to help us meet and negotiate with contractors. For my appointee I had a truly remarkable man in Count Giacomo di Vite de Marco. I have written about him at length and the long-term influence he had on my future interests in a recent paper, *Seeking Classical Manuscripts at Mount Athos and Seiches at Ancient Chalkis (IJMS, 42, 2469–2487, 2000)**, and therefore will not elaborate further, except to say that he arranged for me to meet Ralph Brewster, the author of a well-known book concerning *his* visit to Mount Athos, *6000 Beards of Athos* (1935). At his

---

* See Part IV, Chapter 4.

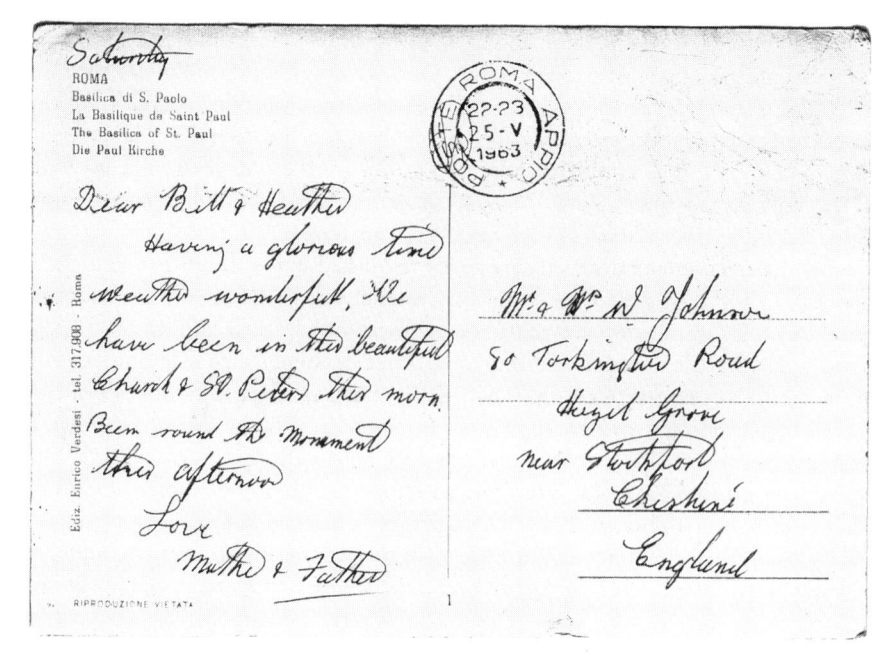

Figure 7(a). Postcard from Rome.

Figure 7(b). The ambulatory of St Paul's outside-the-Walls.

home in Florence, when I met him, we sat in his garden and talked about the war and Athos particularly, whilst eating fresh figs and drinking vermouth.

In the August of 1945 I managed to secure a week's leave in Florence which I put to good use in trying to see much of what I had read about. Only a few years ago I made such a visit again, this time with my wife (paid for by our offspring in celebration of our golden wedding anniversary). But for me there was too much of a contrast with that first visit. In 1945 there were few people around, the atmosphere seemed puritanical and well-fitted to the sparsity of the population and the general silence. There was then very little Italian traffic, though the tramcars which circulated around the Baptistery have now been removed – the atmosphere was quietly academic, not immensely touristic as it is now. Then, museums and galleries etc., were half-closed but a packet of cigarettes was more use than a 100-lire note for persuading guardians to unlock doors! I was very interested to have read about the English population in Florence in the eighteenth and nineteenth centuries – by seeing and reading their names at the English cemetery which is now engulfed in traffic. I had just read, at that time, George Eliot's *Romola*, and enjoyed it very much. Her treatment of her subject seemed to evoke well the atmosphere of the Florence she described.

Most weekends I did not miss the opportunity to travel into Umbria and visit some ancient historical monument or ecclesiastical structure. One occasion I well remember: still under the pressure of feeling that I might suddenly be plucked out of Italy and sent to the East, I did not intend to miss a visit to Assisi. It was out of bounds to troops at the time but, taking a chance, I nevertheless went there. Arriving outside what was obviously San Francesco and there being not a soul in sight, I went to what was probably the Oratory where St Francis (1181–1226) died. I tolled the bell at the entrance, feeling like a lone traveller at the end of a long journey, and a priest answered. I indicated that I would like to see inside and flourished a 100-lire note for the coffers, but he indicated that cigarettes were preferable to lire. (Though a non-smoker I always carried with me a supply of this second currency.) All I remember at this time is being conducted to St Francis's cell – a room containing a bed ready made-up, with a little lighted candle and small portions of food on the little table near the bed. Whilst it was a charming place I could not but wonder at the level of credulity, that St Francis was still being expected, though he had died about eight centuries ago! I remember little about the monastery and church of St Francis, completed around 1250, apart from there being upper and lower level churches much decorated by the frescos of Giotto and Cimabui.

After my visit to Assisi and out of sheer curiosity, I felt tempted to look into the Roman Catholic book, *The Little Flowers of St Francis* (see Figure 8) – something I think Protestants rarely do. I had some simplistic pre-conceptions derived from the title and consequently, received some surprises in finding that it was not wholly about flowers, birds and other small animals that were preached to by St Francis. The book, *I Fioretti* ... was translated from Latin and old Italian manuscripts (some parts of which are clearly fable). It is written by Ugolino Brunoforte (1262–1348); the manuscript is dated pre-1390. It consists of an early portion of 38 short chapters about St Francis himself, his companions and their lives as 'brothers'. The later portion of the book consists of sixteen chapters and describes certain of the brothers of the Marches area near Ancona. This little

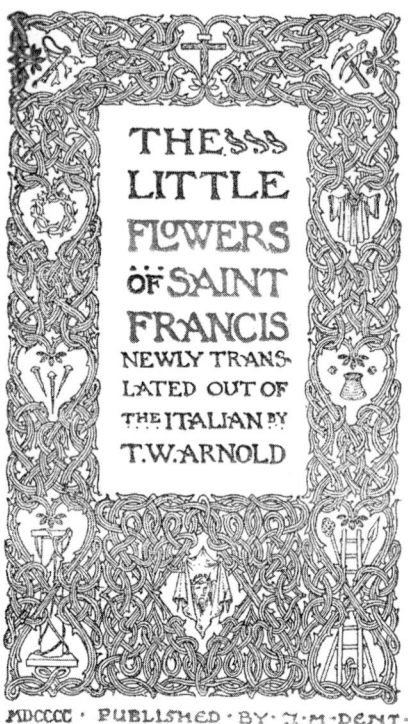

Figure 8. The Little Flowers of Saint Francis.

volume on the patterns of the holy early life of this brotherhood is 330 small pages in length. I give some examples below of the kind of material embraced by this volume.

The opening chapter tells of the founding of the Order of St Francis by his choosing 12 companions who were analogous with Christ's Apostles – even to a dejected one, John of the Chapel, who finally hanged himself. There are also references to certain 'little Flowers, miracles and devout examples of ... Christ and St Francis ...'

An early remark, such as may be met in the Bible, refers to St Francis passing Lent, alone, on an island in Lake Perugia for 40 days and 40 nights, 'taking with him naught save two small loaves.'

Also, we may learn of how St Anthony of Padua preached to fishes and St Francis to 'birds and made swallows hold their peace'. As well, that Brother Bentivoglio carried a leper 15 miles in 'a very brief space' (of time?).

There is a 60-page section on Stigmata and about St Francis's 'most holy miracle' in converting the 'fierce wolf of Agobio', the latter laying his 'right paw' in the hand of St Francis. A little later on we learn how St Francis ... received turtle doves ... into his bosom ... and began to speak tenderly unto them ...' The life of Brother Juniper (a character with whom I had not been previously acquainted), is related through some 25 pages, the first section of which describes, 'how he cut off the foot of a pig to give it to a sick man'. Later, his 'great power over demons', is described and of how he 'played see-saw to abase himself'.

The book is worth perusal if only to see how the minds of the mass of (European) mankind thought and believed in the thirteenth century.

I have written elsewhere of the value I believe attaches to browsing in libraries as an educational activity and I was therefore pleased to find this notion expressed by Leonardo Bruni Arezzo, writing about 100 years after Dante's death, so – '... by the study of philosophy, of theology ... astrology, arithmetic and geometry, by reading of history and *by turning over many curious books*, watching and sweating, he acquired in his studies, the science which he was to adorn ...' (Bruni enjoyed a fine reputation as scholar, historian and as chancellor of Florence, 1411–1444. As well, his elimination of providence as an historical cause, is said to mark the beginning of modern historiography. The importance of the latter topic is discussed in '... *Early Historical Sciences*' (*IJMS* 39 (10), 1077–1116, 1997.)

On the return journey from Assisi to Rome I met up with a vehicle accident and an American was brought to me with a request to take him to the nearest hospital which was in Rome. The poor chap had an eye hanging out of its socket and, accompanied by one of his colleagues, we went out of our way to do what was expected of us. I was a little apprehensive and reluctant to say why I was where I was, in an out-of-bounds area. (I now suspect this was not for any health reasons, but rather another of the unofficial understandings – not to have to attack over a region of great historical value.)

On another occasion, my journeying took me to Orvieto. The car had been parked and the problem was to find the cathedral because the streets were so narrow as to hide even a structure of considerable height. I mention this to explain the astonishment of turning into a square and suddenly being confronted with a huge Gothic cathedral having a many-coloured marble facade and sides of alternating horizontal black and white stone stripes (the latter were of two different kinds of stone). The town was old and dirty, as J. A. Symons had described in his *Sketches of Italy*. The cathedral was apparently begun in 1290 to commemorate the miracle of Bolseno, when the truth of transubstantiation (the emergence of blood from stone) was witnessed. The cathedral dominated the main piazza because it was built on a platform of earth raised above that of neighbouring streets. (See Figure 9.)

I remember that I visited the Palatine Hill in Rome and recalled that this had been a special centre for the homes of the well-heeled in classical Roman times. This was the location to which applies the fable of the crying geese that alerted guards to the danger of an enemy climbing the cliffs behind them.

I spent a day at the Vatican museum and recall G. Bernard Shaw remarking that it was so large that he felt hob-nail boots were required to cover the long distances over which the treasures were displayed. I remember thinking how I myself had hardly stopped walking over a period of three hours!

I pass on to an experience which occurs infrequently. The occasion arose when I was fortunate enough to secure a ticket to hear the performance of a Mass sung by one of the great Italian tenors of the time, in the Belvedere courtyard of the Vatican. I felt transported back into medieval times, when suddenly, the

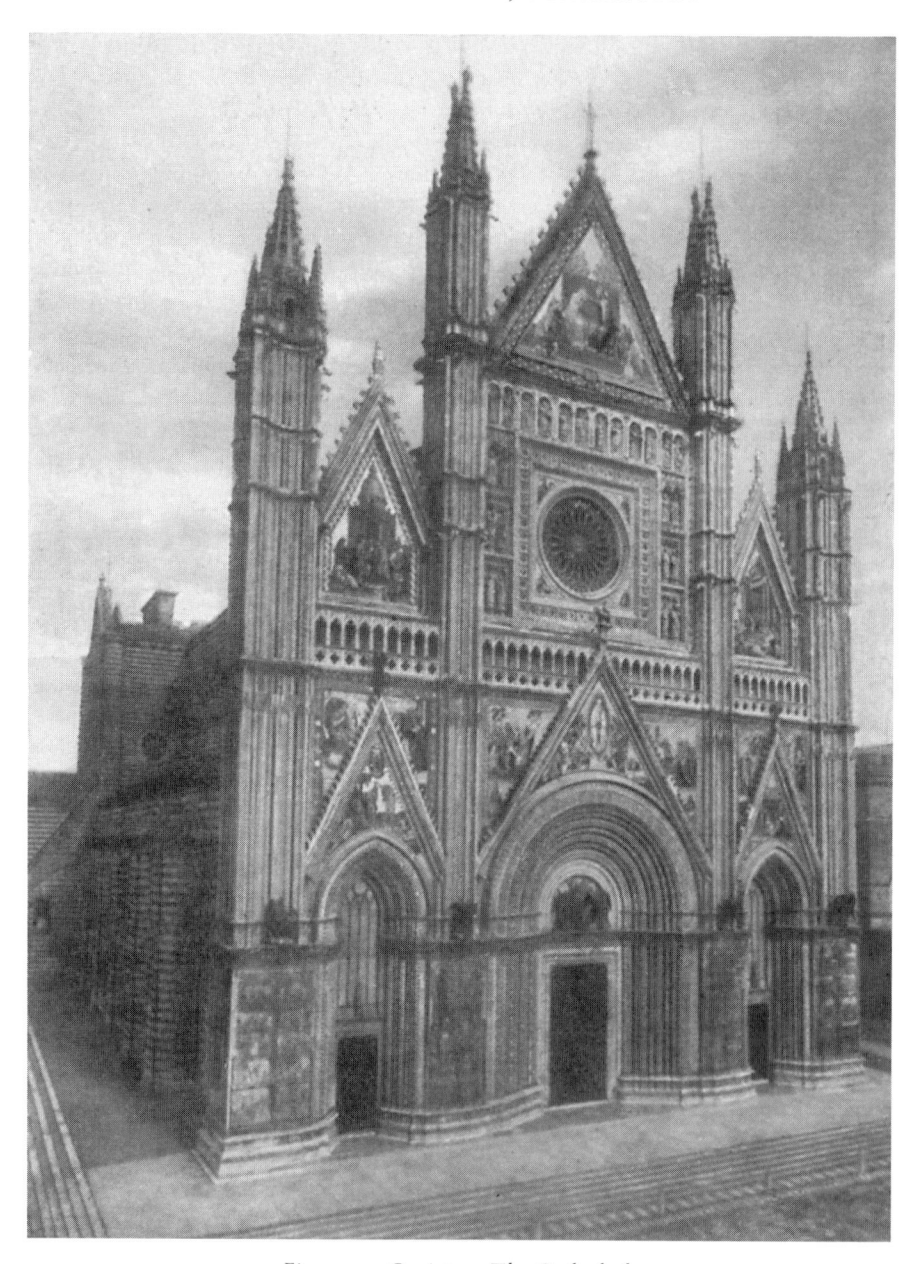

Figure 9. Orvieto – The Cathedral.

Pope appeared, being carried shoulder-high, somewhat unsafely, on a palanquin, down a ramp and into the courtyard – by four huge guards wearing bright uniforms. The crowd applauded loudly but I have little recollection of the singing.

In contrast, a very unpleasant happening occurred about this time – the opening of caves which contained about 300 persons killed during the war. A military truck carrying a platoon of German soldiers had had a bomb of some description thrown into it and more than 30 of them were killed. The occupation force of Germans demanded that the perpetrator come forward and if he did not do so within 24 hours they would round up ten prisoners or civilians from the streets for each soldier who died, and execute them. This threat was carried out and execution was by shooting those collected, in the back of the head, just outside Rome, in the Ardeatine caves. The caves were then sealed using explosives at the entrances. When I came to hear of this, an opening of the caves had been achieved. There was a request to the people of Rome, to visit the site and to identify anyone they could. Inside, one walked through passageways at the sides of which lay the rough coffins containing the dead. Small family groups were gathered here and there, examining bodies from which covering sheets had been thrown back.

Milan

I moved up to the colder climate of Milan, from Rome, just before Christmas 1945, where I found that the populace could predict the onset of snow to within a day or two, at which point all the ladies seemed to sprout fur coats immediately. My first impression of Milan was that it could be any industrial-commercial-banking city in Europe. Remains of its antiquity are not easily visible, save perhaps for the huge cathedral seemingly overrun on the outside with too many pinnacles and a too-sumptuous interior. One reads much about the city as populous and thriving up to about the fifth century AD. The town was then at a very important cross-roads and led invaders down into the body of older Italy. Many invading armies, from the Goths and Huns to the French Kings, passed through the town between the fifth and the twelfth centuries. Of this period, it is recorded that, 'it was besieged 48 times and stormed 28', so that little is left of early Christian architecture. The Dukes of Milan helped the city back to wealth and power, the succeeding Sforzas improving on it and leading a fine restoration through excellent architects, painters, engineers and other craftsmen. All this was fine until the Second World War, when the town did sustain some bombing. Strolling through the streets one day I was surprised to see a wall, adjacent to bomb damage, on which was painted in white, in large letters, 'This is the work of our Anglo-Saxon liberators'!

Often painted on walls too was advice about whom the Italian people should vote for in their elections (see Figure 10). The 'Two Types' were old 8th Army legendary officers – one infantry and one tank corps – here rather remote from their origin, the desert of North Africa.

Not much of historical interest was available to be seen. I tried to gain admittance to Santa Maria delle Grazie, hoping to see Leonardo da Vinci's *Last Supper* (Figure 11), but it too was well sealed off (actually damaged). Neither did I see anything but the exterior of the fourteenth century Castello Sforzesco.

Our Mess for this region was a floor among flats in the via Verdi Guiseppe just behind the Milan Opera House. Only a few days after joining it, at about 7 p.m. in the evening, when we had just sat down to dinner, the table began to

Figure 10. The Two Types from the North African desert.

shake and cutlery and crockery to rattle. It was a quite unique kind of motion for me which only lasted for a few seconds. It was an earthquake, such as one might expect since we were at the foot of the Alps. Our CO, a man with no great claim to culture, looked around and with great seriousness remarked, 'Hell! I haven't drunk that much already, have I?' It was an uncommon Mess as I soon learned. Two young ladies joined us for coffee after dinner one evening. They disappeared from our company thereafter. One retired and stayed the night with the CO, whilst the other – after our cook had been thrown out of his room – was installed there, my room mate going there to join her.

Our office was, incidentally, close by a garage where there had been unpleasant happenings around the end of the war. It seems Mussolini fell into the wrong hands when captured along with his mistress, Clara Petacci. I was told that photographs were offered for sale, of them both hanging from the roof of the garage. Others showed them with their bodies butchered and in unseemly attitudes.

I remember little of our habitual day-to-day work, except that it seemed to be lessening. From it a pleasant journey came my way. I was required to collect a quantity of second-fusion aluminium from a company which was a day's journey away in the foothills of the Alps. (This metal, used for numerous purposes, turned black when tea was contained in a mess tin made of it! – I had used such tins when I was a private, and nobody complained.) We took three 3-ton trucks and went in search of the company. On arrival, due to recent storm damage, the bridge we had to cross seemed terribly unsafe. It was so uncertain that only the driver, without his mate, took his vehicle across it, proceeding with great care. The operation was successful. The return journey by another route with loaded trucks, involved a considerable increase in distance but the delight of the journey was to stay in an old inn and the next day to have a view of Monte Rosso, diminishing with distance as we drove away, glittering in the snow and showing its red colours.

Due to the declining amount of work, I realised that I might be shifted out east or elsewhere in this district and so was prompted to try to make a visit to Venice, for a weekend. It was a long way east for a weekend on the other side of the Italian peninsula. Three of us took a small vehicle, drove in turn and succeeded in reaching Venice late on the Friday night.

The sights were ethereal and theatrical. We had first to park the car in Mestre (the port of Venice) and then walk into the silent and empty city to the Piazza Venetzia. Despite making a few mistakes en-route in crossing the canals, we managed to find 'the Square'. We had booked into the Hotel Danielle, knowing it was on the edge of the lagoon just behind the bell-tower. As I walked by the Basilica I suddenly heard good singing and, turning my eyes to the right saw two gondolas oared and slightly staggered; it was the gondoliers who sang so clearly in the moonlight, something from one of the well-known operas. It was as if some hidden conductor was directing all this as a wonderful stage set, just beyond the piazzetta.

The Danielle, *the* Officers' hotel in Venice, I perceived was an old hotel with a lovely, though uneven mosaic floor. Hitler and Mussolini, I understand, had met here and it didn't surprise me.

We made the usual tourist rounds the next day of the Bridge of Sighs (there never were sighs because prisoners were never held there) and the Library near the campanile, or bell tower. (This tower is copied and distinctive on the campus of Birmingham University, England.) The basilica of San Marco dates from the eleventh century, and is a Christian conversion of a Byzantine structure, being a Greek cross in plan. I looked for the four bronze horses over the central portal, a photograph of which I often looked at as a child in *Cassell's Encyclopaedia*, and saw at least two of them. We then moved on to pay a fleeting visit to two current exhibitions which we had seen advertised. We later crossed the Rialto Bridge which features in one of Shakespeare's plays, of course.

I eventually ended my days in the Army in Padova (Padua) which is but about 20 miles from Venice and was able to make more visits to this unique city.

An association with Venice which I came to have much later in life, concerned James Stirling (1692–1770), who was known as 'The Venetian Mathematician'. There is a book of 200 pages about this man by Ian Tweddle, entitled, *James Stirling: About Series and such Things*, but only two or three pages are devoted to detail about Stirling's life in Venice, as he returned suddenly to England out of fear of assassination in about 1720.

He had learned the secrets of the Venetian art of glass-making and the artisans suspected he would divulge it.

One small final pleasure in Milan was to learn that the English actor, Godfrey Tearle, and his travelling company were performing a Shakespearean play – entertaining the troops. I had last heard and seen Mr Tearle perform in *Julius Caesar*, in a Manchester theatre when I was ten years of age, having been taken

Figure 11. Leonardo da Vinci's painting of The Last Supper.

by my school. He had so powerful an effect on me that I could not forget his performance – it was my first encounter with great theatre companies and audiences.

Sometime early in 1946, I was posted to the Royal Army Ordnance Corps. CP & P had come to the end of its life and was to be closed down. I missed a great evening on the day I left Milan, for it was the very one on which the Opera House, La Scala, re-opened after a long period of closure. On that first splendid evening a musical concert was being held and conducted by a distinguished figure, it being his first appearance in Europe after having spent several war years in the USA.

CHAPTER XII

The 492 Tank Transporter Company[*]

WHEN CP & P WAS CLOSED DOWN I was temporarily 'loaned' to the Ordnance Corps for a few weeks, to a Tank Transporter Company, No. 492, located in the village of Codroipo near Udine (see Figures 1 and 2, and Figure 2 Chapter XI), owing to the local shortage of RAOC officers due to demobilisation. That I had had no training in heavy vehicle convoy work seemed not to matter to anybody. I had had a sixteen-week course on tanks at Arborfield to prepare me for battlefield recovery and the damage repair of tanks, which of course I never needed.

The TT Company transported only three types of tank: Churchill, Sherman and Cromwell I believe, all of about fifteen tons in weight. All the tanks I thought were vastly inferior to the German ones, not only in armour thickness and gun size but in many other ways. For the Churchill in the workshops there was a one-inch thick War Office collection of modifications required. We were responsible for transporting armoured units' tanks and placing them in tank parks at workshops or in positions prior to proceeding into action. In fact at one point we set out a line of tanks in the hills behind Trieste to overlook Tito's territory and intimidate his men. Trieste was totally Italian but the surrounding countryside was Slav. For months it was feared that the Slavs would make some kind of bid to take over Trieste. They had no large port on the Adriatic and needed one.

But now, in peace-time, our job was that of re-locating a.f.v.s (armoured fighting vehicles or tanks), of collecting damaged tanks and preparing them for disposal, though not before the engines had been removed. CP & P then had the large heavy wooden cases made, for the best engines to be returned to the UK. All damaged tanks could present difficult and unusual problems too concerning their manipulation.

For example if the track on one side of the tank had been blown off, it was difficult in some circumstances to manoeuvre it using a cable and just one track to pull it up onto a trailer with the support of chocks.

There was one factor working for us in Italy and this was the preponderance of level crossings; so there were no problems about passing under railway bridges. In small towns, we were often presented with a problem as to where to park for the night when the trailers remained loaded. We had to seek out hard standing.

---

[*] A tank transporter then consisted of a large wheeled tractor which pulled a separate low, 32 wheel trailer on which the tank was carried, chained down and chocked at the rear.

Figure 1. Codroipo – Via Piave

Figure 2. Codroipo: Passeriano; Palazzo dei Conti Mania.

It was not unknown, in medieval towns, especially, to find the tractors had sunk into the ancient drainage systems beneath the road. The morality of some of our own troops also had to be anticipated! A strong steel cable or hawser would be pulled from one tractor and on to it were threaded tractor and transporter spare tyres from all of our vehicles; the end of the cable was then tightly secured to another tractor, the night guard being required to 'keep an eye upon it'. Since the Italians had little of their own motor transport at this time, tyres brought a good price. (I remember, on leaving an Officers' Club in Rome, one evening, seeing an army vehicle jacked-up and short of all four tyres!) There were 24 tyres to a trailer and with them, 'blow-outs' were the principal kind of damage, whereas penetrations and punctures were relatively rare. These heavy vehicles, bouncing over humps in the road, generated high pressures inside the tyres which could burst as the day wore on. It was also common for a unit to record over 20 blow-outs after a two- or three-day operation. Often the instruments on a vehicle's panel which registered levels of fuel were deliberately damaged, so that no record of fuel consumption could be kept, and thus it could be siphoned off and sold.

Another 'personal' feature of the tractor was the erection of enclosed bivouacs or 'bivvies' built on the back of them by their drivers and tractor mates, ostensibly to carry their kit and bedding. However, it was the practice of a fraction of crews to carry 'temporary wives'. The ladies were picked up and off-loaded as circumstances permitted. As well as tyres, tank instruments needed to have a guard set over them for the night. On one occasion, when I had to function without a sergeant, I decided to check the alertness of the guard and went to inspect it. Getting in among the parked vehicles by climbing over a wall from the railway, I was able to penetrate to the centre, with no difficulty. I finally encountered one of the two guards on duty, carrying a rifle for which he had no ammunition. I asked why he did not challenge me and of course got no proper answer. I then asked where the Lance Corporal, who was in charge of this night duty, was, and he replied, 'In his bivvy, Sir'. (I confess, when initially I entered the compound, to having seen a light in one bivvy, which made me suspicious.) I then asked the guard to call out the Lance Corporal by name. After a couple of minutes, I heard a bivvy door slide back, light poured out and a gentle female voice responded, followed by a tousled male emerging from the bivvy ... The female asked, 'Dove la mia cugina?' – 'Where's my cousin?' – and presently, another lady emerged from a neighbouring bivvy! With such a feeble guard, I went then to find the Corporal in overall charge. He was asleep in the tank barracks. I was perhaps outside my own rights to be entering the Other Ranks' barracks alone. When the Corporal was awakened we found he was drunk! I saw the OC (Operational Commander) of the tank brigade and had all my lot locked up in its guard house, the OC supplying the standing guard over our vehicles, for the rest of the night. (However, really punitive sentences could hardly be passed when every man was needed every day. Modest sentences could be passed by our own OC when we returned to base.) It was a poor comment on the quality of devotion to duty of our/my RAOC troops.

There were difficulties also in providing for the motor cyclist acting as 'tail-arse Charlie' for the day. His job was not over until he had seen the last transporter into its destination park. The motor cyclist would either go without food or wait until late for his dinner, especially when one of the tractors had experienced mechanical breakdown. The same misfortune also overtook the technical fitter; they could easily be two hours behind the main convoy. (See Figure 3.)

A big problem with a TT convoy could be loading tractors with a day's fuel. Our daily distance travelled was around 120 miles, since convoys were seldom run at an average of more than 15 mph. The tractors could be made to move at

25 mph – if you knew how to insert a strip of metal or a coin in the right place in the engine! We had always to be careful to load up at a large fuel station, for it would take two hours. I remember at one station they could only fill up using hand-pumps and this took half a day for the whole convoy.

It was important to keep a convoy together, for separation could lead to disaster – drivers could lose their way. The worst case in our Company occurred when two very young crews lost their way totally and without paying due care drove off the main road and into a canal, one man being drowned. The life of officers in convoys was made relatively easy when they had a technical and a general sergeant to help. The behaviour of troops was a consequence of how they lived when outside barracks, by the sea or in the mountains in all kinds of weather. On the road, the officers usually slept in their own 15 cwt truck, but back in barracks and living in their Messes, their life style, as I saw it, could be far more varied than that of the troops. It was truly a bizarre situation in the Officers' Mess of TT 492. There were about ten officers, with a Major OC; but for evening dinner we often had invited in nearly as many women and girls. Our OC Major – he had one eye and how he got accepted by the Army in the first place, I cannot imagine – was always accompanied by a young lady of nineteen and immediately after coffee had been consumed, they unashamedly retired to his room. The workshop's Captain was a 40-year-old ex-owner of a petrol station and he had somehow become attached to a slightly younger well-educated lady. They lived out of the Mess in part, staying in her flat. Their intention was to marry in due course. Other officers brought to dinner their temporary 'ladies of the night', and a good time was had by all. Some of the females could always be found in the kitchens with the army cooks, helping prepare the meal. They

Figure 3. A Tank Transporter – end of column. Near Trieste, August, 1946.

Figure 4. The Education Officer for the 492 TT Company.

also contributed by bringing in several items of food which were not to be had on the open market – real butter, several kinds of quality Italian cheeses, meats such as pork and venison and many fine wines to boot. The Anglo-Italian conversation was always lively and a very pleasant atmosphere was sustained during the whole meal – certainly much better than the usual all-male gatherings. Of course, some officers had a stable relationship with their female partner which was terminated only when demobilisation occurred – or was the cause of a subsequent divorce. Just a few of the officers did not take advantage of this sexual freedom.

I was again Education Officer for this Company (see Figure 4). But by now though, experience had taught me that very few were interested in education at all. Once, having returned from a few days' leave, I enquired whether a load of new volumes on literature and history had arrived, as requested. The authorities were endeavouring especially to cater for the rehabilitation of the troops, but alas I found some two or three hundred books stored with cleaning utensils and materials. My wife, in an educational college in England, was unable to obtain some of these books, even by paying for them. The Army had been given undeserved preference. (Rather than leaving the books to their fate, I packed a selection of them and until recent years they could be identified in my library because each had a number on its spine.) The Army Bureau of Current Affairs (ABCA) tried to do an excellent job for the Forces. They offered to teach languages and produced large coloured maps, 3′ × 3′, and splendid booklets about current international issues (see Figure 2 in Chapter XI).

I seem to remember using these maps and diagrams and daring to lecture about regions of which I had no personal knowledge such as the various states of Yugoslavia and Mao Tse Tung's 'Long March' in China. This was well-intentioned material at the time, but often perhaps too difficult to be attractive to soldiers concerned mainly with demobilisation. One could not help observing that there was little interest in the material and thinking that the great effort put into these publications and activities by the Army Educational Corps went quite unrecognised.

Relationships between commissioned ranks and Italian females were common; I suspect, because the Italian lasses imagined they were associating with members of the English aristocracy! Non-commissioned men intent on marrying Italian women needed to gain a kind of official permission. There was no allowing of quick marriages – a few months had to elapse and there had to be meetings and discussions with the army padre. On the whole it was a sound procedure and it should at least have been applied in some more subtle way, even to officers. One did wonder, however, if some of the Italian girls knew what they were letting themselves in for, when marrying men who, for instance, were returning to some small, sun-less coal-mining town in the North of England or Wales.

Some officers were not always exemplary and I shared a room with one such. He kept a drawer full of condoms and had had VD. He was once accused of being irresponsible in not locking the door of his 15 cwt. truck and therefore making it possible for it to be stolen whilst having a coffee in a nearby bar. Looking into the matter, the Court of Enquiry recommended him to be fined £15. Many judged that he had contrived the theft and so sold his truck cheaply. There were not a few men whose demobilisation was held back whilst enquiries were held into their financial situation; they were not always easy to investigate when they had a married partner to hide money behind.

There were many experiences that would require too much time to relate in detail – of parking a long convoy under the walls of some historical Renaissance castle for the purposes of protection against the weather; of the sight of the snow-covered Alps, glittering in the sunshine, but promising an extremely cold night on the hills; of arriving in some local town early in the evening and finding that a well-known opera was to be performed in the local theatre that same night. Many of the lapses described above were, of course due to demobilisation weariness. Nonetheless, there was enough richness in the situations to make a TV serial!

CHAPTER XIII

Marriage

———•———

Before going abroad to Italy, I discussed with my wife-to-be our getting married. We agreed that we should not, until after the war was over, in case anything serious should befall me whilst abroad. If it did, it would be easier, and she young enough, for her to make a new connection and, whilst the war was still on, we didn't want a child to appear and be without a father all of its life. Thus, now that the war had ended, there was a much-reduced chance of my getting killed. Heather had been fastened into running a post office with her father, which was listed as an essential occupation; she had been in that job since 1939 and now wished to make more of her life. She started to read for her Higher School Certificate (in English, History, Geography and Economics, by Correspondence College and attending part-time lectures at the University) and got it in time to be able to take up the opportunity to become a school teacher. She was easily accepted for a one-year teacher-training course which started at Exhall (Coventry) in January 1945. We agreed to marry when the opportunity came, and in March 1946 I was lucky enough to be given a month's leave in the UK. I had been out of the country for over a year and the atmosphere of war was disappearing.

I had had instructions to take the troop train for Dover and to present myself at a railway mobilisation centre outside Udine at a certain time and date. I was eagerly awaiting the train when over the loud-hailer came an announcement asking for Lieut. Johnson to report back to his Company urgently. I was then the Company Mess secretary and treasurer and, amusingly, toyed with the idea that I had committed some legal or financial crime. However, when I got back to my Company I was told that my leave would have to be postponed for two weeks. My OC required me to go down to Naples and bring up the remnants of a disbanding Transporter Company which was to be assimilated into ours. Units were slowly being closed down with demobilisation though the American forces were much faster to do so. By the middle of the afternoon, with a small amount of baggage and the driver of my car, I was on my way southwards, but not before having written a letter to Heather, to tell her of the misfortune which had befallen me. All the plans for our wedding had been made: for the church service, the wedding breakfast and taxis etc. Though neither of us had any serious religious convictions and would have preferred to marry at a Registry Office, my mother was strongly against such an intention. What would her friends have said? So I capitulated, telling myself that it was not a matter of any great importance, and anyhow that it was the last time I would feel compelled to follow my mother's strong opinions. So, suddenly, all the wedding arrangements and Heather's absence from College had to be re-negotiated.

Some few hundred miles south in Italy, I found the unit to be taken over – about 30 strong, almost on the coast in Naples, near the Opera House. Three 3-cwt. vehicles there had already had their sides built-up to act as containers. There were perhaps a dozen tank transporters and trailers with a driver and trailer-boy to each. There was a water-tanker, two vehicles for food, cooking utensils, stores and items for servicing any breakdowns which might occur. As well, there were two motorcycles, one for road surveillance ahead and the other following up at the rear; there was also my own driver and a 15-cwt. truck. Our convoy would have been nearly a kilometre long – small civilian cars on the road pulled into ditches to make sure they were well out of the path of these moving heavy-weight giants.

For some reason, HQ in Codroipo (about thirteen miles west of Udine) needed to know all the engine numbers and thus with one of my two sergeants, I had to have them recorded rapidly and sent off by despatch rider. Two items I remember clearly were the taking of early morning parade and, particularly, listening to an unusual number of the men who needed to see the Medical Officer. One of these told me he had a pain in his upper right leg; my sergeant whispered to me, 'He's got a dose of clap, sir. He's already had it twice so this is the third time'. (Penicillin had only just become available in the Forces for treating VD. One third of the whole unit had been infected at some time or other.) I found that of my two sergeants, one acting administratively (from an infantry unit) was excellent for getting things done in the unit, the other, a technical man, alas, was useless!

Passing between the tractors, I came to one youngster and said to my Corporal, 'He looks very young'. 'Yes, sir,' he responded, 'It's Driver Joe Stick, Number 123456 ... He's an Italian and speaks a little English. He has an AB 64, Part I and II, his military 'dog tags', and lives in the barracks with all the fellows.' (These former were booklets, the first of which essentially identified the soldier, whilst the second was his pay-book.) 'He's accepted by the rank and file as one of them. They took him into the Company, substituting him for somebody who had deserted. He goes back to the time when the TT Company was operating in the Southern Apennines, sir,' said the NCO, 'he's the longest-serving OR in the Company.' As the men obviously trusted him and he did the job of 'trailer-boy' satisfactorily, I let things stand as they were and said no more.

After a few days we took off for the vicinity of Rome, but not before an Italian 'old dear' came and asked to see me. She wished to know if I could sell the site to her! I could only advise her to see the Allied Town Major.

We could only travel at a maximum of 15 miles per hour with our large and heavy vehicles and so leaving Naples on Monday morning we slogged on beyond Rome and across the Apennines, covering a hundred miles, more or less, each day. I planned that on arriving after four or five days at Mestre – which is effectively the port of entry into Venice – by mid-day, the early afternoon would be given over to vehicle maintenance and the opportunity would then be there for the men to go into Venice, even if only for a few hours. Alas, no one took up the opportunity. The next day we pushed on in the direction of Trieste and on the Friday, reached our destination, Codroipo, in the late afternoon. I reported in to the OC and he seemed pleased that we had 'got home' without difficulty or mishap, though with a few men on charges.

The following morning I was told there had been a ruckus in the village during the night. Apparently the men I had brought up, in celebration of their week's work on the road, had drunk too much and a fight had started with some of the Codroipo citizens in a bar. One poor chap received serious damage to his eye which needed hospital attention. These affairs were not uncommon.

Thus, two weeks late, I again set out for London by train. I journeyed with full kit and kit bag. My pouches, bag and sack carried nylon stockings, lace collars, filigree bracelets, eight bottles of sherry, rum, port and wine as well as being even more heavily weighted by two albums of '78' records, one, containing the whole of *La Bohème*, the other a miscellany of popular Neapolitan songs.

As usual, my 9 p.m. train from Euston was delayed and got to Manchester about 2 a.m.; and again there were no taxis in those early hours, so I had to hump all my baggage home up the unlit main road for three or four miles. I arrived home at about 3 a.m. and had to wake up the entire family. I happened to take out of my kit bag first, many tins of 50 cigarettes (which were freely supplied to all the troops each week – no thought of lung cancer then!). My grandfather's eyes nearly popped out of his head when he saw them, since he knew they were for him!

The next Saturday morning, Heather and I were married in St Clement's Anglican church, Higher Openshaw, my younger brother acting as best man. At the conclusion of the ceremony we were invited to accompany the vicar to the altar. He thereupon said some extra prayers and uttered some words that may well have come to his mind from knowing that a pair of agnostics confronted him. This little extra attention was a subject for comment in the congregation later on!

At the wedding breakfast (for which we paid the maximum price of five shillings for each guest), I remember lifting up the ham to the light; it was so thinly cut that it was transparent! In the late afternoon we took the train to London. We were unsure as to whether we had a room or not at the modest 'B & B' near the British Museum where I usually stayed. The time had been too short to allow for confirmation of new bookings for our wedding night; however, the reservation *had* been made. At some time during the evening we walked the London streets and I excelled myself, said my new wife, by buying her a small posy. For her part, she tried to secure for me some indigestion tablets, explaining blushingly to the landlady, that they were 'for my husband'.

After four days in London, on a Wednesday evening, we were on our way home, me to Manchester and Heather to Exhall Teacher Training College. We said our temporary goodbyes and separated, she alighting at Crewe and taking the bus to College. She had spent the two weeks of her planned Easter leave simply awaiting my return.

Some 25 years later, by contrast, I came to read *As I Remember*, an autobiography by Stephen Timoshenko (van Nostrand, 429pp., 1968) a distinguished and, to mechanical engineers, very well-known author, Professor of Strength of Materials and Mechanics, born in the USSR, exiled and settled in the USA. He wrote a remarkable account of his life which revealed among other details, how little the Second World War impinged upon him and that he did not seem to recognise or care about it. As a young student I knew and admired Timoshenko's books, but Chapters 42 and 43 of his memoir caused me to stop and wonder about him, for I was totally amazed at how secure from the discomforts of the world between 1939 and 1947 he seems to have been – in the USA, un-involved in the worldwide struggle afoot. However, I shall spend no time here in discussing his views but leave the reader to ponder them by reproducing those extracted and given in Figure 1. I found some of my own pencilled comments in the margins of his books against his surprising opinions and have added these to the Figure.

By comparison, the biography of an equally eminent engineer, Theodore von Karman, of Hungarian origin and who, like Timoshenko, had settled in the USA, shows a man deeply committed to the American war effort.

Figure 1.
Reaction to Timoshenko's views. The lines below refer to the winter months of 1947 when Prof. Timoshenko, a very distinguished research contributor to the engineering subject, Strength of Materials, wrote about his experiences in going to London to receive the Inst. of Mech. Engrs' James Watt International Medal. He emigrated from Europe to the USA in about 1923. I wrote some comments about his opinions on the London of early 1947 after reading them in his autobiography more than 20 years later, thus –

From *As I Remember*, 1968, pp. 357–60, S. Timoshenko's Autobiography:

> It was late March (1947), and the weather was abominable. The ship was late and we got to London at night instead of in the morning. The city was dimly lit. Everywhere we saw filth, piles of rubble – and *this two years after the war had ended*. At all restaurants lunches and dinner cost the same – five shillings. Naturally, one could not get a decent meal for that. What was the reason for all this? People blamed it on the policies of the Socialist government. The next day I went to the *Institute* of Mechanical Engineers to find out when I was to deliver my *report*. At the end of April, I was told. Waiting nearly a month in London did not appeal to me. I decided to go to Paris and spend the time studying the literature on the history of strength of materials. I discovered that I could not get to Paris. All tickets had been sold for the next seven days. It was Holy Week, and Londoners were rushing to France to buy food. Not until a week later, the first day of Easter, did I succeed in getting away from London. The train was crammed with real 'bagmen', carrying on their shoulders bags of various goods to be exchanged for food. I finally did reach Paris. After London it looked clean. On the streets was the holiday crowd. I had booked a hotel room in advance and went to occupy it. There was no heating. Everywhere it was cold, colder than in London. The restaurants had everything, just as in the old days, but the prices were fantastic.

My comments:

There were men still in the forces who had already been there for two years. Indeed, at the end of the War there were men in the 8th Army and elsewhere who had served overseas for 4 years and 9 months without seeing their wives and families.

Five shillings was the maximum one could spend on a meal. All in Britain lived by the same rules in rationing. I remember once 'splashing out' and ordering a five-shilling meal at a Lyons' Tea House near Charing Cross railway station and obtained a small, whole, meatless, bony chicken!

What was the reason in fact? – that he was receiving the James Watt International gold medal from the *Institution* of Mechanical Engineers.

Timoskenko:

But the weather remained *cold*, and in the library I had to sit and read in my overcoat and cap.

My comments:

And did he know what it was to find his way home in the dark un-lit streets during bombing raids?

Timoskenko:

I began the summer of 1943 with a fairly long trip around America, going first to the meeting of aeronautical engineers in Los Angeles, where I read a paper on the stability of compressed plates reinforced with stiffeners. Published in Russia some thirty years before, the work had now become timely in connection with the designing of large airplanes. When I had finished my paper, a representative of one of the big airplane manufacturers came to me and suggested my joining his company as a consultant. I emphatically refused, having *no wish to go back into industry.*

My comments:

Lucky man! I had 'joined up' at that time! (Like a few million others!)

Did he not think, first and foremost, simply of making planes to defeat an enemy?

Timoskenko:

We talked of course, of the oncoming war. The Poles were in a martial mood. No concessions to Hitler! 'If Hitler attacks us, our allies, France and Britain, will come to our aid, will crush Germany.' I told them that in my opinion neither France nor Britain would come to their aid, that it was Poland that would be crushed. I advised them to avoid war and *come to terms with Hitler.*

My comments:

The British prime minister, Neville Chamberlain tried more than once to prevent war, but, in effect, it had already started with the Spanish Civil War, 1936–39, or with Mussolini's invasion of Abyssinia and Albania.

Timoshenko:

After settling in at the hotel, I called on Prandtl, who was very glad to see me. Neither he nor his family had suffered during the war. But the present occupation *irritated* him.

My comments:

Did he recall that the Holocaust took 6 million Jewish lives? And that Russia lost more than three times that number in the War, after they had 'come to terms with Hitler' in 1939?

CHAPTER XIV

Austria

———◆———

I WAS FORTUNATE to be given leave to return to the UK to appear before a Civil Service Selection Board. In 1946 I sat a written examination – four or five papers: history, literature, politics etc., and an I.Q. test – for entry into the Administrative Grade of the Home Civil Service. Candidates had to have at least a 2(i) Honours degree. The examination for the Central Mediterranean Forces region was held in Northern Italy and the top 30 per cent of the examinees were at some time later called before a two-day CSSB (Civil Service Selection Board) in the UK. The Board lasted for two whole days of interviews, appearance and questioning before a committee of about ten persons. A month or two after I was demobilised in 1947, I was offered an appointment in the Secretary's Office of the Board of Customs and Excise – a branch of the Treasury – as an Assistant Principal at City Gate House in the city in London. However, I take up this subject again at greater length below in Chapter XVI.

When my period of leave ended, I reported to a transit camp at Ilkley, near Bradford, on the edge of the Yorkshire moors. I 'hung around' for several days until orders came and directed me back to Italy. We travelled by train to Dover, but after crossing the Channel, on boarding a train (for Italy) from the cross-channel steamer, a difficulty arose. The transit party consisted of about 400 ORs and a dozen junior officers. The senior one among us was required to sign a document acknowledging that he had taken over responsibility for the locomotive and coaches. He was a dentist, a Captain in the Medical Corps. He stolidly refused to sign the document. Thereupon, the signing of the acceptance form reverted to any one of us of Lieutenant status; most officers were reluctant to sign such an instrument and it ended up with my signing it. The practice of signing for the train was new to us all, but once this was achieved, the train pulled away from the station and slowly made its way across France, into the Alps, through Switzerland and into Austria, where at Villach, in the early hours of the morning, my train journey terminated. The train itself (disgorging fifty or so persons every few miles) continued down and into Italy, and what happened to it when the man responsible for it had abandoned it in Austria, I do not know! My orders were to travel to a new unit at Leoban (Styria), travelling by 'truck' via Klagenfurt and Graz; Leoban was some fifteen miles short of the border between Britain's and the USSR's occupied territory in Austria at Brüch, or 100 miles from Vienna. By this time I had become aware that I was being directed

123

to an unusual REME 'outfit'. The 492 TT Company I had left behind in Codroipo was in the process of being re-formed to go to the Suez Canal zone, and since I had but a few months left to serve, it was sensible I be left behind in Europe.

My new Unit consisted of a REME Colonel, about eight captains and lieutenants and a small number of men supporting the former as clerks, drivers, cooks, etc. The day after I arrived I had explained to me the function of the unusual 'workshop' in which I had alighted. Roughly 600 German officers and men, as prisoners of war, were supposedly incarcerated on the site, and their function was to re-build or refit Allied-type vehicles or parts that had been damaged in action or by bombing. I was put in charge of stores from which parts could be requisitioned. Each day, groups of German POWs under the control of their sergeants, took themselves and their tools in their own trucks out into the neighbourhood, searching for vehicular wrecks and recovering from them items in good condition. They would return with such items and deposit them into our large stores for passing on to other vehicle 'indenting' units. My main contact with German troops was through my German sergeant major, a tall, lithe, energetic fellow with blonde hair and light blue eyes a true Nordic type. Never did a group sent out with lunch packs in the morning, work so well and return in the evening less than loaded with cannibalised vehicle parts. There were never any disciplinary problems and what difficulties there were, they and their officers took care of themselves. Occasionally, one of them went AWOL (absent without leave), mainly to return to Germany to help his troubled family. I talked to 'my' sergeant major at length when we had occasion to visit other units or engage in discussion about procedures. One evening he drove me in the unit's car to Graz where I went to listen to a Mozart opera. I offered to buy him a seat at the theatre as he proposed to wait near the car until the performance finished, but I could not prevail upon him to accept this. I remember discussing with him what he was going to do at home with his wife and family, when the unit was dissolved. In his best fully intelligible English, he described how he had it all worked out. He knew that he would be able to return to the job he had had before the war, but as well, he envisaged working each evening on domestic repairs since his house was damaged during Allied bombing raids; and at weekends he had a vegetable plot in mind for eking out the prevailing poor rations. His wife likewise had a fully defined role – whilst the children were at school, she would attend to assigned domestic chores. Their school-work was exceedingly important to him and so had to be planned accordingly; and finally, for his sons, there would be engineering at a Technische Hochschule. His description revealed a thoroughly organised life, and with knowledge of him from our engineering co-operation I remember thinking to myself, nothing much had changed in the manner of the German mind, even though the war was lost to them – strict planning and performance, great attention to detail and strong determination. Because of this man I was less than fully occupied in my appointment and, to a degree, I had time on my hands. I went for lonely walks on the neighbouring hills and marvelled at the sad de-energised order everywhere still apparent, though the end of the war was a year past.

The town of Leoban had, and I believe still has today, a renowned Technical Institute, given over to specialising in mining and metallurgical processes such as happens in Sheffield University and Camborne, Cornwall. Surprisingly, I found a second-hand bookshop in the centre of Leoban selling a good many books in English, a few of which I bought during several visits. A nice young lady watched over the shop and after about my third visit, her mother started to appear!

Our Mess was no bright circus of entertainment, either in the officers themselves or those they invited to dinner. Our frosty Colonel saw to it that everything was exceedingly clean, tidy and had all the features typical of Austria. It was organised and systematic, it stood for health and cleanliness. The area around the Mess was thinly populated and there was nothing to excite one – not even good German beer – which they said was currently 'only 2% alcohol'. There was no wine unless it was brought up from Italy and the food missed the hands of a good cook or, as in TT 492, a cook-house in which a few young, bright, female partners happily assisted the army cooks.

Around this time, when I was still thinking about demobilisation, I enrolled for an External London University degree in mathematics. I began to receive, fortnightly, printed papers, books to cogitate upon and exercises to do. My father helped: he had a small wooden chest made and shipped out, to hold my small travelling library. So, in these uneventful days, evenings and weekends, I settled down to studying in my small bedroom. I could not of course keep up with the degree workload, and steadily declined in the matter of answering the problem papers promptly. I had thought of reading economics and/or statistics, or preparing to read for an M.Sc. in engineering in the autumn of 1947, of the prospect of going to the Harvard Business School, or trying to find a post in Switzerland in engineering, so that I could learn French, German and Italian at close quarters. I even gave thought to starting afresh in medicine; but that would be too long a road through a university. Thus, mathematics was a useful tool in all the subjects I contemplated and as the highest common factor I chose it to try to improve my post-army prospects.

One evening after dinner, in a casual conversation with my Colonel, he asked me how I enjoyed Austria as a 'billet'. Without reflecting sufficiently, I answered that Austria was clean and orderly but dull and I preferred the brighter, un-disciplined Italian atmosphere. Two weeks later, I received instructions to join 533 REME workshops in Padova. I have never been clear whether I was being rejected by my Colonel for not valuing Austria or, out of kindness, he was acceding to my simple wish to return south!

Though dismissive of the area around Leoban at the time, I came back to it some seven years later, to walk and climb in the Julian Alps, which ranged east-west, to the south of the town. I had been encouraged by my wife to join a small national climbing club party, making a two-week summer visit which took in the climbing of two of the highest peaks in the range, Prisoniec and Triglav (just under 10,000 feet high, I believe). Regarding the former, I had a little adventure resulting from the fact that our 'leader' had no first-hand experience in climbing the two peaks, only a sheaf of notes to help him. We had started out ordinarily dressed, but heavy rain soaked us through and as the height increased, it turned to snow. Unsure of where we were in the ascent of Prisoniec, because the mist had closed in, obscuring the summit, the party divided into two;

one group set about returning to the hut at the base and the other making for the top. However, having started on the completion of the last portion of the climb, I was suddenly struck by the thought that as a responsible man and father of four children, I shouldn't be taking any such chances. I turned around and went down alone without thinking that that of itself was quite a risky thing to do. However, I got back to our hut without mishap – but on ascending the stairs to the first floor, I slipped and fell from top to bottom! I was very lucky not to have broken a leg, and suffered only a bruised thigh. So much for thinking about sustaining injuries on the mountainside! I later learned I had separated from my three colleagues only 200 yards from the peak. The next day, with the sun returned, and with several inches of hard snow all around, the valleys, the countryside and the chain of seven lakes, were indeed brilliant and beautiful.

CHAPTER XV

Padova and Demobilisation

I DO NOT HAVE strong recollections about the last few months of my military service which were passed, officially, in Padova, an old mediaeval town about 20 miles from Venice, which possessed one of the earliest universities established in Europe. I functioned as a straightforward workshop officer in a REME unit, largely engaged in repairing light military transport for the region between the towns of Padova and Venice. The 7th Armoured Division was congregated in the region of Monfalconi. It was held there so they would be able to respond to any incursions made by Yugoslav military units. It had as its divisional shoulder-patch, a clear clenched fist, wrongly interpreted by our Italian allies as our communist division!

I recall travelling down the Isonzo river valley and being deposited at my new Mess in the centre of the town which turned out to be quite close to the Arena Cappella – on the walls of which Giotto (1267–1337) and his pupils left many of their famous frescoes. It proved to be a comfortable billet composed of two parts: one covered the floor above a large shop, providing a dining room and a sitting room-cum-bar, which was for entertaining and receiving guests, together with several bedrooms. The second part existed on the upper floor of a small building across the road where young ladies were privately entertained. It was spoken of only quietly and one had to have lived in the Mess for several days to recognise the existence of the two-part system and learn which officers lived in each of the two buildings. The whole situation was one of quiet realism.

We ran a simple, straightforward workshop for cars and lorries (now called trucks), for repair throughout an ill-defined area. One had to be shrewdly aware of priorities. If two models of the same vehicle came in at the same time, one belonging to the MO (Medical Officer) and the other to the padre, then you had to know that the drill was, 'to take from the padre's car what is required to put the MO's car rapidly on the road again.' It usually took a couple of weeks to attend to the padre's car! But he did a good 'social' job for men in the unit who had problems, usually at home in the UK. The philosophy was well-intentioned. The town was quiet because there was still very little non-military traffic about and many ecclesiastical buildings and gardens in our vicinity. The university was closed and so its artistic interest to us at the time derived simply from admiring its external form. Founded as a 'daughter' of Bologna University, it was formed through the migration of scholars therefrom, in around 1260. By the end of the fourteenth century, medicine and the arts were studied, with law dominant. Around the year 1500 several colleges, or teaching corporations – *universitas* – came into being.

Padova had developed a reputation in medicine and the English physician William Harvey (1578–1657), discoverer of the circulation of the blood (but published only in 1628) came here to study under the renowned Fabricius and Casserius. A Scotsman, who spent five years or so in this area, was James Stirling; he was a good mathematician well-known to Newton.

I came to realise after travelling in the region that it was about a year since, on a cold, windy night, I had berthed a convoy of tractors, carrying tanks, under the walls of the Castello d'Este about 20 miles away. Time had moved on and life abroad was coming to a close.

Central Europe was an area little valued or recognised in world affairs before 1940, so that the large ABCA maps helped men who had left school at fourteen to see where they were now operating and why. I myself realised how little I knew about central European and Russian republics and, later on, was pleased to read the informative and adventurous book by Fitzroy-Maclean (1911–1998), *Eastern Approaches* (1949) and to follow it up with several other books from his pen, such as *A Person from England*. Maclean was directed by Churchill to be dropped by parachute into Yugoslavia, there to make contact with General (first, resistance fighter and later President) Tito. His mission was to find out what could be done to help Tito's army of partisans by supplying military equipment which could be spared and thus holding down two or three German divisions.

For many years after the war, if there was a political issue to be explained about Yugoslavia, the usual practice was for the BBC to call upon Maclean to expatiate on it. Soon after Tito died, however, his 'one country', Yugoslavia, rapidly disintegrated into independent States and Maclean ceased to be the expert commentator on it.

Shopping in Venice

Many officers used to enjoy shopping in Venice and dining in its hotels and cafés. Some few seemed to enjoy sight-seeing, seeking out its artistic treasures and viewing exhibitions of many kinds. Of course, at this time there were no tourists and the Venetian salesmen had to be content for troops to substitute for them. Saturday evenings could be a busy time for bars and club-owners. I remember one occasion when, as a group of four, we arrived at one of the more questionable clubs. One of our members was unable to come up with the entrance fee whilst keeping a few thousand lire over for other requirements. They gave him five thousand lire but demanded an item as surety against a bouncing cheque. It had transpired that during the afternoon he had purchased a beautiful garment for his fiancée, since he was due to return to the UK in a few days' time, his military service completed. The club first suggested he give his hat as security, but clearly, he could not do this, and thereupon offered the present he had bought for his betrothed.

Having been admitted to the floor show, we found it had virtually ended and thereupon, alas, we shifted to another club and our previous hassle proved unnecessary. At the second club I encountered an inebriated officer with two female companions and recalled that I had seen him only two or three weeks before, in Naples, with his wife. Wives of 'regular' soldiers, not conscripts, were just beginning to be allowed to join their husbands; it was sad to think of this kind of behaviour. This misused evening concluded when around midnight I found myself returning to the car park, after walking over countless small canals and through a maze of passages because there was no transport. We had acquired the company of two hard-bitten females and when we finally left in the car there were only three of us. Arriving back in Padova in the small hours, we parked the car on the road outside our Mess. The next day (Sunday), there was a heightening of 'atmosphere' when it was found that the car had been stolen. It turned out that in fact it was in the hands of the military police, who had encountered three fellows pushing it along the street; they ran away when the police challenged them. The car was returned to us and the police were well-rewarded with the speedy servicing of *their* cars for a week or two!

A more enjoyable weekend was that in which a colleague and I went to Cortina d'Ampezzo, some miles outside Padova, where we had a Vehicle Recovery Unit. The misfortune was that my task was to close down the unit now that the Army had contracted so significantly; it had had a school for skiing and was the sports centre of the Tyrol.

A more cultured weekend followed when I went to Venice having taken the day off, to try to see the library of San Marco. It was built by Jacapo Sansovino (1477–1570) and was established to house a collection of ancient manuscripts presented to the City Council by Petrarch. The library was claimed to have primacy of place in all the Renaissance buildings and it was said to be on the Piazzetta opposite the Doge's palace. It is a lovely small location between the bell-tower and the landing platform. Sansovino was called upon, in the prime of his life, to design and supervise the building of the library. In 1545, the roof of the library collapsed and for this misfortune Sansovino was imprisoned, fined and dismissed from office. However, he was soon set free and restored to his post, due to the pressure of his friends. Besides providing the city with a beautiful library, he also did good service for St Mark's by encircling its famous domes (then decrepit) with bands of iron. I made enquiries about looking through the library, but it was still closed and not ready for public viewing; and for once, cigarettes were not an alternative and effective currency for gaining premature entrance.

In July 1947, my own turn for demobilisation came up. Every soldier was allotted a demob. number which was based on his length of military service and his age. The most common number was 25, in which group were found men who had been called up in 1939 when aged about 21 and had done some six years service; they were released towards the end of 1945. My own number was in the 50s and I was ending with just four years service. I departed by train from Udine which crawled along at a slow pace out of Italy into Germany and on to Calais; it was my second such journey to Calais since April 1946. There were no celebrations for those of us permanently leaving our units in Italy and elsewhere.

The UK at the time was in the hands of a Labour government, re-settlement was afoot and strikes were plentiful. The exhilaration of late 1945 as the majority of the Forces began to return home, had spent itself.

Figure 1 shows four young fellows at play on the Adriatic coast and two aboard the train starting for home. Once in the UK we were directed to the Demob. Centre, where masses of us were 'kitted out' with a civilian suit, other clothing and a hat – which I soon lost by leaving it on the rack of the train on alighting in London. I can still recall 'my civvy suit' which was rather baggy around the hips. (I still retained my smart army raincoat but soon lost it at home to my younger brother, who, like many another young man, appropriated it in order to parade himself in it before his girlfriend!)

I believe all ranks were paid for eight weeks of demobilisation and for any other leave due to them; my wife informs me that the 'docket' I received was for £64, which immediately was contributed to the purchase of the 1946 edition of the Encyclopaedia Britannica. (Our parents had each given us £50 as a wedding present and with this we had already bought a fine Edwardian bookcase, so that the books and EB volumes were indeed well-housed and displayed.)

Some older people being discharged would ask, seriously, the pointed question, 'How does the Government propose to cover us for our years away, in respect of a pensionable job, the contributions to which had stopped?' (Graduates who had worked in Government research establishments for several years did enjoy transferable pensions.)

However, in one matter the Government was thoughtful; it had introduced a scheme for early or 'out of order' release – if a good case could be made, for instance to be present at the start of a new university year, to continue new courses or ones which had been interrupted. Medicine was a very much sought-after subject in universities at the time, in the first year of which could be found mature men (sometimes distinguished with battle honours) competing with young 18-year-old boys just out of school, such as my younger brother.

My wife and I had a fortnight's holiday in Cornwall and spent a week at a Fabian Summer School in Kent, discussing political issues. Particularly, Tony Crossland spoke on Education and the supposed inegalitarian grammar schools. We lived in Heather's parents' home to begin with but the need to live a separate existence was becoming evident. We thought to live in London's central area of culture, but the problem for us was to find appointments there. At this time I was unclear about my own future. I believed, quite erroneously as I see it now, that I had lost the possibility of entering engineering industry. I was turned 25 and the prospect of doing a form of graduate apprenticeship for two years did not appeal to me. My reading for the External London B.Sc. degree in Mathematics seemed to have been a useful start because it would be helpful in many different directions, though I had dropped behind in my reading whilst in Padova. We also even thought of emigrating to Australia, among other alternatives. And there were appointments to be had in the oil industry in Iran and South America! We finally decided that I should try to finish the mathematics degree – which I did, in June of the following year, though the conditions for work then were much less than satisfactory – alone, and in 'digs' outside of London.

PADOVA AND DEMOBILISATION

Figure 1. Four young fellows at play in the Adriatic.

As indicated in Chapter XIV, in January 1948 I was attracted by the range of work which the Administrative Grade of the Home Civil Service seemed to offer. (Its attraction was: to work in the City, have a steady career, work with a varied and intelligent group, and earn a good salary after the age of about 40.) Things did not work out as the next chapter in this biography tells. Adaptation to the requirements of 'civvy street' proved harder than I had expected – indeed, though this latter choice was a soft option, its failure finally left me two years older and with a very hard furrow still to till.

The Civil Service I found was a difficult culture in which to work. I had led a free and varied peripatetic existence at home and abroad for the last four years so that the confines of an office were difficult to overcome. My broad, scientific interests remained strong and short of a definite academic interest to pursue, I registered for the Masters degree course (by examination and dissertation) in the History and Philosophy of Science at University College, London. The course lectures were six hours per week, delivered on three evenings per week in 1948–9; they were a great success. I did a great deal of reading and got a clearer perspective of the growth of the major sciences. I felt that looking at individual sciences with an historical perspective was the best education I ever had.

After starting in London I lived in lodgings first in Eltham and then Lee, about half-an-hour's journey from London Bridge and a short walk to City Gate House, the site of the offices of Customs and Excise. I spent evenings either at UCL or searching for a house of less than £2,500. There was a large house-market for the area and the quality of the property varied greatly. Eventually, I found a large semi-detached house in the pleasant neighbourhood of Sidcup – on an estate with two large parks nearby. Heather and I, with our few months old baby son Philip, took it over in 1949. We had to furnish it and for a couple of years it was indeed very sparsely furnished; the empty sitting room contained just a fine bookcase containing a collection of good books, and a large Indian carpet. To secure this we paid a £500 deposit (given to us by Heather's parents) and obtained a mortgage for £2,000 – and that the repayments were £148 per year (a large fraction of my salary) is indelibly fixed in my mind.

PART III

In Academia

CHAPTER XVI

A Civil Servant Remembers

DEMOBILISATION was not many months away and I was beginning to think about what I would do once I was a civilian again. I was turned 25 years of age and had lost the best years of my life for scientific work; it was about the age when Newton was 'forced from Cambridge by the plague', when Trinity College was 'dismissed'. At my age he had been at home in Woolsthorpe for about two years, during which time he wrote his first papers on the method of fluxions and reflected on the nature of gravity. I had several options open to me – to read for a Ph.D in engineering or mathematics, to take up a job in industry, to read for a degree in economics, to stay in Italy to 'write', or follow many other ideas with which I toyed ...

It so happened that a paper was circulated through Army channels, saying that a written examination for entry into the Administrative Grade of the Home Civil Service would soon be held and potential candidates would be given leave to sit it. The top layer of the examination list would later be called for further examination and interview in the UK. I came to believe that I had fallen too far away from specialised options whilst in the various jobs* I had done in the Forces not to be interested in the Civil Service appointment. Thinking politically, I had the notion that the Civil Service might offer me the opportunity for a useful career. In the Administrative Grade there were only 2000 civil servants and holding these posts could lead to one's having great influence on national social policy through politicians who became ministers of a Department. I had read two special books on the Administrative Grade's composition and its academic standing was as high as that of any university staff. An Executive class of relatively high academic background supported those in Administration and they in turn were backed up by a very large number of staff of matriculation level in the Clerical class; the top class were the 'directors', the other grades were the 'workers'. In the AG there were many with double firsts in mathematics and fine classicists.† This route also

---

* By my eighth decade I no longer believed this!
† Those looking for quality in the (now old) Administrative Grade of the British Civil Service need only recall the name of Sir Thomas L. Heath, FRS (1861–1940), who became one of its permanent secretaries, by 1913 having passed into the service in 1884. He was a Cambridge graduate first in mathematics and then classics. His avocation became ancient mathematics. He wrote two scholarly volumes on, *A History of Greek Mathematics* (1921) and other fine works which stand today as contributions of great authority in mathematics.

offered me the opportunity to settle in London and to serve the community in a socialistic way. If ever one wanted to be politically effective it would, as well, be very helpful to know about the administrative operations in the various departments.

I took the written examination as I have commented in Chapter XIV, somewhere in Italy, and subsequently was fortunate enough to be called to a two- or three-day Selection Board in the UK. It seemed to follow the WOSB (War Office Selection Board) method of selecting Army Officers. The UK Open Civil Service Competition required writing essays, being tested in chairing a committee, and participating in and being stretched in discussions on a variety of unexpected topics by each of three (probably) Oxbridge tutors.

In the latter, I was made very well aware of the self-assurance of some of the competitors who had public school backgrounds and of the advantages of men who had a sound knowledge of humanities and economics. Again, I just squeezed into the final group or top one-seventh who were offered appointments as Assistant Principals. I noticed from the examination marks, as printed, that the quality delivered by Oxbridge was very evident; my 'hit and miss' education from a peripheral Tech. was, I suppose, very obvious.

Early in December 1947, I received a communication from the Civil Service Commissioners, assigning me to the post of Assistant Principal (AP) in the Department of Customs and Excise in the City of London, and took it up in January 1948. This knowledge depressed me, because the department was an appendage to the Treasury and my assignment had no connection whatever with my previous academic training or recent professional occupation. Could not they have better used me in a Ministry which was related to engineering industry and manufacture? – the Ministry of Aircraft Production or the Department of Scientific and Industrial Research? I did not much care at this time to be called a Civil Servant, because the appellation embraced everyone from clerk to Permanent Secretary; it would give rise to the need for endless explanations. But it was public service, it did touch on politics, and I thought I would be able to influence the running of the country, the older I became. The salary was adequate, I could live in the London area and see the inner workings of the machinery of government, which would be a privilege.

I felt the latter was underlined by my going to an advertised meeting on World Government. It took place in a conference hall amid the newspaper companies which at that time were situated at the upper end of Fleet Street. The speakers included Bertrand Russell, Aneurin Bevan and Roger Livesey. I arrived at 6.55 p.m. for a 7 o'clock start. A score or so other people hung around the large doors of the entrance. They were not open and they remained bolted until some time after 7 when we were admitted. Two men carried a table that was put in place in the entrance hall and a lady was seated to receive the admittance charge. They then had to look for someone to take charge in the lecture room and there was a great shuffling of chairs on the stage and a putting of them into lines from a circumferential position in the hall. A jug of water and glasses were also sought and found for the speakers. Clearly, the gathering had not been well prepared and the speakers each arrived late. We were subjected to the characteristic harangues especially from Bevan, he of the thrusting Mussolini jaw. The whole episode was ludicrous. If these were the people who were to play a large part in creating the World Government, we would need heaven to help us! They had no notion of the size of the problems which would confront them, even in the running of a small 50 million person economy like the UK, let alone the several billion multi-national community! Thus was the task of running our country made more apparent to me for having worked in one necessary corner of British Government.

At the head of C & E was a Permanent Secretary and his Deputy, usually both knighted. Below, there were five Commissioners to whom about ten major divisions worked. Each was largely devoted to a speciality – particular taxes, duties, customs and controls – such as the Purchase Tax, Excise Duty on beer, wines and spirits, capital flow and the like.

I was attached to the Division of Exchange Control. Each Division had an Assistant Secretary at its head and was supported by two or three Principals; to the latter were appended Assistant Principals or 'learners'. I soon learned that one did not become a Principal before about 38 years of age and the Assistant Secretaries were appointed on average at about age 45. Salaries in the latter two grades were very good and the people themselves were very much their own masters in the ordering of their own work. I remember an extreme case of one Principal who used to arrive around 11.30 a.m., have an hour's lunch break from 2 to 3 o'clock and finish work close to 7 p.m. He was reputed to be a fast worker in responding quickly to all the files and cases that came his way. However, mostly people arrived between 10 and 10.30 a.m. and departed about 6.30. All the AG usually arrived soberly dressed and carrying a copy of *The Times*. Life was not too arduous.

My misfortune was to start off with an Assistant Secretary who had spent all his life in C & E, and one who had little regard for an engineering background and some years' service in the army. I saw little of him and was the better pleased for that.

My own preoccupations were in drafting replies to people seeking to recover money which had been confiscated from them when they arrived in this country with currency in excess of £20 sterling. (An Exchange Control Act endeavoured to control the import of currency, Britain having capital flow problems at the time.) I remember one agitated correspondent protesting and stating that it was all very unfair and what should he do, having landed at Plymouth and having to travel by train to Aberdeen – it could not be achieved on £20! Apart from these relatively minor sorts of occasions there were rare discussions about the movement of capital by firms and the writing of drafts to Parliamentary Questions to which Ministers had to reply. Mainly the proposed reply was simply 'No sir!' – but accompanied by two or three pages of background to help the Minister anticipate supplementary questions in the House. 'PQs' were always in files marked 'Urgent' and green-flagged. They were passed 'upwards' from AP to P to Assistant Secretary to Commissioner, all adding to or deleting passages from the supporting background proposed. If the askers of questions as tax-payers had realised what the cost of the reply was, they would, I believe, not have asked in the first place!

For the second year of my service I was transferred to the Purchase Tax division. It was more varied than Exchange Control. Here, it befell me at one juncture to compile a list or Schedule of Drugs which were exempt from Purchase Tax, and which was to be attached to a Bill which was going through the House of Commons. My Schedule was required 'to lie on the table' in the House of Commons for a specific number of days before it could be accepted in law. I recall taking the legislation which had been drafted to an elderly legal gentleman in an ancient office near to Westminster Abbey. He was someone apparently who cast his eye over the Instrument before it was laid on 'the table' in the House of Commons – someone who seemed to operate as if it were still the age of Charles Dickens! There was a Solicitors' Office in C & E, to which we often referred cases for legal advice; (they were better paid, rank for rank, than in the Secretary's Office). I recall that in replying to our queries for advice, the ultimate reference seemed always to be the Customs Act of 1868.

As part of my 'practical' training, I accompanied two senior inspectors on a visit to the Coldstream area on the border between England and Scotland for one week. We went to the horse races, a meeting being in progress, to examine physical arrangements concerning entrance charges and the betting tax. We were very well received and entertained to a substantial lunch. Later, we visited breweries and I had the opportunity to see brewery plant – large vats, etc., at close quarters in the act of brewing.

In the Office where I normally performed, all the APs used to come together for morning coffee. Conversation was very good, in fact better than I ever later encountered in university departments, for instance: for the first time I heard of the select novelist Anthony Powell, from my colleague Leighton-Boyce, or heard demonstrated how to go through a menu stating the customs duty on each and every item. Frequently, there would be intimations of an impending budget change by discussing how much one penny on the price of beer would bring to the Exchequer. I was amazed too, to hear two of my colleagues waxing on about the Wagner programme they would hear at next Bayreuth Festival. Amusement often arose from a daily habit of the Deputy Permanent Secretary, Sir Otto Mundy. His AP secretary would have scanned his master's *Times* to note the Latin and Greek texts or tags he had pencilled into the margins alongside the first, second and third leaders. Half of the APs finished their careers in C & E as Commissioners, whilst others were exported as senior civil servants to other departments. For my part, it was clear to me, towards the end of my 'apprenticeship', that I was not ready or fitted for a lifetime in C & E, and I started applying for posts in engineering. I thought that the opportunity to take up the offer of a lectureship at nearby Northampton Polytechnic should not be missed: it was at least a half-way house to engineering industry. I had learned much from being in Customs and without being specific it was helpful in administrative situations in later life.

CHAPTER XVII

Sheffield University

———◆———

My first year at Northampton Polytechnic (1950–51) was a very strenuous one. I had 21 contact hours, face-to-face with students, in all mechanical engineering subjects except thermodynamics and fluid mechanics, and classes which could be 60 or 70 strong. There were students, both part-time and full-time, reading for the London University External B.Sc. degree in Mechanical Engineering and similarly older industrial students who could be up to about 40 years of age working for their examinations for the Institution of Mechanical Engineers professional qualification of (then) Associate membership. This latter required at least five years and the degree three years if the student was a full-time one and five years or more if he was not full-time. (I never recall seeing a female student, incidentally.)

The I.Mech.E. students, particularly, attended my lectures on Strength of Materials on either Monday night or Tuesday: most of them were in their mid-twenties and they were coming along at the end of a day's work: they were seriously minded men whilst the degree students were youths. The evening classes ran from 6.30 until 9.30 p.m. and were the last in a day when I had already been lecturing for four or five hours. I would arrive home about 10.30 p.m. on Monday night, eat a small supper and then settle to work to midnight or 1 a.m. I was on parade behind the lecturing table before 9.30 a.m. the next morning. This first year was so demanding I can still remember the teaching programme details to this day! By Wednesday lunch-time, 1 p.m., I had worked before a class for nineteen hours. (I had only one hour commitments on Thursday and Friday.) I certainly earned my salary! To appreciate what commitment was required of lecturers, the reader should realise that *at least* one hour was required to prepare a one-hour lecture, then one hour to deliver it and at least one hour to select problems and mark them for a typical class of 30 to 40.

I reflected that I had had no contact with these various subjects since graduating, seven years previously. There were times when lecturing in that first year that I noted I was a mere 50 minutes ahead of the class! Of course in my second year it was a matter of repeating the first year and embellishing it! But the final year was daunting. It was all a big change from the Army and the Civil Service!

Northampton Polytechnic had a fine reputation for its lecturers; their capacity for lecturing in many subjects at relatively high levels made them sought after by other colleges. (There were, in my day, in each year of the degree course, three or four classes of forty men proceeding in parallel – perhaps about a hundred in total.) Thus young lecturers did not stay long, but went off elsewhere to less demanding 'environments', on promotion and thus on higher rates of pay. (In Sheffield University in 1955–56, there was only one man in the 3rd Honours course!)

À propos the above lecturing experiences, I may mention that I recently encountered the following extract, taken from a biography of Professor David G. Crighton which appeared in the Biographical Memoirs of Fellows of the Royal Society, Vol. 47, p. 109, November, 2001. Professor Crighton (1942–2000) was Head of the Department (HoD) of Applied Mathematics at Cambridge University (Woolwich Polytechnic was slightly smaller than Northampton Polytechnic, but they provided almost identical degree and I.Mech.E. courses):

(Extract) Woolwich Polytechnic, London, 1964–66

David was appointed, aged 21, as a lecturer at Woolwich Polytechnic, now the University of Greenwich, to teach a wide range of courses in physics and mathematics, for up to 24 hours per week at times. After two years he saw that his talents could not be suitably developed at Woolwich and he sought to attempt research.

At the end of my first full year at Northampton Polytechnic, having survived its over-demanding lecturing schedule, I started to scan the advertised vacancies for a lectureship in Mechanical Engineering in the universities. I had doubts about my suitability and thought I might be over-reaching myself. A pressurising factor in my consideration however was the inadequate salary at the Polytechnic. I was in receipt of a stipend of around £400 per year, some £50 or £60 less than I received in the Civil Service. We were beginning not to be able to make ends meet. As told above, in September 1949, I had, almost by chance, taken on delivering an evening lecture course at Northampton in *Mathematics* and the pay added to what I received when I became a permanent lecturer in *Mechanical Engineering*. Since I started the latter at Easter (1950), I was only allowed to continue the mathematics lectures until the end of the session in June/July. However, the money for it also stopped at that time. The difference between my civil service salary and that from Northampton Poly. or London County Council (LCC) induced my wife to take up the domiciliary teaching offered by the Local Education Authority (LEA), whilst I also took up an invitation to coach a well-paid engineer-neighbour, employed at the Woolwich Arsenal, for his Higher National Certificate. This latter coaching went on for three hours on Sunday mornings for a sum of £1. (In the course of the coaching I used to sketch out the solutions to his homework. Once he had passed his examination at Woolwich Poly, the way was open for him to apply for Associate Membership of the I.Mech.E. – and thus promotion.)

I well remember that the little girl whom my wife taught for two hours on Wednesday mornings whilst I looked after our three-year-old son, brought in a guinea (one pound, one shilling). The little girl, Anne, was a polio victim with paralysed legs, the daughter of an ex-RAF fighter pilot. When my wife remarked on how unlucky they had been, her mother at once brought out a photograph of her husband's wartime unit – some 40 strong – commenting that, on the contrary, she regarded herself as very fortunate, in that her husband was the only survivor from that group. This money too, finished when Anne went to a special boarding school for disabled children within the year.

It was the loss of these fragmentary earnings which necessitated the search for a better-paid job. I alighted on two vacancies, one at Birmingham and the other at Sheffield University and applied for the advertised lectureship at both. In due course, I was informed in a kind letter that the Birmingham post had been filled, a man with Thermodynamics and Heat Transfer as his primary interests having been chosen. However, I also received an invitation from Sheffield University's Registrar to attend for an interview at St George's Square. (See Figure 1.) By chance, I had seen a paper on 'The Deep Drawing of Thin-walled Cups' in the *Proceedings of the Institution of Mechanical Engineers*. It was a subject I knew nothing about but after studying it, it looked to embrace material that I could easily read up and was thus the kind of opportunity I was seeking. (For our purposes we may say that its subject was Plasticity and that that is an extension of the Elasticity of Strength of Materials. A coiled spring, after pulling, reverts to its initial position or shape if the pull is not bigger than a certain amount. This is wholly *elastic behaviour*. If the pull exceeds that certain value, it will only recover elastically by a certain amount. The permanent extension is its *plastic* component).

When I arrived at the Engineering Building, I was still wondering at my audacity in applying for a university appointment, and I walked around it, seriously considering if I should simply pull out of it and go back home to London. However, I could not afford to do this – I was expecting, indeed needed, to be re-imbursed the £2 15s train fare! The interview lasted for no more than ten minutes. Professor Swift introduced himself, mentioned the name of the Professor of Metallurgy and Dean, Dr A. G. Quarrel, on his right, and on his left a Mr Turner, Head of Mechanical Engineering. (Swift was the only Professor of Engineering in the University of Sheffield – i.e. he was Head of Civil and Electrical as well as Mechanical Engineering!) It was soon clear that Swift dominated the other two members of the interviewing committee. The Dean appeared to agree with everything said and indeed only Swift spoke. It was evident that Swift appreciated precisely my position, certainly technically and less so, socially. Swift was an ex-serviceman and after leaving Cambridge it is possible to see that he had had difficulties in the career moves he made. I think too that he knew what a tough institution Northampton Polytechnic was and how hard staff were worked. I later learned that he had acted as the Examiner for the *External* London University B.Eng., i.e. for London University's four major colleges (of which Northampton and Woolwich were two). I remember little of what transpired. I recall saying that I wanted to engage in research but did not know how to proceed; and in my present position, with 21 teaching contact hours per week, two young sons and a garden to look after, I did not have the time. This amused one member of the committee but Swift certainly understood.

We quickly came to discuss money and because there was an imminent revision of salaries in London I had calculated what I might receive and therefore what

Figure 1. The Engineering Building, Sheffield University at St George's Square in 1950, from a painting by Dr S. Bradbury.

I could justify asking for on this occasion. I stated £675; Swift responded with, 'No £25s! £700!' (I well knew that the universities paid £50 per head for each child and thus I would be on £800 per year! – £350 more than I got from the munificent LCC. With all the issues raised by Swift I had no disagreement and indeed we seemed to 'talk the same language' immediately. I was told after a brief exchange between the chairman and his two colleagues that I was accepted and that a letter of appointment would follow. It did and it was, I believe, the month of September 1951.

After the trauma of the Second World War and its aftermath, following on from the period with the Home Civil Service and nearly two years as a lecturer at Northampton Polytechnic (subsequently City University, London), I arrived in Sheffield in January 1952. I was looking to be involved in engineering 'research' but had little idea of where to start, though from reading journals and especially the I.Mech.E. *Proceedings*, I now knew of Professor H. W. Swift's reputation in plasticity or metal-forming mechanics and hydrodynamic lubrication. I counted myself very fortunate to be on his staff. However, the Division Head imposed on me the teaching of Engineering Drawing (and the drawing office classes), the running of Prof. Swift's first year exercise classes in Applied Mechanics as well as laboratory demonstrating in third year Strength of Materials. I had a load of eight (!) rather uninteresting contact hours a week which, after some twenty per week at Northampton Polytechnic, meant that I now had a lot of uncommitted 'brain' time available!

A brief account of Professor Swift's academic life and work is given in Figure 2.

Figure 2.
The centennial year of Herbert Walker Swift, 1894–1960, Professor of Engineering in the University of Sheffield: his life and work*
by W. Johnson†

1. Introduction and early biography

Dr Herbert Walker Swift was appointed Professor of Engineering in the University of Sheffield, UK, in 1936 at the age of 42, see the Figure, and where he directed three sub-departments in mechanical, civil and electrical engineering, almost until he retired in 1955.‡ He himself was closest to mechanical engineering and in his lifetime he was renowned, in the UK, for his analytical and experimental investigations in the two fields of the Mechanics and Tribology of Machines and Applied Plasticity.

Professor Swift, born 15 December 1894, at Deptford, Kent, the son of a civil engineer, this month completes 101 years since his birth. He received an elementary education at West Hill LCC School (1901–06), but then won a place at the famous Christ's Hospital (School) (1907–14). He is known to have remarked that he won his place for answering 'a few sums, and writing an essay, one Saturday morning'. At school Swift specialised in mathematics in his later years. He proceeded to Cambridge having won an Open Scholarship, to become Barnes Scholar in 1915 at St John's College – a college which, with Trinity, is noted for many historical and outstanding names in mathematical research. He read mathematics and physics but from my knowledge of him he insisted that his primary interest was mathematics; at this stage he was not a potential engineer.

The First World War started in 1914 and after being first rejected for active service on medical grounds Swift was later accepted, in 1915, to join the Artillery. He attained the rank of Captain, served in France, was wounded and was mentioned

---

* From a lecture delivered in the University of Sheffield, 6 December 1995. See, Jnl of Materials Processing Technology 65 (1997), 153–164.

† Lecturer in Professor Swift's Department, 1952–56. When I came to know Professor Swift he was 57. Others, such as Dr P. B. Neal, may have heard him lecture when they were undergraduates.

‡ On moving into new premises in about 1954, the three sub-departments became independent and each had its own professor, Professor Swift becoming the Professor of Mechanical Engineering in his last year, 1954–55. Professor Ripper was the University's first Professor of Engineering. He was followed by Professor F. C. Lea (well known for hs book on *Hydraulics*) in 1923. In 1936, Swift succeeded Lea.

in Despatches.* He returned to Cambridge in 1919, aged nearly 25. Initially, he had been an undergraduate in Mathematics but doubtlessly, having regard to the best scientific years of his life having been 'eaten by the locusts of time',† he changed to reading the Mechanical Sciences Tripos, graduating BA with First Class Honours in 1920 and as the Prizeman for that year. He became MA in 1924. It was not an uncommon intention for numerous mathematically capable men to contemplate first reading Mathematics and then switching to the study of Engineering Science.‡ Not only intellectually pre-occupied as an undergraduate, Swift found time to swim in competitions for Cambridge and was awarded a Half-Blue!

After graduating, Swift joined the firm of William Hollins Bros, a company manufacturing hydraulic turbines in Kendal, in the Lake District of England. He soon became Chief Engineer§ of the company but in 1922 he left industry to enter the academic world, joining the University of Leeds as a demonstrator and assistant lecturer in the Department then headed by Professor John Goodman, 1862–1935. It appears that the two men soon became good friends and collaborators, Professor Goodman being a talented experimenter and Swift both a capable experimentalist and an outstanding analyst. Goodman had published a book, some 730 pages long by the time of its 6th edition in 1908 (and extended further for the last edition in 1927) entitled *Mechanics Applied to Engineering*.

Goodman was a Whitworth Scholar and a member of the Institutions of Civil and Mechanical Engineering, but, not unusual for those days, he had no first degree. Some notion of what constituted the core of Engineering Mechanics in the first decade of the twentieth century may be had from a perusal of the contents of Goodman's book.

Whilst at Leeds, Swift met a young lecturer in Botany – Maisie Hobbins – and married her in 1924. She was a great asset to him and a splendid help-mate in the delicate matter of securing pleasant relationships between her husband and members of staff and their families. They had two daughters, the elder one, Mary, a medical practitioner, and Joan, an Arts graduate.

In 1926 Swift was appointed Head of the Department of Mechanical Engineering at Bradford Technical College. This involved a heavy teaching load and substantial administrative responsibility. Around 1924, the Institution of Mechanical Engineers formed a branch of the Institution and Swift became its first hard-working, unpaid, Yorkshire Honorary Secretary. Ability to fulfil competently the latter function was doubtlessly a recommendation of administrative capacity for a departmental Head in the minds of the electors. In 1924, aged 60, John Goodman retired from Leeds and was succeeded by Professor W. David. The latter was a thermo-dynamicist and from

---

* Swift was not without a sense of humour. He remarked about his experience with certain members of a foreign artillery company, 'Bombardo commenso, bombardo intenso et je départ très vite!'.

† Like many ex-servicemen he found the loss of these years could never be recovered. A somewhat similar case concerning Dr R. A. C. Slater is outlined in 'Early Research in Linear Induction Motors' in the *Newcomen Society Trans.* 66 (1994–95) 215–18.

‡ Professor Osborne Reynolds (1842–1912) graduated in Mathematics from Cambridge (as a wrangler) and after about two years experience as a civil engineering consultant took up the Chair in Engineering at Manchester University in 1868, remaining until 1905.

§ I do not know precisely what his company responsibilities were but he once remarked that he had had to examine the top-most collar of the works' high chimney to determine the quality of the brickwork. He had had to climb the outside of the chimney, exposed, up which numerous separate ladders had been connected or assembled!

my conversations with persons who were members of his staff, I gathered that he was insistent that all academics in his department carry out research in thermodynamics. My information is that Swift refused to conform and he was thus put under pressure to relocate himself. My supposition is that, as a mathematician, he would have been directly attracted to Mechanics; he would have acquired little background in Thermodynamics and Engine Performance during his one undergraduate academic year of a few months (1919–20) in the Cambridge Engineering Department.

It was, at one time, a common practice for some Cambridge undergraduates to take London External Degree Examinations in subjects identical with what they were reading at Cambridge and Swift was one such. This was a means of undergraduates checking on their own progress and preparing for their Cambridge degree examinations. It also entitled them later in life to submit for a London University postgraduate degree if the desire and or the need arose. In 1928 Swift successfully submitted four substantial papers for the degree of D.Sc. of the University of London; of the degree he was able to relate that the grant for the equipment on which his research was conducted, was £5!

Professor Swift's very last public lectures were delivered in Cairo, Egypt, in 1956, a few months after retiring – now almost fifty years ago.

Rodney Hill's classic British monograph on *Mathematical Plasticity* (OUP), was published in 1950 and *The Theory of Perfectly Plastic Bodies* by American authors W. Prager and P. G. Hodge appeared in 1951. Though Swift had had plasticity research in progress since joining the Department in 1937, Hill's mathematical formulations and treatments of many subjects were beyond the experience of engineers engaged in research in the Mechanical Engineering Department (MED); it was too mathematical in style. However, I was especially attracted by Slip Line Field Theory (s.l.f.t.) – then a local topic of study in continuum metal forming plasticity, to which Swift encouraged me to devote myself, perhaps because he himself was unskilled in this new esoteric discipline and recognised my mathematical inclinations (for an engineer). By one means and another I learned this new theory and how to apply it, and succeeded in finding some new solutions to slightly different problems. This it was which led me to register for a Ph.D. in Engineering.

My first research work appeared as British Iron and Steel Association (BISRA) reports, a list of which (about twelve), is given in Vol. 1 of my Collected Papers. (All of these I expect to deposit in the Royal Society Archives.) I wrote one particularly long report on the experimental work in Extrusion, done in the Department during the previous few years and tried to explain it with some theory; my own work was a theoretical extension piece, using s.l.f.s to predict extrusion pressure and metal flow patterns. (See Figures 1–8 in Ch.22.) Some of my results were openly published in a quarterly journal recently founded by R. Hill (Professor of Applied Mathematics at Nottingham University at the time), edited by him and published by Robert Maxwell's Pergamon Press. I had had to learn how to write scientific text and present papers. I also learned much from Hill's comments and advice on my early submissions.

At the end of my first year in Sheffield, I asked Professor Swift if I might be allowed to teach some of his third year Honours classes in Plasticity. He bade me come to his home on Friday afternoon at 2 p.m. For three hours we hopped about, but in some depth, over a multiplicity of topics in Plasticity. At about 5 o'clock I was dismissed but he informed me that I could take his classes. (He was within two years of retiring.) Three months later it occurred to me that that afternoon I had been put through an intense oral examination!

Some time later Professor Swift passed to me, for review for the weekly periodical *The Engineer*, a translation of Professor E. P. Unksov's book on *An Engineering Theory of Plasticity*. Initially, it had been made for the Production Engineering Research Association: it was full of 'main' stresses when 'principal' ones were intended! I learned too that what we refer to as Luder's lines (1860) the Russians call Chernov Lines (1884). Many other minor errors and criticisms were noted by me in the review. (I blush to re-read these today, but plead that only a young man could have written them.) Alas, I later reviewed Morley's *Strength of Materials* in a somewhat similarly cavalier fashion. But in those days it was an honour to review a book and besides receiving the book, one was then actually paid a fee of a few guineas!

All my early work was written up in rough long-hand, typed out on a very small typewriter and copied three or four times using sheets of carbon copying paper by my wife. Making drawings and graphs and copying them was not easy – they had to be drawn in Indian ink on special paper, so they could be copied by hand, using a blue-printing machine – a large item which needed frequently to be adjusted. The whole operation demanded lots of time and patience. Thus did my wife become involved in the operation of the writing up of my early work for publication. It brought me to trying to explain to her (without mathematics) the science in a paper in popular or lay man terms so that she would understand what she was about – at least in part! Today, she is a knowledgable woman who surprises engineers sitting next to her at formal dinners with her grasp of engineering ideas and terms such as creep, fatigue, dislocations ...

At the same time as I worked on extrusion I strayed into other problems, as I have mentioned. My second paper, or Note, with all the luck of the beginner, won a small Premium Award from the Royal Aeronautical Society. (In the laboratory on Friday afternoons, the third-year students determined the (elastic) shear centre for two, thin-walled sections, held as cantilevers. I did the same calculations making assumptions that befitted plastic rather than elastic bending and obtained new results.)

By the time I left Sheffield for Manchester, the notion of submitting for a Ph.D. had been completely discarded. There were so many novel problems to be investigated, and due to other commitments I had acquired, spending time in writing a thesis was insufficiently attractive; it also seemed dull to stay investigating one subject for several years.

A major involvement for me whilst in Sheffield was the three-years role as Honorary Secretary of the Yorkshire Branch of the Institution of Mechanical Engineers of about 2000 members, to which I was elected.

Service to my professional institution called for arranging meetings of local committees, the venues and presentation of papers, with responsibility for briefing authors, settling hotel bills and often obtaining reprints – as well as minute-writing and account keeping. It is small wonder that in two consecutive years my wife and I spent Boxing Day preparing the Branch accounts for presentation to the appointed accountants on 1 January!

This whole operation was anything but honorary! Besides organising monthly meetings of the Branch programmes in Sheffield, Bradford, York, Leeds, Huddersfield and Hull, I found myself coping also with between six and seven hundred persons at the 1953 Institution National Meeting in Sheffield. For assistance I managed to recruit two graduates, for a modest fee. I saw nothing of the long vacation in that year, so heavy were the demands on my time. This Honorary appointment however did have a positive side for it brought me into contact with senior mechanical engineers from all the major towns of Yorkshire, from David Brown's at Huddersfield (world renowned gear-manufacturing specialists) to Elastoplast at Hull! My conversance, and indeed almost integration into the everyday plasticity of the steel working industry in Sheffield was very useful and well developed, and among other things made student visits easy to arrange. The pay-off for all this non-University work, in days when University Chairs were few, was the expectation or hope that the Secretaryship after two or three years would lead on to an appointment as Head of Department at one of the major Colleges of Technology, usually in Yorkshire. H. W. Swift, J. C. Oakden, and J. G. Jagger – names once familiar to hundreds of students – had between 1926 and 1950 each been HoD at Bradford and Northampton Polytechnics. (All were First Class graduates at Cambridge in their day.) So, with the thought that I would never make a Chair, the Headship of one of the latter Departments was a post to aim for. If one survived the activity of being an Honorary Secretary it was clear to any selecting body that one would likewise be successful in running a big college department! (And of course some members of our Branch Committee would be on the Selection Committee.) Nonetheless it was all too great a task and when I was appointed Professor in Manchester Tech. in 1960, I only agreed to one of my staff becoming the Honorary Secretary of the area, if the Institution backed him up with a substantial full-time paid appointee.

A great pleasure in all this activity was to meet the Mayors of towns whom we usually invited to dinner when we held a meeting in their territory. Sheffield itself was different however. I learned that in my day it was the Master Cutler who took prime place on many official occasions. The latter was an injured old soldier and company director. I remember him, Sir Somebody-something, standing upright in his fine clothes and saying to my wife and me that he would like a dinner in which 'sausage and mash' was on the menu as he had eaten in excess of 550 lunches and dinners of 'meat and fowl, veg. and potatoes' during his year of office. He was a splendid old soul!

I now come to William Alfred Tuplin (b. 1902) and my first Ph.D. supervision. Alf Tuplin was appointed Professor and Head of the Applied Mechanics Department in Sheffield University, a little before I joined the Mechanical Engineering Department as a Lecturer in January 1952. It was an innovation, the true motive for its establishment I never elicited or understood. Why Mechanics? That was Professor Swift's professional line. Tuplin was a time-served apprentice – and so a professor with a difference – of a company which built locomotives, I believe.

He took a first class honours degree at Manchester University and some years later was awarded a senior doctorate D.Sc., for his published research papers. I once naively asked Professor Swift about co-operation between the two units and got a very dusty answer ... Swift himself was a man with a fine, classical Cambridge reputation for his researches in hydrodynamic lubrication and the plastic working of metals whilst Tuplin was a gear and vibration specialist with David Brown Ltd at the time.

In moving into academia, Tuplin maintained his interest in locos. He wrote popular articles, especially about riding on the footplate of a locomotive across America and Canada, helping the driver and fireman with a shovel. He also had written an article I am told to which he attached a fictitious name, concerning his taking a loco up and down the biggest inclines in the Lake District. Like some of the distinguished ancient engineers of the nineteenth century, he would sketch out proposed designs of equipment, in chalk, on the floor of his departmental workshop – and you had to be careful not to walk over them!

Tuplin had to create his own courses and research school without previous academic experience. He had three lecturers on his staff, to help, but I can now only remember Dr Ludwig Meyer – later Professor at City University – and a person who had been beaten up by the secret police in Nazi Germany. As a new member of the academic staff I had visions of attending some of Tuplin's courses, but this notion quickly evaporated because of professorial stand-offs. Tuplin was a large, dark-haired man, very direct – easy to talk to – and unpretentious. I once complained to him about a professor not knowing something I thought he should have done, only for him to comment, 'Ah, Johnson! You should never be surprised at what professors don't know, it would fill volumes!' However, I had one longer involvement with him that I cannot forget which became a matter of long-term concern to me.

After Professor Swift had retired (in 1955) I was assigned to be the Ph.D. research supervisor of an Egyptian, Mr F. I had only been in Sheffield about three years and had no Ph.D. myself, though I was registered as a candidate at this time. (This situation became possible only because I was a member of staff of the Department.)

Incidentally, the only reward for taking on any Ph.D. candidate is the prospect of being able to publish new findings of research investigation conducted, under joint authorship.

I had attended a one-week lecture course on Plasticity at Imperial College, given by an American (actually, a German refugee), Professor William Prager, in 1953. Apart from that, my knowledge was acquired by reading, especially from translated pre-war German books and Professor Hill's volume.

Mr F. was a pleasant, 50-year old man, released from Cairo University for four or five years, to study in Sheffield. In his first two years he had worked under the supervision of one of Swift's chief technical assistants, designing and preparing his research equipment. The research investigation he was allotted was that of determining the yield loci of some well-known metals, by using thin-walled tubes which could, simultaneously, be pulled in tension and twisted. The technical assistant alas, died and no-one else on the staff was willing to take on Mr F.

Mr F. was supported on a five-year scholarship and three years had gone by. He had to complete his experimental programme and write up his thesis in the two remaining years. With much assistance he succeeded in submitting a 250-page thesis.

He was an intensely hard-working student and frequently he stayed on until the early hours of the morning. Working late myself until about 2 a.m. on one occasion, I joined him by chance in walking home and was astonished to find that policemen on late night patrol would bid him 'Good-night!' as he passed by.

Professor Tuplin was Chairman of the Examining Board, which included a professor from a neighbouring university and one internal senior lecturer. The former was the External Examiner, the latter the designated Internal Examiner (not me as should normally have been the case). I myself constituted the audience of one. Mr F. arrived late for his oral examination. It turned out that he was lucky to be alive, for the gas tap in his bedroom had been left on during the night, he said. The reader can well imagine the situation ... Mr F. was soon upset and nervous and in the face of only a few simple questions he showed that he could not cope with the situation. In less than 20 minutes, the Board closed down the examination, there was some consultation between the Board members, and Mr F. was declared to have failed, but to have done enough to warrant a Master's degree. Returning to Cairo without a Ph.D., I learned, would not allow him to be taken back on to his university roll of permanent staff, and for this reason, he would have no pension to look forward to. It was a rare situation which should never have happened and underlined for me the necessity to ensure, as far as possible, that Ph.D. candidates should have the ability to achieve their objective in the first place. Mr F.'s failure meant that he would have an academic millstone round his neck for the rest of his life.

I left the Department soon afterwards to go to Manchester University as Senior Lecturer. Taken up with selling my home in Sheffield and buying one in the Manchester area absorbed nearly all my time and especially as I would be my new Departmental Head's Deputy, I had much to organise – time-tables, various courses for the new intake of 'Freshers' and responsibility for Stores Control. However, despite these preoccupations, à propos of the Mr F. fiasco, I contacted Professor Tuplin and arranged to go and meet with him at his home in Sheffield, on a Sunday. There I tried to persuade him as Dean of Engineering, to re-consider Mr F.'s failure, but his reply was that there could be no remission – the Examiners had spoken and pleas were of no avail. I had argued that Mr F. had been terribly over-anxious and his age, the magnitude of the event and lack of preparation, had not fitted him well for the oral examination he had encountered. He had not appreciated what a testing situation he would have to endure. But none of this prevailed.

Business over, Professor Tuplin beamed, and said he would like me to see his latest installation. This turned out to be in his garden, where a mass of dials, gauges, taps interconnected by metal tubes and pipes was spread over the lower portion of the wall of the side of his house, with a platform, a foot or two off the ground, carrying steps at one end. There was also a rail at about three feet high along what was obviously the footplate for a loco driver and fireman. A

Figure 3. Alf Tuplin's British Steam.

call to his little son brought him out to us — wearing a black, peaked cap with a larger one for his father. They climbed up on to the footplate and, at father's word of command, the pair then went through the motion of raising steam through the array of equipment. Water gauges were tapped, a low iron door was opened and small quantities of coal were shovelled into what one had to imagine was a fire. Steam pressures were read and called out and finally the Professor cried, 'Steam up, ready to move!' It was, at once, both impressive and bizarre!

Dr Tuplin published an excellent 200 page paperback book, *British Steam since 1900* (Pan Books, 1969), written not for professional designers but for admirers of steam locomotives. (See Figure 3.) Jnl. Japan Soc. Mech. Engrs, 99 (929), 1–3, April, 1996.

The Ph.D. system (which in fact varies from university to university) is almost invariably hard and unremitting. Even for good candidates it is tough going for what can be up to four or five years. Candidates generally start slowly and when they come to the end of their first year they have virtually nothing to show for it. Thereafter the pressures are heavy.

Ten years later as a Head of Department I tried to devise a system to prevent this sort of thing happening. We declared that we would only admit for Ph.D. work men who had gained a Master's degree with distinction. When a research student joined us having only a good first degree we usually registered him for an M.Sc. He then had to attend courses for two terms and these usually provided him with adequate theoretical background to the research which he intended to pursue. These courses were often given by a member of the staff who had specialised in the subject of interest. A written paper was set and those who passed, as nearly all did, then proceeded to pursue some allotted minor M.Sc. research topic. They learned the background literature, got to grips with experiment and learned how to set out a Master's thesis: it often required two years' work but it could be finished and examined in a year and a half. The essence of pursuing what was involved in the Ph.D. was therefore laid out in a minor way. The Ph.D. was a deeper and profounder study with some requirement to produce completely new results – with new territory explored. Only men who had achieved a pass mark of over 65 per cent in our written examination were admitted to the Doctor's degree programme; the system worked well and a well-trained Master could accomplish his Ph.D. in another two and a half years. A candidate was usually rewarded by becoming joint-author with his supervisor (and perhaps Professor) of two or three good papers in well-established journals. Learning the art of writing papers completed the Ph.D. process and stood the candidate in good stead for life.

Words about the above topic were summarised in a Note requested by the Journal of the Japan Society of Mechanical Engineers and my response, in English is given in Figure 4, as follows.

*Figure 4: The Way Ahead – Message from Prof. W. Johnson**

Your future professional life will have been largely decided by your choice of undergraduate course. Thus, I advise you to find for yourself a university where good professors (not stand-ins) still teach undergraduates and take a great pride in doing so. The first years should be science based but with some specialisation later on. Though mathematics is vitally important, today some social science is educationally valuable if only for understanding open ended problems (which engineering science ones are not).

A good Master's degree of advanced lectures is desirable to build up your background training in special subjects – when you know what you really want to do. Your M.Sc project should be good training in concise and accurate reporting.

If you continue for a Ph.D., your choice of supervisor is extremely important, not all of them are equally capable, experienced and helpful. Make some quiet, private inquiries of other research students. You will be with your supervisor for five years, so choose him very carefully – as you would a wife!

If, after the Doctorate, you need a few more years as a 'post-Doc', study something a little different from your thesis work; work to increase your width as well as your

---

* Jnl. Japan Soc. Mech. Engrs, 99 (929), 1–3, April, 1996.

depth – both of which good professors have. At this stage too, you are creating intellectual capital, so your topics of research should be mutually supportive.

When young, consider moving every few years; in new environments you will gain more experience, more friends and contacts. Postgraduate employment with large international companies usually provides the best career opportunities; so foreign languages are important. Small private companies too often make special openings for family and friends.

Visit your university library often. Note the new books in your field and scan relevant journals regularly for articles in your own and neighbouring fields; be able to recall the topics you have glanced at.

In lectures and seminars ask questions. Questioning clarifies the mind and other people's questions reveal weaknesses in presented work and suggest new research topics.

Do not criticise written or oral work destructively but to help construct something better. It will cost you nothing and give you a friend – which is better than making a professional enemy!

You should not always be engaged in professional work. Read for perspective, pleasure and wisdom; try reading about the work of the historical founders of your kind of science and technology.

Do not be dominated by monetary reward. Always give time and attention to your family, the soundest investment you will ever make. Remember your obligations to the country which gave you your education and be thankful for the gifts of good health and intelligence. Happy in these respects, you will be well balanced and reasonable in all your dealings with your colleagues.

In my lifetime I have examined over one hundred Ph.D.s and failed two only. Most complaints would be that no real supervision was given after a research title or topic had been settled. One candidate commented, 'I saw my supervisor at the beginning, I said 'Goodbye' to him when I left and 'Hello' to him once in the corridor!' Poor supervision or lack of interest is a common criticism of the supervisory system. I could write at length on the topic of supervising and acting as an External Examiner (for theses from home and abroad), of the different procedures and of the derisory payment for a job which, properly, required three or four days and pays even today only about £100. Examining is a task professors do for one another.

From my first starting to teach Engineering Plasticity in Sheffield, grew the first postgraduate text book I wrote with (later Professor) P. B. Mellor as co-author, *Plasticity for Mechanical Engineers* (412 pp.). The first edition appeared in 1962 and was reprinted in 1970. It was translated into Japanese in 1965 and is, or was, the basis of lectures on metal forming which Japanese students received in the 1960s and 1970s. (This book extended to 576 pp, was translated and appeared in Russian in 1982.) *Mechanics of Metal Extrusion*, with Prof. H. Kudo (see Figure 5) had been similarly dealt with (but without royalties in 1965). Professor Mellor, who was awarded the D.Sc. degree in 1983, was a doctoral student during my period in Sheffield, as were Dr John Hawkyard and Dr Philip Neal – both later Readers, the former at UMIST. The BISRA Hoyle Street Laboratories were opened during the mid-1950s but we had only slight contact with staff there. Professor Swift received £1,500 per year from BISRA to back

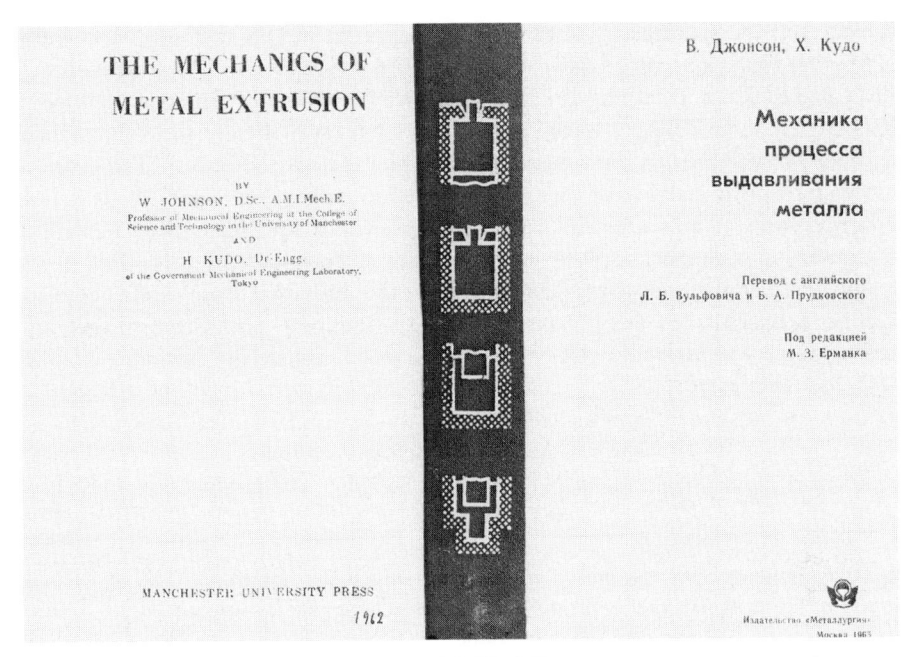

Figure 5. The Mechanics of Metal Extrusion *in Russian.*

his Plasticity researches – it going, mainly, to support research students. I recall with gratitude (and, at the time, surprise) when I was called to his office one lunch-time and informed that in recognition of my BISRA-related researches, I would receive an extra £100 per year from his fund!

Other close colleagues of these years, but in the Civil Engineering Group, were Professor R. M. Haythornwaite (later at Temple University, USA), Professor Henry Cowan (NSW, Australia) and (then to be) Professor N. S. Bolton in Sheffield.

I might add here that a significant source of extrusion problems requiring solutions (without payment of course!) was a local company, who at the time were much preoccupied in extruding turbine blades. Another company in the area had difficulties with the breaking of the cutting edges of the bolt croppers they manufactured. This was a 650-employee firm at the time, in about 1954/5. It had one non-graduate metallurgist of an HNC level of training and one tensile-testing machine, not in working order when I visited it. About 25(!) years later when I was at Cambridge I had a telephone call from one of the 'research' engineers of this company, to ask me for more information about the results of tests I then did. This company put absolutely nothing into the cost, etc., of my work, nor did it pay me personally. It probably did make a small contribution to the university chest, annually.

In the following decade I became very aware of how little British industry does in learning about research in progress in universities and it is no surprise to me to learn how inferior we are in many applied science fields. By comparison, German Technical Institutes are invariably well connected with industry.

During my four years in Sheffield, 1952–56, I wrote some short papers on subjects outside the ordinary research of the department. One such was *Mechanics before Newton*, a lecture I gave to the Engineering Society. The impression is easily gained as an undergraduate that the Three Laws of Motion (and much more beside) were the product of Isaac Newton only. The essay tried to show how much had been contributed to the subject over the previous two millennia. The essay is too long to print and I have therefore reduced it greatly (see Figure 6). It is not produced here as a continuous story, but it conveys major ideas and interesting quotations in four short sections, which I trust readers will appreciate. This effort is appended at the end of this chapter. Note the quotation from Archimedes in Section 4, by Plutarch, for its class attitude to engineers (unchanged to this day in England!) and Galileo's ability to write – which helped get him into trouble with the prelates!

Figure 6: Mechanics Before Newton
Extracts from the Presidential Address delivered to the Engineering Society on 14 October 1954.

1. Every moving body requires a mover to maintain its motion and the effect (the speed of the body, v, say) is proportional to the cause (the 'power' or 'virtue' of the mover, say P) and the resistance encountered (say R). Thus, $v \propto P/R$, summarises symbolically the Aristotelian law of motion. If we accept this expression, immediately it follows that the speed in a void (i.e. R=O) must be infinite; and since infinite speed is unthinkable, hence, argued the Aristotelians, there can be no void. And besides this they argued that the existence of a void would involve a contradiction; there could be no motion in the void because there is clearly nothing by which movement could be applied.

2. A copy of an interesting manuscript of Archimedes, found in 1906, called 'The Method', and it gives an insight into his methods of investigation. This document reveals, for instance, how he found the area of a parabolic segment in the first instance by actually weighing it. The value of this experimental method he acknowledges – but grudgingly so. We obtain a view of the status attributed to experimental and practical work in ancient times from the section on 'Marcellus' in *Plutarch's Lives*. It has reference to Archimedes' use of pulleys to drawn along laden ships and other devices for war-like use. The passage incidentally, throws light on the standing of the engineering profession as well as on one of its origins, thus –

> "Yet Archimedes .. though these inventions had gained him renown of more than human sagacity, he yet would not deign to leave behind him any commentary .. but repudiating as sordid and ignoble the whole trade of engineering .. he placed his whole affection .. in those purer speculations where there can be no reference to the vulgar needs of life .. so it was that mechanics came to be separated from geometry and, repudiated and neglected by philosophers, took its place as a military art."

3. Galileo's success in mechanics is in no small way attributable to his understanding of scientific method. His writings on this point also show clearly his ability in controversy, so that it is not surprising that eventually he should fall out seriously with the Church theologians when their opinions differed.

These points are evidenced by the following extract.

"If it be true, that of one effect there is but one sole primary cause, and that between cause and effect, there is a firm and constant connection, it is necessary that whenever there is seen a firm and constant alteration in the effect, there be a firm and constant alteration in the cause.

If Sarsi wishes me to believe, on the word of Suidas, that the Babylonians cooked eggs by whirling them swiftly in a sling, I will believe it; but I shall say that the cause of such an effect is very remote from that to which they attribute it, and to discover the true cause I shall argue as follows: If an effect, which has succeeded with others at another time, does not take place with us, it necessarily follows that in our experiment there is something lacking which was the cause of the success of the former attempt; and, if we lack but one thing, that one thing is alone the true cause; now, we have no lack of eggs, nor of slings, nor of stout fellows to whirl them, and yet they will not cook, and indeed, if they be hot they will cool the more quickly; and, since nothing is wanting to us save to be Babylonians, it follows that the fact of being Babylonians and not the attrition of the air is the cause of the eggs becoming hard-boiled, which is what I wish to prove."

4. Christian Huygens was born at the Hague, Holland, in 1629.
In 1663, Huygens was elected an FRS and in 1669 delivered before a meeting, a clear and concise statement of the laws governing the collision of elastic bodies. He was actually preceded by Wallis (treating of inelastic bodies) and Wren on elastic bodies but all three showed the importance of (m × v) jointly and probably clarified the concepts of mass, 'm' and momentum, 'mv' considerably.

In 1673 was published what had been said to be 'historically a necessary introduction' to Newton's 'Principia'; it is the famous 'De Horologium Oscillatorio' (The Pendulum Clock). It is in five parts and includes:

(i) A description of pendulum clocks as invented by himself.
(ii) A treatment of the accelerated motion of bodies, falling freely or sliding on inclined planes or on given curves and culminating in the cycloid as the tautochronous curve.
(iii) A complete discussion of the centre of oscillation, and
(iv) at the end of the work gives 13 Theorems relating to Centrifugal Force in circular motion of radius, r; in particular that centrifugal force = mv^2/r and a treatment of the conical pendulum.

For the first three months of my new life in Sheffield I lived in 'digs', separated from my family who remained in our home in Sidcup, London. I spent many evenings searching for a new house. Starting in January was at the worst time of the year for weather. However, I alighted on a small, three-bedroom house that would satisfy our needs, even though it was a come-down compared with Sidcup. It was in Eccleshall, on the very perimeter of the south of the city and where the moors begin. Heather was trying to sell our London home but with Philip, then aged four and Chris aged one, she had a lot to do. (I am reminded too that this was still in the pre-washing machine days!) However she found a buyer, considered it sold and removed to Sheffield. Unfortunately, the sale was unable to be completed, and so for some time we had two houses to maintain, and when we did finally sell Sidcup it was at seven-eights of the earlier agreed price. Selling one at £2,800 and buying the other at £2,000 left little over to buy new furniture for the new home. It was Easter when we were a family again. Having settled in however, my wife soon pointed out to me that I had acquired a home at the top of a hill and though surrounded by park and countryside, she had the laborious task of pushing a perambulator up and down it for shopping! Likewise, young son Philip had to walk it twice a day for school! Here I launched out too into concreting my own drive-way and paths – a task I performed in all the houses we subsequently owned. We had difficulty in assembling our large bookcase – it reached to within a few inches of the ceiling and its length was such that we could barely open the lounge door. But Sheffield was a healthy climate and frequently when Sheffield city was in fog – that is, in the valleys and the town centre – it was clear, in bright sunlight on the hill tops and only half an hour's pleasant walk from the University. It was also the end of a difficult three months, since I had been unable to go home every weekend – the railway fare was too great and too much of the weekend was spent in travelling. Knowing that I was alone, Professor and Mrs Swift kindly invited me on several Friday evenings to accompany them to Sheffield Repertory Theatre for which they had three season tickets.

Whilst moving into our new property, Heather's father, who was helping, had a heart attack and was taken into Sheffield hospital. Fortunately he recovered and for the next nine months I found myself with enough time to think, for the first time for four years.

During this period Philip attended a poor school, had a collar bone fracture and tried to light an electric fire with a gas lighter! I remember that in the lunch hour, once a week, I went into the centre of the city to collect bottles of orange juice – our 'ration' (and free) – provided by the state for both boys. Our good fortune in that first summer of 1952, was celebrated with a one week's happy and healthy holiday at Filey, on the Yorkshire coast, in a caravan, on a farm, at a cost of £5. We also bought ourselves some new clothes for the first time since we married in April 1946!

Around Easter 1953, Helen – a very welcome daughter – was born, but unfortunately at the same time Heather's father died. Grandmother, to avoid living alone, gave up her home and joined with us in buying a large detached house in Nether Edge, Sheffield, in which she had her own flat whilst we had more rooms for the growing family. The partnership arrangement worked well and we all came to appreciate our improvements in house quality and the area surrounding us. The children found their grandmother's flat a fine refuge when they had been errant or if they wished to see a television programme denied them 'downstairs'. Grandma – or 'Nana' – lived in the same house as the family for another 26 years until she died at Ridge Hall, aged 92. In June, a fourth member of the family arrived – Jeremy, a fine, lusty, dark-haired boy. Heather had to spend a week or two in hospital not long after his birth and as term had begun, I was unable to be at hand to help Nana deal with all four youngsters. We had to put the few-months-old baby into the hands of a Care Home, to which I delivered him. This event was one of the hardest and darkest of my life. After a few weeks we recovered him and Heather and, slowly, life returned to normality.

CHAPTER XVIII

At 'Owens', Manchester University

Professor H. W. Swift retired in the summer of 1955 and the search for a successor was afoot. We moved into new buildings during the long vacation with three separate departments of engineering having been newly created – Civil, Mechanical and Electrical. There was no indication that the new professor would be a specialist in the same area as Professor Swift – it might be anything – Engines, Heat Transfer, Tribology, whatever. The likelihood was that the Sheffield pre-eminence in Engineering Plasticity would decline. I also wished to escape from the Secretaryship of the Yorkshire Branch of the I.Mech.E. So there were several reasons that caused me to look around for a change and some degree of enhancement in position and salary. Two advertisements attracted me, a post in the Atomic Energy Authority at Risley and a Senior Lectureship in mechanical engineering at Owens College, Manchester University. (The Victoria University of Manchester developed from a college founded by John Owens (1790–1846) who in 1846 bequeathed nearly £100,000 to trustees for an institution which taught 'learning and science' and was free from religious tests. In my day it was usually referred to simply as 'Owens'.) The latter post I recall had first been advertised a year previously; so they had not filled it and clearly I might stand a chance now. I applied for both posts: I went to Risley, saw the establishment and came away very unsure I would like to live in that built-up area. I had had no decision from Risley when I was called for interview at Manchester University. Only two of us were interviewed, the other candidate being from Birmingham. I was fortunate and was offered the post on the spot – and accepted; the interview with Professor J. Matheson and Professor Jack Diamond had lasted but ten minutes under the Chairmanship of the Professor of Latin. It was just before Christmas and I was appointed as from 1 August 1956. The post had been advertised as being 'on probation'* for three years and this worried me somewhat. I never knew of a *Senior* Lecturer being so appointed. I thus had to give up a permanent appointment at Sheffield for an impermanent one at Manchester. My wife and I went to see many houses which were on sale and a fine one in Wilmslow took our eye. However, we declined it as too expensive and uncertain

---

* Later on, I had reason to believe this item was erroneously included in the advertisement.

a venture for a man 'on probation' or 'on trial'. We finally bought a detached house in Hazel Grove, a region on the outskirts of Stockport. It was spacious but needed a lot of alteration. Wilmslow would have brought many minor immediate advantages but alas I was afraid to go too far out on a limb. We slowly added to the comforts of our new 'Norbury House' and though short of a bedroom we enjoyed our nine years there. We thought we had re-located in a rural district, but soon found the local council having the road outside the house straightened, the trees along it being trimmed of large, thick branches if not actually chopped down. Traffic signals were introduced at the end of the road and it became a busy by-pass to Marple for buses and traffic generally – and a threat to children crossing it. A large, open, green field opposite us was covered with houses two years later.

It was the latter which ultimately led us to move out and into a new home in Derbyshire. However, I concreted a path around Norbury House, as usual, demolished some out-houses, had a room added at the rear which reached out into the garden, and built the usual large sand-pit for our young children.

Our fifth child, a daughter, Sarah, was born to us in February 1959. I joined Owens in September and the tasks to which the senior lecturer found himself disposed were many and varied; there were two such Senior Lecturers in the Civil Engineering sub-division but I was the only one in the Mechanical. I was administrator-lecturer and conceived as a different animal from the two full-time researchers of civil engineering. Affairs became complicated when one of the Owens lecturers was appointed to succeed Professor Swift at Sheffield. (It seemed curious to more than me, how lecturers could exchange institutions, one to a professorial post, the other to a senior lectureship.) I filled this slot and found myself again in charge of first year Engineering Drawing and Design. No-one ever wished to have to lecture this inter-disciplinary subject – a one-hour lecture on the elements of representing a machine on paper – giving all necessary dimensions and detail according to a well established convention; it involved giving three interrelated views or elevations of the object required; practice in doing the latter was obtained through exercises in the Design Office which usually lasted three hours. Lectures included descriptions of common items such as bolt fastenings and kinds of bearings.

I confess that through lecturing this subject at my two previous institutions, I was now re-writing the conventional approach and including simple discussions of the theory of lubrication, of fatigue and creep and stress concentration – topics with which the professional designer is fully familiar – but which students only meet in their third year in an analytical or mathematical fashion. Topics I came to think much needed in design were ones with a few examples about engineering systems as opposed to specific items.

I lectured second year Thermodynamics – a new experience – as was the unusual course I acquired on Engineering Materials (*not* The Strength of Materials) – on types of lubricant and the properties of some metals etc.; it was a veritable miscellaneous collection of subjects. The practice was to bring in an industrial lecturer for many topics. However, in my third time around, I started to give some lectures on Statistics. There was, then, no treatment of elementary statistics

Figure 1.
Professor Osborne Reynolds.

in the Higher School Certificate Examination system or anywhere in mechanical engineering undergraduate studies. One could find engineering doctoral students who had never heard of the theory of drawing the 'best' straight line through a collection of points. This topic was quite successful. (An occasion sticks in my mind when a foreign student objected to an example in which horses in the same race were said to have different chances of winning – one, say, of 2 to 1 and another of 3 to 1; all horses he said had the same chance! All had four legs! And he was not simply being humorous.) Nonetheless, I felt this matter of 'best' straight lines is something curiously omitted from the engineering syllabus, and should be put right. Ignorance on this topic by even Ph.D students was profound.

I ought before proceeding further to make a genuflection in the direction of Owens' first or foundation Professor of Engineering, Osborne Reynolds (1842–1912), see Figure 1, internationally distinguished especially for his work on facets of fluid flow and allied subjects. This is well exposed in a Celebratory Symposium for him, *Osborne Reynolds and Engineering Science Today* (Manchester University Press, 1970, 263 pp.).

An annual job that I acquired was to arrange the programme of lectures for the whole Department – times, lectures and rooms. I was, too, designated Stores Officer – responsible for the efficient running of the Technical Stores – items and staff. I used also to make arrangements for student classes to make visits to industry. In my last two years in Manchester it was agreed that some student groups would carry out projects of a thermodynamical nature in Sheffield, in big steel rolling plants (for example to find the thermal efficiency of the steam engines which actuated some of the rolling plants). My job was to identify subjects of interest to students, to get them started, visit them from time to time and supervise their progress. On one occasion when engaged in determining the quantity of water delivered to a steam plant, we were unable to do so, because the water pipes were walled in and no-one knew how many there were – or their diameters!

In the middle of my time with him, Professor Diamond (see Figure 2) was appointed to the committee to look into the Calder Hall incident. (His post-war

Professor Jack Diamond

JACK DIAMOND, Professor of Mechanical Engineering at Manchester University from 1953 to 1977, devoted his considerable talents in almost equal parts to practical engineering and to the development of engineering as an academic study. At Manchester and outside he concentrated his work principally on the engineering of nuclear projects.

As an apprentice at HM Dockyard, Chatham, he distinguished himself by gaining a Whitworth Scholarship, and it was characteristic of the man that in later years he prized this more highly than many of the honours subsequently bestowed upon him. As a Whitworth Scholar and Senior Scholar he read Engineering at City and Guilds College, London and followed this with a period of research at Cambridge. He served as an Engineer Officer in the Royal Navy from 1939 to 1944. He was seconded from the Royal Navy to the atomic energy project in Canada, before joining the Cockcroft team at Harwell in 1946 where his wide ranging practical experience, coupled with the ability to lead a group of bright young engineers, proved invaluable to the project.

Diamond's move to the Chair of Mechanical Engineering at Manchester in 1953 coincided with a period of rapid growth in the University; to his duties in the Department he quickly added wider responsibilities in the University. His preference for the more practical issues – energy supplies, health and safety, works and buildings – "looking after drains" as he put it.

As Dean of Science, a faculty not noted for lengthy academic discussion at the sparsely attended meetings of its board, he quickly established a record for brevity. While he professed, when faced by a confused situation, to "keep it confused, but keep a clear head", his aims were in fact to clarify and resolve problems, and thus to make more time for teaching and research. It is a testimony to his effectiveness in academic affairs that as a member of the University Grants Committee he chaired its Technology Sub-Committee from 1967 to 1973, and that he served his University as Pro-Vice-Chancellor from 1970 until his retirement in 1977.

In addition to his university duties he participated actively in the affairs of his profession. He served on the Council of the Institution of Mechanical Engineers from 1958 to 1970, and as Vice-President from 1967 to 1970; on various bodies concerned with nuclear science and engineering; on the National Research and Development Corporation; and as President of the Engineering Section of the British Association. He also served as Regional Scientific Adviser to the Civil Defence Service for 14 years, a contribution for which he was awarded the CBE in 1969.

In the midst of all these activities his first priority was the Engineering Department, of which he was immensely proud. His move to Manchester had re-established the Whitworth link; the benefactor Sir Joseph Whitworth, who made possible the beginning of his academic career, was also a benefactor of the university, and had participated in the election of its first Professor of Engineering in 1868. One of his most treasured possessions was a model of Joseph Whitworth's measuring machine, presented to him on his retirement by his technicians. Like Whitworth, his concern was with the complete engineer, skilled in analysis, but able also to design, manufacture and operate engineering plant. He was suspicious of theory disconnected from practice, whose algebraic manifestations he would sometimes dismiss as "flute music". At the same time he would be the first to recognise true intellect in colleagues and students. By them he will be remembered above all as the complete manager.

His marriage in 1943 gave him a lasting firm and happy background. With his wife, Iris, he was much involved with the lives both of his three daughters and of the many students who passed through the department.

W. B. Hall

Jack Diamond, mechanical engineer, born 22 June 1912, Beyer Professor of Mechanical Engineering Manchester University 1953-77, CBE 1969, Pro-Vice-Chancellor Manchester University 1970-77, married 1943 Iris Purvis (three daughters), died 27 June 1990.

Figure 2. *Professor Jack Diamond: Obituary.*

career was all in nuclear engineering; he had worked in Canada at Chalk River during the last years of the War.) For this reason he was often unable to give his first year lectures on thermodynamics. It therefore often fell to me to substitute for him. This was no great hassle as long as I had time enough to make adequate preparation. The highlight of these occasions occurred when I entered the large lecture room where all first year Mechanical and Civil Engineering students were present. Seeing me again substituted they would burst into one chant: 'We want

Jack! We want Jack! We absolutely bloody refuse! We won't be buggered about!' There was only one method of quelling it – write fast on the black-board! They had to copy it into their notebooks and could do but one thing at a time. It was a fine spirited occasion. Today, student audiences are quieter and too serious.

I came to lecture true Thermodynamics to the third year honours students in my last two years at Owens and particularly enjoyed learning more about Thermoelectricity. However, I was not allowed into Heat Transfer for that was Professor Diamond's own province. In 1959, Professor W. B. Hall of Risley became our Professor of Nuclear Engineering and the two professors with a few new lecturers developed a postgraduate School of Nuclear Engineering, also acquiring new experimental facilities. Courses were put on that met the great need of companies then entering the nuclear field; everywhere the lectures were spoken of with great respect. Alas, as the twentieth century progressed, faith in the future for nuclear power stations has declined.

I believe that the emphasis on nuclear work was urged on Manchester by Professor P. M. S. Blackett. (He was Professor of Physics in Manchester 1937–1953.) From the National Nuclear Laboratories we had among others in quick succession to Professor Diamond, Professor Brian Flowers in the Physics Department and Professor P. L. Rotherham who headed up the Metallurgy Department. (Some referred to us as *Little Harwell!*)*

The research interests of my new department turned on Heat Transfer Theory, Nuclear Engineering and Aerodynamics led by (now) Professor J. Livesey (formerly of Salford University). Unexciting Engineering Plasticity I researched alone.

I saw that all the omens were against developing my subject in Manchester and therefore to succeed with it I had to strive to continue to develop it alone. As well, having abandoned my pursuit of a Ph.D., I had now to think in terms of attaining the senior doctorate, D.Sc. I observed that I had got to writing about six papers a year, and that rate I kept up in the four years I was in the Owens Engineering Department. Figure 3 is a copy of a letter I received from Jack in our later years and well reflects his academic and pracitical personality.

Professor James Haddow, a Britisher-become Canadian, came into the Department as a Ph.D. candidate on a special form of scholarship in 1956 and elected to join me to study a plasticity topic – Plastic Indentation and Compression. This he did well and eventually he graduated in 1960. From his thesis we published three papers. Jim returned to Edmonton, Canada and remained there, I believe, until he retired as a full professor, publishing research on mechanics. I visited him in Alberta some years later and know something of his University's renowned location. I was then taken by car down the highway along the foot of the Rockies; the road had only just been opened that spring and there was much snow still about. We journeyed up the 'cleared' Kicking Horse Pass (5329m) and then returned to a beautiful lakeside village (whose name I cannot now remember). No wonder Scotsmen such as Jim Haddow choose to live in these regions!

From quite a different direction at this time came Professor Hideaki Kudo of

---

* Though (now) Prof. A. M. Neville had started his work there on concrete which led to his becoming a world authority on it – witness the events on p. 408.

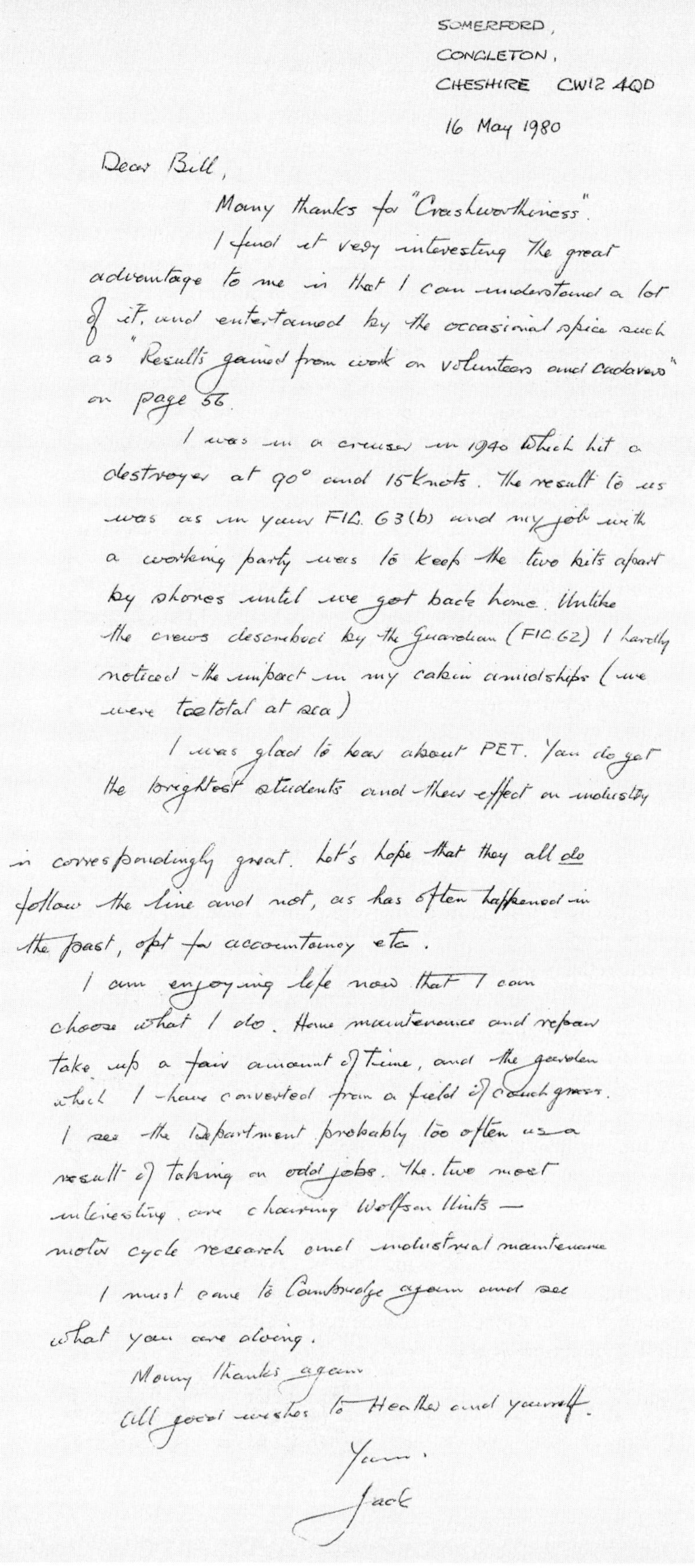

SOMERFORD,
CONGLETON,
CHESHIRE CW12 4QD

16 May 1980

Dear Bill,

Many thanks for "Crashworthiness".

I find it very interesting. The great advantage to me is that I can understand a lot of it, and entertained by the occasional spice such as "Results gained from work on volunteers and cadavers" on page 56.

I was in a cruiser in 1940 which hit a destroyer at 90° and 15 knots. The result to us was as in your FIG. 63(b) and my job with a working party was to keep the two bits apart by shores until we got back home. Unlike the crews described by the Guardian (FIG. 62) I hardly noticed the impact in my cabin amidships (we were teetotal at sea).

I was glad to hear about PET. You do get the brightest students and their effect on industry in correspondingly great. Let's hope that they all _do_ follow the line and not, as has often happened in the past, opt for accountancy etc.

I am enjoying life now that I can choose what I do. Home maintenance and repair take up a fair amount of time, and the garden which I have converted from a field of couch grass. I see the Department probably too often as a result of taking on odd jobs. The two most interesting are chairing Wolfson Units — motor cycle research and industrial maintenance.

I must come to Cambridge again and see what you are doing.

Many thanks again.

All good wishes to Heather and yourself.

Yours,
Jack

Figure 3.
Letter from 'Jack' to 'Bill', dated 16 May 1980.

Tokyo, Japan. We had common interests in research into metal extrusion. He was moving through German universities, staying at one for some time, working and learning whatever came his way in plasticity and then moving on. I do not know quite how, academically speaking, he came to Manchester – I suspect I invited him.

However, he was totally self-financed and constituted the true 'wandering scholar'.

Professor Kudo spent six months with me in the Engineering Department of Manchester University in 1958 from which we formed a life-long friendship. He died alas, in 2001, aged 77. His obituary is to be found in the *Int. Jnl. Mech. Sci.* for 2001. I have chosen to give extracts about him visiting the UK in 1958/9 in Figure 4; this is taken from his autobiography as it stood in 1990, the year in which he retired. Dr Kudo was the foremost researcher in metal forming plasticity in Japan in his day.

Besides his personal motivation and his professional career (Item 1 in Figure 4) the second, No. 2, describes the pleasure he found in Manchester during his six months' stay and how it changed his political outlook. His observations on the social standing of engineers in the UK, No. 3, is remarkable – a situation still evident today. The last extract, No. 4, refers to why German engineering and education have such a fine international standing.

Professor Kudo tells of our joint authorship of our monograph on Extrusion. It was planned in Manchester and it took us about three years to complete. It was published in 1962 by the Manchester University Press and by the Russians in translation in 1965. (See Figure 5 in Chapter XVII.) On the cover of their translation, the Russians showed the four diagrams central to explaining the mechanics of extrusion. Many more copies were sold in Russia than in the UK, but as Russia was not then a signatory to the international rights on publishing we received no monetary reward! However, even from the English sales we received only a tiny sum. But we academics do not publish for profit nor is our book-writing a paying profession.

Figure 4: Some Aspects of My Life of Metal Forming Study
H. Kudo
(Department of Precision Machinery Engineering, Tokyo Denki University, Chiyoda-ku, Tokyo, Japan)

The present author attempts to explain and analyse his personal, historical and social backgrounds of, motives for and execution philosophy in some of his research and organisation work which characterise his professional career. These include developing work of the upper bound approach to bulk forming processes, systematic research project of the cold forging technology, organisation business of Japanese Cold Forging Committee and international co-operation activities, in particular, creation of International Conference on Technology of Plasticity.

1. Introduction

It was really a mystery for me that I was requested by the Organising Committee of the 3rd ICTP to give a keynote lecture. However, I must thank the present Committee for the request which means a great honour. After vacillating among a number of courses, I finally decided to analyse and explain the personal, historical and social background of, motives for and execution philosophy in some selected research and organisation activities of mine which seemed to me rather unique, but not necessarily exemplary.

2. Thanks to Mr W. Johnson, my six months' stay in Manchester became one of my most efficient time of harvest in life. I learned slip-line field and hodograph techniques from him and jointly published papers. He also assisted me in preparing English manuscript of my doctor thesis for International Journal of Mechanical Sciences, which he had just launched. Mr Johnson and I also started a plan of writing a monograph on mechanics of extrusion, which was materialised in 1962. I think that it is these publications that popularised upper bound approach and made my name unduly well-known in the Western circle compared with my Japanese seniors and colleagues.

In the UK, I got to know many metal forming researchers, such as Messrs. J. M. Alexander, P. B. Mellor, P. L. B. Oxley, H. Ll. D. Pugh and D. M. Woo and this have been very helpful for me to exchange information and co-operate internationally until today. I stayed in the home of Mr M. Derrington, the then lecturer at the University. This experience and other contacts with British and German families made my pacifism and internationalism absolutely sound.

3. In the UK, I never came across instances of combination of theory and practice, at least in the field of metal forming, contrary to my expectations. To my regret, I often heard academics say, looking down on industrial engineers, 'They are not scientific,' and engineers say, mocking academics, 'Their papers are useless.'

4. Since my next target institute in Stuttgart had not been instrumented yet, I moved in July 1959 to Hanover by permission of Prof. O. Kienzle. I was astonished there at the largeness of the scale of Die Forging Research Institute and the systematic approach to the die forging system consisting of plant, machine, tool, lubricant, work material, billet, product etc. The second subject I received there was to examine effect of billet dimensions upon the load-stroke diagram in a simple hot die-forging of steel. I carried out an experimental work in hot forging for the first time under supervision of Dr. J. Stöter using new measuring instruments to me.

I leave the account of my interaction with Professor Kudo at this point, simply remarking on the relatively long flow of Japanese men who came to work with members of my teams or myself at Manchester, in UMIST and at Cambridge over the next 15 years or so. Their names can be identified in many joint papers. There was a great reciprocation by the Japanese when I was invited to visit their country, with Heather, to give a few lectures (including one on Mechanics in Games) and to tour their country even down to visiting active volcano Mount Aso in Kyushu. My abbreviated report of that occasion of 1975 is given in Part IV, (perhaps with a few words of repetition, hopefully forgivable).

During my period in Manchester a young fellow recently returned from the USA was Roger I. Tanner, initially a graduate of Bristol University. As he was a very capable analyst I involved him in problems of finding the temperature distribution in fast worked metals, due purely to the work imposed by applied force. There was only one analytical paper on this topic at this time – and a very good one by Dr J. W. F. Bishop.

An interesting topic that came along was the search for somebody in our department to try to build an apparatus which in effect was a heavy pendulum oscillating in a fixed bearing – a ball and socket joint – the lubricant being supplied by Dr John Charnley. The aim was to study the mechanics of the hip joint. Dr Charnley later became well known in the English medical world for his work in hip surgery and in particular performing hip-replacement surgery. This story is continued in the next chapter, but not with Dr Tanner (now FRS), who eventually took up an Engineering Chair in Sydney, Australia, devoted much of his research life to problems in Rheology and become Deputy VC (Vice Chancellor) of his University.

In 1957 I had a long paper accepted for presentation at the 3rd US Congress of Applied Mechanics which was held in Brown University, Rhode Island in June 1958, the Proceedings of which were published by the American Society of Mechanical Engineers (ASME). I was supported in attending the conference by my University who paid my air-fare and hotel expenses etc. Transatlantic flying was no great business in those years. There were only two passengers on the 'plane I flew on and the flight was of about twelve hours duration, i.e. from London to (then) Idlewild (or New York), it was a piston engine 'plane which created a loud unceasing noise. At New York I changed with difficulty to an internal flight to Boston, arriving there at nearly midnight. I then took a taxi to the Brown University campus, some 20 or 30 miles away. Fortunately, the hotel was close by and I registered in at 1 or 2 a.m. This was my first journey by air and at the time, not to be recommended.

The lecture programme as delivered was very efficient and the Special lectures very good. My own lecture was well received. I took the opportunity to visit several universities, including also a visit to the publishers of my forthcoming book with Dr Peter Mellor, *Plasticity for Mechanical Engineers* and to visit people involved in its production, at Van Nostrand Ltd in Princeton. The company was very clear about its objectives and seemed to know its business better than the publishers I had met in England.

Among other things, I eventually got to MIT, missed the professor I had arranged to meet, and spent the whole morning very fruitfully talking with Professor Walter Backofen, Professor of Metallurgy. He later produced a long paper on measuring the friction coefficient between cylindrical specimens and plates when compressing a metal; it appeared as the first paper in the first issue of my *International Journal of Mechanical Engineering Sciences*, in 1960. Only three or four years later, he resigned his Chair at MIT and retired, as far as I know, to private life. I also met Professor Robert Haythornwaite at Brown University, then on the staff. I knew him from my days in Sheffield. He rescued me from the hotel and I went to stay in a University residence. I made many new friends in the States and had some good and useful discussions. One very clear message at the time concerned the length of time it took to get work published through ASME's Journal of Applied Mechanics – at least eighteen months. There was clearly room for a new journal! I eventually arrived back in New York mainly to visit Professor B. W. Shaffer and to return home. I purchased many presents and returned to the UK bearing, principally, a large telescope for use by our offspring! Of course my wife 'held the fort' and governed our four children whilst I was away. These frequent few-week absences were something she was going to have to put up with in the future!

On a different line – a new building for our Victorian make-shift Department suddenly became a possibility on a closeby site, and I got involved in drawing up small plans. The site became possible when the street opposite the University's main entrance and quadrangle were scheduled for removal or change. The area had been a good middle-class one in the mid-1800s, but had declined over the century, gaining a reputation as the centre of houses of easy virtue. That the University acquired the region for expansion gave rise to many amusing comments. A pub at the junction of the street between Ardwick Green and Oxford Road was well frequented by some academics at lunch-time. My professor would call for me, occasionally, in my office and command I accompany him. We would retire to the pub, the Professor's Arms, and for a few minutes before lunch we enjoyed a drink and quickly and quietly despatched matters departmental. We could meet there the notable Professor Graham Cannon (a biologist who seemed to favour Lamarck rather than Darwin) and get involved in arguments with him about student indiscipline (there was a lot of it at the time!). Apparently, he lectured in a room looking into the quadrangle. In the latter was a huge ten-feet high smooth, glacial boulder. Some student made his protest by sitting on the top during daylight hours. In looking through the lecture-room windows, Cannon's students paid more attention to the antics of the exhibitionist than to his pearls of biological wisdom! (Neither Cannon nor his colleague Professor Wood-Jones held to orthodox Darwinianism.)

Deep into the 'creative' aspect of the Theory of Slip Line Fields at this time and reading *James Nasmyth: An Autobiography* (see Figure 5(a)) edited by Samuel

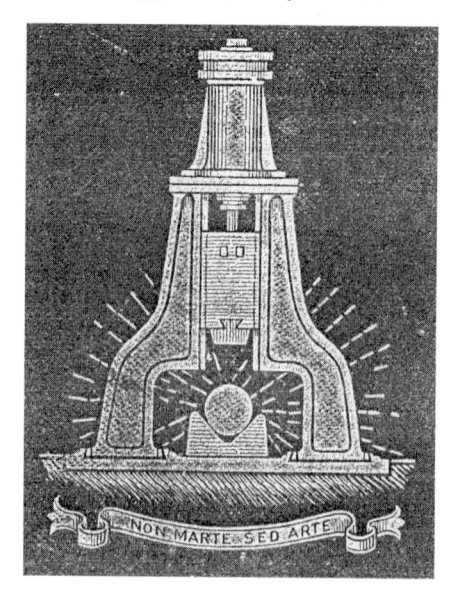

Figure 5 (a). A Vee forging anvil from the cover of – James Nasmyth: An Autobiography, by Samuel Smiles.

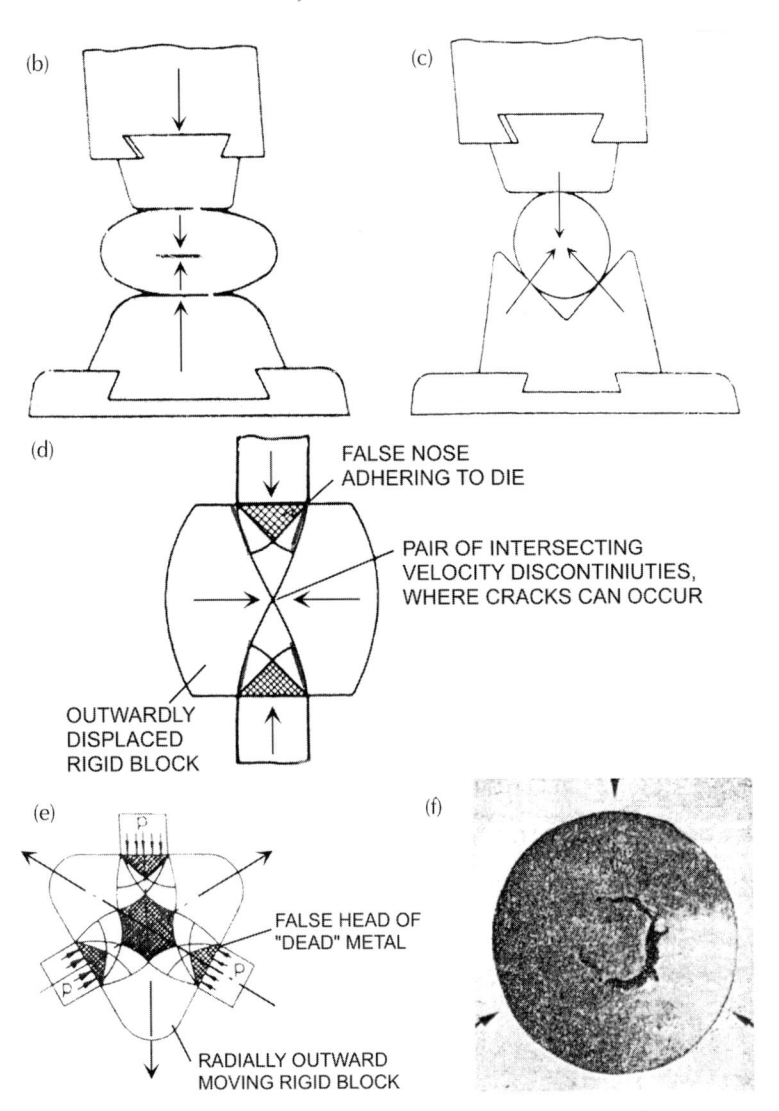

Figure 5 (b) – (f). Analysis of forging between anvils.

Smiles (1855), I was struck by the account of the action of the Vee anvil introduced by him as opposed to the normal flat anvil (see Figures 5(b) and 5(c)). When pressed (or struck) the flat anvil gives rise to a central crack or cavity in the forging, see Figure 5(d), whilst the Vee anvil causes a cavity away from the centre of the forging, see Figure 5(f); the intention of forgers was that the central region of the forging should remain whole. Using Slip Line Field Theory I sketched the diagrams in Figure 5(d) and (e); the slip line field for the flat anvil situation is indicated in Figure 5(d). In Figure 5(e), the central (black) region is left whole, with the cavity surrounding it, if at all. Analysis (and discussion) appeared in *The Engineer* of 7 March 1958, pp. 348–350. Some time later I had the photo, Figure 5(f), from Professor Gene Popov (previously unknown to me) of the Bauman Institute, Moscow verifying the circular region of cracks. So, a small victory!

I began, at this time, to think about submitting my small collection of published works for the University's D.Sc. and made some careful comparisons of what had been required in previous applications. I conformed with the requirements, among other things, writing a small commentary on the whole submission and submitted the collection in January 1959, expecting not to know the outcome until May or June later in the year.

At this time I submitted an application for a Chair in Applied Mechanics at a Scottish University. Professor Diamond said the chair would go to a Scotsman. And it did. Another advertised Chair, at Leicester, went to Edward Parkes. In all I made five attempts to succeed in surmounting the last barrier but the sixth opportunity came from UMIST and six men were invited for interview as candidates. Each of us got an hour's interview from a committee of Dr Vivian Bowden, eight professors from Owen's, six from UMIST and two industrialists – Sir Charles Renold and Mr George Begg. The Vice-Chancellor was not able to be present but a Mr Pariser substituted for him: the latter was a senior solicitor and a chairman of various UMIST committees. (Some years later a UMIST building was named after him, and similarly after the other two mentioned non-academics.) Tired from intense discussion for a whole hour before the Committee, I went to the cinema in the afternoon. I took a train home after some three hours. I called Heather to tell her where I was and to say I would be arriving on the usual train at the usual time. Walking home from the railway station, I was met by my four older children. I saw nothing unusual in the encounter. As we sat down in our customary dinner-time manner my wife raised a glass of wine and the children theirs of the usual juices. I recalled that it was 6 April and our 14th wedding anniversary – which explained the cake at the centre of the table, and Heather proposed a toast to the success of the day. Lord Bowden (Principal of UMIST) had twice been on the telephone to her trying to reach me and had to leave her with the good news. The children had followed their mother's instructions to say nothing about it when we met!

Some months later, and about one before I joined UMIST, I had the pleasure of informing Dr Bowden that his new professor-to-be would be able to flourish the degree of D.Sc. after his name.

During the Easter of 1960, as a family now of seven, we spent the week in a rented house in Fairbourne, near Barmouth in Wales. We saw various castles, walked Snowdon and enjoyed the trip by the small train through the hills and mountains of Snowdonia. Just before I came away, I had been to Risley – the National Industrial Nuclear Power Unit – where I was interviewed by the head of the company (whose name I regret to have forgotten) and, in effect offered the Chair of Mechanical Engineering in the New Institute of Technology in New South Wales, Sydney, Australia. A first letter to the VC of the Institute regretting not being able to accept the offer was responded to by the offer of a new building and services for any research I wished to continue. I recalled, whilst playing chess with one of the children in the railway station, that last week I was not worth one Chair, but this week I was worth two!

On another optimistic note, one of my parents who had become depressed at the thought of losing a member of the family to Australia, rapidly recovered.

On returning from the USA in 1958 I became involved in launching the *International Journal of Mechanical Sciences* in 1960 through Pergamon Press, of which Robert Maxwell was the head. It follows that over the decades I came to have a certain amount of correspondence with him and naturally followed whatever was published about him in the national press. The following excerpt about him from *Robert Maxwell and Pergamon Press*, Oxford, 1988; pp. 146–152 (Figure 6) describes how I came to be involved in a small number of his periodicals and books; it is an Appreciation which gives insight into the world of books and papers as encountered by a typical academic, which readers might welcome the opportunity to read, thus –

Figure 6: Mr Robert Maxwell
An appreciation of him and Pergamon Press, on the occasion
of his 65th Birthday*

I attended the 3rd Congress of Applied Mechanics at Brown University, USA, in the summer of 1958 and continually encountered complaints that journals were taking an unreasonable amount of time to publish papers which had been accepted.

On arriving back in England, I found a letter waiting for me which asked whether I had any suggestions for new journals. My simple and straightforward response was in the affirmative, and explained why. A reply came from Captain Ian R. Maxwell requesting me to provide evidence by writing to about a score of active research workers and asking whether they would be well served if a new journal were to come into existence aiming to print rapidly refereed work. After some weeks I submitted about a dozen supporting letters or replies. His response was to invite me to become Editor of the new journal, for whose name I had proposed the *International Journal of Mechanical Sciences* (IJMS). The professors who had written supporting letters were invited to become members of the Editorial Advisory Board.

At some time in 1959 I remember visiting Mr Maxwell at his office in premises in a London square. We talked briefly but in a rapidly conclusive fashion about many of the details connected with forwarding manuscripts to the Press for the quarterly publishing of the journal. I recall a good lunch (on the premises) and meeting a Lord (who later became Defence Minister in the Labour Government) and his wife, who wished to publish short books about travel and touring visits. Their proposed literary venture dominated the lunch and seemed very exciting, but I do not recall ever having seen the realisation of their idea.

Here I can rightly pose some questions. At this stage, why did Robert Maxwell choose to settle Pergamon Press at Oxford rather than at Cambridge? The reason is certainly neither known nor understood by me. Perhaps it was that London is reached more quickly from Oxford than from Cambridge. Could it have been a subconscious wish for association with Britain's chief training ground for politicians and a desire for proximity to lectures and tutorship in PPE? But can that be all? Heirs to the historical preponderance of scientists and engineers on the sharp, puritanical,

---

* Published in Robert Maxwell and Pergamon Press, Pergamon Press 1988, pp. 146–52, and IJMS, 30, 71–5, 1988.

non-Anglican and non-monarchical East Anglian plain are left wondering. I saw Robert Maxwell only once during a residence of seven years in Cambridge, and that was when he called on us, by helicopter, for a period of two hours to help launch a biography of Mr Chernov.*

I should explain that, when the new journal came into being in about 1959, I was a Senior Lecturer (Associate Professor) in a British provincial university, and, given its typically hierarchical power structure, I was doubtful about the propriety of accepting an editorship: normally only professors were great enough for such appointments. However, I duly informed my Head of Department† about my new involvement when all the details for publication were settled and a date for the first issue had been agreed. He was an understanding man (and wise in the world's ways) but he was a Council member of the Institution of Mechanical Engineers and my actions had repercussions in that sphere. The Institution, learning from my 'boss' of the impending new journal, promptly decided to publish its own journal; unbeknown to me it had been discussing such a development for some months but had been unable to make up its mind about the wisdom of starting up a new venture. Clearly, my seizing the opportunity presented and afforded by Captain Maxwell helped the Council to decide not to be pre-empted. At the end of 1959 the first issue of the *Journal of Mechanical Engineering Science (JMES)* appeared,‡ being published under the auspices of the Institution of Mechanical Engineers. Captain Maxwell's Pergamon Press thus gave birth to one engineering journal in 1959/60 and caused the birth of another.

The IJMS, as the Pergamon Press journal later became, only appeared in the first quarter of 1960 and so was not first into the new field. This, however, was not due to tardiness on the part of the private venturers. Britain was in the grip of one of its usual printing strikes at the end of 1959; the Institution of Mechanical Engineers had its own printing facilities§, but Pergamon Press had to find a foreign printer. Our first issue (and several later ones) thus came from Poland, so it was to be expected that our birth pangs would be protracted, and indeed the birth itself was delayed by some months.

There was no point of direct conflict between the two journals – the Institution as a body of highly respected standing had a ready source of manuscripts and a body of professional workers to hand. The IJMS, in my inexperienced hands, had to find its own way. With hindsight I see that our start was hesitant – one reviewer of our first issue said that one article should not have appeared (or should have appeared) elsewhere, another thought that one paper might well have graced the Proceedings of the Royal Society. I might add that Professor D. G. Christopherson, FRS, was bold enough and kind enough to write a recommendatory introduction for the first issue of the IJMS.

For the first five years it was not easy to keep going, but with Mr Maxwell's continuous and energetic support we did, and by 1965 we were beginning to feel accepted, with our standing established.

At that time, my recollection is of a young publisher with whom it was easy to 'do business'. Mr Maxwell gave decisions – almost invariably supportive and encouraging – by return of post or by telephone. I had a lot to do with publishers in those

---

* Successor to Messrs. Stalin, Kruschev, etc.
† Prof. Jack Diamond.
‡ The JMES ceased publication by this name in about 1980. This was arguably a disservice to authors whose papers had appeared in that journal. The existence of that journal (and a fine journal it was) will quickly become forgotten by older readers and not even known of by younger ones.
§ Or arrangements.

**STRESS CONCENTRATION
AROUND HOLES**

From the Russian by
G. N. SAVIN

Translated by Mr. Eugene Gros for the Department of Scientific and Industrial Research and made available by the Department for publication in book form.

Translation Editor
W. JOHNSON
Professor of Mechanical Engineering in Manchester College of Science and Technology

40 years' service to Science, Technology and Education

Robert Maxwell, MC, Founder and Publisher

Figure 6 (a).

days, and I can only record that to me he seemed to be in a class of competence which was all his own – a sharp mind, ability in several languages and a capacity for almost instantaneous decision-making.

In 1960, I left the Faculty of Science in Manchester University and joined the Faculty of Technology in what was to become UMIST. This was the address from which the IJMS was run, and it continued so until it went with me to Cambridge in 1975; it stayed there until 1982. It was very well placed in Cambridge, in that traditionally the title of Cambridge's undergraduate degree was the Mechanical Sciences Tripos: this I had in mind when searching for a title for the journal in 1959. Somewhere in this period Prof S.R.Reid began to help me with the day-to-day running of the journal and gradually he took on more and more of it, becoming Associate Editor in 1978. He moved to Aberdeen University as Professor in 1980, and the circle was fully completed in 1985 when he returned to UMIST as Head of the Applied Mechanics Division, Mechanical Engineering. Unfortunately, like many of the younger editors of Pergamon journals, it has not been his good fortune to see Robert Maxwell other than at a distance of yards! Perhaps the opportunities for this to happen will be the greater with time and as Robert Maxwell's empire expands.

I cannot record that I myself saw much of Robert Maxwell in person after 1960; all exchanges with him were by letter or telephone. He will not know in detail, though doubtless he is well aware in a general way, that all his ventures make ripples (or tidal waves) in unexpected academic quarters – some of them I think, he will be pleased to hear about.

In the 1950s the major effect of Pergamon Press for me, and for many more of like interest, was the sudden appearance and availability of a flood of first class scientific and engineering treatises, mostly in translation, from the USSR. Without Pergamon, many Russian masterpieces would long have awaited translation. As it was, they quickly became available, and we were enormously gratified to have them. I believe that in that decade and the next, without Robert Maxwell's establishment of a special relationship with the USSR for technical translation rights, the West would have been the poorer in knowledge about the Soviet Union's achievement and

Figure 6 (b).

contributions in the field of Applied Mechanics. I was involved with the production of two fine Russian works; the first in 1961, when I was asked to edit, and check the (first) translation of G. N. Savin's *Stress Concentration Around Holes* (Figure 6(a)): this was a text of 430 pages of small type containing many mathematical equations, tables and graphs. The reader should be made aware that these first translations are (or were) made by non-technical specialists. Normally they did an excellent job, but the editor could encounter unfortunate choices of words*. One I recall was the continuous use, in a 350 page book, of 'main stresses' when what we all accept of course is '*principal* stresses'. However, the translated manuscript of Savin's book was very far from perfect and it cost me a lot of effort to render it readable for engineering specialists. The effort was worthwhile because we then had access to work of great use – in aircraft structural design, for example.

My second involvement was with the translation of Academician I. I. Artobolevski's 278 page monograph on *Mechanisms for the Generation of Plane Curves* (Figure 6(b)) in 1964. On this occasion the translator's script proved well-nigh perfect and I neither bear scars nor have any recollection of encounters with it.

Both translations were beautiful examples of Russian technical scholarship and it was a privilege to see them placed for use on the shelves of western libraries. There were many more such classics made available and – though doubtless there was good business in it for Robert Maxwell – their accessibility to the engineering and academic communities was invaluable, and Pergamon Press served them well.

In being involved in the latter translation, I was of course dealing with a subject in which I did not research. Mechanisms theory was at that time growing fast. Once – in the nineteenth century – Britain had contributed to it substantially, but somewhere in the following decades lost interest in it. By contrast, Germany and the Soviet Union (and perhaps the East European countries too) never did cease to produce fine work in the field. The USA had a number of workers in the area, but there was not a conspicuous national or mass achievement. Australia was beginning to show work of great promise, but the UK was hardly to be seen. Taking on the Artobolevski translation was my technical contribution to generating renewed interest in the topic in this country. To aid this, and at about this time, I invited Professor Erskine Crossley of

---

* The most bizarre was in a paper submitted for the journal, in which what was intended to be a 'hydraulic ram' appeared as a 'water goat'!

Georgia Tech. to spend a term in the Department of Mechanical Engineering at UMIST, to deliver a course of lectures on Mechanisms. This he did very successfully, and our Department subsequently included courses at undergraduate and postgraduate level on the Synthesis of Mechanisms; we thought this probably unique at that time in the UK. Before he returned home, I proposed to Professor Crossley that he might consider becoming the editor of a new *International Journal of Mechanisms*. This was proposed to Robert Maxwell and accepted with alacrity. This journal was started in 1966 and still runs very successfully*; it truly serves an international audience. It now bears no trace of its origins, and alas the UK seems not to have made the substantial contributions once hoped for.

An outcome of the translation of Academician Artobolevski's book and the generation of an awareness of his massive contributions was his selection in 1967 for the triennially awarded James Watt International Medal – the most prestigious of the Institution of Mechanical Engineers' awards.

I should recall here my impression of the very early appearance, in 1953 (further volumes followed later) of Pergamon's *Journal of the Mechanics and Physics of Solids*, under the editorship of Professor Rodney Hill. It had well found its niche by the time the IJMS appeared. It was this journal in its early style which I used very much as a model for the nascent IJMS. I can well remember the excitement with which I looked forward to each issue of the JMPS. In those days plasticity was 'new' and exciting, and almost month by month new theorems, methods and meaningful experimental work appeared. It was a much-needed journal, with which Robert Maxwell, the Press and its Editor splendidly served the early development of the subject.

The late Professor Franz Koenigsberger and the late Professor Stephen Tobias considered, in about 1959, emulating the German schools of machine tool engineering by holding an Annual Conference of Machine Tool Design and Research; their idea was that the venue of the Conference should alternate between their respective Departments in UMIST and Birmingham University. They proposed to me the idea of publishing its proceedings through the IJMS. This was not acceptable to me for many reasons, but the idea resulted in my suggesting that they approach Captain Maxwell with a view to starting their own journal. This they did, and thus was born the *Journal of Machine Tool Design and Research*, a publication still in existence and one which much meets the needs of the times. At the same time, annual Proceedings of their International Machine Tool Conference also started to be published in one large volume per year by Pergamon.

It needs to be said that the latter journal and Proceedings were started by two men trained in Continental schools of engineering design; the UK has had very little to show by way of matching them. The raising of the visibility and importance of manufacturing was of tremendous importance to the laggardly UK in the 1960s. Attention to machine tool design and associated processes was not deemed to concern the universities much in those years. Unfortunately, British industry contributed very little to the conferences, and only in the last few years has the Institution of Mechanical Engineers awakened to the nation's deficiencies in this matter. Koenigsberger, Tobias and Maxwell, in their different ways, each stimulated interest in research in a subject never close to the UK's heart; but now one for which it has come to appreciate the immense cost of years of neglect. See Figure 6 (c).

In the late 1960s, I recall being involved in writing and commissioning articles for that mammoth multi-volume production, the Pergamon *Dictionary of Physics*. In 1968,

---

* Under a slightly different name.

Figure 6 (c). Prof. F. Koenigsberger (first on the left) and Prof. S. Tobias (fifth from the left), at an MTDR Conf.

I published with my colleagues J. B. Haddow and Robert Sowerby the certainly non-profitable monograph, *Plane Strain Slip Line Fields*. Not dismayed, Pergamon were bold enough to publish an updated and much longer version of the book in 1982. Economically this seems to have suffered the same fate as the first version. However, suffice it here to say that taking a chance in publishing books of academic worth and utility, when they are unlikely to be economic in market terms, indeed deserves saluting.

A venture in a similar vein was that concerning the *Bulletin of Mechanical Engineering Education*. It was started in the mid-1950s as a forum for articles discussing the teaching and demonstrating the theory and practice of mechanical engineering, for reviewing undergraduate text-books and for proposing new and improved methods of approach to presenting established topics. Its publication was taken on by Pergamon Press; it resulted in a high quality, professional-looking journal. It was maintained for about a decade by Robert Maxwell after I requested him personally to have it published. It is very much the sort of non-research journal that is needed to enhance the education and training of engineers; it was the kind of journal which one thought would be a staple publication of its professional body. Unfortunately, unable to raise circulation above 400-500 copies, in its then rather voluminous format, it had to be withdrawn. It still continues, but in a much diminished form, which is perhaps a testimony to the lip-service, as opposed to action, devoted to education.

I record with satisfaction, and many still remember with great pleasure, that once a year Pergamon Press was happy to support a dinner for members of the Mechanical Engineering Department at UMIST. The occasion was known as the Pergamon Press Dinner for the Referees of the BMEE. Those attending included wives: it was a rare occasion when their part in their husbands' work was recognised, and it was probably a unique reward for men who normally receive minimal recompense – a thank-you letter – for their free-gift of energy and time spent on refereeing. (The much-vaunted world of economic enterprise only, please note.) (See p. 208 et seq.)

The *International Journal of Impact Engineering* (IJIE) was launched in 1983 with

Pergamon's customary ease and is now an established quarterly with Professor Norman Jones (still) as Executive Editor. Professor Jones, already an established international authority in structural mechanics and impact processes, took the 'return road' to the UK and Liverpool University in 1979, after occupying a full Chair at MIT, in the Department of Ocean Engineering.

The IJIE was pleased to publish in June 1987, as Volume 5, the Proceedings of the First Hypervelocity Impact conference held at San Antonio, Texas, in October 1986; the guest Editor was Dr Charles E. Anderson. (It contained 750 pages; Pergamon produced it at a very satisfactory price.) Including a Conference Proceedings within a regular journal was a step taken to ensure that the former would not be 'lost' in archives; being associated with an on-going journal would help keep it before the eyes of impact engineers more prominently than might otherwise be the case.

In concluding this account of my association with Robert Maxwell as the incarnation of Pergamon Press, I would like to thank him for his services to the part of the academic world I have been concerned with over a period of more than 30 years.

He has been eminently easy to work with, and his Press and organisation enormously efficient and accommodating. The Executive Editor of the *International Journal of Mechanical Sciences*, Professor S. R. Reid, and the Editor of the *International Journal of Impact Engineering*, Professor Norman Jones, join me in congratulating Robert Maxwell on his 65th Birthday. And whether he retires (highly unlikely!) or not, we hope that he will have many more highly energetic years before him, which the Editors hope they will be able to use to the benefit of the mechanical engineering sphere of academia.

W. Johnson,
Editorial Advisor, Founder and Editor-in-Chief 1960–87,
15 October, 1987

The above essay represents an honest account of my dealings with Robert Maxwell. My regret is of his development towards what we saw reported of him in the national press in his last years. Had he been able to contain his ambitions and to have earned the enormous reputation which he enjoyed among academics, he would have been very well remembered. He certainly served the academic community very well in many ways on a national and international scale.

It is curious how from his beginning, there seemed to be persistent attacks on his reputation in the newspapers; it was as if there was always a group of detractors that rapidly denied his special talents. It is also regrettable that the winning of his Military Cross in the Second World War seemed to have to be substantiated by words of verification from his former Commanding Officer.

After his downfall many academics would interject in a conversation, 'speak in a whisper any words of commendation'.

Professor Diamond and I saw little of each other in the years after I left his department in 1960. The letter reproduced in Figure 3, is typical of what passed between us twenty years on – still close friends. (In the letter, 'Crashworthiness (of Vehicles)' is the title of a short book of some 129 pages that Professor A. G. Mamalis and I published in 1978. The reference in his paragraph 2 is made with respect to a paper on ship impact damage I wrote at the time.)

CHAPTER XIX

Manchester College of Technology (later UMIST)

A New Start

I succeeded Professor Henry Wright-Baker whom I had first met as a sixth-form schoolboy in 1940. Wright-Baker kept his double-barrelled name in order to distinguish himself from Professor John Baker of the Engineering Department in Cambridge.

I suppose it always seems to a young newcomer that he does not have the competence of the man who is retiring, measured by his accomplishments and writings. Wright-Baker was professor from 1937 to 1960, and I wrote a seven-page biography of him for the *Journal of Materials Processing Technology*, pp. 66–72, Vol. 94, in 1999. He was best known outside of UMIST for 'unwrapping' some of the Dead Sea Scrolls; he was the first to open two ancient scrolls found in 1952 at Quram,* (see Figure 1), for which he received neither university nor formal public recognition. Briefly, Wright-Baker's prime interest was in internal combustion engines, for research in which he was awarded the University's D.Sc. He also edited several editions of Inchley's *Theory of Heat Engines* – a textbook on which many engineers were raised. He claimed to have developed a degree course with a bias towards Production Engineering, which was unusual and ahead of its time. With one of his lecturers, Dr K. L. Johnson (later Professor at Cambridge), he introduced the *Bulletin of Mechanical Engineering Education*. Wright-Baker was also responsible for the teaching of many day and evening student-apprentices from industry, but only a few undergraduates had, up to about 1950, passed through his hands each year. Finally, he edited two volumes of *Modern Workshop Technology* (1948).

When I joined my new department in August 1960 I found that Prof. Baker had left me about 20 type-written pages of notes about the departmental staff –

---

* This was a contribution to archaeological, biblical scholarship recently recognised by including a description of his work in *Copper Scrolls Studies* (eds G. J. Brooke and P. R. Davies, Sheffield Academic Press, 2000, p. 334).

Figure 1. Professor H. Wright Baker examines fragments of a Copper Scroll.

academic, technical and secretarial. The total number of staff was about 70, there being approximately 30 lecturers. There were thirteen different and sometimes totally isolated areas of laboratories distributed from basement to upper floors in the old six-storey building. There were only three buildings for the MCoT: the original main building put up in 1898 (see Figure 2), an old office block (converted for among other things, the teaching of mathematics),* Velvet House (the basement which was used as a store, even though it was often damp and wet, and a recently adapted or converted old mill, which turned out to be very suitable for labs and drawing offices. Otherwise, there were rows of old dwelling houses and small industrial premises around the main block, still there from the early nineteenth century, when the whole area had been a hive of engineering activity.

A conspicuous feature at the time were academic staff offices housing three and four lecturers; however the principle which was going to obtain in the future, I ordained, was that each lecturer would have his own office.

---

* Mr Frank Bowman, a Cambridge man, was the Head of the Mathematics Department, who had written several undergraduate mathematical texts – some more appropriate for mathematicians than engineers. He was well-known, much liked and highly appreciated by all his colleagues. He it was to whom the Socialist Society tried to sell copies of their magazine. I remember him too for discussing a point with me after a lecture which finished at 12.15 p.m. only being interrupted by audible 'pips' from a radio at 1 p.m.!

Figure 2. UMIST main building in 1898.

In the basement of the main building there were several workshops for training machinists and technicians for industry. Beyond this there was a great need for renovation, except in one area – venture into teaching and research by a Machine Tools group led by Professor F. Koenigsberger (1907–1979) (see Figure 6(c), Chapter XVIII). The Machine Tool Trades Association had chosen to invest in this group and provide money over and above that which had been forthcoming from the Government. Its area and building had originally been intended as part of a steam engine and turbine laboratory. Professors Wright-Baker and Koenigsberger were indeed providing the Machine Tools industry with its first postgraduates in British universities with a one-year M.Sc. course behind them. The course continued as such for many years.

In another part of the basement there was a bizarre situation in which a laboratory housing a large wind tunnel operated openly above a collection of old-fashioned double desks set out for teaching purposes; the whole was covered by a heavily leaking roof and set alongside the departmental workshop – and for a short period we actually used it.

Divisional Structure

Soon after I took up the Chair I learned from Lord Bowden that the department had been allocated two new professorships, so there was a need to decide on the principle for filling them. I could press for having a departmental situation in which all three Chairs were closely linked to one speciality, so that there would be much mutual support and therefore the topic which the three Chairs supported, would then surely bring national if not international reputation. On the other hand, I could argue for a Chair in each of three separate subjects, not mutually supportive but chosen to give across-the-board research standing and teaching. I myself intended to pursue, broadly speaking, the study of metal-working processes and impact phenomena. The department enjoyed a very good Strength of Materials laboratory under the management of Dr J. H. Lamble. I found it to be well run and serviced with a good selection of testing machines. It would constitute a very good back-up therefore to my own current research interests. It is customary when a professor joins a department to support him with relatively small sums of money to facilitate a change of research direction in a department – to be used for new equipment and facilities. I negotiated a senior technician, with two technicians supporting him, an electronics technician, a photographic suite and a draughtsman. These were in part in anticipation of the needs of the two new professors. In the event, Professor Roland Benson joined us in 1962 – then a Reader in Thermodynamics in the University of Liverpool and a time-served apprentice. There was a fairly large laboratory in the basement of the old block for undergraduate use in experiments with steam engines and small steam turbines. It also consisted of gas engines, ignition compression engines and petrol engines. Professor Benson re-equipped and adapted the laboratory to his needs, with the prospect of a new building and laboratory in two or three years' time. Subsequently his teaching and research laboratories were separated and with outside help his large and heavy i.c. engines were re-housed. Other equipment he was able to procure by doing research work for industry. His research work was such that he quickly acquired a world reputation. Unfortunately, he died at the relatively early age of 53. His obituary is printed as Figure 3. (Professor Benson was Jewish, as was Professor Koenigsberger, but the former was strictly orthodox, and with connections to Israel, especially during the Six Days' War.) Heat transfer research was extended, improved and led by Reader, Dr Peter Hatton.

Stephen Tobias (see Figure 6(c) Chapter XVIII), was somewhat younger than Frank Koenigsberger, but had similar professional inclinations despite being appointed to the chair in Mechanical Engineering in Birmingham University in 1959. He and Frank had similar ideas too about collaborating to establish in the early 1960s an annual Machine Tools Conference that would take place in alternate years at Birmingham and Manchester. The annual bound volumes of the *Proceedings* of the Conferences held during their lifetime can be found in technical libraries. These contain accounts of the research work done in their respective departments on machine tools and metal-forming processes. Conferences in the UK annually attracted a little over 100 participants; very few contributions and attendances were made from British companies. In Germany, similar conferences attracted numbers of approximately 1000. It is noteworthy that these machine tool conferences (still held) had had to be created by two men trained on the continent of Europe.

I opted for the three independent divisions. Taking this route, the three professors would not then run into conflict in respect of research requirements

PROFESSOR ROWLAND BENSON

Professor Rowland Seider Benson, one of the most distinguished present-day engineering thermodynamicists, died suddenly on March 30 in Manchester, at the early age of 53. He had been a Professor of Mechanical Engineering at the University of Manchester Institute of Science and Technology since 1962, and he was internationally renowned for his researches on internal combustion engines and radial turbomachines.

His influence on university engineering education at postgraduate and undergraduate levels was enormous. He was a much sought-after engineering consultant and served on many national research committees. He was also very active in working for the Jewish Community in the North-west, by his involvement repaying a debt of gratitude for nine years spent in the Norwood Home for Jewish Orphans.

He served a five-year apprenticeship with Cammell Laird, of Birkenhead. In 1946 he joined Sulzer Bros (London) but after two years he moved to become a research engineer with the British Shipbuilding Research Association, where he spent five years acquiring much of the practical experience in the internal combustion engine field which was later to become the foundation for his academic career and researches. During these years he was a part-time student at Northampton Polytechnic and gained a first class honours degree from London University and the major prizes available; he followed this with a dissertation for the MSc degree on two-stroke cycle engines in 1954.

He returned to Liverpool to take up a university lectureship in mechanical engineering in 1953 and became a Reader in 1961. At the age of 37 he was appointed to a chair at UMIST, where he started and developed the Division of Thermodynamics and Fluid Mechanics, bringing it to a level second to none in academic reputation and experimental and computational facilities.

Rowland Benson received several major prizes from the Institution of Mechanical Engineers (London), the American Society of Mechanical Engineers and other bodies for his papers. In 1977 he received an honorary doctorate from the University of Ghent, with which he had established a cooperative research programme. He published well over one hundred substantial papers — being awarded the DSc degree of London University in 1968—and two notable books. He planned a seven-volume authoritative text on the *Thermodynamics and Gas Dynamics of Internal Combustion Engines*.

Benson was Academic Vice-Principal of UMIST, 1971-73. He served on many university committees and rendered many services to his professional engineering institution. He was, among other things, chairman of the Aeronautical and Mechanical Engineering Committee of the Science Research Council.

Rowland Benson is survived by his devoted wife, Rita, and by two sons and two daughters.

Figure 3. Obituary for Professor Rowland Benson.

and services and there would be opportunity for each of them to grow and diversify independently. In my first year, I had in mind to try to have Dr Koenigsberger appointed so that he would become Professor of Machine Tools Engineering. I hoped that this would indicate that there was at least one university department in the country which was trying to help re-establish Britain's past achievements in machine tools. Dr Koenigsberger already had the essence of a good Division, so that the opportunity opened up for us to have a department in the College/University very different in name and form from what could be found elsewhere in the UK. The chair appointments committee was very understanding and therefore readily elected him in 1961. This was quite successful too in that Professor Koenigsberger had very good connections with the German Machine Tool Departments in Technische Hochschüle.

I should mention that Professor Koenigsberger was a product of the University of Berlin, having close family connections with the well-known Professor G. G. Schlesinger. After completing his doctoral thesis whilst an assistant to him, he chose to take up work, from 1931 to 1934, first in Berlin, then with a company in Belgium and thirdly with Ansaldo S.A., Genoa, Italy. He also married Lili, who I believe was the daughter of Professor Schlesinger. In this period of the early 1930s, he would have had difficulties in his own country because he was Jewish. Around 1939 he elected to emigrate to Britain with his wife, family and their parents and eventually worked for Ferguson, Cooke and Pailin Ltd in Higher Openshaw, Manchester. With his teaching and industrial experience he was therefore well qualified for a Chair. In 1947 he had joined the CoT and later became Reader. (Professor Koenigsberger's autobiography, *Anvil or Hammer?*, 68 pp., printed by Cosmos Verlag, Switzerland, was published in 1980.)

Thus were established the three Divisions of Machine Tools, Thermo-and-Fluid-Mechanics, and Applied Mechanics. Each Division was responsible for its own research programmes and had similar workshop and clerical back-up. This kept the three professors independent to a large degree. The most important matter which concerned us all was the teaching of our 200 undergraduates; to it we gave over-riding attention. All three Divisions served the undergraduates to almost equal degree. Each lecturer in the Department supervised about nine undergraduates (three students from each intake-year) as tutor; besides dealing with problems raised by lectures, tutors were asked to inquire if they had any personal difficulties connected with their academic work. This applied particularly to first year students regarding accommodation problems. (One year we found that six freshers had accepted accommodation in one room over a pub!)

In respect of research Professor Jack Diamond (of 'Owens' in the Faculty of Science) agreed informally to try to ensure that there was no overlap between our undergraduate courses. Nuclear Engineering was a prime preoccupation of both him and Professor W. B. Hall, who had been designated professor of that subject.

Once a year the three of us at the Tech. had to present our recommendations for promotion to Reader, Senior Lecturer or for increases in salary for making an outstanding contribution to the department generally. The order in which the latter were placed had to be agreed so that, as far as possible, the Divisions were

∪L OF TECHNOLOGY, MANCHESTER.

SCHOOL OF TECHNOLOGY
13 MAY 14 ∗ 007345

Memorandum
the Work of the Mechanical Engineering Department
for the Session October 1912 to October 1913

To the Principal

<u>Materials Testing Laboratory.</u> During the period, the usual amount of testing for the Corporation and other outside concerns was carried out in this laboratory. Mr. Popplewell carried out some researches on the effect of repeated reversals of stress on the ultimate endurance of specimens. A paper has just been submitted to the Institution of Civil Engineers, covering this work, and further work on the same lines.

During the Session, the equipment of this laboratory was increased by the addition of an Avery torsion machine.

<u>Machine-testing & Hydraulic Laboratory.</u> The tests on a number of different types of bearings which were commenced in the previous Session for the Unbreakable Pulley Co. were continued during the 1912-13 Session. Designs were completed and work started on a new dynamometer gear for measuring the various forces and reactions on the cutter of a milling machine. Designs were also started for a transmission dynamometer suitable for investigations on the efficiency of rope, belt and other drives.

<u>Heat Engines Laboratory.</u> Mr. Ferguson continued some investigations on cylinder condensation and valve leakage, which, after further work, will be the subject of a future publication.

The equipment was increased by the addition of a Boys gas calorimeter, and of a 2½ in. steam meter presented by the Schäffer & Budenberg Company as a mark of appreciation of the testing work done by the laboratory for them previously.

<u>Visits to Works.</u> Apart from the visits to outside Works under the auspices of the Engineering Society, a visit was organized to the Works of Messrs. Mirrlees, Bickerton & Day at Hazel Grove.

<u>Publications.</u> A pamphlet on Engineers' Estimates by Messrs. D. Smith and P. C. N. Pickford (Emmott, publisher).

During this Session there were no research students, so that no theses have to be reported here.

Figure 4. This figure is interestingly and effectively the Mech. Eng. Dept Report put out at the time of the First World War. Research was done by staff since no research students had been admitted. The memorandum is approaching a century in age.

The following office rules were issued in 1852 by a firm of Merchants and Ship Chandlers

Rules for Clerical Staff

1. Godliness, Cleanliness and Punctuality are the necessities of a good business.

2. On the recommendations of the Management, this firm has reduced the hours of work, and the Clerical staff will now only have to be present between the hours of 7 a.m. and 6 p.m. on weekdays. The Sabbath is for Worship, but should any man-of-war or other vessel require victualling, the Clerical Staff will work on the Sabbath.

3. Daily Prayers will be held each morning in the Main Office. The Clerical Staff will be present.

4. Clothing must be of sober nature. The Clerical Staff will not disport themselves in raiment of bright colours, nor will they wear hose, unless in good repair.

5. Overshoes and top-coats may not be worn in the Office but Neck Scarves and Headgear may be worn in inclement weather.

6. A stove is provided for the benefit of the Clerical Staff. Coal and wood must be kept in the locker. It is recommended that each member of the Clerical Staff bring 4 pounds of coal, each day during cold weather.

7. No member of the Clerical Staff may leave the room without permission from Mr. Ryder. The calls of nature are permitted, and the Clerical Staff may use the garden below the second gate. This area must be kept in good order.

8. No talking is allowed during business hours.

9. The craving for tobacco, wines or spirits is a human weakness, and, as such, is forbidden to all members of the Clerical Staff.

10. Now that the hours of business have been drastically reduced, the partaking of food is allowed between 11.30 a.m. and noon but work will not on any account cease.

11. Members of the Clerical Staff will provide their own pens. A new sharpener is available, on application to Mr. Ryder.

12. Mr. Ryder will nominate a Senior Clerk to be responsible for the cleanliness of the Main Office and the Private Office, and all Boys and Juniors will report to him 40 minutes before Prayers and will remain after closing hours for similar work. Brushes, brooms, scrubbers and soap are provided by the Owners.

13. The new increased weekly wages are as hereunder detailed:

Junior Boys (to 11 years)	1s. 4d
Boys (to 14 years)	2s. 1d.
Juniors	4s. 8d
Junior Clerks	8s. 7d.
Senior Clerks (after 15 years with the owners)	21s. 0d.

The owners hereby recognise the generosity of the new Labour Laws, but will expect a great rise in output of work to compensate for these near Utopian conditions.

Figure 5. Found in a file on Models for Office Staff for around the time of the First World War. Readers will be amused at the directions.

equally served. To this end we used to hold one dinner in one of our homes each year where, leaving our wives to chat together, the professors wrangled over the departmental case to be put forward until agreement was reached – all three of us thus being able to speak with one voice. (Dr Bowden had been heard to say that from one department he had had a different claim put forward by each professor and yet another one when all three spoke as one for the whole Department!)

We had an understanding that each professor would act as Chairman of the Department for two years, in rotation. The Chairman attended to all general issues across the Department and, most importantly, was responsible for all matters concerning undergraduate teaching; during term-time they were to have first call on all staff. Initially, the notion was that power lay in being Chairman (or Head), but quickly it was found that no such advantage lay in that office. It turned out eventually, that Dr John Parker was made Deputy Chairman, attended to most of the Department's day-to-day business and only conferred with the Chairman (for eleven of my fifteen years in UMIST, me!), when necessary.

I might add that we had a significant number of part-time students studying

Cultural Attache,
Royal ——— Embassy,
——— Cultural Interests Section,
Embassy Cultural Department,

London.

Dear —— ———

```
        IBRAHIM ABID    ——X——        (A)
        IBRAHIM ABID    ——X——        (B)
        OSAMA IBRAHIM   ———— X       (C)
        IBRAHEEM ABDUL ———X ——       (D)
        ——— ( ———                    (E)
        I.A.    ——— X                (F)
```

    I thank you for your letter of 23rd May in which you inform me that (F), who I presume to be (C) on whose behalf you first submitted an application on 1st September, if infact the same person as (A). You then say that (E) is the person (B) to whom I wrote in ——— on 23rd March offering him a place on our M.Sc. course. When on 23rd March I wrote to (B) I deduced from his academic qualifications that he was no other than (D) who entered a B.Sc. course at U.M.I.S.T. in 1963.

    I must confess that your letter of the 23rd added to my confusion as the dates of birth, academic qualifications and photographs of Messrs. (B) and (C) do not correspond and so it would appear that we are referring to at least two (if not five) potential students.

    I would appreciate your help in clarifying this matter.

Yours sincerely,

Figure 6. This figure is a copy of a letter concerning Application for Admission by a foreign student to which the lecturer dealing with admissions responded. Photographs could be of individuals who had discarded long hair or beards and for foreign students instead of date of birth could be substituted an estimated date of conception!

for the HNC in engineering. The classes were held mostly in the evenings and were given by part-time lecturers. My responsibility was generally to ensure the classes were well catered for; normally this was carried out by an appointed full-time member of the staff. It invariably proceeded well and without trouble. The Higher National Certificate essentially gave entry to the Institution of Mechanical Engineers after adding some years of industrial experience. This part-time teaching was subsequently taken over by the John Dalton College of Technology. It became, at some point, part of the Manchester Polytechnic. (The story of the development of this is told by its first Director, Sir Alex Smith, in his memoir, *Lock up the Swings on Sundays*, The Memoir Club, 454 pp., 1998.) Dr Ron Kitching and I perhaps then made a small contribution to the start and development of the latter college with advice about equipment and by serving on some of its appointing committees.

X — — — — — has been at this — — — — — — — "public"
school of (new) 150 pupils since it was "founded" in 1970 with
6 pupils and two teachers in an almost derelict town house in
central — — — — whence it was transferred in 1972 to a 100 year
old mansion standing in an acre or so of ground in a fashionable
suburb.

Taught by a growing staff of "moonlighters", raw recruits in the
shape of holiday-makers wanting to extend their days of sunshine
and one or two whose excellent teaching ability was not matched
by the regularity of their attendance or attention to duty, he
battled his way onwards and upwards, aided by much private weekend study, to a reasonable range of success at "O" level in 1972
(headed by Maths (1), Phys/Chem (1), Eng. Lang. (A), Eng. Lit. (A).
He added Additional Maths (2), History (1), French and Technical
Drawing in June 1973 in spite of fearful scenes at the school in
April when the present writer (and new headmaster) appeared on
the scene - to hear the fiery American Chairman of Governors tell
the assembled school that the former (good, kind but overwhelmed)
headmaster was useless, that the Senior Maths master was a rogue
and vagabond and that both were sacked forthwith.

Having restored something like order and with a really good staff
round me I can give him 8 months of first class Maths teaching
and of Physics teaching which would be first class if we had Labs
equal to the job and to the men teaching in them - or rather it.
The fact that the Lab measures 12 feet by 8 and is occupied (often
at the same time) by a D.Sc. Chemist and a D.Sc. Physicist does
somewhat hamper all concerned. Fortunately a friendly greek school
up the road allows us the use of their good Physics Lab once a
week but I think that even the Curies might have jibbed at preparir
themselves for "A" levels and a Cambridge entrance exam in the
prevailing circumstance.

To make things a little more interesting Rodger is of course head
of the School which has been prefectless but not school council-
less for some time and he is also responsible for co-ordinating
all the (new) inter-house games and other activities.

He has risen to the occasion really splendidly and it looks very
much as though he has not only saved the school from disintegratio
but has helped to set on the road towards a future which may well
see it become a mediterranean star of the first magnitude.

To sum up — — —X— — — can be compared as regards ability with
any of the many minor award winners I have sent up to Oxbridge fro
— — — in the past 25 years but I think it would be unfair to
expect him to do more than score Bs or Cs in his 1974 "A" levels.
That I believe he will (if selected) obtain at least a good 2nd
class honours can be taken as read for he has the brains, ambitio
desire and the character to overcome all obstacles; is well read
and enjoys good literature (he has decided to add 1974 "A" level
Engl. Lit. to his qualifications), but he writes rather stilted
English - possibly as a result of working in a 60% — — speaking
school.

I have/have not checked sections 18 and 19. (Delete as necessary)

The academic referee is asked to return this completed form without delay to: The Secretary, Universities Central Council on Admissions, PO Box 28, Cheltenham, Glos. GL50 1HY

Figure 7. Correspondence with referees for testimonials from schoolmasters and the like for enroling candidates for courses, could lead to exchanges which were very remarkable.

In the 1970s, we acquired a new building on the far side of the railway line, which runs between Piccadilly Station and Oxford Road Station; there can be few campuses that can boast of having a line of arches surmounted by a railway, passing through their middle! (And under one arch is a full scale 'statue' of

Archimedes sitting in his bath!) However our new building boasted being a new home for our Thermo. labs, design and drawing offices, some lecture rooms and a display of a fine collection of model engines and pumps manufactured by our own technicians (see item 12 in Chapter XXIII). Solid Mechanics was housed in yet another block with the Civil Engineering Department, whilst Machine Tool Engineering did not move from the old Victorian building. Solid Mechanics was thus in the new Pariser Building and the Thermo-fluids mostly in the George Begg Building. (These two names were those of men on my interview committee who had died – so it was a grateful gesture and record.) In the very centre of the campus were two areas of lawn, one was a bowling green and the other sported a metallic 'artistic' creation from our own workshops which mocked some of the well-known creations found in national art galleries. Along one side of one lawn was a collection of lecture theatres, on the side of which was mounted a copy of a magnificent astronomical structure or clock for informing one of the seasons, year, and time etc. It was created when the Institute started its History of Science and Technology Department. It is still there but the Department it celebrates has shamefully been run down to a near nothing. From the top of one of its buildings one of our Machine Tool lecturers jumped to his death. No-one knows why. Nearby is the Students' Union, called the Barnes Wallis Building; the Institute gave him an Honorary Degree. It is curious that the Union chose Wallis of Möhne Dam fame who is accepted as a war hero. Wallis is widely thought to have introduced the idea of using the ricochet bomb. In fact for three centuries before Wallis, the ricochet firing of large spherical shots had been practised by the Army and Navy. And the damage caused by bombing the German dams only put local German industry out of commission for a few months. The cost of it was the loss of about half the air crews who flew the mission. Despite its intention the total mission was a failure and no such action was ever used again. It did however inspire the people at home with hope.

Annual Reports

The purpose of dividing the Department into three arose from recognising that professors direct research and generally decide on what should be included in the undergraduate programmes and developments in the Department. Difficulties and discordant notes can arise when one professor is set over another. Professors should be the sole directors of their own empires. It was agreed between us that in term time undergraduates must be put first and accordingly that professors should lecture at all levels to make themselves known. The writing of useful Annual Reports was pursued in order to show in some detail what the Department had accomplished in a given year. For example, the book *Theory of Machines* by Thomas Bevan (a recently retired senior lecturer in the Department), served internationally as the most-read textbook on its subject for a generation. That such a contribution had been made and emanated from our Department deserved to be recorded for posterity, yet it never was. An Annual Report should widely proclaim a College's success and, correspondingly, help to raise the national standing of the Department and Institution. Our research work that had been reported in international journals was likewise listed annually and with the same objective in mind. We started an Annual Departmental Report soon after 1960, but it became the practice to issue an Annual Report for the whole Institution soon afterwards. Such material is remembered in Cambridge Reports but trying to learn what had been accomplished in the CoT, since its foundation, was not possible, since no records had been kept. Our aim was to establish a tradition!*

The Divisional structure worked well – professors did not 'get into one another's hair'. I tried to extend this later, aiming to add two new big territories to our three, namely, Polymer Engineering and Metallurgical Engineering. The latter subject would attempt to focus on plasticity or all kinds of metal forming used in processing, covering somewhat machinery and material structure. The former Chair was eventually filled by Professor Stephen Bush but the second one did not mature. It was felt more attractive to combine the University's interest in Metallurgy and that of UMIST in one unit, on the UMIST site.

My hope at the time was to see separate faculties in Science, Engineering and Humanities all on the UMIST site. Figure 8 shows, incidentally, the original Mechanics Institute, built about 1825,† from which the MCoT developed.

The establishment of a Chair in the History of Science and Technology at UMIST is worth describing as being typical of others. The case for a new Chair – assuming there are funds for it – is first made before Senate and a committee of about ten persons is then appointed to examine in more detail, the case for the Chair. I was appointed a member of just such a committee for the above-named Chair of History of Science & Technology at UMIST. The case was deemed sound and Senate then authorised a Committee of Arrangements. The aim here was to find a Professor to fit the Chair. I was not made a member of the latter committee, largely, I believe, for disagreeing with Lord Bowden who seemed to me on that occasion to have many opinions but little detailed knowledge of existing departments in the subject. He had not encountered the department which had been running for some decades at UCL. The first candidate to be offered the Chair was a man from MIT, who had written a short book on the History of Machine Tools. (For an American, a British salary was quite inadequate and the idea of changing from Boston to Manchester was too much – and who could blame him?) The second choice which came up was that of Dr Donald Cardwell, then a Reader at Leeds University. It was a splendid choice, for Cardwell went on to write several sound books on industrial and technical developments

---

* At the time of writing, 2002, the decision has been made to dissolve UMIST and simply to incorporate it in the University. Some regard this as a new opportunity, others see it as an act of suicide.

† The Dict. Nat. Biog. notes one John Watts (1818–1887), a virtually unknown, largely self-taught, educational and social reformer, as a young acting secretary and librarian, at the 'local mechanic's institution'. He had attended the Andersonian University in Scotland and was a lifelong advocate of the new free and rate-supported schools and libraries. He had a great influence on the contemporary Manchester Mayor, Sir John Potter, strongly encouraging him to lead, and succeeding, in securing the first *free* civic library, (Manchester), in England, in 1859.

Figure 8. Once the Manchester College of Commerce, originally the Mechanics Institute, forerunner of the College of Technology.

GEORGE BIRKBECK (1776–1841) *took a leading part in the founding of Mechanics Institutes in the UK.** *He was appointed to the chair of Natural Philosophy in the Andersonian Institution in Glasgow in 1799. He also played a leading role in forming the London Mechanics Institute in 1824. It became known as the Birkbeck Institution and, later on, developed into Birkbeck College.*

in the early nineteenth century in the North of England. As earlier remarked, I had known Dr Cardwell about fifteen years earlier when we were students attending the M.Sc. Course in the History and Philosophy of Science in 1950/51 at University College, London. He himself lectured our own departmental undergraduates and he was greatly appreciated by the staff and students, especially

---

* See, *Science in Victorian Manchester* by R. H. Kargon (Johns Hopkins Univ. Press), pp. 16–25 and W. Johnson in *The Bull. Mech. Eng. Educ.*, 2003/4, 'The Mechanics Institute and The Free Library of Books'.

A One-Third Scale Working Model of The Newcomen Engine of 1712

BY

R. L. HILLS, M.A., Ph.D., D.I.C.

(Read at the Science Museum, London, on 12 January 1972)

The people who suggested originally that Manchester should have a Museum of Science and Technology intended from the very beginning that it must be concerned with historical research and that it should have a strong educational basis to help school and University teaching. When possible exhibits for the steam engine display were discussed, a vital gap in the historical sequence became apparent. There was no atmospheric engine in the Manchester region, and it seemed unlikely that any of the ones surviving elsewhere would ever become available. Atmospheric engines, both pumping and rotative types, played an important role in developing industry in the Manchester area, and a thorough understanding of their performance and characteristics is the essential basis for a true appreciation of James Watt's inventions and subsequent improvements.

Therefore we realised that we would have to build an atmospheric engine, and decided to try and recreate the first engine ever built, the one erected in 1712 by Thomas Newcomen at Dudley Castle. The cost, and lack of space, compelled us to reduce the size to one third, but even so the engine stands nearly fourteen feet high (Plate IX). We also resolved to construct the engine as closely as we could to the sketch drawn by Thomas Barney in 1719. The earlier drawing of 1717 by Beighton depicts the later Griff engine which had some differences. No records or papers have survived to tell us whether the Dudley Castle engine was modified in any way between 1712 and 1719. All we could do was to base our reconstruction as faithfully as possible on Barney's drawing,[1] trusting that the engine had remained virtually unaltered during the intervening years.

There can be no need to describe to Newcomen members the basic layout and parts of the Dudley Castle engine. However, the reduced scale of the museum model and the fact that the museum is housed only temporarily in its present building has led to certain difficulties. For example, because the engine will have to be moved, it is supported by steel girders which will be clad with mock brick and stonework. The reduced size has meant that certain parts of the boiler will not work. For ease of operation, electric immersion heaters generate the steam, giving the added advantage that heat input can be measured easily. Wherever possible, the same materials have been used as in the original, but, for safety reasons, it was felt advisable to make the boiler from copper sheets, tinned to look like lead.

It is impossible to mention all those who have contributed to the building of this engine for so many have been concerned with the planning, drawing, building and erecting. Without the help of Professor W. Johnson at the Mechanical Engineering Department of the University of Manchester Institute of Science and Technology, the project would have been stillborn. Two people in particular, Messrs. G. Needham and G. Robinson worked very hard, not only to build the engine but also to make it run smoothly which they achieved during the early part of 1970. Then the engine was tested by two students, Messrs. K. Cookson and P. May[1] working under the direction of Dr. A. P. Hatton. Some of the performance figures resulting from their tests are given in the appendices at the end of this paper. To my mind, the difficulties that we have had to overcome must have been similar to those which faced Thomas Newcomen, and it is these that I wish to discuss.

[1] K. Cookson, *An Experimental Determination of the Power and Efficiency of a Model of an Early Newcomen Engine* (3rd Year Mechanical Engineering Ordinary Degree, 1970–71, U.M.I.S.T.); P. May, *Power and Efficiency Tests on a Replica of the First Newcomen Engine* (Report in partial fulfilment of Postgraduate Diploma in Technical Science, 1970–71, U.M.I.S.T.).

Excerpt: Transactions of the Newcomen Society
Vol. XLIV, 1971-1972

Figure 9.

those electing to write their third year undergraduate dissertation on a History of Engineering topic. The subject was lectured once a week for an academic year to all our students in their first and second years.

After the Chair was filled there developed a strong expression of opinion for a Manchester Museum of Science and Technology. This has been realised and is now a proud expression of Manchester's devotion to technical scholarship, situated in the vicinity of the city's old central railway station. Many people have contributed to its realisation, none more than Dr Richard Hills. Through the extract in Figure 9 he tells of the building of one unique exhibit (and an account about another on p. 292). Mr George Robinson was a Divisional Chief Workshop Technician who helped with this project and Mr Needham an enthusiastic technician who supported him. It has to be added that work for the production of historical models fell to be carried out by the Applied Mechanics Division; no support or interest was available from elsewhere in the department apart from Dr A. P. Hatton of the Thermodynamics division.

From another small departmental workshop Mr Joe Flowett contributed or supervised a variety of work. During the war he went through the North African campaign, so he was older and near retirement. (Many Ph.D. degree foreign students owed much to him for patient help, suggestions and advice regarding the design of their Ph.D. equipment – sometimes it was an input more valuable than that from their supervisors!)

These few technicians had a value which was priceless. UMIST has (had?) a wonderful collection of historically accurate models that will 'work'. (No electric motors hidden from public view in what should have been steam energised engines – as in some celebrated museums!)

Reader Dr A. P. Hatton, was the devoted academic member of staff who watched over our modelling activities; he may well have been their instigator in the first place. In making these accurate working models there was on many occasions, almost unbelievably, a need for research to find out and reproduce engineering detail; many photographs are especially deficient in showing misleading details.

Medical Engineering at UMIST

I have remarked elsewhere, see p. 172, about getting research work in the Theory of Mechanisms started in the Department in the early 1960s. Dr Jan Skorecki (a senior lecturer) told me at that time he had been asked by a local hospital orthopaedic group if he could design a wheelchair which could be 'straightened' so as to bring a person sitting in it to a nearly vertical position. It was to aid the nurses faced with getting old, heavy men to a position from which they could be better handled. I encouraged him to get involved and to use our small workshop. These were projects that seldom seemed to get finished. But there were some investigations which did. The first was for helping a psychiatrist who asked if he could be provided with a means of measuring bed 'restlessness'! At first sight this appears to be an impossible task; it seemed to be calling for the measurement of a certain quality and variety of behaviour. In brief, a useful solution *was* accomplished by stitching several tubes lengthwise to the sheet of the bed. These were thin, plastic tubes which could be filled automatically with water at the foot of the bed and be expelled at the head of the bed, into a measuring cylinder. The volume of water gathered over a specific interval of time was a function of the tossing and turning of the sleeper and so the squeezing of the tubes. The height of water collected in the cylinder could be monitored automatically. It was simple and effective to a high degree.

Another topic arose from our work on impact problems: this was a study of blows to the head which had relationship to motor car impact injury, boxing and the heading of a football. The aim for the latter was to record and determine the severity of blows and in order to help do this we placed an accelerometer at the back of the head on the opposite side to that from which a blow was delivered i.e. the forehead; the device recorded head acceleration with time. Figures 10(a) and (b) show a human subject and a punch ball being used in a study of slow speed frontal blows in boxing, actuating the ball as a bifilar pendulum; for high ball speeds a kind of gun was used (see Figure 10(c)). An old expression known as the Gadd Severity Index (introduced initially to study damage due to head impact in car crashes) can be used to calculate a recorded impulse (actually acceleration) over a specified time. A GSI (Gadd Severity Index) value of 1,000 is usually indicative of a very serious blow to the head of a subject.

I had always been puzzled as to why footballers do not seem to suffer brain damage from heading a football. As long as they receive the ball in a restricted area of the mid-line of the head, they are not notoriously injured by the end of their careers. From our studies, the GSI sustained from a soft ball is, at most, in the low hundreds. However, there is some doubt about the effects of *repeated* impacts (a kind of 'fatigue' effect)* for which there seemed to be no published research at the time. In boxing, for a typical head suffering a direct facial blow, using a glove, the limits seems to be set by a speed of delivery of about 25 ft/sec. The real 'killers' seem rather to be the 'hook' and the 'upper cut' which rotate the head; the bony skull rotates over its soft internal contents, thus causing internal bleeding where the two were connected. The forward blow tends to cause the opposite side of the head to move outwards, so as to cause a gap between the two parts – a kind of spalling situation. These explanations are, of course, vastly over-simplified. Much American sophisticated experimental work (in the field of head injury in motor car accidents) has been carried out by Professor Werner Goldsmith, Berkeley, California, USA, and he is noted for his outstanding contributions. My early interest in the study of boxing was the result of a co-authored book on *Impotence* by my younger brother, John, and a colleague, both psychiatrists. A number of cases had arisen of marred marriages caused by the onset of impotence in the later life of boxers; it seemed this was due to brain damage accumulation from a lifetime's career.

A third piece of work was performed for the late Sir John Charnley FRS – the design of a gait-measuring machine in connection with hip prostheses; as a subject walks along a 10 ft. platform, the force impressed upon it through each of the feet is recorded and their degree of dissimilarity I believe can then be used as a measure of the degree of recovery of an individual when a prosthesis has been fitted.

At UMIST in our Strength of Materials laboratory, tensile tests were carried out by pulling in tension the bones, tibia and femur. (I could usually tell when a new

---

* Analogous to metal fatigue.

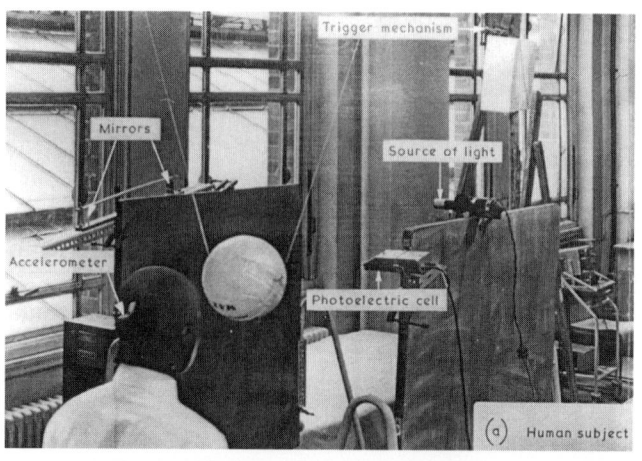

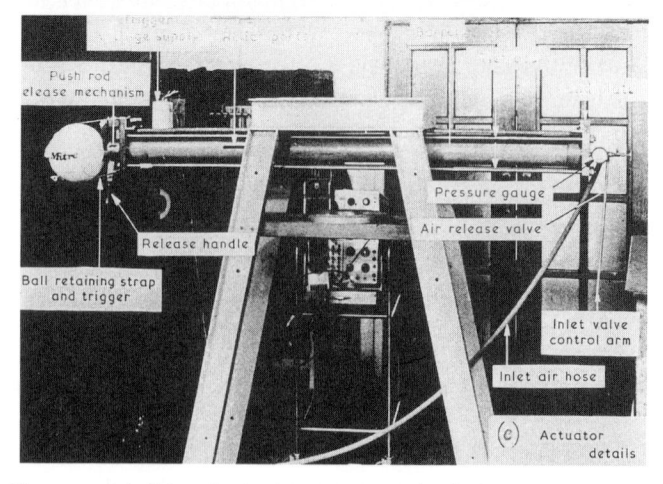

Figure 10 (a), (b) and (c). Arrangements for high and low impact speeds to the head.

batch for testing had arrived, because my secretary used to put them out of the way in a filing cabinet in my office, and a certain odour then pervaded the air.)

A collateral piece of research which was carried out in our Division by Mr R. D. McLeish was to explore the distribution of load or foot pressure under the feet.

We started a Manchester and Salford Medical Engineering Club with monthly meetings. Each commenced with a lecture by a medical consultant describing some of the engineering problems he thought he was confronted with and which might be capable of solution by engineers. The audience was frequently about fifty strong and was a mixture of engineers and medics of all ranks. We had elected Professor J. H. Kelgren, Dean of the Medical Faculty as our first annual chairman. The meetings moved from hospital to hospital in the area, covering Salford and as far afield as Buxton. After a lecture we had a light dinner and then went to view and discuss (if it was possible) something of our useful engineering medical facilities. We usually finished about 8 p.m. Dr Skorecki was our first secretary and later on Dr P. Soden, their period of office lasting for about a decade see figure 11; there was little or no charge for club membership and postage, secretarial work and arrangements were covered freely by the Department. We had fairly steady attendance numbers for several years. I may mention that Dr Soden himself pursued studies in the design of rotational micro-pumps, ones which delivered small quantities of liquid medication over a period of weeks. A more sophisticated study (with Drs Al Hassani and P. Soden), was that of the *Analysis of a Simple Heart-aorta Analogue* (IJMS, *13*, 615, 1970); our simple mathematical analysis predicted the important features of the model's performance.

We had introduced into the Department an M.Sc. degree by Course and Dissertation and progressed to having Medical Engineering as a subject. Members of the Medical Faculty came to give lectures and their patients' problems were a source of engineering dissertations. The examiners were medical and engineering staff. We quickly came also to having one club meeting per year at which students contributed from their dissertations and from which we selected one for a prize.

Interest in living matter brought us (and in particular Dr P. D. Soden) to the study of the squid – work we did in conjunction with the University Biology Department under Professor Ted Trueman. A relatively high velocity jet is produced in the squid by contraction of its mantle muscle so as to expel water from the respiratory mantle cavity through a narrow channel; this was a study of jet propulsion which found reasonable concordance between calculations and experimental results; see Figure 12.

In due course, some time after I had moved to Cambridge, the club secretary-ship shifted to the Electrical Engineering Department and I lost contact with it. I was invited to celebrate the 20th anniversary dinner, but on attending dismayed to learn that the numbers attending meetings were declining. About five years ago I received a letter informing me that it was proposed that the club be closed down for want of satisfactory size of audience and interest. This was a matter of great regret especially as the whole operation had cost the university virtually nothing. Towards the end of the last decade of the twentieth century, the government announced it would put money into ventures such as ours had been.

Continued on page 196.

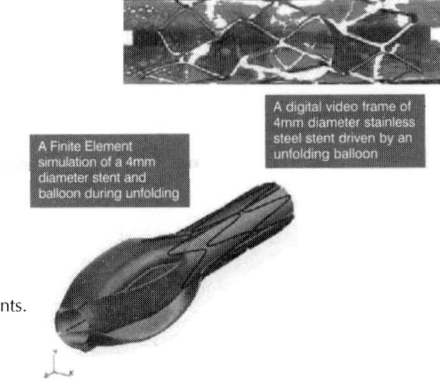

Professor S. T. S. Al Hassani investigates the design of stents.

A Finite Element simulation of a 4mm diameter stent and balloon during unfolding

A digital video frame of 4mm diameter stainless steel stent driven by an unfolding balloon

Dr P. D. Soden

Modern, recumbent bicycles with streamlined fairings are capable of up to 50 mph but are unstable in side winds and at low speeds. Mr Soden has supervised undergraduate and postgraduate projects on three and four-wheeled manpowered commuter vehicles. The photograph shows a four-wheeled vehicle designed and made by a small group of undergraduates. Vehicles under consideration at present include lightweight, robust, aerodynamic, monocoque body-shells made of fibre-reinforced composites.

Dr Jan Skorecki *(BSc Tech Hons Mechanical Engineering 1949, MSc 1957, PhD 1960)* on 17th September 1999.

Dr Skorecki was a former member of staff at UMIST. He studied under Professor Wright Baker and after graduating in 1949 joined Joseph Lucas Ltd as a research engineer. He returned to the Mechanical Engineering department as a Lecturer in 1957 where he gained his MSc and PhD and was promoted to Reader during the period when Professor W Johnson was Chairman. His interests though basically in Applied Mechanics, ranged widely embracing Medical Engineering where he worked closely with Sir John Charnley in the study of aids for disabled.

Dr Jan Skorecki

Jan was a unique person, a solid and reliable friend, popular with staff and students alike; with the latter he was particularly close always having their well-being and interests at heart.

Tribute provided by Dr John Fielding

Figure 11. Extracts from the Annual Report of the UMIST Department of Med. Eng., for 1998–2000.

J. Exp. Biol. (1972), **56**, 155-165
With 4 *text-figures*
Printed in Great Britain

A STUDY IN JET PROPULSION: AN ANALYSIS OF THE MOTION OF THE SQUID, *LOLIGO VULGARIS*

By W. JOHNSON, P. D. SODEN AND E. R. TRUEMAN

Department of Mechanical Engineering, University of Manchester Institute of Science and Technology, and Department of Zoology, University of Manchester, Manchester M13 9PL

(Received 4 June 1971)

INTRODUCTION

Squids and other cephalopods have evolved a remarkably effective form of locomotion by jet propulsion. The high-velocity jet is produced by contraction of the mantle muscles so as to expel water from the respiratory mantle cavity through a narrow funnel (Fig. 1). The animal can repeat the process after water has been drawn into the cavity by the expansion of mantle musculature and may produce a number of jet pulses in quick succession.

The purpose of this paper is to outline an analytical approach to the study of cephalopod locomotion, resulting from one contraction of the muscular mantle producing a single jet of water. The theory and method of analysis is described and results for a simplified model are compared with the results of the experimental studies.

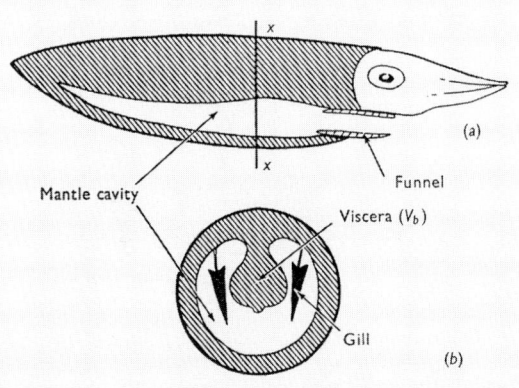

Fig. 1. Diagrams of *Loligo* in (*a*) sagittal section, behind the head, and (*b*) transverse section (line *x–x* in (*a*), showing extent of mantle cavity, viscera and mantle muscles (hatched).

COMPARISON OF THEORETICAL AND EXPERIMENTAL VALUES OF JET THRUST

Figure 12. A Study in Jet Propulsion: An Analysis of the Motion of the Squid, Loligo Vulgaris.

Ours was one which had run on enthusiasm. I believe we were not alone in our medical engineering activities and in particular knew that a very successful venture was operated by Leeds University. The growth of a substantial Medical Engineering Unit was difficult to see in the early days. The engineer had no prospect of a career in the subject for he was always subservient to the medical practitioner who played the pivotal (medical) role – even though the engineer could be quite a talented scientist.

The collapse of the Medical Engineering Club did not however bring about the loss of internal departmental interest in the subject as will be clear from Figures 13(a) and (b); the latter was extracted from the Annual Report of the UMIST Department of Med. Eng., for 1998–2000.

It is interesting to note that the title of Imperial College was adapted to include Medicine alongside Science and Engineering and regrettable that UMIST was not able to do the same.

Figure 13 (a). Scoring a goal from a corner kick. Initially the spinning ball is shot at $5°$ to the dead-ball line.

Using Maccoll's experimental results [5, 8] for the aerodynamic lift generated by a rotating sphere, we may estimate the 'bending' or 'curving' undergone by the ball when 'taking a corner'; similar calculations would apply for a 'banana shot'. By assuming a corner kick to be delivered, about 36 m ($\sim$ 120 ft) from the goal mouth, in a horizontal plane at a constant speed of 18 m s^{-1} ($\sim$ 60 ft s^{-1}) and with a rotational speed of 15 rev s^{-1} about a vertical axis, it may be shown that the aerodynamic lift manifests itself as a horizontal force giving to the ball a transverse acceleration which can deflect it from its original direction by as much as 3 m in its flight-time of 2 s. When crossing the goal mouth, the lateral speed developed would be about 3 m s^{-1}, so that moving at 18 m s^{-1} ($\sim$ 60 ft s^{-1}) across 7.2 m (24 ft) between goal posts, the ball would move transversely by about 1.2 m (4 ft) if delivered as an 'in-swinger'. It is thus easy to appreciate how a goal may be scored from a corner, see Fig. 15.2.

Scoring a goal from a corner kick. Initially the ball is shot at 5° to the dead-ball line.

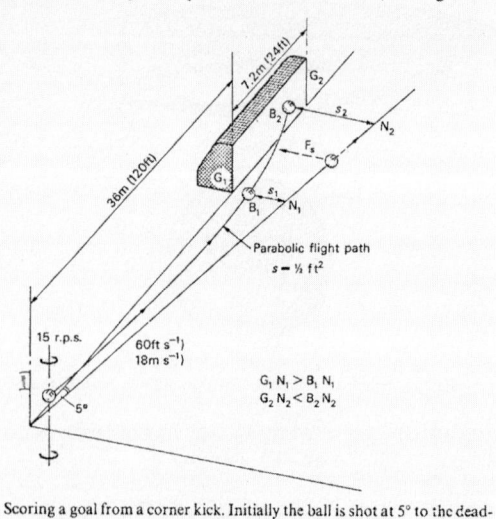

From: Human Body Dynamics, Impact, Occupational and Athletic aspects, ed. D.N. Ghista, Clarendon Press, Oxford, 1982.

A curious Ph.D. examination from the Engineering Department at the University of Salford came my way. It was concerned with a device or structure which was attached to the head in order to help target a surgical instrument at specified co-ordinates deep in the head or quite specifically small regions for the treatment of one of the degenerative diseases. The instrument was lightly clamped to the head and when used, with the aid of diagrams, a specific region could be located. I understand this surgical procedure subsequently ceased and reliance was placed entirely on drugs. The second examiner from the medical school obviously had little experience of Ph.D. examinations, contributed little to the oral examination and I was left to sustain it largely out of a sense of pure curiosity. Only familiarity with one medical consultant and two medics-to-be in my family, gave me the confidence to dare to ask questions.

Mechanics of Sport

The special interest in the Department in mechanics of impact led almost automatically into studying sport. A number of the subjects staff of the Applied Mechanics Division examined were:

(i) with *footballs*, *golf balls* and *cricket balls*, their swerve or 'swing' in air due to their rotation in flight. With footballs, goals could be scored from a corner kick, see Figure 13 (a), and with golf balls, substantial upward lift can be given to the early part of the trajectory;

(ii) *rock-climbing* mechanics considering stances, see Figure 13 (b), rope strength and karabiner design;

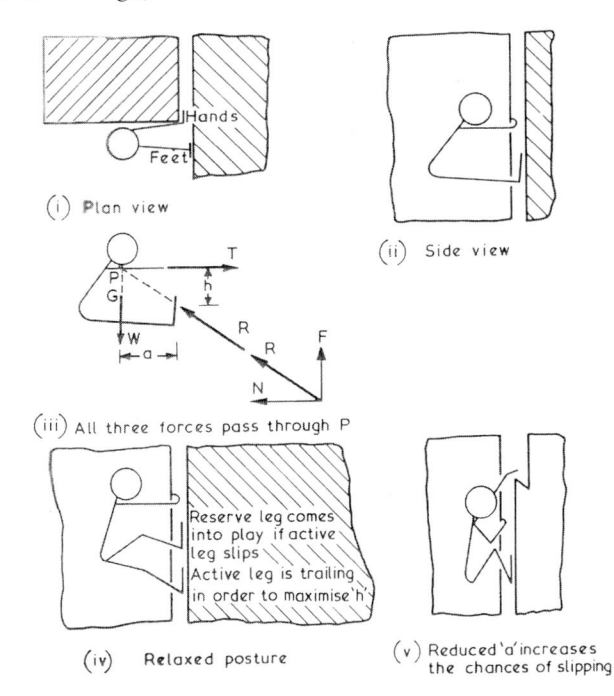

Figure 13 (b). Lay-backing in rock-climbing. Force analysis.

(iii) investigations of *tibia fracture* due to torsion in *skiing* accidents;

(iv) impact from water in *diving* – of 305 suicide jumps from the Golden Gate Bridge, San Francisco, USA, there were only two survivors at impact speeds of about 100ft/sec. on reaching the water;

(v) *pole vaulting*, in which there are two major factors for securing height. The kinetic energy of a running sportsman is converted into potential energy or height and, secondly, added to that is the amount of bend and 'push-up' which can be mustered in the time between planting the pole and crossing the bar. Around 20 ft is all that can be achieved or expected – unless one fits a compressed spring or gas inside the pole, releases it when in the vertical position near to passing over the bar and thus being projected to a greater height!

(vi) the general *ricochet of balls*, but especially spherical shot, which is mentioned elsewhere below. (And ricochet is *not* bounce.)

Figure 14. The Manchester Association of Engineers, Council 1955–56.

'I hold every man a debtor to his profession, from the which as men of course do seek to receive countenance and profit, so ought they of duty to endeavour themselves, by way of amends, to be a help and ornament thereunto.' (Lord Bacon).

The Manchester Association of Engineers

The Manchester Association of Engineers (MAE) was founded in 1856 and existed alongside the Institutional branches of Civil, Municipal, Mechanical and Production Engineers in Manchester. It claimed its mission to be that expressed by Lord Bacon, see Figure 14. As well are Dr J. H. Lamble, Professor H. Wright-Baker and Dr C. A. Sparkes – notable for taking a Ph.D. in Machine Tools at UMIST, after he had retired at age 86.

The names of some well-known engineer-members, who had their own companies are Adamson, Gledhill, Galloway, Hetherington, Hopkinson, Mather,

Nasmyth and Roberts. The membership of the association was at a peak of 844 in 1922, but today stands at about 200. (There was once an Engineers' Club, well-frequented and plush, opposite the Manchester Town Hall. I remember visiting it many years ago during the Second World War. It was my introduction to a gentleman's club. The I.Mech.E. and MAE held branch meetings in it on Saturday afternoons.)

The UMIST Mechanical Engineering Department and the Association have always enjoyed a close relationship and its professors frequently favoured with an Annual Presidency. The long line of men devoted to Manchester engineering will be obvious from the length of chain in the frontispiece!

Details about the founding and history of the MAE are to be found in *One Hundred Years of Engineering in Manchester*, (1856–1956), published by the MAE.

Apprenticeship

This is a subject which often claims the attention of engineering staff and the following reproduced article tells something of its history and importance to them.

*(From The Engineering Industrial Journal,
issue 198, February 1961)*

Professor W. Johnson D.Sc, MI.Mech.E., Department of Mechanical Engineering, the Manchester College of Science and Technology, was asked at very short notice to speak at the North-Western Region Annual luncheon. His talk was so interesting and informative that we have reproduced it in full.

When asked to speak to you at such short notice I was allowed a great deal of latitude in the choice of my subject – indeed I could very nearly address you on any topic I cared to. In these circumstances, I might have been induced to play safe and make the subject 'technical' and this would have been easy – for I could then have delivered any one of my lectures to the undergraduates on the Strength of Materials, Thermodynamics or Heat Transfer. This would not have been well received! You could have tried me on one of my research interests – say the extrusion or the flow of metal through small holes – a process which aims at giving a required shape to a product to the exclusion of machining – and I should then have talked about calculations of local pressure in the metal and the manner in which it flows or doesn't flow. This I would consider only to have been properly presented if I had related this special process to the other major forming processes such as rolling, coining, forging, machining. Again, this is not, I felt, what is expected explicitly or officially, so to speak.

Of course, it could well be that you spend so much of your lives engaged in discussing Apprenticeship Training that you would be pleased and interested to listen to anything that was relatively new to you!

A different species of title might be thought up concerning the history of specific engineering subjects. What of 'Mechanics before Newton'? But I suspect that many of you, in more senses than one, have long since left 'Mechanics' behind. And anyhow the histories of the sciences and technologies can be very difficult to handle once one attempts to do more than relate facts; I refer here to trying to follow the fascinating developments of scientific ideas or concepts. In this particular case, too, on the one hand there are now available five very large volumes on the history of technology, and if you are still interested in the topic then in a few years' time I suggest you invite a Professor of the History of Technology to address you – a post it is earnestly hoped to establish in the fairly immediate future in the College of Science and Technology.

But these meanderings have given me some pegs on which to hang my reflections about a more apposite subject for this afternoon. In the first place it occurred to me that I might educate myself by looking up the facts of the history of technical apprenticeships. In the second place I might examine the growth and development of ideas about apprenticeships. There are, of course, experts on these matters and I am certainly not one. But in an endeavour to approach the matter in the right academic way, I began by considering what is meant by the term apprenticeship. I am hardly more than familiar with the name 'The Carr Report'. My own experiences are with apprentices-to-be who are a pretty uniform bunch and who nearly all, on graduating, take up a form of two years' apprenticeship, generally with the larger organisations. I should guess, however, that the term – apprentice – and its implications are very well circumscribed in that Report. Am I correct in thinking that it deals with plans for technical education, discusses the nature and scope of technical training, and generally seeks to relate such training activities to the needs of the community? If this is the case, then perhaps you will be interested to learn what I found when I looked into the history of such training for, in many ways, the 'problems' with these young people seem to be much the same today as they were five to seven centuries ago.

After quoting the first definite statutory aim about apprenticeship, I shall then continue to fill out with quotations about the obligations and responsibilities of masters and apprentices. You shall see that there has not been a revolution in dealing with these young people.

The object of apprenticeship is defined in an Elizabethan state document of the fifteen hundreds*: 'Until a man grow unto the age of twenty-four years' he has not 'grown unto the full knowledge of the art that he professeth.' Apprenticeship then was a system of technical training under a master by which the craftsman was initiated into the secrets of his craft and was rendered qualified to carry on his calling. There are two amusing records from the fifteenth century in which one master undertook to 'find his apprentice two years to grammar school,' and a second in which an apprentice was covenanted to be sent to France for a year 'to learn the language of France.' There is a report from Exeter in 1562 of a master who was charged with 'refusing to instruct and set forth his apprentice in such sort as he is bound to do' – and the apprentice was therefore set free from his employment.

The master's responsibility did not end with technical training. He was responsible for such matters as, to give several quotations from this period 'for good demeanouring and bearing,' 'for his apprentices good and sufficient workmanship,' to give 'suitable clothing, shoeing, board, bedding and chastisement.' The latter sometimes went too far, for there are records such as that in which an apprentice complained against a master for 'not well-using him in beating him.' Another master exceeded his powers for he chastised his servant, or apprentice, by 'the bruising of his arm and breaking his head.' On that occasion the master had to pay the doctor's bill, the servant's board and a fine to the guild 'for his misbehaviour against the craft.'

A guild sometimes punished an unruly apprentice; in 1572 one was so punished

---

* *Economic History of England.* Volume 1, E. Lipson, A.& C. Black Ltd, 1925, p. 309.

'for his lewd and evil traditions'; he was 'whipped openly in the hall' in the presence of officials and 'divers apprentices.'

The similarity between the behaviour of present-day apprentices and those of four centuries ago are many. But I think your problems with them are now more serious – serious in a different kind of way. Riots were not then uncommon, especially among London apprentices; in 1400 many were killed in disturbances and the King 'wrote' the parents and masters asking them to check assemblies and gatherings. Complaints against them were common, witness the reference to '..the abuses and enormities reigning in our apprentices at these days.' As you will well know, a favourite theme, much in evidence to those who watch pantomime at this season, is the contrast in the fortunes of the industrious and the idle apprentice: the one married his master's daughter and rode in his coach as Lord Mayor of London, the other ended a life of dissipation on the Tyburn Gallows.

The length of apprenticeships at first varied and lasted no fixed period: only until the masters testified that the apprentice or servant was 'able and well instructed.' Soon in the sixteenth century it settled down to about seven years. In 1563 the Statute of Apprentices became law throughout the land and this period was made compulsory. But the period in which to acquire 'sufficient cunning' did remain variable and anything from four to ten years is frequent. Sometimes the duration of the apprenticeship was intended to limit membership of a guild. On this point it was stated that 'the number of this fellowship is so augmented and daily doth increase to the utter destruction of the company.' Cases are recorded in Northampton of boys 'bound' for 11, 13, 14 and even 16 years.

The number of apprentices a master might employ became a subject of great controversy in the fifteenth and sixteenth centuries and some attempt at control was made. When the apprentice had served his time he became a journeyman. A few remarks on these are worth while. In 1380 the Ordinances of the Cutlers speak of 'journeymen who had not been apprenticed in the trade'; in 1389 the Founders ordered an unskilled journeyman to 'be ousted therefrom if he will not become an apprentice'; the Bladesmiths, 1408, forbade anyone to 'teach his journeymen the secrets of his trade as he would his apprentice.'

As I have said, after completing his term of training the apprentice was free to become a journeyman and to seek employment as a hired workman. Many were required to continue with their masters for a further year or so – though in receipt of wages. A few travelled to other towns in search of wider experience. It was unusual to allow an apprentice to become a master until he had served as a journeyman for some time, perhaps three years. The journeyman, however, looked forward to the day when he would cease to be a wage-earner and could take his place among the masters of the guild as a fully qualified craftsman. Sometimes he was required to furnish a masterpiece and this was especially the practice in the seventeenth century. The London Pewterers examined a journeyman as to his 'honesty and behaviour', and required him to produce a sample of his work. These years as a journeyman allowed him time in which he could accumulate capital sufficient to establish his own workshop. Not that much of this was required in the shape of machinery and building, for this played only a small part in mediaeval industry. The basis of industrial life was craftsmanship – tools and technical skill. Circulating capital for the purchase of raw materials and the payment of wages would be necessary – though he might work on the material supplied by his customer.

Numerous crafts made and enforced rules to safeguard the interests of consumers. Night work, in an effort to ensure sound quality in work, was generally forbidden.

For example, no London cutler, in 1345, could work in winter between 6 p.m. and 6 a.m. It was said that artificial light militated against sound work. 'No man can work so neatly by night as by day.'

Sunday labour was also prohibited. And wages and prices were regulated by the guild. The London Blacksmiths (1434) ordered that if a stranger came to London to serve in their craft, he must give service for two weeks – presumably to provide assessments of his ability – and then had to enter into a covenant for three years during which he received a yearly salary of forty shillings.

Many craft guilds seem to have started as religious fraternities, brought together by common devotions. Many guilds, as a rule, maintained lights on the altars of their patron saints and annually exhibited a pageant in different parts of their city on movable stages drawn by horses. In York, the Armourers represented Adam and Eve driven from Paradise, and the Shipwrights the Building of Noah's Ark.

Distress was relieved in the Middle Ages by the craft guilds; as friendly societies they contributed to the support of the poor.

Disputes between members of a craft were resolved by the guilds, if it was at all possible, before allowing legal action to proceed. A feature of the guild was that none should seek unfair advantage over his fellows.

Some attempt was made to find employment for those without work. In the year Columbus discovered America, 1492, at Worcester, labourers who needed work were instructed that 'they with their tools in their hands should daily stand at the Grass-Cross on the work days within the said city, and be there ready to all such persons that will hire them.'

Much may be said against the mediaeval craft guild, but the institution of apprenticeship was its most admirable feature. It bequeathed the ideal of technical training and sound craftsmanship.

Guild apprenticeship declined in the eighteenth century. The introduction of machinery in the great new manufacturing industries was outside the scope of the apprentice laws, and the rise of capitalism led to the repeal in 1814 of the important parts of the 1563 Statute. A man might then exercise any craft or trade he pleased whether he had been an apprentice or not. But long before 1814, in trades outside the scope of the apprenticeship laws, a new kind of apprenticeship had come into being. The apprentice ceased to live under the personal control of his master; he served a strict contract, lived with his parents and received wages.

Despite the introduction of machinery and the increasing sub-division of labour, apprenticeship in its new form persisted as an important element in the industrial organisation of the country. At the end of the nineteenth and the beginning of the twentieth centuries, the *Encyclopaedia Britannica* tells us that apprenticeships were threatened from other quarters. Employers, it says, became less willing to spend time and money on the training of apprentices, which the specialisation of processes and the speeding up of production had rendered more difficult and more expensive. The trade unions, realising that the employment of cheap juvenile labour needed protection, called in aid the time-honoured methods of the guilds and the apprentice laws, and imposed restrictions on the number and proportion of apprentices and the conditions of their employment – which bear a curious resemblance to those which were imposed by guild officers some six or seven hundred years before.

The late eighteenth and nineteenth centuries do not present a pretty picture. Let us look at them from two very different points of view.

One aspect of the industrial scene in the early nineteenth century is described by Dr Cook Taylor; he refers to the conditions in 1842 in the vicinity of Burnley which were such that weavers 'were haggard with famine, their eyes rolling with that fierce and uneasy expression common to maniacs.' These men said, 'We do not want charity, but employment.' In Accrington, of 9,000 inhabitants not more than 100 were fully employed and many, we are told, kept themselves alive by collecting nettles and boiling them. There was much hostility to – as it was put – 'The melancholy mad engines which feed on water or burning coals.' Such was the comment on England's industrial supremacy. I do not need to remind you, too, that Engels and Marx found their raw material, in all senses of the words, in this age and in this area. It was the age of Malthus, and there was great concern over the growth in population. This is typified at this time by Cobbett, who wrote *A Surplus Population Comedy*. Two quotations from it will appeal to you.

Squire: Pray, young friends of procreation

Thimble: Of breeding children, shun the woes. Check the surplus population, Restraint! that's moral interpose.

A dialogue continues:

Squire: 'But, young woman, cannot you impose on yourself a "moral restraint", for ten or a dozen years?'

Betsy: Pray, what is that, Sir?

Squire: Cannot you keep single till you are about thirty years old?

Betsy: Thirty years old, Sir! Am I a saint? (*She leaves, stifling a laugh*!)

A vastly different, and a far more pleasant picture of the era is provided by James Nasmyth, inventor of the steam hammer, who was long resident in these parts. A reflection on the industrial scene in all its aspects is gleaned from briefly looking at his career and noting some of his remarks.

The start to his working life is revealing: 'I unpacked my working model of the steam engine .. (and) had it conveyed to Mr Maudsley's next morning on a handcart. I was allowed to place my work for his inspection in a room next to his office .. he received me in his library and asked me to wait until he and his partner, Joshua Field, had inspected my work ..'

Thus Nasmyth found a post as Private Assistant to that great machine tool maker, Henry Maudsley, in 1829. Many practical instructions did the young Nasmyth receive. He tells us that he, Maudsley, 'considered no man a thorough mechanic unless he could cut a plank with a gimlet and bore a hole with a saw!'

Nasmyth began business on his own account in Dale Street, Manchester, in 1834, removed to Patricroft in 1836 and invented the steam hammer in 1839. He was born in 1808 and in 1856 he retired from business 'to enjoy the rest of my life in the active pursuit of my most favourite occupations.' The latter included astronomy and Egyptology.

The severe picture of industrial unrest at this time is clear from the following: 'When the Union delegates called in upon me to insist that none but men who had served seven years' apprenticeship should be employed in the Works, I told them that I preferred employing a man who had acquired the requisite mechanical skill in two years rather than another who was so stupid as to require seven years' teaching.' Clearly things have changed somewhat.

Nasmyth's approach to training might easily be your own: ' ..we had some indenture-bound apprentices ..who paid premiums ..some caused a great deal of annoyance and disturbance ..they were irregular in attendance ..careless in their work and set a bad example to others ..But the arrangement which we greatly preferred was to employ intelligent, well-conducted lads, the sons of labourers and mechanics and advance them by degrees .. they took charge of the smaller machine tools by which the minor details of the machines in progress were brought into exact form without having recourse to the untrustworthy and costly process of chipping and filing ..'

In respect of an employment policy, he says: 'I believe that Free Trade in Ability has a much closer relation to national prosperity than even Free Trade in Commodities.'

Nasmyth's comment on his management problems – for he obviously had some – are enlightening: 'Notwithstanding his mechanical intelligence, Hutton was of too cautious a temperament to have acted as a general foreman or manager .. A man may be admirable in details but be wanting in width, breadth, and largeness of temperament and intellect. The man who possess the latter gifts becomes great in organisation .. he soon ceases to be a "hand" and becomes a "head".'

Though the economic condition in England seems to have been one in which there was no economic ultimate, yet there were clearly a number of men who were manifestly dissatisfied with the situation – probably from a variety of motives. The insecurity of our place on the international stage was probably grasped and their foresight was materialised in a deliberate attempt to educate for industry. The history of the College of Technology reflects this. Its brief history is interesting:

In 1824 a Mechanics Institute* was established in Cooper Street, Manchester, being inaugurated in the belief that there is no mechanical employment and no manual art 'which does not depend more or less on scientific principles.' In 1827 eleven Manchester businessmen each lent £634 15s. to buy land and erect the first building in England to be built and planned as a Mechanics Institute. Though the Institute took on educational functions it never forgot that its primary aim was to 'instruct the working classes in the principles of the art they practise.' This motive secured financial support from many Manchester industrialists. In 1882 it was proposed to raise funds to turn the Mechanics Institute into the Technical School. In 1883 day and evening courses in engineering, chemistry and textile subjects, etc., were planned. In 1889 the City was empowered to levy a two-penny rate for technical education. In 1890, the Government helped financially and the City Council sent five people to the Continent to examine the Continental approach to technical education. The aim was to set up a Technological College comparable with the Polytechnikum of Zurich, institutions designed particularly to teach the application of science to industry. Zurich science, however, aimed at the highest level of theoretical training and finding this, new quarters for the Technical School were arranged and the name was to become the Municipal School of Technology. In 1918 it took on the name of the College of Technology.

I think, gentlemen, I do not need to go further. The remainder of the events and histories up to today are well documented and well known to you. Taking apprenticeship in its broadest implication to mean training the young – I am as much involved as any of you. It embraces nothing less than the whole educational system – and here you are entitled to ask if what is being done is adequate. From the side of the educationalist, the clear answer is No! Let me put it to you in the following way, taking my cue from my Principal, Dr B. V. Bowden.

In recent years many observers have complained that our national productivity is lagging behind that of almost all other Western countries.

It is not easy to make precise comparisons between different countries, but there

---

* See Figure 8.

is a considerable amount of evidence available. However one interprets the figures, or however one may argue about their accuracy, they seem to show conclusively that British Industry is growing more slowly than it should. Between 1938 and 1958 the gross national product of the United States increased by 125 per cent, that of Western Germany grew by 128 per cent; the average of all the OEEC countries grew by 64 per cent and that of this country grew by only 34 per cent. In the post-war period from 1950 to 1959 Western Germany increased by 125 per cent, France by 78 per cent, Italy by 100 per cent, the Netherlands by 58 per cent, the average of the OEEC countries by 64 per cent, and this country by only 29 per cent. It is true that the population of some of these countries is growing faster than ours, but the gross national product per head increased in Western Germany by 71 per cent, in the OEEC countries on average by 39 per cent and in the United Kingdom only by 22 per cent.

It is true that we have spent £20,000 million on defence since the war – enough to rebuild the railways, the roads, schools, universities and scores of cities – more in fact than any of our commercial rivals except America, France and Russia. This may have prevented us from investing enough new capital in industry. Nevertheless, even when one has allowed for this we still have not explained why our economy has not grown more rapidly during the last twenty years. Capital investment per worker in our country has, in fact, been quite comparable to that in either Western Germany or the United States – why has our industry grown so slowly? Our investment have not been as efficient or as productive as similar investments have been elsewhere. Why should this be?

It is very probable that one of the most important causes of our relative inefficiency has been the inadequacy of our educational system and the consequent shortage of competent well educated engineers at all levels.

The Government seems to be congratulating itself on the developments which are now taking place in our educational system, but they never seem to compare our efforts with those of our industrial competitors, sufficiently closely. It is not enough that we should be better than we have been; we must hold our own in a competitive world.

How does our educational system compare with those of other countries? I will remark on that aspect of the system with which I am familiar.

Both theory and practice have a vitally important part to play in industry today. Theory may become even more important in future. We teach our students all we can about engineering and technology while they are with us. We expect them to learn that nothing is so practical as good theory, but we know that they will become good technologists only by practising their profession for years after they have left us.

The pattern of world trade is changing fast and it is the new industries which are growing more rapidly and changing the world as they grow. Most of the new commodities and the new gadgets which brighten our homes and change our lives have come to us in the last two or three decades; few of them had even been heard of forty years ago. Most of these new industries depend almost entirely on well qualified scientists and technologists.

It is our job to see that our young men are well trained, practically and theoretically, for such contingencies as the next fifty years may bring. Both aspects of this task have not been over well done this last century. I hope that together we shall do better. Facilities for training in every sense of the word which are nowhere bettered anywhere else on the face of the earth should be our objective.

Why does our educational programme always seem to lag behind? People have been complaining about the inadequacies of our educational system for 150 years and many pamphlets written in Queen Victoria's time could be re-issued today.

A hundred years ago Thomas Henry Huxley was trying to persuade the Government to provide better facilities for scientists and engineers; he wrote 'We are now entering upon the most serious struggle for existence to which this country was ever committed. The latter years of the century may well see us in an industrial war of far more serious import than the military wars of its opening years; to those of us who reflect how serious a customer famine could be, the situation appears grave.'

Until recent years these industries owed little or nothing to laboratory science – they spent very little on research, but some of them have begun to change fast; they might have been revolutionised by modern science.

It is deplorable that this country which pioneered the Industrial Revolution should so often have been so slow to apply the results of scientific research. It is true, of course, that for many years science owed far more to technology than technology ever owed to science, but far too often in British Industry there has been no contact between the brilliant theoretical work of a man in the laboratory on the one hand and the inspired empiricism of the industrial designer on the other. Far too many practising engineers think of theory as 'more theory' and believe that the words 'theoretical' and 'impractical' are synonymous.

Addenda with comments:

1. Of course, the English word apprentice is associated with the French word, *apprendre* to learn.
2. In the records of ancient Egypt and Babylon there were enforced long apprenticeships in such skilled crafts as making jewellery, in gold, silver and bronze ware. Perhaps in every age apprenticeships have been a fact of life in working with precious metals and other substitutes.
3. The term *journeyman* reflected the notion of a man who has fulfilled his apprenticeship or is 'out of his time' but has not yet become a master; somewhat, the idea of *wanderjahre* fits his style of life in mediaeval times.
4. The *Universitas* was a mediaeval corporation in which undergraduate students were taught by masters licensed to teach. The degree of MA given in our older universities about five years after graduation, indicates the relationship of master and pupil.
5. Vacation Apprenticeships

   This article and its views derive from my own period as a vacation apprentice on three occasions of three months, once with Metro-Vickers (on steam-turbines) and twice with Crossley Brothers* (on 2-stroke, loop-scavenge internal combustion engines†). We took up these long vacation apprenticeships in order to gain some knowledge of the every-day practices in industry – tools, machines, testing and seeing something of the variety of interpersonal relationships created and the physical conditions of workshops. (Some undergraduates came away from such experiences having come to the conclusion that they were wandering into the wrong profession.) There was competition for work at MVs and one was accepted only

---

* Both companies, as such, no longer exist.

† The Chief Engineer, Mr Desmond Carter, M.I.Mech.E., wrote a fine paper on this subject, see the *Proceedings* of the I.Mech.E., about 1943.

after a competitive interview. In 1941/42 Crossley Bros, had never heard of vacation apprenticeships. In anticipation of internal combustion engines as one of my two specialities in my forthcoming third year (Hons.) course, I wrote to the Chief Engineer requesting an appointment adding, 'I received 25 shillings per week in my previous employment with MVs.' He took me on at 30 shillings per week!

My Lower Openshaw environment was 'full of apprenticeships' which were regarded as a normal thing to do. After leaving school at 14 years of age, boys quickly became men and discontinued friendships with clerks. Their first year, however, seemed heavily devoted to becoming 'tea boys' – brewers and conveyors of tea for the many 'fitters', morning and afternoon; they usually received, then, wages of 10 shillings per week or in today's terms 50p. in their first year. Apprentices were always poor until they had 'completed their time', when, on moving to journeymen's rates at 21 years of age, they were able to marry. It was not unknown, however, for some of them to have their association with the company terminated – jobs on becoming 'time-served' men were not assured.

6. A term occasionally referred to was 'premium apprentice' – apprenticeships were paid for or bought for their sons by families who could afford them, but they died out in the early years of the twentieth century. The liberties they took were decried by employers: there is some account of the indisciplines which prevailed in Smiles' biography of James Nasmyth.

7. The recollection of the experiences of my first vacation apprenticeship (on large steam-turbines) are still clear in my mind and always seemed to me to have been of great value, to such a degree that I tried hard to encourage our own undergraduates to take them up. At MVs in my first month I was supposed to fettle (roughly, file), steam turbine diaphragms; it was a totally boring job which prompted me to tour the 'shops' to talk to any machinist or fitter about their work, e.g. with the operator cutting the large, heavy turbine rotor shafts several feet diameter and some 30ft. in length; one also saw 'nuts' as big as one's head – but very much heavier – for holding down turbine casings. I also encountered a peace-time salesman working as a machinist – draft-dodging? (It was the second year of the Second World War.)

My second month was spent on turbine assembly and the third on testing. It was excellent experience to see how rotors were 'centred up' between bearings, to actually handle Kingsbury bearings, to see the marking-out processes on large metal castings prior to machining using whitewash and dividers but *not* following Euclid's geometrical constructions!

8. For university teaching departments, these two or three short periods in workshops were thus naturally to be encouraged. By the early 1970s our own UMIST Mechanical Engineering Department actually required that first-year men should take up a vacation apprenticeship in the UK, and for their second one they should search for one abroad; one half in fact, succeeded in doing so. Students worked in Denmark, Australia and the USA – an experience they were not able to repeat in later life. We even went so far as to require them to submit a 1500-word essay on their experiences.

9. Due to a down-turn in trade, the mass of companies ceased to take up these youngsters in 1971/72. Just how widespread was this change I only learned of from my son, who at the time, was reading Engineering at the City University, London, because he had been unable to sign up for a vacation job. The value of vacation work for men who had joined the department at 18 years of age, without

any workshop training, seemed so important to me that I thought it should have been more formally organised in conjunction with the I.Mech.E. It always seemed deficient in the Institution not to have a magazine or journal through which matters of education could continuously be discussed. When our own Bulletin of Mechanical Engineering Education had to be taken away from Pergamon Press, it was offered to the Institution but they declined it.

10. Female students, no less than male ones, we required to engage in engineering practice for these short periods. I recall one of our women students who was later voted President of the Engineering Society, having not long returned from working in a Swedish shipyard.

11. I do not know what practices applied in the USA, Germany and elsewhere. It revealed my own ignorance and brought me to thinking it was an item in engineering education of international proportions and therefore deserving of discussion through a journal such as described in 9 above.

12. I might mention that excellent college apprenticeships were run in companies such as Metropolitan-Vickers and English Electric. Selected *graduates* were given a 2-year apprenticeship at a reasonable salary which included besides the technological trades, an introduction to production control, and selling etc. It was a system for which many foreign graduates especially were grateful.

A Partner in Print at UMIST

This section is one which reveals some aspects of my life which involved my wife, Heather. I let her speak for herself, but first I must explain ...

The Bulletin of Mechanical Engineering Education was produced for many years by Captain Robert Maxwell's (see Chapter XVIII) Pergamon Press and the refereeing of its papers was carried out by the teaching staff of the MED. As a recognition of their freely and willingly given efforts, we started to give an Annual New Year's Dinner, covering the cost of academic staff and partners by expenses allowed us by P.P., though charging a purely nominal amount for all the pairs who came – lecturers, technicians and administrators. It proved to be a very popular celebration which did something to bind together members of the department as a unit. My wife continues ...

'On one occasion, Bill was asked by John Parker (who always organised all the Department's social programmes), if he thought I would be willing to give a speech – responding to the 'Welcome to the ladies'. Bill said yes, and after the first one – given below – I gave one every year thereafter, always starting with a humorous preamble and 'thank you', and ending with a humorous (I hoped) verse ... I remember a few of them and have found one or two notes ... but most are, of course, entirely forgotten; though people I met in later years nearly always recalled them, seemingly with pleasure.

Of course, many of the so-called jokes were 'inside' ones, but I think the following give a flavour of the sort of themes I used and the academic politics of the time; the first year was that in which Harold Wilson made the Principal of UMIST a peer – 1964.

The poem was presented as a paper – with sly references to its title, 'On the raising of Heads of universities, colleges and faculties to higher status ...', 'I do like long titles, don't you?' and 'the author wishes to thank ... you know who ...' for my privileged knowledge of papers etc., having spent ... 'many years between the sheets with the Editor-in-Chief ...' and 'frolicking in slip-line-fields ...'

PROMOTION

There's commotion at 'the Tech.'*
And it's all aflame, by heck –
'Cause they've gone and made the Principal a Lord!
So it's clear this government – if it's not indifferent,
May perish by the word, if not the sword ...

We can understand the need to bring the strength up –
With Sir Alec and poor Quintin† now both gone,
And we certainly won't quarrel
With whoever draws the moral –
That the two of them are worth just one Beau-don‡ –

We in Tech are now right full of expectations –
Since we've got a voice to speak out in the Lords –
What with James' and Bowden's voices –
We should soon all have Rolls Royces –
When they tell them what our choice is – in the Lords!

All the CATS and all the SISTERS§
Have to put up with just plain Misters –
Only Barons and bold Knights will do for us
And if the people *down* at Owens want to keep up with the Jones's
We don't mind, we feel there's room for all of us!

We know Bowden's dedication,
To the cause of education –
And we feel he can't do anything but good –
But we'll criticise like mad, because he'll still be *our* lad,
If he restricts himself to only throwing mud!

We look – now he is ermined, for a policy determined –
To give Industry the engineers it needs.
Now we've given them the man,
We shall hope to see a PLAN –
And to see some words which really lead to deeds!

---

* UMIST was originally the College of Technology; Tech. in short.
† Sir Alec Douglas Home and Quintin Hogg.
‡ I spelt Lord Bowden's name as Bow-don in those days, wrongly.
§ Acronyms for the new Colleges of Technology.

I was overwhelmed with praise at the end of that speech – a previous HoD said the poem reminded him of Kipling (alas, much as I would have liked to believe it, I knew my Kipling too well!). One man said it was the best after-dinner speech he'd heard, and now he knew where Bill got some of his strength from ... (that latter *did* please me; I didn't get many compliments). The poem was apparently sent to a UMIST Professor who had retired to India (that worried me because I had mis-spelt Lord Bowden's name) and others wanted to publish it in the IJMS – but the editor (you know who) turned that down flat!

'Mr Chairman,
Some experiences take a lot out of you and others put a lot in ... Well, these occasions undoubtedly put the fear of God into me ... but since you *have* put a very nice meal into *us* this evening I'm very happy to reply on behalf of my fellow-guests and myself ...

Incidentally, I'm sorry that these speeches seem to have developed into a cross between Vaudeville and a commercial for the AUT.[*] I hope you'll be relieved to know that it's Vaudeville's turn tonight!

VOTE OF THANKS
(Given in a broad Lancashire accent ...)

Seated one day at my type-writer,
I was weary and ill-at-ease –
For I'd been asked to give a Vote of Thanks –
And I'm always that anxious to please ...

Now a vote of this kind is not simple –
Not like voting for Harold or Ted[†] –
There's a nice-looking lad called John Parker –
'You just speak when you've fed' – so he said.

Well, I'm not one to talk when I've got nowt to say –
Tho' there's some 'ere who might not agree –
I said, 'Talk of what?' He said 'Oh – this and that –
Then say, 'Thanks for a very nice tea ...'!

Well, even *I* knew as I'd 'ave to say more,
For I'd been around more than 'e knew ...
Most of the voters of thanks that I'd heard –
Told long stories, and most of them blue ...

It's a limiting thing being a lady;
A lady is always discreet –
And although I'm a woman for most of the time –
Alas! I'm a lady toneet!

---

[*] Association of University Teachers.
[†] Prime Ministers Harold Wilson and Edward Heath.

So, I sha'nt tell you any blue stories –
You'll hear all of those from the men –
And all of us ladies won't listen –
Till we get home and are told them again!

There's those who go sailing and such-like,
Such tales of the briny they tell ...
And folks from exotic Newcastle,
Must know rich Geordie ripe 'uns as well.

And everyone knows that the golf club,
Is the place where one lets down one's her
But here there are so many egg-heads –
I doubt if there's much her to sper!

There's men here who go in for writing –
Sending papers far over the sea –
At times they go with them (in case folk can't read) –
Each one is a Hero to me ...

But I'm just a lass from up-country;
And I live in a sort of retreat
And tho' I've succumbed to temptation at times
I'll not tell you about that toneet ...

I'll just say that it's been a real pleasure –
To meet all you folks from the town,
And having said nowt about owt for so long –
I'll just say, 'Thanks a lot!' and sit down.

BIGGER BOXES

(With apologies to Pete Seeger (pop singer) who had a very catchy song 'Little Boxes ...' which was popular at the time, and to BBC television's programme, 'Men and Materials' 6 March 1970.)

Bigger Boxes on the hillsides
On sites known as campuses –
Some are old ones, some are new ones –
And they don't look quite the same ...
Built of old stone or of red brick
Of plate glass and coloured concrete –
They are all called universities –
So they all sound much the same.

And inside those universities
Are lots and lots of lecturers –
Some old brains, some young brains –

Who have not yet drained away ...
They are all made of super-plastic
Strong and workable materials
Life can bend them, work can stretch them –
And they mostly stand the strain ...

Down in London there's a Clearing House
With computers working over-time –
Sorting students, little students –
Who nearly all look much the same –
Tubes of plastic materials
To be filled up with education –
To be made into intellectuals –
By adding letters to their names ...

So the teachers feed the students
With lots of information
Little pieces, bigger pieces –
Which shouldn't cause much strain –
Some work hard, others argue,
Sit and protest to the Vice Chancellor –
But it's all part of the System –
And we pay for it just the same ...

After three years, examinations
Holding up The Revolution –
There are high marks and low marks,
(For which the teachers get the blame) –
There are B.A.s and B.S.cees –
And other sorts of batchelors –
Even spinsters turn into batchelors,
So it's all part of The Game ...

CHAPTER XX

Ridge Hall

HEATHER AND I DECIDED THAT as our five children moved into adolescence, we needed to provide them with their own rooms for privacy and homework and Norbury House was too small for eight people, despite the extension we'd had built on. Heather's mother needed her own bathroom and the two younger boys currently shared a room as did the two girls. The local council had recently straightened Torkington Road and had removed many trees along it. Buses also ran up and down it to the Grammar School at Marple and traffic lights were installed where it joined Stockport Road – all of which changes encouraged traffic to use our road as a short cut to Marple. The housing estates in recent years had displaced the farms which used to surround us, which now meant that we had moved from countryside-living back to urban dwelling. We started to look for a big old house, one that would easily accommodate all of us and be capable of improvement. In an estate agent's window in the centre of Manchester, I noticed that a 'Ridge Hall', see Figure 1(a), was for sale, a property on the periphery of Chapel-en-le-Frith, twelve miles further out than where we lived then – but close to a railway line into Manchester, Stockport and Buxton. The Hall had a total of about seventeen rooms and the asking price was £7,000. We could expect £6,250 for Norbury House according to my wife, so it seemed well within our grasp. Heather and I went to see it. It was owned by a Major Ramsay, who was a director of a company in Stockport. He was a well-made fellow with bright white hair and military moustache. I later found that his forbears were artillerists in the Peninsular War (1808–14). We were pleasantly received, quickly shown over the house, and then left alone to look around while the Ramsays went out shopping ... When we asked about locking up after we left, they said, 'Oh, we never bother to lock up!' He seemed to spend most of his time in the lounge, sitting by the open log fire, enjoying a whisky and watching his little daughter at play while his wife was outside, mowing the lawns! (The Hall was indeed untidy, many of the stairs had small heaps of books on them and numerous elephant's 'feet' (from service in India?) were used as containers for literature and poetry.) This fireplace was at one end of the lounge – some 20ft. by 18ft. – but about 40ft. in total. All the rooms in the Hall were large, some of them were almost entirely stone walled and evidently if they included electrical night storage heaters, as well as radiators working off the central oil-fired boiler, the dwelling should everywhere be pleasantly warm. Outside, there were regions for storage

Figure 1 (a). Ridge Hall.

Figure 1 (b). Ridge Hall in the Wood.

Figure 1 (c).
The Bagshawe coat of arms.

Bagshawe

Bagshawe. Ridge Hall (Chapel en le Frith). *Or a buglehorn stringed sable between three roses gules (pierced of the field)*; crest: *a cubit arm erect proper holding a buglehorn sable enguichy or* (Vv. 1569, 1611, 1662; only Harl.MS 6104 of the latter supplies the tinctureless crest). This is the oldest and senior branch of the Bagshawes, recorded as early as 1141.

– too many to mention, but especially attractive was the fact that the curtilage of the whole Hall was two acres, around which there were castellated old stone walls. Japanese visitors later reported us as 'living in a castle'! One first floor room over a garage, which we later converted to a kitchen-diner was given over to hens and the floor was covered in 'deep litter' (for which Major Ramsay apologised). In the courtyard outside the front door were several stacks of wood and much building rubbish; the rear garden was a tip – not touched, I believe, between 1939 and that day. During the war, troops had occupied the premises, ostensibly as a precaution against German paratroops landing on the moors a few hundred yards behind us. Horses – said to be more reliable than vehicles over our land in the various kinds of weather – had brought up supplies and stores from the station during the war.

We found, about a hundred yards away, our own covered reservoir, up the hillside; it would have been 40ft. by 20ft., and probably 8ft. deep. (If one had fallen into the water in there, there were no ladders attached to the wall to facilitate escape.) It was filled by run-off water from the moors and perhaps in Victorian times supplied the water for both cattle and human beings; it was filtered by iron machinery which now no longer functioned. In one outhouse, the ash from fires had been dumped – perhaps 5ft. deep, underneath which lay an ancient boiler and its equipment. There were six glass-houses; each of them had lost many panes of glass, none of which was I able to recover, and indeed, I eventually removed them all. In the boiler room there was a single 'slop-stone', 6ft. by 3ft., on which butchered cattle meat had obviously been washed and in a neighbouring room there were two 400-gallon oil tanks. And the hall was in the Wood, see Figure 1 (b).

It was clear we would have to think hard before taking on these premises – it was no 'ordinary house'. We thanked the Major and promised to let him know if we were seriously interested in buying. I hesitated to buy the property because of the big demands it would make on Heather. She would be isolated with only the farmer at hand and one other large property, perhaps a hundred yards away, called 'The Ridge'. The roads to our front door were rough and we were over a mile outside of the (now) town of Chapel-en-le-Frith ('church in the forest', see Figure 2). The name derived from mediaeval times when foresters guarded the hunting region around; no forests are of course to be seen today – so much for not changing the nature of the countryside! We had also to take note of the fact that the property was at 1100ft., but below the moors which were at about 1500ft. (We later noticed that often when it rained in Chapel it presented itself, to us, as snow.) The views across the valley beyond Chapel, were magnificent – Mount Famine's edge was always in view and the 500ft. upsweep to the moors behind our house provided a splendid backdrop to the Ridge Hall property.

We next saw a few other houses – none of which compared with Ridge Hall according to Heather. She telephoned the Ramsays to ask if it was still on the market and it was. However, another couple was very interested but haggling over the price. Thus two weeks after our first visit we returned to Ridge Hall with our five youngsters and mother-in-law, on a glorious day when we were capable of driving only half way up the road because of the deep snow! At first, I thought that these conditions would provoke outright repudiation of purchase by the family, but it proved not to be so. At the Hall, the Major declared that the children could go anywhere in the house they liked, open any door – mainly because I had warned them not to be too inquisitive. When all the family came together after half an hour, there was a unanimous and resounding 'YES!' when I asked them about coming and living there. It was even declared an 'excellent' home by Nana herself. So, I agreed to pay the price set by the Major and no problems were later encountered by either side to the transaction. (The Ramsays left a magnificent dining room table – too large to move into their new home – they said.)

On the day we moved in, I had to be in London, my secretary having unfortunately omitted entering the appointment in my diary. Nonetheless, without me, Heather and the three boys (Helen was at Guide-camp and Sarah stayed at Norbury House with her grandmother) moved in and neatly arranged our little furniture around the property. I arrived home from London at about 9 p.m., only to find Heather and Chris busy vacuuming but no sign of the other two boys. Chris said, quite casually, that Philip and Jeremy were out climbing on Castle Naze, a notable spot for rock-climbers on the edge of the moor. It was

Figure 2. Market Place monuments, including the old stocks at Chapel-en-le-Frith.

nearly dark and I set out, apprehensively, to search for them, only to meet them, a hundred yards away, striding cheerfully down the lane. They said they had had a great time!

(On the top of Castle Naze it was possible to make out two lines of ditches right across it; these were punctured at intervals with holes in which sharpened wooden poles had once been placed to deter invaders. Between the palisade and the rocky face, an ancient settlement would have been contained. A lake lay half a mile away, perhaps 500ft. lower and around it in ancient and peaceful times there would have been a settlement (see Combs Lake, Figure 3). Under threat, there would have been a rapid retreat on to the Naze. Much of this history was researched at the end of the nineteenth century.)

We remained in Ridge Hall for precisely 34 years and 4 months – more than one third of a century. It became the delight of our lives and our true home as we improved and organised it, and filled it with our own belongings. Affection for the old Hall made us very reluctant to consider ever relinquishing it, even when we went to Cambridge for 7 years and later, to the USA for about 5 years. When we were emptying the house of its contents in 1999, Jeremy spoke for us all when he said he wept.

Some History

There are many volumes in county libraries on the country houses in the various shires of England, and Ridge Hall is no exception for Derbyshire. It is one of

Figure 3. Combs Lake.

the smallest in the county but almost the oldest building in the neighbourhood of 'Chapel-in-the-Forest'. It was built in 1142 on Ridge Hill and known as *The Ridge Hall*. In *A Derbyshire Armoury* by M. Craven (Derbyshire Record Society, Vol. XVII, 1991), it is said that the Hall was the home of the senior branch of the Bagshawes, see Figure 1 (c). An account of the early history of Ridge Hall is given in Bunting's *Chapel-en-le-Frith*. In the sixteenth century it is recorded that there were eleven old Halls within a radius of three miles of Chapel's church. The first owner was a Bagshaw and changes in the spelling of that name, Bagshawe, Bagshaugh ... reflect changes in our language with time. A Professor Newton of Sheffield University has spent much of his time in tracing members of the Bagshaw family (his wife being one), and has found there were/are enough of them to fill a small book which he had completed.

The Bagshaw family lived in Ridge Hall seemingly from the time of the first foundation of the house in the twelfth century into the sixteenth century when the line at Ridge Hall ceased. The Gisbourne family followed and inhabited the Hall until around the eighteenth century. Various families inhabited the house from then on and as it passed from family to family, each put their little stamp on it.

In our property there were four sets of stone mullion windows – one set would appear to have been blocked in completely at the time of the Window Tax (introduced in England in 1697 and abolished only in 1851), whilst another set of four had two windows closed up; to have opened up the other two of the set would have led to them appearing over our library mantelpiece! (The second

Figure 4 (a). Old Stone fireplace.

Figure 4 (b). Tudor fireplace, notice also the pew door to the left of the picture.

set of four on the first floor has just been opened up by the present owners, to much improve the house's appearance.) The original fireplaces are fourteenth and fifteenth century, some strong and resolute, see Figure 4 (a), but another – on the first floor landing, see Figure 4 (b), of shapely Tudor form. (One Saturday afternoon I took an old coating of plaster from the wall under the stairs to reveal a magnificent old fifteenth-century fireplace.) There are many doors unchanged since the eighteenth century and a fine seventeenth-century entrance to the house from the boiler room. In parts of the property, ships' timbers have been found, fitted into the roof. One ancient 'pew' door from the local Anglican church (removed during restoration), adorns the landing.

The internal shape of the house has changed much and often as room shapes have been changed; the original axis we found had been altered from overlooking Chapel, i.e. north, to west, towards Combs valley. Our structure had a strong cellar with a recently added ceiling now forming the lounge – the story was that at some time the cellar had been a refuge for cattle. Heating the Hall was accomplished by almost every means – burning wood and/or coal, electrical space-heaters and by steam pipes from an oil-fired boiler; we also kept three mobile gas heaters and numerous electric fires. We had to be able to cope when power failures occurred, as they did – once or twice – each year.

The Combs valley is still lovely and 'undiscovered' with a fine pub at the centre of the village. I took some American visitors over to it for lunch once and received a letter many years later, recollecting the occasion, when I had almost forgotten it.

For the first time in my life I was able to have a roomy study/library with lots of storage space and our parents' wedding present – the Edwardian bookcase – could be handsomely displayed. Off our courtyard there was a line of four stables which had been roughly converted into two garages (four in all).

The opportunity came, and was taken, in 1967 to buy for £200, six acres of woodland which stretched for half a mile and was cut by two valleys through which streams ran. Grass cutting was always difficult as we failed to get regular help. Early on, we could buy eggs and milk from the adjacent farm until the owner retired and the farmhouse became a middle class professional home. I recall finding a first floor hay-loft (dimensions 20ft. by 40ft.) on my property which an adjacent old farmer, a Mr Garner, still owned. For £5 I bought it from him! Access to it was by a fixed wooden vertical ladder 20ft. in length from the former stable (later garage) beneath. This hayloft became a room in which our adolescent children held their parties. Chris and Jeremy made a great effort with it, fitting a false ceiling, whilst curtains were made by Sarah who was also caterer; the loft had window seats and was furnished with second-hand articles bought by Sarah under Chris's financial direction. Chris had the floor carpeted and called the place, 'The Second Hand Joint'; many of their friends still remember it with great affection. And there were and are still, old buildings and stout stone walls to be encountered outside the house well below the surface of the soil.

A problem we never surmounted was to get repairs done to the property; the prospect of driving across the neighbouring railway line seemed to terrify many of the workmen although Heather and Sarah used to cross it four times daily when the latter was at the Infant/Junior schools. Afterwards, schools were no great problem, despite snow often 3ft deep. The trains were very reliable and conveyed the boys down the line to Stockport Grammar School and the girls up to Buxton Grammar – when Sarah became old enough to join Helen there. Similarly, with universities. I travelled to Piccadilly Station, Manchester, and after

Figure 5. Simba.

a 45-minute train journey was but five minutes walk from UMIST, whilst Philip, when at Medical School and Helen in the Law Department at Owens College, Manchester University, required about 15 minutes.

During our first 15 years in Ridge Hall there was indeed deep snow 4 and 5 feet deep every winter; after that in our opinion there was a definite climate change which meant a reduced amount to 6 to 8 inches. Such hazards as these necessitated our buying in and being prepared for many obvious eventualities. Wet, heavy weather led to us having walking parties calling on us and asking permission to be allowed to rest and eat their sandwiches under cover and occasional campers sought to set up their tents in our wood. The latter could be a little hazardous in that our neighbour bred prize goats of which the 'billy' was of a height to look one straight in the eyes and use his head to butt anyone to whom he came too close! My daughter Sarah kept one or two goats which led to Philip and I at one point delivering kids. Jeremy at some time also kept a pig with whom he became too friendly. His initial intention was to rear it, then to sell it, and use the money to buy a telescope. However, he found it hard to help in getting his pig into our neighbour's van in order to take it to the sausage factory! Helen tried to keep hens and was very successful at first, but then the foxes proved superior and all she had left were bunches of scattered feathers. We adopted, and perhaps regretted adopting, a Dalmation dog from an elderly neighbour. On occasion it could escape over our 6-feet-high-stone walls to travel sometimes 15 miles, and Heather only become aware of its absence when a telephone call from a distant farmer asked her to come and collect 'Simba' (see Figure 5). Once, Simba landed me in court on a charge of her attacking sheep. There was an account in the local newspaper carrying the headline, 'Professor's dog attacks sheep'! I only learned about this a week or two later, Heather and the children having deliberately kept it from me. It cost me a fine of £20, a day's absence from the University and using Sarah and Jeremy as witnesses in defending the animal from being destroyed.

The Bagshaw Family

The published pedigrees at the Ridge begin with Thomas Bagshaw, son of William Bagshaw of the Ridge; it was the home of the Bagshaws for more than 400 years. Ridge Hall was shown as a house of major importance at this time in sketches on the contemporary Duchy of Lancaster maps. It seems to have declined somewhat in the nineteenth century when portions of the original Hall were pulled down. The Bagshaws lived there but married 'out' and into various Halls in the neighbourhood. During this period and indeed beyond it, it produced several men who have merited some record in the Dictionary of National Biography. The senior branch of the Bagshawes at the Ridge died out in the sixteenth century, but the name was carried on prominently in the neighbouring Ford Hall. One such individual in whom I developed a special interest was Colonel Bagshaw (see Figure 6). He was in charge of the 39th Royal Regiment of Cork, Southern Ireland and was expecting to serve in India. He was described as 'a good and careful officer' and his regiment was the first Royal one to enter India in 1754. At the time he was not in good health but he nonetheless recovered sufficiently to sail to India, well recognising that he was entering a sub-continent in which there was cholera, smallpox, malaria, enteric fever and dysentery; dying within a year of landing was common. This happened to the distinguished engineer-mathematician Benjamin Robins about whose work I have written much elsewhere.* Robins died in 1751 in Fort St David on the Coramandel Coast, India. He had taken up a post as Engineer General responsible for restoring several of the forts which were held by the East India Company (EIC). This was the period in which Robert Clive, and the contemporary but now forgotten General Stringer Lawrence, fought the French and the Marathas. I thus chose to look closely at Colonel Bagshaw's service in India because I thought it might reveal some information about the previous professional preoccupations of Robins. I recognised that Samuel Bagshaw had had his origin in Chapel-en-le-Frith and must have known Ridge Hall well. Bagshaw, despite his health risks, hoped for an independent command in India and a reputation which would provide him with 'a few thousand pounds'. Such a sum would have met the upkeep expense of his house and property in England. However, this did not happen and he had to be allowed to go home in 1757 because he was seriously ill, without having surmounted his domestic financial problems. Bagshaw is in fact remembered on a wall tablet in the church in Chapel-en-le-Frith; however, I found nowhere any mention of Robins in Bagshaw's letters.

The second man in whom I developed the greatest interest – one about whom an interesting volume could still be written for the first time – was Christopher Bagshawe, 1552–1625, born in Lichfield, 'of a Derbyshire family'. He graduated from Balliol College, Oxford in 1572 having matriculated in 1566 from St John's College, Cambridge. He was later caught up in religious polemics as a Protestant,

---

* *Collectd Works on Benjamin Robins and Charles Hutton*, Phoenix Publishing House, Delhi, India, 2003, 540pp.

COLONEL SAMUEL
BAGSHAWE AND THE ARMY
OF GEORGE II

1731-1762

EDITED BY
ALAN J. GUY

PUBLISHED BY
THE BODLEY HEAD
FOR THE
ARMY RECORDS SOCIETY
1990

Lieutenant-Colonel Samuel Bagshawe, 39th Regiment of Foot
(oil on canvas, artist unknown, c.1750)

Figure 6. Colonel Samuel Bagshawe and the Army of George II.

with the well-known Robert Persons (or Parsons), who was Head of Gloucester (later Worcester), College, Oxford. Bagshaw secured the latter's expulsion and replaced him as Head, 1579–81. Obviously, he was a great agitator, for he himself was soon compelled to resign. He went to Paris in 1582 and took doctorates in Divinity at both Paris and the Sorbonne, having become a convert to Roman Catholicism and a Jesuit.

Evelyn Waugh's *Edmund Campion* (1540–1581) (Penguin Books, London, 1954, 173 pp.) can be recommended for a detailed account of a scholar and missionary who was made a martyr in 1581. Christopher Bagshaw followed Campion's life in several respects. He was a fellow at Oxford and was at the religious centre at Douai, France, before going to Rome in 1572.

An English cardinal, William Allen (1532–1594), who had refused to take the oath of supremacy to Elizabeth, escaped to France, establishing a college or seminary at Douai which was so successful that it had in excess of a hundred 'pupils' and teachers. The Pope invited Allen to create an English College in Rome. Bagshaw journeyed to Rome but failed to establish good relations with either Pope Pius or Cardinal Allen and indeed he was again expelled. The issue appears to have turned on his refusal to agree that the Pope had a right to call for tyrannicide or the assassination of the English monarch; to Bagshaw this was a sin. By this time, he was becoming known as 'doctor erraticus' or 'doctor per saltum' (by jumps); he was said to be, 'a devil incarnate', being 'an Englishman Italianate'. At some time he had apparently helped to produce Catholic literature for circulating in England. He had returned to England in 1585, was eventually 'taken' and imprisoned, first in the Tower but later in an 'open' prison at Wisbech Castle. The reader will appreciate that the political antagonism between Rome and Spain against England built up to the sea battle of the English with the Spanish Armada in 1588.

Bagshaw was subsequently released, in 1601, and returned to Paris where he died in 1625.

Edward Bagshaw, the elder (d. 1662), was another who was at loggerheads with authority and changed from being Protestant to Catholic at the time of the Civil War. He was a member of the Long Parliament, was taken prisoner in the Civil War and incarcerated at Southwark, but released in 1646, dying in 1662.

Edward Bagshaw, the younger (1629–71), a divine and a controversialist, seems to have been most notable because he was second master at Westminster School in 1656 at the time of the first master, 'the terrible' Dr Busby!

A very interesting Diary by James Clegg (1679–1755), was written between 1708 and 1755; it consists of three volumes which have been edited by V. S. Doe. He was a preacher and country medical doctor, typical of the early eighteenth century. He had a congregation around Chapel and wrote accounts of farming practices, the state of the weather and the crops, the sick and the place of dissenters in the locality. He was succeeded by William Bagshaw, well-known as 'The Apostle of the Peak' and noted as 'the author of an enduring chapbook'. (This was a small pamphlet of popular tales, ballads and tracts, hawked by chapmen or pedlars.)

I continue here with the mention of Dr O.C. de C. Ellis whom I first introduced on p. 34. At that particular time I was a youth of about 17. Now, many years later, a letter addressed to O.C. de C. Ellis arrived at Ridge Hall. This explained his seeming to come from afar in my school days. He obviously had had rooms in the Hall just before the Second World War with his wife and small son. From school I remember acquiring a booklet of his called, *'Shakespeare as a Scientist'*, which I found difficult to follow. Thus I now tried to learn more about him and did indeed find he was, 'a minor poet and a friend of Walter de la Mare'. The British National Biography lists about twenty of Ellis's works on poetry, literature *and* 'flame or combustion'. From reading a recent obituary[*] of a Fellow of the Royal Society (J. D. Birchall), I learned that Ellis had been this man's scientific mentor. They had worked in industry together and Dr Ellis had been the senior specialist in combustion; indeed he was awarded a Manchester D.Sc., for his researches in 1936. As well, he had Ph.D. and M.A. degrees. He was long a noted colleague of the distinguished professor of English Literature at Manchester, Professor H. B. Charlton. Ellis had been described as a great polymath, but alas, too little is known of him. Professor Anthony Kelly, a former Vice Chancellor of the University of Surrey, wrote to me of him as having been, 'a legendary figure at ICI'. So, it was indeed a remarkable coincidence how our paths should cross for the second time at Ridge Hall.

A Maturing Family

Norbury House in Hazel Grove and, especially, Ridge Hall on the outskirts of Chapel-en-le-Frith, were our two consecutive homes which were central to

---

[*] Biographical Memoirs of Fellows of the Royal Society, Vol 43, 89–104 (1997).

bringing up our family. We took up residence in Ridge Hall in 1965 and departed from it in 1999. The children's ages then, in 1965, ranged from 6 to 17, and when we (Heather and I) left they were middle-aged and had families of their own. It would require a book of quite a different character from this one to tell of our family's vicissitudes; it would be too long a story to tell here. However, I have hinted at events in other parts of this book and perhaps it will suffice (and I be excused) for simply outlining major events in all our lives, below. (Heather, my wife, will give a more intimate picture of our internal family life in her imminent book, *A Family Anthology*.)

I have told elsewhere about our getting married and the difficulties of staying together when I was demobilised. It was only late in 1948 with the purchase of our first house in Somerhill Avenue in Sidcup, Kent, that we began to have a settled married life. It was a house we were too poor to fill and at a time when it was hard to make ends meet. Nonetheless, our first child, Philip James, was born in May 1948 to a mother who had until very recently been a school teacher. Philip was a happy, healthy, inquisitive and very active child with a great tendency to climb. The area of Sidcup was a quite delightful one and we were very happy there, even though money was scarce. My young brother John and his girlfriend

Figure 7. Our small family, about 1960 at Norbury House.

stayed with us for a short period and I learned from John many years later that Margaret, his wife, had noted in her diary that we seemed idyllically happy and rich! An outstanding event too, in that home, was the birth to us of a second son, Christopher John in July 1951. He came into the world after labour problems but turned out to be a model baby and an independent, determined child.

Helen was born in our first house situated at the top of the hill, in Sheffield, in April 1953. She was a quiet little bundle, quick and full of fun. At this stage we thought we had learned a lesson! Philip as a baby was typically a noisy, first-born boy – it was the parents who did not know how to handle him. Chris had a babyhood quieter than did Philip. We said to ourselves it is the parents who make the difference – they do not know well enough about the baby's requirements etc. After Helen came she was 'so good' we hardly knew we had her. Then came Jeremy William in June 1954! Our whole notion that it was all a matter of parenting went for nothing. Downstairs, when he was born, I heard his first cries and turned to my mother-in-law to say, 'It's a boy!' Helen went to sleep at well-defined times but Jeremy could stay awake until midnight! Their eating habits and forms of play contrasted sharply too. Helen became much attached to her grandmother but Jeremy was always a centre of action on his own. The two grew up and were very close in adolescence; she was 'big sister' and moderator whilst he was her protector. Sarah was our last child, a girl whose protector was mostly Chris. They went to football matches where at times she was bid, 'Put your hands over your ears!' – to obliterate the bad language. When he left grammar school, Philip chose to read Medicine at Manchester University, lived on the campus and early became a rock-climber. He used to bring groups to take soup in our kitchen when they were climbing on Castle Naze (which was more or less outside our rear entrance). He seemed to disappear into various hospital appointments and eventually went to a Liver Research Unit in London. He took up a Chair appointment in a liver unit in Hong Kong for about 9 years but recently returned to the UK to join a Cancer Research Unit in Birmingham University. Chris and Jeremy both went to Stockport Grammar School; then Chris went on to read Mechanical Engineering at City University and Jeremy read Metallurgy at UMIST. Chris became attached to computer programming at Simon Carves Ltd, Stockport and developed his own personal style. After several moves he settled in Sheffield with a company where his own programs are developed and sold for some large sums of money. Jeremy worked with British Nuclear Fuel but during its first depression he left and passed through several companies until he became a senior executive in buying and manufacturing in Cambridge. Chris incidentally is an ardent Socialist still – an equally ardent supporter of Stockport Football Club and a recent adopter with his wife of two young girls. Jeremy is a strong mountaineer with about 200 Munros to his credit – a Munro is, effectively, a Scottish peak of over 3,000ft. – and a committed extra-mural lecturer with the Open University.

Figures 8 (a) and (b) show the origin of the mountain walking and climbing interests of the boys.

Helen read Law at Manchester, worked for several companies and at the old LCC she met John Ryan whom she married in 1989. They started their own

Figure 8 (a). An Teallach in North West Scotland. (b) Father, Chris, Jeremy (and Philip, photographer) in the vicinity of An Teallach, about 1963.

Figure 9. Our extended family on the occasion of our 50th Wedding Anniversary.
The present generation in the top rows.
The past generation (left to right: Elsie, Heather, William, Margaret and John).
The next generation along the front row.

legal practice and today have a successful business in Isleworth and live in Chiswick, London, Helen specialising in family law. Both girls were at Buxton Grammar School. Sarah spent three years at Manchester Metropolitan University and after working in banking became a chief legal cashier in St Austell, Cornwall, and married Roy Purlan, an engineering manager. Chris married Sarah Philomena Lowery who runs her own massage, reflexology and chiropody unit. Jeremy, 'Jem', a company buying and production manager, married Tracey Fenton, a company secretary, and Philip's wife, Susan, was a medical secretary.

All our children have their own children – we have eight granddaughters, two grandsons and two adopted granddaughters, with ages from six to twenty-one, three of them graduating in 2003.

We have been fortunate in generating book readers, without ever applying pressure, and persons of liberal persuasion. All our sons and daughters-in-law are splendid complements to their spouses and Heather and I believe we have been very fortunate to be surrounded by such successful partnerships.

Advanced age, unfortunately, prevents me from continuing to discuss philosophies for maintaining good family life.

There was a short period of perhaps five or seven years when the family, spread over eleven years of age, encompassed infancy to adolescence. We were fortunate in these years to enjoy a salary which allowed us good domestic help and to buy a Dormobile (seating for twelve), which besides everyday use in and around Ridge Hall, gave us the possibility of ranging relatively far afield for holidays. We had Easter holidays in the UK and summer villa holidays in Europe.

The spring holidays were usually a week or ten days, spent in Wales, the Lake District or north-west Scotland, mountain climbing. Scotland was our great success. We stayed in Ullapool and walked some of the well-known range of An Teallach, over Stac Polly and later in parts of the Red Cuillins in Skye. See Figures 8(a) and (b). I took the lads and we enjoyed our little expeditions, often struggling up through snow; Heather had the girls and usually found a 'little Stac Polly' to conquer. The glorious feature of north west Scotland was its emptiness – and surprisingly good weather for Easter – one could walk all day and encounter no-one.

In summer, bathing was the objective, plus a few museums. We enjoyed three-week tours to Austria, Southern Spain, Brittany, Yugoslavia, the Loire Valley from the sea to Paris, a special stay in Rapallo, Italy, and several other itineraries. Our Dormobile conveyed us all, full of provisions, games and mattresses – and never a breakdown!

It would take too long to detail our adventures. I can only regret that time and age now preclude that option. Figure 9 best summarises us now.

CHAPTER XXI

Cambridge

———◆———

Soon after I joined the grammar school and for want of something to do during the lunch hour, I found it was possible to go into Manchester's Central Reference Library which was only five minutes' walk away from school, there to trawl the bookshelves for whatever science I was able to understand. I learned the names Jeans, Thomson, Darwin, Wells, the Huxleys and the Haldanes, Russell, Hogben and those of many other distinguished scientists. This practice continued in a casual way from age 12 to 16, until I started reading science seriously for HSC physics. I began to think my boyish dream was that I might get to become a research student at that premier institution, Cambridge. It was not unconnected to the fact that Manchester University had supplied Cambridge with many of its finest physical scientists – Thomson, Blackett, Bragg, Rutherford, etc.

My first visit to Cambridge was made in about 1941. There was a National Conference of Students about ... what? I cannot remember. But doubtlessly something political or social. Despite the cost, I must have gathered sufficient to cover rail fare, conference charges and enough for a small hotel for three or four days, and I went alone. I remember queuing outside the city council building on the edge of the market square, where the plenary meetings were held, and getting into conversation with a small group of young people from Bedford College. I recall walking on Trumpington Street and encountering J. D. Bernal accompanied by a small flock of young and seemingly adoring young ladies. I learned later that his research colleagues always referred to him by the name of Sage – wise, knowledgable. By this time I had heard him speak in Manchester, read his well-known book *The Social Function of Science*, and I knew a little of him as a crystallographer. In his book he was very dismissive of engineers and seemed not to recognise engineering science as a worthy study; he was, politically, quite left wing. However, the first sight of Kings College Chapel and Trinity, of Pembroke and Peterhouse and other colleges, rendered them unforgettable. It was comparable with Saul's transformation to (St) Paul on the road to Damascus! The contrast with Manchester too, was stark. And Cambridge then was not in all its glory but dull and half shut-down in that third year of the war. I went to some lectures in Mill Lane, then frequented by the mathematicians – a building inadequate for Cambridge's reputation. I recall listening there to a confident Cambridge under-graduate arguing with a military officer lecturer and deriding service in the forces. Nonetheless it all had a very profound effect on me, producing a feeling of reverence for that ancient centre of scholarship.

Apart from a short visit from Colchester where I spent several months in Army workshops, I cannot recall that I saw Cambridge again until the 1960s and 1970s, when several International Engineering Conferences were held there. I remember my young colleague, Geoffrey Needham, presenting our work (the first academic effort) on Ring Rolling, and Frank Travis describing our efforts in the Explosive Forming of Metals. I recall too, meeting there Professor Pericles Theocaris, from Greece, for the first time. By the end of the 1960s too I had had several papers on Extrusion and other metal forming processes published in Professor Rodney Hill's journal, *The Mechanics and Physics of Solids*, as well as in 'my' own *IJMS*.

I believe the only interaction I had with Cambridge before about 1970 was in the capacity of External Examiner for Ph.D. students, a function I had fulfilled twice. (I have already described the examining process, somewhat, at Sheffield University (see Ch. XVII p. 149). I hasten to add that in the course of a lifetime, I calculate I have examined more than one hundred of these – sometimes six or eight a year. On the first occasion from Cambridge, I received a large thesis, but, contrary to practice elsewhere, my first task was to write a report on it, making a recommendation, of Pass or Fail, of perhaps two or three pages. One is usually then called upon to make at least a day's journey to the department and there, spend, typically, three hours engaging in an oral examination of the student, with an *Internal* Examiner – a member of staff, but *not* the student's supervisor. (And for my part, I used to ask to be taken to see equipment in the lab., alone with the candidate.) It should not be forgotten, that an engineering science thesis of 250 pages requires about eight hours of reading; a second reading occurs around points at issue or requiring clarification and questioning. A last requirement was for a report on the Oral Examination. It will be clear that in total, some four days' work was involved, for which the fee would then be of the order of £60 or £70. Of course, if the recommendation was against passing the student, and requiring a re-submission, the time and effort would be even further extended.

I may interpose here, that for a long time, I entertained the notion that the American system or approach to Ph.D.s was better than the British. I always favoured a requirement of students to attend selected postgraduate courses relevant to their subject of research. It would be the case that the current research frontier and the papers related thereto, could be identified. This method suggests a uniform approach and treatment of a topic rather than the British system which leaves everything to the candidate, to be done on his own and to the degree he thinks fit. My view is that it is possible to help a candidate and to save time in acquiring somewhat more than an immediately relevant background. Perhaps it is that the American system is more economically geared, because it has to deal with larger numbers of students or postgraduate schools.

From participating as a member of examining Boards in the USA, I found it to be a weakness to have, say, half-a-dozen such persons gathered together. No one person seemed to me to feel himself to be responsible for the candidate. Most members of the examining committee, I thought, tended to believe that detailed examining was someone else's responsibility. The British system, with one External Examiner, ensures that the latter is totally responsible for all the facets of the process – he has to and cannot avoid difficult issues simply by keeping quiet.

At a much lower level, undergraduate projects always tend to give rise to problems. What is suitable for undergraduates and what for postgraduates is not always clearly identified. The importance attached to projects is of course different in different departments and they may count for much more in one circumstance than in another. The best projects I ever saw were those from the City University, London, but I was also left with the thought that too much was being asked for.

In about 1973, Professor Ted Parkes was appointed Vice Chancellor at the University of Leeds, which would leave his Cambridge Chair (Engineering Mechanics) vacant. I thought much about applying when applications for it were advertised but I decided not to pursue it. (In fact a very interesting appointment had been advertised by the Central Electricity Board concerning one of its big research laboratories and I was attracted by this too and therefore hesitant.) However, Professor Ken Johnson came up to UMIST, in order to deliver a lecture, and in the course of his visit he encouraged me to put myself forward as a candidate. I believe at this time that I also had conversations on the topic with persuasive Professors Andrew Scofield and Jacques Heyman. In the event, I duly submitted an application and was later invited to visit the Department and meet a few people – which I did – and which included Jacques Heyman taking me to a delightful lunch at Peterhouse. (I also paid a visit to the Department because a member of the Election Committee asserted he would not vote 'for a person he hadn't seen'!) Appointment or Selection Committees apparently met twice, usually on successive days – Friday afternoons and Saturday mornings – the second occasion aiming to confirm what had been decided on the first.) There was no interview but one Saturday morning, quite unexpectedly, I received a 'phone call from the Vice Chancellor, to say, briskly, that the Committee was prepared to appoint me and could I say, on the spot, that I was prepared to accept? As indeed I was. Later, after appointment, I saw an announcement pinned on an unassuming notice board outside the Vice Chancellor's college, Sidney Sussex, on half a sheet of notepaper. It announced that, 'Mr W. Johnson has been appointed Professor of Mechanics in the Engineering Department', *sans* title and degrees! I believe that strictly, the University only recognises, besides its own, the degrees of Oxford and Dublin!

At a simple ceremony, in January 1976, I was awarded an MA 'by incorporation' (that is, not as a graduate student). The occasion was almost mediaeval and contrasted sharply with what happened in a provincial university; yet it seemed appropriate to the circumstances. At my college I had joined a small band of students about to receive their degrees and walked with them, in academic dress, through the streets of Cambridge. In the Old Schools building, adjacent to the grounds of Kings College Chapel, I was presented to the Vice Chancellor by a Fellow of my College-to-be – Fitzwilliam. I knelt, with hands as if in prayer, and the VC covered them with hers. Graduated, I passed on to a cadaverous, black-cloaked figure who foraged in a large black chest and then handed me a scroll – the M.A., the historical certificate or licence to teach. All this took place in an atmosphere of serious simplicity, with Heather and Sarah watching from one of the balconies.

On the mechanical side of the Engineering Department at Cambridge,* Dr Ken Johnson was well known for his work on friction and contact stresses, and Professor Ted Parkes and his research student had worked, principally, in thermal stresses and dynamic plasticity. I knew little about the achievements in electrical engineering apart from Professor C. W. Oatley, whose work in developing the electron microscope was known world-wide. Research in civil engineering, was conspicuous and widely known – led by Professor (later Lord) J. F. Baker and at that time, ably supported by Professors Jacques Heyman, C. R. Calladine and also, earlier, Michael Horne; Professor Ffowcs Williams, now Master of Emmanuel College, enjoyed an outstanding reputation for his work in noise and vibration whilst Sir William Hawthorne was a previous Head of Department, and later, Master of Churchill College. At the time I joined the Department, Professor W. Austyn Mair (an authority in aerodynamics) was Head; he had been the Director of the Fluid Motion Labs at Manchester (1946–52). I learned there was only one salary level in 1975, for all the professors who were not HoDs. Thus, I took a reduction of some 15 per cent in my UMIST salary. (Today, there are many more professors about and I understand that their salaries increase according to the monetary support they bring in with their research programmes.) and compares, fascinatingly, with the picture of him in the writers article, see IJMS, 39, 1231, 1996.

Not a College Man?

At Cambridge, as opposed to Oxford, after appointment, a College Master writes and invites one to become a Fellow of his College. If one has been a student at one college it seems usual for newly appointed professors to be invited to return. The modern or most recently raised colleges tended to take the absolutely new members of the university, of which I was one. I was asked to dinner by the Master of Fitzwilliam College (meeting a college-fellow, the University Registrar, on the same occasion), for a pre-prandial sherry and invited to be a Fellow – which I promptly accepted, seeing that there was no offer from any of the older colleges. Edward Miller† was Master, a mediaeval historian, a former lecturer in Cambridge and then Professor of History at Sheffield University. (He has written an enjoyable volume,‡ *Portrait of a College: A History of the College of St John the Evangelist*, of which he was a Fellow.) The college room I was

---

* Much detail about the Department and the men who have served it, will be found in *Engineering at Cambridge University*, 1783–1965, by T. J. N. Hilken, CUP, 1967 – an excellent history of the department.
† He died in 2000.
‡ Pages 87/8 describe how I. Todhunter appeared to the mass of his college fellows, and compares, fascinatingly, with the picture of him in the writer's article, see IJMS, 39, 1231, 1996.

assigned, I shared with the only other professor, then, in the College (in the biological sciences and with Charles Darwin in the title of his Chair, I believe.) After he retired, I believe that, like him, I was then the sole professor left at the college. I met him once only while in Fitzwilliam when we exchanged a pleasantry at a Council meeting. The Fellowship was composed predominantly of young lecturers, i.e., a generation younger than me. The twice-a-week formal dinners I attended scrupulously in my first year but I did not, or was unable to, establish a close relationship with anyone. In subsequent years my attendances grew more and more infrequent. I tried attending lunches, but that too failed to improve relations, and anyway, the college was too far away from our Department at a half-hour's walk. I attended religiously the monthly Council Meetings but rapidly found I had little or nothing to contribute to them; they were, principally, about undergraduate arrangements. I found it surprising and interesting to note how, as in the departments of provincial universities, some of the older fellows were central to the running of their colleges but had little interest in the day-to-day research or scholarship work going on in their Departments; they are never greatly lauded by the outside world but their commitment inside was invaluable.

In my first year or two, professors were not required or even allowed to be tutors; that rule was changed but I neither became, nor wanted to be, a tutor. College business was of little interest to me and I can only recall two items worth remembering. One occurred when bequeathed money was offered to the College and promptly refused. There was no discussion and the Master was brief and downright in his rejection. The bequest was made from the will of the Indian, Chandra-Bose. The latter had been an ardent advocate of Indian nationalism and was associated with a sizeable army body of Indian POWs who joined the Japanese Army and fought against the British in Burma in the Second World War. Men from the College had been killed in Burma, fighting the Japanese. And the second event took place whilst I was at Fitzwilliam when the Master retired and a new one was sought; the situation reminded me of C. P. Snow's novel, *The Masters*. Alas, the processes of selection had no semblance of similarity to the ordered approaches described by Snow.

Fitzwilliam, alas, had relatively little history and – of much more interest to me – no great library of historical books, as had St John's and Trinity. Eventually, I was asked officially to improve my attendances, which I could not do, because in my last years in the University I had a weekly third-year class, late on Wednesday afternoons, which clashed with the council meetings. I suppose I had become too old and set in my ways for the system in which I found myself. My habits were formed in a different Institution. To most colleges, professors seemed functionally unimportant except as future Masters or as committee-chairmen. There is of course a great deal of difference between individual colleges; a few are very wealthy and some impecunious.

The *IJMS* published a technical paper on a subject in the Mechanics of Sport in which I was then actively engaged – the flight of a spinning cricket ball – by a Dr A. M. Binnie, FRS (Reader in Fluid Mechanics) and at the end of our correspondence in saying that my journal would publish his article, I added that

I had never been inside Trinity. He read the message and there upon invited me to dinner the following Sunday! I found that he had a suite of rooms on the first floor of a block lying along one side of the main court – it seemed to consist of a lounge, a workroom or study with many bookshelves, two bedrooms and other necessitous items. I arrived at his rooms half an hour before going to dinner and was served with a fine glass of sherry. After a pleasant exchange we ambled *across* the court (which was not allowed to ordinary pedestrians) en route to the dining room after the sound of a single bell, just in time to be able to attach ourselves to a small procession heading for the dining hall, on the walls of which was an intimidating array of portraits of distinguished scientists deriving from the College. I enjoyed a good dinner, taken with two glasses of wine. I learned that bachelor Dr Binnie had joined Trinity soon after the end of the Second World War, and thus his suite had been his home all the subsequent time. I was told that the college was responsible for all the meals of aged Fellows, so that some of the kitchens were at work during bank holidays when everywhere else was closed down. For all these advantages, at the time of his death, Dr Binnie left a bequest of almost one million pounds for the foundation of a College Hall.

A few colleges, such as St John's, Emmanuel and Gonville and Caius, invited all new professors to one of their feasts and particularly I remember, with great pleasure, the many-coursed dinners and good conversation. I think it was at Caius that the feast was arranged like undergraduate degrees, i.e. in two parts. About 10.30 p.m., when we had a 15-minute break, I went outside to meet my wife who had come to collect me, and explained that she should return at about 12.30, as I had only just passed Part I!

I think that I was generally disappointed with the inaccessibility of college libraries when I had need of them for historical materials. It always seemed very hard – and with reluctance on the librarian's part – to borrow books. This is of course a widespread phenomenon – I have tried to gain access to survey the books in the libraries of some of our stately homes – only to be refused. I have the notion, acquired over the years, that librarians are happiest when books are locked away and not loaned out. (Many of the old Halls of England have large and fine libraries. But they can seldom be touched without setting off alarm bells – as I know from personal experience!) It doesn't seem to matter if no-one ever sees or touches them, provided they are safe!

It was both infuriating and amusing to go over to Oxford to consult the great Bodleian Library, only to find myself in a queue being interviewed at ten minute intervals, by a black gowned Fellow conducting an interrogation for personal details and allowing nothing for the fact that I was a professor engaged in archival work at the sister university. I still had to swear an oath regarding conduct in the library and have my photograph taken.

I thought to try to start a Medical Engineering Club in Cambridge such as we had at Manchester for several years. The coming together of members of staff of all grades for lunches and in the Common Rooms in Manchester made for wider acquaintanceship with people across the university than that which seemed possible in Cambridge. I knew a few lecturers in College from almost every Department but not those necessarily who have influence enough to launch new projects. The latter would also likely require critical surveillance from Colleges as well as Departments and Councils. In UMIST, with the help of Lord Bowden, it was easy to enlist the interest of the Dean of the Medical Faculty and professors therein; but the task of doing the same thing in Cambridge seemed altogether too formidable.

We took up residence in Cambridge in a university block of flats for the first six months, commenced the search for a new dwelling but ended up buying a small modern terraced house in Chesterton. (We did inspect some larger houses being built on the edge of Midsummer Common and would probably have bought one had not a Fair arrived with all its paraphernalia and noise to repel us. We thought later on that we made an error of judgement for the Fair only came once a year!)

Each day, I walked to the Department from my new home and en route passed through Pembroke and Corpus Christi; my attention was always attracted by the order and beauty of their courts and I greatly regretted not being in such a college (which was one of my great disappointments in going to Cambridge). The feeling however that I had been unloaded of all the departmental responsibilities I had at UMIST was almost a physical sensation. It was a pleasure most days too, to have uncommitted afternoons when one could stay at home and work. It was indeed a great boon, especially when one had lived ten or twenty miles (by railway) outside the big industrial city of Manchester, which absorbed so much time and energy in travelling in or out of it each day.

Cambridge: other aspects

In the first half of the 1970s in quick succession, three UMIST professors went to Chairs in the Engineering Department in Cambridge. Andrew Schofield from Civil Engineering effectively returned whence he had come, to devote himself to Soil Mechanics; Alistair MacFarlane of Electrical Engineering went to lead a team in Automatic Control and allied topics. I, from Mechanical Engineering, the oldest and last to depart, went to a Chair in Mechanics. (Yes, the entire realm of mechanics!)

It was a semi-fortunate change for me at the time but I think an unqualified success from the beginning for the other two. I suffered from 'adaptation' difficulties for over two years but in my last years, I increasingly enjoyed my role and I separated at the end of seven years rather sadly.

All engineering is carried on in one Department at Cambridge; almost anywhere else the Department would be a Faculty. It is nearly all on one site and it possesses and is embedded in a legalistic structure not easy to change. Judged by A-level and Scholarship standards, it enjoys the best entry standards to engineering in the UK (and if this reflects reality, which is arguable, then such a quality of resource means that it is very important to deal with it carefully and well). The students are rewarded with expensive and very good undergraduate teaching. One educational columnist in an article in a quality daily newspaper recently, giving advice to would-be freshers, told them how teaching quality varied from university to university. (How he could know this he did not reveal.) According to him, Cambridge 'passed'. But as a teacher in several UK and North American universities, I know that Cambridge engineering teaching is second-to-none. Students are served by a truly dedicated staff. As for the quality of staff, it would be invidious for me to say anything but that the mass of appointments tends to be made from such staff – mainly in other universities – as are 'available'.

To the efforts of departmental teaching, there is the back-up of a College supervision system. I cannot speak of that in depth because I was, initially by statute, not allowed to supervise and later, when it was changed, I chose not to engage in it. Colleges select their own undergraduates, *not* the Department, and the latter as part of the University entity, is obliged to provide lectures and laboratories and to examine. I believe that Cambridge is not one entity in the sense that UMIST is: it is made up of many Venn-like intersecting circles having differing concerns.

Examination paper production is the outcome of an enormously tedious process and a Part II three-hour paper can easily require a week's work. It results in models of conspicuous clarity, their disadvantage being that they may lead students to expect that the real problems they will encounter in later life are always easily perceived and defined and amenable to tidy solutions!

At the senior academic level I believe that individual research thrusts there are always less easily developed, supported and encouraged than they are elsewhere. Direction can be much less clear than, say, at UMIST.

For various reasons I was deeply involved in helping to start a new Tripos – the Production Engineering Tripos – a four-year Dainton course in Manufacturing Science. Now that Cambridge (and Oxford) openly and officially embrace manufacturing at the undergraduate level (and the Cambridge course certainly is a very good one with most of the fourth year of 38 weeks spent in industry), the whole subject has become academically respectable. Such courses should have been available in the UK fifty years ago. (Though Cambridge was one of the few universities which did not then possess a Department of Management.) Had manufacturing received the attention it deserves from the higher echelons of the tertiary educational system two generations ago, perhaps the UK would be in less of a parlous state than it now finds itself. However, academic staff tend not to be the ones most perceptive of the need for change and innovation; responding to the need for new directions, in the UK, usually sits ill alongside tradition and academic attachment to time-honoured 'disciplines' and 'rigour'.

I visited the newly founded Robinson College in Cambridge a few weeks ago; it was built with a gift of £18 million. Also, at least three full-time College Fellowships were established by Ford, British Aerospace and Metal Box, for supporting the new manufacturing course. The bequest of a new laboratory worth about £1 million has recently been received by the Engineering Department. Many such wonderful 'tokens' of support find their way to the oldest universities. 'To those that hath' more is given. The wonder is that the marginally supported civic universities do so well in turning out the quality of student they do. It is astonishing that so many of those (individually and corporately) who are disadvantaged in early life, when the opportunity to distribute wealth comes their way, tend not to support their peer class but choose that which is already advantaged.

College life in a small, neat, picturesque market town is a gift to students of great value. The colleges and the name of the university confer life-long privileges and benefits; among many other things they 'open doors' and 'ring bells'. It is curious that grammar school élitism should have been expunged from secondary school education (for the lower classes – not for the public schools) and that no-one should have yet (fortunately?) suggested the same approach to the whole of tertiary education. But enough said on that score.

Cambridge's geographical situation is atypical of Britain as a whole – and certainly the industrial North; it is not reminiscent of industrial, working class Manchester! There in UMIST one cannot fail to encounter managers and engineers every day, engaged in productive industry. In Cambridge it is a rarity and then they are visitors; in UMIST companies are usually a few minutes' drive away. Technical association meetings too are plentiful, there few. In my day I felt that Cambridge was ideal for science, but not for intersection with the real everyday working world. Its psychological impact and influences on would-be engineers are worth reflecting on. (This has become less true in the past three decades.)

[From a Presidential Address in 1983, to the Manchester Technology Association.]

The Royal Society

In 1973 I was asked by a mathematician if I had been proposed for Fellowship of the Royal Society. In those days one had to be proposed, seconded and supported by four fellows. The proposer, incidentally, was asked to enquire of the candidate if 'he is prepared to pay the annual Society fee for membership': there was a lot of 'confidentiality' to election twenty years ago! The colleague who approached me may have had to find an engineer proposer because I was being put up through the Engineering Sectional Committee – in which case he himself would act as Seconder. The Proposer and Seconder would have needed to find at least four more supporters. It is no small task to undertake seeking supporters, so one is very grateful to the initiators of the process.

In the provincial universities or ones other than Oxbridge, Imperial College and University College, Fellows are rare and it is generally difficult to find enough 'names' to complete the four required after the proposer and seconder. All this was a totally unexpected accolade – even to be proposed – let alone elected. To this day I do not know for certainty the names of the other four. Thus I supposed that I was first considered in 1974 but I later deduced that it was, in fact, only in 1975. The Royal Society Annual list of candidates shows the names of the persons proposed, a short citation of about 200 words making the case for election, with a statement of degrees and current affiliation. Further names supporting the case may be added in succeeding years. About five hundred candidates are considered each year, forty being elected. Candidates stand for seven years, at the end of which time their names are removed from the list if not elected. As with many other persons proposed, I affected, at the beginning, not to set too much store by election, but to be pleased even to have got up to the starting-line. However, as the years passed by I seemed to become increasingly concerned; one looks at the list of successful candidates published each year and makes comparisons!

One large task which had to be accomplished by candidates was to send to the Society's librarian a complete list of books and papers as well as the items themselves, where they may be kept and consulted or read by members of the election committee.

For election purposes the Society recognises (or did) about ten 'Sections' of science, each one of which is charged with selecting four new fellows – in my case, the category of engineering science and metallurgy or materials science – and recommending them to Council for election. The committee chairman takes steps to determine or enquire how candidates are perceived, scientifically, by colleagues. (I write all this incidentally, without having been a member of one of these sectional committees.)

In due course not having been elected – after six years, beyond 1974 – in early autumn of 1981 I wrote to the Librarian in such disappointment that I asked him to return all the latter papers and books to me. It also so happened that in the late autumn of 1981, the university had circulated terms for the early retirement of professors, for which I would be eligible in 1982; university money was becoming 'tight'. I studied the financial details and having decided that my research life had come to an end I opted to retire. I thereupon submitted my resignation to the University in January 1982 and accepted their terms. I had had many invitations to visit overseas institutions to give lectures or for short term appointments and they would pleasantly occupy me for the next few years. And recognising my incompatibility with college life only reinforced my decision. However, in March 1982, on a Monday morning while I was discussing a matter with one of my research students, the telephone sounded and the voice of my seconder said, 'Congratulations Bill, your name is on the list of those elected'. I was of course astonished when he went on to express surprise that I did not know, since the information was three days old. Thus I owed him a great debt of gratitude for bringing about my election.

In December 1981 my wife had taken a curious telephone call from Dr D. G. Christopherson (recently deceased, then Master of Magdalen College and previously Professor of Mechanical Engineering at Leeds University and Vice-Chancellor of Durham University) for a list of my books and papers – which I acceded to without reflecting on why they were requested. I did not make any connection with the RS, supposing that matter to have been closed. I now believe that at the time either he must have been Chairman of the appropriate Sectional Committee or that my Proposer or Seconder was.

A letter came advising me of my good fortune on election and requesting me on one of two dates, 1 or 29 April, to visit the Society and sign its Charter Book of Signatures; I was also informed that I could bring visitors to witness the event. The 1st April seemed an inappropriate date to me and therefore I went to the simple ceremony at Carlton House Terrace on the 29th. A thoughtful feature on the latter date was for each new member to be welcomed by a member of the Society's permanent staff, whose task was to conduct one through the RS building explaining details of the Society's administration and facilities and being introduced to some of its administrators. However, *my* receptionist was the Librarian and on shaking hands with me he observed that I was perhaps the first Fellow ever to have been elected without a set of his papers being on the premises. I reflected on this for a moment or so and decided not to comment. In the afternoon, after we had been entertained to a happy lunch, the simple ceremony of induction was performed, it being witnessed by Heather and our two older sons and their wives. It was all a great about-turn in my fortunes! But I was then a retiring man who had burned his bridges.

Each year, I receive a handsome book of the biographies of Fellows who have died in recent years, usually written by current Fellows. Volume 46, published in November 2000, contains 614 pages and covers 33 Fellows, or about 20 pages per individual, plus a list of their published work.

After 'retiring' I spent many periods abroad and was not therefore available for becoming a member of a Section Committee. Thus I have seen little of the internal problems of selection which must occur. (And, incidentally, busily I wrote one third of all I have published after retirement!)

In reading the biographies of Fellows I was surprised to notice that fewer members of the RS hailed from the well-known public schools than I had expected, and this prompted me to make an analysis of their origins by reference to the schools as given in these annual biographical memoirs. It appears that each year about one half had a state grammar school education, one sixth came from the lesser public schools and a third were foreign Fellows.

(Another curious triviality seen in the Society's Charter Book relates to the signatures themselves. Almost all in the eighteenth and nineteenth centuries until the First World War are written in an inclined hand and thereafter change to the upright form. Why the change?)

CHAPTER XXII

Some Research Activities

━━━━◆━━━━

I THOUGHT THAT I SHOULD TRY to give some idea of the subjects I have worked on primarily for the non-technical reader. This is not straightforward, since a lot of mathematics often lies behind each investigation. I have had to content myself by describing what I have been involved in, using photographs and figures from books and papers published in conjunction with colleagues. (In looking back through the researches I have been engaged in, I find I can recall the writing of earlier ones better than I can the later ones. This I assume reflects the loss of short term memory with age! It is also an astonishing fact that of the actual writing of books I now recall almost nothing.)

During my time at Sheffield and Manchester, my research work was narrowly confined to the metal-forming processes of extrusion, compression and cutting with wedge-shaped tools such as pliers. Simple experimentation was backed up by traditional plasticity theory, slip line fields and upper-bound solutions. (I shall not elaborate here on the latter two subjects.) Appointed to the Chair in UMIST, I continued along the same lines but determined I should address myself to problems of a more immediate industrial nature. This was possible too, because several Ph.D. students became available.

Plasticity in Extrusion

My first research work was in the plasticity of metals. Most of us observe how, having lightly pulled a spring that on removing the actuating force, the spring recovers its initial shape or form: this is referred to as *elastic* behaviour. If a large force is applied and removed, the extension enforced may well not be recovered: there is a *permanent* change in form or length which is referred to as plasticity and the latter succeeds the former.

In industry, many operations are performed to permanently change the shape of blocks of metal to some other required useful shape or size by extrusion. Figure 1. shows a diagram of a set-up to change a short cylindrical block (or slug) of metal to one longer but of smaller diameter. Applying sufficient force to a punch causes a thinner cylindrical solid to be *extruded*. The investigator may wish to be able to calculate the force that must be applied to make a slug of a certain metal and dimensions, in the given circumstances, achieve the new shape desired;

Figure 1.   *Figure 2.*   *Figure 3*

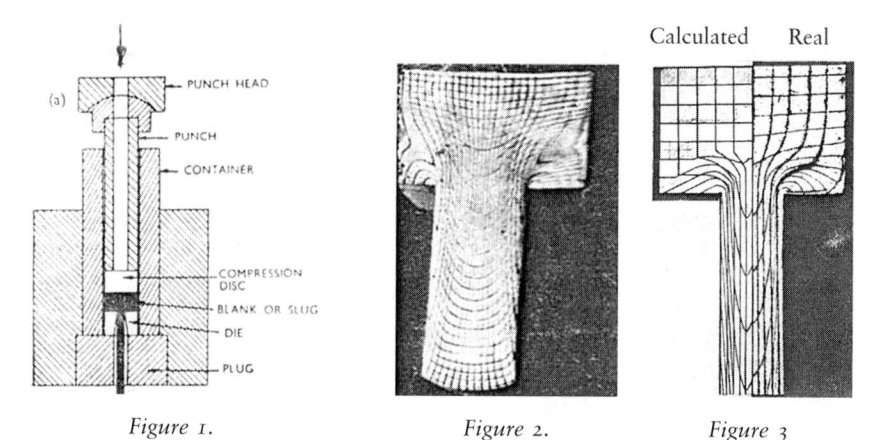

he tries to find a 'formula', based on slug dimensions, the kind of metal and certain laws governing plastic behaviour. He may also need to know how the metal flows inside the slug in going from one shape to another, e.g. in changing from a given width to one which is smaller, see Figure 2. (Friction between tools and the moving slug may become an important factor in shaping operations.) This internal flow of metal may be shown up by first stamping a square net of lines down the centre plane of a slug split (on a diametrical plane) before extruding. In Figure 3 a real and a calculated internal deformation are compared. In Figure 4 an example is given of three same-diameter 'wires' being extruded; the holes are centred on one diameter. Their length may change according to the hole *positions* and the friction present, that is whether it be smooth (a) or rough (b).

Figure 5 refers to extruding one, two or three sheets from one slug; the *total* thickness of the extrusion in each of the three cases is the same.

In Figure 6 two thick sheets are obtained from one block and the internal flow is made evident. Figures 7 and 8 show the effect of displacing an exit orifice away from the central position – extruded sheets emerge oblique or in rotation; Plasticene is extruded here simply to help study various circumstances of flow.*

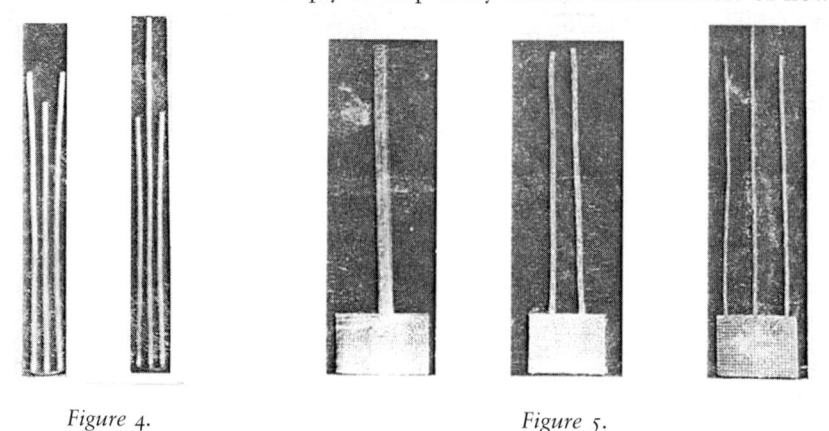

Figure 4.   *Figure 5.*

---

* Research for circular geometries continues to be done by Dr N.Chitkara.

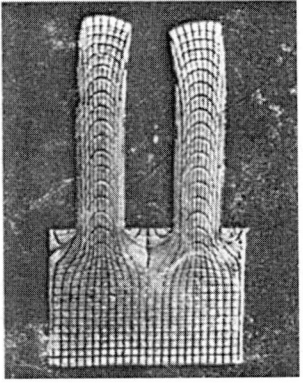

SOME RESEARCH ACTIVITIES 243

Figure 6. 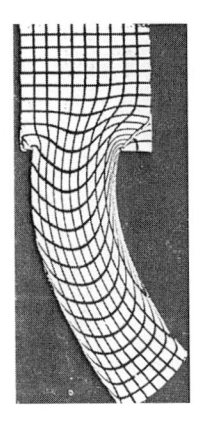   *Figure 7.* 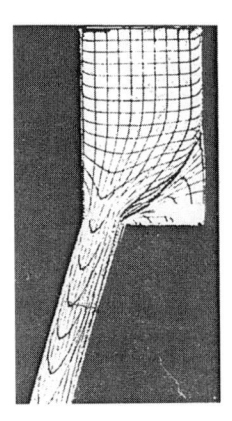   *Figure 8.*

Plastic hinges

When a mild steel cantilever is end-loaded thin black lines are developed in it and show a kind of plastic 'hinge', see Figure 9. A ring loaded by forces at the ends of a vertical diameter, forms four hinges of two different kinds; examine the quarter points carefully in Figure 10. The black plastic zones are brought out using an etching technique.

Figure 9. 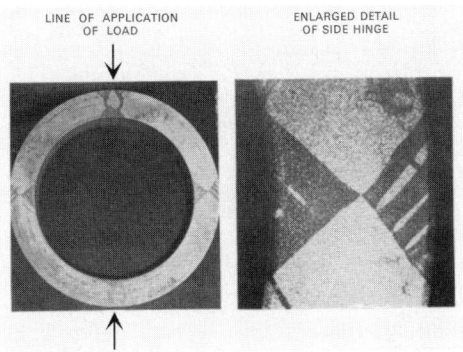   *Figure 10. Diametral compression by a point load.*

New Kinds of Machine

We later expanded our work with the study of three kinds of new machines:
  (1) The Linear Induction Motor.
  (2) Ring Rolling Machines.
  (3) Rotary Forging Machines.

First, some facts surrounding the mechanism of moving large masses (as with electric trains) using a Linear Induction Motor (LIM) – a technique to which Professor Eric Laithwaite was to devote much of his life. We see here too one aspect of the difficulty there always was in getting a new device 'off the ground' from university circumstances and into manufacturing industry and everyday usage.

1. Early Research in Linear Induction Motors for Manufacturing Machinery*

Introduction

The recent article on 'The Tracked Hovercraft Project' in the Newcomen Society's *Transactions*, Vol. 65 (1993–4),[1] about early work on the LIM at UMIST in the early 1960s, drew the attention of the writer and stimulated him to set down his own experience in relation to the article. For the historical record it is important to describe one early development and field of application of the LIM albeit with some emendations to the aforementioned article and also in respect of UMIST and Professor E. R. Laithwaite.

Where the name of UMIST appears in ref.1, it was in the early 1960s, The Manchester College of Science and Technology (MCST) and officially it became UMIST only in 1966.

Initially, the MCST Linear Induction Motor research team included, principally, myself, Dr Eric Laithwaite and (later Dr) R. A. C. Slater. I was Head of the Department of Mechanical Engineering at MCST and Director, Dr Laithwaite acted as an unpaid consultant and R. A. C. Slater, a new research investigator. Nearly all our work is reported, essentially, in five papers and two British Iron and Steel Association Reports (BISRA).[2–7] The late Dr R. A. C. Slater conducted all our experimental investigations, first for his Master's degree and subsequently for his Doctorate.

Our first three-author report to BISRA appeared in 1962 as ref.2(a) and was converted to ref.2(b) appearing in *Sheet Metal Industries*, in April 1963, under the title, 'An Appraisal of the Linear Induction Motor Concept for High-Energy-Rate Metal Forming'. My own research in those days was in the field of metal working plasticity and received about £1,500 per year support from BISRA, which included £400 per year to support Dr Slater. To understand the origin of our work it is necessary to know that I moved in August 1960, from the Department of Engineering in the Faculty of Science, Owens College (which is physically located in the main body of Manchester University) to the Department of Mechanical Engineering in MCST, which constitutes the Faculty of Technology in the University. (The existence of two distinct Engineering Departments in the one university has always been a source of much confusion.) Of course, at this time there were also two quite separate departments of Electrical Engineering, the one in the Faculty of Science being directed by the late Professor F. C. Williams, FRS.

---

* Early Research in LIMs for Manufacturing Machinery, The Newcomen Society, Vol. 66, pp. 215–218, 1994–95, by W. Johnson.

IMPACT BLANKING TOOL | LINEAR INDUCTION MOTOR

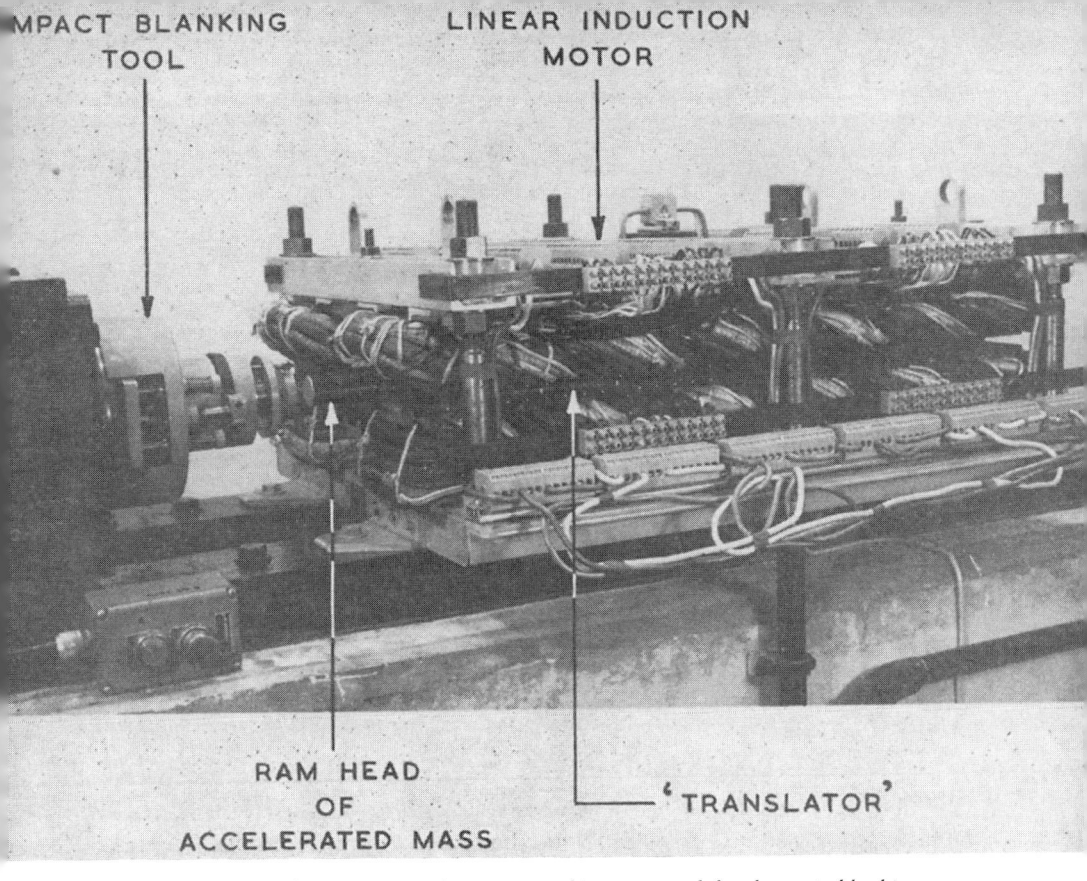

RAM HEAD OF ACCELERATED MASS | 'TRANSLATOR'

Figure 11. The experimental impact machine arranged for dymanic blanking.

The latter's principal research work (with Professor Tom Kilburn, FRS) was in the building of computers; the 1950s had been the days of electronic valves before the development of the 'chip'. However, in the late 1950s Professor Williams, Dr Laithwaite and their collaborators also became engaged in the development of Spherical Induction Motors (*Proc. I.E.E.*, 1959) and Brushless Variable Speed Induction Motors (*Proc. I.E.E.*, 1957). Nikola Tesla (1856–1945) first had the idea for an induction motor in 1887 when at the Technical University of Graz, Austria. Separately, to my knowledge, Dr Laithwaite had produced papers on LIMs in *Proc. I.E.E.*, for 1957 and 1960, from the Owens College Department.

At no time was Professor Laithwaite ever a member of the MCST, or at UMIST as shown in ref.1. As well as in *Proc. I.Mech.E.*, ref.4, in 1964/5, Professor Laithwaite is clearly noted as 'lately Senior Lecturer ... Owens College, Manchester'.

LIM: Origin of Manufacturing Interest

In 1962, LIMs were 'in the air' of engineering and it was then that I thought to use an opportunity to investigate and develop them for the field of metal forming, possibly as a new form of high speed press. My aims at the time were two-fold and are stated clearly in refs. 2 and 4; they were:

(i) to learn how to design LIMs and to describe the electrical principles for their employment by mechanical engineers;

(ii) to obtain experimental data about the feasibility and limitations of high speed metal working in such processes as extrusion and blanking.

High energy Rate Forming* processes in the 1960s were much publicised, notoriously drawing attention to themselves especially in the shaping of plate of large area. Under-water high explosives were detonated to constructively deform flat plate into large dies to form, for example, submersible pressure vessel ends. As well, the same explosive phenomena were studied using underwater high voltage electrical discharges in these years.

My early aim was to examine the possibility of quickly executing repeatedly some new forming processes for the purpose of achieving cheaper production at the same time as securing certain new features in the items produced.

Dr Laithwaite attended our first planning meeting along with some BISRA representatives, one consequence being, in brief, that Mr Slater as he then was, would spend several weeks in the Owens College laboratories learning practically of the intricacies and building of electrical machines. Personally, I believe that I did not again meet Dr Laithwaite, though three articles on LIMs were published by us and Mr Slater.

First experimental results

Our first significant paper was a long one describing our first experiences in building and experimenting with the machine fully described in ref.4. The LIM we had designed and built was a two-sided stator system of constant pole pitch. The latter consisted of two wings which operated in the stator gap, both being fastened to a hammer head. This rotor in a distance of two feet could be accelerated to nearly 50 ft/s, its total weight being nearly 22 lb. The hammer impinged symmetrically upon a punch or ram which forced a steel pad to press a small lead slug through a die and thus secure an extrusion of given reduction in area; the amount of reduction secured was, of course, a function of the input kinetic energy. Extruded lead rod though produced by an essentially compressive process, was yet frequently found to be fractured or showed regions of deformation in certain locations; this was due to stress wave propagation and reflection and typified an adverse consequence of *impact* forming. Among other things, the results of our tests showed that a much larger machine would be needed to secure the extrusion of any product of significant industrial value.

Our overall process efficiency was only about 2 per cent – that is to say but 2 per cent of the electrical energy put into the device for securing metal deformation really did so, the remainder simply heated the slug and the machine! However, we *had* built a system and secured the required deformation.

Certain useful electrical design calculations were made in 1963 and 1965 and these are described in refs. 3 and 5; Dr Laithwaite was a co-author of the former of these papers.

---

* See pp. 253–56 below.

An improved machine

Our sixth paper, on work by myself and Slater, was produced in mid-1964, Dr Laithwaite having by then taken up his Chair at Imperial College. It describes our building of a *variable* pole pitch machine (see Figure 11). It was a common sense expectation that this should be more efficient than the uniform pole pitch machine and so it turned out. At the very best it now achieved an efficiency of 6 per cent. We also took the opportunity to investigate the high speed blanking of 1 and 2 in. diameter circular metal discs. This process required far less energy than did the extrusions we performed previously so that the machine worked at an appropriate energy level, well within its capacity.

Our seventh and final paper which followed in 1966 was predominantly devoted to comparing the energy required to blank rapidly as against that required for quasi-static production; the edge quality of the product formed by the fast blanking process with an LIM was much improved though there could be an unwanted 'doming' of the actual discs blanked out.

The next machine

It was realised that for many practical manufacturing operations, much more energy would be required to be available than that provided by the first machine and indeed the second improved one. Accordingly, plans were drawn up and after we had submitted an outline to SERC,* £10,000 was awarded for research into a machine capable of delivering 10,000 ft/lb of work as against 1000 by our earlier ones. (We were also grateful to ICI for the donation of a sum of money for purchasing a very useful transformer.) Besides providing for an increase in energy of one decade the new machine would also be double-acting, i.e. employ a double-headed rotor-hammer for forming specimens at either end of the stator, running continuously and therefore probably needing to be force convection cooled. Our belief too, was that the newly designed system would prove to be cheap to manufacture, because so much of it consisted simply of metal stampings – as opposed to the high quality machining usually required in conventional presses.

At this stage I invited Metropolitan Vickers Ltd, an electrical machines producing company of international standing in neighbouring Trafford Park, Manchester to see a display of our two early machines, and to make any comments they wished concerning our new proposal. It was only after many efforts that the company was induced to send two representatives but, in truth, when they visited us it was evident that they had no interest in our endeavour. Around this period the company in fact changed hands and parts of it were relocated.

The end

In 1966/7 Dr Slater took up an appointment as Senior Lecturer in the Mechanical Engineering Department at Salford University and as we were unable to find a

---

* Science and Engineering Research Council.

successor to him, with his kind of maturity and enthusiasm, the UMIST LIM project was discontinued and the grant not taken up.

In the following few years I read of LIMs being developed for several new purposes such as a dynamic rope-testing device and as an overhead gantry. Dr Slater and I liked to think that our work encouraged the production of such new devices as these and found it hard to believe that some real quantity of machine innovation could not have been achieved.

Dr R. A. C. Slater

No obituary notice about Dr R. A. C. Slater was published at the time of his death in 1990. It therefore seems opportune to present here the following brief account of his life in the context of one of his major research investigations, the LIM. His sudden death after retirement was long unknown and he received no proper public appreciation.

Robert Arthur Charles Slater (1920–1990), was London born and schooled, entering the engineering profession at sixteen and gaining the old Higher National Certificate in 1939. On joining the Army in the same year at the outbreak of war, he soon found himself an Electrical and Mechanical Engineer in the region of Palestine and later engaged as a Light Aid Detachment Commander, in tank recovery maintenance and repair with the 8th Army in North Africa and later still in Italy. He served for six years, was mentioned in despatches and demobilised in 1945 having achieved the rank of Major. For several years after demobilisation he was a lecturer in mechanical engineering at the Borough Polytechnic, London. Accepted as an Associate Member of the I.Mech.E. he joined the MCST in 1961, being registered as a candidate for the Master's degree. Dr Slater was assigned to research into the potentiality of the LIM as a high speed metal forming tool, the results of which have been outlined above. A mature student, he appeared to be well capable of coping with what was a difficult task. Rapid promotion to a lectureship at MCST, with special responsibility for part-time students in 1963, enabled him to continue research for a doctorate after gaining his master's degree, by developing a variable pole pitch machine and using it to explore the mechanics of high speed blanking at room and high temperatures in several different metals. Having earned his Ph.D. in a difficult field, Slater then turned his attention to developing a Rotary Forging Press, to a degree in conjunction with S. & J. Massey Ltd. Subsequently he obtained an appointment as senior lecturer at Salford University where his own first research student was Ernest Appleton, presently Professor in the University of Durham. Later he joined the new City University, London and there significantly developed the Rotary Forging Press* in conjunction with industrial sponsors. Thereafter he was soon promoted to a Readership. In 1973 he also achieved his life's ambition of publishing a well-received textbook for senior undergraduate and postgraduate students entitled *The Theory of Plasticity*. Dr Slater retired 30 September 1980 and died 16 February 1990.

The quality of Slater's work was well recognised by the award to us of the

---

* See p. 251.

T. Bernard Hall Prize of 1965 for the improved LIM and its associated investigations in blanking.[6]

Dr Slater was a modest, enormously hard-working bachelor, well liked and totally reliable in all that he was called upon to do. Given the time available to him his contributions to engineering academia were outstanding.

References

1. M. R. Bailey 'The Tracked Hovercraft Project', *Trans. Newcomen Society*, Vol. 65 (1993–94), pp. 129–145.
2. R. A. C. Slater, W. Johnson and E. R. Laithwaite 'An Appraisal of the Linear Induction Motor Concept for High-Energy-Rate Metal forming', a) BISRA Report, MG/G/13/62; b) *Sheet Metal Industries*, April 1963, pp. 237–243.
3. R. A. C. Slater, W. Johnson and E. R. Laithwaite 'An Experimental Investigation Relating to the Accelerated Motion of Various 'Translators' in the Air Gap of a LIM', BISRA Report MG/G/55/62; *Int. J. Mach. Tool Des. Res.*, Vol. 3 (1963), pp. 111–135.
4. W. Johnson, E. R. Laithwaite and R. A. C. Slater, 'An Experimental Impact-Extrusion Machine Driven by a 'Linear Induction Motor', *Proc. Instn. Mech. Engrs.*, Vol. 179 (1964/5), Pt. 1, No. 1, pp. 15–36.
5. R. A. C. Slater and W. Johnson 'Some Considerations Relevant to the Design of a High Rate of Energy Transfer Machine Employing a LIM', *Proc. 5th Inter. Machine Tool Design and Research Conf.* (1965), pp. 267–293.
6. W. Johnson and R. A. C. Slater, 'A Comparison of the Energy Required for Slow Speed and Dynamic Blanking Using an Improved Linear Motor', *Proc. Instn. Mech. Engrs.*, Vol. 179 (1964/5), Pt. 1, No. 7, pp. 257–263.
7. W. Johnson and R. A. C. Slater, 'Further Experiments in Quasi-Static and Dynamic Blanking of Circular Discs from Various Materials', *Proc. Instn. Mech. Engrs, 180*, Part 31, Pa 5, Appl. Mech. Conv. 1965–66: 19 pp. Figs. 1–8

2. *Ring Rolling*

Figure 12 shows a method of manufacturing rings or wheels of large diameter or differently shaped cross-sections. An initially thick ring is at once steadily compressed and rotated between a Driven Roll and a Pressure Roll; as the ring is thinned in compression, its roll diameter is increased.

Because of an invitation from Mr John Ellis to visit the firm of which he was Chief Engineer, located in Trafford Park, I became interested in ring-rolling. It was impressive to see a hot 'cheese' of steel about one foot diameter have its centre pressed out, be threaded into a ring-rolling mill and then rotated, squeezed and expanded to form a ring of perhaps 6 ft. diameter, the ring heating up to orange-red brightness as it was plastically worked. Large railway wheel tyres were hot-formed in this way. Mr Ellis complained that virtually nothing scientific was known and recorded about the process, i.e. concerning the magnitudes of the forces and torques on the rolls, so that he never knew quite what size of motor or power was needed to energise his equipment. Accordingly, Dr Geoffrey Needham (later Head of Mechanical Engineering at Newcastle Polytechnic) made

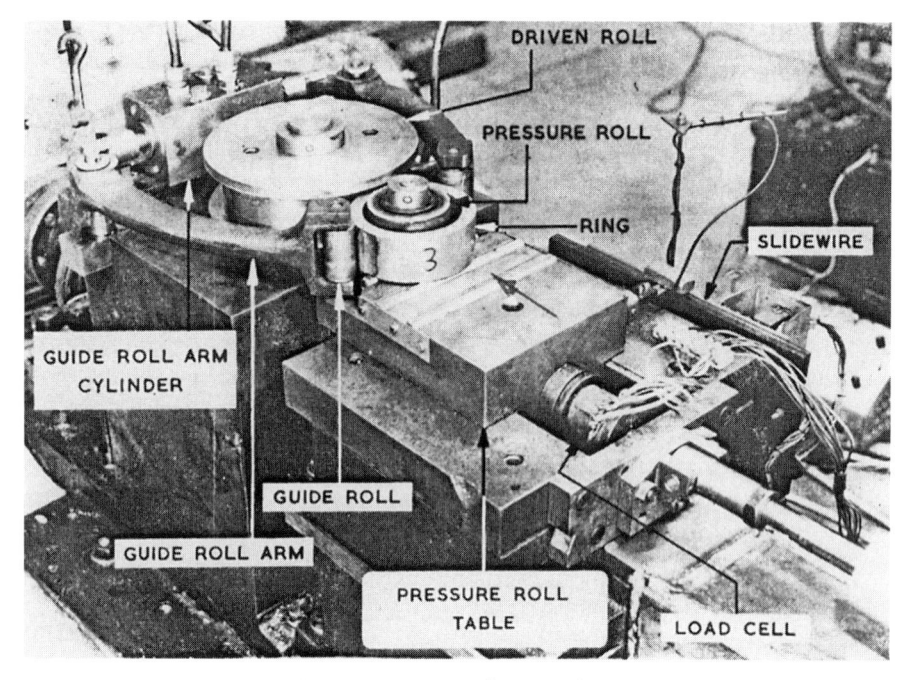

Figure 12. Ring Rolling Machine.

the first academic investigation of this process, in about 1967. Later the work was carried on by Dr John Hawkyard (then Reader in the MED, UMIST) and A. G. Mamalis (now Professor at the Athens Polytechnic). Interest in this and related work took me to Greece in December 1978, to lecture first at the Greek Institution of Mechanical Engineers in Athens and second in Salonika at the Hellenic Steel Company (Japanese owned).

How long did the ring rolling with which I started last? Through NRDC* I was involved with a small group of enterprising young men who developed machines for *cold* rolling small ball-bearing races. After successfully setting up their own company (their metal-shaping replaced and was cheaper than a metal machining or cutting process for a while) they were bought out and it was, I understand, closed down! In respect of *hot* ring-rolling, we had visits from a few groups of Germans to see our work. After some time a programme backed by German companies was set up. Later in Aachen T.H.,† I saw a fine, large investigation in progress; it was backed with DM 5,000,000! Dr Hawkyard later developed a machine for the sound precision ring-rolling of bicycle wheels for an interested British company.

---

* National Research and Development Council
† Technische Hochschule

3. *The Principle of the Rotary Forging Machine*

In Figure 13 the large spinning conical angle die makes contact with a workpiece top which is compressed but only a sector at a time. The die rotates about its own axis while simultaneously revolving about the vertical axis. Not every sector is spread at the same time, but it is sector by sector.

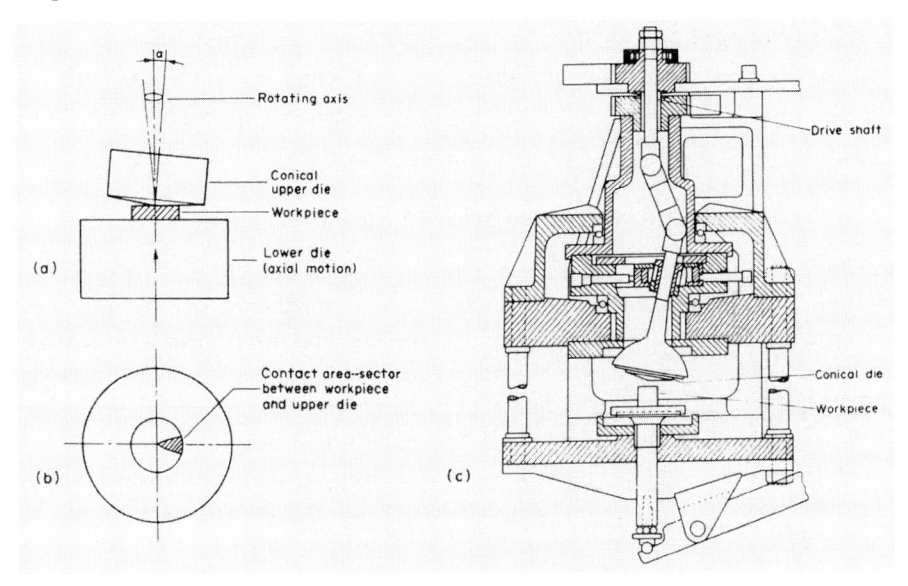

Figure 13 (a), (b) and (c). Princples of rotary forging.

Figure 13 (d). Rotary Forging Machine.

Using Explosives

Shaping or reshaping metals by using chemical explosives is only one method of many which can be used. We also employed water waves (water hammer), magnetic discharges or pulses, exploding gases and electrical discharges* etc. As a class all these techniques constituted High Energy Rate Forming (HERF) and all had some detail which recommended them.

One consequence of our HERF work was for it to lead to a general interest in Impact Engineering: on the one hand, looking into its destructive aspects – and therefore being neighbour to military research – and on the other, to studying constructive ends, such as the mitigation of damage due to impact in vehicles and structures or for helping in the construction of metallic articles.

Simple Explosive Waves Causing Fracture

In Figure 14 (a) on the extreme left, we see one straight thin bar of Perspex and to the right of it, several curved bars of lesser radii. A small explosive charge, when detonated at the top end of a bar, leaves a 'ragged' tip but, surprisingly, a clean break or fracture plane just visible at the other end. The lengths of the latter pieces in specimens (a) to (j) are all about the same. A compressive wave is sent along the bar by the explosion, but on reaching the distant end it is returned, as a wave of tension which can grow to be large enough to effect a clean break; in fact at the bottom, tips, called spalls, are 'blown off' at speed. It is evident that despite curvature, all the bars involve the same 'mechanisms', at least until the radius of a curved bar is relatively acute or sharp. The same applies in the other two top sets of bars.

With thick plates, see Figure 14 (b), an explosive detonated in contact with the bottom faces causes a smooth depression. However the other or opposite free face shows a tendency to be 'blown off' and to leave a jagged surface, or a crack. Figure 15 shows structural surfaces where there has been an explosion on the

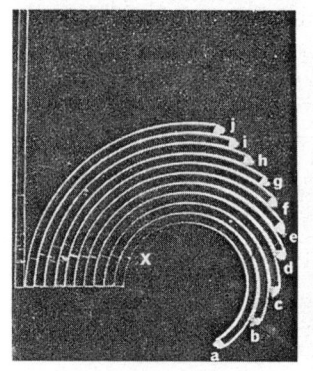

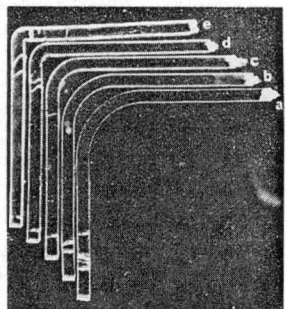

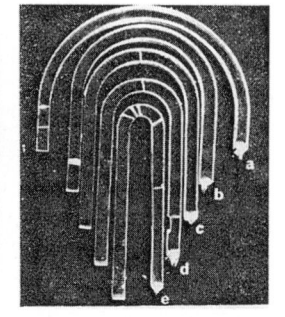

Figure 14 (a). In the left-hand picture X marks the fracture line.

---

* As Prof. D. Williams showed in compacting powders and happens naturally when lightning forms fulgerites.

unseen, far side, whilst the near side shows brick and concrete structural surfaces, clearly damaged and flung off.

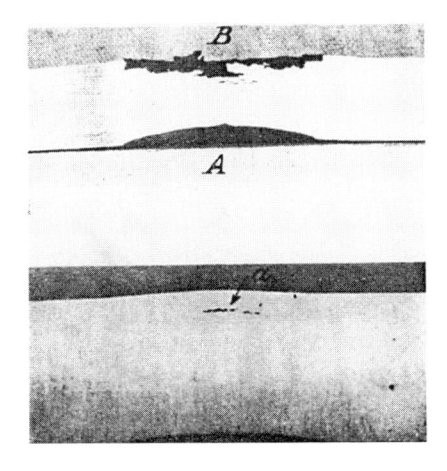

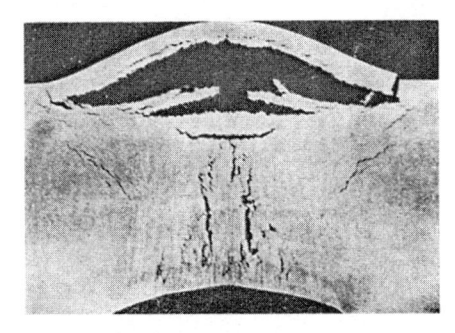

Figure 14 (b).

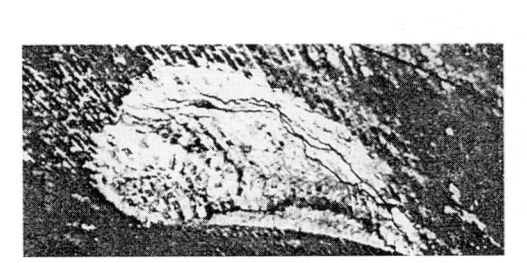

Figure 15.

Constructive Explosive Forming

In the middle of Figure 16, no.2 is a tube about 2m long, 26cm original outer diameter and 2.6cm thick. It was required to show that this tube could have its diameter increased by 30% acceptably, using explosives. The system for doing this will be clear from Figure 17. Lines of explosive, Cordtex, were stretched along the tube axis. With the ends of the tube covered by wooden plugs the tube was filled with water. After detonating the Cordtex, the wall of the tube was almost uniformly increased in diameter. The tube radial speed was about 130 m/s at the beginning of expansion. The tube No.2 was expanded to what is shown in No.1 and No.3 in Figure 16.

Explosive forming using a point charge in a tank of water as in Figure 18, can be used to form plates or dishes as will be evident in Figure 19; plate, of about 1″ thickness and about 15ft diameter has been formed for the dished ends of tanks. It will be obvious that there are many complexities in these processes. However, these methods – *without machinery* – are very cheap to perform.

Figure 16.

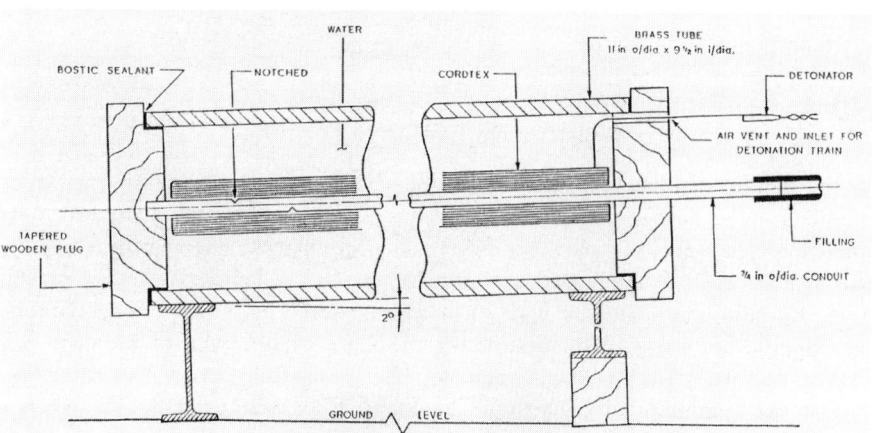

Figure 17. The set-up used to expand cylindrical tubes.

There are several methods of achieving high speed metal forming processes, such as using exploding gas, high explosives for plate welding and certain sophisticated electrical and magnetic techniques.

SOME RESEARCH ACTIVITIES 255

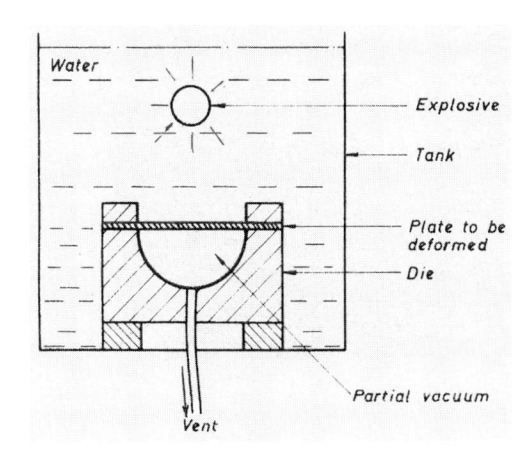

Figure 18. Set-up used to dish plate.

Figure 19. A dished pressure vessel end about 4 ft in diameter.

As intimated earlier, it is not possible to delve into details about the mass of items mentioned here. However, I may add that interest in these fields of work drew little or no interest from British industry. Japan, Germany and the USA, evidently followed our published research, and indeed I began to think it was all being done for the benefit of the latter three countries.

Explosives can be used for accurately fracturing ingots and the like (see Figure 20). I must add that Prof. Frank Travis was responsible for all our explosive forming work.

Figure 20.

ROD IMPACT AND PENETRATION: PHENOMENOLOGY

In Figure 21, note at the top 1–4: parts of the gun; 5 is the target plate.

The Figures show (in section) how flat-ended solid cylinders fired at high speed at right angles into relatively thick plate are deformed. Both plate and cylinders

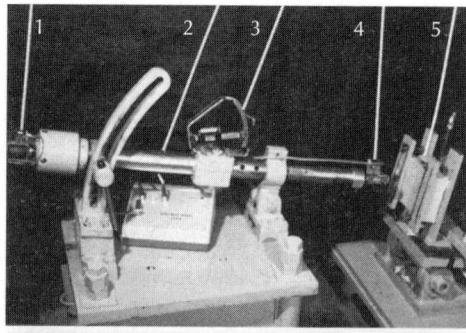

Figure 21.

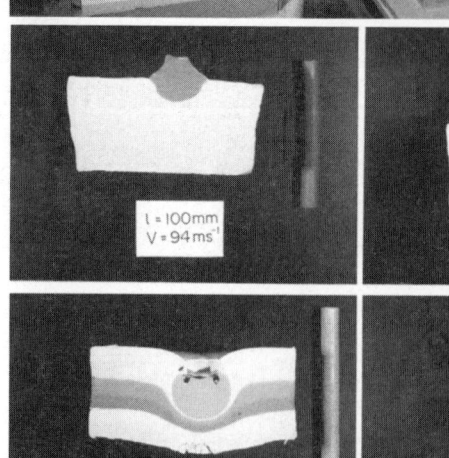

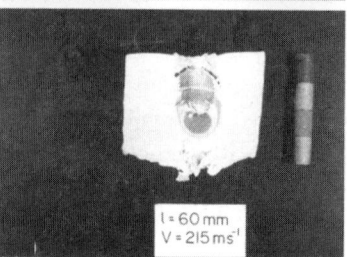

are of the same Plasticene (or modelling clay); this material is used to simulate the deformational behaviour of metal missiles and plates of the same strength. Different forms in penetration and perforation are encountered, as shown in Figure 22. With metal, speeds of about 1000 m/sec are employed, but only about 100 m/sec using clay. Different coloured clays are used to show the details of internal deformation. A simple stud-firing gun suffices to shoot the clay projectiles into the clay mass.

Note that the volume of the craters is many times larger than that of the impinging cylindrical projectile. (This applies to craters made by micro-meteorites.) Note that the top of the projectile is at the bottom of the crater – it is literally turned inside out during the impact process. See Figure 23.

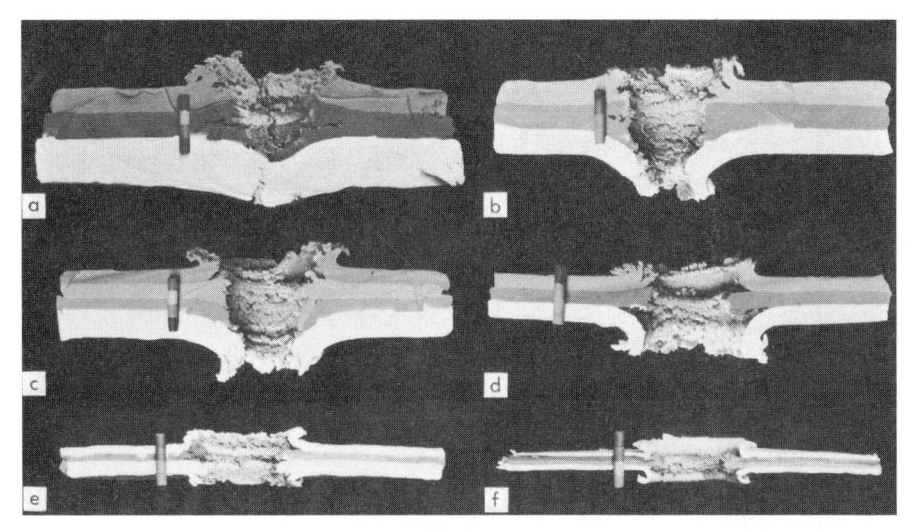

Figure 22. The initial speed of the plate-entering rods is about 500m/sec; the shape of a hole is characteristic of the high speed.

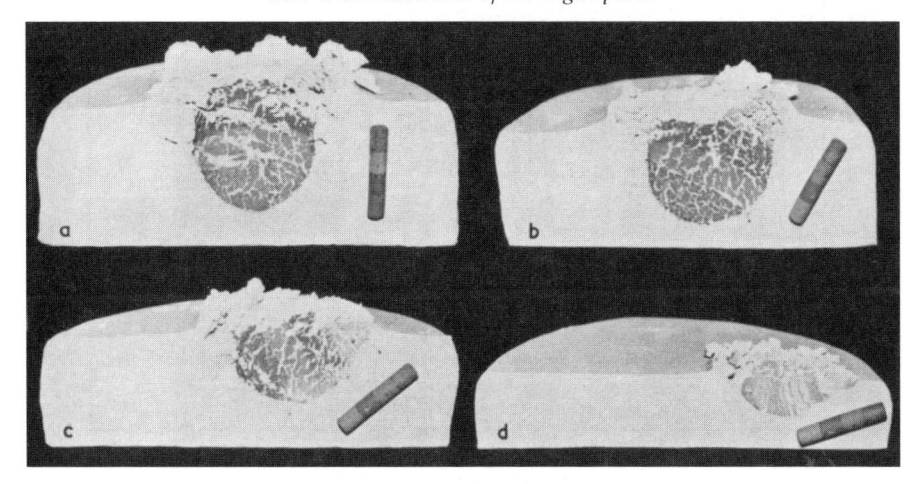

Figure 23. Showing the effects of obliquity by using a penetrating missile.

A charge exploded in a large block of Plasticene forms an egg-shaped cavity (a camouflet), see the bottom of Figure 24. The nearer the surface (the charge being kept to the same amount), it is, the greater the tendency for the surface to be broken. Such cavities are much studied and formed in 'rock' using nuclear bombs. (And then used as test chambers for such.)

The study of Impact Engineering needs more exposure in our undergraduate and postgraduate schools. One conspicuous value of Impact Engineering flows from the spectrum of energy levels engaged in impact processes. At one end of the range there is the subject of elastic stress waves and near the other end, hypervelocity impact. It is astonishing how deficient is the teaching of these topics in the mass of books and courses in Strength of Materials.

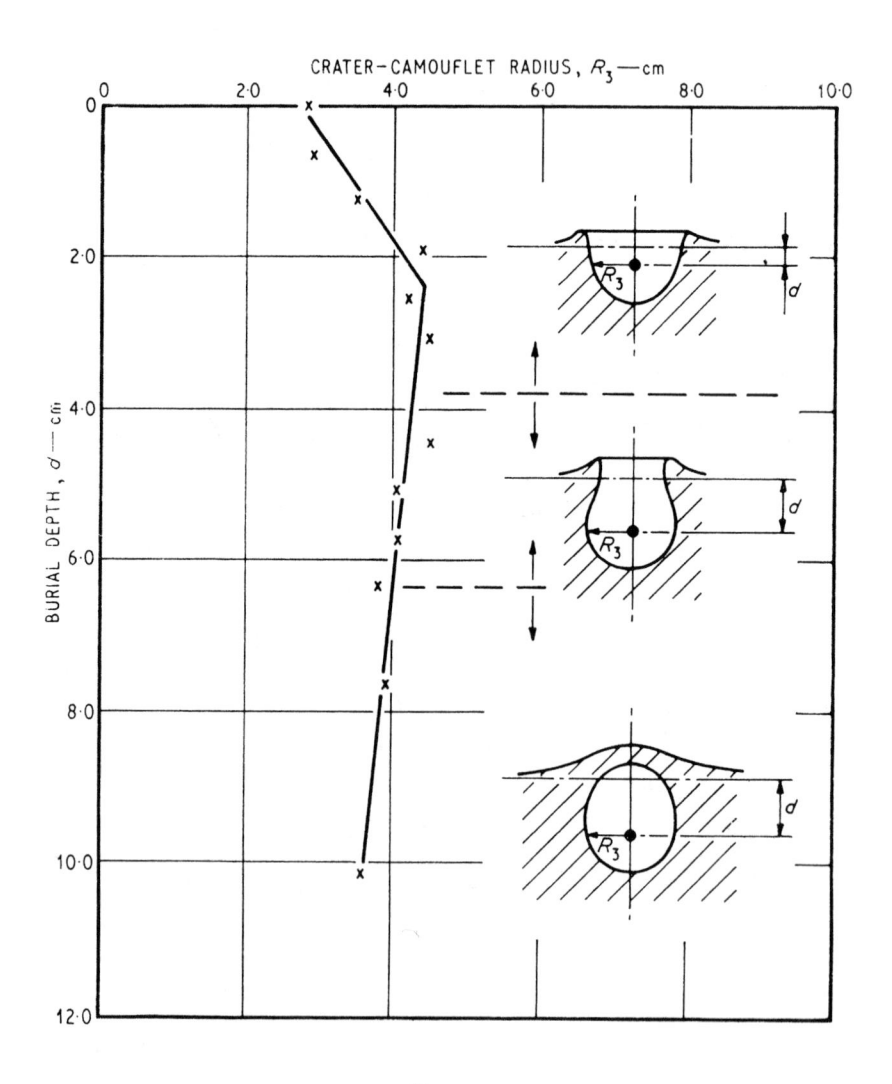

Figure 24.

Ricochet

Colleagues (principally Professor S. R. Reid, research students and visitors and I) co-operated in writing a number of papers about the ricochet of spherical shot, from water, sand and soil. *Bouncing is due to projectile compression and reassertion, but in ricochet the projectile undergoes no significant change of shape*; as it progresses over a flat surface, liquid or solid; it generates a kind of furrow by which 'lift' is generated; material is pushed up around the front of the projectile and flattened behind it; the maximum angle (with the water surface) for ricochet in impact with water for a steel ball is 7° and 9° for aluminium; for ebony it is 15°.

Ricochet was introduced in the late seventeenth century by French artillerists and particularly by navies in the eighteenth and nineteenth centuries. Using 54 lb. spherical shot, up to about 30 'grazes' or 'hops' were counted in tests (see H. Douglas's *Naval Gunnery*, 1855). Low-angle shot, by virtue of its many grazes, reaches, relatively, to large ranges. Though target penetrating speed is steadily lost over distance, yet damage to sails and crew on crossing the deck of a ship, were, militarily, very effective. Sometimes, shot was fired at low angle over the walls of forts to attack troops, buildings and equipment in the same way.

No general *theoretical* understanding of ricochet was available up to about the time of the Second World War. Dr Barnes Wallis had the British Air Force use large 'bouncing' cylindrical bombs in an attack on the Möhne and other dams in Germany. In too much modern literature on ricochet the Möhne dam epic is presented as if it was the first time the ricochet phenomenon was ever employed!

I continued studying many subjects especially the history of engineering mechanics. This led on to examining the work relating to early guns, of Benjamin Robins and Charles Hutton, especially the former, to such a degree that, in 2001, I had about 30 papers on the work of these two men, written by myself and colleagues published as a book in India in 2003.[*]

Benjamin Robins was born in Bath, England in 1707, the only son of a poor tailor and was brought up a Quaker – a strict religious Christian sect. After completing his schooling, Robins was recommended to Henry Pemberton, in London, editor of the final edition (1724), of Newton's *Principia*. Robins, then aged 20, had published work on the calculus acceptable to Newton.

Very little is known of Robins' private life but, principally, he is remembered for the use of the ballistic pendulum to measure bullet speed and the study of air resistance. He also explored the Magnus effect and wrote about ricochet. (The Magnus Effect was identified and studied by Robins a century earlier than Magnus: it causes the swerve in a David Beckham-style of football kick.) Robins came to be widely recognised for his book, *New Principles of Gunnery*, published in 1742, after which he acted as a consultant engineer and did work for some aristocratic politicians. In 1749 he was offered the post of Engineer General by

---

[*] *Collected Works on Benjamin Robins and Charles Hutton.* Phoenix Publishing House Ltd, New Delhi, India. 540pp.

London's East India Company to make secure their forts and ultimately protect their trading territory in India; he landed in Madras, India in July 1750. However, like many foreigners in India at that time, he was overcome by a fatal disease and died in Fort St David, near Cuddalore, one year later at the age of 44; he had travelled to Fort William, Calcutta, seeking supplies of building material. His official residence was Fort St George, Madras.

Crashworthiness

Another topic on which effort was expended was studying the plastic deformation of metals in the collision of vehicles (see Figure 25) in a short book of 120 pages in 1978. Figure 25 (c) is referred to by Prof. Diamond in his letter, Figure 3, Chapter XVIII, p. 162). The book did not attract the attention the subject deserved. However, a later paper in 1990 on *Crashworthiness*,[*] did gain more attention, see Figure 26. Ralph Nader's *Unsafe at Any Speed* (Bantam, London, 1973), early made the case for securing increased safety in motor cars. My aim with

CRASHWORTHINESS
OF
VEHICLES

An Introduction to Aspects of Collision of
Motor Cars, Ships, Aircraft, and Railway Coaches

W. JOHNSON and A. G. MAMALIS

Department of Engineering
University of Cambridge
Cambridge, England

MECHANICAL ENGINEERING PUBLICATIONS LTD
LONDON

1978

Figure 25 (a). Book title

[*] Proc. I. Mech. E., 204, 255–273, 1990.

SOME RESEARCH ACTIVITIES 261

Figure 25 (b). End impact on a coach.

Figure 25 (c). Two ships after a collision.

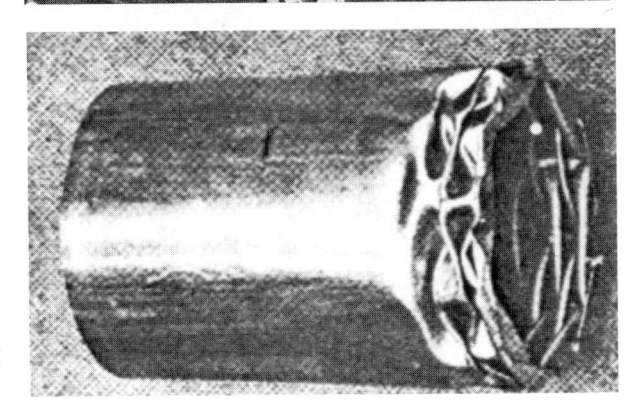

Figure 25 (d). A tube after suffering high speed impact at one end.

Professor Mamalis was to introduce material suitable for two or three hours of undergraduate design; it was probably the first book to attempt to do this. In fact, I believe the paper referred to was more successful than the book simply because it came out as a referred paper in one of the Inst. Mech. Eng. own periodicals. The book was initially offered to the Institution for publication, believing that that would have a wide engineering audience. Alas, it seemed not to have been properly advertised at all. The I.Mech.E. paper made a significant reference to fire – see Figure 26 for a summary – a topic which (then) found no place at all in Thermodynamics or Design but was highlighted among the disasters of the Falklands War.

Figure 26. The Elements of crashworthiness: scope and actuality
W. Johnson
(A. A. Potter Engineering Research Center, Purdue University, West Lafayette, USA)

An across-the-board survey of several aspects of crashworthiness is attempted, being in part an update and an improvement to the balance of an early monograph on the subject of The crashworthiness of vehicles *of which the writer was a co-author with Prof. A. G. Mamalis. Attention is given to perceiving this subject as three interconnected disciplines – materials engineering and design, combustion and fire, and medical engineering or biomechanics – but only after discussing some general guiding principles and the engineer's responsibility for the vehicles he or she produces.*

The latter subjects, together with short separate sections on head injury, fire fundamentals with broad allusions to vehicle fire situations and studies of kinetic energy absorption systems, comprise Part 1 of the paper.

Part 2 reviews some types of collision concentrating on those involving road vehicles but with some attention to the other main types identified. Some useful and provocative conclusions are finally drawn.

The author has tried to provide a useful list of referees, the needs of students and non-specialists being kept in mind throughout.

CHAPTER XXIII

Varia

---◆---

FINALLY, I INCLUDE, in no special order a number of miscellaneous extracts from papers which were written out of purely intrinsic interest in my seventh and eighth decades, the kind which could only emanate from an educational establishment. They have no straightforward economical value but are, I hope, ones from which the reader will derive interest and pleasure and enjoy some educational surprises.

1. Isaac Todhunter: The Elements of Euclid

I judge that today, few people below about 40 years of age, know much of 'Euclid's geometry' which has been taught in schools and universities for at least 150 years until recently. There has always been some controversy between its serious students and those who would remove it totally from the mathematical teaching curriculum – as has now happened; it has taken the twenty-first century to do it. The (reduced) paper below contains part of the case against the change. Apart from its overall purpose there are passages which are of inherent historical interest and some surprising opinions to be learned about. The reproduced *portion* of the original paper, describes the movement in time and place of translations of 'Euclid'. To be able to describe this when teaching a class, as with other 'pivotal' books, provides new educational dimensions of importance and historical understanding that makes for increased interest from students.

Isaac Todhunter and ... the greatest textbook of elementary mathematics that there has ever been ...
(From T. L. Heath's Introduction to Isaac Todhunter's 1862 Edition of *The Elements of Euclid**)

Abstract – The historical 'journey' from pre-Christian times to Todhunter's accurate nineteenth-century text-book on *The Elements of Euclid* via many previous researcher-editors over 2300 years is described and some of the latter's Contents are discussed.

Introduction

It seems that the discovery or beginning of geometry is attributable to the Egyptians and arose through the annual necessity to survey the flooded lands along the Nile. It is held that the Egyptian rules only became a science after they had passed through the hands of the Greeks and when the quantitative properties of lines, areas and volumes had become part of deductive science; principally the process began in about the sixth century BC, mainly with Thales of Miletus in Ionia. Engineer's drawings rest on geometric representation. The engineer will recall his early introduction to the subject through geometrical drawing. His debt to Euclid, the architect of formal geometry, is very great and his need for some acquaintanceship with Euclid's Geometry is mandatory. In the Sections below we outline the book's history over more than two millennia, describing how it came down to us.

---

* AMPT Conf. (Dublin) 1995, 1013–1016, Vol. II.

Origin of Paper

The writer recently completed a short biography and review of the works of Isaac Todhunter (1820–1884), coach or teacher and historian of mathematics in the University of Cambridge in the mid-nineteenth century.

Todhunter produced 4 large histories on (i) *The Calculus of Variations* (1861); (ii) *The Mathematical Theory of Probability from Pascal to Lagrange* (1865); (iii) ... *Theories of the Attraction and Figure of the Earth from Newton to Laplace* (1873) and (iv) *The History of the Theory of Elasticity* in 2 volumes, with K. Pearson (1886). Also, Todhunter produced about 25 volumes on a variety of mathematical topics that once met the requirements of high schools and the early years of undergraduate courses in mathematics; the quality of his output was always of the highest standard. From domination of the English-speaking market for his books before the First World War, they had moved by the time of the Second World War, like his own reputation, to one of almost total neglect. Todhunter's Euclid, one among his many textbooks, deals with this most celebrated and distinctive of subjects, elementary geometry, plane and solid; it treats of an ancient subject which has been an object of keen attention by all civilised societies since it was written in about 300 BC. Euclid took the texts of several predecessors and organised them into an ordered whole so that one proposition logically followed and depended on previous ones. Sometimes Euclid worked as an editor and at others as a researcher, filling in gaps where connecting material was wanting.

Several men bearing the name of Euclid existed in the ancient world. For long it was thought, wrongly, that we were dealing with Euclid of Megara. It is likely that our Euclid came from Tyre or maybe even from Alexandria itself. The political period under discussion is that of just post-Alexander the Great, the corresponding civilisation being dubbed Hellenistic. Seventeen Alexandrias were established in the ancient world by the Great conqueror, that in the Nile delta being pre-eminent. The world's first great library – a centre for manuscript conservation and research – was established by Alexander's Macedonian general Ptolemy in this Alexandria, Euclid becoming its Head in the early third century BC. Importantly, Alexandria was the great commercial entrepôt to Egypt for Greece and its territories overseas.

Euclid, as the work on the *Elements of Geometry* came to be known, spread into Europe by two routes at very different periods in time. First, it spread through the Arabic civilisation in, roughly, the eighth to the thirteenth centuries and only later was it acquired by a mathematically emerging Western Europe. The book of Euclid had to be translated from Alexandrine Greek into Arabic and penetrated Europe in late-mediaeval times through the universities of Spain and less so, through Siciliy and South Italy, then being rendered into Latin and later perhaps into a national language. In some cases the translation into Arabic came via the Nestorian Greeks of Syria. Thus, in early Europe there would have been several successive translations of an original text before it reached Latin readers – the European educated class of the late Middle Ages.

The second route into Europe followed the collapse in 1453 of the Eastern

Roman Empire, centred in Byzantium. Ancient original Greek manuscripts were taken westwards by scholars, into central Italy, studied directly and there translated for wider circulation. Clearly, the rendering of original manuscripts directly into Latin was to be preferred to a practice of translation through successive languages.

It was recognised that the study of Euclid's geometry provided a good mental training and discipline for scholars and the senior administrators required by Christian Church and State. Adherence to the original order of the subject was continuously advocated, by men such as Todhunter, into the nineteenth century. Seen as a too-severe approach at that time, some teachers tried to simplify or relax the classical mode of presentation, only to be severely castigated by older colleagues who knew the original Euclid. Indeed, in the mid-nineteenth century, rival confrontations on this issue were common ...

Below, we give some details about Todhunter's Euclid and learn that later T. L. Heath championed the same approach. To these latter men the history of the 'descent' of Euclid, with all its surrounding studies, caused them to enthuse about the pleasures which may be had from a careful reading of Euclid's geometry. First however we describe the credentials of English 'scholar' Heath.

T. L. Heath

Thomas Little Heath (1861–1940), is perhaps recognised as the most outstanding mathematical Hellenistic scholar this past century (nineteenth century). He graduated from Trinity College, Cambridge, twelfth in the Mathematics examination list and first in the Classical one (Latin and Greek). He entered the Treasury of the British Civil Service in 1884, having come first in the Open Competition for entry. (We thus underline here the excellence of Heath's preparation for studying mathematics written in ancient Greek.) Nearly thirty years later he was made Joint Permanent Secretary (or Head) of the Civil Service* in 1913 – the same year as that in which he was made a Fellow of the Royal Society of London. Appointments in the British Higher Civil Service were then, partially, sinecures which afforded time to would-be scholars. Mostly they came from Oxford and Cambridge and were recruited to serve the British public and politicians. The small demands then made upon them were such that there remained ample time and opportunity for them to pursue research outside their professional occupation if they wished. Thus, Heath specialised in studying ancient Greek mathematics, writing scholarly books on *Diophantus* (1885), *Apollonius of Perga* (1896), *Archimedes* (1897) and *Euclid* (1908); other publications of his are, *Greek Astronomy* (1932) and *A History of Greek Mathematics* (1921) in two volumes together of over 1000 pages. His Euclid is compelling reading for those who would obtain an in-depth view of our present subject. It was thus a topic on which both Heath and Todhunter wrote authoritatively, the latter to produce a sound text book for students, the other to perform the role of true scholar with respect to texts, annexed references, background and so forth.

---

* What was known in my day as the Administrative Grade was known in Heath's day as the First Division of the Home Civil Service. Recall Chapter XVI above.

Heath's Recommendation

In the introduction (dated 1932) to Todhunter's *The Elements of Euclid* in the great series of *Everyman* books in an edition of 1933, Heath on p.viii, remarked in glowing terms, what few of us would ever have realised as being at all the case, after the minimum kind of introduction to Euclid's Geometry which we received in school,

> ... it is safe to say that no alternative to the Elements has yet been produced which is open to fewer or less serious objections ... it is unsuitable as a text-book for very young boys and girls who are just beginning to learn the first things about geometry ... it is not written for schoolboys or schoolgirls but for the grown man who would have the knowledge necessary to appreciate highly contentious matters ... to be grappled with ... as a strictly logical system ... My advice (is when) the very young have shown a taste for the subject and *attained the standard necessary for passing an honours examination* let them then be introduced to Euclid in the original form as an antidote to the feeble echoes ... in ordinary school text-books ... I should be surprised if (they) did not find it fascinating, a book to be read in bed or on a holiday, a book as difficult as any detective story to lay down when once begun ... Any intelligent person ... should feel a real thrill in following its developments ... everybody ought to read it who can ... that is, all educated persons except very few who are incapable of mathematics.

From an extract in Todhunter's original Preface we gain an interesting historical insight into an older view of the advantages of the study of geometry as against arithmetic and algebra. Of the latter it is written, '... a beginner spends much of his time in gaining a practical facility in the application of rules to examples whilst (in Geometry) he is wholly occupied in exercising his reasoning faculties from the beginning.' He must argue a case (that of the proof of a theorem say) from the very first line and not depend on operating a prescribed symbolism and set of rules.'

The demonstration is a process of reasoning in which we draw inferences from results, earlier or already obtained. Thus –

> '... the letters Q.E.F. are placed at the end of a discussion of a problem and the letters Q.E.D. at the end of the discussion of a theorem. Q.E.F. is an abbreviation for *quod erat faciendum*, that *which was to be done*, and Q.E.D. for *quod erat demonstratum*, that *which was to be proved*.

When King Ptolemy asked Euclid if there was an easy road to learning geometry through the Elements, he replied, 'There is no *royal* road to geometry!'

The late Bertrand Russell has recorded his delight, noting it as 'one of the great events in his life', when he first 'began Euclid'. After 2300 years the body of deductive knowledge, which is elementary geometry stands as a great landmark in Greek and world mathematical achievements, albeit rescued from obscurity by dispersion in many texts through the efforts of later natural philosophers.

2. Isaac Todhunter (1820–84): Textbook Writer, Scholar, Coach and Historian of Science*

Abstract An outline of Todhunter's life history is first given and we then consider (unequally however) his contributions to mathematical scholarship through his extensive, weighty books, see item 4 in Contents below. These are followed by short accounts of some of his score or more well-known textbooks at junior and sophomore level, mostly written in about the middle third of the nineteenth century. A number of Todhunter's miscellaneous yet mathematics-related books are also discussed and finally, his success as a private tutor and a coach of undergraduates for mathematics degrees at Cambridge in the late nineteenth century.

Today, Todhunter's books have disappeared from library shelves and his activity as a historian of applied mathematics has to be recognised as now more or less forgotten. Todhunter is seen to have been a man of great influence in his time, a highly respected college and university man, greatly honoured at the time of his death but now almost universally neglected. The purpose of this paper is to try to revive appreciation of his contributions in their several dimensions.

Contents

1. Origins of this essay
2. Events in the life of Isaac Todhunter
    (a) Biographical
    (b) College education course at the time of Todhunter
3. Todhunter's many books in chronological order
4. Todhunter's four significant historical research works:
    (a) *A History of the Calculus of Variations during the nineteenth Century* (1861)
    (b) *A History of the Mathematical Theory of Probability* (1865)
    (c) *A History of the Mathematical Theories of Attraction and the Figure of the Earth, from ... Newton ... to Laplace* (1873)
    (d) *The History of the Theory of Elasticity and the Strength of Materials* (with Karl Pearson) (1875)
5. Todhunter's textbooks.
6. Todhunter's miscellaneous books.
7. Three mathematics coaches: similarity in career development
8. Opinions and comments on Todhunter's *Elasticity*
    (i) General
    (ii) Pearson, and Pearson on Todhunter

---

* *IJMS*, 39 (11), 231–242, 1996.

(iii) On diagrams and translations in Todhunter's writings
(iv) Tenacity of purpose and references
(v) James Bell on Todhunter and Pearson
(vi) Miscellaneous remarks
9. The funeral and burial of deeply Christian Isaac Todhunter (See below)
10. Valediction
11. Note 1: Lincoln
    Note 2: Professor Karl Pearson, 1857–1936: Elasticity and Biometrics
    Acknowledgements
    References

The Funeral and Burial Of Deeply Christian Isaac Todhunter

I obtained from the County Archivist, Mr J. Michael Farrar, of the Shire Hall, Cambridge, the following extract from an account of the burial of Dr Todhunter which appeared in a local newspaper: Todhunter died on 1 March 1884.

The funeral of Dr I. Todhunter FRS, Honorary Fellow of St John's College was solemnised yesterday. Shortly before noon those members ... who had intimated their intention of being present, assembled in the College Hall. The procession was formed, headed by the Vice Chancellor and Heads of Houses, Doctors, Professors and officials of the University ... There were several hundred persons present. The body, enclosed in a polished oak coffin, which was completely covered with floral wreaths, was attended on either side by the Fellows and met at the principal gate by the Senior Dean, ... who recited the opening sentences of the burial service. While the long procession was passing into chapel, the choir ... sang ... in the chapel the choir chanted the 19th Psalm ... A large proportion of those present, including the choir, proceeded to the Mill Road cemetery where the remainder of the burial service was performed. The ... order of the mourning carriages:- 1st, Mr G. Todhunter ... 2nd, the Master of Pembroke, Professor Cayley ... 6th, Professor Sylvester and Mr W. H. H. Hudson ... other prominent members of the University who followed were, the Vice-Chancellor, the Masters of Peterhouse, Clare, St Catherine's, Christ's, Trinity and Emmanuel; the President of Queen's; Professors ... Stokes ... Many of the tradesmen in the streets through which the procession passed had their windows partly closed.'

It was obviously a sad but splendid occasion. In view of the splendour of the funeral procession, I visited the burial ground at Mill Road in May 1993, in anticipation of finding the grave for Dr Todhunter's remains and expecting to see a correspondingly impressive memorial. The large cemetery, in the past, has served about 14 Cambridge parishes; it has along one side the newly established City of Cambridge University. The surrounding area is one of the poorest in the town and run-down to match. Most of the graves are totally neglected with many tablets and 'crosses' overthrown; it is not an uplifting sight. The cemetery chapel that was once at the centre of it has been taken down and any recall of its previous existence is minimal. A small number of gravestones for teachers from

St John's and one or two other colleges can be found at the north end of what was the circle of earth on which the chapel once stood. Some tombs are totally overgrown with ivy so that it is impossible to identify them, without seeming to desecrate them. In short, I did not find Todhunter's grave on my first visit, nor yet on the second one, a year later when I gathered correspondence about the site from obvious sources.

I learned from the County Archivist that it is believed that Todhunter would have been interred in either of the segments allotted to St Botolph or St Clement; these are the parishes for members of St John's College and for those who had homes in Brookside, respectively. Today, there appear to be no records of who were buried where, not even ecclesiastical documents seem to be possessed by the church authorities.

The neglected state of this huge burial ground is a very sad reflection on Cambridge – the City, the University and responsible religious bodies.

3. An Engineer Hoist with his own Petard?

Abstract The paper* describes the results of the author's efforts to comprehend more fully a passage of five lines in which the title above, taken from two lines of Shakespeare's *Hamlet*, is found.

Introduction

The full quotation of interest is to be found in *Hamlet*, Act III, Scene IV, lines 207–211:

> For 'tis the sport to have the enginer
> Hoist with his own petard: and't shall go hard
> But I will delve one yard below their mines
> And blow them to the moon: O, 'tis most sweet
> When in one line two crafts directly meet.

The first part of the second line provides us with a common metaphor used frequently in contemporary English conversation. It gives rise to two questions which many must have put to themselves. What is a 'petard' and could an 'enginer' be 'hoist' by it? An endeavour to answer these questions certainly caused the writer to expend considerable energy, especially as associated with the succeeding three lines.

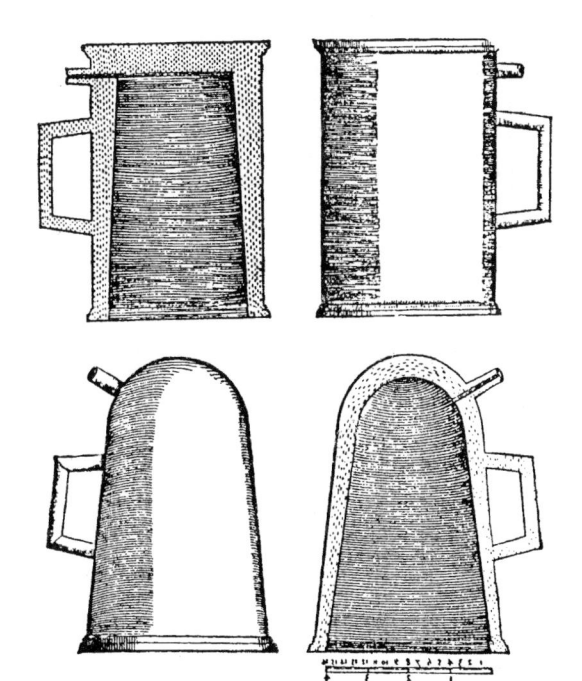

Figure 1. Two Spanish pêtards of the early seventeenth century in outside view and section. From Discusso de la Artilleria as printed in Stone's book (p. 495).

* IJMS, 29, 587–600, 1987

Figure 2. Two methods of using a petard.

The petard is an explosive device for blasting open the doors of fortified structures and some details of it are given below.

At the time of the Civil War,* Prince Rupert† was said to have expressed to Charles I, great surprise that no-one in their army had used, or even knew about, Petards!

---

* The Civil War in England, 1642–46.
† Prince Palatine, 1619–82.

4. Heat Lines

Fig 3(a) represents a slab of metal being plastically compressed between rigid parallel dies or platens, the width to thickness ratio being 3 to 1 and the depth (normal to the page) supposed large. The situation in Fig 3(b) is fundamentally the same, so the description for (a) suffices to explain the *notions* concerned in (b). The force which must be applied to achieve some degree of plastic compression is calculated by considering the three crosses sketched inside the metal: we imagine the metal inside each triangle to move as a rigid body in the directions indicated by the arrows. However as the material at the edges of the triangles traverses the lines of the crosses, it *abruptly changes direction*. The force to impose this

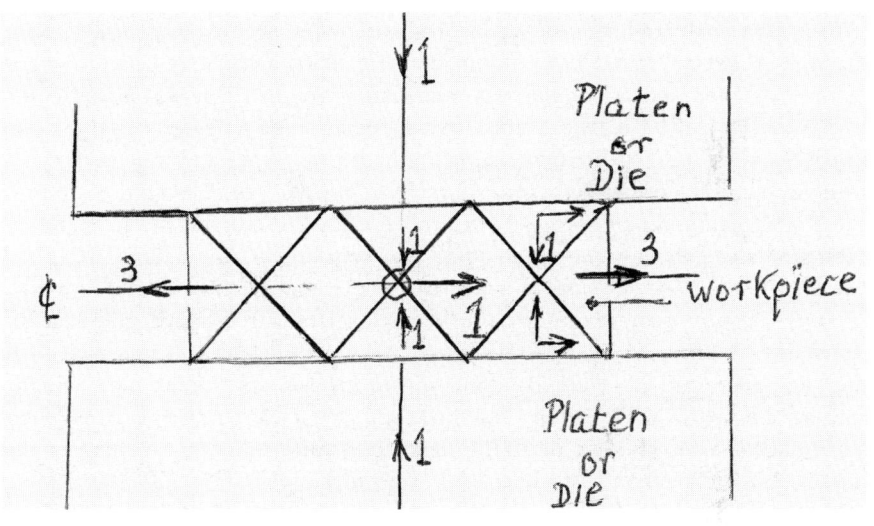

Figure 3 (a). 'If a bar be hammered when at a dull red so as to nip-down a short piece at each blow on the edge of the palletts, as shown, bright lines will be seen where each new portion has been hammered-in as indicated at (A), perhaps two or three being visible at once'.

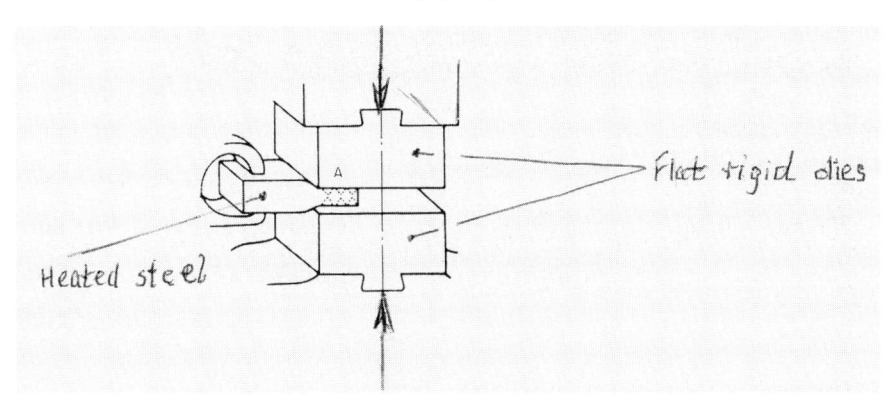

Figure 3 (b).

motion on the steel specimen is supposed due to the metal being suddenly sheared as it changes direction. In terms of mechanics the energy being applied by the platens is dissipated *in the lines of the crosses only* and reappears as heat. Thus, there are 'heat lines' in the body of the metal block. This explanation though greatly simplified should convey the notions used in making the analysis. Having done this elementary piece of work I felt suspicious of what I had found and I could not easily believe it. After setting it to one side, I began to look for mention of the phenomenon in the literature on forging. At the time (it was in about 1963) I came into contact with the two centuries-old forging company, B. & S. Massey Ltd of Openshaw, Manchester. (It was situated on Ashton Old Road, Manchester. I passed it on the bus almost every day when I was young (before 1934); it was about a mile further on to my home. Lying quietly in bed, some nights one could feel the shake of the ground and just hear the thud of hammers.)

We were then looking into doing research on a new type of roll-forming machine. However, I raised a question about Harold Massey, once Chief Engineer of the Company, and a booklet was immediately produced. It was a written-up lecture he had given to the Manchester Association of Engineers in 1921, i.e. nearly 40 years ago. At home that evening I read his paper and in it is shown a forging containing *bright and distinct lines in triangular form*. I could not suppress some strong remarks of surprise! – Here were my crosses and the temperature generated along them had been seen and was very bright. A few days later I had occasion to visit Massey's again. I referred to the lines of thermal discontinuity. *No one had ever seen them* – not the Managing Director, Chief Engineer or his Assistants. (None of them remembered what was in Harold Massey's paper – if they had ever read it!) I asked permission to go and talk to the men actually forging the metal in the 'shop. Our little group – G. L. Baraya, R. A. C. Slater and myself – trooped down on to the shop floor and I talked to the 'man on the hammer'. All concurred – no heat lines were to be seen! To verify this a piece of steel was then heated clearly red. The hammer hit the work-piece several times but nothing visually exceptional happened. However, the metal was in fact cooling and so became dull red. Hitting it again, bright lines suddenly arose and then faded. This happened several times for each strike. Clearly the heat lines were not early visible because the contrast with the colour of the whole block was not strong enough for easy visibility.

It transpired that a French worker in 1868, H. Tresca, had reported on the phenomenology of 'heat lines' but his paper or report had been forgotten and their significance not appreciated. This subject is told of in greater depth in the two articles in the *Int. Jnl. of Mech. Sci.*, 7, pp. 1–14, 1965 and 29 pp. 301–310, 1987.

It remains to add that the ability to predict the existence of these heat lines using a new and very simple and obvious theoretical approach was an event in a day worth remembering in my academic research life.

5. Dr Moshe Barash: From the Technion to Purdue: the British Connection*

Dr M. M. Barash went from UMIST, soon after I joined it, to a Chair at Purdue University, Indiana, USA. He was primarily responsible for my five years or so in his Department (1984–89). Over many years he and I have been close friends and have enjoyed working in the same field. The paper below tried to do homage to him, Manchester and its University. Lack of space allows but a few extracts to be given from the paper. (*Journal of Materials Processing Technology*, 40 (1994) 1–32 Elsevier.)

Manchester – late nineteenth century – 'a ghastly place, and I feel sorry for anyone who is condemned to profess and teach in its murky atmosphere.'

YET,
'What Manchester thinks today ... the world does tomorrow ...

Manchester, UK: statistics

	Population	Cotton (millions of lbs)
1773	about 24,000	approx 2.5
1801	70,000	25
1841	300,000	366
1940	760,000	–

The basis of an appreciation

I believe that the purpose of writing a paper as a contribution to the *Festschrift* of a scholar is to underline his contribution to the development of a subject. This may mean the identification of an original or seminal paper on a topic not previously addressed – for instance, some new idea or concept or some thoughts that suggested new lines of development – or a paper may alternatively have constituted a constructive criticism interjected at a critical time. An alternative to a critical appreciation of a scholar may be an attempt to identify some of the unique factors which worked upon him at an early time of life when the direction of his thoughts were being established: this can aid the understanding of his life's work and make possible the perception of the direction taken in that work.

---

* A contribution to the Symposium – Advances in Manufacturing Processes and Systems – 1992 in honour of Moshe M. Barash, Ph.D., Ransburg Professor of Manufacturing.

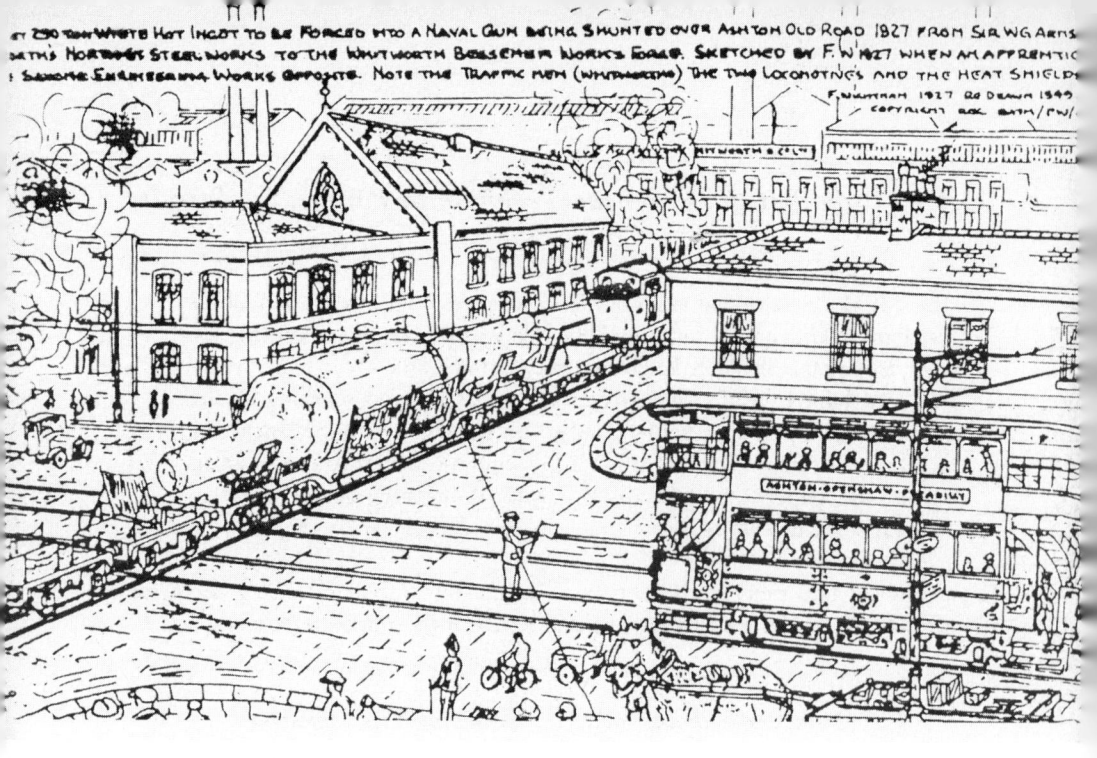

Figure 4. The last 250 ton 'white' hot ingot to be forged into a naval gun being shunted over Ashton Old Road in 1927 from Sir W. G. Armstrong Whitworth's North Street steel works to the Whitworth Bessemer Works forge. Sketched by Frank Wightman when an apprentice at Saxon's engineering works opposite. Note the traffic men (Whitworth's), the two locomotives and the heat shields. (Courtesy F. Wightman). The above was a sight typical of what the author often saw, as a child in the working-class area of Openshaw.

An American recommendation

Robert H. Kargon, professor of the History of Sciences at The Johns Hopkins University, wrote an outstanding book of some 283 pages in 1977 entitled *Science and Victorian Manchester* (published by The Johns Hopkins University Press).

Manchester from 1830 to 1900 is Professor Kargon's period of exploration. A shorter book, none the less absorbing, is *Manchester in the Victorian Age; the Half-Known City* by Gary Messinger, another American Professor (first published in 1943; reprinted in 1985). Messinger quotes at the beginning of his book from a novel, *Coningsby* (1844), written by our distinguished Prime Minister-novelist Benjamin Disraeli (1804–1881).

'Rightly understood, Manchester is as great a human exploit as Athens'. In war-torn Florence, Italy, in the summer of 1945, I remember thinking that for Athens, above, I might well have substituted Florence.

Clearly, Manchester constitutes a subject of some distinct sociological attraction in its own right for US students: this is not to be found regarding any other British city (London, excepted) as far as I know. Thus, if two American professors, within a period of a few years, found the development of Manchester so attractive a topic for historical research of a technological nature, can there be any doubt that the city is assuredly outstanding and worthy of further study?

Correspondence

The Magazine of The Cambridge Society
From Professor W Johnson

Dear Sir,

I was surprised to read about the claim for Cambridge of physicists Thomson, Rutherford, Blackett, Chadwick, Cockcroft and Bragg, since I myself had used the same names to urge Manchester's claims to excellence in a similar manner in an article published last year (see Ref. 1).

So, after reading Mr McCrum's review of *Cambridge Minds* I was left wondering if there is indeed significance at all in this notion, without an impossibly tight definition. Some minds are polished and honed in Cambridge and achieve fame elsewhere, others educated elsewhere ripen in Cambridge and for many it is six of one and half-a-dozen of the other.

We must surely recognise too that Cambridge and Oxford, from the antiquity of their foundations, must have a long edge in this matter on the Manchesters and the Leeds. True, no Milton in Manchester, but a lot of inspiration (!) for Dickens, Disraeli, Mrs Gaskell and George Gissing. There are, too, the Hallé Orchestra, *Manchester Guardian*, Rylands Library, Manchester Lit and Phil Society and Manchester Grammar School ... and no end of engineers of great consequence!

It was surely a help too for a University of Stamford (Ref 2) to have been suppressed in 1333 by Edward III (at Oxford's insistence), for had it survived, Newton from his home in Grantham – a mere 15 miles away and therefore only a good walk (or easy horse ride) – might well have enrolled there ... and then ... Trinity, what?

Yours sincerely,

References
1. Moshe Barash: From the Technion to Purdue: the British Connection. Jnl of Materials Processing Technology, 40, pp. 1–32 (1994).
2. *The Importance of Newton's Birthplace*, Int. J. Mech. Sci., 33 (8), pp. 679–685 (1991).

Manchester

In this city Engels collected material for his book, *The Condition of the Working Class in England*, which contributed politically to Marx's *Das Kapital*.

Some of Manchester's distinguished men and women were:
Scientists, John Dalton, James Chadwick, J. J. Thomson and James Joule.
Engineers, Joseph Whitworth, James Nasmyth, William Fairbairn and Osborne Reynolds.
Authors, George Gissing, Thomas de Quincey, Howard Spring, Elizabeth Gaskell and Anthony Burgess.

Reynolds, Manchester's first Professor of Engineering, *inter alia*, performed original work in the operation of journal bearings, fluid flow and heat transfer. (See p. 159, Ch. XVIII)

Figure 5. Sir J. J. Thomson: 1902. Thomson discovered sub-atomic particles.

6. A Pair of Mechanical Innovators

Figure 6 (a). Photograph: James Nasmyth (1808–1890) invented his famous steam hammer. In 1834 he made the first machine in the world for manufacturing industrial gears, cutting gear wheels for textile machines and soon after designed a power loom, marketing it to the burgeoning textile industries of the region. His self-acting spinning mule was in mainstream industrial use into the twentieth century.

Figure 6 (b). Richard Roberts 1789–1864. He was renowned for his famous punching machine for iron sheets.
(See Richard L. Hills' *Life and Inventions of Richard Roberts 1789–1864*.)

Nasmyth and Roberts were founder members of the Manchester Mechanics Institute in 1824. (See Ch.XIX, p. 188)

7. Part 1: Unfinished Military History

The following extract is taken from the 1993 Karunes Lecture entitled *Unfinished Military History, Plate Cutting and Heat Lines* (Wiley Eastern Ltd, pp 1–27). It was given by the writer in order to encourage a full study of Fort St David, Cuddalore, India. (See also: Part IV.11)

Fort St David and its Environs: A Case for Military Archaeology

In the Proceedings of the Institute of Metals' International Symposium for Advanced Technical Systems which was held in Tiruchirapalli in November 1990, – Dr P. Rama Rao's Presidential year – there will be found an article entitled, *Benjamin Robins: A Neglected mid-eighteenth-century Military Engineer–Scientist*. [2] He is called the Father of British Gunnery Science, which soubriquet causes him to have been the subject of biographical study by several European students of the History of Engineering-science. He is, none-the-less still a shadowy figure, and facts beyond those given in James Wilson's 40-page scientific biography of him, which prefaces Vol. 1 of the two which Wilson assembled entitled, *The Mathematical Tracts of the Late Benjamin Robins*, [3] are not easily come by. I set down in the above-named easily accessed article, a list of his major achievements or contributions which I therefore need not repeat here. Robins' scientific precocity was recognised by his election to the Royal Society of London at the tender age of 20 and for some further 10 years he worked in, and published, on the foundations of the Differential Calculus. (See *The History of the Calculus*, by C. B. Boyer, Dover Pubs), turning eventually to problems of a physical nature and particularly to the study of the flight of cannon balls and their launching.

Military work and membership of the Royal Society, led Robins to conversations with distinguished military men and politicians, he needing their financial support and they his advice. Once past the age of 40, Robins appeared to be much in need of a permanent position to support his lifestyle but because it did not mature he accepted the offer of an appointment from the Honorable East India Company and went to the Coromandel coast as Engineer General, there to function as the third in command for the Company, but specifically to put into good condition, several of the forts which had been established at Bombay,

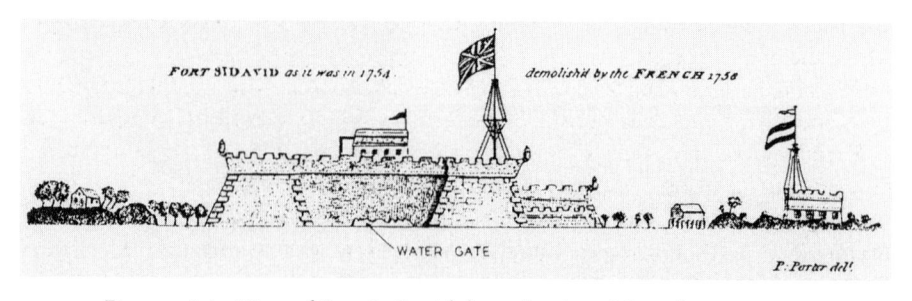

Figure 7 (a). View of Fort St David from the river. Note the watergate.

Calcutta and St Helena, as well as St George in Madras and St David, Cuddalore, by the year 1750. He landed at Madras on 13 July 1750, but spent much time around Fort St David. Unfortunately he contracted fever two months after landing and died in July 1751; his time in India was so short that his impact militarily was miniscule. Robins, by upbringing a Quaker, was a pacifist, but soon after moving to London from the place of his birth, Bath, he seems to have put un-warlike thoughts out of his mind.

Once in London he ceased to wear the Quaker garb. He never functioned as a soldier in combat but his inclination left no doubt that he thought and hankered after a reputation such as had been possessed by Frenchman Vauban and Dutchman Coehorne. To complete a biography of Robins I felt compelled to examine his activities and motives during the year in which he was in India and to this end I made visits to Madras and Cuddalore in December 1990. The time available for doing this was, naturally, very limited. There is a fine collection of early eighteenth-century documents in the museum and offices at the Madras fort and in the archives of the oriental and India Office Collections in London. As interest in biography declines with time and because there is a seemingly inevitable wastage of archival documents, it is only by visiting the regions where events actually occurred that deterioration can be compensated for to some degree. Generally, at a *mise en scene*, questions are prompted and answers found which conspire to extend appreciation and understanding.

Below, I describe some features and ask some questions about the Fort that once existed near to Cuddalore, that might well be able to be easily answered by those who find interest in military technology. I venture to propose that the identification of many significant landmarks at Fort St David, including its own extent, would provide a splendid exercise for Civil Engineering students in practical surveying, during a long vacation!

A representation by the eighteenth-century artist, Porter, of Fort St David as it was in 1754, which the French destroyed after taking it from the British in 1758 and a visit to the site, reveals the central square and walls still in good repair, but there remains to be clearly specified on the ground, the extreme boundaries before destruction took place.

Figure 7(b) is a copy of a sketch of Fort St David made by Robert Clive at a time of its defence in 1746 when Fort St George had already been taken by the French General La Bourdonnais. (It was supplied to a grateful author by the India Office archives in London.) It is Commander Clive's sketch of physical and artillery dispositions against attack from without. In Figure 7(c) I have emphasised by lining-in where the outer protective works might be expected to have been on an ordnance-survey map of 1945. Figure 7(d) is a sketch taken from Orme's Vol. I, made in 1758 and shows the clear outline of the Fort. This was copied on to Figure 7(c).

Various facts, questions and surmises may now be listed as follows about the Fort and its environs by reference to the figures.

It may be inserted here but cannot be pursued, that impact investigations and results were made known to fortifications expert, Vauban, by French military engineers generally. They had rules for camouflet and crater size according to weight of charge, type of soil and charge location; Belidor is quoted as giving

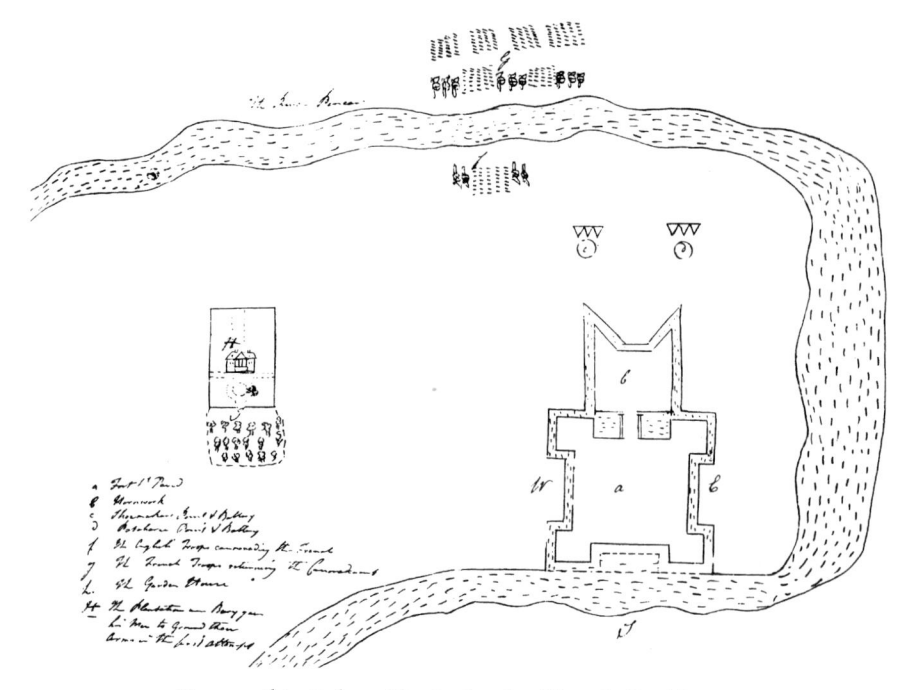

Figure 7 (b). Robert Clive's sketch of Fort St David, 1746.

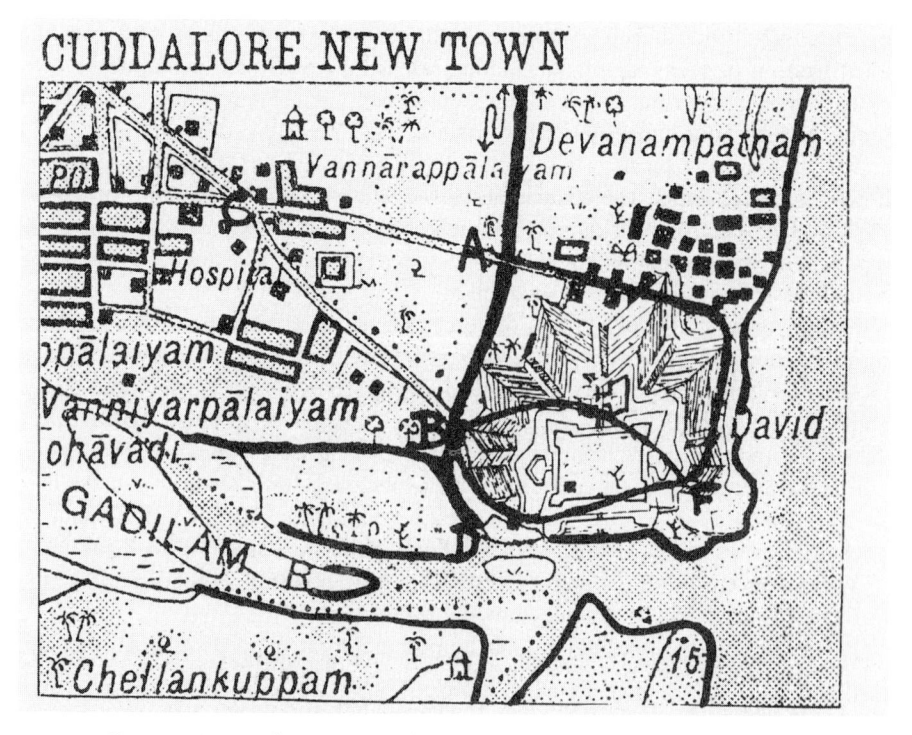

Figure 7 (c). Ordnance map of 1925 to which is added Fort St David.

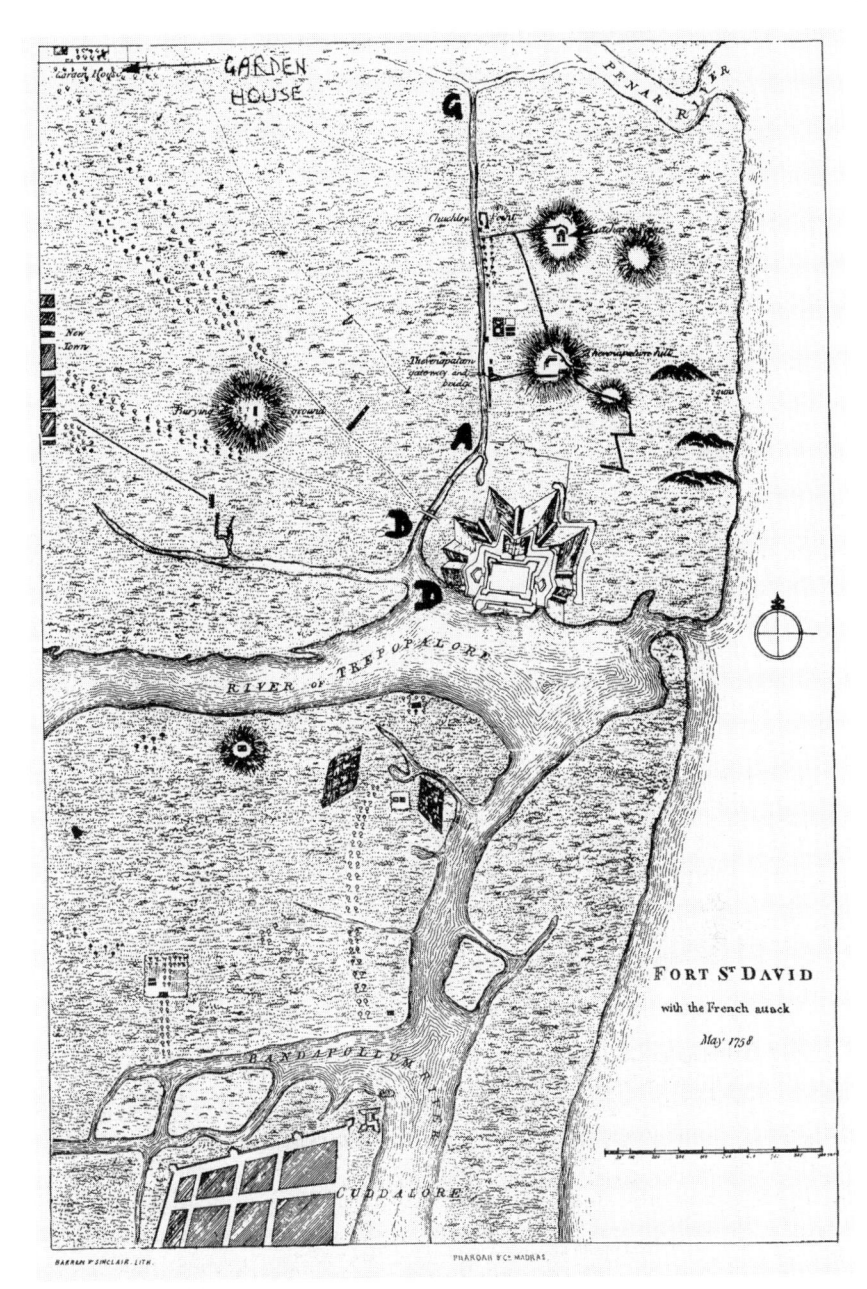

Figure 7 (d). Orme's sketch of Fort St David as it was in 1758.

seven crater diameters with corresponding powder charges – work of a kind seldom researched and reported, but see for instance work on camouflet (closed underground cavities in Figure 24 p. 257), knowledge of ricochet off water (see p. 253), and the design of castle architecture, particularly walls and gateways.

After two French attacks failed to take Fort St David in the years 1747–49 peace was declared. However, one sees that the defensive arrangements described above (and below) were obviously of little value as regards deterring a determined commander such as was du Lally in 1758.

The French in the Locality in the Years 1746–60

A brief review of the history of past and present day small town Pondicherry, neighbour to St David, is called for. It has a small museum clearly consisting of artifacts from previous decades and centuries. It might be useful to examine it at length for interesting items of historical importance which specifically relate to the Fort St David period. (There may also be items in public and rich local residences dating from those years.)

Du Lally, whose men captured Fort St David with relative ease, razed it to the ground in 1758, but he himself was captured by the British in 1761 in Pondicherry. He was sent to Britain but chose to return to Paris to face impeachment for the loss of 'French India', and was eventually executed. Voltaire secured an exoneration for him in 1778, having induced Louis XV to have his impeachment re-examined, this having been promoted in the first place at the request of du Lally's son. It seemed to lead Voltaire into writing his *Historiques sur L'Inde*, 1773, a book of 128 pages. I have not read this untranslated book but I would not be surprised if it did not provide a fascinating historical and social background to du Lally in India. (Arguably, Voltaire was an originator of *social* history.)

I might suggest that information about the conflicts around the forts, between the British and French in the Carnatica might well be found in Paris, since servants of the Crown and a (French) EIC would have had to report to directing officers or superiors there exactly as happened with the British in London. Specific to maps and sketches of forts, the advice given by the British Library is that there are at least four fine map collections in Paris, well worthy of consultation. (Letter to author dated 7 August 1993, 010C/109/82).

The Military Engineer in India by E. W. C. Sandes, 1933, p. 55

The military preparedness of Fort St David around 1758 is referred to in the above-named book. Sandes writes that ten years earlier Commodore Griffin advised the Governor (of Madras) to improve the fortifications of Fort St David without delay. It would have been captured by the French in March 1747 had not Griffin arrived in time with a British naval squadron, causing besiegers to withdraw. George Jones was thereupon directed to submit a scheme and improve its defensive posture. When he did so he prefaced his recommendations with the remark that Fort St David was too weak and defective to offer any effective resistance to the French, being merely a rectangular enclosure with four small bastions, a *fausse-braye** and a wide ditch – which was then the standard design of early fortifications.

---

* See Quentin Hughes, *Military Architecture*, 1991, 256pp. I.J.M.S., 39, 1077, 1997

8. Edward Gibbon FRS: Early Historical Sciences, Maurist Erudition and Related Scholarship 17th–20thC

Abstract – Edward Gibbon (1737–1794) prepared over many years to write his classic six-volume history, *The Decline and Fall of the Roman Empire*. The indisputable quality of his work (at the time) rested first, on his choice of reliable references and second, on the excellence of his English prose. Some elements of the former, when described, have the imprint of natural philosophy or early science – for example, the taking of collections of manuscripts and carefully comparing details to establish what is true or false (or often fabulous) and thus leading to the creation of palaeographic science. This kind of procedure led to a great output of Maurist (Benedictine) erudite work through the late seventeenth and into the early eighteenth century. A huge academic 'industry' developed over the years and gave rise to a large research body of scholars. Relatively little about this Maurist activity is to be found in English language historical writings so here we endeavour to raise the curtain on it for the benefit of scientists-engineers who have come to have an interest in the historical sciences. The works of scholars with different monastical and other backgrounds contemporary with that of the Maurists, which Gibbon made great use of, are referred to. As English historiography seems somewhat reticent on the topic of Maurist learning, we include a short account of the life and works of Benedictines Mabillon and Montfaucon, and less so, we take note of a score of other *érudits* such as Muratori, Tillemont, Cluwer, D'Anville and less well known scholars.

"... The Decline and Fall could never have been written without the French ecclesiastical scholars and antiquarians who supply so many of its footnotes ..."*

The paper concludes with an account of the works of E. C. Butler and M. D. Knowles – English-writing historians who, in the middle of the twentieth century independently endeavoured to spread knowledge of the Maurists.

INTRODUCTION

At the foot of p. 143 of Gibbon's *Memoirs of My Life*, he remarks that during his visit to Paris in 1763, he saw there the *Cabinet of Medals* and that 'the public libraries opened a new field of enquiry ... the view of so many manuscripts of different ages and characters induced me to consult the two great Benedictine works, the *De Re Diplomatica* (1681) of Mabillon and the *Palaeographica Graeca*

---

* From *IJMS*, 39, 1077, 1997. Betty Radici, Editor's Introduction to Edward Gibbon's *Memoirs of my Life* (MCMXCI, p. 20)

(1708) of Montfaucon.' These two distinguished scholarly monks had developed theory and methods for determining the truth or validity of the contents of ancient classical manuscripts, the first in Latin, the second in Greek texts. Thus, wrote Gibbon, 'I studied the theory without attaining the practice of the art; nor would I complain of the intricacy of Greek abbreviations and Gothic alphabets ...'. Gibbon's awareness of this kind of esoteric knowledge surprises and mystifies the average educated English scientist, for neither the subjects initially researched by the two monks, nor any of the details of the scholarship worked out by their successors, seem to have meant much to the professed English writers of European history.

9. A University at Stamford

THE BEGINNING – AND SUPPRESSION – OF A UNIVERSITY AT STAMFORD

(Int. J. Mech. Sci. Vol 33(8). pp.675–678, 1991)

Abstract – Political changes and fighting between the students of 'nations' in universities or with townfolk in mediaeval times was common enough. Disaffected students, scholars and tutors would then leave their university and migrate to another suitably receptive town. One secession from Oxford occurred in about 1332 when dissatisfied scholars transferred themselves to Stamford, Lincolnshire and sought to help establish a university there. Unfortunately, or not, King Edward III quickly banned it.

If a university at Stamford had been allowed, then by Newton's time it would very likely have been as well-developed as was Cambridge!

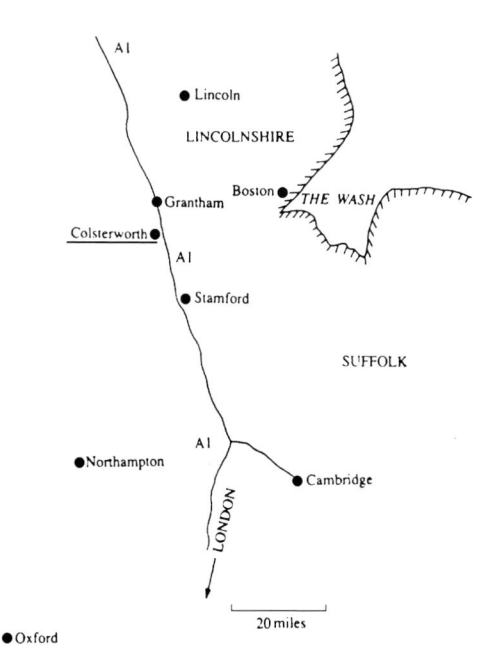

Figure 8.
Map showing the position of Stamford in Lincolnshire.

Concluding note about a university at Stamford and Francis Peck's *Academia Tertia Anglicana: The Antiquarian Annals of Stamford*

(Int. J. Mech. Sci. Vol. 35, No.8, pp. 715–722, 1993)

Abstract – The author herewith concludes his work [*Int. J. Mech. Sci.* 33, 675(1991); 34, 831 (1992)] on the subject of a university at Stamford – a university which 'there never was' – but an institution of which there was promise in the early fourteenth century. When one did seem likely to be realized, it was suppressed by the then-King of England. This association, mostly in 'halls', was within 13 miles of Newton's birthplace, Colsterworth, Lincolnshire and so might well have been attended by him had it existed in the mid-seventeenth century. Reliable details of this potential centre of learning are difficult to come by, but a major source of information chanced upon by the writer has the title given above and is a large volume of several hundred pages, *Academia tertia Anglicana* (The Third English Academy), composed by Francis Peck in 1727. The author gives, briefly, some items from the latter work which should help those who might henceforth wish to penetrate more deeply into this subject; for the mass of readers it provides a simple though partial picture of how some European universities started early in this millennium.

The reader interested in Stamford's academical history, will find much additional material in *The Myths and Legends of Stamford in Lincolnshire* by M. Smith (1991). See also the *IJMS*, 32 (10), 831, 1992.

10. The State Lottery

I happened, in mid-1998, to be writing about Benjamin Robins and in searching for information about his engineering activities I found a fascinating account of a National Lottery which was being held in support of a new London Bridge. There was great interest in lotteries in the UK in 1998, and because of this, I made a copy of what I had found in J. R. Green's *A Short History of the English People* (1894, Vol. iv, p. 1606), and accompanied it with a letter to *The Times*. Unfortunately, it was not possible for the illustration to be accommodated, even as a contribution to current interest. However, it transpired that Benjamin Robins was one of a group of six proposed by the Royal Society to advise on improvements to London Bridge in 1746. Figure 9 overleaf is a copy of the advertisement which appeared in 1739.

Politicians and bishops exclaim about the National Lottery but would seem not to be aware that lotteries are of quite some antiquity. In fact, the history of legal lotteries is at least two millennia old and was used by the Emperor Augustus and his successors for helping to finance building projects no less than to-day.

England's first recorded lottery was patronised by Elizabeth I in 1567 though they were held in Europe as early as the fifteenth century and in the seventeenth in America. They were mainly used for benefiting church, school and public works.

Count C. B. Cavour referred to lotteries as 'a tax upon imbeciles' according to A. H. Moorhead and as being a desperate attraction to the poor who could least afford them. As well, safeguards against deception could not be provided, since ticket-holders could not then easily be present at a draw – as TV now permits. Whilst private lotteries were tolerated, those run by the state were not, because corruption was thought to be so easy. England prohibited private (un-licensed) lotteries in 1698 and until recently none was licensed after 1824.

THE STATE LOTTERY.

The Name of a LOTTRY the Nation bewitches, / The Footman resolves, if he meets no Disaster,
And City and Country run Mad after Riches: / To mount his gilt Chariot, and vie with his Master:
My Lord, who already has Thousands a Year, / The Cook-Wench determines, by one lucky Hit,
thinks to double his Income by vent'ring it there: / To free her fair Hands from the Pothooks and Spit:
The Country Squire dips his Houses and Grounds / The Chamber-maid struts in her Ladies Cast Gown,
For Tickets to gain him the Ten Thousand Pounds / And hopes to be dub'd the Top Toast of the Town:
The rosie-jowl'd Doctor his Rectorie leaves, / But Fortune alass! will have small Share of Thanks,
In quest of a Prize, to procure him Lawn Sleeves / When all their high Wishes are bury'd in Blanks:
The Tradesman, whom Duns for their Mony importune / For tho' they for Benefits eagerly watch'd,
Here, hazards his All, for th' Advance of his Fortune: / They reckon'd their Chickens before they were hatch'd.

Engraven By B. Roberts & Sold by him at his Shop in Ball Ally Lombard Street. Price 6ᵈ

STATE LOTTERY, 1739.
Contemporary print in British Museum.

Figure 9. The State Lottery.

11. The Taj Mahal

From a distance, the Taj Mahal – built 1630–53 by Shah Jehan as a mausoleum for his consort – is undeniably a beautifully attractive Moslem construction of white marble; quintessentially a building in Persian style which we westerners conceive of as Eastern, in contrast with our own Gothic architecture. I found it heart-warming in recalling that it was raised by a man to the memory of the woman he loved – explicitly a marriage of affection, one not grounded in wealth.

As I wandered around the tomb in 1994, I became slightly less agreeably impressed; the tomb inside and under the dome seemed to show ageing and want of a little more care in presentation.

The adjacent Red Fort of Agra, built about 1570, is of red sandstone, well proportioned, up to 70ft high in some places and has a walled perimeter of over one mile. I found it much more interesting than the Taj and wished I could have given it more time. The fort on the bank of the Jumna river is picturesque. In surveying the situation, I caught sight of the single figure of an old man, only partially clothed, bathing. He had entered the water, knee deep, and was looking away from me down the Jumna; he raised his arms, palms upwards, and seemed to appeal to the heavens. It was a true expression of the age of India, the sight of an aged man at prayer, in isolation, in this huge cosmos.

Reduction of Traffic Congestion and Air Pollution in Manchester

The Taj Mahal in Agra, India, has been suffering deterioration due to pollution from motor vehicles so that, in 1994, all such transport was banned from a four kilometre square area surrounding the building. But tourists still needed transport and had to be catered for somehow. Existing traditional rickshaws were too often crude and had no springs, as well as being constructed dangerously. So a new pedal rickshaw has been designed with springing which takes into account passenger comfort as well as being safer. The new design weighs about 30 per cent less than the traditional ones so making the task of the driver much easier, needing less effort. These new pedal rickshaws have been a great success, not only in Agra but in many other Indian cities as well. Both drivers and passengers prefer them. Perhaps they should be introduced into Manchester to ease both traffic pollution and congestion. I am sure volunteers to drive them could be found from among the numerous sellers of the Big Issue.

(From a recent publication)

12. Blenkinsop

John Marshall, a flax spinner, who also made linen, built up a great business and became a millionaire. He employed Matthew Murray, an engineer and inventor of Leeds, who built four locomotives in the year 1812; one of them pulled trucks from Middleton Colliery to Leeds. This was 13 years before the famous 'Rocket'. (John Blenkinsop (1784–1831), British railway pioneer, in 1811 patented rack-rails which meshed with a cog-wheel on the locomotive.)

Since there was no great body of mechanical engineering experience available in the first years of the nineteenth century, then whether or not smooth, loaded, metal wagon wheels could be driven over smooth metal rails was not clearly known; to do so would require sufficient tractive force. Blenkinsop's rack-rail locomotive was developed to ensure that the latter pulled itself along, positively, via a gear-wheel and rack-rail, the former being actuated by a steam engine. (There was, incidentally, no such word as locomotive then, and it was simply called a wagon.)

Mr Joe Flowett and Mr George Robinson, Chief Workshop Technicians in my Division, along with a small body of other keen technicians presented to me,

BLENKINSOP

One of the first railways in the world	Rack and gear on one side for driving
Engine self-starting	Capable of pulling 90 tons
Reversing cranks at 90°	Weight: 5 tons
Water tank with boiler feed pump	Cast iron boiler
Wood frames	Two vertical cylinders, 9' bore by 22' stroke
Flanged wheels	Plug valves

Int. J. Mech. Sci. Vol. 33, No. 8 pp. 679–685, 1991. Printed in Great Britain, 1991 Pergamon Press plc

Figure 10. The Blenkinsop Model.

un-announced, late one Friday afternoon, the model shown in Figure 10. (A second model of 'Blenkinsop' will be found in the museum of the Mechanical Engineering Department, UMIST.)

The mechanical details of the full-size Blenkinsop engine given in Figure 11, were supplied by departmental staff.

WJ/JH
Mr J. W. Flowett, May 1968
UMIST

Dear Mr Flowett,

I was extremely pleased with the engine which you and the staff made, and my wife also would like to send her very best thanks for such a wonderful model.

I wonder if you would be kind enough to have a simple cover made for it, shall we say a rectangular thin plastic covering?

Could you also let me have some words about the history of the engine and a note of its special features?

With many thanks,
Yours sincerely,
W. Johnson.

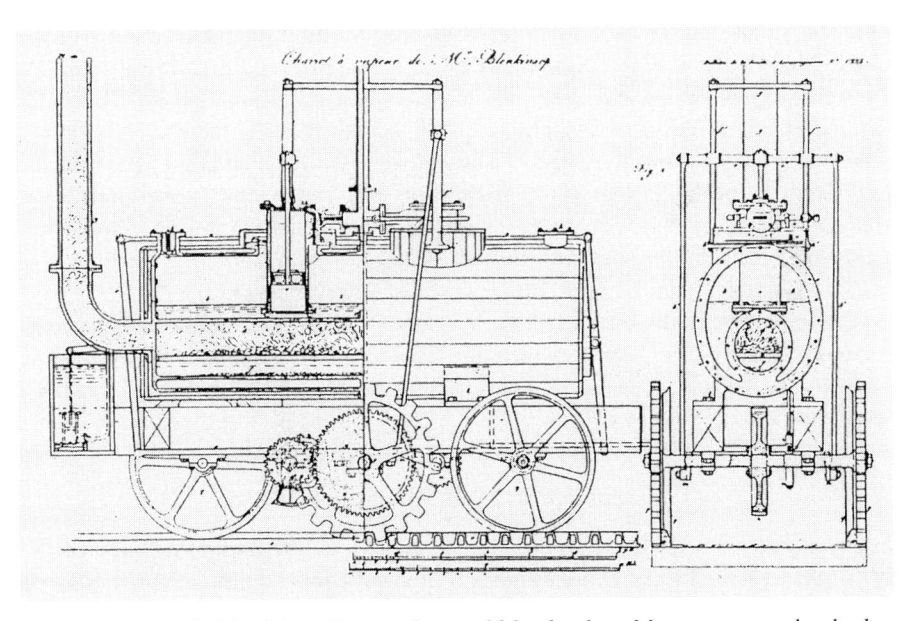

Figure 11. Doubtful of the adhesion that could be developed between smooth wheels and rails, Blenkinsop designed this rack railway engine.

13. The Importance of Newton's Birthplace*

Abstract – From often travelling past Colsterworth the author came to wonder if Newton's birthplace, Woolsthorpe Manor, is not too little recognised and promoted. How, when and why the property came to be in the hands of Britain's National Trust is described. A brief note about our knowledge of Newton's home and the surrounding territory is made followed by an expression of thoughts asking if more might not be made of the Manor as a vehicle for promoting interest in mathematics, science and the latter's importance in the lives of young people.

A guess is hazarded at what might have been the future of Cambridge University had Newton attended a University of Stamford which had not been suppressed.

Introduction

Woolsthorpe Manor, see Figures 12 and 13, was the birthplace of Isaac Newton; it is in the parish of Colsterworth some 7 miles south of Grantham and was one of a few small cottages and farmsteads around the time of the beginning of the Great English Civil War (1642–1646) in an area of some agricultural richness. Colsterworth is on an old route earlier known as the Great North Road (or Ermine Street, London to Lincoln) with the parish being somewhat less than a mile to the west of the motorway. Thus anyone with the slightest reason to be interested in the history of mathematics and physical science travelling on the well-designated A1 highway south (or north) to (or from) Cambridge should feel tempted to take the opportunity to visit Woolsthorpe Manor, the birthplace of England's greatest contributor to the world of physical science.

This note essentially derives from the author's reflections about the seemingly curious status of the Manor which he learned about after frequently passing between the ancient towns of Chapel-en-le-Frith (see Ch.XX) and Cambridge a few years ago.

The acquisition of Woolsthorpe Manor

In the middle and darker years of the Second World War the President of the Royal Society, Sir Henry Dale, wrote to Captain Herbert Turnor, M.C., of Little Ponton Hall, Grantham, about correspondence which had passed in May 1941, between him and Dr C. S. Orwin of Oxford concerning Woolsthorpe Manor. That correspondence explained. 'The Royal Society in this tercentenary year (1942) of Isaac Newton's birth have been speculating as to the possibility of acquiring the house and property (from Captain Turnor) to ensure its preservation in perpetuity in commemoration of the birth there, of one of the greatest of Englishmen'. Sir

---

* From I.J.M.S., 33, 675–678, 1991.

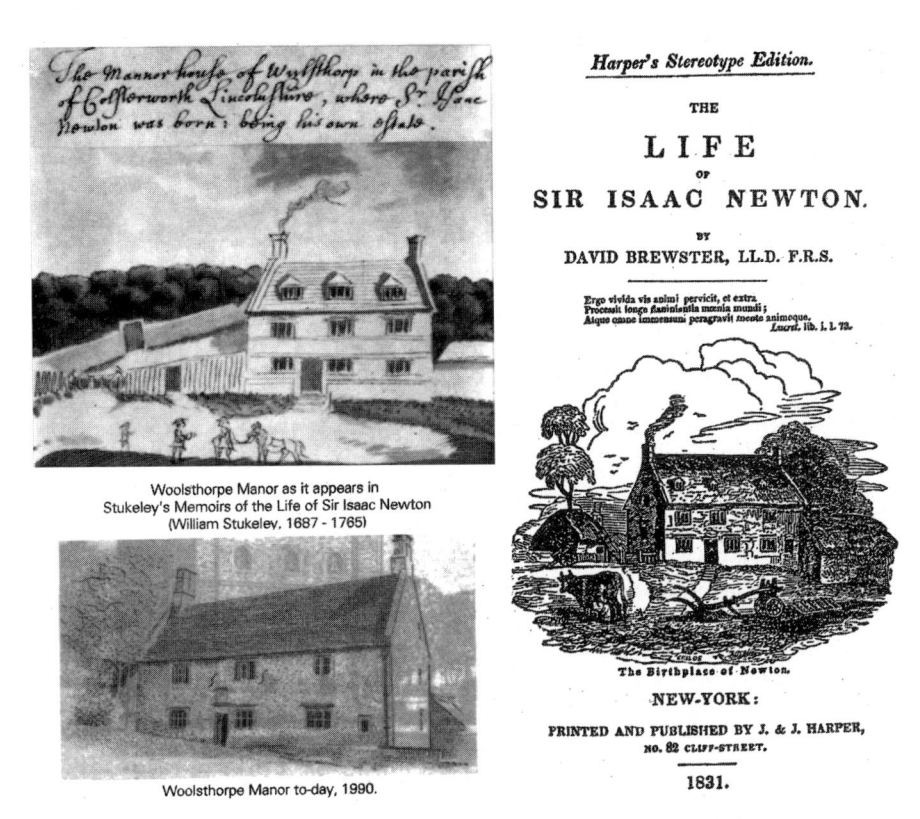

Figure 12. Colsterworth – Newton's birthplace and home in Woolsthorpe Manor.

Henry continued by writing that though the Society had 'no funds which would enable it to make an offer for the property (yet because) of the interest shown in the matter by your letter to Dr Orwin (he ventures) to ask whether you could give him an idea of the sum for which you would properly consider transferring it (and so that the Society) might give further and more detailed consideration as to the possibility of acquiring it ... arranging for it to be held by the National Trust or some other appropriate body as a perpetual memorial'.

Captain Turnor replied on 28 August indicating an interest in releasing Woolsthorpe Manor and helping the Royal Society in the matter of its acquisition. The President then stated in a letter of 1 September 1942, that what the officers of the Royal Society had in mind at that time, 'was to give an additional and more permanent assurance of the preservation as nearly as possible in the condition in which Newton knew it ... and where he in fact laid the foundations of most of his great discoveries'. It was explained that the intention was to secure the freehold of the house with the farm buildings and the actual fields which formed the farm as it was operated in Newton's own time.

The President in this letter also observed that Captain Turnor had raised another possibility and that was the transfer to the Society of only the house and by implication the small and historic garden and orchard in front of it. It was in the mind of the Royal Society, and Sir Henry, to restore the interior of the Manor – room divisions and fireplaces, etc. – with the aid of a learned architect sympathetic to the conditions which prevailed in Newton's lifetime.

The President thus put to Captain Turnor two different schemes saying that he would be glad to know the terms on which he would be prepared to negotiate.

Independently of the above correspondence an approach to the Pilgrim Trust had been made during the last months of 1942 for a grant for the Royal Society to purchase Woolsthorpe; it resulted in a letter from the Secretary of the Trust dated 8 December 1942, the President added that he was considering whether a special trust should be appointed to hold the property or whether he should approach the National Trust requesting it to take the responsibility and possession of the property into its hands.

A letter of 18 December to Major Turnor from Sir Henry recalled that at a meeting held on the 15 October it was explained that the fields then representing the land farmed by Newton's family 'had been entirely leased to the Ironstone Company and that in the near future (it) would inevitably be made unfit for cultivation'. Thus in the circumstances, the opportunity of acquiring only the house, orchard and land immediately around it were on offer. In this same letter it is remarked that the agent for Major Turnor, Mr Purchase, had expressed the opinion that the house with the orchard attached was worth £1500, but that Major Turnor would be prepared to sell the freehold to the Royal Society for £1000. Further, wrote Sir Henry, the Pilgrim Trust which was contemplating assisting the Royal Society in the acquisition, asked 'for evidence of the extent to which the vendor would be willing to assist the project'. The Royal Society's agents, Messrs Bidwell and Sons of Cambridge, had then independently been set to inspect the property and had reported on 27 November that it valued it at £1250. The Pilgrim Trust, when informed of the latter figure, accepted that the price of £1000 did indeed 'involve a substantial and generous contribution ... to the memorial enterprise'. In this same letter of 18 December it was stated that, 'It is probable that it will be most suitable for the Royal Society not to become the freeholder in its own right, but to arrange for the transfer of the property to a Trust charged with the duty of holding it in the public interest and that it is possible that the National Trust for Places of Historic Interest and Natural Beauty will be willing to accept the responsibility'.

In due course, to judge from a letter of 31 March 1943, the Royal Society later agreed to a direct transfer from Major Turnor to the National Trust and so saved double conveyancing fees!

It is of interest to note that an Edward Turnor purchased Woolsthorpe Manor and certain lands from Thomas Alcock in 1733 for £1600.[1] See p. 300.

In concluding this section, the author observes that though Woolsthorpe Manor is secure in the keeping of the National Trust, it has always been surprising to him that the Society allowed to pass out of its hands an item that would be thought of as, indisputably, one of its most treasured possessions. It is all the more surprising too, because it happened at so critical a time in the nation's history.

Newton and the manor, in brief

Isaac Newton senior, having married Hannah Ayscough, died after 6 months, young Isaac being born 3 months later and premature on Christmas day 1642; he died in his 85th year. In 1645, Mrs Newton was re-married to a clergyman (an M.A. of Oxford of 1604) Barnabas Smith, rector of a parish about 1 mile south of Colsterworth.

Mrs Newton, now Mrs Smith, went to live with her husband and left her young son in the care of her mother. Part of the marriage agreement was that the widow's son would receive 'a parcell of land' which was worth about £50 a year. This together with a paternal inheritance from Woolsthorpe brought him a total of some £80 per year.[2] An average income from land for families in those years in this area was then about £50.

Newton maintained contact with the Manor and its region throughout his life. He was at Woolsthorpe until turned 12 years of age when he left for Grantham to attend the Free Grammar School of King Edward VI and where he was put into lodging with an apothecary whose brother was said to be a mathematical master at his school. He remained at the Grammar School until he was about 18½ years old. This type of grammar school then taught mostly Latin, a little Greek but apparently only a small amount of arithmetic or mathematics. The school had been founded in 1343 as had many more of the same name,[*] such schools were re-established under a new charter in the mid-sixteenth century (due to a Reformation upheaval), 'Free' being dropped from the previous title.

Whilst there are no stories of precocity associated with Newton there is an abundance of examples revealing a distinct inclination to mechanical model-making which doubtlessly developed in him a capacity he was later able to put to good use for making scientific instruments such as telescopes. At about 15 years of age his mother recalled him to take charge of the family estate at Woolsthorpe seemingly aiming to train him to be a yeoman farmer. The endeavour failed and Newton was returned to Grantham school. It seems that the school's headmaster, Mr Stokes, had detected in his pupil great promise that it would require a university to give opportunity to and he strove hard to prevent his star pupil from becoming apprenticed to the land. He took the boy into his own home as a boarder and as the story is, when the time came for him to leave for college, they separated having been as close as any father and son could be. Thus, at just turned 18 years of age, Newton left Woolsthorpe on 20 March 1661 and went to Trinity College, in the University of Cambridge.

Newton, when effectively a graduate research student, returned from Cambridge in 1665 to spend about 2 years at Colsterworth, this being the beginning of the plague years 1665–1667. 'It had pleased God to send a two-year visitation of the pestilence starting during the summer of 1665.' He left Cambridge before 7 August 1665 and returned late in April 1667. The 2 years of the plague, during

---

[*] In an attempt to identify where military-engineering scientist Benjamin Robins (1707–1751) was educated, see *Int. J. Impact Eng.* 9, p. 503, 1990, the writer alighted upon a school of precisely this name in Bath.

which men were sent away from Cambridge, he spent in Woolsthorpe, and they have been called his *anni mirabiles*.[3] During this period of detachment he came by many of the ideas which were to sustain him in scientific enquiry for the rest of his life. When he finally went back to Cambridge in 1667, broadly it is said, he had already laid aside mathematics as such – calculus and algebra – and was deep into physics – gravitation, more optics and other subjects. It is fair to add that Westfall in *Never at Rest*[4] has argued that Newton's intellectual development was continuous, and not suddenly enhanced in 1665–1667 as compared with that of other years. Readers may make their own assessment after perusing the relevant entry in Gjertsen's book.[5]

It seems that Newton returned to Woolsthorpe to attend to rent collections and similar matters every few years and especially in 1679 when his mother died he was there for several months. All the records show that he did good deeds, for all members of the family and others too, especially in his last decade or two. He helped find employment or settled debts for some and arranged marriage portions on females. He had become a man of property, prosperous or even wealthy, and certainly one of social distinction. 'Charity', writes Westfall, 'supplied a constant background to Newton's last years'.[6] Always he was fond of Lincolnshire and genuinely concerned with the activities of his native village and his estate in it.[7]

Reflections

When I have visited Woolsthorpe Manor it has often been closed and if open the number of visitors small.* One reflected, 'it should do better than this'. Thinking of Shakespeare when visiting Stratford-on-Avon, one naturally compared it with Woolsthorpe. There, one encountered a situation which is perhaps overly successful.

I spoke on this subject with a professor of mathematics who gave it as his opinion that the matter of birthplace was unimportant, after all, he said, 'they' believed Newton had done all of his great work in Cambridge in Trinity. This despite Newton's own remarks about the '*anni mirabiles*',[8] and the useful lionizing of Newton for the purpose of promoting him as a scientific exemplar for young people. Does Trinity have a monopoly of Newton, binding him to the courts and the Wren Library and not developing his reputation more widely as a national asset?†

I have met few mathematicians (and fewer engineers) who have visited Woolsthorpe though in my experience not many are to be found who show serious interest in the history of mathematics or physics [Indeed have we now not seen the emergence of a new cadre of historians into whose hands has fallen the critical chronicling of the Queen of Sciences (pre-eighteenth century?).] There are few

---

* In recent years there has been an improvement.
† I acknowledge that the new Issac Newton Institute for Mathematical Studies whose Director is the Master of Trinity, Professor Sir Michael Atiyah, is a kind of recognition of this.

men in the practice of medicine who are unaware of the outstanding contributors to the history of their profession and the same view applies in law, philosophy and for many subjects. Knowledge of predecessors is no less desirable in the engineering sciences so that we should do all we can to improve matters, especially so as the men concerned are heavily socially committed by profession. Bertrand Russell argued, surely incontrovertibly, for 'history is an essential part of the furniture of the educated mind'; through it he rightly says that one derives a 'new dimension to life'.[9] Without the history there is no sense of a stream of continuity in subject matter or of feeling part of a vast and important army of past and indeed future scholars. Subjects provide deeper insights when we become aware of the origins and developments of ideas; ideas have histories as much as do events. To operate purely in the skin of time leads to a limitation of outlook which can be the very enemy of education. For a lecturer to know the history of his subject is for him to be able to infuse his lectures with a humanity which protects him and his students against scientific and engineering endings which are a kind of Chaplinesque '*Modern Times*'.

The Royal Society and the Fellowship of Engineering try hard to raise interest in science and engineering among young people especially.[*] Might not even more be done to this end by more vividly prompting Woolsthorpe?[10] Perhaps present-day Woolsthorpe could be made a more attractive mechanical sciences shrine for the children or youth of to-day; and it would not need great cost. Among other things, lectures might be given about how matters have progressed since Newton's day, perhaps having shown something of the work of his distinguished contemporaries, for example, Sir Christopher Wren. It could also be demonstrated that the scientific world did not stop with his death. (In a sense, as indeed did tend to happen and against which Charles Babbage so loudly proclaimed in the early nineteenth century.) Progress might even be charted so far as to explain the relationship of Chaos (theory) to Newtonian gravitation!

Interestingly, Derek Gjertsen on p. 29 in *Let Newton Be!* (OUP, 1989), records: '*In 1796 Champlain de la Blancherie denounced the English for their failure to honour Newton's divinity properly ... and that Newton's home at Woolsthorpe*' [but only his birthplace and residence till he went to Cambridge; of which Derek Gjertsen writes of as home for over 30 years (p. 39) '*should be turned into a Sanctuary.*']

Newton and a University at Stamford

When Newton went to Cambridge, presumably he did so because it was nearer to his home than Oxford: it was 70 miles down the Great North Road. But supposing a university of Stamford had been established in the 1330s, scarcely 15 miles south from Colsterworth (merely a good afternoon's walk or an easy horse ride), might not Newton have registered himself there? That there was no university of Stamford to attend in the 1660s is the subject of a companion paper,

---

[*] The writer takes this opportunity to recall the government's fine support in establishing the Manchester Museum of Science and Technology in the Greater Manchester area.

see item 9 above. Had it not been for King Edward III's edict, by which a university of Stamford in 1333 was suppressed, and despite the aims and efforts of a few Oxford secessionists, such a university (earlier called a *studium generale*) would have been close at hand.

Cambridge's reputation till past mediaeval times was said to be inferior to that of Oxford and indeed, Hastings Rashdall,[11] wrote originally that it was 'third rate', though this remark is footnoted by present editors of Rashdall's book claiming that it is 'too sweeping' a comment. However, in all probability by Newton's time, it is very likely that a University of Stamford would have enjoyed a status somewhat similar to that of the University of Cambridge: it would have had more than three centuries in which to mature and develop a reputation. [It might conceivably have come to possess an early inclination to science drawn from the reputation of the once, not too far north, distinguished Bishop Grosseteste (c. 1175–1253) of Lincoln cathedral (and some time Chancellor of Oxford).[12] Of any outstanding scholar that Cambridge had before 1660 we might well consider whether he may not have chosen Stamford had it been in existence. Surely there would have been something of a sharing of talent between the two, if not the three, universities?

The reader is left to reflect that King Edward III, in suppressing the Stamford experiment set up by Oxford dissident scholars, made an absolutely pivotal decision for facilitating Cambridge's bright future.

Note

Annus mirabilis, *1666*, or Anni Mirabiles, *1665* and *1666*

The following passage is said to be Newton's written recollection concerning the years 1665–1666, recorded about 50 years later.[13]

'In the beginning of the year 1665 I found the Method of approximating series and the Rule for Reducing any dignity of any Binomial into such a series. The same year in May I found the method of Tangents of Gregory and Slusius, and in November had the direct method of fluxions and the next year in January had the Theory of Colours and in May following I had entrance into ye inverse method of fluxions. And the same year I began to think of gravity extending to the orb of the moon and ... I deduced that the forces which keep the Planets in their Orbs must be reciprocally as the squares of their distances about which they revolve ... All this was in the two plague years of 1665–66. For in those days I was in the prime of my age for invention and minded Mathematics and Philosophy more than at any other time.'

Acknowledgements – I am grateful to Mr N. H. Robinson, former librarian of the Royal Society, for copies of some of the letters mentioned in the second section. I am also grateful to Heather Johnson for the typing of this manuscript and Professor Donald Cardwell for reading it.

References

1. R. S. Westfall, *Never at Rest*. Cambridge University Press, Cambridge, 1980.
2. H. D. Anthony, *Sir Isaac Newton*. Abelard-Schuman Ltd, London, 1960.
3. Westfall, *Never at Rest*, Chapter 5.
4. Westfall, *Never at Rest*.
5. D. Gjertsen, *The Newton Handbook*. (The *Annus mirabilis* entry, p. 24). Routledge and Kegan Paul, London, 1986.
6. Westfall, *Never at Rest*, see pp. 857 et seq.
7. Ibid., p. 851
8. Gjertsen, *The Newton Handbook*.
9. Ibid.
10. W. Johnson, *The Beginning – and Suppression – of a University at Stamford*, Int. J. Mech. Sci. 33(8), 675 (1991).
11. H. Rashdall, *The Universities of Europe in the Middle Ages* (edited by F. M. Powicke and A. B. Emden), Vol. III, Oxford University Press, Oxford, 1936.
12. C. B. Boyer, *The Rainbow*. Princeton University Press, New Jersey, 1987; and A. C. Crombie, *Robert Grosseteste and the Origins of Experimental Science*, 1100–1700. Oxford, 1953.
13. B. Russell, *Portraits from Memory: History as an Art*. Allen and Unwin, 1958.

14. *The New Dictionary of National Biography*

An unsought pleasure and accolade for writing about the lives and discoveries of some British scientists and engineers, was to receive an invitation to contribute about a dozen biographies for the new DNB, which is to appear in the year 2003. One half of the new entries I wrote were to be articles of some 1500 words long, whilst the other half were to be revisions from the now, old DNB. The old DNB, up to 1900 AD, was deficient in respect of its coverage of the engineers and scientists of the nineteenth and twentieth centuries and the New DNB will spread new light on them. As far as I could determine the editors were satisfied to include Engineering under Science.

The articles or potential entries were not quickly dashed-off and were written to a certain pattern; they were carefully scanned by dictionary researchers and the whole approach could be said to be salutory. Former classicists and literary names, as mentioned in *The Dons* (by Noel Annan) for instance are seen as much more important than engineers, such as Whitworth, Maudsley, Bazalgette, and the like by reference to length of entry.

The New DNB deserves to be much better known and mentioned to research students than is presently the case. Engineering and technology history should indeed be thrust before them to increase their all-round knowledge, and, it may be added, that the DNB and the old Encyclopedia Britannicas (full of excellent articles), are far too little used.

PART IV

A Wandering Scholar

CHAPTER XXIV

The USSR and Russia

(i) A Visit to the USSR, 22–31 May 1968

Introduction

My visit to the Soviet Union took place under an Anglo-Soviet Cultural Agreement and I was one of the agreed twelve-day Professorial Exchanges; in particular, I was the guest of the Bauman Technical School (or University). My host was Professor E. A. Popov,* whom I had met a year before and with whom, as with nearly all the professors mentioned below, I have corresponded and exchanged reprints and books. The invitation to make the visit came from the Russian side, but I must record that I never determined precisely how my visit was inspired. A Russian representative came to my office one day in 1967 when I was away and left a message asking if I would care to visit Moscow. When the visit was agreed I wrote to all the Russian professors in Moscow I knew, or have met, and advised them of the period during which I would be in the USSR expressing the wish to see them and their laboratories. The British Council staff in London seemed to set no store by my efforts to pre-arrange my visit. They advised me that since the visit would be made under the auspices of the Soviet Ministry of Higher Education the procedure would be for me to travel to Moscow and to discuss my programme with their officials on arrival there. However, as described below, this did not happen and, indeed, for all I saw of the Soviet Ministry, it might not have existed. I was never dealt with in any official way and I seemed to escape all formal contacts. I was also informed that it would be very difficult to make visits to Institutes under the direction of the Academy of Sciences or similar bodies because I was sponsored by the Ministry of Higher Education. I now have the opinion, however, that given good personal contacts in Moscow there is as little difficulty in arranging these matters as there is in the United Kingdom.

I have confined my report to a simple chronological non-technical account of my experiences and observations; the report is more of a memorandum than a literary product.

---

* Now deceased. His obituary is given in the *IJMS* 38, 1037–1041, 1996.

Because of a misunderstanding at the Soviet Embassy in London I received my visa late and I proceeded to Moscow on Wednesday, 22 May, two days late, so that my stay in the USSR was for 10 days and not as previously arranged, 12 days.

Wednesday

On arrival I was met by Mr Jocelyne, who was the British Assistant Cultural Attaché. I was also met by Professor Eugene Popov of the Bauman Institute who was accompanied by three of his assistants. I left the very quiet Sheremotovo Airport – such a contrast to the busy, amorphous, never-finished Heathrow – in the car brought by Professor Popov and this was all I ever saw of the British Embassy officials. I was conveyed to the Hotel Russia (said to be going to have 5,000 bedrooms!) where arrangements for me to stay had been made. From my bedroom window I had a wonderful view of the gold covered cupolas in the Kremlin. I received about 70 roubles which was money to meet all sorts of contingencies and for meals, etc. Professor Popov and I had an excellent dinner in the Hotel Russia which lasted until 11 p.m. and during it we discussed some of the probable details of my visit. (For my first four dinners and lunches I had the equivalent of Crimean champagne, and I had begun to wonder if this was the national beverage!) A very full and interesting twelve-day programme had been worked out and arranged by Professor Popov but in view of my late arrival this had to be abandoned.

Thursday

On Thursday morning at 8.30 I endeavoured to take breakfast in the restaurant of the hotel but this took approximately one hour so I was half an hour late for my first appointment. I mention this particular incident because it was the only occasion on which I had experience of a meal taking a long time to be served. Thereafter, each morning I breakfasted in a Buffet, one of which was to be found on each floor of the hotel where I found the service excellent and the breakfast quite satisfactory.

I accompanied Professor Popov to the Park of Exhibitions where he was an official judge of students' exhibits – some of which I was able to see also. The Park of Exhibitions contains a large number of excellent exhibition halls which are used for displaying equipment, goods, models and films for visitors. I was very greatly impressed by the Kosmos Hall, which contained a huge selection of the space and geophysical rockets, satellites and capsules put up by the Soviet Union, liberally illustrated with diagrams, maps and explanations and with portraits and descriptions of the contribution to science of Soviet space scientists and astronauts. At the entrance to this hall was Gagarin's original rocket. I also spent a lot of time in the hall given over to the display of models of steam turbines and hydroelectric power plant. One of the young ladies in charge was kind enough to run through three or four film loops about engineering projects in the Soviet Union, one of which was in English. I also saw the exhibition hall for electronics and another devoted to consumer goods. The Park was of tremendous size, beautifully laid out, clean, and most impressive even though it was 'dated' architecturally. We had a very good lunch at one of the restaurants in the park and then proceeded to the Bauman Institute (see Figures 1, 2 and 3). The Baumann Technical Institute was established in 1830, and the first two Figures are copied from the volume which celebrated its 150 years anniversary. Besides being a history of the Institute, the volume of 320 pages is a bibliography of its most well known engineering scholars. Not a few Englishmen and Scotsmen visited and served Russia in the Navy in the eighteenth and nineteenth centuries.

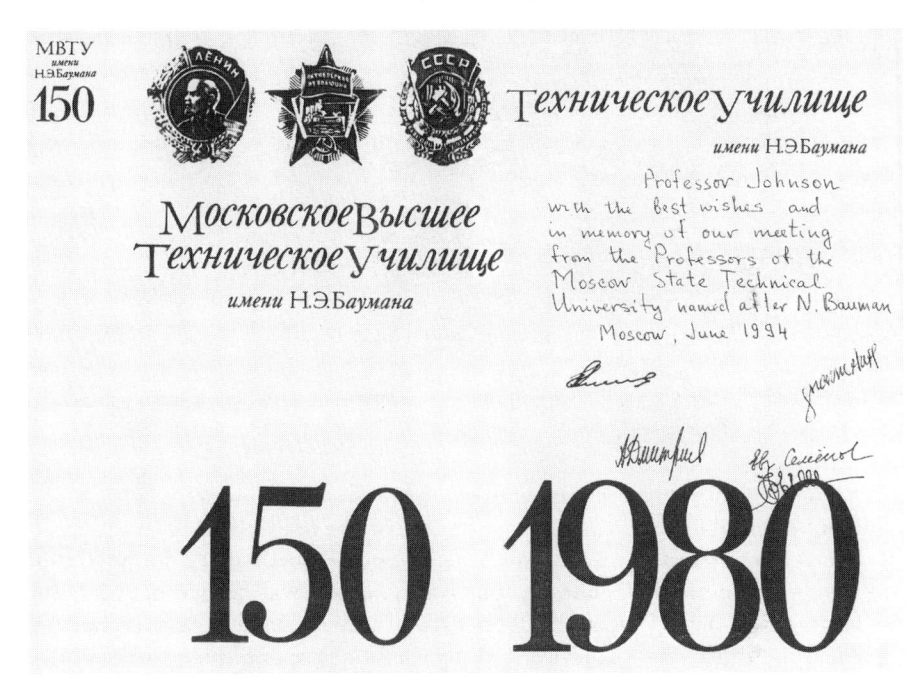

Figure 1. The form of the Bauman Institute Anniversary Volume, 1830–1950, with dedication.

Figure 2. Views of the Institute, then and now.

Figure 3. Honouring Baumann.

The mechanical engineering laboratories of Professor Popov were being renovated but I was able, nevertheless, to see some of the research work in progress. Of special interest to me was the work on electro-magnetic metal forming; this was being conducted in a very confined area sandwiched between two large presses. Many of the exhibits of electro-magnetic swaging were mounted on cards. They had used 'drivers' – appropriately referred to as sputniks – to compel the deformation in thin mild steel tubes. The equipment was obviously got together without special monetary help, and I suspected that Professor Popov was engaged in this work, more out of a spirit of enthusiastic enquiry than one of specially oriented research. (Later I learned that this was indeed the case.) Professor Popov's research interest was in 'sheet metal' and most of his teaching was in this field, too; his reputation and his standing were very high. Research work into oscillatory deep drawing was about to start and a problem on the automatic handling of parts for a press was being investigated. Professor Popov's laboratory was very crowded; he was certainly not over-endowed with space or new equipment.

Arrangements were made, after visiting this laboratory, for me to lecture the following morning. In the evening I was taken to see an Austrian Ice Revue.

Friday

On the Friday morning I used Professor Popov's office for preparing my lecture. His office accommodation was the most trying of any I saw; it was half the size of my office (the UGC standard is about 250 sq. ft. for professors) and was

Figure 4. Discussion at the Baumann Institute, Moscow, May 1968.

shared with two docents. I gave a lecture purely on the research work my group had been doing in Manchester over the previous two years, and after it held a discussion; the session lasted from about 10.15 a.m. to 2.15 p.m. with a break of 10 minutes. I had the help of two interpreters and an audience which seemed to be very interested in the kind of work I (or we) had been doing, see Figure 4. I got through about 70 slides and showed two short films, but had to cut out much that I had hoped to cover. There were, particularly, questions on our practical Explosive Forming work – and no doubt some of the ideas will be tried out by Soviet engineers. There was also a lot of interest in my description of our as yet unpublished (and therefore cautiously circumscribed) magnetic-hydraulic investigations: as yet there are no reported experimental or theoretical results in the literature. The audience in discussion was also very much interested in the British methods of financing research in universities.

After an extended (protracted?!) lunch, from about 2.30 to 4.00 p.m., I was eventually taken to the Strength of Materials Chair which was under the headship of Professor S. D. Ponomarev – nearly two hours late! Professor N. N. Malinin, somewhat younger than Professor Ponomarev, was present and we started on a quite formal level by my being informed of some of the details of the courses in the Department. This stilted dialogue persisted only until we had engaged in what I found to be the usual Russian practice, which was to exchange one's books and research reprints and thereafter declare opinions in a very free and friendly way. I was presented with three very large volumes on the subject of the Machine Design, which had won the Lenin Prize in 1959. (I knew of these three volumes – about 2,500 pages! – because they are world renowned, and one sometimes reads of their excellence in books describing Russian technical education. I had tried, unsuccessfully, to persuade Pergamon Press to translate and market them in about 1961.) I was able to present a good number of research reprints of my own and from my Department. With the formality of our meeting evaporated I was taken to see the laboratories of Professor Malinin. His Materials and Creep Laboratory contained the usual standard testing apparatus, but of great interest was a rig for investigating deformation under *triaxial* loading. As with Professor Popov's laboratory the equipment was good, and in going around the laboratories nothing appeared to be hidden from me. Our discussion of problems and equipment was uninhibited and it was evident to both of us that the problems in our own teaching profession were much the same on both sides of the Iron Curtain.

I left the Department at about 6.30 p.m. and barely had time to arrive at the Moscow State Circus at 7.00 p.m. with Dr Tolya Ovchinnicov. (Dr Ovchinnicov was especially interesting as he was a member of the Joint British-Russian Pamirs' Expedition of some years ago. Dr Ovchinnicov was hoping to be able to spend a year or so in this country in the near future and his Institute had asked that he should spend the time in my Department. Asked what he thought of Sir John Hunt as a climber, he replied, 'Not so bad for an old man'. All these climbers are alike! (My son at 17, also a climber, made the same remark about another well known climber aged 22!)

Saturday

Arrangements were made on Saturday, 25th, for me to meet Academician A. A. Ilyushin of Moscow University, who is internationally known for his work in Applied Mathematics. Originally our appointment was to last half an hour, but there was considerable discussion of his current mathematical research interests and our meeting went on until after 1 o'clock.

I did not see much of the university itself though I was impressed by one or two of the many halls which are to be found on the lower floors. As on other occasions the university architecture, typical of about 1930, was referred to in disparaging terms. However, as with all the meetings I had with scientists in the Soviet Union, they were very pleasant and the exchanges were very useful. I ought to add that a book by Ilyushin and Lensky (I was not able to make contact with Lensky, much as I would have liked to) on Strength or Materials (for students of Mathematics, *not* Engineering) has recently been translated into English, and after examining this I wrote to the authors making some complimentary remarks about their book and offering a number of reprints.

At the termination of our meeting and after having viewed Moscow from the Lenin Hills (see Figure 5), I returned by Metro to the Hotel Russia with Professor Popov, where we had lunch. The Metro is, of course, more impressive than the London Underground in its spaciousness, but as the stations have a distinct architecture, they also appear dated.

Saturday afternoon I spent in the Tritskoya Gallery again with Professor Popov. As something of a painter, he was very happy to impress me with an appreciation of some of the relatively unknown Russian painters. This was a little hard to do because I was spoiled by being in Italy for two years.

Figure 5. Professor 'Gene Popov and I overlooking the river in Moscow, on my first visit, 1968. (It was cold!)

In the evening I went to the Palace of Meetings where I saw the usual wonderfully directed and marvellously executed folk dancing. This palace, as must have been thought by many others, was to me the finest I have ever been in. It is, of course, used for the All-Soviet meetings and required therefore to be something of a show-place. The seating was superbly comfortable with lots of room for one's arms and legs. (There was also a facility for receiving simultaneous translations.) I was as well very impressed with the cloakroom facilities since these were organised on a scale I had never witnessed before! The arrangements for refreshments on the top floor of this building were likewise most impressive.

Sunday

Sunday was my 'day of rest' and was devoted entirely to 'cultural' activities. (Why did we have to categorise our visits as 'cultural'? Were we afraid we might enjoy them?!) We returned to the Lenin Hills to survey Moscow and to take photographs on Sunday morning, then drove along Kalinin Prospekt to take in the sight of some of the fine new buildings which had been recently erected. I had expressed a wish to see the Moscow Planetarium – an obligation laid upon me by my youngest son, a keen astronomer – said to be the largest in the world.

The planetarium was, of course, much like other planetaria, the main hall being surrounded by small exhibitions relating to particular astronomical phenomena of current interest. Since we had only a limited amount of time I was conveyed and introduced to the Director of the planetarium who asked the lecturer and operator of the projector to put on a short display. The capabilities of the planetarium were exhibited over some ten minutes and, in particular, a quite interesting and novel introduction was the simulation of the movement of satellites against the sky and the introduction of earth into 'the sky' to facilitate an appreciation of the heavens from the surface of the moon. (This special effort was made on my behalf since I would otherwise have had to wait an hour for the next show.) From the planetarium we drove to Professor Popov's flat for coffee.

Further sightseeing of Moscow followed and, in particular, as I had expressed a wish to try a real Borshch I was taken to the Hotel Ukraine where we had lunch at about 5 o'clock in the afternoon. I was assured that the Borshch I was served was the best that could be had in Moscow – short of going to the village in the Ukraine from which our waitress derived. After this leisurely lunch we moved to the flat of one of Professor Popov's assistants, Dr Colya Lyapunov. (Mr Shubin drove us everywhere in the High School car.) There I was entertained with Russian music for an hour or two until the next alimentary trial started, with dinner at about 9 o'clock. Dr Lyapunov's flat was one which he was buying through one of the Moscow Co-operatives. It was apparent that as a young married couple they were very similar – as ambitious and houseproud – as those in the West. Their flat was rather small, not awfully well finished, but brightly painted (paint there is rather rare, except when being used for the restoration of buildings) and had new, sparkling furniture.

Monday

We departed for the night train to Leningrad at about 11.30 p.m. on a Sunday. I was in a state of contented repletion, having consumed and drunk enough to sustain me for the next three days. The train departed precisely at 11.55 p.m. Dr Lyapunov was to accompany me on my two days' visit to Leningrad. We had two bunks in a four-berth compartment, one of whose occupants was a female.

I let fall to the floor from my upper bunk, Laurence van der Post's *Journey into Russia*. It was picked up and returned to me by a traveller below. When I switched out my light in the dark he asked to see the book. He returned it the following morning without comment.

The train arrived promptly in Leningrad at 8.15 a.m. on Monday, the journey having been uneventfully covered at an average speed much less than that of a comparable Manchester to London journey; for this reason it was possible to sleep more comfortably. Dr Lyapunov and I had had accommodation booked for us in the Hotel Octuabzskay which, at this time, was very full because a film festival was in progress. A good many people congregated about the hotel entrance because many Russian film stars were to be seen. The accommodation was perfectly satisfactory and on this occasion I had a television set!

I would like to insert at this point a few thoughts and facts which I had accumulated at this time.

(i) I learned that there is no compulsory age of retirement for professors.

Apparently they are at liberty to choose when they retire (after 65) and, if they wish to, may remain in harness until they die or are incapable of getting themselves to their office! The head of Professor Popov's department in Moscow was aged 75. I think some of the young assistants were inclined to wonder if Professors should indeed be allowed to remain 'active' and 'in office' for so long.

(ii) There are departments of Machine Building in the Soviet Technical Universities; I do not know of any equivalent in the UK This is certainly one of the shortcomings which we would do well to improve.

(iii) Before departing for the USSR I had read Stephen Timoshenko's autobiography *As I remember* and an American book about the Soviet system of technical education. The American opinion seemed to be that the Soviet text book writers are encyclopaedic. I think this term was used to indicate broadness of coverage rather than quality of work. As I knew at least one of the American engineering professors concerned it did not surprise me to find that I could not agree with his assessment. From the Russian books and papers I have collected, and from my own previous knowledge, it is not simply that the Russians are collators. I suspect that, historically, due to their state of comparative isolation they have had to be far more concerned to produce books which cover all aspects of work and they have not felt able to rely on foreign sources.

Russian books in my field are second to none,* both in extent and in depth. Their scholarship in engineering has, traditionally, been great. I acquired 20 kg of books and papers, etc., during my journeys, and after examination and discussion with a good number of Russians my conclusion is that the Russian work is certainly very thorough. (As I have remarked, I did not need this visit to confirm this opinion.) On this visit I was also impressed by the uniformly high standard of knowledge and experience which the Russians – the professors – bring to their academic departments, though in Moscow I may have been encountering the cream of the Soviet educational system and to this extent my views may therefore be lacking in balance. There is certainly not the same uniformly high degree of professionalism and soundness to be found throughout the UK.

The Soviet system demands a very high degree of engineering specialisation from its professors and teachers; in Britain our practice is such as to promote the wider view, and to give a wider research opportunity. (I prefer our system which allows me to pursue my own research interests, to change direction if I wish and to work with the energy and enthusiasm which comes to the 'self-starter' granted the right to self-guidance or complete independence.)

(iv) It is a little hard for an Englishman to grasp how greatly the Russians respect learning. This manifests itself in very many ways. For example, in exhibitions for children, the respect of the university students for the professors (!),

---

* Pergamon Press published, in translation, many Russian engineering science classics – due to Maxwell! See Chapter XVIII.

competitiveness for university places, the attention paid to book learning, and so on. I would like to have discussed with the Russians the general usefulness of Universities and to ask if they do not seriously over-value academics. After all, many profitable engineering industries do not derive much of value from Universities or, indeed, Engineering Departments (e.g. most of the American automobile industry). Perhaps to the Soviets engineering is basically a science, whilst the mass of the West sees and practises it as an art, a technology or a craft.

I was first introduced to Professor Smirnov, Rector of the Leningrad Polytechnic, which has about 30,000 students though no one seemed to know to within plus or minus 6,000). Some details of its activities are obtainable in the Battelle Memorial Institute volume on Soviet Research Institutes, etc. Professor Smirnov, besides being Rector, was a Professor of the Rolling of Metals, part of the field of Metal Plasticity, an area of great interest to me) yet he still managed to find time to direct a number of Aspirants (in effect, Ph.D. students). Our initial meeting around the table was, as usual, somewhat formal, and it was only later that I managed to move the conversation onto his current work and interests in rolling theory. My persistent questioning of Professor Smirnov led to his presenting me with a copy of his book. I do not believe that he had intended to do this and I think it was given as something of a palliative. Whilst I was conducted around the laboratory of Professor Smirnov, the most interesting experimental feature I learned of was the design of a rolling-mill which was able to cross-roll, i.e. with the roll axes set at a particularly large angle to the sheet-moving direction.

Before visiting Professor Borgovolensky's laboratory I was taken to lunch in the Staff House and found myself competing with him in consuming Georgian brandy.

In Professor Borgovolensky's laboratory I was very interested in a piece of work dealing with the roll forming of small turbine blades. The blades were accurately formed, bent and twisted in a small two-high mill. Some very interesting work had also been done on the design of a sheet bending mill and I was shown a model consisting of eighteen stands.

It was then late afternoon and at the conclusion of the visit, I went with Professor Borgovolensky and his assistant to see the Leningrad Cemetery, where many of the one million people who starved to death during 900 days of the Second World War are buried. Following this we separated and with assistant Dr Lyapunov I went to see the Isaki Cathedral, which has been beautifully restored, and then the Winter Palace and the Summer Garden of Peter the Great. This was followed by a tour of the City in general and a walk along the Nevski Prospekt. Certainly Leningrad was a fine and gracious city – probably looking westward! By contrast, however, Moscow had the attractive air of mystery and orientalism.

Tuesday

On Tuesday morning I asked Dr Lyapunov to make arrangements for me to see Professor Stepanov who was in the Department of Technical Physics in the

Leningrad Polytechnic. I had met Professor Stepanov in Czechoslovakia two years previously when I had to share a bedroom with him. (I was the only Englishman in this Western party and there were three Americans. It would have been unthinkable for one of them – especially the one from the Navy Department – to share a bedroom with a Russian – the implications to the CIA would have been enormous!) Professor Stepanov had worked in the field of high speed indentation, and since I had also been occupied in this line of research, there was a good deal for us to talk about. After an hour's telephoning, Dr Lyapunov was able to make an arrangement to see Professor Stepanov at 3 o'clock in the afternoon. Thus, at 11.00 a.m. we departed for a visit to Petrogorf, which was a Summer Palace of the Czar. In many ways the Palace, with its multiplicity of beautiful fountains, was very reminiscent of the Villa D'Este at Tivoli, near Rome. The whole of the Palace had been beautifully restored and was a very delightful spot to visit. It was about 30 kilometres from Leningrad, and on this occasion we were led on tour by another of Professor Borgovolensky's assistants and his wife.

A consequence of my visiting Professor Stepanov was to lose the opportunity of visiting the Hermitage, but as I had by now become convinced that I would be visiting the Soviet Union again in the course of the next year or two, it did not seem so terrible an omission from my itinerary.

More than Professor Stepanov, I would have liked to meet a Professor Zlatin because we had recently been doing work – the high speed impact of hot metals – somewhat similar to some he did some years before. Whilst his results and interpretations were very enlightening for certain processes, they appeared to be incomplete for others. It would have been worthwhile to have had the chance of hearing Professor Zlatin comment on our own results. My visit to Professor Stepanov was also very useful in that I learned of the work of Professor Zusman which dealt with fracture and cavity formation in polymers.

Further enquiries at points in my visit showed that there seemed to be as little intercommunication between the students of Physics and Engineering in the Soviet Union as there was in the UK and USA.

It was of interest for me to note that in the Leningrad Institute there was a department devoted to Artillery Science, and I was intrigued to see them taking guns into a particular laboratory. I wonder if the Leningrad Polytechnic was founded by Frenchmen on the Napoleonic École Polytechnique model and that, by tradition, Artillery Science was still taught?

Later on Tuesday evening Dr Lyapunov and I strolled in the Palace of Pioneers; we also drank a lot of mineral water since the evening had become hot and sultry. I was surprised to hear some of the BBC overseas programmes being listened to on transistor radios in the Leningrad parks. We took the night train back to Moscow at 11.40 p.m.

Wednesday

I spent some time making notes about my visits, but between 10.30 a.m. and 12.00 noon I made the first of three visits to the Kremlin with Professor Popov.

We were unable to visit the Museum of Armoury and contented ourselves with visits to the churches. These had, of course, been very well renovated and, as all visitors observed, the Soviet Union was making a tremendous effort to stimulate the tourist industry. I found, generally, that the Soviet people had little interest in their churches unless they were classified as national monuments, but I was very surprised to note that on the wall of the Hotel Russia the style of depicting a Soviet woman and her child gazing into the future was almost identical with that to be found on many of the diptychs in the churches.

I had some small discussion with Professor Popov about the place of the church in the USSR. This was not very profound but only of factual interest. (All attempts to discuss religion in a wide context seemed to founder in references to 'the Jesus'.) There was clearly a conference of members of the Orthodox church in session, because the Hotel Russia was accommodating many ecclesiastics. These men looked very well fed, seemed buoyant and confident, and certainly gave no impression of persecution. According to Professor Popov – who made the observation – such a conference was not reported in the Russian press. Apparently there was a body which was composed of representatives of the Church and the State which discussed matters of mutual interest. Of course, the State did not contribute to the upkeep of the Church, which seemingly existed on gifts. These must have been handsome gifts because, as I have remarked, the ecclesiastics seemed to live very well. It would appear that permission for the church to exist owed a lot to Stalin, who apparently had not forgotten the part the church played during the last war in helping to achieve national solidarity, and when it was therefore at one with the Soviet State in opposing the Germans. It would appear that many of the Russian people were well aware of the fact that only certain things were reported in their newspapers. On other matters political, the only comment I could draw when I referred to the Chinese as now possessing an atomic bomb was an observation that 'The Chinese possess a bomb but they have no pants'. This was in line with another observation when one of them remarked to me somewhat shamefacedly that 'we have sputniks but no brown shoes'.

The English *Morning Star* was easily bought in the Hotel Russia. It surprised my friends to find I had little time for it; also the opinion that I could do without political information for ten days, because the world would still be as confused when I departed for home as when I arrived, was beyond comprehension.

At mid-day Professor Popov and I went by taxi to the flat of Academician Artobolevskii, in the centre of Moscow. My connection with the Academician was of five or six years' standing. I was the Translation Editor for one of his books which was published by Pergamon Press on 'The Synthesis of Plane Mechanisms'. Academician Artobolevskii and I had exchanged letters and I had written a preface to the English translation of his book expressing the hope that an area of research which was once well pursued in this country (the UK) would be revived by being brought to the attention of English readers. The backwardness of the UK in the Theory of Mechanisms was monumental and had not much improved over the years.

The following November, Academician Artobolevskii and his wife were invited to London as the guests of the Institution of Mechanical Engineers, and he was presented with the James Watt International Medal, a triennial award to outstanding foreign engineering scientists. I was present on the occasion of the award and later, when he visited various parts of the country, he visited UMIST and gave a lecture at an Institution of Mechanical Engineers branch meeting held here. Academician Artobolevskii and his wife were entertained to lunch by one of my staff, Dr J. Parker, and by my wife and I to tea, in our homes. A very pleasant relationship was built up, and I think that on the occasion of my visit to Moscow, Academician and Mrs Artobolevskii wanted to show their appreciation for our efforts.

After half an hour's technical discussion and an introduction to various engineers, we sat down to lunch at 12.30 p.m. I should add that I was pleased to note a picture of Professor Osborne Reynolds (see Figure 1 Chapter XVIII.) (the first Professor of Engineering in the University of Manchester) on the wall of the Academician's study. This was presented to him whilst he was in Manchester. The lunch continued until after 3 o'clock and was a very happy affair. Apparently Academician Artobolevskii had many friends amongst the 'artistes' and so at his table there was one singer from the opera, one from operetta and one folk-singer. Soon after the lunch commenced the opera singer sat down at a grand piano in the dining room and sang a selection from *The Merry Widow*; a little later the operetta singer did likewise and later still the folk-singer had his turn. All were, of course, excellent. This was a very unusual experience, especially as Mrs Artobolevskii felt constrained to present each singer with a small bouquet of flowers after his contribution.

Academician Artobolevskii's research work was, of course, not identical with mine, and clearly his Institute was very deeply involved in problems of automatic control and automation. Academician Blagonravov, the head of the Institute at which Academician Artobolevskii worked, had been conspicuous in the Soviet Space Programme. Throughout the lunch I had an interesting conversation with Academician Artobolevskii's sister, who was (I believe) a professor at the Marx-Engels Institute; she appeared to know the city of Manchester well, having visited it for 'material'. Towards the end of the lunch (I counted twelve bottles of spirits in circulation at one juncture) both the lady to whom I talked and the opera singer had to depart, but the other two singers remained, forsook the grand piano, and acquiring a large balalaika commenced to sing gypsy duets until the lunch was terminated. I think that there were eight toasts – as far as I can recall!

Professor Popov and I returned to my hotel at 4 o'clock so I was pleased that my next appointment was not until 6.30 p.m. when I went to a performance of Swan Lake, which was given in the Palace of Conferences on this occasion. As all who have seen the Bolshoi Ballet know, their rendering of classical ballet is near perfection. It was a very delightful evening. Many impressions of this day remain with me – too many to record.

Thursday

On Thursday morning, the 30th, Professor Ye. P. Unksov and Professor Popov arrived by taxi and took me to the Central Scientific Research Institute of

Technology and Machine Building, of which Professor Unskov was the Director. This Institute was started in 1931 and was one of the largest in the Soviet Union; it was very well known to mechanical engineers and it enjoys a very high reputation. Some account of it and the senior staff attached to it can be found in the Battelle Memorial Institute volume. I had known Professor Unksov for several years by name and reputation. His book 'Engineering Plasticity' was, among other things, badly translated when published by PERA.* – and unfortunately (for me now) I had said so when reviewing it. I recall also that it was written in the early 1950s when Stalin was alive, and I suspect that some of the nationalism which it displayed was due to his remote pressure.

Professor Unksov had been a member of the Editorial Advisory Board of the Journal I edited† for about two years and for this reason our meeting was disposed to get off to a good start. (Professor Popov and Professor A. D. Tomlenov are likewise on this Editorial Advisory Board.)

I was struck, however, by the similarity of treatment on visiting this Institute and that which I received when I visited the Leningrad Polytechnic and elsewhere. Again, we all sat around a table and I had first to be regaled by general but often uninteresting remarks about the Institute – all of which were translated to me by a female translator, with Professor Unksov speaking in Russian, even though his English was better than that of the translator! The whole time I was at the Institute the translator was present and she had the unfortunate, and frequent, experience of being corrected by Professor Unksov and others from time to time. Exactly why this poor woman was made to sit through our meeting and accompany us through various laboratories, I do not know. I indicated to Professor Unksov that I was only interested in visiting the laboratories concerned with metal working and Strength of Materials. We confined ourselves therefore to these: both laboratories in his Institute were very large. This was the *only* Institute which I visited where I felt that I was capable of really learning something – and that Professor L. V. Prozadorov there should be more widely known.

(In my full Report I described eleven subjects of research, all extremely interesting to the engineering-scientist only and thus they must regrettably be omitted here.)

When we returned to Professor Unksov's office at the conclusion of the tour we found that one of his post-doctoral students had set out a great number of very large graphs and diagrams concerned with investigations he had been pursuing over 2½ years into the determination of the coefficient of friction in the forward extrusion process carried out at different ram speeds. This was, of course, especially interesting because Dr J. H. Lamble‡ and I had had a research student do precisely this same investigation some years before, and we had published our results in two papers which appeared in the *Proceedings* of the Machine Tool Design and Research Conference for 1964 and 1965. We had used 'pressure pins' for measuring the container wall normal stress and the container wall frictional

---

* Production Engineering Research Association.
† The *Int. Jnl. of Mechanical Sciences*.
‡ Reader in Mechanical Engineering at UMIST

stress. We had also explored the possibility – and shown it to be quite feasible and reliable – of obtaining the same information using photo-elastic techniques; it was this which the Russians had used to carry out their very extensive investigations the results of which were now laid out. I had some discussion with the young engineer who had been responsible for the work. It was gratifying to learn that they had obtained very similar results to those we had – even to the extent of obtaining seemingly *negative* coefficients of friction in some regions!

I had considerable discussion with Professor Unksov about publications in Russia and, in particular, it appeared that one large Russian book on Plasticity which he had despatched to me had, in fact, never arrived. This latter book would have been very useful. It was published in 1959 and would have afforded me a view of the status of Slip Line Field work in Russia round about 1960 when I was engaged in writing my two books. In discussing publications with Professors Unksov and Popov it came to light that my monograph with Professor Kudo on *The Mechanics of Metal Extrusion*, which had been translated into Russian, mainly on the recommendation of Professor Tomlenov, published and had been sold at about 7s. 6d. (90 Kopecks) per copy. They had printed 2,650 copies in 1965 and apparently the edition was sold out within a matter of two weeks. This monograph, in English, first published by the Manchester University Press at 40 shillings (or £2 in late 1962, had only just sold about 1,000 copies!

Throughout this conversation we were eating cake and drinking brandy, and as it was turned 1 o'clock I had begun to believe that this was lunch. However, it was not, because at 1.30 p.m. Professor Prozadorov and Professor Unksov decided that they would like to take me to lunch and we moved to the Hotel Russia. This was a very pleasant lunch where, for once, the drinking was not predominant. The conversation touched on many matters other than those concerned with engineering and science. I think that I sensed here, as on several occasions, that the Russians are critical of the West for seeming to take so little interest in its cultural achievements. At one point in the lunch I was challenged to name eight Russian writers, and failure to have done this would have been evidence that the Western intellectuals neglect, and are indifferent to, Russian art and literature. (I was allowed to include Boris Pasternak!) A particular point of the discussion which remains in my mind concerned with the way the world is developing with respect to the appearances or interests of the younger generation. Professor Popov had many times observed that his daughter failed to appreciate the difficult times through which he and, in particular, the Russian people had lived. I have had much the same impression regarding British youth. The hardships and economic and political upheavals which all peoples have lived through but which have largely disappeared since about 1950, are little known or appreciated by our children. Certainly the relatively high standards of living to which all the present generation in the West is habituated is taken for granted and any thought about what some people may still need is a light-hearted matter for many of them. I expressed the opinion that as the older Russian generation passes, the young ones, who would not have been familiar with the Revolution and the hard times of the 1920s and early 1930s, will not understand the policies which have been pursued in the past, and I ventured to think that youth everywhere will find many of the difficulties and troubles which have existed between nations – Britain, America and the Soviet Union – rather silly. They will have no memory of the difficulties which they have all endured and the problems will seem very unreal. That all industrial nations are moving in much the same direction and will produce much the same sort of civilisation was not an idea with which Professor Unksov was able to agree. It seemed to me, however, to be a very obvious evolutionary development.

I departed at about 3 o'clock for the Institute of Machine Science to see Professor A. D. Tomlenov. His research interests were predominantly in the field of the plasticity of sheet metal and plate. I had been in touch with Professor Tomlenov for a longer period than with any other Russian and I had, over the years, received copies of Russian books from him; it was thus a great pleasure to meet him. As he had no teaching function he was able, naturally, to devote very much time to research problems, and I found him in charge of perhaps half a dozen post-doctoral students to each of whom was assigned a research problem. For brevity I describe only one research – the experiments being conducted on water-hammer forming. Professor Tomlenov had been engaged on this project for six or seven years. A column of water 'sits' on a diaphragm, which is held on a thin circular steel disc firmly clamped around its circumference, so that when a weight falls on to the top of the column of water, a shock wave is transmitted which, in impinging on the thin metal sheet, causes it to move with a high velocity. The kinetic energy acquired by the metal is dissipated in doing plastic work, the diaphragm taking up its appointed convex shape in a female die provided. I learned that an industrial machine embodying this principle was expected imminently. I was very interested in this investigation because my (UMIST) Division – it was quite an original idea with us, i.e. Dr Donaldson and myself, in 1962 – had published three papers on this subject and we subsequently gave up further exploration of it due to lack of industrial interest. I might mention that later I received a brochure from Tokyo, emanating from the Tokyo Car Manufacturing Company which had produced and marketed a machine using the water-hammer principle for the efficient forming of sheet metal, the surface of the metal formed in this fashion being extremely good.

Friday

On Friday morning I again endeavoured, with Professor Popov, to visit the Armaments Museum in the Kremlin, but it was closed – it being a 'rest day' for the staff. And for exactly the same reason I was unable to pay a visit to Lenin's Mausoleum. I did, however, pay visits to a number of churches in the Kremlin which I had not previously visited. This was our last 'cultural visit'. Professor Popov was heard to say that in the course of the last nine days he had completed his cultural programme for the next two years; for my part I had completed my alcoholic programme for the next five years!

At about noon I went with Professor Popov on a small shopping expedition and was able to gain some impression of the goods available to the Muscovites, especially in their renowned Universal Stores (GUM). I found quite a lot of articles which it would have been interesting to purchase – which was contrary to information given me at other times, namely, that there was nothing in the Russian shops which would be of interest to purchase. I bought fur hats for my three sons and a few other mementoes. Later, I purchased a number of records, all remarkably cheap. Of the 'pop' records I brought home, 'Gorod Spat' was quite a success.

Late in the afternoon I endeavoured to complete my packing, but found that I had acquired an excess of books, papers and journals. Nonetheless these were securely packed up by Dr Lyapunov and armed with a letter from the Rector of the Bauman School, we departed for the Airport. The purpose of this letter was to ask the airline people to carry the books free of charge! I thought they were over-optimistic, and indeed they were. I believe Professor Popov paid something like £15 excess baggage charge to BEA to carry them home.

We arrived at Sheremotovo Airport at 5.50 p.m. for the 'plane which was supposed to leave at 5.55 p.m. Fortunately, the take-off was delayed by half an hour and I was able to take the 'plane as planned. We arrived at London Airport at about 7.55 p.m. and the usual immigration facilities were completed very easily. I caught the Manchester 'plane, only to find on arrival at Manchester there was a strike in progress and some difficulty about unloading the baggage. The passengers and air crew did the unloading. I mention this latter point, since, if it had occurred in reverse, that is, on my arrival in Moscow, it would have been entirely in line with many of the reports one reads in our newspapers and books. This is just to record that when seen in reverse such events can present a very different picture.

On reflection I found that my experiences in the Soviet Union did not tally with those I had read about.* I am quite prepared to believe that my own experience was unique and that it was entirely attributable to the fact that in Moscow I went to friends and was never at any time entrusted to the bureaucracy. It is fitting to add that on three visits to Czechoslovakia and two to Hungary – to or with the help of friends – I have also never encountered difficulties. My troubles always started on reaching home base.

The visit to the USSR was very enjoyable and, though hard on my stomach, was thoroughly worthwhile.

---

* I tried to recall some of the books – regardless of articles, radio and television programmes and films – that conspired to prepare (or prejudice) me for what I encountered in the Soviet Union. I have tried to read Das Kapital (did not get beyond p. 50), Peter Kropotkin's 'Mutual Aid', something by Plekhanov, Lenin's tract 'On the State and Revolution', Burnham on 'The Managerial Revolution', 'I Choose Freedom' by Kravchenko, Souvarin's 'Stalin', 'Darkness at Noon', 'The Dark Side of the Moon', 'The God that Failed', Silone's novels, Fitzroy Maclean's 'Eastern Approaches', something by Odette Keun, Wells on *Russia*, Morehead's 'The Russian Revolution', Geoffrey Gorer's psychological analyses of the Russians, the spurious The Long Walk Home, Shokolov, Ehrenburg, Tolstoi, Gogol, Turgenev ... and Noel Behn's recent 'Kremlin Letter'.

(ii) Impressions: Visiting Ekaterinburg and Perm in the Urals, Russia, 1994*

To see something of Moscow and St Petersburg is common but a journey into the middle part of the Ural mountain region is something of a rarity for an Englishman and as an opportunity presented itself to me, it was quickly grasped. My short visit to Russia of about 17 days was naturally made in warm weather, so I was there in early June, 1994. (My host early prepared an attractive thermographic diagram!) The prime purpose of my visit was to meet members of the Ural Branch of the Russian Academy of Sciences – of which esteemed body I had had the honour to be an elected member.

I thought an account of the high points of my journey and of some details about actual travel to and around western Russia as I encountered it might, in different ways, help and encourage others to make such a journey.

I flew from Manchester to Moscow by Aeroflot, (the fare being £300 return as opposed to BA's £425), some of the difference in cost being attributable to less comfortable conditions of seating and other arrangements, but ones by no means representing hardship. The meals served were, if anything, superior to BA's oft-repeated servings.

Ekaterinburg, (henceforth designated E), is at the middle of the 2000 km. N/S mountain range (just inside Asia) which constitutes the boundary between the European and the Asiatic geological continental plates; it is along such a common boundary that metals are found. Thus Russia's great metallurgical industry is distributed along this line.

The flying time to Moscow was almost four hours and I elected to make the on-going journey of about 1,000 miles to E, almost due east of Moscow, by train enjoying a first class comfortable compartment with sleeping arrangements (and bedding) for two.†

Until relatively recently, E was Sverdlovsk, the name of the local revolutionary leader of 1917. As in pre-Revolutionary days and since 1992, the town has again become that of (Czarina) Catherine, of Ekaterinburg. A shrine was in process of being erected in memory of the last Czar, and family when we were there.

We departed Manchester at 10.30 a.m. and arrived at Sheremetievo airport at 5.30 p.m., local time. In respect of volume of traffic it was not to be compared with Heathrow and correspondingly we were efficiently passed through the Immigration and Customs barriers. It was impressive to watch the lines of *'camels'* passing through Customs. These were individuals arriving home from abroad carrying large quantities of goods, intentionally imported for sale on the domestic market. Soon picked out by our host, Corresponding Member of the Russian Academy Prof. V. L. Kolmogorov, we were carried off to a Russian Academy of Science's hotel, Uzkoe, on the quiet outskirts of Moscow, an hour's hard, pot-holed road journey away! This was a nice large and airy hotel by our standards, of rather average price, having a restaurant with meals which were certainly adequate and well served. All our costs in Russia were everywhere

---

* Advances in Materials Processing Technologies, Dublin City University Press, 223–235, 1995.
† Though I write here mostly in terms of myself, my wife accompanied me throughout the whole of the visit.

paid for by the ailing Russian economy through their Academy of Sciences. One train per day departs form Moscow for E, at 6 p.m., reaching it at about 10.30 p.m. the following night; the railway stations are sad, dilapidated places and, like the roads, in need of much money spending on them. The western media leads the visitor to expect crime but we saw none of it, though we did see people with evident drug problems but no more so than in London.

Figure 6 gives a sketch of the rail route which we followed. Over the thousand miles which we travelled (outside of the towns) there was little change in the countryside with an endless stream of small wooden cottages dotted about, some given over to farming but the mass, seemingly, being weekend self-built dwellings around which numerous vegetables and flowers were grown. The country was everywhere green, neat, mostly empty and impressively large.

I remember gazing at the mighty Volga river, with tributary the Kama, (and indeed so wide that Peter the Great had his Caspian fleet built hereabouts for his campaign against Persia) and the onion-shaped cupolas of Kazan – easily visible from the railway coach and by then perhaps a 7 hour ride East of Moscow. For this sight we were prepared by an early call at 4.30 a.m. It is astonishing, on reflection, how little we seem to know of Russia, thinking of ancient towns such as Kazan and Novgorod. The Kazan of Middle Russia is made up of Russians and Tatars, respectively Greek Orthodox (70%) and Moslem (30%). On a hill in Kazan is the Kreml or citadel, built 1437, with its walls of view towers, surrounding a cathedral from 1562 and several churches, a monastery and arsenal. (Seemingly, remarkably similar to the Moscow Kremlin, this city is noted for its oriental scholarship and its Kazan State University founded there in 1804.) In passing, literally, it was recalled that N. Lobatchewsky was here the university Rector; to him *'the honour of being the effective discoverer of non-Euclidean (hyperbolic) geometry must be assigned'*; his first publication was dated 1826.

I may insert that before reaching Kazan we had stopped – probably at P'yanski Perevoz – a town noted for glass manufacture, the platform being packed with many people selling sets of crystal glassware at low prices.

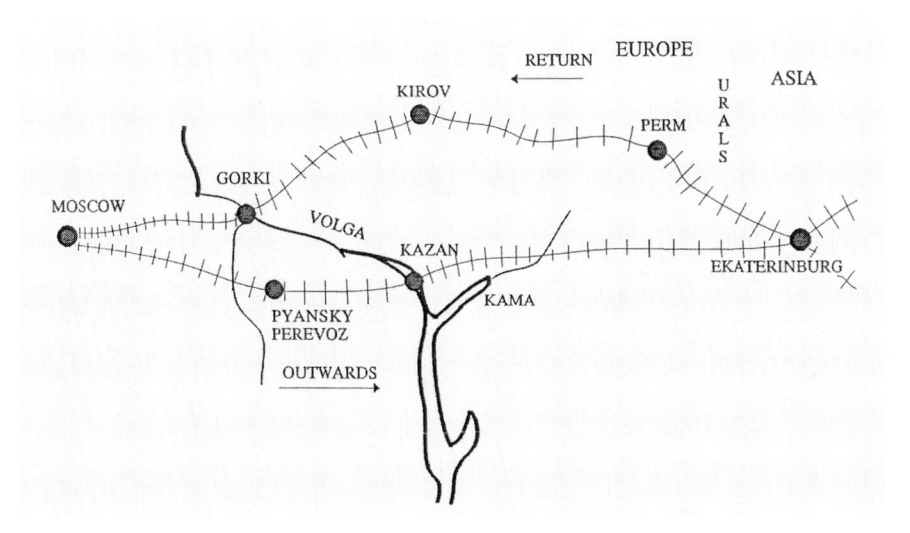

Figure 6. Moscow to Ekaterinburg (1000 miles).

We checked in at the Oktyabrskaya Hotel E, – large and with a good restaurant – at nearly midnight on Sunday. It is on the edge of a park and very close to the Scientific Institute and similar bodies we were to visit.

The next morning – notably it was the 6 June, the 50th anniversary of D-Day – we were received at the Ural Branch Presidium by Vice-President Academician Prof. V. Koroteev and his senior staff of Academicians and Professors. After some formalities, information was exchanged about the Russian and British Academies of Science. At some point we enjoyed a little light refreshment and then a meeting with the Leaders and the Scientific Council of the Institute of Engineering Science under Professor E. S. Gorkunov's direction for an account of its work. Among other encounters I recall a meeting with some of the professors at the Institute of Mathematics and Mechanics, headed by Acad. Prof. A. Sidorov, when several professors made short speeches of welcome in English (!) and spoke in some detail of the work they and their research student were carrying out (See Note 1). Particularly interesting was an exchange I had with Acad. N. Krasovskii about a short book on Computer Games and Puzzles he had written for the serious teaching of computational methods and mathematics by means of examples for young teenagers. Apparently he had already written a number of such books and they had sold very well; (I brought home a copy of his latest book and showed it to a British publisher, recommending it for translation and publication in English. This was accepted but is a project not in process of fulfilment alas.)

At this latter meeting we had some discussion about the possibility of making accessible in the West some of the Institute's results which they believed could form the basis of patents. I next visited some of the laboratories but language problems made exchanges about metal-forming research difficult. This first day was long and full of intense discussions which went on for several hours.

Scientific seminars were held from 10 a.m. to 2 p.m. for the next three days. Typically, I had some lunch with the UPI professors after 2 p.m. There was much discussion of programmes concerning grants, research outlets and co-operation with the UK. One significant outcome was that an unofficial programme for mutual help was able to be drawn up and signed by the Institute President and myself, with Prof. A. Bogatov, Head of the Metal Forming Department, UPI making strong contributions to our exchanges.

In the late afternoons during these latter days I was able to see something of the sights of E mainly under the knowledgeable guidance of the English-speaking Dr M. Vierb (of the Urals State Forest Academy). It is a large town of about one and a half million population with of course its people housed in massive blocks of flats and many, alas, now needing serious renovation. The streets and boulevards are wide and extensive and the centre seems very well serviced by a tram car system, motor cars being a comparative rarity, see Figures 7 and 8. Conspicuously in a town centre square in the open air, was a permanent exhibition of large ancient engines and metal-forming equipment, rolling mills and tilt hammers for example, see Figure 9. It reminded me of Sheffield and particularly of a visit not three months before, to Wortley Old Forge on the occasion of the award to the City of a certificate of excellence by English Heritage.

On consecutive evenings we saw first, Tchaikovsky's ballet *Sleeping Beauty* at the Opera House and secondly, a production of the musical *Oliver!* rendered in Russian, and as the programmes noted, 'After Charles Dickens'! Both productions were at least three-hour shows! The ballet, as one would expect in Russia, was beautifully performed before a packed audience which consisted mostly of mothers and small daughters in

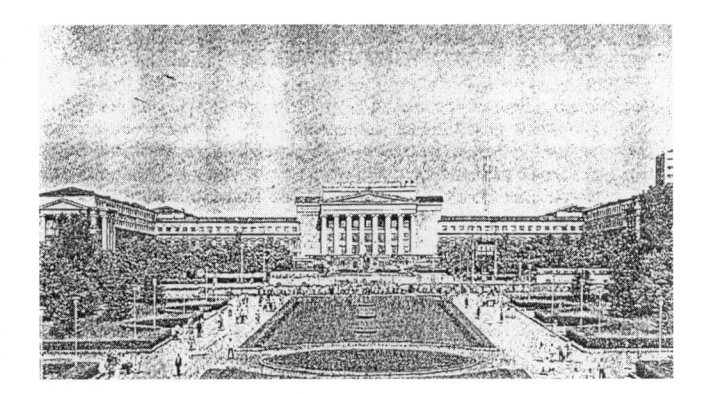

Figure 7. Illustration, The city centre, Ekaterinburg.

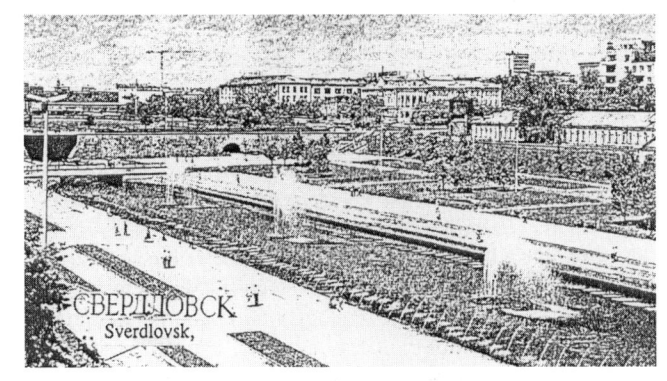

Figure 8. Illustration, The city centre, Ekaterinburg.

Figure 9. Illustration, Exhibition of an early pump, Ekaterinburg.

ballet-like attire. The production of *Oliver!* followed the British film closely, except for the introduction of a trio of French-style mummers and an adaptation of the hanging of Bill Sykes. I had the opportunity to talk to the Director of the production after the show and was astonished to learn that it was not to be put on in other parts of Russia (or offered for presentation/sale, in part, to the BBC!) The costumes were superb for both productions and one was at a loss to understand how they could be staged for the minuscule admission charge of 20p. In Moscow, tickets for ballet cost pounds, these being intended, I suppose, to be bought by visitors, whilst the 20p in E, one imagines, simply matched the level of income of the average Russian in that town. See Figures 10 and 11.

Of special scientific interest to me, in E, was a visit organised to the Geological Museum where I soon recognised that a great effort had been put into establishing it; I do not know what could compare with it in the UK outside the British Science Museum in South Kensington, London. Of specific interest to me were volcanic bombs and fulgarites and I enquired if they had any on display. I was directed to an upper floor where a fine collection of many sizes and kinds of bombs had been assembled. A number of them were not shown and I took the opportunity to handle them and therefore, to compare different types. Unfortunately, the female geological curator had no English and therefore, discussion was difficult. I tried to buy a bomb, was refused, but in compensation was given, freely, a small specimen which I still possess. I endeavoured to engage one of the custodians in a discussion of the details of the extensiveness/ stratigraphy of various kinds of rock in the south Urals area and in the presence of maps and models, but alas, this was again linguistically difficult. Any visitor to the Urals with the smallest knowledge of geology who encounters the name Perm will also instantly call to mind the term, the Permian Layer. The latter comprises *'the youngest and uppermost system of strata of the Palaeozoic series situated above the Carboniferous and below the Trias'*. The term Permian derives from the Russian province of Perm where these rocks are extensively developed and were, apparently, so identified by Sir Roderick Murchison (1792–1871) of Scotland who made three visits to Russia. During the second visit in 1842, made with a Dr de Verneuil, they started from Moscow and *'struck off for the Ural mountains, followed them southwards to Orsk (at the bottom of the Ural chain) and then went west to the Sea of Azov.'* (Encyclopedia Brittannia, 13th edn, 1926 pp. 176–8.) In April 1845, *The Geology of Russia and the Ural Mountains* was published by Murchison, von Keyserling and de Verneuil. (In this region seemingly, interpretation of rock stratigraphy presented fewer difficulties than in Great Britain where circumstances were more complicated.) For this work Murchison received the Russian *Order of St Anne and of Stanislas*.

I half-expected to see the name Permian Layer mentioned on Russian geological maps, but this was not so. I also enquired if Murchison's visit of a century and a half ago was known, but seemingly not. It could be that the term Permian is replaced by a name that I would fail to recognise.

In brief, we also saw the Museum of Art which included a very special, worthy display of cast-iron work for which the region is well-known. What I can only describe as an ornate house with sculptures beautifully designed, all rendered in cast-iron, was assembled in the centre of a large exhibition room, as it was originally displayed in 1851 at the World Exhibition.

It may be of some interest to record that small artistic items which had come from palaces and the like were allowed to be bought (cheaply) in this museum and exported from Russia; many attractive; specifically manufactured souvenirs such as enamelled trays and delicate filigreed tea glass holders were also on sale.

Figure 10. Illustration, Ekaterinburg Theatre.

Figure 11. Illustration, Perm: Opera House.

I visited a large military museum which, however, was limited to the display of equipment (and photographs) from World War II, particularly that which had been designated and built in the steel plants of Ekaterinburg and Perm. The latter were the great centres of production located always at a great distance from any fighting front.

It was a great pleasure for us to be entertained in the apartment of several of our professorial hosts and their wives and we cannot speak too highly of their hospitality. We also acknowledge the very cordial manner of the women interpreters, in Moscow, (Anne Ovchinnikov), Ekaterinburg and Perm (Yelena Verstikova and Tatyana Domilovskaya) who served us; not only did they perform their professional function exceedingly well but they also welcomed us into their homes, despite the economic difficulties of the times.

One of our cherished memories is that of being conveyed into the country out of E, to a region of many wooden *'cottages'* where Professor Komogorov retired to relax, to listen to music and to write some of his papers. He had built his substantial wooden log cabin or cottage and separate sauna with the aid of his sons. Equally remarkable was his surrounding garden and greenhouse containing flowers, vegetables and herbs. It was clear to us that the ability to supplement purchased daily diets with home-grown produce made life for many families much easier. The Kolmogorov family (sons and grandchildren) made us a lunch which was taken *al fresco* and with several toasts (typically Russian) rendered the occasion all the more memorable. See Figure 12.

Perm

After one week in E, we started our return to Moscow, by train, with a two-day visit to Perm a local town only 7 hours railway journey(!) to the West – to the Institute of Continuum Mechanics which is under the direction of Professor Matvienco. The hotel was perhaps the most splendid we stayed in whilst the Institute itself was located in quiet rural surroundings. Lack of time prevented us from seeing much of the town. The one full day I had in Perm was devoted to one session of four hours of technical presentations – made to me in English. The meeting had obviously been carefully arranged with some fifty or so professors and postgraduate students being present. I found their material new and was regretful that much of it was not known, or better known, in the West. The best way in which I am able to respond to this situation, as indeed is also the case at Ekaterinburg, is to offer to put active workers in touch with persons, conferences, journals and book publishers in England.

In the latter part of the day we were taken to what was one of the highlights afforded us by the Perm region, namely a visit to the unique Khohlovka Museum of Architecture and Ethnography. This large, outdoor museum, is located on the bank of the majestic river Kama, which is the fourth longest river in Europe – some 40 miles or so outside of Perm. Khohlovka is a branch of the Perm Museum of local lore in the Prikamye area; for the facts below I am indebted to the Director.

'The Khohlovka Museum was founded by a well-known Perm architect, A. V. Terekhov. It is remarkable for its collection of the most typical Russian style ancient wooden buildings, dating from the seventeenth-nineteenth centuries, the impressive buildings of the Church of the Virgin (1694), and the Hipped Roof Bell Tower, (1781) (see Figures 13 and 14) were brought to Khohlovka from the Suksunsky region. The original building of a village fire brigade of 1920 and the building of a brine-lifting tower had also been brought in from the Perm region and Solikamsk. The church of Transfiguration (1702) has been transferred from the Cherdynsky region. The churches of the Virgin and the Transfiguration represent the highest point of wooden architecture in old Russia, and are masterpieces in their fascinating combination of complexity and simplicity. The ancient buildings of the Khohlovka Museum are surrounded by a beautiful pine and larch forest, frequently visited by visitors to Perm.'

After returning to Perm we had a fine opportunity, over a special dinner, to engage in technical discussions and to get to know our hosts better.

On the morning of our departure we visited the Meeting House of the Ural Academy of Science. As with many Russian institutions the fine quality of the interior is in no way foreshadowed by a plain exterior.

Departure for Moscow after lunch and the presentation to us of a student painting

THE USSR AND RUSSIA

Figure 12 (a). Professor and Mrs Kolmogorov, Professor and Mrs Johnson.

(b). Professor Kolmogorov, his secretary, Elena, myself and Mrs Johnson, June 1994. Early evening in Professor Kolmogorov's 'dacha!'. All their own produce!

Figure 13. Illustration. Ancient Wooden Church Tower: Khohlovka.

Figure 14. Illustration. Ancient Wooden Bell Tower: Khohlovka.

of Khohlovka was memorable, as was the stirring music relayed through the railway station as our train, The Kama, pulled out. We arrived the next day at 4 p.m. and again registered at the Uzkoe hotel.

Moscow

The following morning we travelled to the Bauman Institute or the MGTU by car. (The Moscow State Technical University, was founded in 1830*. The visit was organised by Prof. A. Ovchinnikov, until recently a mountaineer/climber, once a colleague of Sir John Hunt.) We were entertained in his flat with the help of his family, son-in-law and especially his daughter Anne, who acted as an interpreter as well as hostess, whilst we were in Moscow. It was twenty-five years since I last visited the Institute and a great pleasure to see once again several old friends – with whom we had kept in touch despite the vicissitudes of years. However, the first ceremony that had to be performed, was that of receiving an official welcome from the Russian Academy of Science and MGTU. This was a simple, pleasant occasion and was all the more delightful for the presence of a reception committee of colleagues old and new, especially Prof. N. Malinin, Prof. E. Popov, Academician Kolesnikov and Professor E. Semonov. At the conclusion of this I was taken to see the metal-forming laboratories but especially was I treated to a very interesting hour in the museum devoted to the achievements of Russian rocketry in, and since, the Second World War from Acad. Kolesnikov. By confining themselves to this period only, the early history of rockets

---

* See Figure 3, p. 308 in previous section.

and especially the work of William Congreve and others in the early nineteenth century is not noticed – Russia, Austria and other countries in that century actually purchased patents for Congreve (and perhaps Hale) rocket manufacture from England.

My old friend Prof. Malinin, now turned 80 years of age and a Lenin Prize winner some 35 years ago, was reluctant to talk about his work until he was able to deliver himself *'from his Chair'*. As I remember, this was in fact just his desk in a room shared with several others. Clearly, his sense of pride and tradition as reflected in his attachment to *'his Chair'* at MGTU is well worthy of one; I think few professors today would appreciate the honour and responsibility he felt himself to have to uphold. Gathered around his chair, perhaps ten of us sat and listened to him while he explained some of the research and writings in which he was currently engaged. Especially interesting was his account of the book he has been writing for many years on the subject of the History of Strength of Materials,* there were perhaps 100 large portrait photographs of his chosen distinguished contributors spread in straight lines across the wall of the room, behind him. I was surprised to find no more than three or four of them British!

The touring party had perforce to visit an auditorium in which a Doctoral examination was taking place; I seem to remember that Professors Popov and Ovchinnikov were designated examiners and needed to make a visit to the gathering. All the party were accommodated in a specially prepared side *'box'* and for 10 minutes or so we tried to take in the proceedings. What was going on was clearly quite different from the procedure for Ph.D. examinations followed in the UK so much so that I thought to write a special note about it and to describe therein the Russian examining procedures for, in effect, Ph.D.s and D.Scs. A written account of this, as provided to me by Prof. Kolmogorov, is Note 2, affixed hereto.

One of the last buildings I saw – not previously seen during my visit of 1969 (if it existed then) was the splendid headquarters of the Russian Academy. This was a fine building in its own grounds having many beautifully decorated and imposing staircases; it had been the home of a wealthy merchant built one or two centuries ago.

A final impression for the record is that the mass of young men and women with whom we talked were of the opinion that the old system of government *'was probably to be preferred to the present one'*. On the one hand this was sad, but on the other, remarkable, for it was generally uttered as a community on the lack of youthful idealism which the new system seemed able to arouse – it is seen now as a totally money-based ethic. It is not always realised in the West that to embrace the academic life even in engineering, in Russia was, and is, to choose a career in which professors are paid less than bus conductors! It was evident to me that a choice in favour of a life in academic work was breaking down for one heard many accounts of men with Ph.Ds taking to the life of merchants.

On-Going

Relationships between the former Academy of Sciences in the Soviet Union, now Russia, and the academies of foreign countries have, in fact, usually only taken place with the branches of Moscow and Leningrad/St Petersburg. In a small way, my visit to Ekaterinburg, Urals Branch, was to do something to correct this. A consequence

---

* Actually, a 'Who's Who'. See IJMS, 2000. (In process of translation.)

of my visit has been to try to establish better long-term contact with the pre-eminent engineering centres of Russia in the Urals and similar centres in the UK. The Ural cities, since they are 1,000 miles East of Moscow have always been at a great disadvantage when endeavouring to build *'bridges'* with technological centres abroad. One endeavour presently being pursued is that of bringing about a *'twinning'* of Ekaterinburg and Sheffield, because they both have similar metallurgical features; they both are *'steel'* cities, especially are their engineering research centres in Ekaterinburg (and Perm), and in the universities of Sheffield and Hallamshire. Already some visits have been made by professors form Ekaterinburg to the UK (and Dublin) and it is to be hoped that the number of these will grow. There is also a keen desire to have scientists from both countries at the international conferences they both hold, for easier access to publication in each other's journals and for the facility to be able to publish books for a world-wide readership. Many other forms of co-operation, interchange and exchange can easily be imagined, with great potential benefit to both.

Note 1

I may mention that whilst visiting the Institute of Mathematics and Mechanics in Ekaterinburg I had the opportunity to see a copy of (MATHEMAT K MEXAHH K) or *Mathematicians and Mechanists* by A. N. Bogolubov, (1983), 637 pp. This is a volume in Russian, of short biographies of some 1,400 persons. It is now more than twenty years old but is nonetheless a very useful and absorbing book to those who have at some time been engaged in research in mechanics. The book describes mainly Russian males but several women and quite a number of distinguished foreign scientists are included. The average entry contains a head portrait with vital dates and is, in length, about 150 words.

The volume should be very helpful to persons who need Russian biographical references or to those who wish to know more about Russian contributions to the two fields mentioned.

I received a copy of this volume from Professors A. Sidorov and V. Berdishev of the Institute of Mathematics and Mechanics, on 25 January, 1995. I am very grateful to them for their kindness in obtaining this volume for me.

I take this occasion to add that I was the proud recipient of many other books and papers acquired during this tour and thank the authors for their gifts.

Note 2
Procedure for Examining Doctoral Students in Russia

I was fortunate enough to be able to be present for a short period of time at the examination of a Doctoral candidate in the Bauman Institute in Moscow. The circumstances seemed so dissimilar to those followed in the UK that I thought it worthwhile to describe what I encountered physically and what are the legal or administrative procedures involved.

The setting

The physical circumstances for the examination of candidates are not unlike those with which we associate the proceedings in a law court. These take place in a large room, the candidates and the examining body appearing on a raised platform at the front. The body of the hall on the occasion I was there contained a gathering of perhaps 30 persons; I do not know if there were any restrictions as to who could be present and whether members of this audience could, at some stage, intervene to comment or put questions. On the platform in the centre, at a table, sat the Chairman (President) of the proceedings, with the Vice President and the Scientific Secretary on either side. To one side, as if *'in the dock'* sat the candidate, whilst on the opposite side an appointed member of the *'court'* appeared to be publicly discussing the thesis. Twenty to thirty large sheets were set high up above the heads of those on the platform; these were made by the applicant and illustrated his work; this made it possible quickly to judge its value. Members of the Scientific Council sit among the audience; the members are responsible for making all the arrangements of the meeting.

All these arrangements contrasted very sharply with our British system of one External Examiner (from a university not associated with the one in which the doctoral programme had been carried out) and one or perhaps two Internal Examiners, sitting alone with the solitary candidate in an empty classroom or the Internal's office/study conducting an inquisitorial investigation. Slightly differently, I remember that at Oxford University an Internal Examiner appeared robed and in formal attire, black dress and bow tie, etc. At Cambridge, the practice is/was for the oral examination to take place only after the submission of the report and interim recommendation to the examining faculty; in effect, the oral examination would confirm the written recommendations. The practice also was to exclude the Internal Examiner since he had been the candidate's supervisor.

Russian Consideration Concerning Students for Doctoral Theses

Candidates for Doctoral Degrees must have previously graduated from universities. There are two kinds of academic degrees – Candidates of Sciences, seemingly the equivalent of the British Ph.D. and Doctor of Science. It would seem that at the same time as that of securing the latter two academic degrees, the status of associate professor (or senior research workers at the research institute) and a professor, may also be applied for. These academic degrees are conferred on applicants after defending theses at candidate or doctoral level. To confer academic degrees, the Government Supreme Attestation Commission (SAC) establishes Scientific Councils at the most authoritative universities or academic institutes. The Council consists of 15–20 members. As a rule, all of these are Doctors of Science and professors. The Candidate degree is conferred on *'beginning scientists'* (mainly working for 3 to 5 years and simultaneously taking graduate courses) after they have defended a thesis before a meeting of the Scientific Council. The defence is preceded by conducting research and passing three obligatory examinations: in the major subject, a foreign language and the philosophy of science in general. The candidate thesis generally consists of a manuscript of 120 to 150 typewritten pages containing the results of the study of a specific scientific problem. Before the defence is conducted the thesis material is required to have been published in the form of journal articles. The thesis is now defended in a succession of stages, the first being a preliminary one *'at the university Chair'*. If the prima facia case is positive then on report to the Scientific Council, it will appoint independent official opponents (one doctor and one candidate) who are required to familiarise themselves with the submitted work in detail and prepared to present a public analysis of the work before a session of the Scientific Council. An applicant is required to make about 100 copies of this thesis in outline in the form of a small pamphlet and to send it to a list of addressees, interested in the subject-matter, forwarded to him by the Scientific Council. After a month or so another session of the Scientific Council is held at which the candidate and the official opponents make their presentations. A general discussion ensues and finally a decision about the award of the degree of Candidate of Sciences is taken by secret voting. The Council's decision is final.

The Doctor's degree is conferred upon those who have a Candidate's degree, after they have defended their doctoral thesis. The latter is supposed to be a treatise embodying scientific generalisations which can be acknowledged to represent *'a new trend in science or a theoretical description of certain topical scientific problems'*; I suppose that we would refer to the latter as being *original* contributions to knowledge. The requirement for Doctoral thesis is that of a manuscript of up to 250 type-written pages, the content of which is required to have been published as a monograph or in reputable journals. The first stage in considering the doctoral thesis takes place at the appropriate *'Chair'*, the procedure being similar to that followed for a Candidate's thesis except that three Doctors of Science opponents are appointed. Council decisions are again taken by secret vote but this is not final and is required to be confirmed by the SAC. The administrative machinery of the SAC in fact examines the defence proceedings to establish proper conformity with laid down procedures. Attached to the SAC are Expert Council members from among the most qualified of professors and members of the Russian Academy. One of the EC members examines the essence of the thesis and reports on it. The Doctor's degree is able to be conferred on an applicant if the latter procedure is in conformity with the finding of the earlier examination.

Conferment of the Candidate and Doctor's Degrees is certified by diplomas and these are required for further promotion. Only a candidate may become an Associate Professor (or lecturer) and only a Doctor of Science may be given the title and position of a Professor.

The titles of Professor and Associate Professor are conferred by the Scientific Councils of universities or academic institutes again by secret voting but without further thesis defence. However, candidates must produce evidence of ability to teach, some knowledge of teaching methods and with all, be able to justify themselves as an authority in public. The Diploma is given by a higher body (either SAC or the Ministry of Education) which also oversees the activity of the Scientific Councils.

Some recent statistics which apply for the Ural Branch of the Academy of Science are:

Total number of staff	7222	10	(These – extreme right – apply
Number of scientists	310	9	in Prof. Kolmogorov's laboratory)
Doctors of Science	830	1	
Candidates of Science	1588	3	

Acknowledgements

The author wishes to thank the Royal Society of London and the Russian Academy of Sciences (Ural Branch) for funding his visit. He also expresses his gratitude to the many persons who happily gave their help towards making it a success and who looked after his welfare in many different ways. Particularly we are indebted to Yelena Verstankova for her great help with all translations, correspondence and conversations. A special debt of gratitude is owed to Professor A. Ovchinnikov (and members of his family) for the arrangements and unfailing kindness in Moscow. Finally, I cannot speak highly and gratefully enough of Professor and Mrs V. L. Kolmogorov's efforts on our behalf. Besides making the overall plans for our visit whilst in Russia, Prof. Kolmogorov travelled four times between Moscow and Ekaterinburg, chaperoning us on all occasions with unfailing good humour.

For the contents of Note 2 which were supplied entirely by Prof. Kolmogorov, I remain deeply indebted.

(iii) Connections with the USSR and Russia

1. Translations into Russian of:
   - (i) *The Mechanics of Metal Extrusion* (W. Johnson and H. Kudo) 226 pp., initially published in English by Manchester Univ. Press in 1962. In Russian since 1965.
   - (ii) *Engineering Plasticity* (W. Johnson and P. B. Mellor), 620 pp., initially published in English by Van Nostrand Reinhold in 1973. In Russian since 1979, published by Mashinostroyeniye, Moscow, 567 pp.
2. Editor of translations from Russian of:
   - (i) *Stress Concentrations Around Holes* by G. N. Savin, 430 pp. Published by Pergamon Press, 1961.
   - (ii) *Mechanisms for the Generation of Plane Curves* by Academician A. A. Artobolevski, 278 pp. Published by Pergamon Press, 1964.
   - (iii) *Superplasticity of Metals and Alloys* by A. A. Presnyakov, Published by the British Library, 1971.
3. Chapter Contributions to an Encyclopedic Book: *Theory of Plastic Deformation of Metals*: Chapter 5, pp. 121–211, entitled *Slip Line Field Methods* (in Russian and with co-authors R. Sowerby and R. D. Venter.) Published by Mashinostroyeniye, Moscow, 1983.

   Book also re-issued and enlarged in 1992 as *Theory of Forging and Stamping*, 719 pp. Article in Part II, pp. 187–267, again published by Mashinostroyeniye, Moscow.

   (And shown as one of the Editors in these books.)
4. (i) British representative at the founding of *The International Federation for the Theory of Machines and Mechanisms* (IFFTOM) held at Drubsha (Black Sea Coast), Bulgaria, July 1968(?). (I was invited to represent Britain by Academician Artobolevskii. See below).
   - (ii) Pergamon Press established in the 1960s (a) *The Int. Jnl. for the Theory of Machines and Mechanisms*, with Prof. Erskine Crossley (Amherst University, USA) as Editor. To start the Journal and have Prof. Crossley as Editor, were both my suggestions.
   - (iii) In view of 2(ii) above, for which I wrote a small prefatorial recommendation, I came to know Acad. Artobolevski well and I visited him in Moscow

in 1969. Then, I also made good connections (which by correspondence still function).

(iv) Several of the above Russians have at some time been members of the Editorial Advisory Board of the *Int. Jnl. Mech. Sci.* (*IJMS*)

(v) My latest close contact (started about 1990 – to date) has been with the Russian Academy Technological Research Institute in Ekaterinburg, formerly Sverdlovsk (Urals) and in particular with Professor Kolmogorov.

(vi) I have and have had many (irregular) contacts with Russians on a variety of technical subjects, particularly:

(a) I published my analysis of Vee-anvil forging in *The Engineer*, Vol. 25, pp. 348–50, 1958. Prof. Tomlenov sent me a *photograph* confirming the analysis.

(b) I reviewed the English translation of Unksov's book (in *The Engineer*), in about 1955.

(c) Research with the staff and students of my Department at UMIST on the coefficient of friction in forward extrusion took place slightly before that of Prof. Safarov under Prof. Unksov. (I was shown this work on my visit to Moscow in 1968.)

Addendum

1. Professor Artobolevskii was the I.Mech.E.'s winner of the James Watt International Medal for 1967. It was the year Mr Hugh Conway was President of the I.Mech.E. (I was invited to join the Russian Ambassador on the occasion of the presentation having urged the case for the chosen recipient upon the President, as against German contenders.) Mr Conway had had special undergraduate student interests in Mechanisms. Since there was then no evident interest in the topic in the UK, I thought to try to secure an award in this field which would help towards the resurrection of a subject which had a high profile in the UK eighty years ago but had since virtually died; in this endeavour I did not succeed. (I knew Mr Conway from at least ten years earlier when I was at Sheffield University, as Branch secretary of the Institution and I had secured him as an evening lecturer for our Yorkshire Branch.) Academician Artobolevskii repeated his London lecture at several other centres besides Manchester (see the Institution's Proceedings for 1967).

2. I agreed to attend the meeting at Drubsha, Bulgaria and in acceding to the request to edit the Academician's translation (see 2(ii) above) my thought was to be able one day to establish a research group in this area. It never materialised though it did give rise to a post-graduate lecture-course in the Theory of Mechanisms for our new M.Sc. course in UMIST in the mid-1960s. Spokesman for Mechanisms was a task I later passed into the hands of Professor Maunder of Newcastle University; financial support by the Royal Society was given to the IFFTOM (see 4(i) above).

For many years my name appeared as a member of the Honorary Editorial Board of the Journal of Mechanisms, but at some stage it was removed and all traces of my involvement with it also disappeared – due to my inactivity in the area.

3. Elected to the Russian Academy of Sciences (Urals Branch) in April 1993 and formally made a Foreign Member on 6 June 1994.
4. Helped Prof. Kolmogorov secure overseas funds to attend a one-week Conference on Metal Forming at Dublin University, Ireland in August 1993.
5. Had as a research student, L. B. Aksenov who worked on 'The Plane strain Pressing of Circular Section Bar to form Turbine Blades' – which resulted in a nice, first research paper with Dr N. R. Chitkara, see *IJMS*, Vol. 17, pp. 681–691, 1975.

Some time after the formality of election to the Urals Branch of the Russian Academy of Science, 1994, I received, month by month, the regional newspaper, Nauka Uraly, see Figure 15, about science, its news and recent achievements. In particular, I found my own scientific career and articles, outlined in Russian through about five issues! It is remarkable that interest in science in Russia is able to be sustained so easily.

At the time of the newspaper publication I was reading the biography of one of England's outstanding Second World War Generals, Sir Brian Horrocks, from

Figure 15. Ural Science, monthly newspaper, January 1996, front page. In the lower right corner General Horrocks is shown with his dog!

which I learned that he had seen service in the Ekaterinburg region of Russia, as a junior officer. Around 1920 there was internecine war between monarchists and communists. General Horrocks was sent in from Vladivostok, by Britain, to help in the supply of arms to the monarchists and to assist in their struggle. I mentioned the latter in a letter to Professor Kolmogorov and apparently it had aroused great interest in today's people, despite the fact that it had all happened nearly 80 years ago. Ekaterinburg, incidentally, was where most of the Russian royal family who had escaped from Moscow at the time, were murdered. We saw the supposed actual site of the latter deed. It was thought in the West, that a memorial was to be put up, but no such event has happened.

CHAPTER XXV

Japan

I USED TO MEET PROFESSOR KUDO,* of whom I have told much in Chapter XVIII, at many international conferences but in 1975 I had the experience and pleasure of going to his own country. Over a period of one month, I made a quick tour of Japan and in particular met many academics, saw a lot of the research in some Japanese companies and enjoyed various cultural features.

Prof. Kudo was at the heart of my visit to Japan in the pleasant, mild month of November of that year. The reader may judge of the very full programme set out for us from Table 1 and Figure 5. I wrote a report of this visit, which ran to 42 pages; it is available in my archival papers. I propose therefore simply to highlight some of the non-technical events we enjoyed.

My wife, Heather and I stayed for our first four nights in the Grand New Otani Hotel, Tokyo. We had a quick tour of the city (including a visit to the Kabuki theatre), conducted by Prof. and Mrs Jimma, being the official guests of the Hitachi company. The following day I visited Prof. Kudo at Yokohama National University, saw his experimental work in progress and learned how the Government, industry, national conferences, research and teaching, were co-ordinated – a considerable lesson for the UK which helped one understand something of Britain's decline in motor-car manufacture at the time. (The latter is Table 3 in my Report and Table 4 (likely of value for the History of Technology) shows the succession – pupil and master – in the country's research workers in metal-forming from 1935 to 1970.)

Later that same afternoon, I visited the Technical Research Centre of NKK (Nippon Kokon Co.,) which had a staff of about 500. This visit was far too short. Later, an NKK technical director favoured us with an invitation to visit his very expensive home. Typically, it had both traditional and western-style rooms and a very small garden. He showed us volumes of photographs of the marriages of his young company researchers in which he appeared. To judge from his position in them, he was more important than the parents! Employers played a very patriarchal role at that time in providing homes for their employees.

At the Institute of Physics and Chemistry, I met its distinguished Director, Prof. S. Fukui, whom I had known for over 25 years, and discussed technical

---

* Prof. Kudo died in 2001. His obituary, by Dr W. J. Bradley-Dodd, appears in the IJMS for 2002.

TABLE 1

Nov	Movement	Visit Company/University	Lecture	Sight Seeing	City/Stay	Local Programme Controller
2 (Sun)	Dep. London about mid-day					
3 (Mon)	Arr. Tokyo about mid-day				Tokyo	
4 (Tues)				City of Tokyo Kabuki Theatre	Tokyo	Prof. Kudo Dr Jimma Dr Nakagawa
5 (Wed)		(i) Yokohama National Univ. (ii) Nippon Kokan Co. Central Research Lab.	Slip line field analysis applications (30 persons)		Tokyo	
6 (Thurs)		(i) Visit to Seiko Watch Co. (ii) Inst.Phy.Chem.Research			Tokyo	
7 (Fri)	Tokyo→Hakone	(i) Inst.Ind.Sci.Univ.of Tokyo (ii) Tokyo Inst.Tech.			Hakone	
8 (Sat)	Hakone→Fuji →Nagoya (Express Train)	Amino Iron Works		National Park & Mount Fuji	Nagoya	Prof. Kasuga Prof. Tozawa
9 (Sun)	Nagoya→Toba Toba→Nagoya			Toba Pearl Island	Nagoya	
10 (Mon)		(i) Nagoya Univ. (ii) Toyota Motor Co. (Forging & Sheet Forming Plants)	Some plastic newer forming techniques (50 persons)		Nagoya	
11 (Tues)	Nagoya→Kyoto (Express Train)	Symposium on Super Plastic Forming (in Kyoto)	Super-plastic forming in UK. (150 persons)	Evening party (Technical plasticity club)	Kyoto	Prof. Hirai
12 (Wed)	Kyoto→Toyama	Japanese National Congress of Plastic Working	High speed forming (300 persons)	Imperial Palace Gardens	Toyama	
13 (Thurs)	Toyama			Japanese Alps	Toyama	
14 (Fri)	Toyama→Kyoto	Nachi Bearing Co. (Bearing Plant & Forming Plant)	Ring rolling & rotary forging (60 persons)			
15 (Sat)	Kyoto	(i) "The Doshisha" (ii) Kyoto University		Kyoto Old Imperial Palace	Kyoto	Prof. Hirai
16 (Sun)				Nara	Kyoto	Prof. Saga
17 (Mon)	Kyoto→Kyushu (Express Train)			Kumamoto Castle	Kumamoto (Kyushu)	Prof. Hirai and
18 (Tues)		High Energy Rate Forming Inst.		Mt. Aso (active volcano)	Beppu (Kyushu)	Prof. Kiyota
19 (Wed)		Nippon Steel Plant	Mechanics and Sport (30 persons)	Beppu (Hot spring)	Beppu (Kyushu)	
20 (Thurs)	Ohita→Tokyo (Plane)				Tokyo	Prof. Kudo Dr Jimma Dr Nakagawa
21 (Fri)		Kagushima Space Centre		"Sayonara" party (Good-bye!)	Tokyo	
22 (Sat)	Tokyo→London Arr. Saturday mid-night					
23 (Sun)	London→ Cambridge					

problems with him. Again, the visit was too short, though somewhat continued by our being taken as guests to a private, expensive, traditional dinner party. Sitting at a low table in stockinged feet we enjoyed the full attention from both the diners and the servers, bedecked in traditional dress. There seemed to be one waitress to each person; our lady watched our faces while we ate and there was no opportunity to avoid eating and swallowing octopus! During the dinner, we had a Geisha 'girl' sing and dance for us.

The next day, I visited Prof. Tom Nakagawa, an ingenious user of technology,

Figure 1. Prof. Kudo and an English visitor (who did much work with him) Dr W. J. Bradley-Dodd, and myself in rapt attention watching a film of a research machine in operation.

who was trying to compact iron powder using a ring-rolling machine in an effort to form a solid, porous, ring bearing. The first test had been delayed for me to witness because Tom knew of our early studies in ring rolling. The experiment I witnessed was not successful – though it was soon to be so, and indeed it was later adapted to form blocks of cattle feed!

I was introduced to Prof. M. Mori, now widely known for his toy animals which move around and do not cross certain perimeter lines when they have been 'seen' by an 'eye' in the machine which initiates changes of direction. These performing animals have been seen on TV many times.

We were taken by courtesy of Amino Co., I believe, to Mishima and booked into a typically Japanese hotel, where the furniture and fittings were sparse but tasteful. For just one night we were moved to a traditional Japanese house opposite the hotel. Notably, our bed was a comfortable mattress on a very clean floor and the room also had a bath which was a 3 ft. cube wholly let into the floor. (Arising from or descending on to the mattress (i.e. literally, getting in or out of bed!) was difficult for us Westerners, and indeed, we found that many Japanese preferred the western style or height of bed.) The following morning when we awoke and drew the curtains, a wonderful view of snow-capped Mt. Fuji met our eyes. Breakfast was also something of a new experience – raw eggs in soya sauce, cold omelettes and raw fish! A walk in the National Park, on the lower slopes of Fuji, was a disappointment, it being a huge cinder heap. Moving on to Nagoya, we could not but admire the 'bullet' trains' precision in coming to a halt at a pre-determined position on the platform. It helped in making it

Figure 2. Prof. Tom Nakagawa (centre) and myself inspecting a trial ring-rolling-compaction machine.

easy for our hosts to find us. Train seats were spaciously separated, we had foot-rests and coffee and tea were carefully served; from time to time, uniformed collectors of trash came through the coach, each wearing gloves, uniform and a mask. An impressive way to run a rail service in 1975!

Dr Kunogi, general manager of a small American-owned company, Oilgear Ltd, greeted us on arrival at Nagoya and conveyed us to the Nagoya Castle Hotel. Our room overlooked a well-kept moat surrounding a picturesque castle about a century old! Castles we seemed to find were everywhere built of wood and seemed to burn down, on average, once every century!

Early on Sunday morning we departed for Toba Pearl Island. En route we had lunch at Matsuzaka and were introduced to its famous and expensive beef. (We paid a visit to the stock-yard close by to see the artificial feeding of a cow with a bottle of beer and the rubbing-down of its flank with spirits – said to be traditional pre-requisites for providing good beef!)

Pearl Island is the home of the cultured pearl, the name and statues of its great creator, Mr Mikimoto, being everywhere to be seen. Equally prominent was a tribute to Queen Elizabeth II's visit earlier in the year; a large section of one museum was given over to a photographic record of it. The science of pearl-culturing was explained in detail in a museum whilst an adjacent large store did a great business in pearls and associated marine jewellery and display-ware.

Despite the cold and very choppy sea, a dozen or so *women* divers equipped with baskets took to the water from a boat just offshore and dived to show their ability.

The manner of pearl collection was demonstrated to us on film.

At tea, in a special foreign visitors' room, we were treated to a private showing of a tele-recording of our Queen's visit.

Pearl Island is beautifully situated and kept and was a joy to visit; the fresh air was a tonic.

Unfortunately the three-hour return journey was very tiring and an evening meal in a 'native' Japanese (raw) fish restaurant taxed us greatly, though our greeting from the cooks and their bonhomie was memorable!

The next morning, an hour late journey from the hotel brought me to the Engineering Departments of Nagoya University but after lunch with Professors Tozawa and Kasuga I was taken to the Toyota Car Co., a company only established in 1937 and now about the third largest in the world. Immediately on arrival, i.e. at 2.00 pm, I delivered the second lecture of my tour to about 70 engineers; it was one about our work on 'Newer Methods of Metal Forming'.

For an hour I was shown through the metal forming plant, i.e. manufacturing mild steel components by extrusion, forging and upsetting, by the works director. All my questions were freely answered and nothing was concealed. We concluded with a meeting (including the serving of saki) with several engineers mainly brought together to answer any questions I may have. Notably, and without conceit, they pointed to 30 years of activity without a strike!

We were the guests of the Company for a regal dinner at 6.30 and in particular our host was the Engineering Director. (Could this happen to a professor in Britain?!) Our discussions were fairly free ranging, though I found the director to live a life totally absorbed in his company – and he had served with Toyota about 35 years, since graduation! He revealed that his company was negotiating about the exchange of technical information with China. My understanding was that officially there was *no* exchange between Japan and China; I was assured that all contacts thus far were quite unofficial!

We travelled from Nagoya to Kyoto early the following morning and were met by Professor Hirai. After registering in at the Grand Kyoto Hotel he promptly took us on a fast tour of this ancient city, the capital of Japan until about a century ago. (Tokyo is an anagram of Kyoto). This rapid visit included a special exhibition of the art of painting on silk (the Yuzen process) – with lunch in the Conference Hall. At about 3.00 pm I gave a 35-minute lecture on *The Present Position of Superplastic Forming in the UK*; this was one of several papers at a one-day national conference on Super-plasticity attended by, I suppose, some 150 engineers and metallurgists.

In the evening, my wife and I were guests at an annual dinner of the Technology of Plasticity Club. All the Japanese professors of note in plasticity or metal processing were present – perhaps 40 in all. It was the evening before the commencement of an annual National Congress on Plastic Working and was the occasion for electing club officers. It fell to me to respond to some kind remarks which were addressed to me and to thank them for their hospitality. This body was responsible for many of the internal arrangements made on my behalf in Japan. Over a period of fifteen years I have accommodated many Japanese students in my Department and this was their acknowledgement and expression of gratitude. It was a very happy and relaxed dinner with Japanese respect for

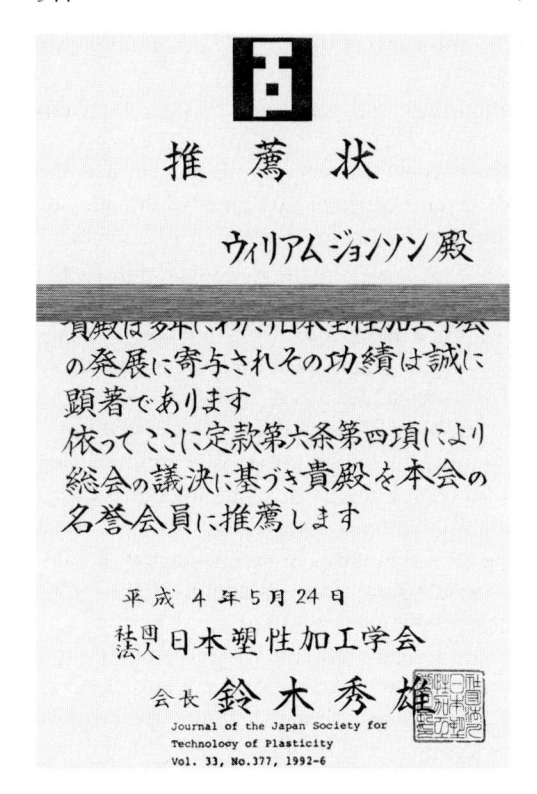

Figure 3. Letter of Election of the author, to the Society!

age clearly making inter-relationships very easy to manage! Somewhere in these proceedings I was elected to the Japan Society for the Technology of Plasticity (see Figure 3).

Early in the morning, and because Professor Hirai had obtained special permission, we were able to visit the very beautiful gardens in the Sugakuin Imperial Villa. Later, at noon, I gave the Congress general lecture, for one hour, on 'High Speed Forming and Associated Mechanics', to a packed (indeed overflowing) hall of about 300 – and it seemed to be well received. Due to not having been sufficiently precise when agreeing the lecture title before I arrived in Japan, some misunderstanding occurred and the lecture given was not as prepared; indeed my lecture was nearly extemporé (with many slides of course), but seemed none the worse for it and indeed the spontaneity may have added something to it. After the lecture I met many new and old friends and it was hard work and tiring to talk to all who wished to further discuss some of the contents of the lecture or to exchange pleasantries.

At this point, half-way through the tour, I confess that I was beginning to feel the pressure from the demands on my energy and time and I was therefore very pleased to be put on the train for Toyama after lunch. (Toyama is at nearly the same latitude as Tokyo but on the west coast of Honshu, that is, on the 'other side' of the Japanese Alps.)

An uneventful three- to four-hour rail journey deposited us in Toyama at about 7.00 p.m. and after being met and installed in a good hotel, we were mercifully left to ourselves until the following morning, after agreeing arrangements for the next day.

The next morning a large athletic young man, dressed in climbing gear, arrived in a car of Nachi Bearing Ltd at 9.00 a.m. and carried us off in the direction of the mountains. (We had expressed a desire for exercise by walking, and fresh air in the Alps, if it could be arranged. Our young guide was instructed to look after his middle-aged 'hikers'. After some twenty miles of travel up a valley to Tateyama station we took a cable rail-car with our guide part-way up a mountainside on to a plateau at Bijou-daira and then transferred to a bus which conveyed us nearly to the top of Mount Tateyama at Muro-do. Our mountain guide brought along with him socks and anoraks for both of us; he alarmed us because he also carried an ice axe! The tourist hotel provided us with climbing boots and all three of us set off for a two-hour walk amid the snow and ice. The area is highly volcanic and hot geysers abound. The hot springs and ponds are fully utilised for providing hot water to the large hotel. It was our first close acquaintanceship with volcanic activity and we spent much of the time examining the hot sulphurous springs. The weather was excellent and the day gave us a very refreshing and much needed change. We were especially well catered for by the hotel with a huge lunch after our walk; we only just made our return connection. We got back to our hotel by 5.00 pm taking in a visit to a temple en route and in the early evening were graciously entertained to dinner by Mr Fujii, the local Director of the Nachi company.

I spent the following morning touring the Nachi Bearing and Tool plant; this company is noted for its precision engineering.

We returned from Toyama on the 3.20 p.m. train and arrived at Kyoto at 6.50 p.m., to be received and conveyed away again by Professor Hirai to hotel, dinner and bed.

Early the next day we were privileged in being given special permission to visit the Old Kyoto Imperial Palace, after which Professor Hirai insisted on showing us around his University, 'The Doshisha'. This was a large private foundation, started as a Christian school in Kyoto in 1875 by Neesima (1843–1890), after graduating from Amherst College USA, in 1870. The Chapel and Faculty House I visited were recognisably American in style. The connection with the USA was severed during the Second World War and, alas, the beautiful colonial-style rooms were visibly neglected. The extent of private university education in Japan greatly surprised me – said to be about 80%! See the article in Figure 4.

Figure 4. History of Japanese Universities.

It was early in the Meiji Era (1868–1911) that the basis of Japan's modern education system was established with the inauguration of the national, then called Imperial, universities in major cities, including Tokyo and Kyoto.

The national universities were established following the issuance in 1886 of the 'Imperial University Order' which emphasised the necessity of educating people and imparting knowledge and skills the nation needed.

The Tokyo Imperial University was founded the same year, followed by the Kyoto Imperial University in 1895.

By the year 1939, a total of nine imperial universities had been set up in Tokyo, Kyoto, Osaka, Hokkaido, Tohoku (Sendai), Nagoya, Kyushu (Fukuoka), Keijo (Seoul) and Taihoku (Taipei).

The private university was recognised officially as an education system after the promulgation in 1918 of the 'University Order'.

Most private universities in Japan were set up by the nation's pioneer educators who had hopes to educate students in the principles of humanism, religious ideals and individual dignity – rather than produce talented manpower for the building of a modern state, the purpose of the national academies.

Yukichi Fukuzawa founded Keio Gijuku, a private institute (predecessor of the present Keio Gijuku University) in 1868 on the basis of 'independence and self-reliance.'

Jo Niijima, a devout Christian, established Doshisha, the predecessor of the present Doshisha University in Kyoto in 1875 in the spirit of Protestant Christianity after returning from studies in the United States.

Likewise, Shigenobu Okuma, a liberal statesman of the Meiji Era, who opposed the 'reactionary' government created by the people who engineered the Meiji Restoration (1868), organised in 1882 a politico-economic institute called Tokyo Semmon Gakko, which became Waseda University in 1902.

In the course of time, various other private universities were established according to their own principles.

They include Rikkyo (St Paul's), Aoyama Gakuin, Sophia, and Kwansei Gakuin universities, as mission schools, and Meiji, Chuo, Hosei and Ritsumeikan universities as politico-economic and law schools.

Universities created on the basis of Buddhist principles are Otani, Ryukoku, Koyasan and Toyo universities. Schools that live up to Japan's traditional spirit are, among others, Kokugakuin and Kogakukan universities.

Women's Education

Another significant aspect of education in Japan is the fact that women's education was started by private schools as early as the 1890s when the predecessors of Tsudajuku Women's University, Nihon Women's University, Women's University of Arts and Tokyo Women's Medical College were established.

Miss Umeko Tsuda, founder of Tsudajuku Women's University, was one of the first Japanese women to study in the United States after the Meiji Restoration.

The woman educators' zeal to upgrade women's social status, which had been unduly suppressed under the feudalistic ethics in the old social systems, drove them to do all they could to set up these institutions.

The government policy of educating competent youths to produce specialists for the building of a new country according to the European education system (mainly German and French) served its purpose well. But in some respects, it made the education system too rigidly formalistic and, in this way, it tended to control the thinking of the people and hampered the growth of democratic thought. The principal idea of the pioneers of private universities, such as Fukuzawa, Okuma and Niijima, was to oppose government control of individual thought.

The spirit of these forerunners prevailed for some time after their deaths, but nearly a century later the brilliant colours of their independent spirit seem to have faded, giving way to the uniform education which now is spreading throughout the country.

Government control over the private universities became inevitable after the promulgation in 1918 of the University Order and private universities were 'officially' recognised as part of the nation's education system.

But, until the end in 1945 of the Second World War, the number of universities, including private institutes, was only 47 across the nation – and both the state and private universities had retained much of their individual characteristics at least to a certain extent.

The obvious trend toward uniformity and standardisation of university education came into existence in 1949 when the New University Order was enforced. As a result, higher schools in the pre-war Japanese education system were upgraded to universities and colleges.

Seeing the mushrooming of new universities and colleges in post-war Japan, one critic remarked on the trend and coined a new word; 'Ekiben Daigaku,' which cynically implied that Japan now had as many universities as railway stations, and their academic standard is as 'cheap' as box lunches sold at the stations.

With the increase of universities and colleges, standardisation of education began to take shape in the name of democratisation of education. Thus, the curriculae of the universities and colleges were rigidly regulated.

The formalism on the part of the government, caused a number of shortcomings to emerge. Many universities have lost their characteristics stemming from their 'spirit of foundation,' although the new trend contributed to the diffusion of university education.

Under the New University Order, standards for curriculae were regulated to the extent where private universities could not pursue their own ideals of education.

Financial Gap

In addition, the ever-widening gap in the financial scales between national or public schools and private institutes frustrate the latter. But, still they are obliged to absorb an increasing number of students.

In Japan, in fact, nearly 80 per cent of the students receiving higher education do so at private universities, which depend for funds almost solely on tuition fees from their students and donations from their parents and graduates.*

This gives rise to various problems that cry for early solution. The problems include the so-called 'Mizumashi Nyugaku' (inflated admission of students) and the resulting lowering of the 'quality' of students.

In some universities, especially in medical colleges, the admission fees and compulsory donations are too high for ordinary applicants, even if they are fully qualified scholastically.

As for the 'inflated admission,' the poor financial conditions of private universities are to blame. To ease their plight, they are obliged to collect necessary funds by enrolling as many students as possible.

More than 30 per cent of high school graduates now go on to colleges and universities – a ratio third highest in the world, next only to the United States and the USSR.

But, do all of them really need higher education? There is no denying that there is a considerable number of students who 'do not deserve' university education.

The rush of Japanese youths to universities results from the fact that Japanese society tends to attach too much importance to educational background.

---

* The following few paragraphs mirror the situation in the UK, today, 2003.

How should Japan's private universities solve all these problems now facing them? One suggestion seems to be that each private academy should have its own education philosophy and special character, attractive enough to the students. And it is also requested that the government and private universities co-ordinate their efforts to tackle these problems.

The second half of the morning I spent at Kyoto University visiting Professor Yamada (not the same professor as at Tokyo) to see his Impact laboratory. I saw a two-stage light gas gun in process of construction (length 5.28 m and bore dia. 22 mm); this was to be a high speed, fast loading device.

Shock waves were generated by the impact of a plastic or metal projectile against water to bulge-form metal tube. (Again, it was first done in UMIST, and is described above.) I was told about, but did not see, their innovative system for bonding stainless steel tube to the inner surface of steel tube.

Around noon we were taken to have another traditional Japanese meal in a temple – a return gesture of Professor Yamada, to repay me for taking him to a Manchester 'pub' for sandwiches and beer; the meal included 'bean curds boiled in water'. After lunch we visited the Heian Shrine, the Kinkakuji Temple and the Saihoji Temple.

An hour or so was spent in a visit to the most famous of all such establishments, that of the Urasenke of Mr Sen, to partake in the tea ceremony. (Mr Sen is seventeenth grand-master in a line started in the seventeenth century). The ceremony was conducted by the elegant Madam Sen; mainly it consisted in correctly and ceremoniously bringing a bowl of thick, unsweetened, luke-warm green tea to our lips. This was not my kind of tea! An apprentice ceremoniously made the tea with water at only about 60°C, I was informed; they said three years are required to train a proficient tea-master!

From 7 to 9.30 pm we were entertained by Dr Okomoto and Professor Yamada to a Gion* party. A long meal was served by hostesses and interrupted for a performance of Geisha singing and dancing. Later the hostesses took over again, and, with one of them playing a simple guitar-like instrument, we proceeded to the end of the evening with childlike sing-and-act games performed by our companions.

Time was too short for me to be able to visit Osaka University, but Professor J. Saga (accompanied by the accountant-cum-national-poet Mr Taneka of Sanyo Ltd, the company which loaned us their car for the day) kindly met us at Nara (30 miles south of Kyoto), an ancient capital of Japan in the eighth century AD. Professor Saga and I had met some weeks earlier at Brighton, at the International Cold Forging Research Conference. Between discussions of cold forging research problems we exchanged (amateur!) opinions on archaeology, literature and poetry. (Professor Saga I found to be a very knowledgeable Japanese person whose 'hobby' was travelling in Europe – when he could afford it.)

Nara is located in a very pleasant region where the weather is extremely mild. We visited the stone tomb and palace excavations presently being made, slowly went

---

* Gion is an area of Kyoto in which all the traditional restaurants (with entertainments) are, or were, to be found.

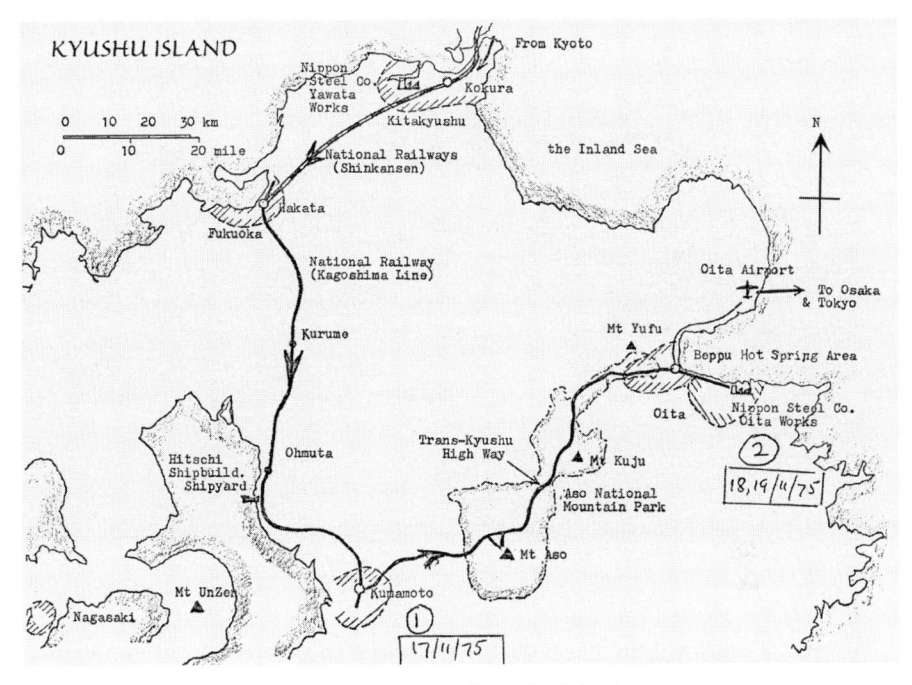

Figure 5. Map of Kyushu Island.

around the museum and carefully examined several temples and shrines; with lunch and dinner this took up the whole of a very pleasant and relaxing day.

We departed by train from Kyoto at 9.53 am for Hakata on the Island of Kyushu (passing Hiroshima on the way – with a notable historical symbol on the hill overlooking the town) – where we were met by Professor I. Tatsukawa, director of the Kumamoto High Energy Rate Forming (HERF) laboratories. (A map of our route in Kyushu is shown in Figure 5.)

Changing to a local train, we proceeded to Kumamoto to arrive at about 3.50 p.m. and immediately made a tour of the ancient castle grounds.* This beautifully sited, mainly wooden structure was of some antiquity though, as now built, was but barely a century old; previous castles on the site had at some time been burnt down, as we guessed. We were accommodated at the Kumamoto Castle Hotel and sumptuously entertained that evening. The host party consisted of persons nearly all of whom had some connection with HERF.

A short morning's visit of 1½ hours to the Kumamoto University High Energy Rate Laboratory was arranged (and allowed) by its Director Professor I. Tatsukawa. (A touring party of six included members from departments other than mechanical engineering.)

Among projects studied were the following:

(i) Shock waves in solids

---

* Auld Lang Syne was broadcast; this is very frequently played in Japan at the end of term at schools and university graduation ceremonies!

Figure 6. The Crater: Mount Aso.

(ii) Shock wave transmission due to explosion in the atmosphere aiming to *reduce* nuisance effects

(iii) Experiments into generating ultra high magnetic fields.

(iv) The study of explosion-induced phase transitions in carbon. (Diamond had been produced in a 4 m dia. spherical chamber.)

(v) A weld-forming technique by underwater explosion had been successfully developed so that in particular the inside of pressure vessel bottoms could be clad.

(vi) The metallurgical properties (fatigue and residual stress) of explosive stainless clad steel had been investigated.

(vii) A 'machine' for explosively forming dental plates was demonstrated, first introduced by Prof. Sir Bernard Crossland and his team.

Project (vii) had earlier been carried out at Queen's University, Belfast. Details of (iv) and (v), they would not reveal to me.

We departed from Kumamoto about noon for the Beppu site of the Ohita Works of the Nippon Steel Corporation but made a long stop first in the Aso Kanko Hotel National Park in order to visit the crater of the *active* volcano, Mount Aso. (See Figure 6.) The sight of such a huge active volcano was magnificent, in spite of heavy rain. It was daunting to see the concrete bomb-proof shelters near to the crater – shelters for visitors to resort to when large clouds of hot ash were ejected!

We were delivered into the hands of a Mr H. Katoh of Nippon Steel, and proceeded to the Suginoi Hotel, Beppu.

A small dinner party (Japanese-style again with hostesses and lots of warm saki) was arranged during the evening and 'conducted' by Mr Katoh, manager of the Nippon Plant. Mr Katoh both sang (a Japanese lullaby) and danced for us! (Imagine similar behaviour by a British plant manager!)

On arrival at the plant on the morning of the 19th, the Union Jack, along with the Japanese flag, was gaily flapping at the top of a pole at the main entrance where we were officially received. A film about the establishment and development of the Ohito works was shown to us, the General Manager, Mr Kurass, being present to answer any questions. We discussed technical and labour problems for 40 minutes – especially Britain's steel manning difficulties. In his opinion this was mainly attributable to craft unionism. The tour of this very large plant occupied an hour and a half. The plant was built on land reclaimed from the sea, of extent several square kilometres, and from the beginning of planning to production only four years elapsed. The cleanliness, good order and sparsity of men about was very obvious. The plant is heavily computer-controlled from one central building, and they were greatly exercised about its security from sea attack; if it was seized (e.g. for ransom) the whole of it could easily be put out of operation.

We were conveyed to see the off-shore berth for the 300,000 ton ore carriers, the blast furnaces (a third one was planned but held back because of the recession) and the continuous casting process plant. The rolling plant was not in operation but we were conducted through the computer room which controlled the furnace output. We scarcely ever got close enough to anything to be able to distinguish or identify detail! Official catwalks etc. were always far from the theatre of operations!

After lunch I gave my sixth and last lecture in Japan, on 'Mechanics in Sport' – as requested – to the works engineers, some thirty in all. This seemed to be a

Figure 7. Mrs Johnson eats Japanese style.

great success especially those parts which dealt with golf, football and pole vaulting!

Returning by 'plane from Beppu to Tokyo, the day was overcast and thus we lost the opportunity to see much of the country from the air. From Haneda airport we travelled out on the monorail to a suburb of Yokahama to spend our last two days in the home of Professor Kudo. See Figures 7, 8 and 9.

We spent a portion of the day, 9.45 a.m.–1.00 p.m., at the Kagoshima Space

Figure 8. At the entrance to the Kibuki theatre with Prof. and Mrs Jimma.

Figure 9. Departure for the UK from Haneda Airport with Prof. and Mrs Jimma.

Centre (part of the University of Tokyo). To visit it was not straightforward for reasons of security but Professor Fukui as an ex-director of the Japanese space programme was instrumental in securing permission. I was certainly carefully passed from one group to another.

I was shown the satellite CORSA and had explained to me by Professor Oda, the Japanese instrumentation for the collection of atmospheric X-ray data. My main interests were in, and useful discussion was obtained on, (a) high velocity impact work, (b) axial cylindrical tube plastic buckling and (c) the use of photo-plastic coatings.

This visit was one of the most useful and interesting of any I made in Japan and it was only a pity it was so heavily surrounded by security considerations.

Our route back to the UK was via Moscow, with Aeroflot, on the same route as that on which we went out, landing at Heathrow at about 10.30 pm. We motored home to arrive early Sunday morning in Cambridge and en route had a fire in the car (due to an electrical short). It took a few days for our physiology to adjust to being 12 hours out of phase.

Some General Observations

1. I was immensely struck by the large number of universities and institutes devoted to, or involved in, Industrial Science. This stands in contrast with the position in the UK. Industrial Science in Japan occupied a wide conspicuous area of university study and activity – much greater I thought than that given to civil engineering. In the UK universities the latter receives the same amount of resources for teaching and research study as the whole of mechanical engineering (which I take to include Industrial Science). This difference in teaching and research resource allocation (seemingly 'directed' as SRC was endeavouring to impose here) reflected perhaps the industrial and production successes and failures of Japan and the UK respectively. (Civil and Structural engineering in the UK were regarded as gentlemanly whilst manufacturing industry was somewhat inferior and 'working class'.)

2. Engineers were enormously attached to their companies – we have all heard of the patriarchal nature of Japanese firms – which submerged their personality and character. One felt that they appreciated that their jobs were connected with keeping it successful. Their feeling of security in their particular companies was very evident too. Also one sensed no rivalry between old and young professional engineers whilst promotion battles or fears were, as far as I could ascertain, non-existent.

3. At all the factories or plants I visited (Nippon Kokon, Toyota, Nachi Bearing, Nippon Steel) *management* and workers wore a 'uniform' of grey cloth jacket (and often cap). The most senior man on the plant was dressed to be identical with the shop floor workers; no manager was at pains to distinguish himself in dress from his subordinates as would generally be the case in the UK. *All* the senior directors and managers I met in companies

4. The fraction of the age group in universities was said to be 25–30% – which made me reflect about Japanese engineering, science and commerce vis-a-vis the UK. Asked to say some words about postgraduate build-up to Ph.D., I made some general remarks which later became a 500 word article on the topic – see Figure 4 Chapter XVII – one among a small series by other authors.

5. Questions asked by me were seldom avoided and indeed I was surprised at the honesty of some of the replies. I concluded that the Japanese were not afraid to learn from anybody or anywhere. Their well known habit of copying should, I felt, be looked at more in terms of willingness to learn than a desire to get something for nothing or steal ideas.

6. The quality and quantity of the work performed in my field was as good and indeed perhaps better and in advance of ours in the UK. (Of course the population of Japan was twice that of the UK.) This overtaking of the UK has happened in my lifetime. I felt that professors and others in universities in the UK involved in metal working research could well have followed the example of the Japanese professors by coming together for the purpose of defining and co-ordinating their specific spheres of research, thus making for economy, efficiency and greater concentration, as well as reaping the benefits of specialisation for themselves and industry.

Acknowledgement

I was enormously grateful for financial support for my visit to the Royal Society, the Japanese National Congress of Plasticity and many Japanese companies and friends.

CHAPTER XXVI

China
and
Women in Mathematics

China

One of the nicest occasions I ever enjoyed followed from receiving a letter from Professor R. Honeycombe, when Head of the Metallurgy Department in Cambridge, asking me to join him in receiving a Chinese visiting party; a political thaw had not long started with China. The visit had been organised by BISRA. Some twenty or so of us listened to speeches of reception and at the close of it the leader of the visitors announced that he had a letter for Professor Johnson and would he please contact him. It was a surprise and in any case, I thought later, the letter might not have easily survived the normal channels of communication. It proved to be from Professor Ren Wang of Beijing University, saying that he wished to send a Mr T. X. Yu to me for postgraduate work and would I receive him – which I answered in the affirmative.

I had known Professor Ren Wang for many years and we had exchanged research publications; he had produced new and useful results using Slip Line Field Theory, many of which were similar to mine. He had spent several years in the USA but returned to China in 1956 despite the 'cold' political climate. It transpired that Mr Yu had been fifth in the Mathematical Olympiads held in his country. He had spent about a decade performing menial work in the countryside in the days when intellectuals were unwanted during the Cultural Revolution. After a first degree he had spent some years on courses in Applied Mechanics and Plasticity. In particular when he joined me in the Cambridge Engineering Dept., I quickly found him to be easy, pleasant and hardworking and moreover he spoke English well. Further, like many Chinese students, he was always reluctant to question his supervisor. I set him to research successively various problems and found him to be very competent indeed. He moved to being able to discuss the problem and then he would disappear and return later, with a theoretical solution. In his first year with me, 1981, we co-authored several papers. We went on at speed throughout 1982 and our combination was very fruitful. I have forgotten whether or not he was finally accepted as a Ph.D. candidate at this time, and anyway, it didn't seem to matter to him too much.

Heather and I had Mr Tong X. Yu over to our house in Cambridge for dinner along with several other students. Afterwards, I received an invitation to dinner at a house in the poorer part of Cambridge in which he resided with other Chinese men; it seemed to be a kind of commune for researchers. On arriving at Mr Yu's 'residence', Heather and I were seated alone at a small table set for four in a sparsely furnished upstairs room. It was intended that Mr Yu and his helper-colleague, a Physics post-graduate student, would sit with us. We later learned that all the foodstuffs prepared for us and a nice collection of Chinese wines, had been purchased from Chinese shops in London. Each of the two men kept a menu in the back pocket of his jeans and took turns alternating between the basement kitchen and the dining room, in cooking and serving each other, as well sitting with the two of us, during a next course. This was a sort of oscillating dinner party which we had not encountered before!

A conference came up in the USA for which one of our papers was suitable, and – thinking to give Mr Yu more knowledge of the western world – I sent him to present it, which he did efficiently. Unfortunately, while he was away, a letter arrived from his brother which proved to be serious. The letter, from Beijing, could not be passed on because neither his colleagues nor I knew Tong's precise whereabouts in the USA. The letter was opened and contained the information that his wife was very ill – it turned out to be cancer. The procedure for Chinese students going abroad was for them to report at the Chinese Embassy before and after any proposed visit abroad. It must have been ten days or so before Tong actually returned and when he did so he came up to Cambridge by bus, having just learned from the Embassy of his wife's terminal condition. Heather and I met him at the Cambridge bus station, tried to comfort him, taking him back to our house and then to his rooms. He made arrangements for returning to Beijing and was away several months, among other things, making arrangements for his young daughter to be cared for. His wife had died of throat cancer – a common form of cancer in that part of the world. I was somewhat surprised that he ever returned, but he did and then continued working as hard as ever.

By 1982 when I retired we had written 16 papers! I had lost contact with Tong, during which period he acquired his Doctorate. He became closely connected in the department with Dr W. J. Stronge, who had joined us as a lecturer and who came, unusually, from California. Subsequently, they co-authored a book which appeared in 1993, *Structural Plasticity*. Later, Tong moved to Manchester where he worked for a period with Professor S. R. Reid. Today, it is Professor T. X. Yu of the University of Science and Engineering, Hong Kong! He had married Shying, she too, having lost her first partner and having been left with a daughter. They were living on a strikingly beautiful campus at the edge of the sea. Heather and I visited them in their elegant university apartment, some time later. We have kept good contact this last decade and presently, he seems to be forging strong academic connections with Beijing.

Conferencing in China

In 1986, my wife and I were invited to the 30th Anniversary of the Institute of Mechanics, in Beijing. Two conferences or events were held, one in Beijing itself and the other in a hotel on the outskirts. The total period of my visit to China was about three-four weeks and the train of events which befell us was quite atypical for visitors.

After leaving Heathrow on our way out to Beijing, our plane landed unexpectedly at Rome. We were grounded there for twelve hours and some passengers became very aggressive with air-line staff, because no information was forthcoming about the reason for, and the duration of, the delay. In the course of having a meal at the Rome airport I lost an artificial front tooth, which not only marred my appearance, but registered in my speech as something between a whistle and a lisp! Later, on arriving over China we were told that the plane could not land in Beijing before 7.30 a.m., and accordingly we spent some time I believe, in Singapore airport. After continuing and landing in Beijing we were met by Tong and Shiying Yu, still smiling and welcoming despite the long wait they had had – we were a day late. They conveyed us to an apartment on the Beijing University campus. We discussed the lecture programme which was set to start the next morning at 8 a.m. There was a good audience for it, but I came to doubt if half of them could understand English, and I think, less, were familiar with plasticity. I remember that my slides were shown upside down and/or back to front, but I did not let it trouble me. My wife came to meet me near the end of the lecture and heard me say, 'This slide is upside down but you can easily up-turn it mentally'!

We were visited by Dr and Mrs Bai, who enquired about our arrangements and condition. Mrs Bai, on learning of my 'dental misfortune', promptly announced that she, 'was on intimate terms with her dentist, and believed that he might be able to help'. (I had had visions of being treated in the Dentistry Dept. in the university hospital, by a series of learner undergraduate dentists!) The couple departed, having informed me of some new arrangements for the next few days, each on a bicycle – no cars here! Mrs Bai returned later with her dentist, a retired gentleman who proceeded to examine my teeth and then took impressions of them by having me bite into clay before he left. A second appointment was made for me to see him the next day, Sunday, at 11 a.m. In mid-morning, we were duly walked to the dentist's surgery, passing through a maze of narrow passages or lanes passing by what were clearly every-day dwellings. I noticed from time to time communal water stand-pipes; I got such a view as is seldom seen by the average tourist who generally sees only the well-planned main roads, hotels and exhibition features they are meant to see.

I arrived at an orderly small dwelling, where, in a home-made surgery, after a short examination, the old dentist commenced to use an ancient drill on the stub of my tooth. The low – as opposed to the usual high – speed whir of the drill, became very hard to bear – it seemed to say, 'you are now very far from home!' I just about survived the experience and eventually a replacement cap was fitted and dressed, all very easily and painlessly. At one juncture when my head was laid back on the top of the chair, I became aware of people who had come to the window immediately in front of me to stare in at the dental subject! Looking around me I noticed that the water for the mouth wash was delivered from a black kettle. At once, when I rose from the chair, the dentist apologised for the colour of the teeth not quite matching; I couldn't see any difference and the tooth felt fine. I asked 'How much? American dollars?' 'No payment', he responded and the answer to the question remained the same, try as I would to have him receive a fee. The impasse was broken when my wife suggested 20 dollars for presents to his grandchildren. A year later, my Buxton dentist examined the tooth and noted in a general survey that it was in good order (as it still is), and was astonished to learn of the Chinese competence which had been displayed which was certainly no less than his own.

Mrs Bai was a plasma physicist in her own right, whilst Dr Y. L. Bai, whom I had known and worked with for several years was then the Deputy Head of one of the Chinese Government's Impact laboratories; we had earlier exchanged research papers on Impact problems. Like Dr Yu he very obviously was well trained in theoretical mechanics. Altogether we published a total of seven papers, two of which were on *Plugging (high speed expulsion of very short metal cylinders from a plate, due to normal impact by a punch)* and on *Ricochet*. (See Chapter XXII, p. 259 for a definition and some remarks on this topic).

I well recall the formal evening dinner arranged in the Great Hall in Beijing, which marked the beginning of our first Conference when perhaps 300–400 people sat down to what was a general celebratory occasion, with television cameras present. A number of us were received and welcomed by a government minister before entering the dining hall. On being shown to our places at the top table we found the first course of the dinner laid out before us, covered with plastic film. After the Chairman had formally welcomed the whole gathering and another course or two served, he again rose and called on an American professor to speak. There were, in fact, participants from two independent conferences present! Behind the top table there was what resembled a lectern, but raised to a height of some three or four metres. The American addressed the diners from the top of the lectern for a few minutes and then returned to his place. The chairman stood up again and announced, 'Professor Johnson will now address the gathering ...' I had not been forewarned and so mounted the stairs, slowly, thinking what I should say. I mentioned visiting China for the first time, the Conference occasion and China's future in the field of Mechanics. It seemed to be well received but took no more than five minutes to deliver. It was not a totally pleasant experience.

The next day at the first Conference location, as a special lecture, I contributed a paper entitled *Topics for Research in Mechanics in the next 15 years*. Predicting is a subject in which one can be grossly incorrect. I always remember reading for example what H. G. Wells wrote in *Anticipations* (1902) – '... the coming of flying ... I do not think ... that aeronautics will ever come into play as a serious modification of transport ...'! However, my paper duly appeared, in Chinese, I am told, in 1986 and at length, subsequently, in English.

At the second Conference, I gave two papers in a Symposium on Materials and Structures, entitled *Oak Targets and Naval Gunnery in the early nineteenth century* and *Wood, under Impact Load*. There was only a modest degree of interest in these topics; indeed nothing connected with history sparked a response reflecting China's own experiences.

This Conference at Beijing took place at a beautiful hotel on its perimeter; several of the buildings which comprised it were said to have been where visiting Russians only stayed when their political relationship with China was closer.

At the conclusion of the latter Conference, my wife and I were taken to a quite remarkable lunch arranged by Professor Ren Wang and in memory of this special occasion, he gave me an inscribed book of 450 pages, full of photographs of eight large earthquakes in his country. See Figure 1. (Unfortunately, the captions to all the prints were in Chinese.) This was a splendid occasion, and a unique one for us. We dined in what seemed to be a prestigious and once royal palace; our dining proceeded on (or near) a boat carved in stone, on the edge of a small lake. The lunch consisted of many, many varieties of foods and Chinese wines – but the final serving was soup!

地震出版社
1 9 8 3. 北京

中国八大地震
震害摄影图集

国家地震局地质研究所

The Photo Album

of Eight Strong Earthquake Disasters in China

Institute of Geology, State Seismological Bureau

PREFACE
In this photographical album, we have collected 434 pictures showing disasters from eight strong earthquakes (6.8 ≤ M ≤ 7.9)* which occurred in China during the period of 1966 to 1976.

Figure 1. The Photo Album of Eight Strong Earthquake Disasters in China. Institute of Geology, State Seismological Bureau.

---

* M: On the Richter scale.

One other evening, we were taken to see a Chinese circus and were highly impressed, especially with the acrobats.

On yet another occasion we paid a visit to the National Museum and there, particularly, I was drawn to a History of Technology display. (One recalls, the memorable volumes by Joseph Needham, on *The History of Science and Technology* in China.) I was informed that Chiang Kai Shek had taken many of the best exhibits to Taiwan and I understood why China was incensed! What I encountered and particularly remember were two long remarkable parallel rows, one above the other, of descriptions on the wall of the exhibition room, stating the dates at which various engineering or technological developments were made, in chronological order, as between the cultures of the West and those in China. They gradually converged but with some decades in time between them at certain points in time; the East was sometimes first and sometimes the West. But, conspicuously, a diversion took place in the seventeenth century when Europe seemed to take off on a quite different track which was obviously due to the beginning of modern Science; no comments were made but a hiatus was clearly demonstrated.

Two further occasions remain clearly in my memory from this visit: one was of being taken to see the astonishing Buried Army of life-size statues of ancient soldiers when it had not long been exposed in Sian and the other was walking along a portion of the Great Wall of China (with Professors S. K. Ghosh and M. S. J. Hashmi), which could be compared in width with a typical main road but with gradients which were surprisingly severe at some points.

At the conclusion of the conferences, we travelled by air to Harbin where we met Professor H. Wang with whom again, I had exchanged published research papers. It had so happened during the Cultural Revolution, that Professor Wang had been directed to a brick-making factory. Contrary to the experience of most 'directed intellectuals', he had enjoyed his work and even made many useful suggestions and improvements, all of which led to him becoming highly influential in the enterprise. Thus elevated, he took off into academic life and climbed the ladder to a chair in metal forming. I was taken round his laboratory to see his experimental work and indeed his facilities were better than mine; also his research was quite different in kind to anything else I saw in China.

Our return journey to Beijing was by train and much more comfortable than that by air; it had not been possible to book return by air. Thus we travelled by rail and were able to see something of the countryside.

As a consequence of my visit to China and the cultivation of several new acquaintances and associations, the following shortened paper resulted and appears to have started (or tried to start) a new line of interest there on the subject of Women in Mechanics.

ACTA MECHANICA SINICA, Vol. 11, No.3, August 1995

The Chinese Society of Theoretical and Applied Mechanics
Chinese Journal of Mechanics Press, Beijing, China
Allerton Press, INC., New York, USA

A SHORT ACCOUNT OF SOME WOMEN IN MATHEMATICS, ENGINEERING AND ASTRONOMY
W. Johnson

Editor's Note: This paper may serve as a greeting to the United Nations Fourth World Conference on Women, to be held in Beijing in September, 1995. It is also the first paper contributed to the new column 'The History of Mechanics' in our journal, which was set up also at the suggestion of Dr Johnson. We will welcome further contributions on that line.

We begin by pointing out that up to 1960 it is not easy to find outstanding women in the scientific fields embraced by the title above. The writer felt prompted to attempt this after working on a paper about Newtonianism entering France widely, in the eighteenth century and for which **MME. du CHATELET** (1706–1749), served as a notable vehicle. She was encouraged by Voltaire to translate Newton's *Principia Mathematica*, which had first been published in England in 1687 (the third edition appearing in 1724), after living with him during the years 1734–1748; her book appeared in 1759, ten years after her death. The author's aim was to search out other notable women mathematicians and scientists. In the first instance, he restricted his aim to women of more than about two generations ago, because there would be now so many to consider in the fields surveyed and because it takes at least half a century for new distinguished persons to emerge and be recognised.

Besides Mme. du Chatelet the author has selected some fourteen other women and presents a short biography about them and their contributions. It is necessary to identify and appreciate these women because they are hardly to be distinguished from among very many men. Once we know the women we can then begin to study them as a class and perhaps draw generalizations about them and the work they have done and why there are so few of them. Bringing to the fore the names I have chosen, finds more than one half who would be on everybody's list charged with the writer's task. A small number I have included and who they are, will be obvious to the reader. I therefore review all these women in brief but for a fuller account of each, the reader is referred to the writer's longer paper of the same title in the *Journal of Materials Processing Technology* (Elsevier, 1994, 40(1): 37–71).*

By many centuries is **HYPATIA OF ALEXANDRIA** (c.370–415 AD), the earliest and most prominent female who claims our attention. She was the daughter of the Head of the famous museum established at Alexandria on the Nile delta, living during the collapse of the West Roman Empire. She was trained by her father and her major interests were astronomy – descriptions of the planetary system, and pure mathematics – conics and arithmetic or the theory of numbers and of reckoning. The Christian church in the fourth century AD was in the throes of sectarian conflict and since

---

* Received, 10 April 1994.

Hypatia was non-Christian, under Bishop Cyril of Alexandria a mob was incited to attack and kill her. Her story is told by Charles Kingsley in his novel, *Hypatia*, 1853. This 'Christian' act is seen by Edward Gibbon in the *Decline and Fall of the Roman Empire*, as a great stain on the history of the early church.

LAURA BASSI (1711–1778) was a Professor of Anatomy in the University of Bologna who also lectured mathematics and a kind of experimental physics. She published very little – she had twelve children – but clearly left behind a remarkable reputation so that when wishing to become a member of the Bologna Academy of Sciences, even Voltaire courted her support.

A contemporary of Bassi was **MARIA AGNESI** (1718–1791) who published her two-volume book in 1748, *Instituzioni Analitische ad uso della Gioventu Italiana* (Analytical Principles for the use of Italian Youth). This work, highly acclaimed in Europe, was translated into English by Professor John Colson, a successor to Isaac Newton in the Lucasian chair at Cambridge during the last twenty years of his life. To do this he learned Italian, his purpose being to make available to Cambridge undergraduates reading mathematics, much material which was then widely dispersed. The subject matter was mostly analysis and differential equations; it treated Leibnizian methods of analysis as well as Newtonian fluxions. Unfortunately, the translation – *Analytical Principles for Italian Youth* – lay unpublished until 1802. Pope Benedict XIV, effectively the Head of Bologna University, in recognition of her claim, pronounced Agnesi 'an honorary professor of Mathematics and Philosophy'. Agnesi was precocious but one always drawn to the life of a nun. After her father's death in 1752 she returned to Milan and thereafter lived the life or a recluse, abandoning mathematics.

One specific item on which Agnesi's name is imprinted is a cubic equation, $y = a^3/(x^2 + a^2)$, which, plotted, has the appearance of a witch's cloak. This is popularly known as 'the Witch of Agnesi' and referred to as such by engineering students of mechanisms. Rather than a 'Witch', Agnesi seems to have been a saint. She devoted herself to the welfare of the poor, sick and aged, from 1752 to the end of her life, in a 'Benedictine' hospice. See Figure 2.

ELIZABETH CARTER (1717–1806), a well-educated eighteenth-century English lady, is included here more for tradition than originality. She was an accurate translator, widely known for her intelligence, hard work and perseverance. This lady translated from the Italian, Francesco Algarotti's *Sir Isaac Newton's Philosophy explained for the use of Ladies in six dialogues on Light and Colour*. It went through six editions between

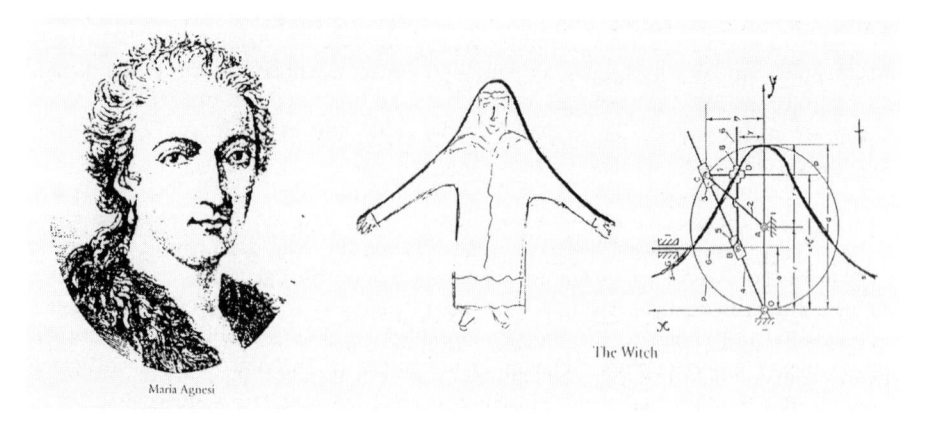

Figure 2. Maria Agnesi.

1739 and 1772. Mrs Carter received £1000 for translating this book. She wrote many other items and her conversation made her of interest to such national writers of the day as Bishop Butler, Edmund Burke and Samuel Johnson.

Our next notable woman is **EMILIE DE BRETEUIL, Marquise du Chatelet**, much of whose relevant biography we have told in our Introduction. As well as her translation of Newton's *Principia* she produced an influential volume, *Institutions de Physique* (Principles of Physics), many of the ideas here being Leibnizian and contrary to Newtonian attractionist theory. Emilie also had an interest in the nature of Fire and its propagation. She died in 1749, in childbirth.

CAROLINE L. HERSCHEL (1750–1848), was a sister of (later Sir) William Herschel, the much-acclaimed observational astronomer and was, like him, born in Hanover, Germany. Both came to England as musicians but William deviated to become private astronomer to King George III. Caroline also changed to become his valuable co-operator, 'sweeping the sky for comets', performing long, laborious calculations and cataloguing hundreds of stars and nebulae. For her work she received the Royal Astronomical Society's gold medal in 1828, the Prussian gold medal for Science in 1846 and the King of England settled on her a life pension of £50 per annum.

A curious place is held in the history of Vibrations by **SOPHIE GERMAIN** (1776–1831), of France. A thin metal plate covered with a fine, uniform layer of dry sand, when caused to undergo vibrations at right angles to its own plane, sets the sand in different patterns according to the form and the frequency of agitation of the plate and its material properties. Emperor Napoleon (engineer trained!), intrigued by E. F. F. Chladni's experimental results as just described, offered a prize for its explanation in mathematical terms, putting the conduct of the competition into the hands of the French Academy of Science. Only one prize essay was received by 1811, and that was submitted by Mme. Germain. It was shown to be incorrect by Lagrange and a supposed corrected solution was given by Mme. Germain in 1813. The latter was however again unsuccessful but a third submission by this lady was deemed worthy of the Prize in 1816 despite some small criticisms remaining. The view taken by the distinguished examining body of mathematicians was that Sophie had made a very substantial contribution to what they all regarded as a difficult problem in engineering science.

MRS DR MARY SOMERVILLE (1780–1872), a British woman, first expounded in English, Laplace's five-volume *Méchanique Céleste* in the *Mechanism of the Heavens* in 1831. This was unquestionably a 'college text book for the next century'. It was followed in 1834 by her *On the Connection of the Physical Sciences*. Dr Somerville wrote several more expository books on Optics, on the Form and Rotation of the Earth and on Molecular and Microscopic Science, among other works.

In 1879 a hostel for women students was opened at Oxford University and named, after her death, as Somerville College. This lady eschewed all claims to scientific originality but nonetheless was zealous in seeking the proper emancipation of her sex in nineteenth-century Britain. There are a small number of biographies of Dr Somerville which describe her life and deal with her various scientific contributions at length.

The daughter of the well-known English poet Lord Byron, **AUGUSTA ADA-LOVELACE** (1815–1852), in whom he took no interest, displayed mathematical ability and learned advanced mathematics despite 'official' obstacles being put in her path. She came to know Charles Babbage well and translated work on the Analytical Engine for him in about 1843. She wrote a notable fundamental paper which embodies the essence of

Figure 3. Augusta Ada-Lovelace.

a modern successful, commercial digital computer. The story of her contribution is told at some length in an article. *The Language of Computers* by the late Lord Bowden of Chesterfield (sometime Principal of UMIST) in *Mathematics*, Vol. 3, p. 5, Wadsworth International, California. See Figure 3.

Probably the most original female mathematician up to the twentieth century was **SONYA KOVALEVSKI** (1850–1891). A Russian, she was brought up in St Petersburg and while young entertained romantic feelings for Dostoevsky whom she met, but these were not reciprocated. Her emotional dependence on men cannot be shortly told and anyway, its history is interwoven with her intense researches into mathematics.

The principal director of Sonya's researches was then Professor Karl Weierstrass of Berlin. For a period during the 1880s she held an appointment, first as lecturer and then professor in the department of Professor M. G. Mittag-Leffler of Stockholm, Sweden; he was interested in 'the woman question' and wanted to secure 'the first great woman mathematician'. Her work included research into the refraction of light in crystalline media, establishing the now-called Cauchy-Kovalevsky theorem (in 1875), work on Abelian integrals, the shape of the rings of planet Saturn, work on the theory of gravitational potential and the problem of the rotation of a rigid body. She died at the early age of 41, having been made a member of the St Petersburg Academy and receiving a research prize from Sweden. She later had a monument erected to her by the women of Russia. As the great Professor Weierstrass remarked, 'My faithful pupil was not a frivolous marionette'. See Figure 4.

EMMY NOETHER (1882–1935), the daughter of a professor of pure mathematics, was born in Erlangen, Germany and enjoyed an excellent education in a stable home to become as different temperamentally from Sonya Kovalevsky as could be. Her remembered work on 4th degree equations was accepted for a doctoral thesis in 1907. She transferred to Gottingen where she heard and was encouraged by eminent Professors Klein and Hilbert. But she went to work under Professor Wegl and in 1920 proceeded to change the 'aspect of algebras' in a series of papers. Though not an

Sonya Corvin-Krukovsky
Kovalevsky
1850–1891

Figure 4. Sonya Kovalevski.

adequate lecturer she seems to have been kept down in Germany and when racial laws were introduced in 1933 she emigrated to the USA, settling finally at Bryn Mawr women's college. She died, unexpectedly, in 1935. The work for which she will be remembered deals with certain formulations for relativity theory, a so-called 'general theory of ideals' and non-commutative algebras.

Englishwoman **HERTHA AYRTON** (née Marx) (1854–1923), read mathematics at Cambridge, 1877–1881, but performed poorly in examinations through heedless preparation. She early showed some design talent, an item of hers being patented. She married Will Ayrton (1847–1900), whom she met at Finsbury Technical College, London, whilst attending an evening lecture course in science. Subsequently he became Professor at Imperial College, London and was elected a Fellow of the Royal Society in 1881 for pioneering studies on high voltage electricity transmission. She read a technical paper to the Institution of Electrical Engineers in 1899, but her paper on this topic to the Royal Society in 1901, had to be read by Professor *John* Perry!

Hertha's next work was on ripple marks in sand made by water and she read a paper on it before the Royal Society in 1904; two further papers were presented and these were the first ever delivered by a woman before the Society. For this, and other contributions, this lady received the Society's Hughes Medal, however a proposal to elect her as a Fellow in 1902 failed. A second endeavour to elect her was made in 1920 but this too failed since all her supporters, but one, had died. During the First World War she invented the Ayrton Fan or Flapper and this materially aided the shifting of poisonous gas from war trenches; about 100,000 such fans were used on the Western War Front. Hertha Ayrton died in 1923 and was forgotten until recently when an article by Joan Mason about her and the non-admission of women to the Royal Society appeared in *Notes and Records of the RS*, 1991, 45(2): 201–220.

The engineering profession has generally been entered by women from its 'light' side through minor management, work measurement and work organisation. **MRS LILIAN GILBRETH** (1878–1972), of the USA was a famed industrial engineer and wife of work measurement innovator, Frank Gilbreth, who died in 1924. She acquired her interest in the subject from him and greatly developed this facet of industrial engineering until her death. The life of this couple has been greatly popularised by the book and film, *Cheaper by the Dozen* which related to their twelve children.

ANNE SHAW was a slightly later researcher and a distinguished ergonomicist of the Metro Vickers Company and later AEI Ltd, Trafford Park, Manchester. She made some original advances in this field during her two generations of active employment, particularly in the Second World War when the 20,000 labour force of the company had to make Herculean production efforts.

The last lady we mention, who, like Anne Shaw had local associations*, is **DAME KATHLEEN OLLERENSHAW** (1915–). Dr Ollerenshaw was an Oxford graduate of Somerville College and a postgraduate in mathematics. During her lifetime she has had a considerable involvement in Manchester politics and education but with Sir Herman Bondi in 1982 she co-authored a very substantial paper of about 100 pages which appeared in the *Philosophical Transactions of the Royal Society of London*, A306, 443–532, on *Magic Squares of Order 4*. Such a square is shown below.

7	12	1	14
2	13	8	11
16	3	10	5
9	6	15	4

The above square is 'magical' in that the total of the integers in each line or column as well as the two major diagonals always totals 34. These squares have had a fascination for mankind since legendary times. This subject belongs in the difficult field of the Theory of Numbers.

In my longer paper there will be found a short *Bibliography* which leads into the fast-growing field of literature about women in science associations.

---

* 'Local associations' applies to Manchester.

CHAPTER XXVII

Turkey, Greece and Mount Athos

———◆———

I WAS FORMALLY INVITED by the British Council, in November 1977, to visit Greece but also persuaded to visit a neighbouring country which I chose to be Turkey, even though I had met only a few Turkish professors at conferences.

(i) Turkey

I departed for Istanbul by Turkish Airlines and found myself on a full plane of passengers of whom one half were members of a Lucky 7 Club bound for the Istanbul Hilton! A game of Bingo was played during the flight for a prize of £500. There were lots of loud calls for such as 'legs 11' and 'blind 60', with photographers from *The People* taking photographs of the club members with their arms raised, crying out, 'House!'. I was amazed that Turkish Airlines encouraged this kind of activity, which was to the displeasure of the other half of the passengers.

When changing planes and airports at Istanbul for Ankara everything seemed to be in pandemonium, and I was grateful to a teenage, worldly-wise porter for helping me to carry some of my baggage (which contained a lot of 2″ × 2″ glass slides) to the national airport, 500 m away, and finding an empty coach which took me out over the tarmac to a waiting plane! Once arrived at Ankara, at 11 p.m., I was met by the British Council Assistant Director who had arranged accommodation for me in the Kent Oteli.

I was introduced the next day, to several Turkish engineering professors at a cocktail party and lunch. In particular I renewed an acquaintanceship with Professor Kraftanoglu of METU (Middle East Technical University), Ankara. I went off with him to see his technical laboratories and then made a swift tour of the Citadel (a hill of 'houses erected in the night' they said), to the Hittite Museum housed in a converted market but displaying some lovely metal work, the Temple of Augusta, the pillar of Julian the Apostate (a second Marcus Aurelius for some) which was sadly neglected, and we paid our respects to Kemal Ataturk at his Memorial. Overall, I gave three lectures, two on HERF (high energy rate forming) – fast shaping metal forming processes accomplished using explosive-like methods, and one on ring rolling, rotary forging, superplasticity and like forming processes. There was a good audience of senior academics and doctoral students, keen to know about the former subject, since, apparently, it was neither known nor practised in Turkey. In the evening, I was delighted to attend a mixed dinner party arranged by the British Council. Ladies were too often missing on such occasions but most of the wives I met on this one were good conversationalists.

I was later scheduled to visit the Bosphorus or Bogazici University (BU), formerly Robert College, founded by an American a century ago; it is at the other end of the sea of Marmora. Here, I gave my two usual lectures, somewhat truncated. Among the audience, unexpectedly, I observed many females listening in rapt attention in a lecture room so full that many were sitting on the stairs. At the end, I was requested to speak for a further 15 minutes on the Ph.D. system and its level in the UK. There were some very intelligent questions and all went well. At the conclusion, I had the unique experience of being presented with a large bouquet of gladioli and a card, 'From the engineering seniors of BU'.

On Thursday, at 5.30 a.m., I set out to see something of the not-so-well-known region of Cappadocia. The taxi fare to the bus station was 20 TL, but the public bus I embarked on for Ürgüp, over 250 km. south east, cost only 15 TL. The well-used coach was full of 'the people' carrying children, several parcels and food; en route a bottle of perfumed water was circulated for rinsing our hands and dabbing on our faces. We also had five hours of Turkish music. The bus journey passed along the Tuz Golu (salt lake), via Nevsehir, along the Anatolian plateau, finally arriving at Ürgüp at noon. The occasional sight of large herds of goats and wandering asses, enlivened the journey. However, I did feel for one woman with a baby in her arms, running to catch our bus without help from surrounding men. (Are the male and female sexes still so strongly divided in Turkey?) At my destination, with the aid of a little French, I was transported by taxi to a British Council-booked hotel. I checked in, was quickly served lunch and then whisked away by the same taxi driver to Avciler across a tributary of the Kiziliramak (Red River?) to be shown around an alabaster and onyx factory. Shamefacedly, I did not purchase anything, but the trip was obviously on a popular tourist route – though in fact no tourists were in evidence. Our next call was to Zilve which counted among its ancient exhibits a dozen ninth and tenth century churches and some 'fairy chimneys'. I spent an hour or so walking up the nearby valley, searching for the site of old wall paintings in the caves alongside the river, reached after scrambling up the sides of the river bank. Greek anchorites would appear to have lived in these ancient caves until the 1920s when they were evicted by Kemal Ataturk (1880–1938). He was the first soldier-President of Turkey; he overthrew the sultanate in the upheavals of 1919–1922 and returned non-nationals to their original countries as Turkey became westernised. I found little evidence of painting on cave walls and began to wish I had visited Bogazkoy – the well-known capital of the ancient Hittites. I continued my journey to Uchisar (three castles) and Goreme – a site of four or five rock churches set in some remarkable landscapes; the latter site was clearly kept up for visiting tourists.

The following morning in my hotel, I was awakened at 6 a.m., by the (electrical or mechanical) call to prayer of the muezzin from the top of a tower; for a moment I was transported into the world of Omar Khayyam ...

> Awake! for Morning in the Bowl of Night
> Has flung the Stone that puts the Stars to Flight;
> And lo! the Hunter of the East has caught
> The Sultan's Turret in a Noose of Light.

The breakfast was unusual, almost biblical – of olives, goat's cheese and honey.

My first visit that day was to Kaymakli but unfortunately, all the electricity was cut off and entry to a troglodyte or underground 'city' was not feasible. We pressed on, southwards for 9 km. to Derinkuyi where I was delivered to another underground city on several levels, 85 m. deep, much larger than that at Kaymakli. It was said there was a 9 km. long tunnel between the two 'cities'. The manner of hewing out these structures in stone and tufa (solid lime carbonate mud), immediately posed questions about structural strength and techniques, for which no answers were available. The 'city' was entered after removing a horizontal grating and indeed one felt a certain hesitation about descending into the first floor chamber. Apparently human beings had lived in the upper levels, while store and refuge rooms and those for live animals were lower down. I tried hard to find out more about these old structures later, when in the UK, but encountered nothing, except to learn there was a book about it all in German – German scholarship ahead once again?

Another day I went to the Ege (Aegean) University, being booked into a magnificent hotel, mainly to deliver up-dating lectures in my areas of research. I was shown around the university laboratories but was not particularly welcomed by the university staff who seemed overworked and indeed happy to see me leave, though without any discourtesies – there were few points of common interest between us. However, I had contracted to deliver my usual lectures but including elementary material on impact mechanics. I started lecturing but immediately had projector difficulties and this delayed us. I had, to begin with, an audience of perhaps a dozen, but after a few minutes a block of, perhaps 30 students entered, interrupting my flow of words. Some 35 minutes or so into the presentation, the electricity was cut off, so we waited for several minutes and with no indication of when it would return and no suggestions as to what we should do, the mass decided to take over an adjacent theatre where only chalk and a blackboard were available. More students arrived too and, doing the best I could, with chalk and talk, I finished my lecture. Perhaps it had got round that I was talking about the creative use of explosives or the students simply wanted to hear English spoken. It was indeed a very attentive undergraduate audience and the questions were plentiful and well-aimed. I had avoided many of the technicalities of my subjects and wondered how useful it was for them. This visit into the Turkish hinterland was not 'technical' time well spent, but perhaps it was that I expected too much from them all. Current research problems were evidently of no interest to the staff. My respect for Ege was due entirely to its youngsters.

I reflected that for my own education I ought to have tried to spend time at famed, historical Efes (Ephesus), and Izmir (Smyrna). Better than that, I should have travelled up and down the whole of ancient Ionia's coastline, which I have still not done – and furthermore, I had half-hoped to get to the southern coast of the Black Sea and visit the region of Colchis, from where Jason stole the golden fleece but I suppose there would be even less there of technical interest that I could do to promote the UK and science. I had mentioned making a journey to visit Samsun and then extended it to Colchis, but the idea was clearly not encouraged.

More detail about the sights and area I visited may be found in John Freely's *Guide to Turkey*, published six years after my visit.

I might note for contrast, that when returning to Ankara I was amazed to encounter an example of modern culture – for, when passing two motor coaches, there were pasted on them notices of a football game, Derby County v Kayseri.

(ii) To Athens

I returned to Ankara the next day and subsequently flew over the Aegean, to Athens. Surveying a litter of sunny islands from the plane made me understand how, on a journey from Greece to Ionia, the Ancients could make land and obtain provisions, every night. Professor Pericles Theocaris was supposed to meet me, but instead I was picked up by a British Council officer, Mr Fraser, and conveyed to the Galaxy Hotel. He told me that he wanted a few words in private about the current political situation in Greece. There was a ban on assemblies exceeding four persons and the Polytechnic was closed. A week previously a clash had occurred between demonstrating students and the Army, and some students had been killed or injured. There was a curfew in force which was steadily being relaxed and for the present Saturday night, it stood at 1 a.m. That evening however, at 10 p.m., I was taken to dinner at an exclusive restaurant, outside Athens, well dined and returned to the hotel by 12.55 a.m.

The next day I set off for a Sunday morning walk just before 10 o'clock, the weather being wonderful, but remembering after a few yards that Mr Fraser was to telephone, I started to return to the hotel. My view of the road as I turned around thus re-directed to the other end, 100 metres or so away, alighted on a military tank and a sprinkling of soldiers. I then tried to telephone Mr Fraser but learned that no telephone communication had been possible since 5 a.m. My Greek phrase book contains phrases, as they always do, for the most unlikely events but not, 'Have you had a coup d'état this morning?' I therefore had a coffee and attempted to do the best I could in a conversation with the barman, from whom I had a guarded, 'Revolution'!

My impression from what he had said was that Mr Fraser lived in Kolonaki Square which was only 'around the corner'. In order to find out more exactly what was happening (if anyone knew) I decided to walk through the back streets and seek Mr Fraser's explanation but, of course, I found that in Kolonaki Square there was only a locked-up British Council office. In the Square, knots of ten or twenty men stood about – waiting for something to happen and perhaps to take part in it. On the way back police were stopping the few people in the streets

Figure 1. Professor Pericles S. Theocaris

and talking to them. I avoided this potential pleasure, but when I got back to the hotel little information was available or offered. At 10.55 a.m. a few planes flew over the city. Standing on the pavement contemplating the dreadful waste of a lovely day, I observed two car loads of soldiers, just thirty yards away. By design, or otherwise, the hotel room radio was 'out of order', but I had brought a hand-size radio and on tuning in at about 11.15 I heard the end of a proclamation being put out by a local radio station. It was in English, but later repeated in French and German. I gathered that a new President had been installed, that only ambulances were allowed on the streets and that we all had to stay 'at home'. Stirring words about forces on land, in the air and on the sea then followed.

This dreary Sunday ended with the good news that the curfew was to end at 5 a.m. on Monday morning.

I was grateful to Mr Fraser for two telephone calls during the day, anxious for my safety and concerned to keep me informed about the progress of events.

Some time later, I learned from my wife in Derbyshire (UK) that she had had a telephone call to our home, from the Foreign Office, to make sure that she was not with me in Athens.

I gave my lectures in the university. The first was delivered on Monday evening, before an obviously well-informed audience of about forty; however, there were three finely bedecked police officers, sitting and listening on the back row – presumably there because of the restrictions in force. Despite the political situation, the subject of Explosive Forming was not prohibited and surprisingly, it drew no comment. Two days later, at my second lecture, no police were present.

I have known Professor Theocaris for more than a dozen years and he was on the Advisory Board of the *IJMS* (which always confers some degree of celebrity on members). I visited his many laboratories and quickly appreciated that he had some of the best equipped ones in the world for Experimental Stress Analysis and the study of the Properties of Materials. Prof. Theocaris died in September,

2000, aged 79, having published 23 books and about 945 papers (see Figure 1). He was a very determined man with much political influence, and, perhaps because of some of his competitive successes, he would say, 'Some of the American professors have become my enemies'.

I spent one day with Prof. Theocaris visiting the well-known monastery at Daphne, the starting point of the Olympic Marathon and the battle mound of the Spartan dead from Xerxes' invasion of the country. The encounter at Thermopylae occurred when the sea only allowed for a narrow battle ground; today, the coast is some kilometres away.

I had been handsomely entertained and welcomed by Prof. Theocaris and a young Professor Paipetis, and was pleased therefore to be able to present them with a copy of my just-published book (with Peter Mellor), *Engineering Plasticity*.

(iii) Other encounters in Greece

The Athens National Academy which includes literary men, artists and historians etc., as well as scientists, elected me a member in 1982. On the visit to be initiated I had scarcely got out of Athens airport when encountering Prof. Mamalis, who announced that I had to respond in Greek in the first 500 words of my reply after my citation for election had been read out. The only thing I could do was not to panic but to write the first 500 words in English, then ask a bi-lingual colleague, Professor Mamalis's nephew, to translate it into Greek and to transcribe it phonetically for me; and then to practise reading the latter until I could utter intelligible Greek sounds to an audience. In the Academy hall, quite full of men and women, with their eyes and those of the busts of Plato, Hippocrates, Aristotle and others looking down upon me, I delivered my Greek response in accepting the honour. The Falklands war had recently started and my spoken words were about war, democracy and freedom before passing on to give an ordinary lecture. I was sure, at the end of my performance, on looking at the bust of Aristophanes that I saw him turn his head and wink! Asked how my modern Greek was received, people said with a wry smile, it was intelligible.

The Athens theatre is very impressive and Heather and I on a later occasion enjoyed seeing and hearing, if not understanding, a very powerful performance of Sophocles' King Oedipus, in Greek. Some time later, travelling outside Athens we chanced to come across a small town where a performance of one of Aristophanes' plays in modern dress was taking place in a tiny outside theatre.

The area in the vicinity of Epidaurus is associated with the healing god, Aesculapius and indeed the countryside seems ideal for patient recovery. One branch of the Aesculapids studied medicine without admitting religion. We also heard a play delivered in the much celebrated theatre of Epidaurus to a packed audience. (There is a spectacular small outdoor theatre at Minack on the Cornish coast where recently, we heard a French play by Molière delivered in English; it strongly recalled Greece to us.)

Towards the end of another visit to Greece we stayed in Professor Mamalis's splendid seaside home at Chalkis. He had invited Professor Theocaris to come from Athens for lunch and they co-operated in trying to roast, on a spit on the patio, a kid (which turned out to taste more like an old goat!) On another occasion in the same area, we went with Prof. Mamalis (uninvited) to a wedding 'breakfast'. All the males danced collectively in a line, the littered state of the table they vacated indicating they had first eaten and drunk very well! It was a happy and unusual experience.

A single visit for us to Meteora (near Kalabaka, in Thessaly) was well worthwhile. Once remote, it is now spoilt and crowded with coaches and cars. It is at the top of a cliff which once rendered the monastery nearly impregnable; roads have been made to approach it from the rear thus making it available to everyone. The old method of entry was by basket or large net and winding rope, raised up vertical cliff faces; it is the height from the cliff side which suggests the name, Meteora – among the stars. On the parking side, there is now a simple short path into what was once a religious or reclusive area.

I am reminded of visiting the monastery (I believe) at Iviron, Athos. A walk along the cliff top brought us to a notice which told us that if one wished to see the holy man who lived alone there in a cave, all one had to do was to ring the bell on the wire netting, and wait. My two Greek colleagues rang the bell, thinking they would have a unique and unforgettable experience. After 15 minutes there had been no reply to our several calls and we departed, they somewhat disappointed, but I, astonished at myself, an uncompromising scientist, hanging about waiting to see an uneducated magus, was not. At the other extreme, while I was in Athos, a young man acting as a driver and conveying Heather to various local sites in the vicinity of Salonika, when asked what he would like as a token of gratitude for his service, answered, 'A Manchester *City* tie!'

A young American I encountered on Athos was contemplating joining the monastic community. I got into long and deep discussions with him on history, science and religion. It was 50 years since I was so intellectually and spiritually exercised.

*(iv) Seeking classical manuscripts at Mount Athos and Ancient Chalkis**

Introduction to Athos

The official end of the Second World War in Europe was declared to be 8 May 1945 but the war in the Far East still seemed a long way from being concluded. There was an intention ultimately to invade Japan which would require a build-up for that event with massive troop transfers from West to East and it was highly likely that many in Italy would be transferred eastward. Whilst the war in Italy was in progress, any encounter with art, architecture, an historical ruin or cultural

---

* Extracts from a paper in *IJMS* 42, 2419–87, 2000.

feature was of minor importance, but with the end of the war, for some of us, the encounter became one of good fortune. We have remarked earlier about rich mid-eighteenth century Martin Folkes (President of the Royal Society, 1741–52)* taking his family to travel around the Mediterranean for more than two years in order that they should be educated at first hand about classical Greece and Rome. Thus, here in the mid-twentieth-century 'undistinguished' persons such as I were provided with the same opportunities by the State – unintentionally and free!

Contriving to see and read all one could, the availability of cigarettes, chocolates, sweets and food (especially 2 lb tins of beef), were currencies then as strong as gold for gaining entry to ostensibly still closed historical sites and museums.

The opportunity to visit Florence for one week presented itself and for a pittance I enjoyed a room, with all meals provided in an internationally prestigious hotel. Italian roads in 1945 were empty of all civilian vehicles so that despite war damage, the journey from Rome to Florence was a pleasure.

In Rome, my military function required the use of colloquial Italian for which purpose I had been allotted a 50 year old Italian aristocrat, il Marquese Giacomo ('James') d'Viti de Marco, as interpreter. He was a product of an English public school – Merchant Taylors' I was told – and spoke a quality of English I could not match. He wore well-cut English suits and a bowler hat. During the First World War at Capporetto he had been a young Italian officer who suffered a head injury, which led to his long stay in hospital. A great anglophile, in 1921 he is alleged to have opposed Mussolini and his Fascisti; for calling out words of opposition at a meeting, the opportunity was taken to incarcerate him in an asylum for the brain-damaged; he was thus removed from the political scene without attracting attention. A court eventually released him, but declared him a minor for his supposed unreliable mental state, attributed to his First World War injury. D'Viti's father was a government financial minister at some time in the early 1920s. On the death of his father the family estate was divided between James and his two sisters, it being alleged that by collusion with solicitors it was contrived to keep him restricted and a minor so that the sisters remained principal beneficiaries. Anglophile James, throughout his years of incarceration insisted that, when the British came they would free him – and this is precisely what happened when British troops helped liberate Rome. However, though freed, and put in receipt of a good pension in those years, Italian law was not then able to be used to lift him out of his status as a minor. Acting as an interpreter was James's own method of helping the new Italian war effort.

In a good quarter of Rome, I several times dined with him and a lady of similar age who was, in effect, I learned, his common-law wife; as a minor, he had not been permitted to marry and they had remained 'affianced' for more than 20 years. Dining with the couple off beautiful crockery, on items unattainable on the Italian open market, served several kinds of wine from various family vineyards across Italy – Cambridge college feasts alone provided comparable situations – was quite an assault on the mind of a young man only recently a member of the officer class. Two decades ago, James had enrolled to read for

---

* See *IJMS* 21, 604, 1998.

a degree in Engineering at Rome University and having resurrected this plan, I became his unofficial tutor. However, our discussions covered not only engineering theory but politics, ancient history, opera, architecture and mathematics.

When learning that I was to go to Florence for a week, James interceded, saying he had a good friend there and would give me a letter of introduction to Ralph Brewster, who lived close by the Ponte Vecchio. James thought I would benefit greatly from meeting him – an author and a pre-war graduate in Classics from Cambridge University. He had recently written one of the first travel books to be published by the English Company, Penguin Ltd, in 1935, *Six Thousand Beards of Athos*, price 6d.! I might mention that the Ponte Vecchio was the only bridge allowed to stand intact across the river Arno throughout the war. It would not have been able to carry army equipment and seems to have been perceived as an historical architectural structure, spared by both sides, Allies and Germans, unspokenly. I met Brewster in his mother's many-roomed home; it had several rooms full of books and one wholly devoted to music – the home of an educated family of substance. Some time later we sat in the garden but there was little to eat and we contented ourselves with a few green figs. Among the many items that our conversation touched upon was Athos and in particular I was enthralled by his descriptions and comments, not having previously heard of it. Making a resolution to visit it one day, I little realised that another 30 years would elapse before the opportunity to do so arose.

Transferred, I left Rome for Naples in September 1945, said farewell to James and never saw him again. Around 1948 I made an attempt to have some of the relations he had in the London area try to intervene on his behalf, but my efforts yielded nothing.

In 1966, a handsome book on Mount Athos by John Julian Norris and Reresby Sitwell was published and attracted wide acclaim. It rekindled my feelings that I should try to make a serious effort to visit the site in Chalcidici, Greece.

Visiting Athos

It is proper that it should be mentioned how, through the help of two Greek colleagues, arrangements came to be made for me to visit the site where lived the 'Six thousands beards of Athos', aiming to satisfy my old wartime-inspired curiosity; these were Professors Mamalis and Theocaris.

Athanasius G. Mamalis (b. 1941) was a slightly older than average postgraduate student in the Applied Mechanics Division of the Mechanical Engineering Department, UMIST, during 1972–1975, publishing his first research paper in English with Dr J. B. Hawkyard and the author in 1975 on ring-rolling. He had been chief engineer and technical manager at a Steel and Pipe plant in Thessalonika (1967–1972) and desired to work towards entering the academic profession. During the years 1975–1980 we became close friends and co-operated in Metal Forming research and writing two technical books.

Professor Dr Pericles Theocaris, (b. 1921) – who had retired from being Director of the National Technical University of Athens, Greece (1981–1987) and professor there in Applied Mechanics – and I had come to correspond in the 1960s. We

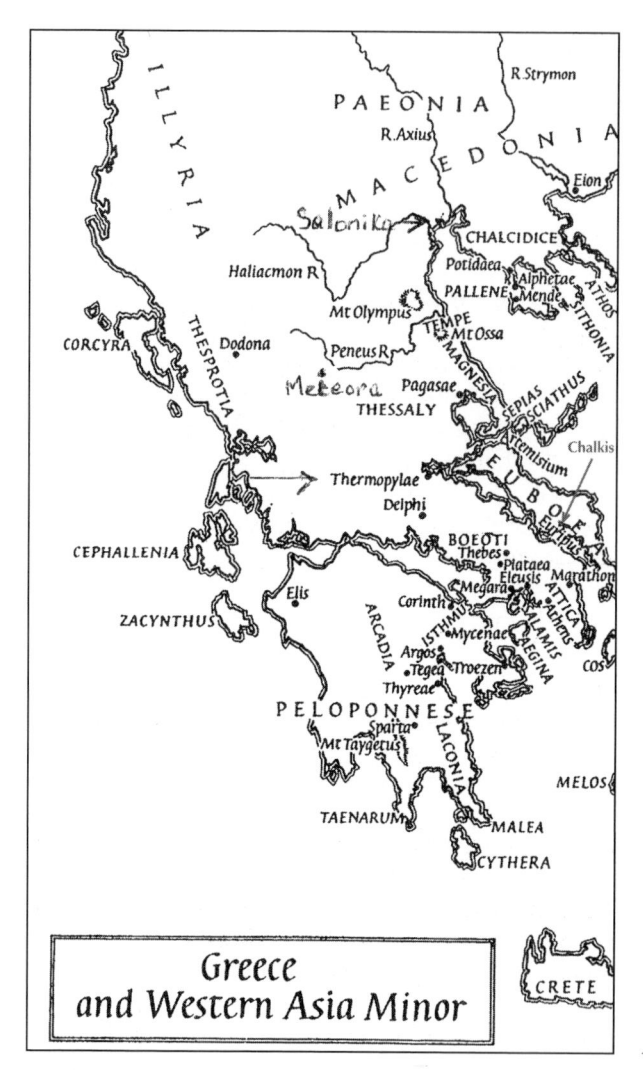

Figure 2. Map of Greece.

met personally in 1966 at a conference in Cambridge and with the passage of years became well acquainted. It was Professor Theocaris who introduced and recommended Dr Mamalis to me.

In short, through close acquaintanceship with Dr Mamalis, I ventured to mention to him the subject of Mount Athos and in 1974 hazarded the suggestion that we might try to visit this special site – 29 years after my meeting Ralph Brewster. (Dr Mamalis had a villa at Chalkis on the road to Athos, via the city of Thessalonika.) He applied formally through an influential ecclesiastical 'friend' about visiting this region and in due course matters were arranged – a letter of introduction was forthcoming via his local bishop and the help of the works medical officer for the staff of the steel plant in Thessalonika; the latter happened also to be medical officer to the Monastery Philotheou on Athos, to which we were specifically directed (see Figures 2 and 3).

TURKEY, GREECE AND MOUNT ATHOS 377

Figure 3. Monasteries on Mount Athos.

When the Christmas term at Cambridge was completed, early in December 1977, I delivered two lectures in Greece – at Athens and Thessalonika – but had in mind the intention to proceed to Athos, to stay there for two winter nights. A second visit in Summer 1982 ran to one week.

On both occasions the approach was the same – by car from Salonika to Ouranoupolis (see Figures 2 and 4), but diverging to the small town of Stagira en-route, where we paid our respects to it as the birthplace of Aristotle. The captain of a hired motor boat took us half-way down the rocky peninsular to Daphne and after landing we had a rough bus ride up to Karyes, which is virtually on the mid-line of the promontory – up and down mere tracks and often along beaches. We presented our credentials to the bishop at the central governing point, in his comfortable palace from where he ruled this independent 'Kingdom' (Greek-backed and claiming to be the oldest republic in the world!). He issued us each with a visiting permit, or a *Diamonhthpion* (Greek), free of charge, see Figure 5.

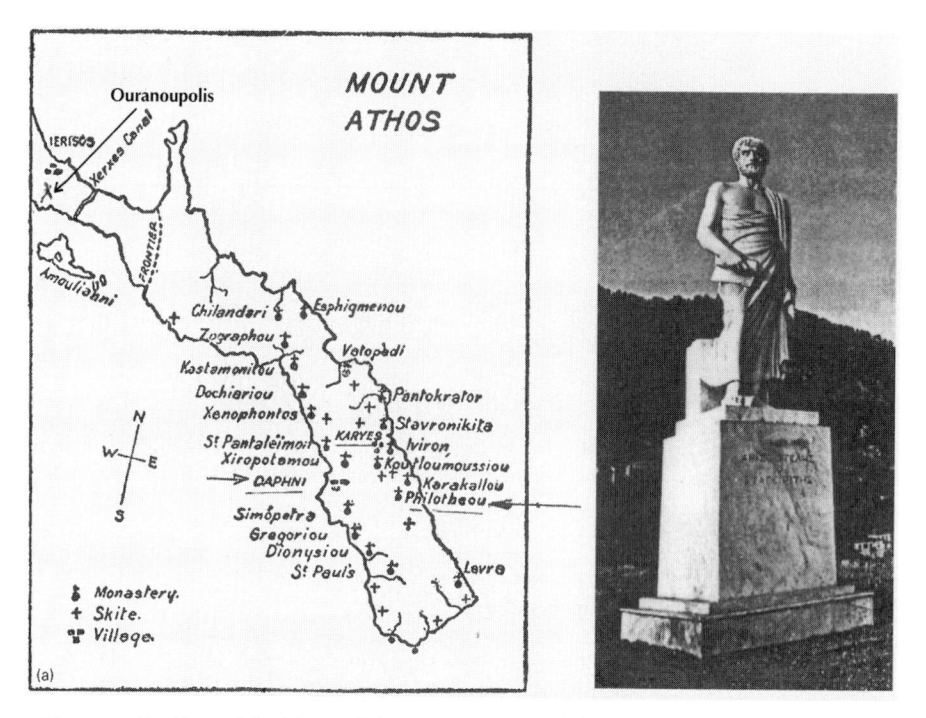

Figure 4. Position of the Mount Athos monasteries and the Statue of Aristotle at Stagira.

On our first visit we received the traditional welcome of a spoonful of jam, some loukoumi (Turkish delight), ouzo and a small coffee. Our permits, when presented at any monastery, seemed to entitle us to a bed, meals and free roving within the monastery. (In Brewster's book he gives a table assessing the quality of 'board' in the monasteries he visited, in no half-terms; in one, regarding his bed, he did not hesitate, under the heading 'bugs', to enter, 'millions!' – however, that was in the 1930s.) My first permit, 1977 (see Figure 5), is notable in that it was dated for 28/29 November, as per the Julian calendar, by which almost all monasteries then kept their records – though not so today. This was then about 12 days behind our Western European calendar; it was 10 and 11 December on our Gregorian calendar. In all the monasteries but one (Vatopedi), 12 o'clock was not regarded as mid-day; this is not a fixed point but varies with the season. Clocks were changed every few days. I will not describe our many experiences; these were typical of what the few visitors 'enjoyed' and for my part are described elsewhere in books and 'official reports'. Besides Brewster's own book, the volume of Norwich and Sitwell (containing many photographs) is perhaps the best for western Europeans to read, whilst the volume by Sidney Loch, *Athos 1957*, is by a Scotsman who had a home in the region, knew the monasteries intimately and lived there 1928–1954.

Much that is related on monasteries, for instance that 'everything' female is banned from Athos (see the newspaper report in Figure 6 below), brings to mind what was encountered in the colleges of the older universities in the UK and

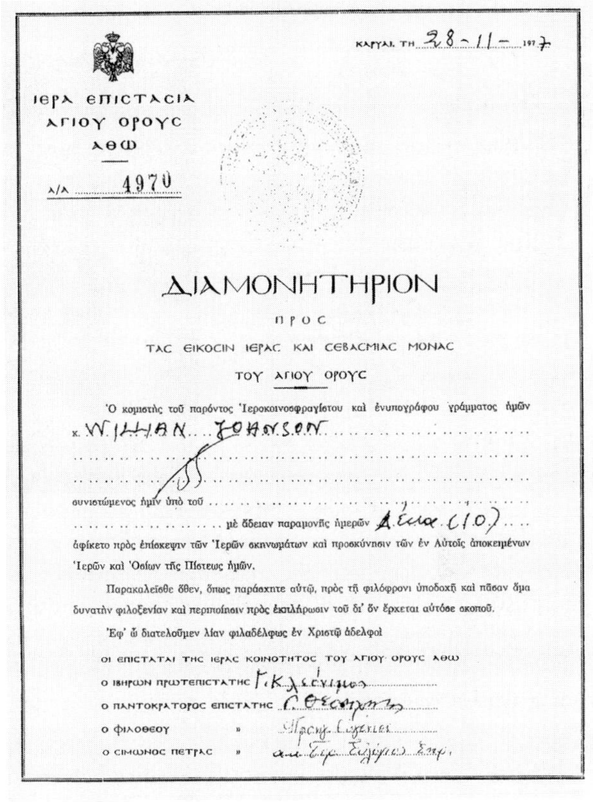

ΚΑΡΥΑΙ ΤΗ 28-11-1977

ΙΕΡΑ ΕΠΙΣΤΑΣΙΑ
ΑΓΙΟΥ ΟΡΟΥΣ
ΑΘΩ

Α/Α 4970

ΔΙΑΜΟΝΗΤΗΡΙΟΝ

ΠΡΟΣ

ΤΑΣ ΕΙΚΟΣΙΝ ΙΕΡΑΣ ΚΑΙ ΣΕΒΑΣΜΙΑΣ ΜΟΝΑΣ

ΤΟΥ ΑΓΙΟΥ ΟΡΟΥΣ

Ὁ κομιστὴς τοῦ παρόντος Ἱεροκοινοσφραγίστου καὶ ἐνυπογράφου γράμματος ἡμῶν

κ. WILLIAM JOHNSON

συνιστώμενος ἡμῖν ὑπὸ τοῦ ……

…… μὲ ἄδειαν παραμονῆς ἡμερῶν Δέκα (10) …

ἀφίκετο πρὸς ἐπίσκεψιν τῶν Ἱερῶν σκηνωμάτων καὶ προσκύνησιν τῶν ἐν Αὐτοῖς ἀποκειμένων Ἱερῶν καὶ Ὁσίων τῆς Πίστεως ἡμῶν.

Παρακαλεῖσθε ὅθεν, ὅπως παράσχητε αὐτῷ, πρὸς τῇ φιλόφρονι ὑποδοχῇ καὶ πᾶσαν ἅμα δυνατὴν φιλοξενίαν καὶ περιποίησιν πρὸς ἐκπλήρωσιν τοῦ δι' ὃν ἔρχεται αὐτόσε σκοποῦ.

Ἐφ' ᾧ διατελοῦμεν λίαν φιλαδέλφως ἐν Χριστῷ ἀδελφοί

ΟΙ ΕΠΙΣΤΑΤΑΙ ΤΗΣ ΙΕΡΑΣ ΚΟΙΝΟΤΗΤΟΣ ΤΟΥ ΑΓΙΟΥ ΟΡΟΥΣ ΑΘΩ

Ο ΙΒΗΡΩΝ ΠΡΩΤΕΠΙΣΤΑΤΗΣ ……

Ο ΠΑΝΤΟΚΡΑΤΟΡΟΣ ΕΠΙΣΤΑΤΗΣ ……

Ο ΦΙΛΟΘΕΟΥ » ……

Ο ΣΙΜΩΝΟΣ ΠΕΤΡΑΣ » ……

Figure 5. Visiting permit or Diamonhthpion.

elsewhere, and similarities can be quite remarkable. The refectory at one monastery possesses fixed stone tables at which one eats and simultaneously from a lectern a 'brother' delivers simple stories aimed to elevate faith and action. Every monastery has its own library but, as we saw, most were ill-secured and not very impressive; generally, they contained a few illuminated manuscripts and codices of no great antiquity. Today, nearly all the books in Athos have been catalogued and are known in Athens.

Sleeping was imposed by nightfall, in winter at about 7 p.m.; there was no artificial lighting, windows were often broken and dormitories very cold. My two colleagues rose at 11.30 p.m. to celebrate a midnight mass of four hours with the gathering of the whole monastery brotherhood. Not being Orthodox, I was suspect and barred from participating in, or even seeing, the ceremonies. Breakfast, again alone, was nearly the same as dinner. Meals I took alone in a refectory – only olives, fish caught off the coast, hard bread, coarse red *un*-fermented wine and some thin vegetables.

In the chapels there were many religious ikons but they can be the cause of some social discomfort when monks around one suddenly prostrate themselves before them. Outside monasteries, one is likely to encounter heaps of neatly sorted, arranged human bones as ossuaries or collections of tibia, femur, etc., in charnel houses. Saints' bones and ancient religious raiments of distinguished ecclesiastics, perhaps several centuries old, are frequently taken out of cardboard boxes and shown to one.

The four following notes will be of interest to readers.

1. Philotheou monastery was the most recently built monastery (1747–65). When lecturing at the steel company in Salonica (the company had recently been financially taken over by the Japanese), I inquired of the company medical doctor about the life expectancy of monks, believing, I said, that I would suppose it to be much above average, due to the ethically superior nature of life in a monastery. I was told that it was not so and he averred that for the most part, life expectancy was as it had been in the 1950s. Too little physical exertion and exercise, along with a lack of substantial food and female friendship, meant that the road was hard for many.

2. As a gift in 1628, a copy of the *Codex Alexandrinus* was sent to King Charles I of England by Patriarch Lucaris. This codex rates fifth in importance after the Codex Sinaiticus in establishing an authenticity for the New Testament. Whilst at a monastery in Athos, I was shown a copy of the Codex Sinaiticus and on expressing surprise and saying I thought the original was somewhere in Europe, a scholarly Father replied that he had not thought it was important enough to mention but it was indeed true that what we were looking at was a replica, and the original fourth-century manuscript was in either a Russian or a British museum!

3. Euripides (480–406 BC), the Greek dramatic poet, wrote in his classic *Iphigenia in Aulis* about 'Artemis claiming a sacrifice before adverse winds can fall'. King Agamemnon, having assembled his fleet for Troy, offended the goddess Artemis so she prevented it from sailing and according to a soothsayer, Calchas, she could be appeased only by the sacrifice of the King's daughter – to which he yielded. Alas, when I visited this region of Aulis it was dominated by a large cement-making factory, though the earth around it seemed to abound with archaeological artefacts.

4. The town of Chalkis was a very early manufacturer of bronze artefacts and pottery, an exporter of arms and a coloniser of Sicily in the seventh and eighth centuries BC. It exported, particularly to Cuma (near Naples) – the port which then imported tin from Cornwall, England.

Figure 6. *Newspaper report: Mount Athos* ban on women upheld.*

From Mario Modiano
Athens, June 8
The Greek Parliament has decided to conform to the wishes of the 1,500 Orthodox

---

* There are 11 coenobian (community) and 9 iddiorythmic (oligarchical) monasteries in all, on the Holy Mountain. About one half the total number of monks live in the monasteries, many in small groups or skites and some in caves as hermits.

monks on Mount Athos by upholding the ban on women entering the self-governing peninsula of 20 monasteries in Northern Greece.

Mr Ioanis Koutsoheras, a poet and Socialist member of Parliament, had invoked the new constitution which grants equal rights to men and women, in objecting to the discrimination against women. He said: "We must free Mount Athos and the Greek women of restraints reminiscent of the Middle Ages."

According to the Mount Athos charter, no woman, no child, and no female animals are allowed to disturb the monastic calm of the men who have withdrawn to the mountain to seek communion with God.

Mr Koutsoheras said: "Let us limit this ban to the monasteries – not the entire peninsula. Mount Athos is dedicated to the Mother of God. It is a place that shelters a universal treasure that cannot be denied to women who, after all, were an integral and continuous part of Christ's life."

Most speakers argued that the ban on visits by women to the monasteries could hardly be regarded as a violation of human rights – just as women's beauty parlours were out of bounds for men.

Even Mrs Virginia Tsouderos, an Opposition deputy, who advocated that women Byzantinologists should have access to the treasures of the Mount Athos monasteries, agreed that the ban should not be entirely lifted.

Mr Constantine Stavropoulos, the Foreign Under-Secretary said that a revision of the Mount Athos charter to allow visits by women would inevitably bring Greece into conflict with the Oecumenical Patriarchate of Constantinople which has suzerainty over Mount Athos.

The ban on females on Mount Athos has been violated deliberately on two or three occasions by women who later wrote books about their experiences. There are no hens on the peninsula, and no eggs. There are no female cats, with the result that the mouse population – inevitably male and female – thrives in the monasteries.

There is a nationwide campaign to bring all the treasures of Mount Athos together in a museum to protect them and make them more accessible to the public. The monks are resisting this effort.

Figure 7. Mount Athos. The more precipitous monasteries.

CHAPTER XXVIII

Taiwan

OVER A PERIOD OF THREE MONTHS at the end of the Summer Semester (1988) at Purdue, I ran into a very heavy period of work. I had agreed to give a lecture course in Taiwan (or Formosa as it was known when I was a boy) of two hours each evening for two weeks (the intervening weekend excepted) at the University in Taipei. My course was to be *Engineering Plasticity* – Outlines of Metal Forming and Impact Strength of Materials – really rapid reviews of my postgraduate lectures at Purdue and that given in Baltimore. I was also committed to a one week lecture course (in a programme put on by well-known Prof. John Zukas, with Professor S. R. Reid and I sharing the course lectures in Baltimore, USA on Impact Mechanics. It was arranged to be given two weeks before going to Taiwan. Lecture notes for the class in Baltimore were required and hence had to be mailed to the US at least two weeks before it started. Both courses were programmed for the weeks after my postgraduate lecture course at Purdue had ended and an examination been conducted. It came about that at this time my elder daughter Helen was in labour in London with her third child when news came through that she was experiencing difficulties and we were advised by my medical doctor son to comfort her however we could. After a brief discussion with Heather we decided she must go to the London hospital immediately and be with Helen. Heather was booked in on the next 'plane from West Lafayette to Chicago and then on to Heathrow, London. She arrived the following morning and was supporting Helen before midday. It turned out that she would be needed for some weeks and so her return to the USA was out of the question. The latter decision left me alone at Purdue to shift for myself and to cope with the lectures as best I could. The next two months turned out to be stressful. The Purdue postgraduate course ended in good style as did the one at Baltimore, but the venture to Taiwan was not so easy. The flight was made to Anchorage (Alaska) and then down to Tokyo and on to Taiwan. It was a long, tiring journey and arrangements at Taipei had not been confirmed; my time of arrival there was known only as 'late evening'. Emerging from the terminal, I managed to see a taxi-driver carrying a small red card bearing my rank and name: there was no one from the University. Once swept up and on into the town, the taxi-driver offered me a bottle of beer – a first time experience! He delivered me to a splendid hotel indicating it was just a one night stand and I would be collected the next morning about 10 a.m. Picked up on time I was delivered to my host and then taken and registered in a very trim little university flat – close to the lecture room they said. I asked why no one had met me off the 'plane. 'Because no one would have been able to recognise you', was the reply. "But I was the only Caucasian face in a small sea of Chinese people", I replied. The subject was dropped and I was advised that my next task was to go out shopping with one of the secretaries if I wanted to have breakfasts and perhaps dinners. Lunch I was assured could be had at the university restaurant. Breakfast-making was a must and dinners a matter of chance since I lectured from 6 p.m. to about 8.30 p.m. each day. Most of each day I prepared the evening's lecture, took a walk and found bookshops selling cheap English books. But some evenings I was too tired to go out to a restaurant and soup and cakes sufficed in my own room. My class was around 40 and its size did not reduce as the course progressed. One evening a member of the audience came to me after the class and said his wife had made a bag of puddings for him to give to me! It was a very nice gesture. At the end of the course they put on a celebration in the lecture room after the last class and we ate cakes, had ice cream and drank wine. A few speeches were made and it all ended in good friendship.

I may add that, typically, this class of south-east Asians asked very few questions. No doubting the older man!

One evening I was invited to take dinner with the Head of Department; he was American and on leave from his University, Yale.

At the weekend, I was chaperoned everywhere I went. First, I made for the seaside but the traffic was heavy and unpleasant, and the atmosphere heavily polluted. I did enjoy walking in the city and visiting the temples: it was like Japan and very peaceful. I also required to be taken to the Museum. This was stocked by what General Chang Kai Shek had removed from the museum in Beijing when he retreated to Taipei from China – or was pushed out by the Communists some years ago.

I should have liked to see more of Taiwan and had only seen the tip of the island. I had the impression from the newspapers that the people were very contented in that the region enjoyed a sensible and fair culture. The owners of a few large estates had been relieved of them and the land shared among many small-holders.

CHAPTER XXIX

The USA: Two special visits

I WOULD WISH TO RECORD two substantial periods in the USA, one in about 1979, and the other living there during the two two-year periods of 1986–87 and 1988–89, both at Purdue. (Absence for the middle year of the five, was required for taxation easement purposes.) For the first one we flew the long journey from Manchester to San Francisco to spend several weeks in the Mechanical Engineering Department at Berkeley, California. Professor J. Frisch was the Section head whilst Profs. Kobayashi and Thomson were major plasticity personalities. (With a Professor Yang, they had just published a well received volume on Engineering Plasticity.) Professor Iain Finnie was Head of the whole, large Department at the time. Outstanding there was Prof. Werner Goldsmith, for his life-long work (and book) on *Impact*. He still is very active though his laboratory, due to his health limitations, is not as large and full as it once was. I also met a young Dr Bill Stronge, then working close by in one of the local Government Research Laboratories on projectiles. After one of my general, open lectures he came over to me and said he was keen to come to England. After some discussion I encouraged him to apply to Cambridge and within the next year he had become a lecturer – and later, Reader and Fellow of Jesus College. He has written two books on Impact and Dynamic Structural Plasticity (one with T. X. Yu) and is still a keen student and director of Ph.D. work in the field in Cambridge engineering.

Throughout our stay in the States we were excellently entertained and never short on political news because of the many demonstrations against the Korean War on the Berkeley campus. (Fixed in my mind too is a punctuation by my younger daughter made in a dinner party we were giving by her telephoning and asking if we could 'lend' her £500 towards buying a house near Eccles; she had not long been married!)

My second period in the US was one brought about by Prof. Moshe Barash (see p. 275) who persuaded me to take up a two-year visiting professorship in 1984 and '85 in Purdue University (40,000 students strong) at West Lafayette, Indiana, where he had been for more than 20 years. He had moved there from UMIST early in the 1960s. I had retired from British University life in 1982, spent time travelling the world and wanted to settle somewhere quiet and reclusive to read and write as I wished. Dedicated only to postgraduate lecturing and no administrative use to anyone in Purdue, for the first time in my life I was free!

Thus came the opportunity to study the history of the physical sciences in the eighteenth and nineteenth centuries, relating to engineering. At home for the year, 1986–87, my return was brought about by Dean Henry Yang who secured funds for two years for a United Technologies Distinguished Professorship in Engineering which he kindly offered to me. He provided me with a good work room, Heather with a separate compartment to type in and a large copying machine. I had 'the run' of the departmental library – given my own key to it, to enter and work when I wanted – the special and valuable, normally locked-up sections too. This was the greatest encouragement I ever had. The use it was put to can only be assessed by looking through my list of papers in those years.

The university region and town of West Lafayette had many very good second hand bookshops, to which Heather and I resorted on Saturday afternoons when the University team was playing football (not soccer) and many regions of the town deserted. I finally came home from Purdue to the UK with 16 mail bags of books at the end of 1989!

We made many very good friendships in Purdue with all of whom Heather especially still corresponds regularly. Henry Yang became the President of a University on the Pacific coast whilst Moshe Barash at 80 continues to lecture when 'they' find a need arises. I should add that the *IJMS*, which publishes 3000 pages per year and the *IJIE* (about 1500), gave me a welcome entré to many universities in the USA because they service mechanical engineering research so well.

Whilst in Purdue, Heather elected to fly north from Indiana to Winnipeg, Manitoba, Canada to spend a week with an old widowed friend (initially from Hazel Grove, Cheshire). The day after arrival she found herself in pain in the lower part of her leg and since the friend was a nurse, they both diagnosed a blood clot or D.V.T. and decided that she should go to hospital immediately for investigation. Their opinion was verified and she was detained in hospital for five days. To visit her in hospital and be near at hand for those few days I had to travel on a Sunday – and thus went indirectly by small 'plane from West Lafayette to Toronto and then Toronto to Winnipeg, arriving at the hospital late in the evening. For the return journey I decided we should travel Business Class and to effect the change went to the counter to explain the reason for it. They kindly made the change of tickets and declined to charge further payment. En route home, with our lunch, we were given champagne and a compliments slip which read, 'To Heather and Bill with best wishes'.

CHAPTER XXX

Australia

———◆———

I HAVE TOLD ABOVE of flying from Singapore to Melbourne, but on the way somewhere across the Cape York Peninsula we landed at a lightly populated town. On coming to rest we were instructed to remain in our places. After a few minutes the 'plane doors opened and in walked an official in beautifully laundered white open-necked shirt and shorts. He carried with him a cylinder, raised it high and walking down the centre of the plane, proceeded to fumigate us and the atmosphere. It seemed a risible antic. But this done we were guided off the plane and into a motor coach which took us on a tour of the neighbourhood. There were homes on wooden stilts, it all looked truly tropical. The tour was thoughtfully laid on to occupy us whilst a little maintenance and re-fuelling went on.

My relationship with Australia has always been tangential, in that on several occasions I have come close to emigrating there only to be finally deflected. In 1947/8, when just demobilised I thought to apply for an engineering post with the Snowy Mountains Hydroelectric Scheme. When at Sheffield University I also considered applying for an advertised chair at a new Tech. in New South Wales in the 'steel' city of Wollongong and lastly, through the recommendation of the Director of the Risley Nuclear establishment I was offered the post of a new Chair in the University of New South Wales early in 1960. Each time the thought of fracturing our relationships with families caused us not to proceed. The days of fast 15-hour flights had not yet come. In the days of the journey to Sydney by boat the sailing time was measured in weeks – this was why sabbatical leave to return to Europe had been invented for academics. But from Manchester University in the 1960s I knew four academics depart for Australia. Two left the Engineering Department, one for Monash and one for Melbourne (Dr Morgan and my once close colleague Dr Arthur Williams); Prof. Sir James Matheson left his chair at Manchester University to become VC of Monash and then Dr Roger Tanner F.R.S at some stage clearly settled there and not in the USA. (Today he is Deputy VC of the University of Sydney.) Dr Peter Oxley (now deceased) too, left UMIST for a Chair in that continent. Besides these, good fellows from other universities took the road to the land of opportunity and Mediterranean weather. (And two from UMIST later went from Senior Lectureships to Chairs in New Zealand – one being my old colleague John Duncan.)

The Conference at Melbourne went well and from there I went on to Adelaide.

Melbourne was an attractive town but Adelaide I found to be quiet and somehow Edwardian. There was little discussion at the University and I was disappointed. Mostly I remember watching the kangaroos bounce through the fields! I would like to have made a journey to Perth, 'the town with a perfect climate', but engagements in Sydney claimed me, where I talked to a number of professors who had come out from Cambridge where they had been lecturers, now men with a name in their discipline. In Australia there is nothing of the claustrophobic, densely populated, industrial towns of England. The weather and purity of the wooded countryside in the south east of the country made it an attractive country in which to bring up children.

In the environs of Sydney I met my wife's aunt. She had been a Queen Alexandra's nurse during the Second World War. She had travelled and nursed around the world during the war and declared she had found a very agreeable home in Australia and that she and her ex-army husband had no desire to return to his native Poland. Of all the people I know who went out to Australia, not one has returned to the UK.

Prof. A. G. Mamalis and I had published a book on the *Crashworthiness of Vehicles* (for most kinds of transport and now rather limited in some respects) in 1978. Prof. Noel Murray published *When it Comes to the Crunch (or The Mechanics of Car Collisions)* in 1994. I knew him in the late 1950s when he was in the Civil Engineering Dept. at Manchester University. Only a few days ago I received notice of a one-week Crashworthiness Conference in 2002 in Australia. It was heartening to see that this subject, early addressed by us in book form for undergraduates, had been ahead of the field for once!

CHAPTER XXXI

Israel

I WAS INVITED to be one of a small panel of four asked to report on the performance of the Mechanical Engineering Department at Haifa, Israel. It required a week of discussion and examining on all the usual facets of the life of a major technological institute. My travelling expenses were paid as was hotel accommodation but there was no mention (or expectation) of fees. For five days we put in a lot of effort under the Chairmanship of Prof. Dan Drucker of the University of Illinois, Alabama, USA and ended in writing, collectively, a short review of the teaching and research quality which came our way. We found the unit efficient and its plasticity research output – already well known, internationally – of a high standard. The occasion made it possible to make the personal acquaintanceship of various individuals whose names I knew well from the published literature. We also surveyed work on topics unknown to us, none more surprising than that on solar panels. Of course it was a topic for which there was no call in Manchester! In contrast a subject obviously engaging them was some aspects of ship performance, a topic not actually brought up for review. Their professors occasionally came to Manchester and then went on to Barrow-in-Furness ship-yard where they participated in ship trials at sea; presumably they progressed some special naval requirements. An impressive visit also took us to a vineyard where a large amount of agricultural science was tried out and then employed for securing good grape production.

The temperature here was so high at this time that one of our party collapsed but fortunately it was no more than a faint.

I took the opportunity to see at close quarters the running of a kibbutz – the accommodation, the food and mess halls, and general family living; it was not attractive. I have several times observed that women are less attracted to emigration to Israel than men. Aids for household work and culinary activity etc. are far fewer than they are in the West.

The two-day weekend rest I enjoyed enabled me to make the common round of religious sites in Jerusalem – the Wailing Wall, the mosque and churches, wells and on the Mount, archaeological museums. I walked several Stations of the Cross but having no guide did not make much of them. I recall making a short journey down the coast from Haifa, to find a holiday village which served a splendid 'St Peter's fish' and wine.

When I returned home to the UK, I greatly regretted that I had not planned my journey better by including a trip down to St Catherine's monastery at Mount Sinai or walked the region of Petra.

The 'political peace' in this area was uneasy at the time so getting down to the Dead Sea was unsafe as was visiting other towns such as Damascus.

I did go to see the British cemetery of war graves as was my custom and was mindful of how well they were kept, here, in Singapore, Malta and in India. By comparison the university residence or student hostel nearby which had few or no ground floor windows, appeared built in the style of a prepared fort! However, despite some lost opportunities and with political instability in the air, I had tasted the land of the Bible, the Crusades and the Templars.

CHAPTER XXXII

Nigeria

I HAD TWO AFRICAN STUDENTS on one of our M.Sc. courses at UMIST. One returned to Lagos and the other to a new university in northern Nigeria, west of Zaire. The former became a professor in his university, but the other subsequently migrated to the Caribbean. I was probably suggested by one of them as Internal Examiner for the undergraduate course in the north of Nigeria. However, the country was very unsettled when I went there. Passing through passport control after landing at Kano, a soldier with a machine gun strapped over his shoulder and unsure in handling passports admitted me. Arriving at the university we found confusion, as the VC's residence was under threat of attack. When the committee for examining the Final Year results was convened, I learned that the Head of Department was away in England at a conference, and two other senior members of staff were abroad (all three were East Europeans), and the other professor in the department, because he was not nominated Senior Examiner (he was of a strong religious persuasion) would not act or chair the staff meeting for classifying the degree results. It puzzled me that so many of these lecturers could be allowed not to attend or be absent at such an important time. So, nominated Visiting External Examiner, it fell to me to chair and lead the meeting – which I did without much difficulty. Normally, the External simply observes and verifies that proceedings are fair and accurate, especially regarding degree classification; there were about 40/50 undergraduates.

I stayed with the religious professor and his wife but had to remember that their house was 'dry'. The university Club House was well-intentioned but badly needed a strong manager. I did walk through and around the town but it did not seem safe. Eventually I was pleased to return home. Mostly, I felt sad that the whole place seemed abandoned, and of no great concern to anyone.

CHAPTER XXXIII

Singapore and Hong Kong

I TRAVELLED TO AUSTRALIA to present a paper and participate in an Engineering-Metallurgy conference near Melbourne, at a time when the UK had a nuclear weapons centre near there. We travelled out, passing Israel at the time of the Six Day War in 1982, on an ancient Ministry 'plane conveying only individuals on secret work carrying lockable brief-cases. Also we did not fly from a public airport. Once at Singapore we were unloaded for half a day's rest but travelled on the next morning across the islands and central Australia at about 10,000 ft only, the views being wonderful. At Singapore I remember the sight of many junks on the river, the smell, and staying at the Raffles Hotel, once the base for novelists such as Somerset Maugham, when 'out East'. And English tea at the Raffles was appropriately accompanied by the playing of Noel Coward's *Mad Dogs and Englishmen*.

I visited Singapore again some years later in the second year of my appointment as External Examiner for the undergraduate course. I gave some lectures but detected little research interest. There was only one lecturer then engaged in research and the department seemed to close down at 4.30 p.m. It clearly needed re-energising – which it did subsequently enjoy.

New Singapore University, beautifully situated on the sea coast, was clearly of great interest to us (my wife accompanied me). The Raffles Hotel was still there but the town centre had been shifted or rebuilt on a new site nearby. There was now a fine set of buildings, housing blocks, superb hotels and large shops etc.

We walked the parks, zoos and museums and studied the orchids for sale. I had read of the poor British resistance put up against the invading Japanese forces in the Second World War and wondered at how little fortification could come to have been erected to withstand them. The General in charge seemed to have shown very little imagination. All the big guns faced the sea! Why no slit trenches? No mine fields …?

'The people' were very well catered for in Singapore whilst the professional class seemed to have to look after itself in respect of housing. Workers' flats with play centres for children in the block, could teach parts of the UK how to organise themselves. Talking to staff and students it was always difficult to bring them into a dialogue. Both had too much respect for authority! In the town by 9 p.m., many restaurants were beginning to close and, if there was an item on television,

Figure 1. From the left: Profs Reid, with my three 'academic sons', Hashmi, Ghosh and Yu, which they are pleased to call themselves, and Mrs Johnson and I.

e.g. a football match, which was scheduled post 10 p.m. it was difficult the next day to find anyone who had seen it!

There was an issue in the university common rooms which needed, as I saw it, a response from the staff; however, they had no organised structure for representing themselves. I asked, 'Have you no AUT (Association of University Teachers)?' No! They had not. Why not form one, I suggested? It was clearly not a done thing. It could well be the reason I was never invited to Singapore again ... A piece of comedy was to read in a handout we received on entering Singapore: a note to the effect that if you are a male whose hair reaches down over your coat collar, you will be put at the back of the queue!

But Singapore was pleasant, clean, well run and very safe and orderly. It was a credit to its new directors who succeeded the British.

I have visited Hong Kong twice, to stay with my eldest son, Philip, his wife Susan and family, for a one-week holiday – Philip was Professor and Head of Oncology in the University for about 10 years – and secondly to attend a Materials Processing Conference at which I gave the opening lecture in November 1996.

CHAPTER XXXIV

India

From 1960 on, and during my time at UMIST, I had a constant supply of Ph.D. students from the Indian sub-continent and conspicuous in the early years were Commonwealth scholars. When they ceased to come it marked the sad termination of a long chain of good researchers. However, matters took quite a new and unexpected turn for the better in the late 1970s.

Dr B. Karunes (1925–1978) was an Indian professor well-known for his wide-ranging contributions to Plasticity and the Properties of Engineering Materials who had taken his doctor's degree at Yale University, USA under the supervision of Professor E. T. Onat. Having returned to India, Prof. Onat visited UMIST in 1977 and after a day in discussion we found we had much the same approach to our technical problems. Through this conjunction I soon came to know of young Dr N. K. Gupta of the Institute of Technology at New Delhi. Unfortunately in 1978 Prof. Karunes died and to Dr Gupta fell the task of organising a Symposium in memory of him in December 1979. I gave the keynote address and along with Profs S. R. Reid, T. Y. Reddy, S. K. Ghosh, P. E. Rees and A. N. Singh delivered five papers. In all 42 papers were read and well received by an audience of about 200 persons. Accommodation for the foreign visitors in the Institute residence, including meals and special dinners, was excellent. (The House Rule against serving alcohol – beer – on the premises was kindly set aside for the few days we were there.) The area around the Guest House is very interesting walking country, especially when one can encounter such a huge figure (100 foot tall?) as that of Siva, the god of destruction, see Figure 1.

A Symposium every four years was started after the first, and still continues. Now, twenty years later, Prof. Gupta directs mostly Impact Engineering Research in several laboratories which can compare well with any in Europe. I have been present at four of these symposia but a session of one, held at Trichinopoly, was special. Prof. Gupta invited Prof. N. Jones, Prof. S. R. Reid and myself to be his guests and proposed that the three of us should fly to Madras and then drive by car southwards to Trichinopoly. By this means I would have the opportunity to visit 'Robins country', the Carnatic, by-passing through Cuddalore and Fort St David, see Figure 2, where, Benjamin Robins had died in 1751 after serving as Engineer General for the East India Company for almost precisely one year. (See Chapter XXIII, pp. 280–284 above). It gave me the opportunity also to use the Fort St George library and archives at Madras, and then travel 90 miles south

Figure 1. SIVA, the Destroyer, Delhi December 1996.

to explore the region of Fort St David. What I learned I have written up in *In Search of the End of the Life, in India, of Benjamin Robins*. (IJIE, 11, pp. 121–134, 1991 or my *Collected Papers on Robins and Hutton*, 2003, South Asian Pubs. PVT, New Delhi, India). Before reaching St David's we called into Pondicherry for lunch – a town sometimes held in the eighteenth century by the French. It is still French in style, very pleasant and with a museum and library. I imagine no one has explored the latter for Robins' material or the French view of the wars between our countries in India in this town in the eighteenth century – an opportunity waiting to be taken up? I have had many offers of help in searching this area but none has ever matured – alas. I think this could also be the case for St George's too. The latter has (had) a magnificent ballistic pendulum on show, some intriguing small paintings – by Army artists of more than a century ago – and indicating the origin of British interest in the catamarans of that coast.

Figure 3 is a memorable photograph of 'Three Editors on the walls of Fort St David'. In Cuddalore I searched in vain for a gravestone or plaque indicating Robins' burial in the churchyard. Robins, in conformity with his Quaker upbringing, asked for a plain grave when he died and that he seems to have got.

After having made the most of a half day in the St David's region we hurried on only to arrive in Trichinopoly late for dinner. The following morning we were conducted through the Rock of Trichinopoly, a geological structure rising 270 feet above the city. It was honey-combed with chambers and passage-ways to Buddhist temples and religious activities, inscriptions and carvings from the fifth century AD. It was a very complicated geological structure that seemed to serve many functions – praying, teaching and for discussions. At one point in the heart of the Rock I came upon two old elephants, chained at their ankle to rock and clearly very seldom moved to judge from the pile behind them on the ground below. We completed our tour and then gently walked (it was November, 1990) to a hall where, with others I gave a General Lecture to the Indian Institute of Metals on, *Robins – an Early Fortification Engineer at St David's near Cuddalore*. At the conclusion we were bid to remain seated if we were foreign visitors. After ten minutes a waiter passed in front of us, laying a very large green leaf on the desk; this was presumably a substitute for a table mat. He was

THE CARNATIC

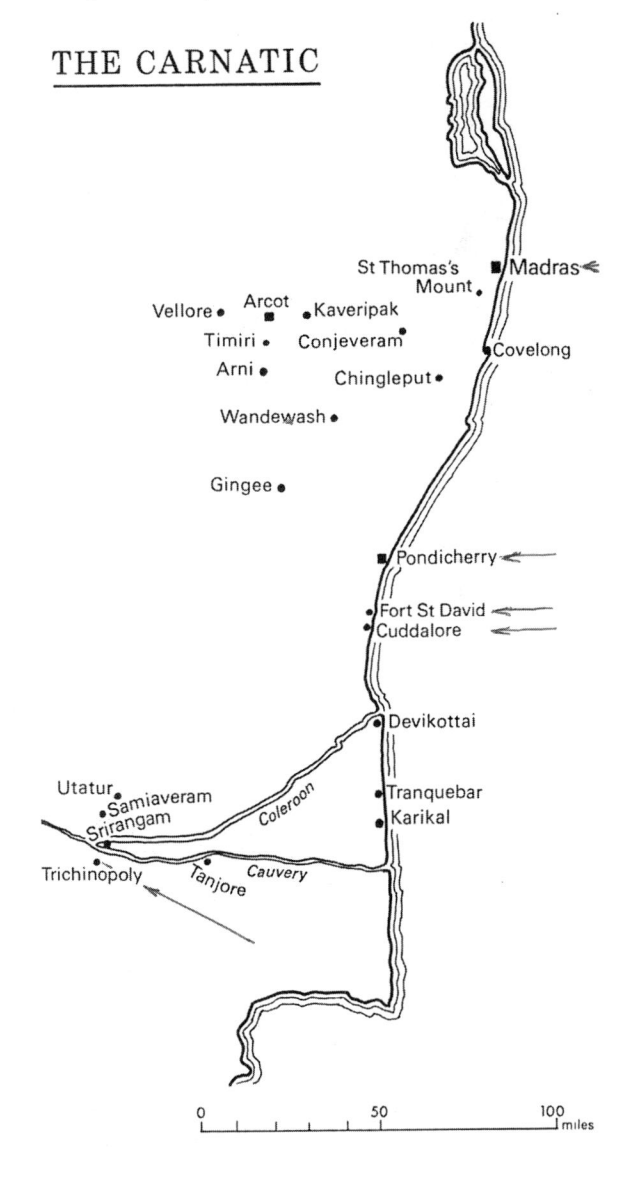

Figure 2. *The Carnatic Coast.*

Figure 3. Three editors at Fort St David, Cuddalore, India, Professors N. Jones,* W. Johnson and S. R. Reid.†

soon followed by two waiters all in white, one laying a dish on the leaf, the other following with a pail and ladle. We received a huge helping of a white sauce (gravy?) and chicken or meat and some vegetables (I presume.) Each of us made what we could of our meal in the following half hour, that is until the bus arrived when we were driven to the airport. We took the 'plane on to Bangalore, India's Silicon Valley. Most of the airline passengers were young men all similarly attired in beautifully ironed white shirts. Looking around it was difficult to believe I was not in the UK especially as cricket was the subject of conversation and on the television – and the refreshment everywhere was orange juice. The little I saw of Bangalore – was one of wide clean streets. Most surprising of all was to observe lots of small male gatherings listening to orators on 'soap boxes', addressing them. I soon learned that a National Election was in the offing – and what I saw was a democracy in action!

---

* I. J. Impact Engineering.
† I. J. Mech. Science.

CHAPTER XXXV

Iran

———◆———

WHEN Kazil Kormi became Professor of Mechanical Engineering in Tehran University, he invited me to visit his country to give some few lectures to his small staff and to see and comment on the work his research students were engaged in. I had a second invitation some years later when he became Head of the Technical University at Abadan, only this time I was able to have my wife accompany me. Political conditions as known to us in the West were not clear and internally we understood there were difficulties. But my professional trips were, as usual, unforgettable, some of them being made with Dr G. H. Daneshi and his sister – another of my Ph.D. men whom I later lost to the USA.

Early in my first visit, Prof. Kormi drove us to the Elburz mountains, just south of the Caspian Sea, on whose shores I had hoped to stand. The colours of sky and earth were more brilliant and clearer than I have encountered anywhere else. My experiences in the latter respect were identical with those of Sir John Chardin,* who visited Persia in the 1670s.

> There is such an exquisite Beauty in the Air of *Persia*, that I can neither forget it my self, nor forbear mentioning it to every body: One would swear that the Heavens were more sublimely elevated, and tinctur'd with quite another Colour there, than they are in our thick and dreary *European* Climates.

At a new unfinished hotel in the mountains we had lunch; the hotel was being built by Koreans, though how they came to be there, I could not determine. We did not reach the Caspian Sea which was unfortunate. There is no shortage of volumes about Persia and many Europeans have written about it in past centuries. On my return to Tehran I was taken to attend a traditional wedding ceremony and to enjoy the celebrations afterwards, witnessing some unusual forms of dress and dancing – older men dancing alone, surprisingly elegantly; despite their age and corpulence they struck me as not unbecoming. I had my fortune told by a professional soothsayer in a small hotel where the bread was freshly baked around a circular oven situated in the dining area; I was also presented with jars of caviare and sturgeon.

We left Tehran and flew down to Isfahan in the centre of the country and once its capital, arriving about 6.30 a.m. Dr Kormi took me to his friend's house,

---

* *Travels in Persia*, by Sir John Chardin (Dover, 1988)

Figure 1. Traditional Persian Male 'Tea'-party, 1970, smoking hashish, Shiraz.

where we awakened him. After a little breakfast the three of us took off for a colleague's property outside the city. We drove slowly for perhaps an hour out into the desert, aiming for what seemed to be a small oasis. On arrival, under some palms we came to a rectangular pool. A dozen women and children were seated at one corner and six men diagonally opposite (see Figure 1). One man was French (with a broken leg) and another I was introduced to as, 'The greatest living poet in Persia'! The other two were smoking, but not cigarettes; one of them later bragged that he had smoked hashish in a London park. The fifth person sat cross-legged with a small silver grate on his lap in which he had a very small fire. He possessed a long pipe with a conspicuous hole in the exterior of its bowl and into the latter he pressed a short quantity of what looked like white cord. (I am quite innocent in the matter of drug-taking) He would take up a hot coal and apply it to the cord, to render it plastic. At one side of him he had a very small kettle which he used to make 'tea'. He strongly inhaled from his pipe, gazed upwards and then proceeded to drink a small cup of the 'tea'. After several drafts he offered each of us a 'pull' from his pipe. I was the only one who declined. From time-to-time he would take out a small tin box, and having selected a different coloured cord, proceed as before. I supposed it was a collection of different drugs – opium and the like. The chief user of the opium said he was involved in securing the prohibition of drugs in his country! Whilst all this was going on, I several times observed a labourer in a long white gown moving to a large 'shed' in an area outside the oasis; he made several journeys, each time carrying a large circular tray on his head. Though we were becoming worried about lunch and getting back to the airport on time, eventually our host bade us follow him into the 'shed'. On entering, I saw a large cloth on the ground

Figure 2.
Naqsh-e-Rostam.

on which were set large bowls and plates of yoghurt, fresh chapattis, rice, goat's flesh, fruits and weak tea. We sat around the perimeter of the cloth, cross-legged; there were adults, young and old, and children. We helped ourselves to whatever we wanted from the array of foods – mostly using our fingers; I reflected this was how Abraham had lived! I supposed that I would later suffer internally from this primitive feast. Eventually, once finished, I thanked my host for his hospitality, regretted we could stay no longer and departed. No misfortune concerning my stomach overtook me.

On another occasion we were booked into the Shah Abbas Hotel (in Isfahan, I believe), later destroyed in a riot – an incomprehensible act to my mind – for it was surely one of the most beautiful, colourful and unique in architectural style, anywhere; indeed it was said to be one of the three best hotels in the world. It was there, I remember, that I crossed the path of Teddy Kennedy of the USA and his group of assistants, doubtlessly here on business and not vacation. We saw the blue Mosque off the Maydan-e-Shah, the bazaars around it, the old wooden palace and the Khwaju Bridge.

Heather and I were next taken to Shiraz where we stayed in the home of Dr Vojdani whose son had worked with me for his Ph.D. at UMIST. The experience of living in a private residence in this ancient city was something to be remembered. Shiraz of course, was called, historically, 'the city of roses' and indeed these flowers bordered the road leaving the airport. Dr Vojdani Jr, kindly conveyed us to the rock carvings and paintings on an open but hardly accessible hill-side

Figure 3. Persepolis.

at Naqsh-e-Rostam (see Figure 2), a lonely place apart from goatherds and their flocks. From there we went on to the ancient and elevated Persepolis (see Figure 3), the Summer Palace of King Darius the Great, apparently abandoned when it was set on fire after a drunken party, some time after its capture by Alexander the Great in 330 BC.

Frequently, in flying between cities in Iran we would marvel at the sight from the air of long straight lines of qanats. (See the representation in the Figure 4.) From a 'plane above, they had a resemblance to a line of bomb craters. These well-like drillings intercepted an underground channel of water in which *Blind White Fish in Persia* were said to live. The notion is for the horizontal channel to convey water collected from an aquifer in the earth below. The bored holes are for giving access down to the channel to keep it clear of mud.* (The above is the title of a book by Anthony Smith (Geo. Allen and Unwin, 1953). Among other things, Smith and his two Oxford undergraduate colleagues were sent to Persia on a student project to find out whether or not these blind white fish existed.)

Our final destination was Abadan where Prof. and Mrs Kormi lived in one of the many spacious bungalows erected when the British had oil interests there.

---

* See the article on qanats in Donald Hill's *A History of Engineering* (1996, Routledge), pp. 33–36.

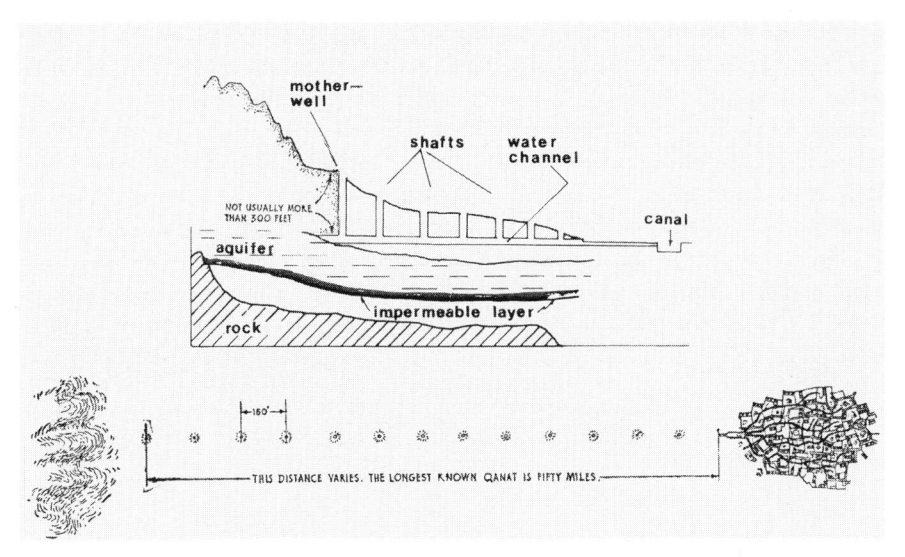

Figure 4. Qanat diagram.

Whilst I was delivering two lectures at the Abadan Technical College, Mrs Kormi took Heather shopping. The pair of them were accompanied by a strong, masculine 'butler', Abraham, who, to the embarrassment of my wife, walked behind her, carrying her small purchases in a stately manner up the magnificent staircase of our hotel.

Our last diversion was to fly down the Arabian Gulf on a small plane of the National Iranian Oil Company to the port and coral island of Kharg, so much in the news at the start of a recent war with Iraq. I was invited to sit by the pilot and to have a wonderful view into the sea along the coast. On alighting, Heather asked humbly for a small piece of coral for her marine collection; she repeated this request from time to time, fearing that it had been overlooked. The tour of Kharg Island and all its oil installations was most impressive. At its conclusion, Heather was presented with a hemispherical 'piece' of coral of about one foot in diameter! Because of its fragility she had to hold on to it on her lap for most of the return journey to the UK. On leaving Abadan, an American passenger paused and asked, admiringly, 'Gee, Honey! Did you swim for that?!'

We said goodbye to Dr and Mrs Kormi, little expecting that in a few months, the Shah would be deposed and they have to leave the country. The ageing and ill Shah was not allowed to stay in the UK or the USA and died quietly in some distant corner of the world. From what I could infer about this old man, *in his last years* – despite his family – he had worked hard to improve his country's future.

Dr Kormi and his family left for the UK, where they have settled. It took him some years to re-establish his career and, despite ill-health, to become a Professor of Engineering in Leeds Technical University. He has made his mark in the subject and until a few years ago he was often to be found, with his assistants, presenting papers at conferences.

It would seem from Omar Khayyam's writings that in his day, his country had been a land of wine and flowers. This Persian epigrammatist and distinguished mathematician-astronomer, who died in 1123, was made popular in 1859 by Edward Fitzgerald, who made a loose translation of his Rubaiyat (quatrains). Fitzgerald (1809–83) presented the Rubaiyat – a small book – so colourfully and attractively, that his work has been widely and continuously acclaimed since the time it was written. I believe I have savoured another four translations of the original verses and found it hard to believe they were indeed translations of the same poem. I think it will appropriately conclude this chapter to quote two of Omar's free-thinking quatrains for their evocation of the atmosphere of their land.

> Dreaming when Dawn's Left Hand was in the Sky
> I heard a Voice within the Tavern cry,
> 'Awake my Little ones, and fill the Cup
> Before Life's Liquor in its Cup be dry.

> And, as the Cock crew, those who stood before
> The Tavern shouted – 'Open then the Door!
> You know how little while we have to stay,
> And, once departed, may return no more.'

CHAPTER XXXVI

Germany

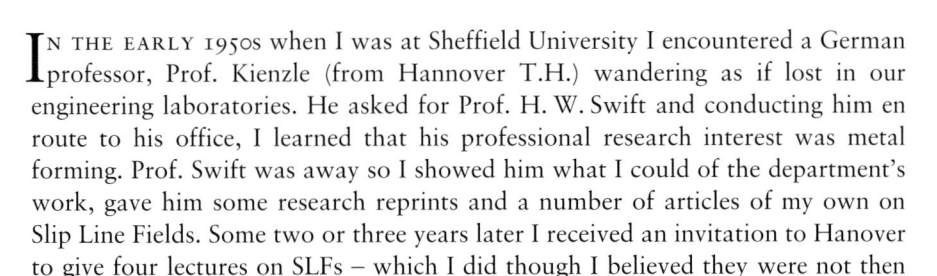

———◆———

IN THE EARLY 1950s when I was at Sheffield University I encountered a German professor, Prof. Kienzle (from Hannover T.H.) wandering as if lost in our engineering laboratories. He asked for Prof. H. W. Swift and conducting him en route to his office, I learned that his professional research interest was metal forming. Prof. Swift was away so I showed him what I could of the department's work, gave him some research reprints and a number of articles of my own on Slip Line Fields. Some two or three years later I received an invitation to Hanover to give four lectures on SLFs – which I did though I believed they were not then well appreciated in Germany even though initially introduced there.

None-the-less it was a good connection to have made with Hanover and I should have treasured it far more than I did. But then I was a busy young man in a hurry. A young assistant of Prof. Kienzle was Dr Horst Lippman, a graduate in mathematics with whom I made good friends. Helpfully, though I had no real quantity of equipment, Prof. Diamond (see Chapter XVIII) provided funds for Lippman to come over to Manchester for a month or so, in order that we should be able to collaborate in plasticity projects. This worked well and in due course, 1960, we produced a substantial piece of work on temperatures developed due to the fast working of metals. The following year Dr Oskar Mahrenholtz collaborated with us on other investigations; he was another assistant of Prof. Kienzle's. He also spent a short period in Manchester, with which city he was not greatly impressed. My association with Lippman and Mahrenholtz has stood the test of years. I saw Lippman advance to a Chair in Mechanics at Munich T.H. and Mahrenholtz to succeed to Kienzle's Chair in Hanover a few years later. My long relationship with these three (including Prof. Eckart Doege, see below, p. 404), alas, can only be noted here in respect of a few major circumstances.

Kienzle was Jewish. How he survived the war intact I never determined. I believe he lost his Chair but was restored to it after the war. He visited me at UMIST and saw our research facilities and current work. I was proud to think we had something original to show him and as a consequence I was elected to membership of CIRP (International Research in Production Engineering) – in effect then a select club limited in membership to ten persons per country. Dr Galloway, once Director of PERA, was a founder member, the French being the originators of the club under a General Nicolau. I write 'club' because at that time it did not publish papers, it only discussed them. The club was also a good facilitator for exchanging postgraduate students for short periods and meeting other professors seriously interested in our subject. One annual conference of CIRP was held in Germany, in the town of Hamlin (or Hameln) – of Pied Piper fame. It was excellently organised and a great pleasure to attend for both work and relaxation. Equally memorable was a general conference on Plasticity convened in an ecclesiastical centre set in the beautiful surroundings of Tutzing, Wurzsee, near Munich, by Prof. Lippman. However on this occasion, to me the most outstanding contribution was an invitation to members to propose young men who would have something original to contribute. Lippman had financial support enough to pay all their expenses – air fare as well as accommodation. I proposed a young man from Korea with whom I had been exchanging letters – now Prof. Dong Yol Yang of the Korea Advanced Institute of Science. He made a very useful contribution to our programme and subjects. Such generous action by Prof. Lippman's backers deserved acclamation. The event is still an unforgotten beautiful experience for my wife too.

I have written of some of my encounters with Prof. Mahrenholtz elsewhere in this volume, as well as a special one which occurred by chance in Madras, India. We got to arguing about scholastic contributions to science and classics (excavations, Greek translation and scholarship generally). I held to the supremacy of England, he to Germany. Our exchange took place at a time when I had begun to be able to give more time to the History of Science and was therefore much concerned with original references. Since that time I have changed my opinion and I now agree with him. The scholarship in quantity and quality developed by German workers in the nineteenth century especially, is massive and profound. This is reflected in the number of 'famous names' from England who went to German universities to expand their scientific knowledge in those years. It is also very enlightening to read the articles on classical scholarship and archaeology in the Encyclopaedia Britannica (for 1926) and to note in the references how much is German.

In the early 1960s Eckart Doege, a young student from Hannover came over to UMIST for a term and chose to work with (then) Dr Frank Travis on the Explosive Expansion of Unrestrained Tubes; this is depicted and referred to in Chapter XIX, Figure 16; it was an endeavour which was a great success. Doege joined the group which not only worked hard but enjoyed one another's company at weekends particularly in supporting Manchester United! It has now been Professor Doege at Hanover (or Kienzle's) University for some twenty or more years.

Mutual regard for one another's work extended to having a German group visit UMIST to see our efforts in ring-rolling, especially those of Dr John Hawkyard who had put so much effort into decreasing the thickness and hence increasing the diameter to which rings could be rolled. This rolling technique was more accurate at the time than the competitive technique in which rings were manufactured by machining. A lot of good work was also done in putting together theory (where there had been little or none before) for calculating the roll forces etc. involved. A German unit was started to research this method of ring production by the investment of many thousands of Deutschmarks. The scale of German research support by industry in comparison with ours (British) was astonishing.

It has always surprised me that a few such large independent Technical Institutes have failed to be established in the UK in the manner of the German ones. The Robbins Committee recommended establishing, in 1962, a few special Institutes for Science, Technology and Engineering Research (SISTERs) which could well have taken the German Technische Hochschule as an example. There were only about eight in West Germany at the time but fewness helps concentrate quality in people and research facilities. This line was not followed in the UK. Much could be said these days about the British inability to establish a public educational system and of its inability to remain committed to it without change for more than a few years.

CHAPTER XXXVII

Canada

———◆———

IN CONTRAST with Germany, I had no technical contacts with France. I did go to Paris to present a paper at an International Conference on Nuclear Engineering, which attracted I believe about 1500 persons. There were eight parallel sessions! The most novel feature was the circulation of preprints with no numbers inserted. (Clearly papers were prepared before experimental results came to hand.) It was difficult to see how conclusions could have been drawn before numbers had been inserted and results considered.

Likewise I failed to establish research relationships with Italian colleagues post-war. No temporary staff exchanges were ever made or postgraduate student visits even contemplated. Only two occasions arose when there was a reason to produce a paper. One was given in Turin whilst the second found a 'home' in Bologna. I was unable to locate the Conference Lecture Hall in Bologna. I asked a stationary bus driver outside the railway station where the Hall was located and in response he simply collected me and my baggage and drove to the Exhibition Hall where the meetings were being held – and not proceeding along his everyday route or charging a fare! (At the time Bologna was noted for its Communists.)

In 1969, through the efforts of Prof. Michael de Malherbe, see Figure 1 (an ex Second World War injured air gunner), I was able to spend a short sabbatical leave in McMaster University, Hamilton, Ontario, Canada. The department was not demanding in its teaching commitments – though my class was large, with three lectures per week, and a weekly problem class as specified in the formal Schedule.

By 1968 my parents had died and I was glad to have the opportunity of changing my physical surroundings from those typical of Manchester. Heather enjoyed the break too, for Philip was in medical school in Manchester, Christopher had started Engineering at City University and Helen, Jeremy and Sarah went to appropriate schools in Hamilton, Canada – Sarah happily, Jeremy less so and Helen, as a teenager, reluctantly. One thing stood out – all were about one foot shorter than their friends! We all first visited Niagara Falls and then went on to Western Canada to pay visits to Canadian friends, among whom one was an old Manchester University colleague (now at Vancouver) Prof. Jim Duncan. (He had been elevated to Head of Department in Sheffield in the late 1950s. See also p. 161, Chap. XVIII for a connection with Prof. J. B. Haddow.

It was at McMaster that I met Dr R. D. Venter, who had moved to Toronto

Figure 1. Prof. M. C. de Malherbe, Carleton University, Ottowa, Ontario.

from South Africa following Prof. de Malherbe, I believe to read for his Ph.D. under his supervision. We became closely acquainted and after finishing two papers with Prof. Malherbe and me he agreed to become a third author in the second edition of our *Bibliography of Slip Line Fields*. Bob Sowerby became second author of the latter volume. In the late 1960s he had joined the Department at UMIST, acquired a skill in s.l.f. theory and together we made some contributions to the subject. In the 1970s he emigrated to Canada and settled finally in McMaster. (He died in 2001.) We lost contact in the late 1980s and 1990s. In his final years at McMaster he seemed to have a great burden on his shoulders with M.Sc. student numbers. Prof. de Malherbe and his wife Rada remained close friends with us for many years and indeed we spent an excellent holiday with them in Rome and Switzerland. When they married they did so in Buxton, Derbyshire, with our family the sole and total audience. My final recollection of Canada turns on Quebec. In the middle of writing on various kinds of disaster, whilst wasting time waiting in one of the airports in Quebec province, I came across a volume entitled *Disasters from the pages of The New York Times* published by ARNO Press, 1976 – and later up-dated. The event of 11 September 2001 – the Twin Towers Disaster – was long reported before reference was made to a similar disaster in 1945, see Figure 2. The volume is an enormous source of primary information for students of engineering disasters and deserves to be widely known.

Ronnie Venter eventually became the Head of the Mech. Eng. Dept. in his University but, unfortunately, suffered problems due to his wife's illnesses.

Dr S. Meguid who carried out work for his Ph.D. at UMIST in the mid 1970s on Shot Peening, Peen Forming and Impact Erosion caused by small spherical particles, went on to Cranfield Institute of Technology, UK, thence to Canada and some time later he too became a Head of Department.

All the universities I have visited, or lectured at, have always provided good audiences and their buildings and departments were well supported. I suspect that in recent years financial support has not been what it once was – as indeed Bob Sowerby gave me to understand. I had encouragement to move to two Canadian universities and would have been content to go, for it seemed to promise well for young people, i.e. my family. In the event, domestic complexities prevented it.

Figure 2. 'Times' newspaper article, 'Bomber hits Empire State Building ...

PART V

Coming to Rest?

CHAPTER XXXVIII

Removing to Cornwall

———◆———

WE PUT RIDGE HALL on the market in 1999 and quickly sold it to Mr and Mrs John Franklin who owned a house close by in the centre of Chapel. They developed the property and land so that it became a small business and hotel as well as a home; as a result of the various improvements and extensions it came to merit a 5-star rating.

Our treasured pieces of furniture we sold either to the new owners or passed on to our children; our library we likewise dissolved – half of it went to Philip, our eldest son, some smaller fractions went to our other offspring and some of the technical books were sold or given to colleagues. The remaining few hundred have had to be housed in a small chalet in our present garden.

Heather had been diagnosed in the early 1990s as having a Parkinsonism and as the years passed we considered increasingly the matter of removing from our large home. Chapel proved difficult for securing steady domestic help – contrary to Cornwall. One always had to be fit and mobile to surmount the problems continuously presented by the hard weather of the Peak district. Buxton, only four miles away, was frequently cited on the radio and TV as the coldest or wettest town in England! We thus decided to remove ourselves and chose Cornwall so as to be near to family help from our younger daughter Sarah, who was living in St Austell. Here, the temperature is nearly always 5°C warmer than elsewhere in England. The county is scenic, there is virtually no heavy industry, relatively little heavy traffic and a low noise level. Its disadvantages are its distance – from London, Lancashire and Yorkshire and Cambridge. It also has no outstanding university, no conspicuous football clubs, good libraries or second-hand bookshops.

We found Cornwall to be a land of writers, ancient history, mining and early engineering innovators – Arthur Quiller Couch, Daphne du Maurier, A. L. Rowse, Isambard Kingdom Brunel, Richard Trevithick and the like. Brunel is remembered every time one drives a car or comes by train into Cornwall. On crossing the River Tamar one traverses the huge, magnificent bridge designed and erected under Brunel. Trevithick developed the steam locomotive first for the road in 1801 and next, in 1804, on rails. (The Stephensons installed their locomotive only in the late 1820s.) As for A. L. Rowse, we found he had lived about two miles from where I now write. I tried to learn more about him. He was an 'historian of promise', wrote Noel Annan, 'a Shakespearean scholar and at one time leftist politician'; he was defeated by John Sparrow in his attempt in 1951 to become Warden of All Souls, Oxford, having been a Fellow of that postgraduate College many years. The mathematician associated with this geographical area was John Couch Adams (1819–82), memorialised in Truro Cathedral and remembered mainly for his prediction of the existence of the planet Neptune.

I believe it was at Purdue University, USA, where we went to a lot of trouble to hear John Sparrow deliver a short lecture, but it turned out rather to be a talk for 30 minutes on nothing in particular and we were very disappointed. Again, Annan in his *The Dons* (Chicago Press, 1995) headed a chapter on him with the title *The Don as Dilletante*, p. 193. Perhaps I write with some asperity for about this time, applications were invited for professional fellowships of All Souls, Oxford. I submitted an application, thinking I might have had something unusual to contribute and looking to have the opportunity over a year or so to browse and make use of the Bodleian Library for some non-technical work I had in mind. I am afraid I received a very discouraging answer. Of Sparrow, Annan wrote that he 'had no interest in ideas but played on the outer periphery with marginal triviality.'

I recall visiting the National Maritime Museum in neighbouring Plymouth, Devon (about twenty miles away) and being disappointed in one small part of its structure on the Hoe until I saw, on a circular frieze, the names of the many theatres of war in which men of the UK and Commonwealth had died. I had not previously had much regard for this factor, but the en-bloc display of so many territories was quite astonishing. What is sometimes very frequently referred to as 'the repulse of Germany from Russia on a single front' contrasted very sharply with what was shown here – a veritable world-wide engagement.

A Journey to Cornwall

One truly outstanding memory associated with my period of lecturing at Northampton Polytechnic, London in 1950–51, recently overtook me in September, 2000. A particular young student had been in one of the mechanics classes I had lectured to in 1951/52. He had settled in the USA and when I came to know him personally he was Professor Euan Somerscales of Rensselaer University. He wrote to me in the 1990s to say that he had been following my various historical publications (see Figure 1) and proposed to put my name forward for the American Society of Mechanical Engineers Award of Engineer-Historian. This actually matured in 2000. I was personally unable to travel to the USA for health reasons and instead Professor Somerscales made the journey to the UK, came down to Cornwall and in St Austell, at the Carlyon Bay Hotel, which is near to my present home, presented me with the Award, in an empty room. There was an audience of just two wives (see Figure 2). However, the manager of the Hotel kindly encouraged us to celebrate the occasion by sending in four glasses and a free magnum of champagne.

Figure 1. Prof. Euan Somerscales and I on the occasion of his presentation to me of the ASME Engineering-Historian Award for 2000, for 'many publications on a wide variety of technological history subjects, including projectiles, the life and works of Benjamin Robins, manufacturing technology, and steam hammer forging.'

Figure 2. Mrs Heather Johnson, one half of the audience, looking on.

1. An Epitaph from Jonathan Swift (1667–1745)

When preparing an article on Jonathan Swift (*IJMS* 37, 499–521), who incidentally was no friend to science, I came across the following satire which seems eminently fitted for reproducing at this moment in the life of the writer.

> See, how the dean begins to break!
> Poor gentleman! he droops apace!
> You plainly find it in his face.
> That old vertigo in his head
> Will never leave him till he's dead.
> Besides his memory decays:
> He recollects not what he says;
> He cannot call his friends to mind;
> Forgets the place where last he dined;
> Plies you with stories o'er and o'er –
> he told them fifty times before.
> How does he fancy we can sit
> To hear his out-of-fashion wit!
> But he takes up with younger folks,
> Who for his wine will bear his jokes.
> Faith, he must make his stories shorter,
> Or change his comrades once a quarter:
> In half the time he talks them round,
> There must another set be found.
>
>   For poetry he's past his prime,
> He takes an hour to find a rhyme:
> His fire is out, his wit decayed,
> His fancy sunk, his Muse a jade.
> I'd have him throw away his pen –
> But there's no talking to some men.
>
> And then their tenderness appears
> By adding largely to my years;
> 'He's older than he would be reckoned,
> And well remembers Charles the Second.
> He hardly drinks a pint of wine
> And that, I doubt, is no good sign.
> His stomach, too, begins to fail
> Last year we thought him strong and hale;
> But now he's quite another thing;
> I wish he may hold out till spring.'
> They hug themselves and reason thus:
> 'It is not yet so bad with us.'

In such a case they talk in tropes,
And by their fears express their hopes.
Some great misfortune to portend
No enemy can match a friend.
With all the kindness they profess,
The merit of a lucky guess.
(When daily How-d'ye's come of course,
And servants answer: Worse and worse!)
Would please them better than to tell,
That, 'God be praised! the dean is well.'
Then he who prophesied the best,
Approves his foresight to the rest:
'You know I always feared the worst,
And often told you so at first.'
He'd rather choose that I should die,
Than his prediction prove a lie.
Not one foretells I shall recover.
But all agree to give me over.

   My good companions, never fear;
for, though you may mistake a year,
Though your prognostics run too fast,
They must be verified at last.

   Behold the fatal day arrives
'How is the dean? 'He's just alive.'
Now the departing prayer is read;
'He hardly breathes.' 'The dean is dead.'

   Before the passing-bell begun,
The news through half the town is run;
'Oh! may we all for death prepare!
What has he left? and who's his heir?
'I know no more than what the news is
'Tis all bequeathed to public uses.'
'To public uses! there's a whim!
What had the public done for him?
Mere envy, avarice and pride:
He gave it all – but first he died.
And had the dean in all the nation
No worthy friend, no poor relation?
So ready to do strangers good,
Forgetting his own flesh and blood!' ...

Now Curll his shop from rubbish drains:
Three genuine tomes of Swift's *Remains!*
And then to make them pass the glibber,
Revised by Tibbalds, Moore, and Gibber.
He'll treat me as he does my better,
Publish my will, my life, my letters;
Revive the libels born to die,
Which Pope must bear, as well as I.

Here shift the scene, to represent
How those I love my death lament.
Poor Pope will grieve a month, and Gay
A week, and Arbuthnot a day.
St John himself will scarce forbear
To bite his pen, and drop a tear.
The rest will give a shrug, and cry:
'I'm sorry – but we all must die!' ...

One year is past; a different scene!
No further mention of the dean,
Who now, alas! no more is missed,
Than if he never did exist.
Where's now the favourite of Apollo!
Departed; and his works must follow;
Must undergo the common fate;
His kind of wit is out of date.

Some country squire to Lintot goes,
Inquires for Swift in verse and prose.
Says Lintot: 'I have heard the name:
He died a year ago.' 'The same.'
He searches all the shop in vain:
'Sir, you may find them in Duck-lane.
I sent them, with a load of books,*
Last Monday to the pastry-cook's.'

---

* The last two lines here are not just literary license as is exemplified by the following paragraph from *Brief Lives* by John Aubrey (1626–97), when writing about Sir Charles Cavendish (1591–1654):

> He had collected in Italie, France, &c, with no small chardge, as many Manuscript Mathematicall bookes as filled a Hogges-head, which he intended to have printed; which if he had lived to have donne, the growth of Mathematicall Learning had been 30 yeares or more forwarder then 'tis. But he died of the Scurvey, contracted by hard study, about 1652, and left an Attorney of Clifford's Inne, his Executor,, who shortly after died, and left his Wife Executrix, who sold this incomparable Collection afore-said, by weight to the past-board makers for Wast-paper. A good Caution for those that have good MSS to take care to see them printed in their lifetimes.

2. The Book title derived from a letter of Yester-year

```
                                    THE WAR OFFICE,
                                    STANMORE,
                                    MIDDLESEX.
                                    1 February, 1950.
P/320085/1 (Records))

Sir,
        With reference to your letter of 17th January, 1950
I am commanded by the Army Council to furnish, from the
records of the Department, the following particulars of
the military service of Lieutenant William JOHNSON:-
```

Enlisted into Territorial Army under National Service Acts, 1939 to 1941, and posted to General Service Corps.................................	5.	8.43
Transferred to Royal Electrical and Mechanical Engineers..	20.	1.44
Discharged on appointment to a commission..........	5.	5.44
Appointed to an emergency commission as 2nd Lieutenant, Royal Electrical and Mechanical Engineers..	6.	5.44
Promoted War Substantive Lieutenant...............	6.	11.44
Released with effect from	9.	9.47
and granted honorary rank of Lieutenant.		

Served overseas.

His record and services were satisfactory.

                    I am, Sir,
                        Your obedient Servant,

                        (signed) L. Sumner
                    For
                    Permanent Under-Secretary of State.

Figure 3.

3. Errors and Author's Apologies

The author apologises for the errors he will be found to have committed in his writings in this Memoir. He only takes comfort from the fact that other, greater writers have done likewise in the past, as Figure 4 reveals.

Figure 4. From Isaac Newton's Mathematical Principles Appendix by Florian Cajori

Sir Isaac Newton's
MATHEMATICAL PRINCIPLES
OF NATURAL PHILOSOPHY AND HIS SYSTEM OF THE WORLD

Translated into English by Andrew Motte in 1729. The translations revised, and supplied with an historical and explanatory appendix, by

FLORIAN CAJORI

Volume Two: THE SYSTEM OF THE WORLD

UNIVERSITY OF CALIFORNIA PRESS
BERKELEY, LOS ANGELES, LONDON

4 (p.xix). *Alterations and corrections made in preparing the second edition of the Principia.*

In preparing copy for the second edition of the Principia, Cotes took great care to remove errors and imperfections. Newton wrote to him on Oct. 11, 1709: "I would

not have you be at the trouble of examining all the Demonstrations in the Principia. It's impossible to print the book without some faults and if you print by the copy sent you, correcting only such faults as occur in reading over the sheets to correct them as they are printed off, you will have labour more then it's fit to give you."*
In 1713, after the second edition had appeared from the press, Newton sent Cotes a list of errata, perhaps intending it to be printed as a table of errata. To this Cotes replied, Dec. 22, 1713: "I observe You have put down about 20 Errata besides those in my Table. ... I believe You will not be surpriz'd if I tell You I can send You 20 more as considerable, which I have casually observ'd, and which seem to have escap'd You: and I am far from thinking these forty are all that may be found out, not-with-standing that I think the Edition to be very correct. I am sure it is much more so than the former, which was carefully enough printed; for besides Your own corrections and those I acquainted You with whilst the Book was printing, I may venture to say I made some Hundreds, with which I never acquainted You."†

---

* J. Edleston (1816–95), op. cit., p. 5.
† Edleston, op. cit., pp. 167, 168.

Index

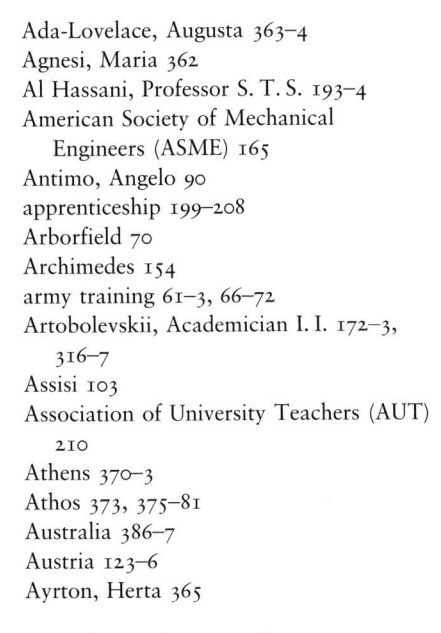

Ada-Lovelace, Augusta 363–4
Agnesi, Maria 362
Al Hassani, Professor S. T. S. 193–4
American Society of Mechanical Engineers (ASME) 165
Antimo, Angelo 90
apprenticeship 199–208
Arborfield 70
Archimedes 154
army training 61–3, 66–72
Artobolevskii, Academician I. I. 172–3, 316–7
Assisi 103
Association of University Teachers (AUT) 210
Athens 370–3
Athos 373, 375–81
Australia 386–7
Austria 123–6
Ayrton, Herta 365

Backofen, Professor Walter 165
Bagshaw(e) family 218, 222–4
Bai, Dr and Mrs 357, 358
Baker, Professor J. F. 233
Barash, Professor Moshe M. 275, 384, 385
Baraya, G. L. 274
Bassi, Laura 362
Baumann Institute 307, 332
Beijing 357–60
Bell, Jack 43, 44
Belle Vue 23, 29, 30
Benson, Professor Roland 179, 180
Bevan, Thomas 44, 186
Binnie, Dr A. M. 234–5
Bishop, Dr J. W. F. 165
Blackett, Professor P. M. S. 161
Blackpool 45–7

Blenkinsop, John 292–3
Bogatov, Professor A. 324
Bogolubov, A. N. 332
Bolton, Professor N. S. 153
Borgovolensky, Professor 314
Bowden, Lord 168
Breteuil, Emilie de *see* Chatelet, Marquise du
Brewster, Ralph 101, 376, 378
British Iron and Steel Association (BISRA) 145, 152–3, 244
Bulletin of Mechanical Engineering Education 174
Bush, Professor Stephen 187

Calladine, Professor C. R. 233
Cambridge University 232–8
Canada 161, 406–8
Cannon, Professor Graham 166
Capri 93
Cardwell, Dr Donald 187–8
Carnatic *see* Fort St David; India
Carter, Elizabeth 362–3
Casey family 58
Charnley, Dr (Sir) John 165, 191
Chatelet, Marquise du 361, 363
Chernov lines 146
childhood and youth 6–7, 8, 9, 12–13, 14–15, 21–4; elementary school 15–16, 17, 18, 24–7, 25, 26, 28; grammar school 35, 36, 37, 38, 40–1, 42; sports and pastimes 27–9, 30–1, 32, 33; wartime experiences 42, 45–8, studies 43, 44, 49–54, 51–2, 55–7, 84, 125, 130; marriage 117–118, 119
Chitkara, N. 252
Christopherson, Professor D. G. 170, 239
climbing 125–6, 227
CIRP 401

civil service 123, 131–2, 135–8
Codroipo 111, *112*, 117, 118
Colchester 71–2
Collyhurst 10
Cowan, Professor Henry 153
crashworthiness 260–2
Crighton, Sir David G. 140
Crossley, Professor Erskine 172
Cuddalore *see* Fort St David

Dale, Sir Henry 294
Daneshi, Dr G. H. 397
David, Professor W. 145
demobilisation 129–30
Diamond, Professor Jack 157, 159–61, 162, 166, 181, 401
Dictionary of National Biography 302
Doege, Professor Eckert 401, 404
Domilovskaya, Tatyana 327–8
Dong Yol Yang, Professor 404
Drucker, Professor Dan 388
Duncan, Professor Jim 406
Duncan, Professor John 386
D'Viti de Marco, Marquese Giacomo 'James' 374–5

Ekaterinburg 322–8
elasticity 141, 241
Elliott, Professor Doug 43
Ellis, Oliver Coligny de Champfleur 36, 224
engineering plasticity *see* plasticity
Euclid 264–7
explosive forming 231, 252–8, 349–50
extrusion 145, 163, 241–2

Fitzroy-Maclean 128
Finnie, Professor 384
Florence 103
Flowers, Professor Brian 161
Flowett, Joe 190, 292–3
Fort St David 280–4
Frisch, Professor J. 384
Fukui, Professor S. 339, 353
Furber, Dr Ben 43

Galileo 154–5
Galloway, Dr 401
Germain, Sophie 363
Germany, links with 403–5

Ghosh, Professor 392, 393
Gibbon, Edward 285–6
Gibraltar, siege of 85–7
Gilbreth, Lilian 365–6
Goldsmith, Professor Werner 191
Goodman, Professor John 144
Gupta, Professor N. K. 393

Haddow, Professor James 161, 174
Haldane, Professor J. B. S. 50, 51
Hall, Professor W. B. 161, 181
Harvey, William 128
Hashmi, Professor 392
Hatton, Dr A. Peter 43, 179, 190
Hawkyard, Dr John 152, 250, 404
Hawthorne, Sir William 233
Haythornthwaite, Professor R. M. 153, 165
heat lines 273–4
Heath, Sir Thomas Little 135, 266–7
Herschel, Caroline L. 363
Heyman, Professor Jacques 232, 233
high energy rate forming (HERF) 252, 349–50
Hill, Professor Rodney 145–6, 173
Hills, Dr Richard 190
Hirai, Professor 343, 344
Hogben, Lancelot 51–2
holidays: Isle of Man 9–10; Blackpool 55–6; Filey 156; North Wales 168; Scotland and elsewhere 229
homes: Lower Openshaw 11, 21–3; Higher Openshaw 16, 55; Sidcup 132, 225; Eccleshall 155–6; Nether Edge 156; Norbury House 158; Ridge Hall 213–221, 411; Chesterton 236; Cornwall 411
Honeycombe, Professor R. 355
Hong Kong 392
Horne, Professor Michael 233
Hutton, Charles 259
Huygens, Christian 155
Hyde family 57–8
Hypatia of Alexandria 361–2

Ilyushin, Academician A. A. 310, *311*
impact engineering 252–8
India 393–6
Institute of Electrical Engineering (IEE) 245
Institution of Mechanical Engineers (I.Mech.E.) 146

International Journal of Impact Engineering 174
International Journal of Mechanical Sciences (IJMS) 165, 169, 170, 274
Iran 397–402
Israel 388–9
Italy (wartime): journey to 80–2; Naples 88–97; Rome 97; Florence 103; Assisi 103; Orvieto 105, *106*; Milan 107, 109, 406; Venice 109, 128, 129; Padova 127, 128

Jagger, J. G. 147
Japan 339–54
Jimma, Professor and Mrs 339, 352
Johnson, Bella (*sister*) 16
Johnson, Catherine ('Kit') (*aunt*) 3, 4–5
Johnson, Christopher (*son*) *15*, 155, 216, 220, 225, 226, 227, 228, 406
Johnson, Elizabeth, *née* Riley (*mother*) 5, 6, 9, 13–14, 15, 18, 31, 32, 56, 406
Johnson, Heather *née* Thornber (*wife*) early life 19, *20*, *64*, 64–5, 117, marriage 119, family 132, 140–1, 146, 155, 168, 216, 220, 225, 228, 229, *351*, *352*, 356, 382, 385, 391, 399, 400, 401, 406, 411, *413*; conference verses 208–212
Johnson, Helen (*daughter*) 156, 216, 225, 228, 382, 406
Johnson, James (*father*) early life 3, 5–6, 9, 13–14, 16, 18, 31, 32, 42, 49, 54, 56, 99, 100, 406
Johnson, Jeremy (*son*) 156, 216–7, 225, 227, 228, 406
Johnson, John (*brother*) 7, 16, 17, 45, 47, 225–6, 228
Johnson, John (*uncle*) 3, 4
Johnson, Ken (Professor) 176, 232, 233
Johnson, Margaret (*sister-in-law*) 225–6, 228
Johnson, Philip (*son*) 132, 216–7, 225, 228, 392, 406
Johnson, Sarah (*daughter*) 19, 158, 216, 225, 228, 384, 411
Johnson, Sarah *née* Cartwright (*grandmother*) 5, 6, 7, 8–9, 13, 31
Johnson, Thomas (*cousin*) 3
Johnson, Thomas John (*uncle*) 3, 5
Jones, Professor Norman 175, 393

Journal of Machine Tool Design and Research 173
Journal of Materials Processing Technology 275
Journal of Mechanical Engineering Science (JMES) 170
Journal of the Mechanics and Physics of Solids (JMPS) 173
Judy (*dog*) 22

Kargon, Professor Robert H. 276
Karman, Theodore von 120
Karunes Professor B. 393
Katoh, Mr H. 350–1
Kay-Shuttleworth, Sir James Phillips 33–4
Kelgren, Professor J. H. 193
Kienzle, Professor 401
Kilburn, Professor Tom 245
King's Royal Rifle Corps 80–1
Kitching, Dr Ron 184
Knott's Iron Yard 24
Kobayashi, Professor 384
Koenigsberger, Professor Franz 173, 178, 181
Kolesnikov, Academician 330
Kolmogorov, Professor V. L. 322, 328, 329, 332–5
Kormi, Professor Kazil 397, 400, 401
Koroteev, Professor V. 324
Kovaleski, Sonya *364*, *365*
Kraftanoglu, Professor 367
Krasovskii, Academician N. 324
Kudo, Professor Hideaki 152, 161–4, 339, 352

Laithwaite, Professor Eric 244, 245, 246, 247, 249
Lamble, Dr J. H. 179, 198, 318
Leningrad 312–315
Leoban *see* Austria
linear induction motor (LIM) 244, 245–8
Lippmann, Professor Horst 401, 404
Livesey, Professor J. 161
lottery 289–90
Luder's lines 146
Lyapunov, Dr Colya 312, 315, 321

MacFarlane, Professor Alistair 236
Machine Tool Trades Association 178

Malherbe, Professor M. C. 406, 407
Mahrenhotlz, Dr Oskar 401
Mair, Professor W. Austyn 23
Malinin, Professor N. N. 309, 310, 330, 331
Mamalis, Professor A. G. 250, 372, 375, 376, 387
Manchester 275–8
Manchester and Salford Medical Engineering Club 193
Manchester Association of Engineers 198
Manchester College of Technology (MCoT) 37, 39; 176–9, 181–93
Manchester Mechanics Institute 279
Manchester Museum of Science and Technology 189
Manchester University *see* Owens College
Marshall, John 292
Massey, Harold 274
Matheson, Professor Sir James 157, 386
Matvienko, Professor 328
Maxwell, Robert 169–75
McGrath, Mr 57
McLeish, R. D. 193
mechanics of sport *see* sport, mechanics of
medical engineering 190–4
Meguid, Dr S. 407
Mellor, Professor P. B. 152–3, 165
Messinger, Gary 276
Metropolitan-Vickers 50
Meyer, Dr Ludwig 148
Milan 107–110
Miller, Professor Edward 233
Mittag-Leffler, Professor M. G. 364–5
Mori, Professor M 341
Moscow 305–312, 315–21, 330–1
Murchison, Sir Roderick 326
Murray, Matthew 292
Murray, Professor Noel 387
Mussolini 108, 109
Myers, Sir John 52–3

Nakagawa, Professor Tom 340–1
Naples 88–97
Nasmyth, James 279
Neal, Dr Philip 152
Needham, Mr J. 190
Needham, Dr Geoffrey 249
Neville, A. M. 161
Newcomen Society 244

Newton, Sir Isaac 135, 294, 297–8, 300
Nigeria 390
Noether, Emmy 364
Northampton Polytechnic 139–40

Oakden, J. C. 147
Oatley, Professor C. W. 233
Ollerenshaw, Dr Kathleen 366
Onat, Professor E. T. 93
Openshaw, Higher 29, 57
Openshaw, Lower 21, 23, 57–8, 276
Orvieto 105, *106*
Ovchinnikov, Professor T. 310, 330, 331, 334
Ovchinnikov, Anne 327–8
Oxley, Professor Peter 386
Owens College 157–61, 166

Padova 101, 127–8
Paestum 91–2
Paipetis, Professor 372
Parker, Dr John 183, 210
Parkes, Professor Ted 232, 233
Pergamon Press 145, 169–175, 335
Perm 328
Petard, 'hoist by own' 271–2
Piatrowski, Nell and Jan 20, 387
plasticity 141, 241–2
plasticity in extrusion 145, 146, 231, 241–3
Pollitt, Harry 50–1
Ponomarev, Professor S. D. 309
Pope, the 105–106
Popov Professor E. A. 167, 305, 306, 308, 310, 316, 318, 320, 330, 331
Prager, W. 145
Proceedings of the Institution of Mechanical Engineers 141
Prozadorov, Professor L. V. 318, 319
Purdue (USA) 382, 384–5

Quarrel, Dr A. G. 141
Queen's Own Royal West Kent Regiment 66

RAOC: Italy 111–116, 117, 118–119; 127, 129; Austria 123–5
Reddy, Professor T. Y. 393
Rees, Professor P. E. 393
Reid, Professor S. R. 171, 392, 393

REME: training, Arborfield 70,
    Colchester 71–2; prisoner guarding
    73–9; Central Purchase and Production
    (Italy) 88–96, 97–99, 107, 108, 110
Reynolds, Professor Osborne 37, 144, 159
ricochet 259–60
Riley, Elizabeth/Isabella (*grandmother*)
    10, 11
Riley, George (*grandfather*) 6, 7, 10,
    11–12, 13, 31, 32, 56
Riley, Willie (*uncle*) 10–11, 12
ring rolling 249–50, 341
Roberts, Richard 279
Robins, Benjamin 259–60, 280–1, 393, 394
Robinson, George 190, 292
rolling theory 314
Rome 97–102, 105
rotary forging 251
Rotherham, Professor P. L. 161
Royal Society, The 238–40
Russia and USSR (work with universities)
    335–8

Saga, Professor J. 348
Sansovino, Jacapo 129
Savin, G. N. 172
Schlesinger, Professor G. G. 181
Semonov, Professor E. 330
Schofield, Professor Andrew 232, 236
Shaffer, Professor B. W. 166
Shaw, Anne 366
Sheffield University 141–2, 142
Simba (*dog*) 221
Singapore 391–2
Singh, Professor A. N. 393
Skorecki, Dr Jan 190, 194
Slater, Dr Robert A. C. 244, 246, 247,
    248–9, 274
slip line field theory (s.l.f.t.) 145, 166–8
Smirnov, Professor 314
Snow, Dr C. P. 61
Soden, Dr P. 193, 194, 195
Somerscales, Professor Euan 412, 413
Somerville, Dr Mary 363
Sowerby, Robert 174, 407, 408
Sparkes, Dr C. A. 198
sport, mechanics of 196, 197–8
St Francis of Assisi 103–105
Stamford 287–8, 299–300
Stepanov, Professor 315

Stirling, James 128
strength of materials 141, 179, 318–19
Stronge, Dr W. J. 356, 384
Swift, Professor Herbert Walker 141, 142,
    143–5, 147–8, 153

Taiwan 382–3
Taj Mahal 291
(492) Tank Transporter Company *see*
    RAOC
Tanner, Dr Roger 164–5, 386
Tatsukawa, Professor I. 349
Taylor, Mr 9, 10
teaching topics: applied mechanics 142;
    engineering drawing and design 142,
    158; engineering materials 158;
    thermodynamics 158, 159, 160–1;
    strength of materials 139, 142, 179;
    statistics 158–9; machine tools 178;
    nuclear engineering 161; history of
    engineering 154–5, 187, 188–90
Tesla, Nikola 245
Theocaris, Professor 371–2, 375–6
thermodynamics 158
theory of machines 186
Thiépval (cenotaph) 3, 4, 11
Thomson, Professor 384
Thomson, Sir J. J. 278
Thornber, Jack B. 20
Thornber, John B. (*father-in-law*) 15, 18,
    19, 156
Thornber, Mildred *née* Baker
    (*mother-in-law*) 18, 19, 156, 216
Timoshenko, Professor Stephen 120–2
Tobias, Professor Stephen 173, 179
Todhunter, Professor Isaac 233, 264–70
Tomlenov, Professor A. D. 318, 320
Travis, Professor Frank 255
Tresca, H. 274
triaxial loading 310
Trueman, Professor Ted 193
Tuplin, Professor W. Alfred 147–50
Turkey 367–70
Turnor, Captain Herbert 294

University of Manchester Institute of
    Science and Technology (UMIST) 244
    see also Manchester College of Technology
Unksov, Professor Y. P. 317–18, 319

Venice 109, 128, 129
Venter, Dr R. D. 406–7
Verstikova, Yelena 327–8
Vierb, Dr M. 324
Vojdani, Dr 399

Wales (army training) 68–70
Wang, Professor H. 360
Wang, Professor Ren 355, 359
War office selection board 61–3
water hammer 320
Weierstrass, Professor Karl 364
Williams, Professor D. 252
Williams, Professor J. Ffowcs 233
Williams, Professor F. C. 245

Wilshaw, Esther and family 7, 58
'Witch of Agnesi' 47 *see also* Agnesi, Maria
Woodward family 57
Woolsthorpe Manor 294–9
Wright-Baker, Professor Henry 39, 61, 176, 177, 198
writings (author's) 96, 101, 121, 145, 146, 151–2, 154, 161, 167–8, 173–4, 195, 231, 244, 246, 249, 259, 260–2, 277, 319, Russia 335–6; Japan 345; women in Mechanics 361–6; Benjamin Robins 394

Yamada, Professor 348
Yang, Henry 384, 385
Yu, Professor Tong X 355–6, 357, 392